D0846897

Familie
ALLWEIN

Familie
ALLWEIN

Hans Jacob and Catharina Allwein and Their Descendants

Volume II

Journeys in Time and Place

Part 1—Southeastern Pennsylvania

Duane F. Alwin

With contributions by

Edward F. Allwein, Doug Alwine, Patti Keefer Billow, Peter Hill Byrne, Jim Hoffheins, Donna Wagner Koons, Patricia Alwine Lawver, Cheryl Alwine Lutz, Madeline Paine Moyer, Nancy Allwein Nebiker, and Tommy Sims

Copyright © 2013 by Duane F. Alwin.

Library of Congress Control Number: 2013909728
ISBN: Hardcover   978-1-4836-4732-6
               Softcover   978-1-4836-4731-9
               eBook   978-1-4836-4733-3

All rights reserved. No part of this book may be reproduced or transmitted in any form or by any means, electronic or mechanical, including photocopying, recording, or by any information storage and retrieval system, without permission in writing from the copyright owner.

This book was printed in the United States of America.

The cover art for this book is based on a photograph of a Fractur drawing commemorating the birth and baptism of William Allwein, son of Philip Allwein and Barbara Frantz.

Rev. date: 12/11/2013

To order additional copies of this book, contact:
Xlibris LLC
1-888-795-4274
www.Xlibris.com
Orders@Xlibris.com
126178

Dedicated to
the Allwein Families of
Southeastern Pennsylvania

CONTENTS

Volume II

Journeys in Time and Place
Part 1—Southeastern Pennsylvania

LIST OF EXHIBITS

FOREWORD

This book continues the family history research reported in volume 1 of *Familie Allwein—An Early History*.[1] That work established an historical basis for understanding the lives of our immigrant ancestors Johannes (Hans) Jacob Allwein and his wife, Catharina. It began with Han Jacob's immigration to America from Germany, reaching back into his European origins and chronicling his settlement in Pennsylvania. In addition, that work traced the first four generations of the Allwein family in America through to about 1880.

This second volume, titled *Familie Allwein—Journeys in Time and Place,* and its companion third volume, *Familie Allwein—Western Migrations,* cover Allwein families in America over the roughly 70-year period from about 1870 through to 1940, and in some cases beyond that. In many ways these 2nd and 3rd volumes represent an update and extension on the families covered in *An Early History*. In addition, however, they also present or reference many new collections of facts—marriage records, draft registration records, death records, census records, geographic atlases and local histories—as well as new insights concerning the history of the Allwein family in America.

The second and third volumes are organized according to the geographic locations of family members. Volume 2 covers Allwein

---

[1]   Duane F. Alwin, *Familie Allwein—Hans Jacob and Catharina Allwein and their Descendants.* Volume 1: *An Early History of the Allwein Family in America.* Bloomington, IN: Xlibris, 2009.

family descendants who settled east of the Allegheny Mountains in Pennsylvania. This 2nd volume is contained in two parts—Part 1 contains three chapters covering the following areas: Lebanon County (chapter 11), Philadelphia County (chapter 12), Berks County (chapter 13) and Part 2 contains chapters on Dauphin and Lancaster Counties (chapter 14), York and Adams Counties (chapter 15), and Blair County (chapter 16).

Volume 3 covers those Allwein family descendants who settled west of the Alleghenies, including those who settled in western Pennsylvania and those who moved farther west. It contains six major chapters, covering the following areas: Cambria, Bedford and Somerset Counties (chapter 17), Westmoreland County (chapter 18), Beaver and Butler Counties (chapter 19), the state of Ohio (chapter 20), the states of Indiana, Illinois and Michigan (chapter 21), the states of Iowa and Minnesota (chapter 22), the states of Kansas and Nebraska (chapter 23), and the state of California (chapter 24). Volume 3 ends with a recapitulation of the history of the Allwein family (chapter 25), providing a summary of what is known about the family in America and Europe. There is also a volume 4 planned, which will cover related families—such as Arnold, Shartle, Eckenrode, Seifert, Lorentz, and many others.

This work has benefitted greatly from the contributions of others. I have listed some of the main contributors on the title page, and in addition, there are others who I have listed in the Acknowledgements section at the end of this volume.

Duane Francis Alwin
July 2013
State College, Pennsylvania

INTRODUCTION

German Emigrants to America

In the 18th century, before the Revolutionary War, thousands of German-speaking people came to the American colonies through the ports of Boston, New York, Baltimore, Philadelphia, Charleston and Savannah. Only in Philadelphia did the governmental authorities insist on the preparation of careful and detailed lists of arrivals. Given the large numbers of immigrants entering the port of Philadelphia, the government of Pennsylvania required them to sign a "Declaration of Fidelity and Abjuration" which was an effort to maintain loyalty to the colonial government and the British King. Despite these efforts to keep track of them, the German immigrants were in no way considered a threat to anyone and were viewed as hard-working and industrious in character and good for the economy of Pennsylvania.

Lists of many of the early arrivals in Pennsylvania may be found in *Pennsylvania German Pioneers: A Publication of the Original Lists of Arrivals in the Port of Philadelphia from 1727 to 1808*, Volume I (1727-1775). The original lists were published by Ralph B. Strassburger, and the work was edited by William J. Hinke, for the Pennsylvania German Society in 1934. There was a second printing of this work in 1966 and a third edition in 1992.[2]

---

[2]   See Ralph B. Strassburger and William John Hinke, *Pennsylvania German Pioneers: A Publication of the Original Lists of Arrivals in the Port of Philadelphia from 1727 to 1808*, Camden, Maine: Picton Press, 1992.

Pennsylvania had offered asylum since the early 1700s to Protestant groups fleeing persecution in Germany, as well as other parts of Europe. This of course does not mean that everyone who came to Pennsylvania came for that reason, but it was often the case. Between 1727 and 1775, more than 324 ships brought thousands of German-speaking immigrants to Pennsylvania. These people came, not only from Germany, but the German-speaking areas of France and Switzerland. Although few of them were from the Netherlands, these immigrants were called *Dutch* because the German word *Deutsch*, which means *German*, was misinterpreted by their British neighbors in America, and hence were called "Pennsylvania Dutch," simply meaning German immigrants to Pennsylvania.[3] This included many German Brethren, Lutherans, Reformed Protestants (i.e., Calvinists), Catholics, Mennonites, and the Amish, the more conservative branch of the Mennonites who settled in Lancaster County. Regardless of the high degree of religious diversity, these early American settlers shared a common language and culture and helped build an American nation together with immigrants from other lands.

Regardless of their origins, however, these German immigrants thought of themselves as Americans. In the 2002 book, *Foreigners in Their Own Land*, author Steven Nolt tells a story about a German visitor to eastern and central Pennsylvania in the middle of the 19th century who encountered some Pennsylvania Germans and introduced himself to them as a fellow countryman. They responded with quizzical looks, as they did not think of themselves as Germans at all. Two women, for example, were quick to inform him, in a German dialect, that they were "Americans."[4] Despite their origins, the tendency to assume that the German immigrants to the American colonies were Germans and not Americans, especially second (and

---

[3]   See Charles F. Kerchner, Jr., "Pennsylvania Dutch Are of German Heritage, Not Dutch," at the following website--http://www.kerchner.com/padutch.htm.
[4]   Steven M. Nolt, *Foreigners in Their Own Land—Pennsylvania Germans in the Early Republic*, University Park, Pennsylvania: Pennsylvania University Press, 2002, page 1.

later) generation immigrants, was risky, especially given the ways in which national identities typically develop.

While this may be true, one of the remarkable things about these German immigrants is that many of them held on to their German language and culture over several generations. Even into the third and fourth generations, some Allwein family members were still using the German language. For example, some of the early wills of Allwein family members were written in German, as were the inscriptions on gravestones of Allwein family members, and some of the early schools that Allwein family members attended were conducted in the German language.

Coming to America

On October 2, 1741, Johannes (Hans) Jacob Allwein arrived in America. We know this because his name is listed in the premier source mentioned above on immigrants to the port of Philadelphia in the Pennsylvania Colony. The *Pennsylvania German Pioneers* lists "Hans Jacob Alwine" as a passenger on the St. Andrew, commanded by Charles Stedman, which arrived in Philadelphia on the above date. That volume provides access to the records of tens of thousands who entered the port of Philadelphia during the 18th century, and is the earliest record of Hans Jacob Allwein in the Pennsylvania Colony.[5] This is the beginning point of any narrative of the Allwein family in America.

As noted above, originally published in 1934, *Pennsylvania German Pioneers* was printed a second time in 1966, and again in 1992. It was published in three volumes in 1992. The first volume contains the actual ship lists and lists of signers of the Declarations of Fidelity and Abjuration, the second and all-important volume contains facsimiles of the signatures and marks of those male

---

[5]   William J. Hinke (Ed.), *Pennsylvania German Pioneers: A Publication of the Original Lists of Arrivals in the Port of Philadelphia from 1717 to 1808*, published by Ralph B. Strassberger for the Pennsylvania German Society, Camden ME: Picton Press, P.O. Box 1111, Camden, Maine, 1992, Volume I, page 304.

passengers who were aged 16 and upwards, and the third provides an index of all passengers entering the port of Philadelphia during that time.[6] It is important to note that there is *neither* a signature given for Hans Jacob Allwein, *nor* is his name listed on the Strassberger and Hinke reports of the signers of the Declarations of Fidelity and Abjuration. Specifically, in the 1992 edition of *Pennsylvania German Pioneers*, the passengers lists for the St. Andrew (list 85A) arriving October 2, 1741 appear on pages 303-305 of volume I. "Hans Jacob Alwine" is listed on list 85A, the passenger list, but *he does not appear on lists of signatories to the loyalty oaths*—lists 85B and 85C (see *Familie Allwein*, volume 1, pages 21-23).

My theory for why he did not sign the loyalty oaths is that he was Catholic, and that to sign such oaths, which swore allegiance to the Protestant King of England and abjured (or renounced) the authority of the Roman Catholic Pope, would have been to deny his Catholic faith. In fact, as I explained in *Familie Allwein*, volume 1 (pages 22-23), it appears that at that time Catholics could enter Pennsylvania without compromising their faith. Correspondence from Father Wappeler, one of the early Jesuit priests who served the Lancaster area, gave an account regarding his entry into the port of Philadelphia, which indicated that Catholics were not required to take the usual oath that contained an abjuration of the Pope.[7] Concessions of this sort were also made to the Mennonites and members of other plain sects, who did not believe in swearing oaths to governments, on their arrival from Europe.

In contrast to these findings, some sources suggest that Hans Jacob Allwein was among those who took the oaths of loyalty to the

---

[6]   In the 1992 edition of *Pennsylvania German Pioneers*, the passengers lists for the St. Andrew (list 85A) arriving October 2, 1741 appear on pages 303-305 of volume I. Hans Jacob Alwine is on list 85A, the passenger list, but he does not appear on lists of signatories to the loyalty oaths (see *Familie Allwein*, volume 1, pages 21-23).

[7]   Edgar A. Musser, "St. Mary's Church, Lancaster, 1785-1877," *Journal of the Lancaster County Historical Society*, 1969, vol. 73, pages 97-98.

British King, but I am convinced that there is nothing to this.[8] I do not go into this here because his failure to sign these loyalty oaths, as well as the possible reasons for it, are thoroughly discussed in volume 1 of *Familie Allwein* (see chapter 1, pages 20-23). It can be noted here that, according to William J. Hinke in his introduction to the *Pennsylvania German Pioneers*, some people confused ship lists of passengers with lists of those who signed the loyalty oaths, and there is no evidence from the actual authentic lists that Hans Jacob Allwein in fact signed any such loyalty oaths.

Once in America, many German-speaking immigrants became naturalized citizens of the British Colony. However, according to one historian, "the surviving records testify that only a minority of eligible Germans in colonial Pennsylvania chose to become naturalized British subjects."[9] A search of the available information yields no evidence that Hans Jacob Allwein became a naturalized Pennsylvanian, or if he did, there is no known record of it.[10]

---

[8]   See William Henry Egle, "Names of Foreigners Who Took the Oath of Allegiance in the Province and State of Pennsylvania, 1727-1775, with Foreign Arrivals 1786-1808," *Pennsylvania Archives*, Second Series, Volume 17, Harrisburg, Pennsylvania, E.K. Meyers, State Printer, 1892, page 215. This source is cited in James Sidney Hammond's entry on "The Alwine Line" in Wilbert Jordan (Editor), *Colonial and Revolutionary Families of Pennsylvania—Genealogical and Personal Memoirs*. New Series, Volume XI. New York: Lewis Historical Publishing Co., Inc., 1948, pages 536-558.

[9]   See Charles Glatfelter, *Pastors and People: German Lutheran and Reformed Churches in the Pennsylvania Field, 1717-1793*, The Pennsylvania German Society, 1981, pages 5-8.

[10]   See William J. Hinke's introduction to *Pennsylvania German Pioneers: A Publication of the Original Lists of Arrivals in the Port of Philadelphia From 1727 to 1808*, pages xxxix-xlv (Baltimore, Genealogical Publishing Co., 1980). For further confirmation on this point, see the 1992 edition of *Pennsylvania German Pioneers*, published by Ralph B. Strassburger and edited by William J. Hinke (Camden, ME: Picton Press), Volume II, which contains the facsimiles of all the signatures to the oath of allegiance as well as the oath of abjuration (pages 313-315).

Familie Allwein in Europe

Hans Jacob Allwein's origins were clearly in Europe—as indicated by the presence of his name in the records of the *Pennsylvania German Pioneers*, cited above. The voyage of the St. Andrew to Philadelphia was from Rotterdam, one of the northern ports in Europe, but how he got there (and from where) is still somewhat contested. I discussed the possibilities of which I am aware in the first volume of *Familie Allwein* (pages 6-18), but I believe the best evidence to date suggests that he came from the Lower (or Northern) Palatinate region of Germany. Reference in the Strassberger-Hinke volume mentioned above for the group that Hans Jacob Allwein travelled with was to "Palatines," a part of the historical record that is often overlooked. On the one hand, this might have correctly referred to the region of Hans Jacob Allwein's origins, or it could simply be a general reference to Germans, which was sometimes the case, given that the vast majority of the German-speaking immigrants to Pennsylvania came from the Palatinate.

The "Palatinate" was the name of two little countries in the old German empire, one of which (called the Upper Palatinate) became part of Bavaria and the other (called the Lower Palatinate) is now part of the Rhineland-Pfalz. The latter lies west of the Rhine River south of Bonn, bordering with Belgium, Luxembourg and France to the west. The capital city is Mainz, which is situated on the left bank of the Rhine where it is joined by the River Main. This fertile area has always been known for its agricultural products, especially its wine. The Lower (or northern) Palatinate was the origin of thousands of German immigrants to the American colonies during the 18th century. Hans Jacob Allwein was in all likelihood from this region. In fact, we have reason to believe that Johannes Jacob Allwein originated from the northern (or Lower) Palatinate, specifically from the village of Fürfeld (Bad Kreuznach) in the present-day Federal State of Rheinland-Pfalz, near Mainz. His family may have migrated from the province of Brabant (today divided between Belgium and the Netherlands), and/or had relatives living there (see *Familie Allwein*, volume 1, Chapter 1, pages 10-18).

This view of Hans Jacob Allwein's origins has the benefit of some documentation. In the first volume of *Familie Allwein*, I introduced important evidence indicating that church registers maintained at the Catholic Diocese of Mainz contain entries of the christening (on August 8, 1717) of "Johannes Jakob Alwenz" and "Nikolaus Jakob Alwenz," sons of "Johannes Jacob Alwenz" and his wife from Fürfeld, a village in what is today the Federal State of Rheinland-Pfalz. I presented photographs of the entries (written in Latin) in two sets of church books, from Fürfeld and Freilaubersheim, where these baptisms were recorded and a narrative from what is referred to as "the Schmahl report," a report commissioned by an Allwein family member in the United States. The documentation provided in that report and confirming information obtained from the Diocese of Mainz is sufficient to suggest that Hans Jacob Allwein, immigrant to Pennsylvania, is the same Johannes Jakob Alwens (or Alwentz) from Fürfeld in Germany.

The Schmahl report goes on to suggest that a "Johann Peter Alwentz from the province of *Brabant* (today divided up between Belgium and the Netherlands), later a resident of *Winnweiler* in the northern Palatinate, was a relative of the Alwentz family in Fürfeld." The baptism of a third child, Johannes Petrus (Peter) Alwentz, born to Johannes and Maria Elizabetha Alwentz appears later on May 5, 1720. The baptism of Johannes Peter was witnessed by his uncle Johannes Peter Alwentz (that is, brother to Johannes, the father of Peter, Jacob and Nicolaus) from Winnweiler (a town about 30 kilometers to the south of Fürfeld). [Notice the German Catholic custom of naming children for their godparents.] This Johann Peter Alwenz (or Alwens), a drapery merchant living in Winnweiler, was the son of Johann and Maria Alwens of Lommel in Brabant and brother to Johannes Alwentz, father of Johannes Jakob (Hans Jacob). This lends some credibility to the claim that has been made that earliest origins of the name Allwein probably came from the

Netherlands, where the name may have been spelled as *Alewijn* or *Halewijn* (see above).[11]

In any event, I believe there is sufficient documentation in the Mainz Catholic archives to warrant serious consideration of the view that the Johannes Jacob Alwentz / Alweins listed in the Frei Laubersheim and Fürfeld church books was the same "Hans Jacob Alwine" who immigrated on the ship St. Andrew, which sailed from Rotterdam and arrived at the port of Philadelphia on October 2, 1741, and who settled in Bern Township of what would become Berks County, Pennsylvania. There are several things that are consistent with such a view. I do not pursue the evidence for these claims further here, as it is fully described in volume 1 of *Familie Allwein*. I return to these matters in Chapter 25 of volume 3, where I review past results and present new findings regarding the European origins of Hans Jacob Allwein.

Familie Allwein in Colonial Pennsylvania

Whatever his point of origin, there is little doubt that Johannes (Hans) Jacob Allwein came to America prior to the peak of the German immigration, which began in 1680 and lasted through the middle of the next century.[12] Along with large numbers of other German immigrants he settled in an area that would eventually become Berks County, Pennsylvania, northwest of Philadelphia. Berks County came into being in 1752. Hans Jacob's descendants over the next century would be dispersed largely into an area of southeastern Pennsylvania that would be known as the land of the "Pennsylvania Dutch." Eventually through the 19th and 20th centuries these descendants could be found throughout the United States.

---

[11]   See entry for "James Sidney Hammond" in Wilbert Jordan (Ed.), *Colonial and Revolutionary Families of Pennsylvania—Genealogical and Personal Memoirs*, Vol. 11, New York: Lewis Historical Publishing Co., Inc., 1948, pages 555-556.

[12]   See Aaron Fogelman's *Hopeful Journeys: German Immigration, Settlement, and Political Culture in Colonial America, 1717-1775*, Philadelphia: University of Pennsylvania Press, 1996.

I have already thoroughly discussed what is known about Hans Jacob and Catharina Allwein's settlement in Pennsylvania in the first volume of *Familie Allwein* (see Chapter 1), and I will not repeat that material here, except to summarize the broad outlines of what we know and supplement that with some new information. First, we know that Hans Jacob Allwein settled in Bern Township of what would eventually become Berks County. He is listed among the "taxables" of Bern Township in 1754 soon after the formation of the county.[13] Tax records for all available years between 1767 and 1781 also list him in Bern Township.[14] Bern Township actually existed prior to Berks County as part of Lancaster County. It became part of Berks County when the latter was formed from parts of Philadelphia, Chester and Lancaster Counties in 1752. In the northern part of Berks County, Bern Township contained all of the present-day townships of Bern, Upper Bern (formed in 1789), Penn (formed in 1841), Centre (formed in 1843) and Tilden (formed in 1887).

Second, land records for the Commonwealth of Pennsylvania record several land warrants obtained by Hans Jacob Allwein for land he claimed in Bern Township. In Chapter 1 of *Familie Allwein*, volume 1 (pages 24-31) I reviewed all of the available land warrant information that allowed us to pinpoint the location of Hans Jacob and Catharina's land.[15] Bern Township was later subdivided, and although their property was in Bern Township when they acquired it, the land warrant records indicate that according to more recent

---

[13] Morton L. Montgomery, *Historical and Biographical Annals of Berks County Pennsylvania Embracing a Concise History of the County and a Genealogical and Biographical Record of Representative Families.* Volume I. Chicago: J.H. Beers & Co.

[14] This information was published in "Proprietary and State Tax Lists of the County of Berks, for the Years 1767, 1768, 1779, 1780, 1781, 1784, 1785," *Pennsylvania Archives*, Third Series, Volume 18, edited by William Henry Egle. Harrisburg PA: W.S. Ray, State Printer of Pennsylvania, 1898, pages 81, 108, 199, 318, and 446.

[15] Kenneth D. McCrea, *Pennsylvania Land Applications—Volume 1: East Side Applications, 1765-1769*, Strasburg, Pennsylvania: McCrea Research, Inc., 2002.

demarcations of townships they were located in Upper Bern and
Tilden Townships.

The land where Hans Jacob and Catharina Allwein settled lies
in the foothills of the Blue Mountains in northern Berks County.
The Blue Mountain is a ridge that forms the eastern edge of the
Appalachian mountain range in Pennsylvania, running about
150 miles from the New Jersey border in the northeast to the Big
Gap west of Shippensburg at its southwestern terminus. What is
today known as the Appalachian Trail follows this ridge along the
border of Berks and Schuylkill Counties, and as mentioned above,
Hans Jacob Allwein's land can be located amongst the fertile
farmlands to the south of these mountains, a few miles due east
of Shartlesville, Pennsylvania, a settlement named for the Shartle
family who established an Inn at that location in 1765. The land
to the north of the Allwein property, east of St. Michael's Church
Road, was land held by the St. Michael's Lutheran congregation and
is the present-day location of St. Michael's Lutheran Church and St.
Michael's Union Cemetery (see Chapter 13 of the present volume).

Third, we know that Hans Jacob Allwein died in October of
1781. Estate records for "Jacob Allweins" begin with a document
dated October 22, 1781 filed after Hans Jacob's death by (in the
words of the document) "Catharina Allweins of Bern Township
widow of Jacob Allweins deceased and Philip Smith son-in-law
of the said deceased."[16] Philip Smith was the husband of Mary
Elizabeth (or Elizabeth) the eldest daughter of Hans Jacob and
Catharina. Philip was her second husband whom she married after
the death of her first husband Joseph Obold. This document sets
forth that Catharina Allweins and Philip Smith were administrators
of the estate and had the responsibility (again in the words of
the document) "to make or cause to be made a true and perfect
inventory of all and singular the goods, chattels, rights, and credits,
which were of the said deceased" and to provide an accounting of
the estate within one year. On the tenth day of November, 1781 they
filed an inventory of Hans Jacob's estate consisting of all of his

---

[16]   As I mentioned in *Familie Allwein*, volume 1 (pages 32-33), in colonial
Pennsylvania the original name may have been spelled ALLWEINS.

and his household's personal property. Subsequently on March 7, 1783 they filed an accounting of the estate with the court, and after Catharina's death, Philip filed administrative reports with the Court again on July 3, 1790 and finally on October 14, 1799.

Estate Records of Johannes Jacob Allweins[17]

For family historians, wills and estate records are an important source of information on kinship and the property of the deceased. Even if there was no will filed with the county authorities, often the available estate records can help provide information on a number of things, including heirs, kinship relations, and the property of the household. They also reveal a great deal about the nature of society during the historical period involved and a glimpse into the legal system and inheritance norms that operated in early colonial history. When complemented by other information from additional sources, estate records can help develop a narrative of family history and a fuller appreciation of one's ancestors and family heritage.

When a person has made no legally valid will before death, as was the case with Hans Jacob Allwein, he is said to have "died intestate." This term, *intestate*, is a legal one simply referring to the fact that there was no will available to direct the disposition of property. The absence of a will, however, does not mean there are no records of the estate, because regardless, the court must probate the estate of the deceased, if there is one.

These records mention, in addition to Hans Jacob's wife Catharina Allweins, six surviving heirs to his estate: John and Conrad Allweins (his sons), daughter Mary Elizabeth (and her husband Philip Smith), and daughter Catherine (and her husband Joseph Seyfert). It is in the nature of these records that they provide hardly any information about birth date and/or age of the persons of interest; however, among other things, they do clarify the nature of

---

[17] This section is based on the author's article "The Dower Chest of Johannes Alweins," *Journal of the Berks County Genealogical Society*, Volume 32, number 3, Spring, 2012.

the kinship relationships. They can also verify information about the personal property owned by the deceased.

The following provides a list of the "goods and chattels" from the estate of "Jacob Allweins," appraised down to the pence.[18]

Inventory of Jacob Allweins which was appraised by Hieronymus Hennig and John Shartle (Bern Township 27th October 1781) as follows:

	£	S	P
a cow for	2	10	0
a cow for	2	0	0
Hay for	3	10	0
Hemp, some bound and some not broke yet	2	0	0
some unbroken Flax	0	10	0
Wheelbarrow for	0	7	6
Mattock and Dungfork	0	4	6
Two Flax Breakes	0	1	0
Hog for	1	0	0
Hog	0	15	0
Cow chain	0	2	0
a Bell with a string of iron for	0	4	0
a Sythe for	0	2	0
an Indian cornhoe for	0	3	0
two old Indian cornhoes for	0	1	0
a little Garden hoe for	0	0	9
a Shovel for	0	1	6
a Tub for	0	5	0
a Churn	0	2	0
a Grinding stone	0	2	0
a Watering Pot	0	5	0
a Spade for	0	2	6
Ten pots and a Butter tub for	0	4	0
an Ax for	0	5	0
a large Iron Pot	0	10	0

---

[18]   Inventory for Estate of Jacob Allwein, deceased, Exhibit, Nov. 10th 1781, Berks County Register of Wills and Clerk of the Orphan's Court, Reading, Pennsylvania.

an Iron Pot with a Cover	0	10	0
an Iron Pot with a Cover	0	8	0
a Lime Can for	0	2	6
a large Iron Plate	0	7	6
a Pot hook and Shovel for	0	1	0
a Tea Kettle	0	10	0
a little Pan	0	2	6
a Frying Pan	0	2	6
a Iron and Cucumer plane	0	0	6
a deep Pan	0	3	9
a Cake Pan	0	3	9
a old Coffee Pot	0	0	6
Five Iron Spoons and a Fork	0	5	6
a Copper Kitchen Flask	0	2	0
a Pepper Mill	0	5	0
Nine Trenchers	0	1	0
a large and two smaller Dishes and a little Mug	0	0	9
a Flask	0	5	0
Three Pails	0	2	6
An old Washing tub	0	4	0
two little tubs	0	4	0
an old Pail	0	0	6
a Salt box and a Mealbox	0	1	0
an Oil Flask and a Lamp	0	2	0
a Candlestick	0	1	0
Four Dishes of Pewter	1	4	0
Two Dishes of Pewter	0	15	0
Eleven pewter Plates	1	5	0
Eleven pewter Spoons	0	5	0
One Tea Pot of pewter	0	6	0
Two pewter Cups	0	6	0
Two old pewter Cants	0	2	0
Candle Molds	0	2	6
a Pair of Scales with Weights	0	5	0
a Hammer and a Chisel	0	2	6
a Steelyard with Weights	0	15	0
an Iron	0	3	9
a Heckle	0	12	0
two old Sickles	0	0	6
an old Hatchet and old Witchet	0	1	0

a Glass	0	1	0
a Bowl and a Mug	0	1	0
a Teckfel	0	3	0
a Honepick and a Croe	0	10	0
a Hammer	0	6	0
3 ¼ Yard of Wollen Cloth	0	16	0
Pieces of Deer skins	0	5	0
a Pair of Serspenticles	0	2	0
a Brass Crane	0	1	0
two Razors with a box	0	3	0
a Box with some toels	0	0	6
two Bottels and two Ink Glasses	0	2	6
a Razorstone	0	1	0
a Hand Saw	0	3	0
Four Gimlets	0	1	6
two Augers	0	2	0
two Augers	0	4	6
a Drawknife	0	5	0
three Chisels and a Plane	0	2	0
a Chest out of Wallnut Wood	1	10	0
a Looking Glass	0	2	0
a Chest	0	15	0
a Box with Shoemaker Toels	0	9	0
a pair of Wool Charts	0	2	0
a Sickle a Brush and a little box	0	1	0
a Gun	1	0	0
a Fire Shovel and Tongs	0	4	6
a Stove with Pipe and Foot	5	0	0
five new and two old Shirts	2	2	6
Three Table Cloths and four Towels	0	15	0
Six pair of linen Breeches	0	2	6
a Parcel old linen Cloth	0	2	6
two Coverlets and a Sheet	0	10	0
Three pair of Stockings two pair of Gloves and an Iron cloth	0	2	0
Four Knifes and four Forks	0	5	0
a Table out of Wallnut Wood	0	15	0
a Table	0	15	0
Seven Chairs	0	14	0
an old Chest	0	3	0

Three Sieves	0	6	6
Seven Bee baskets	0	0	6
Five Bake baskets and a Kneading trough	0	3	0
Two old Spinning Wheels and a Reel	0	2	6
Two old spinning wheels	0	1	6
Indian Corn	1	5	0
Two old Baskets	0	1	0
a Feather bed and Strawbag	0	10	0
a Feather Bed with Curtains	2	0	0
a Bedstead	0	5	0
Tow yarn which is spun	0	9	0
two Bags with unclean Flax Seed	0	7	6
Some Buck Wheat	0	5	0
Seven Books	0	10	0
Two old Copper Kettles	0	12	0
a Calve	0	10	0
a Grubbing Hoe	0	5	0
a Cabbage tub	0	2	6
a Hogshead with Vinegar	1	5	0
a Clock	13	0	0

Note: 12 pence make up a shilling and 20 shillings make up a pound.

In some historical periods, the issue of "dower rights" comes up in the probate of a person's estate. In legal terms a "dower" or a "widow's dower" is the portion of a deceased husband's real property allowed to his widow for her lifetime. The meaning of this term is related to that of "dowry," which refers to "the money, goods or estate that a wife brings to her husband at marriage," and the two terms are often used interchangeably.

Dower rights are the rights that a non-owner spouse has in the real property of his or her spouse—a common law that entitles a widow to a portion of her husband's estate in absence of a will. These laws were originally set up at a time when the husband was the only real property owner. And even when there was a will, a widow could typically choose to reject the will of her deceased husband and enforce her dower rights under the law, regardless of provisions in his will.

The provision of dower allowed the widow to provide for herself and any children born during the marriage. In most circumstances, the widow is granted up to one-third interest in her husband's assets. Dower provides a woman with a measure of financial security if her husband dies. In some states, a woman forfeits her right to dower if she becomes the guilty party in an annulment or divorce, usually caused by adultery. In modern times, inheritance rights are more prevalent, making dower laws obsolete.[19]

Even though we may reasonably think of the above list of material goods as belonging to both Hans Jacob and Catharina Allwein, they were principally considered *his* property, not *hers*. However, there is evidence in the estate records for Hans Jacob Allwein that indicates that Catharina "inherited" the necessary economic means of support from the estate of her husband.

We do not have estate records for Catharina Allwein. She appears to have died prior to October of 1799, when Philip Smith filed the final papers in the estate of Hans Jacob Allwein. Some sources indicate that she may have died in 1790.[20] On the other hand, she is listed as receiving a disbursement of more than 115 pounds from Hans Jacob Allwein's estate on July 3, 1790. She is not listed as a household head in the 1790 Federal Census, but she very likely was living in the household of her son John Alwein at that time.[21] We suspect she died sometime between 1790 and 1799.

---

[19]   See http://www.answers.com/topic/dower#ixzz1EVTPrgQ2

[20]   See http://freepages.genealogy.rootsweb.ancestry.com/~stobie/index.htm.

[21]   See *Heads of Families at the First Census of the United States Taken in the Year 1790, Pennsylvania*. Washington, D.C.: Government Printing Office, 1908, page 27. There were five females listed in the household of "John Alwein" in that census enumeraton. We surmise that these were very likely his wife, Eva Christina Alwein, his mother Catharina Allwein, and his three daughters, Catharine, Elizabeth and Magdalena Alwein. See *Familie Allwein*, volume 1 (page 71-72), for a discussion of John Alwein's family.

Exhibit 1—Dower chest of Johannes Alweins, Berks County, Pennsylvania

The Dower Chest

One of the items that may have been on the above list of property is the dower chest shown in the accompanying photograph—a chest belonging to Johannes Alweins. This dower chest may have belonged to Johannes Jacob Allweins, or, if not him, it might have been the property of one of his sons, the 2nd Johannes Alweins in Pennsylvania. The latter may be the more likely of the possibilities. The fact of the matter is that we do not know to whom it belonged, but the name on the chest is relatively clear: JOHANNES ALWEINS.

What do we know about such dower chests? According to *Webster's New Universal Unabridged Dictionary*, a "dower chest" is "a Pennsylvania Dutch hope chest bearing the initials of the owner." In this case it bears the entire name.

The following are excerpts from Dean Fales' book on *American Painted Furniture*.[22] He had this to say about Pennsylvania German furniture:

> Shortly after the founding of Pennsylvania the first German immigrants arrived. In the eighteenth century they came in the thousands, eventually settling in southeastern Pennsylvania. They made their land incredibly rich through their sober industry. Perhaps a compensation for their plain, devoted ways, their spirits sang forth brashly harmonious songs of design and color. Their furniture combined Continental inspiration with more than a whiff of the English on occasion. This, plus their own inventiveness, resulted in an exciting and lively folk art that was truly American. It could be as stylized as it was symbolic, but it was always vibrant. [p. 255]

---

[22]   See the section titled "Pennsylvania German Furniture," Dean A. Fales, Jr., *American Painted Furniture 1660-1880*. New York: E.P. Dutton, 1979, pages 254-273. See also Donald Shelly, *The Fractur Writings or Illuminated Manuscripts of the Pennsylvania Germans*, Allentown, Pennsylvania: Pennsylvania German Folklore Society, 1961

Symbols were rife. The unicorn was the symbol of purity, and the peacock signified resurrection. Fish, living in water, were linked with baptism, while griffins and pelicans represented Christ. All sorts of flowers, animals, and birds had their special connotations. However, it must be borne in mind that decorative symbols can rapidly lose their meanings and become stylized. Thus, the true meaning of a tulip was sometimes little more than a love for the new plant; and six pointed stars had long since become conventional motifs, before masquerading as hex signs on later barns. [p. 256]

Decoration could be done by professionals or by amateurs, by stay-at-homes or by itinerants . . . the daubings could be of many colors and could be glorious indeed. [p. 257]

Frequently, the decorative designs were lightly scribed onto the bare wood before the freehand decoration was applied. Many of these colorful chests were used as dower chests by their owners. [p. 257]

The decorative art on this chest is related to a style of drawing known as Fractur Art, which is something unique to Pennsylvania Germans—it is a style of folk art that involves artistic lettering and drawing to commemorate events and to decorate objects. Common artistic motifs were drawings of birds, flowers and hearts. Fractur drawings were commonly used for birth and baptismal certificates—*Taufscheine*—in which the drawings were made in ink and/or watercolors (see Chapter 11).

Will of Johannes Alweins

In addition to its possible appearance as one of the chests on the above list of property in Johannes Jacob Allweins' estate, it was also likely mentioned in his son's (the 2nd Johannes Alweins—aka: John Alwein (M02-0102)) will and estate records as well. The will of Johannes Alweins, written originally in German, was dated February 21, 1809.[23] The English translation of his will was reproduced in

---

[23]   Will of Johannes Alwein, dated February 21, 1809, Berks County Register of Wills and Clerk of the Orphan's Court, Reading, Pennsylvania.

Familie Allwein, volume 1 (pages 106-110). This will included the following:

> I give and bequeath to my dear wife, Magdelena, two hundred pounds of current money of Pennsylvania, which my executors, to be hereafter named, shall pay to her as here made known; one hundred pounds one half year after my death, and the second hundred pounds one year after my death.

> I give and bequeath to my dear wife, Magdelena, two beds and bedsteads; the cloth and the cloths, and pile of cloth; the flax with the tow; a room stove with what belongs thereto, namely, pipe, doors, and tongs; all of my kitchen utensils, namely iron, copper, tin, wooden, pewter, and earthen utensils; two chests; a spinning wheel, a table, a baking trough; two chairs; the scales. Two cows; two cow chains; two sheep, and the wool that I yet have; two swine and the meat that I yet have; a wood axe; and the books that she had brought to me. All of these bequests she shall have instead of the third share of all of my assets. Besides all of the above named, my wife shall have fifteen bushels of wheat and five bushels of barley.

A codicil to the will, dated October 30, 1809, added the following:[24]

> A codicil to my will that I have made last February Twenty First. In this codicil I bequeath to my wife, Magdelena, besides all of that which I have already bequeathed, as follows:

> First, I bequeath to my beloved wife, Magdelena, all of my cloth; Linen, half linen, and wool, except my clothing; all of my hay and grains; all of my potatoes and the corn; the buckwheat; a barrel cask full of cider; a Heiffer; all of my tow and wool spun yarn; the dried apple schnitz; her saddle; two equal—; the old kitchen

---

[24]   Codicil to the will of Johannes Alwein, dated October 30, 1809, Berks County Register of Wills and Clerk of the Orphan's Court, Reading, Pennsylvania.

cupboard; five bushels of barley; two corn hoes; a spade; a small chest; a spinning wheel; two clothing irons; and a flax hackle.

After his death on February 29, 1816, John Alwein's will was probated and "a true and correct inventory of the goods and effects of John Alwein deceased in this Township of Bern in the County of Berks taken this 2nd day of March A.D. 1816" was submitted to the court. This inventory (not reproduced here) included a number of items explicitly designated as property of the widow, most of which were mentioned in the will. In addition, although not explicitly included among the items bequeathed in his will, on this list was the specific mention of "a dow chest," along with many of the other items of furniture. This may refer to the same dower chest in the photograph above.

For many years, the collector who owned this chest thought that it bore the name "Johanne Salweins" and the connection to the Alweins family was not made until recently. In fact, it appears that the keyhole was in the way, and the person who painted it had to separate the word "Johannes" as "Johanne . . . S," so it seems to read "Johanne Salweins" instead of "Johannes Alweins." It is now believed to be one of the chests owned originally by the Alweins (now ALLWEIN, ALLWINE, ALWINE, or ALWIN) family, but we do not yet know exactly whose chest it was.

The Religious Faith of Familie Allwein

In *Familie* Allwein, volume 1 (pages 35-43), I discussed several strands of thought regarding the religious faith of Hans Jacob and Catharina Allwein. There is a lot known about the religious affiliations of their descendants, but less is known about their own religious affiliations. Some of their descendants were affiliated with the German Reformed Church, some descendants became Mennonites, but most were Roman Catholic. Although I discussed this in the first volume of *Familie Allwein*, I review these various possibilities again here, because some new information has come to light.

One of the early indications we have for the religious affiliation of Hans Jacob and Catharina Allwein was the record of the baptism of their son, John Alwein, in a German Reformed Church. Specifically, we know from *Höhn's Church Records, 1745-1805* that a son was baptized on April 24, 1748 at St. John's Reformed Church in Heidelberg Township (now Lower Heidelberg Township) in Berks County to a "Jacob Alwein and wife."[25] This is often cited as evidence that they were affiliated with the German Reformed tradition, and there are additional facts that are consistent with this possibility. Specifically, John Alwein's first wife, Eva Christina Alwein, and at least one of their children, Johannes Alwein (III), were buried in St. Michael's Reformed Church Cemetery, which is adjacent to the land owned by Hans Jacob Allwein.[26] Moreover, although the eldest son of John Alwein, Philip Alwein, converted to Mennonism (see below), Philip and his wife Sarah Miller, were married in a German Reformed Church in Exeter Township, Berks County (see *Familie Allwein*, volume 1, pages 163-164).[27]

Despite the baptism of Hans Jacob and Catharina's son John Alwein in a German Reformed Church and the connections of his family to this religious faith, the strongest evidence for the religious affiliation of Hans Jacob and Catharina Allwein is their connection to the Roman Catholic tradition. The marriage of Hans Jacob and Catharina's son Conrad Allwein to Catharine Weibel was recorded in the *Goshenhoppen Registers* as taking place on May 16, 1773 at Christian Henrich's house at Sharp Mountain in Albany Township of Berks County.[28] Conrad and Catharine Allwein raised their children in the Catholic faith, and all of their children followed the Catholic

---

[25] The source of this is *Pennsylvania Vital Records from the Pennsylvania Genealogical Magazine and the Pennsylvania Magazine of History and Biography*, Volume I, Baltimore: Genealogical Publishing Co., Inc., 1983.
[26] See Luann Seaman and Betty Seaman, *Saint Michael's Cemetery Burials 1766-1991*. St. Michael's Church and St. Michael's Cemetery, 529 St. Michael's Road, Hamburg, Pennsylvania 19526.
[27] Donna R. Irish, *Pennsylvania German Marriages: Marriages and Marriage Evidence in Pennsylvania German Churches*, Baltimore, Maryland: Genealogical Publishing Company, Inc., 1982, page 77.
[28] *The Goshenhoppen Registers, 1741-1819*, reprinted from the *Records of the American Catholic Historical Society of Philadelphia*, Baltimore, MD: Clearfield Publishers, 2002, page 105.

faith. These facts, coupled with the findings of the Schmahl Report mentioned above regarding the likely baptism of Hans Jacob Allwein in a Catholic parish in Fürfeld village of Fürfeld (Bad Kreuznach) in the present-day Federal State of Rheinland-Pfalz, near Mainz, strongly suggests that Hans Jacob and Catharina Allwein were Catholic. There is additional circumstantial evidence supporting this view.[29]

The Catholic branch of the family, on the other hand, automatically assumes that the immigrant ancestor was Roman Catholic. But here, too, one must be skeptical. Early on, I confronted a volume on the "founding Catholic families of Pennsylvania," called *Catholic Trails West*.[30] This book is a hodgepodge of historical facts; it is not well documented, and I could not verify much of the information it contained. It is a secondary source at its worst. I contacted both authors to try to find out where they got the information they had published on our ancestral family—they could not tell me!

We noted earlier that the eldest son of John Alwein, Philip Alwein, became a Mennonite and many of his descendants lived in the Mennonite communities of Somerset and Cambria Counties in western Pennsylvania (see Chapter 17). This has led some people to believe that Hans Jacob Allwein was born to Mennonite (Swiss Anabaptists) parents. There is very little evidence that this was the case, but there are those who believe that the immigrant ancestor was born to Mennonite parents in the Alsace-Lorraine region of France, who moved to Germany in the early 1700s to escape religious persecution in France, and then emigrated to the Pennsylvania colony from there. The published narrative is as follows:[31]

Hans Jacob Allwein was born April 16, 1719 of a Mennonite family who moved from France (Alsace Lorraine) to Germany

---

[29]   See Duane F. Alwin, *Familie Allwein—An Early History of the Allwein Family in America*. Bloomington, IN: Xlibris Publishing House, 2009, pages 10-18.

[30]   Edmund Adams and Barbara Brady O'Keefe, *Catholic Trails West—The Founding Catholic Families of Pennsylvania*, Baltimore, MD: Gateway Press, Inc., 1989.

[31]   See http://freepages.genealogy.rootsweb.ancestry.com/~stobie/index.htm.

because of religious persecution. The family was granted asylum by the King of Wittgenstein, Germany, and they worked for him while living in Schwarzenau.

There is no documentation provided for any of these claims, and as far as I can tell, someone made up this story. However, if one is inclined to believe that the immigrant ancestor might have descended from families that were involved in the Swiss Anabaptist (Mennonite) movement, it has a certain attraction to it, and for this reason, it tends to be promulgated, despite its questionable veracity.[32] In Chapter 25, I examine this "Mennonite narrative" more closely, but for present purposes suffice it to say that these claims are historically inaccurate and not supported by any factual information.

In making the assumption that our immigrant ancestor was among the members of a group that fled France (Alsace-Lorrain) to Germany, and eventually emigrated to Schwarzenau, Germany, and then to America, they may have confused the Mennonites with the Dunkards (Dunkers, Tunkers or Taufers), a Brethren group known for its trine baptism.[33] Their founder was Alexander Mack, a radical Pietist, who withdrew from the Reformed Church in Germany and in 1700 sought refuge in Schwarzenau, a village in the county of Wittgenstein (Westphalia) in North Rhine-Westphalia, Germany, now incorporated into Kreis Siegen-Wittgenstein. This is in the present-day Federal State of Westfalia in Germany, an area to which many French Protestants (or Hugenauts) fled the Alsace-Lorraine region of France in the early 1700s to escape religious persecution. Presumably, the area was under the rule of a King of Wittgenstein (there may have been more than one King of Wittgenstein). There

---

[32]   Someone has in fact registered the name "Hans Jacob Alwine" with the Statue of Liberty-Ellis Island Foundation, Inc. on their "American Immigrant Wall of Honor [URL:http://www.ellisisland.org] certifying that he came to the United States of America from Schwarzenau, Germany. Of course, there was no United States of America when Hans Jacob Allwein immigrated—he came to a British colony—and the claim that his origins were from Schwarzenau is dubious at best.

[33]   Martin Grove Brumbaugh, *History of the Brethren in Europe and America*. Elgin, IL: Brethren Publishing House, 1899, see chapters 1-4.

may have been some Mennonite groups that sought refuge in Schwarzenau, but little is known about them. According to Sydney Ahlstrom, a religious historian, the community at Schwarzenau grew (along with another one at Marienborn in the Palatinate), and Mack continued to develop his radical brand of religion.[34] Decreasing tolerance of the Dunkards caused the two communities to move. Mack moved his Schwarzenau group to West Friesland in 1720, and from there Mack emigrated to America on September 15, 1729, settling in Germantown, Pennsylvania.[35] The Marienborn group, under the leadership of John Naas, moved to Crefeld (Creyfeld), and this group settled in Germantown even earlier, in 1719.[36] There is a connection of some Mennonite groups to Crefeld, which is where the earliest group of Mennonites who came to Pennsylvania originated from, but that was in 1683, nearly 60 years prior to the emigration of our immigrant ancestor.[37] In short, it is not known if our immigrant ancestor descended from one of these families, since he emigrated to America much later—in 1741.[38] And, of course, if his religious origins were Roman Catholic, as many believe, it is unlikely that he would have come from Schwarzenau, in any event.[39]

On the other hand, if one were seriously interested in the facts about one's possible Mennonite origins, s/he might consider several other things. First, Mennonites came to America in groups and there are certain ships that can be identified as passage for groups of

[34] Sydney E. Ahlstrom, *A Religious History of the American People*, New Haven, CT: Yale University Press, 1972, pages 239-241.

[35] Martin Grove Brumbaugh, *History of the Brethren in Europe and America*. Elgin, IL: Brethren Publishing House, 1899, page 93.

[36] Martin Grove Brumbaugh, *History of the Brethren in Europe and America*. Elgin, IL: Brethren Publishing House, 1899, page 48.

[37] Sydney E. Ahlstrom, *A Religious History of the American People*, New Haven, CT: Yale University Press, 1972, pages 239-241.

[38] *Pennsylvania German Pioneers: A Publication of the Original Lists of Arrivals in the Port of Philadelphia from 1727 to 1808*, Volume I (1927-1775), Picton Press, P.O. Box 1111, Camden, Maine, 1992, pages 303-304.

[39] See Duane F. Alwin, *Familie Allwein—An Early History of the Allwein Family in America*. Bloomington, IN: Xlibris Publishing House, 2009, pages 10-18.

Mennonites. Our immigrant ancestor did not come on one of these ships. In fact, he did not come during the major waves of Mennonite immigration.[40]

Second, one might ask whether there were any records indicating the immigrant family members were affiliated with Mennonite groups after arriving in the Pennsylvania colony. On this score, although there were Mennonites in Berks County, Pennsylvania (where he settled) in 1741, most of the immigrant ancestor's family members were either Catholic or Reformed Germans.

Third, one might ask whether the family name ALLWEIN was linked at all to Mennonite history? In other words, is it a name present in Mennonite groups in the latter part of the 18th century America? Again, on this score, there is little support for the fact that the immigrant ancestor was linked to Mennonite history. One source lists "Philip Alwine" as one of the "first decade Amish residents of Mifflin County."[41] Philip Alwine was the grandson of the immigrant ancestor. This is, however, not independent information, as the author (Stanley Duane Kauffman) infers this from the 1800 Census records. Mifflin County is located in central Pennsylvania, south of Centre County and to the east of Huntingdon County. Union Township is where the towns of Belleville and Kishacoquillas are located. From the 1790s Amish Mennonites settled in this area, and today there are three different Amish groups and at least one Mennonite congregation.

The fact that we find Philip Alwein in Mifflin County as early as 1800 strongly suggests that it was around this time that he *converted* to the Mennonite faith and that he was part of the westward migration of Amish Mennonites at the turn of the 19th century (see *Familie Allwein*, volume 1, chapter 4). As noted earlier, he and his wife Sarah Miller were actually married in a Reformed

---

[40] See Table 4.2 in Aaron Fogelman's *Hopeful Journeys: German Immigration, Settlement, and Political Culture in Colonial America, 1717-1775*. Philadelphia: University of Pennsylvania Press, 1996, pages 104-105.

[41] See Stanley Duane Kauffman, *Mifflin County Amish and Mennonite Story 1791-1991*, Mifflin County Historical Society, 1991.

German Church in Berks County, so it appears that he came into the Mennonite faith, not by birthright, but through conversion. By 1810 Philip and Sarah Alwein had migrated farther west to Somerset County in southwestern Pennsylvania. There is considerable evidence of Mennonite communities in southwestern Pennsylvania in contemporary life, which had their roots in the early 19th century. The Southwestern Pennsylvania Conference (renamed the Allegheny Conference in 1954) included settlements as early as 1780.[42] An early history of Somerset County mentions three Mennonite churches in Conemaugh Township, near Davidsville, one situated in the southern part of the township, one in the west and one in the east. This, in addition to one Amish Mennonite church, located northeast of Davidsville.[43] Today several Mennonite Church congregations are located in Holsopple, Somerset, Davidsville, Blough, Seanor and Johnstown, communities in Somerset and Cambria Counties, Pennsylvania, in the area in which Philip and Sarah Alwein and their descendants settled.[44]

To complicate things even farther, in *Familie Allwein*, volume 1 (pages 42-43), we entertained the possibility that Hans Jacob and Catharina Allwein were members of the Church of the Brethren. According to Michael Lau's extensive compilation on Alwine families in York County, Hans Jacob and Catharina Allwein were apparently christened in March of 1749 at the White Oak Brethren Church in Lancaster County, Pennsylvania.[45] This suggests that whatever their original religious orientations, they were involved with the Brethren faith community at about the age of 30. After further research into this possibility, I have concluded that this is not really based in fact. The names given in the major source

---

[42] See *The American Mennonites: Tracing the Development of the (Old) Mennonite Church*, prepared by the Eastern Pennsylvania Mennonite Church, Ephrata, Pa., 1998.

[43] *History of Bedford, Somerset and Fulton Counties, Pennsylvania*, Chicago: Waterman, Watkins and Co., 1884, page 526.

[44] See C. Nelson Hostetter, *Anabaptist-Mennonites Nationwide USA*. Morgantown, Pa: Mastoff Press, 1997.

[45] See Michael Lau, *Alwine Families of York County, Pennsylvania and Surrounding Areas*, York County Historical Library, 1996-1999, page 29.

on Church of the Brethren baptisms gives the names "Jacob and Margaret Alewein," baptized on August 6 and August 21, 1749, respectively. These appear to be different people, and given the surnames connected with this part of Lancaster County, these were very likely Jacob and Margaret OHLWEIN, not Jacob and Catharina ALLWEIN.[46]

Rather than being a Mennonite or a convert to the Church of the Brethren, it is far more likely that the immigrant ancestor was either of the German Reformed or the Roman Catholic faith. As indicated earlier, however, the best evidence for our immigrant ancestor being Catholic rests instead on information I found in the baptismal records archived at the Diocese of Mainz, in Germany, which suggests he was baptized in a Catholic parish in the village of Fürfeld (Bad Kreuznach) in the present-day Federal State of Rheinland-Pfalz, near Mainz, on August 8, 1717.[47]

Organization of this Volume

As noted above, the remainder of the present volume is published in two parts—largely because of its size. I already noted that volume 2 deals with those Allwein families who settled east of the Allegheny Mountains; volume 3 covers those families living in western Pennsylvania and locations farther west. Part 1 of the present volume contains Chapters 11, 12 and 13; Part 2 contains Chapters 14, 15 and 16, the contents of which are described below.

Chapter 11 focuses on the Allwein families of Lebanon County. It extends the work begun in the earlier chapters of *Familie Allwein* devoted to the Allwein families that settled in Lebanon County at the end of the 19th century.

---

[46]   See Martin Grove Brumbaugh, *A History of the German Baptist Brethren in Europe and America*, Elgin, Illinois: Brethren Publishing House, 1899, page 311.
[47]   See Duane F. Alwin, *Familie Allwein—An Early History of the Allwein Family in America*. Bloomington, IN: Xlibris Publishing House, 2009, pages 10-18.

Chapter 12 covers those Allwein families who settled in Philadelphia County. Philadelphia was the port through which our immigrant ancestor, Hans Jacob Allwein, arrived in America in 1741, although he did not spend much time there. Instead he settled in Bern Township, some 80 miles inland, in what would a decade later become part of Berks County. There were members of the Allwein family who settled in Philadelphia County in the late 1800s and early 1900s. Those who came from Lebanon who were descendants of Philip Allwein used the ALLWEIN spelling. There were also several families in Philadelphia from 1844 through 1930 that used the ALWINE or ALLWINE spelling of the name. Some of these are perhaps descendants of another family that used the ALWINE or ALLWINE spelling, but whose origins are in the Ohlwein families of the region. Others using these renderings of the family name are descendants of John Allwine of Dauphin County, and some are descendants of Conrad Alwine and Samuel Allwine, who settled in the Adams and York County areas of Pennsylvania.

Recall that Hans Jacob and Catharina Allwein settled in Bern Township of Berks County and several of our early records about their children come from Berks County. In Chapter 13 we review the early history of Berks County and some of those early records. In addition, although most of their Berks County descendants moved farther west, there were some Allwein descendants with roots in Lebanon County who were located there at the end of the 1800s and into the early 1900s.

Chapter 14 focuses on several related Allwein and Allwine families of nearby Dauphin and Lancaster Counties. Virtually without exception, Allwein and Allwine residents of these areas of central Pennsylvania during that period were descendants of Conrad and Catharine Allwein (see Chapter 3 of *Familie Allwein*, volume 1). Two of their children specifically—sons Philip Allwein (M03-0405) and John Allwine (M03-0404) did much to establish the Allwein families we find in the three-county area in the late 19th century. Indeed, each of these men did much to help populate the area with the ALLWEIN, ALLWINE and/or ALWINE name in Lebanon, Dauphin and Lancaster Counties. Chapter 11 highlights the descendants who settled in Lebanon County, and Chapter 14 focuses on those living in Dauphin and Lancaster Counties.

Chapter 15 reviews the family histories of those Allwein descendants living in the York and Adams County areas in the late 19th and early 20th centuries. This is an extension of the work in two previous chapters (Chapters 8 and 9) of volume 1 of *Familie Allwein*. Virtually all of these families used the ALWINE or ALLWINE spelling for the family name, but they nonetheless descend from the ALLWEIN family of Lebanon County. Three of Conrad and Catharine (Weibel) Allwein's children migrated to these areas from Lebanon Township at the turn of the 19th century: Maria Magdalena "Mollie" Allwein (1777-1856), who married John Orendorff, along with her brothers, Conrad Alwine II (1783-1846) and Samuel Allwine (1792-1865). In Chapter 15 we focus exclusively on the descendants of Conrad Alwine II and Samuel Allwine, and trace the roots of the families in Adams and York Counties who descended from these men. We discuss the Orendorff family in a later volume, where we discuss related families (see *Familie Allwein*, volume 4).

Chapter 16 covers those families that settled in Blair County (chapter 16). Several Allwein families migrated to Blair County with the opening of Horseshoe Curve and the development of Altoona, and as the Pennsylvania Railroad became a major presence in the region.

This volume also includes an appendix providing a detailed description of the sources of information on which we have based much of the detailed facts about vital events, such as births, marriages, residence, and deaths, as well as an appendix of cemetery abbreviations.

CHAPTER ELEVEN

Allwein Descendants in Lebanon County[48]

Introduction

LEBANON County was formed from parts of Dauphin and Lancaster Counties and was established as a separate county on February 16, 1813. It is situated in the Lebanon Valley in central Pennsylvania, noted for the fertility of its soil and its prosperous farmlands. The Lebanon Valley lies between the Blue Mountains on the north and the Cornwall hills to the south, and stretches from the Schuylkill (pronounced "SKOO-kull") River in the east to the Swatara Creek, west of Hummelstown, in Dauphin County. The land area of the county is approximately 360 square miles, an area once covered by Lebanon Township, the governmental unit of the area established when Lancaster County came into being.[49]

---

[48] Nancy Allwein Nebiker and Patti Keefer Billow have done extensive research on many of the families discussed in this chapter. Anyone interested in following these family lines should consult their work. Their contributions to this and other chapters have provided enormous improvements to the extensiveness and accuracy of the information presented.

[49] Information presented here on the history of Lebanon County relies on the following sources: A. Howry Espenshade, *Pennsylvania Place Names*, Detroit: Gale Research Company, 1969; Hiram H. Shenk and Esther Shenk (Eds.), *Encyclopedia of Pennsylvania*, Harrisburg: National Historical Association, Inc., 1932; Hiram H. Shenk, *A History of the Lebanon Valley in Pennsylvania*, Harrisburg: National Historical Association, Inc., 1930; and William Henry Egle (Ed.), *History of the County of Lebanon in the Commonwealth of Pennsylvania*, Philadelphia: Everts & Peck, 1883.

Lebanon, the city and county-seat of Lebanon County, is located about 66 miles northwest of Philadelphia, 23 miles northeast of Harrisburg, and 25 miles north of Lancaster. Lebanon was settled as early as 1700 by German emigrants. The Borough of Lebanon was laid out by George Steitz, in 1750, and was first called "Steitztown," but its name was changed to Lebanon when it was incorporated on February 20, 1821 and chartered as a city in 1885. The name, Lebanon, comes from the Hebrew word meaning "white mountains," but we do not know what it was about the area that inspired this use.

This chapter focuses on the Allwein families of Lebanon County over seventy years, from about 1870 through to the early 1940s. It extends the work begun in the earlier chapters of *Familie Allwein—An Early History* devoted to the Allwein families that settled in the Lebanon area at the end of the 18th century. Chapter 14 focuses on several related Allwein and Allwine families of nearby Dauphin and Lancaster Counties. Virtually without exception, Allwein and Allwine residents of these areas of central Pennsylvania during that time were descendants of Conrad and Catharine Allwein (see Chapter 3 of *Familie Allwein*, volume 1). Two of their children specifically—sons John Allwine (M03-0404) (see Chapter 6 of *Familie Allwein—An Early History*) and Philip Allwein (M03-0405) (see Chapter 7 of *Familie Allwein—An Early History*) did much to establish the Allwein families we find in the three-county area in the late 19th century. Indeed, each of these men did much to help populate the area with persons having the ALLWEIN and ALLWINE surnames in Lebanon, Dauphin and Lancaster Counties.

The present chapter highlights the descendants of Philip Allwein (M03-0405) who settled in Lebanon County. In chapters 12 and 13 we cover the descendants of Philip Allwein who migrated to Philadelphia and Berks Counties, respectively. As noted above, Chapter 14—which focuses on Dauphin and Lancaster Counties of central Pennsylvania—places an emphasis on the descendants of John Allwine (M03-0404). Depending upon the particular family, the typical spellings of the family name were variously ALLWEIN, ALWEIN, ALLWINE and ALWINE. The majority of Allwein/ Alwein/Allwine/Alwine family members resident in all of these areas were descendants of one or the other of these two men.

The Origins of Lebanon County

Originally part of Lancaster County, Lebanon Township had existed from the time the Commonwealth of Pennsylvania established Lancaster County—in 1729. From early land warrants and surveys in this township, it was early known as Quitopahilla Township—named for the Quitopahilla River (now called the "Quittapahilla Creek": see GNIS—http://geonames.usgs.gov) that flowed within its boundaries—but "Lebanon Township" was the official name given to it when Lancaster County was formed from part of Chester County in May 10, 1729.[50] At that time, Lebanon Township contained most of what we now know as Lebanon County. The township would be later divided into Bethel (May, 1739), Heidelberg (1757) and Annville (1799) Townships, and later it would be subdivided even farther.[51] In March 4, 1785, Dauphin County was formed from the northern townships of Lancaster County, which included Lebanon Township, and thus, from 1785 until Lebanon County was formed in 1813, the Lebanon Township was part of Dauphin County.[52]

On February 13, 1810, the following petition from "divers inhabitants of the Counties of Dauphin, Berks and Lancaster" was submitted to the Senate and House of Representatives of the Commonwealth of Pennsylvania meeting in General Assembly:[53]

> THAT your petitioners labor under great inconvenience by reason of their great distance from the seats of justice of their respective counties, many of them residing upwards of forth miles from

---

[50]   Franklin Ellis and Samuel Evans (Eds.), *History of Lancaster County, Pennsylvania, with Biographical Sketches of Many of Its Pioneers and Prominent Men*. Philadelphia: Everts & Peck, 1883, page 219.

[51]   William Henry Egle (Ed.), *History of the County of Lebanon in the Commonwealth of Pennsylvania*, Philadelphia: Everts & Peck, 1883, pages 128-133.

[52]   William Henry Egle (Ed.), *History of the County of Lebanon in the Commonwealth of Pennsylvania*, Philadelphia: Everts & Peck, 1883, page 111.

[53]   Historical papers of Lancaster County, Historical Society of Pennsylvania, 1300 Locust Street, Philadelphia, Pennsylvania, page 149.

the county-town, which either as suitors, jurors or witnesses, renders their attendance very expensive and burthensome; they therefore humbly pray your honorable body to lay off and erect, by law, a new county within the following bounds, composed of part of Berks, part of Dauphin and part of Lancaster counties; to wit, BEGINNING at the south-east corner of Dauphin county, where it intersects the Berks county line, about four miles from Numan's-town; thence through Lancaster county, to the great road leading from Lebanon to Manheim, where the great road leading from Cornwall furnace intersects the said road; from thence to Snyder's mill on the Conewago creek; thence northerly to Racoon creek, on the Blue Mountain; thence along the said mountain to the middle of a great road leading from Roehrer's-town to Uhler's mill; thence through Bethel, Tulpehoccon and Heidelberg townships, in the county of Berks, to the place of beginning.

YOUR Petitioners beg leave to represent to your honorable body That, altho' the said boundaries compose but a small tract of country, yet it is fertile, populous and wealthy, and will be the means of bringing justice as near to every man's door as in the nature of things is practicable;

AND further That, your petitioners have already raised, by subscription, between six and seven thousand dollars, for the purpose of erecting public buildings, and they hazard little in assuring your honorable body, that they can raise a sufficient sum, by the same means, wholly to erect them, without burthening the inhabitants generally, with a tax for that purpose. Your petitioners, therefore, confidently hope that, as the granting of the prayer of their petition will confer much advantage on them, without injuring any person, and as their request is founded in reason and justice, they will not ask in vain.

YOUR Petitioners further pray your honorable body, to make the Borough of LEBANON the Seat of Justice of the said proposed county, it being the most central part of the same.

AND they will pray etc.

As a result of this petition, Lebanon County eventually came into being on February 16, 1813, and as we noted, was formed from lands that were formerly part of Dauphin and Lancaster Counties. Establishing the boundaries that still exist today, it borders Dauphin County on the north and west, Berks and Schuylkill Counties on the east, and Lancaster County on the south.

Philip Allwein (1781-1855)
Lebanon County, Pennsylvania

There were hundreds of signatories to the above-described petition—some 1,343 in total—and among them was Philip Allwein, a resident of Lebanon Township.[54] Philip Allwein (M03-0405), the son of Conrad and Catharine (Weibel) Allwein (see Chapter 3 of *Familie Allwein*, volume 1), was born in Berks County January 30, 1781. Philip Allwein's parents, Conrad and Catharine (Weibel) Allwein, settled in Lebanon Township in the 1780s, and purchased land there. Conrad Allwein was listed in tax assessments for Lebanon Township, County of Dauphin, for the years 1785, 1786, and 1787, and also appeared in the enumeration of that county in the 1790 Federal Census. As I described in *Familie Allwein*, volume 1, Conrad Allwein was a prominent member of the Roman Catholic faith community in Lebanon and played an important role in the erection of St. Mary's Church dedicated in 1814.

After his parents settled in Lebanon Township, this area was the lifelong residence of Philip Allwein, until his death on December 18, 1855. He purchased a farm in Lebanon Township, an area that would later become North Lebanon Township, and later on he purchased another farm in Bethel Township, where he lived for the remainder of his life. He is listed in the Federal Censuses of Lebanon Township in 1810 and 1820 and in Bethel Township in 1830 through 1850.

Philip Allwein married Barbara Frantz in Lebanon on March 25, 1804, with whom there were ten children. She died during the birth of their tenth child, Jacob Allwein, on April 28, 1826, who also died

---

[54] Historical papers of Lancaster County, Historical Society of Pennsylvania, 1300 Locust Street, Philadelphia, Pennsylvania, page 189.

in infancy. Soon thereafter, in 1827, Philip Allwein remarried to Elizabeth Arentz, and there were eleven children born to this union. Of the 21 children born to Philip Allwein and his two wives, 16 were known to have lived into their adult years, and most of these children remained in the Lebanon area.[55] This chapter is devoted to many of these Allwein descendants living in the area of Lebanon County from the 1870s to the early 1940s.

Lebanon County in the 1870s

In 1870, the population of Lebanon County numbered 34,096. Its population size would double in the next 60 years—the population numbered 67,103 in the 1930 Census.[56] In another 60 years it would nearly double again—in 2004 the population of Lebanon County contained about 125,000 residents.

As in other parts of Pennsylvania and American society in general, the Lebanon County of the 1870s was experiencing a societal transformation from one largely dependent upon subsistence farming to one organized around industrial production. The industrialization of American society was accompanied by the vast movement of families out of the agricultural sector and into cities where production was organized around factories and small firms. Whereas two centuries ago almost three-fourths of children in America lived in two-parent *farm* families, after the Industrial Revolution this began to change rather dramatically. By 1870 about one-half of children lived in such families, and this number would decline to under 30 percent in the 1930s. By contrast, in 1870, slightly less than 40 percent were living in what we now consider the traditional "father breadwinner, mother homemaker" type of *nonfarm* family. The latter, called the "nuclear family" by sociologists, had accounted for hardly more than ten percent

---

[55]   See Chapter 7 of *Familie Allwein—An Early History* (pages 357-363) for a discussion of the life of Philip Allwein and his family.

[56]   Hiram H. Shenk and Esther Shenk (Eds.), *Encyclopedia of Pennsylvania*, Harrisburg: National Historical Association, Inc., 1932, page 299.

of families in the late 1700s, but would eventually become the dominant type of family in the 1930s.[57]

Similar changes have been witnessed by other societies undergoing the shift from agricultural to industrial production, and such historical shifts are related to the numbers of children parents desire to have. Hence, with time, the typical family in the Lebanon area and elsewhere was more likely to be living in the cities and towns and was more likely to have been one with far fewer children than had been the case in earlier times.

At the end of the 19th century, the largest part of the wealth of the County came from the quarries and mines of the vicinity. The iron mines in Cornwall Township about five miles south of the Lebanon Borough, the limestone and brownstone at the base of the mountains to the north, the brick clay, and the iron ore, all contributed to the industrial wealth of Lebanon County. Thus, when it moved from being chiefly an agrarian economy to an industrial one, its main industrial establishments were the furnaces and foundries, rolling mills, steel plants, machine shops, nut and bolt works, and chain works. Lebanon also excelled in shirt, hosiery, paper box, shoe factories, and food, such as the well-known Lebanon bologna.[58] These were the factories and mills in which the 5th and 6th generation Allwein family members would spend their working lives.

Lebanon County Townships

When Lebanon County came into existence, there were six major township divisions taken from Dauphin County—the entire townships of Heidelberg, Bethel, Lebanon, Annville, East Hanover, a large portion of Londonderry, and a small strip of West Hanover

---

[57] Donald J. Hernandez, *America's Children—Resources from Family, Government and the Economy*, New York: Russell Sage Foundation, 1993, pages 101-105.

[58] Hiram H. Shenk and Esther Shenk (Eds.), *Encyclopedia of Pennsylvania*, Harrisburg: National Historical Association, Inc., 1932, page 299.

west of Racoon Creek.[59] Swatara Township was created at the
time of the formation of the County from parts of the existing East
Hanover and Bethel Townships. The main original Townships would
later be further subdivided. Lebanon Township (see present-day map
of the Lebanon area reproduced below in Exhibit 11.1) would be
split into North Lebanon, South Lebanon, Cornwall, West Cornwall,
and North Cornwall Townships, as well as the Borough of Lebanon.
Heidelberg Township would be subdivided into Heidelberg, Mill
Creek and Jackson Townships. Annville Township would be divided
into North Annville and South Annville Townships. Union Township
was created from East Hanover Township in 1842, and Cold Spring
Township in the north was formed from parts of Union and East
Hanover Townships in 1853. Exhibit 11.2 depicts a map of the
area of Lebanon, Pennsylvania, showing the Borough of Lebanon
and present-day townships within the *original* Lebanon Township
boundaries

Lebanon County Atlases

Two important sources of information used in this chapter are the
early Lebanon County atlases. These are valuable for reconstructing
the lives of Allwein families in Lebanon in the latter part of the
19th century. One of these was an 1875 *County Atlas of Lebanon*,
published by F.W. Beers.[60] There was a second atlas, published in
1888 in conjunction with the charter of Lebanon as a city in 1885.[61]
These documents are useful because they provide maps designating
the residences of heads of households (primarily, but not exclusively,
men) and provide indexing by surname.

---

[59] William Henry Egle (Ed.), *History of the County of Lebanon in the
Commonwealth of Pennsylvania*, Philadelphia: Everts & Peck, 1883,
page 58.
[60] F.W. Beers, *County Atlas of Lebanon Pennsylvania from Recent and
Actual Surveys and Records*, Reading & Philadelphia: F.A. Davis, 1875.
[61] Frederick B. Roe, *Atlas of the City of Lebanon, Lebanon County,
Pennsylvania/Compiled, drawn and published from official plans and
actual surveys*. Philadelphia: F.B. Roe, 1888.

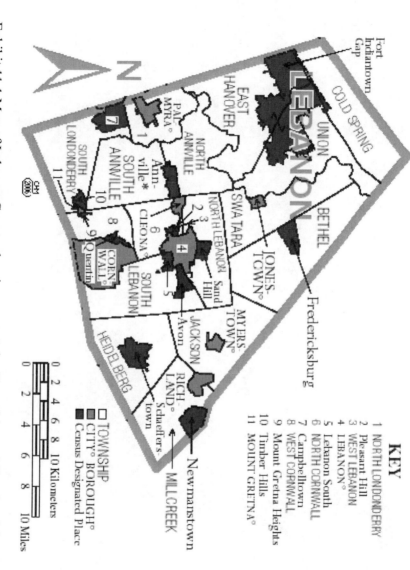

Exhibit 11.1 Map of Lebanon County showing present-day Townships and Populated Areas

KEY

1 NORTH LONDONDERRY
2 Pleasant Hill
3 WEST LEBANON
4 LEBANON°
5 Lebanon South
6 NORTH CORNWALL
7 Campbelltown
8 WEST CORNWALL
9 Mount Gretna Heights
10 Timber Hills
11 MOUNT GRETNA°

☐ TOWNSHIP
▨ CITY° BOROUGH°
■ Census Designated Place

0 2 4 6 8 10 Kilometers

0 2 4 6 8 10 Miles

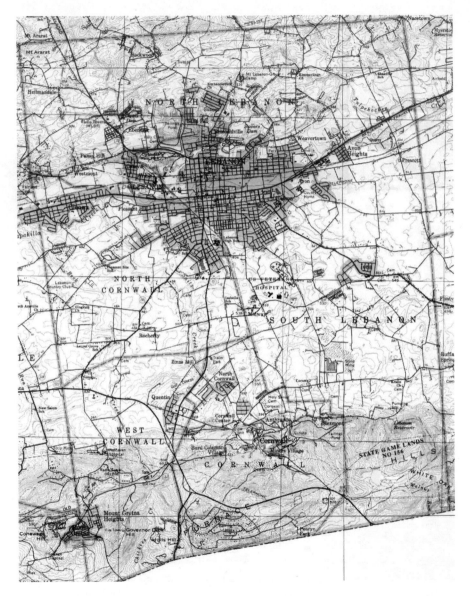

Exhibit 11.2 Map of the area of Lebanon, Pennsylvania, showing the Borough of Lebanon and present-day townships within the original Lebanon Township boundaries

Using the maps contained in these atlases make it possible to recognize there were three main clusters of Allwein families living in Lebanon County toward the end of the 19th and beginning of the 20th centuries: (1) within the Borough of Lebanon; (2) the townships—North Lebanon and Bethel Townships—on the northern perimeter of Lebanon Borough, and (3) the townships farther to the northwest, including principally Union, Swatara and East Hanover Townshps.

With regard to the first location, from about 1840 onward many Allwein families were living within the Borough of Lebanon, specifically in the 5th Ward. This is an area that Philip Allwein also had connections to, in that this is where he built his retirement home in the Borough—at Main and Mifflin Streets—although he never actually lived there. As shown in the 1875 *County Atlas of Lebanon* specifically, there is a cluster around 9th and Mifflin street where John Allwein, Sr., had his carriage shop. John Sr. lived across the street from his carriage shop, and there are others with addresses on 9th street: John Allwein, Jr., H.A. Allwein, V.H. Allwein, and Aaron Allwein. Augustus, son of John Allwein, lived a few blocks to the north and west of his father's shop location. Joseph B. Allwein lived on Spruce street, and there were several Allwein families with addresses on Lehman street: Mrs. Allwein (wife of Samuel Allwein) and Frank M. Allwein. On Church between 10th and 11th was located the residence and carpenter's shop of John Adam Allwein (see Exhibit 11.11 below). I reference these maps where they are relevant in the discussion of each of the Allwein families in Lebanon during this period.

With regard to the second location mentioned above, clusters of Allwein families can be found in parts of North Lebanon Township and southern parts of Bethel Township. This is the area where Philip Allwein originally settled, and it is where several Allwein descendants can be located in the mid 1870s. There were several Allwein families living in close proximity—brothers Edward Allwein, John Allwein, and William Allwein, all owned farms in this area (see Exhibit 11.22 below), in addition to William's son Isaac Allwein, and the widow of Philip Allwein (the younger, b. 1819, d. 1856). The third location, the upper reaches of the township, were settled later, and eventually Samuel Allwine, the son of John

Allwine of Dauphin County (see Chapter 6 of *Familie Allwein—An Early History*, pages 293-294), settled there.

Joseph B. Allwein (1834-1922)
Lebanon, Pennsylvania

We begin the narrative of the descendants of Philip and Barbara (Frantz) Allwein with Joseph B. Allwein (M05-0405-0301), a member of the fifth generation of Allwein descendants in Pennsylvania.[62] He was a lifelong resident of Lebanon County. Strangely, he is not listed in Jerome Allwein's *Genealogy of the Allwein-Arnold Families*. His father was Joseph Allwein (1810-1873), the oldest surviving son of Philip and Barbara (Frantz) Allwein. As it turns out, Joseph B. Allwein was born out of wedlock and raised by his aunts and uncles. Thus, his lacking a "legitimate" parentage may have kept him out of the Allwein *Genealogy*, although we do not know that for sure.

Of Joseph Allwein, the elder (Joseph B. Allwein's father), the Jerome Allwein *Genealogy* had this to say:

> Joseph, son of Philip and Barbara (Frantz) Allwein was born on his father's farm March 6, 1810. He learned the trade of tanner. He operated a tannery at Lebanon, Pa. for some time but owing to financial difficulties was obliged to close out. His father Philip rendered assistance, taking over the stock of Leather etc. on hand and adjusting the claims of his creditors. After this Joseph went to Johnstown, Pa. where he started in business again, operating a boat line, known as "Bingham's Line" from Johnstown to Pittsburg, Pa. He was never married and died at Johnstown in 1873.[63]

We cannot locate Joseph Allwein in the 1850 Federal Census, and it may well be that as a boatman his transience may have

---

[62] Note that for every Allwein family descendant mentioned in this book, I supply a "code number," described in *Familie Allwein*, volume 1 (page 569), to uniquely identify each individual.

[63] Jerome Allwein, *Genealogy of the Allwein-Arnold Families*, Philadelphia, Pa., 1902, pages 26-27.

caused him to escape the notice of the Census enumerators. The 1860 and 1870 Federal Census records for Conemaugh Borough, Cambria County, Pennsylvania, indicate the presence of "Joseph Alwine" working as a saloonkeeper in the 2nd ward of the Borough of Conemaugh.[64] In the 1870 enumeration, Joseph Alwine (age 60) appears with John Alwine (age 16), who may have been a son, but at this point we do not know his exact origins, or what became of him. Joseph Alwine is also listed in an 1869 City Directory for the Johnstown area in Conemaugh Borough, again as a saloonkeeper, on Portage Street.[65] There is no Conemaugh Borough today, since after the flood of 1889, Johnstown incorporated many of its surrounding boroughs, and Conemaugh Borough became the 9th and 10th wards of what is present-day Johnstown.

There was a Bingham's Line, owned by William Bingham, that operated a canal boat line between Johnstown and Pittsburgh, Pennsylvania in the 1840s, but we have not been able to establish Joseph Allwein's connection to it.[66] He may likely have been employed as a boatman with this firm.

Joseph B. Allwein was born January 25, 1834 in North Lebanon Township, Lebanon County, Pa.[67] From all indications he was conceived out of wedlock, as I noted earlier, the son of Joseph

---

[64] *Eighth Census of the United States* (1860), *Inhabitants of Conemaugh Borough, Cambria County, Pennsylvania*, page 23, and *Ninth Census of the United States* (1870), *Inhabitants of Conemaugh Borough, Cambria County*, page 170.

[65] George T. Swank, *General and Business Directory of Johnstown Including Conemaugh, Cambria, Millville, Woodvale, Coopersdale, East Conemaugh, Franklin and Prospect*, 1869.

[66] There are a number of sources that mention Bingham's Line. See the following:

http://www.pghbridges.com/articles/canals/canal_history_wilson.htm
http://www.pghbridges.com/articles/canals/canal_history_boucher.htm

[67] This and other information contained here is based on reports by Joseph B. Allwein and his wife Angeline Eisenhauer Allwein to the Bureau of Pensions, U.S. Department of the Interior. These records are preserved at the National Archives and Records Administration (NARA), Washington, D.C.

Allwein and Anne Beber. If this were the case, given the social norms of the time, it would have likely brought about a marriage between the parents, unless there was a reason to prevent this from happening. There is no evidence that such a marriage took place, and we have no knowledge of the circumstances that prevented it.

The earliest *public* record of Joseph B. Allwein's existence is the 1850 Federal Census of North Lebanon Township, where he is listed in the household of Philip and Catharine "Alwine," his uncle and aunt.[68] That record contains the following household listing:

Philip Alwine (Philip Allwein, M04-0405-07), age 30, farmer
Catharine Alwine, age 30
Maria Alwine (Mary Allwein, F05-0405-0701), age 9
Jared Alwine (Jared Allwein, M05-0405-0702), age 3
Sarah Alwine (Sarah Allwein, F05-0405-0703), age 2
Joseph Alwine (Joseph B. Allwein, M05-0405-0301), age 16, labourer

Philip Alwine (or Allwein) (M04-0405-07) (b. May 6, 1819) was the son of Philip and Barbara (Frantz) Allwein of Lebanon, Pennsylvania, and thus, the younger brother of Joseph Allwein, father of Joseph B. Allwein. Philip's wife Catherine (b. January 16, 1819) was the daughter of Peter and Margaret Arnold.[69] (See the discussion of Philip and Catherine Allwein in Chapter 7 of *Familie Allwein*, volume 1, pages 402-403, as well as later in the present chapter).

The report of Joseph B. Allwein's age in the above Federal Census document is consistent with the birth date given in the NARA pension records. Despite his residence with Philip and Catharine Alwine, it was clear given their ages, he was not their child.

---

[68]   *Seventh Census of the United States* (1850), *Inhabitants of North Lebanon Township, Lebanon County, Pennsylvania*, page 151.
[69]   Jerome Allwein's *Genealogy of the Allwein-Arnold Families*, Philadelphia, Pa., 1902, pages 29-30.

When I began the search for Joseph B. Allwein's parentage there was initially no clear indication of it in the available materials. Initially, it seemed natural to consider the possibility that he was born to Philip Allwein and his second wife, Elizabeth (b. March 4, 1807), daughter of George and Rebecca Arentz. They married in 1827 and eleven children were born to them between 1828 and 1849. This did not seem likely, however, given the thoroughness with which Jerome Allwein's *Genealogy of the Allwein-Arnold Family* treated the offspring of Philip Allwein, and given the birthdates recorded for those children. If the information regarding Joseph B. Allwein's date of birth—January 25, 1834—was accurate, it made no sense that he was their son, given the birth of their son George Elijah Allwein, born November 3, 1833.[70]

Through some further research, however, a baptismal certificate surfaced.[71] This record indicated the following:

1) Joseph was born out of wedlock (*infana ex matrimonis*);
2) Joseph was born on January 25 (*viginti quinta Januarii*), 1834;
3) The parents were Joseph Allwein and Anne Beber;
4) Joseph was baptized on March 9 (*nona Martii*), 1834;
5) The baptism was witnessed by (*levantes*) Joseph Beber.

In the priest's Latinized record, Joseph's name is *not* followed by the phrase "*filius legitimus*"—"legitimate son"—as would be typical for an infant boy whose parents were married, which further suggests that he was born out of wedlock (or at least to a marriage not recognized by the Catholic Church). Finally, the baptismal record suggests that a relative of Anne Beber was the "godfather" of Joseph—perhaps a father, an uncle or a brother. It is logical to surmise, the middle initial B in Joseph's name may stand for Beber. I was curious about the surname "Beber" and tried to locate such

---

[70] Jerome Allwein's *Genealogy of the Allwein-Arnold Families*, Philadelphia, Pa., 1902, pages 10-13.
[71] This record was obtained by Nancy Allwein Nebiker from the Assumption of Blessed Virgin Mary Church in Lebanon, and a copy was forwarded to the author, June 20, 2003.

a family in the area. I found several Beber families in the 1840
Federal Census, but none in Lebanon County—the nearest locations
were Berks and Union Counties—so there is not much to go on with
regard to his mother's family origins. In any event, we concluded
that the line of descent linking Joseph B. Allwein (M05-0405-0301)
to the Johannes Jacob and Catharina Allwein, progenitors of the
Allwein family in colonial Pennsylvania, is as follows:

Generation 1: Johannes Jacob and Catharina Allwein—Berks County, Pa.
Generation 2: Conrad and Catharine (Weibel) Allwein—Dauphin County, Pa.
Generation 3: Philip and Barbara (Frantz) Allwein—Lebanon County, Pa.
Generation 4: Joseph Allwein and Anne Beber—Lebanon County, Pa.
Generation 5: Joseph B. and Angeline (Eisenhauer) Allwein—Lebanon County, Pa.

As noted above, Joseph B. Allwein was living in the household
of his uncle and aunt, Philip and Catharine Allwein, at the time of
the 1850 Federal Census. Philip Allwein died October 7, 1856, and
Joseph B. Allwein then went to live with another family, his uncle
John Edward Allwein (b. April 27, 1828) and his wife, Elizabeth
(Arnold) Allwein, who lived in Bethel Township. He is listed with
this family in Federal Census records for 1860 and 1870.[72]

During the Civil War, at the age of 28, Joseph B. Allwein
enlisted in the Union Army in Philadelphia on October 22, 1862. He
served as a private in the Light Battery H in the 3rd Regiment (Heavy
Artillery) of Pennsylvania Volunteers for nearly three years.[73] Among
other things, this regiment participated in the Battle of Gettysburg.
He was honorably discharged on July 25, 1865.[74]

---

[72] *Eighth Census of the United States* (1860), *Inhabitants of Bethel
Township, Lebanon County, Pennsylvania*, page 10; *Ninth Census of the
United States* (1870), *Inhabitants of Bethel Township, Lebanon County,
Pennsylvania*, page 13. There is some question regarding the accuracy of
the 1860 Census report.

[73] Samuel P. Bates, *History of Pennsylvania Volunteers 1861-65*, edited
by Janet Hewett, Wilmington NC: Broadfoot Publishing Co., 1994,
Volume 8, page 738.

[74] Civil War pension records for Joseph B. Allwein, National Archives
and Records Administration, Washington, D.C.

Exhibit 11.3 Reproduction of photograph taken of Joseph B. Allwein in his Civil War uniform (circa 1865) (contributed by Nancy Allwein Nebiker)

Joseph B. Allwein married Angeline Eisenhauer on March 23, 1876. Angeline Eisenhauer was born December 13, 1854 in Lickdale, Lebanon County, just to the north of the Borough of Lebanon.[75] The marriage was performed by Rev. A.F. Kuhlman at St. Mary's Church in Lebanon, Pa. Together they had the following eight children, six of whom survived to adulthood:[76]

Eugene Daniel Allwein (M06-0405-0301-01), b. July 8, 1876, d. October 15, 1969 (SM), unmarried

Raymond Martin Allwein (M06-0405-0301-02), b. November 19, 1879, d. July 16, 1969 (BW), m. (1) (October 6, 1904) Elsie M. Irey (b. January 1878, d. January 28, 1944), (2) Olive I. Hess (b. October 14, 1887, d. January 2, 1959)[77]

Monica Ellen Allwein (F06-0405-0301-03), b. April 2, 1882, d. November 12, 1886 (SM)[78]

Emma Arabella Allwein (F06-0405-0301-04), b. September 19, 1883, d. November 6, 1954 (CE), m. (January 21, 1908) George Albert Raub (b. March 1, 1882, d. February 25, 1971)

Joseph Ignatious Allwein (M06-0405-0301-05), b. May 21, 1887, d. March 15, 1959 (ML), m. (April 12, 1920) Anna Houtz (nee Reifsnyder) (b. 1874, d. January 11, 1936)

Mary M. Allwein (F06-0405-0301-06), b. July 9, 1890, d. December 29, 1954 (HC), m. (January 20, 1910) William Peter Wentling (b. October 11, 1890, d. September 19, 1959)

Charles A. Allwein (M06-0405-0301-07), b. May 13, 1892, d. December 4, 1892

---

[75] Civil War pension records for Joseph B. Allwein, National Archives and Records Administration, Washington, D.C.

[76] Civil War pension records for Joseph B. Allwein, National Archives and Records Administration, Washington, D.C. Some information for Eugene Daniel Allwein, Raymond Martin Allwein and Joseph Ignatious Allwein was obtained from their draft registration cards, obtained from Ancestry.com.

[77] Additional information on Raymond Martin Allwein was obtained from the Social Security Death Index and the California Death Index, 1940-1997. Ancestry.com.

[78] Following my practice throughout this book, the names of children mentioned here who did not survive to adulthood are given in *italics*.

Christina Maria Allwein (F06-0405-0301-08), b. December 16, 1894, d. April 17, 1984 (SM), m. (September 9, 1913) Stephen Benedict Gress (b. August 31, 1896, d. February 13, 1957)[79]

Joseph and Angeline Allwein are listed, along with their two children Eugene (age 3) and Raymond (age 6 mos.), in the 1880 Census living in the 5th Ward of Lebanon. Their ages are given as 42 and 30 respectively, and Joseph's occupation is given as shoemaker.[80] Joseph and Angeline Allwein resided in Lebanon for the remainder of their lives, as indicated by later Federal Census records, but most of their children moved to other places.[81]

Both the 1875 *County Atlas of Lebanon* and the 1888 *Atlas of Lebanon County* list the residence of "Jos. Allwein" on Spruce Street between Lehman and Monument streets, across the street to the east from the Soldier's Monument Park (see the extract of the 1875 map in Exhibit 11.5 and the extract of the 1888 map in Exhibit 11.23).[82] This is where the residence of Joseph B. Allwein was located for many years, as documented in census reports cited above.

The following six Allwein family residences can be found on this map, reading from the top down, beginning on the lefthand side (spelling as given on the map): P. Allwine, H.A. Allwein, Dr. V.H. Allwein, H.A. Allwein (this is H.M. Allwein), A. Allwein, and Joseph B. Allwein. Notice that on this map there is a listing of the

---

[79] Obituary in the *Lebanon Daily News*, Lebanon, Pennsylvania, Thursday Evening, February 14, 1957.
[80] *Tenth Census of the United States* (1880), *Inhabitants of the 5th Ward, Lebanon Township, Lebanon County, Pennsylvania*, page 329D.
[81] *Twelfth Census of the United States* (1900), *Inhabitants of the 5th Ward, Lebanon City, Lebanon County, Pennsylvania*, E.D. No. 129, page 284A; *Thirteenth Census of the United States* (1910), *Inhabitants of the 5th Ward, Lebanon City, Lebanon County, Pennsylvania*, E.D. No. 155, page 220A; *Fourteenth Census of the United States* (1920), *Inhabitants of the 5th Ward, Lebanon City, Lebanon County, Pennsylvania*, E.D. No. 174, page 253B.
[82] F.W. Beers, *County Atlas of Lebanon Pennsylvania from Recent and Actual Surveys and Records*, Reading & Philadelphia: F.A. Davis, 1875, page 48.

Exhibit 11.4 Reproduction of photograph of Joseph B. Allwein, Lebanon Borough, circa 1875 (contributed by Patti Keefer Billow)

residence of "H.A. Allwein" on Eighth Street between Lehman and Monument streets, across the street to the west from the Soldier's Monument Park (see map in Exhibit 11.5).[83] This probably should be "H.M. Allwein" for Henry Mars Allwein, a cousin of Joseph B. Allwein. The 1888 map gives this same location for "H.M. Allwein." We return to a presentation of information on Henry M. Allwein later on in this chapter. Notice that in the 1888 map (see below) there is also a separate listing of "H.A. Allwein" at Ninth Street and Mifflin (this is John Henry Allwein, son of Philip and Elizabeth (Arentz) Allwein, who went by the name Henry A. Allwein).

Following his retirement, Joseph B. Allwein received a pension for his Civil War service, under the Pension Acts of June 27, 1890 and May 9, 1900. He initially filed an application for a pension on July 29, 1890 at which time he was living in the Borough of Lebanon. He listed his occupation as carpenter. His initial application was witnessed by Henry M. Allwein and Henry A. Allwein, who were his relatives (a cousin and uncle, respectively). Further information on his claim was filed February 29, 1892, at which time George Hubler and John M. Allwein (a cousin) witnessed his submission. In addition, affidavits were filed by George Arnold (age 65) and Edward Allwein (age 67) (an uncle) both of Lebanon, indicating they had known Joseph Allwein from boyhood where they attended the same Sunday school and Church. They noted that they were intimate friends with Joseph Allwein and that he was "a man of good habits and a first class citizen." Finally, on July 21, 1903 he made an application for an increase to his pension, a claim that was witnessed by F.M. Allwein (a cousin), and Daniel W. Brandt.[84]

In the 1900 Federal Census enumeration of the Borough of Lebanon, most of their children were still at home. The 1900 Census listing is as follows: Joseph B. Allwein (age 66), Angeline

---

[83] F.W. Beers, *County Atlas of Lebanon Pennsylvania from Recent and Actual Surveys and Records*, Reading & Philadelphia: F.A. Davis, 1875, page 48.

[84] Civil War pension records for Joseph B. Allwein, National Archives and Records Administration, Washington, D.C.

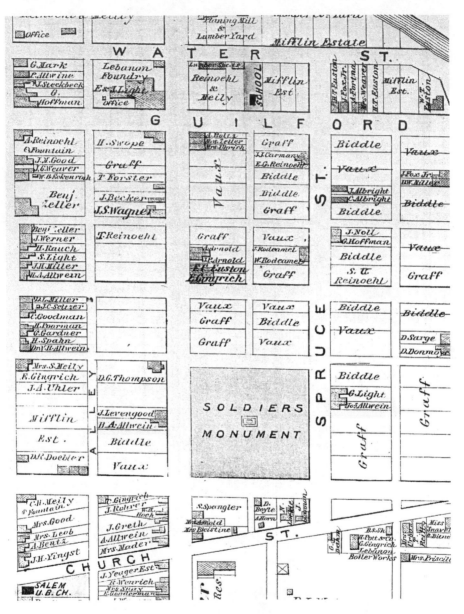

Exhibit 11.5 Extract of 1875 map of Lebanon Borough of area surrounding the Soldier's Monument Park

C. Allwein (age 47), Eugene Allwein (age 23), Emily (or Emma) Allwein (age 17), Joseph Allwein (age 13), Mary Allwein (age 9), and Christine Allwein (age 5). At that time, Raymond Allwein was living elsewhere.

In the 1910 Federal Census, two children were living at home—Joseph Allwein (age 23) and Christine Allwein (age 15). By that time, Emma A. Allwein was married to George Albert Raub, and they lived in Lancaster County, Pennsylvania; Mary M. Allwein was married to William Peter Wentling and they lived in Lebanon.

In the 1920 Federal Census report, Joseph B. and Angeline Allwein were living with their two sons, Eugene Allwein and Joseph Allwein. Eugene Allwein (age 42) owned his own tailor shop, and Joseph Allwein (age 32) was a waiter in a restaurant.[85] By that time, Christina Maria Allwein was married to Stephen B. Gress and they lived in Lebanon.

Joseph B. Allwein died May 16, 1922 at the age of 88, in his home at 420 ½ Spruce Street, Lebanon, Pennsylvania, where he had lived for many years. He is buried at St. Mary's Catholic Cemetery in Lebanon Pa.[86] His widow, Angeline Allwein filed for a Widow's Pension on July 3, 1922 shortly after his death.[87] She died in January 3, 1927 and is buried beside her husband in St. Mary's Catholic Cemetery (see Exhibit 11.6).

---

[85]   *Twelfth Census of the United States* (1900), *Inhabitants of the 5th Ward, Lebanon City, Lebanon County, Pennsylvania*, E.D. No. 129, page 284A; *Thirteenth Census of the United States* (1910), *Inhabitants of the 5th Ward, Lebanon City, Lebanon County, Pennsylvania*, E.D. No. 155, page 220A; *Fourteenth Census of the United States* (1920), *Inhabitants of the 5th Ward, Lebanon City, Lebanon County, Pennsylvania*, E.D. No. 174, page 253B.

[86]   Obituary from the *Lebanon Semi-Weekly News*, Lebanon, Pennsylvania, May 18, 1922.

[87]   Civil War pension records for Joseph B. Allwein, National Archives and Records Administration, Washington, D.C.

Exhibit 11.6 Gravestone for Joseph B. and Angeline C. Allwein—St. Mary's Cemetery, Lebanon, Pennsylvania

Eugene Daniel Allwein (1876-1969)
Borough of York, Pennsylvania

Eugene Daniel Allwein (M06-0405-0301-01), eldest son of Joseph B. and Angeline (Eisenhauer) Allwein, was born July 8, 1876 in Lebanon, Pennsylvania. The lineage for Eugene Daniel Allwein connecting him to the Johannes Jacob and Catharina Allwein, progenitors of the Allwein family in colonial Pennsylvania, is as follows:

Generation 1: Johannes Jacob and Catharina Allwein—Berks County, Pa.
Generation 2: Conrad and Catharine (Weibel) Allwein—Dauphin County, Pa.
Generation 3: Philip and Barbara (Frantz) Allwein—Lebanon County, Pa.
Generation 4: Joseph Allwein and Anne Beber—Lebanon County, Pa.
Generation 5: Joseph B. and Angeline (Eisenhauer) Allwein—Lebanon County, Pa.
Generation 6: Eugene Daniel Allwein—York County, Pa.

Eugene Allwein lived in Lebanon with his parents during his early adulthood.[88] The 1920 Federal Census indicates that he operated his own tailor shop. He moved to York, Pennsylvania, where he is listed as a tailor in a dry cleaning business in the 1930 Federal Census.[89] His name appears in York city directories from 1931 through 1943, most of this time working for the Oliver Cleaners, Tailors and Dyers Company and living at 634 East Philadelphia Street.[90] As far as we know, he did not marry. He died October 15, 1969 and is buried in St. Mary's Cemetery (SM) in Lebanon.

---

[88]   *Twelfth Census of the United States* (1900), *Inhabitants of the 5th Ward, Lebanon City, Lebanon County, Pennsylvania*, E.D. No. 129, page 284A; *Thirteenth Census of the United States* (1910), *Inhabitants of the 5th Ward, Lebanon City, Lebanon County, Pennsylvania*, E.D. No. 155, page 220A; *Fourteenth Census of the United States* (1920), *Inhabitants of the 5th Ward, Lebanon City, Lebanon County, Pennsylvania*, E.D. No. 174, page 253B.
[89]   *Fifteenth Census of the United States* (1930), *Inhabitants of City of York, York County, Pennsylvania*, E.D. No. 99, page 81B.
[90]   *Polk's York Pennsylvania City Directory*, vol 18 (1931-32), vol 19 (1933-34), vol 20 (1935-36), vol 21 (1937-38), vol 22 (1939-40), vol 23 (1942), and vol 24 (1943).

Exhibit 11.7 Gravestone for Eugene D. Allwein—St. Mary's Cemetery, Lebanon, Pennsylvania

Raymond Martin Allwein (1879-1969)
Lebanon, Pennsylvania and Oakland, California

Raymond Martin Allwein (M06-0405-0301-02), second son of Joseph B. and Angeline (Eisenhauer) Allwein was born November 19, 1879 in Lebanon, Pennsylvania. The line of descent connecting Raymond Martin Allwein to Johannes Jacob and Catharina Allwein, progenitors of the Allwein family in colonial Pennsylvania, is as follows:

Generation 1: Johannes Jacob and Catharina Allwein—Berks County, Pa.
Generation 2: Conrad and Catharine (Weibel) Allwein—Dauphin County, Pa.
Generation 3: Philip and Barbara (Frantz) Allwein—Lebanon County, Pa.
Generation 4: Joseph Allwein and Anne Beber—Lebanon County, Pa.
Generation 5: Joseph B. and Angeline (Eisenhauer) Allwein—Lebanon County, Pa.
Generation 6: Raymond Martin and Elsie M. (Irey) [and Olive I. (Hess)]
    Allwein—Lebanon County, Pa. and Oakland, California

Raymond Martin Allwein married Elsie M. Irey, daughter of George and Abbie Irey, on October 6, 1904 in Lebanon and they had five children as follows:[91]

Signa May Allwein (F07-0405-0301-0201), b. April 17, 1905, d. July 1, 1990 (AG), m. Alfred Edmund Field (b. August 11, 1901, d. July 23, 1993)

George Irey Allwein (M07-0405-0301-0202), b. October 22, 1906, d. September 11, 1975, m. Beatrice A. Auclair (b. July 19, 1907, d. March 5, 1997)

Robert H. Allwein, (M07-0405-0301-0203), b. est. 1908, d. November 7, 1913 (ML)

Dorothy I. Allwein (F07-0405-0301-0204), b. March 2, 1910, d. November 15, 1967 (ML), m. (October 5, 1928) Robert W. Emerich (b. est. 1907, d. April 22, 1963)[92]

---

[91] The first four of these children are listed in the Federal Census report for 1910. See *Thirteenth Census of the United States* (1910), *Inhabitants of Lebanon Ward 5, Lebanon County, Pennsylvania*, E.D. No. 155, page 223B.
[92] Marriage announcement from the *Lebanon Daily News*, Lebanon, Pennsylvania, Monday Evening, October 8, 1928; Obituaries for Robert W. Emerich and Dorothy I. Emerich from the *Lebanon Daily News*, Lebanon, Pennsylvania, Tuesday Evening, April 23, 1963 and Friday, November 17, 1967.

Joseph B. Allwein (M07-0405-0301-0205) b. est. 1913, d. March 8, 1913 (ML)

This marriage dissolved, perhaps in part under the pressure of the tragic deaths of two children in 1913—young Joseph Allwein died of measles and Robert Allwein of diphtheria. Elsie Allwein was granted a divorce from Raymond Allwein in January of 1919 on the grounds of desertion.[93] The two oldest children—Signa May Allwein and George Irey Allwein—were placed in an orphanage in Jonestown, Pennsylvania.[94] Dorothy Allwein remained with her mother.

Raymond M. Allwein remarried to Olive Irene Hess in Lebanon, although to date we have not found the marriage record. The following children were born to this marriage:[95]

Pauline Allwein (F07-0405-0301-0206), b. February 15, 1917, d. February 23, 2011, m. (1951) Paul Vincent Bennett (b. February 4, 1918, d. March 29, 2007)

Darrell L. Allwein (M07-0405-0301-0207), b. June 27, 1918, d. July 28, 1999, m. (1) (1940) Darlene Ellen Hutchins (b. September 20, 1920, d. October 26, 2009 (MF)), (2) (May 29, 1976) Margaret Allene Oakes (nee Palmer) (b. April 3, 1931, d. July 16, 2009)

Raymond Allwein (M07-0405-0301-0208), b. est. 1922, d. December 15, 1928

In December 1928, Raymond Martin and Olive Allwein moved their family from Pennsylvania to Oakland, California.

---

[93]   See divorce notice in the *Lebanon Daily News*, Lebanon, Pennsylvania, Thursday Evening, January 9, 1919.

[94]   See *One Hundred Years of History—The Church Home, 1881-1981*, a document on the Jonestown Lutheran Church Home compiled by Evelyn L. Isele. This document was obtained from Nancy Allwein Nebiker, January 5, 2010.

[95]   Obituary for Pauline Allwein Bennett obtained from the *Tooele Transcript Bulletin Online*, March 3, 2011. See http://transcriptbulletin. com/ Obituaries for Darlene Ellen (Hutchins) Allwein and Margaret Allene (Palmer) Oakes Allwein can be found at: http://www.pricefuneralchapel. com/ogp/index.php.

In California, their son Raymond Allwein was killed, and his sister Pauline was seriously injured, in an accident in which they were struck by a truck as they were walking along the side of the highway. We cover more of the family of Raymond Martin Allwein in Chapter 24 of volume 3, where we present information for families that settled in California.

Emma Arabella Allwein Raub (1883-1954)
East Donegal Township, Lancaster County

Emma Arabella Allwein (F06-0405-0301-04), oldest surviving daughter of Joseph B. and Angeline (Eisenhauer) Allwein, was born September 19, 1883 in Lebanon, Pennsylvania. The line of descent connecting Emma Arabella Allwein to Johannes Jacob and Catharina Allwein, progenitors of the Allwein family in colonial Pennsylvania, is as follows:

Generation 1: Johannes Jacob and Catharina Allwein—Berks County, Pa.
Generation 2: Conrad and Catharine (Weibel) Allwein—Dauphin County, Pa.
Generation 3: Philip and Barbara (Frantz) Allwein—Lebanon County, Pa.
Generation 4: Joseph Allwein and Anne Beber—Lebanon County, Pa.
Generation 5: Joseph B. and Angeline (Eisenhauer) Allwein—Lebanon County, Pa.
Generation 6: Emma Arabella Allwein and George Albert Raub—Lancaster
    County, Pa.

Emma Allwein married George Albert (aka Albert George) Raub, son of Simon and Martha Raub on January 21, 1908 in Lebanon. They lived in East Donegal Township (near Marietta), Lancaster County, Pennsylvania.[96] He farmed and worked as a signal and switch repairman for the railroad.

---

[96] *Thirteenth Census of the United States* (1910), *Inhabitants of East Donegal Township, Lancaster County, Pennsylvania*, E.D. No. 28, page 211A; *Fourteenth Census of the United States* (1920), *Inhabitants of East Donegal Township, Lancaster County, Pennsylvania*, E.D. No. 30, page 43B; *Fifteenth Census of the United States* (1930), *Inhabitants of East Donegal Township, Lancaster County, Pennsylvania*, E.D. No. 36-27, page 16B; *Sixteenth Census of the United States* (1940), *Inhabitants of East Donegal Township, Lancaster County, Pennsylvania*, E.D. No. 36-27, page 499A.

Based on Census reports and other archival materials, this is the information available on the three children born to them, as follows:[97]

Archie Maxwell Raub, b. July 2, 1909, d. May 24, 1987 (CE), m.
   (1953) Frieda Wright (b. May 7, 1912, d. December 4, 2003)
Charles Albert Raub, b. May 22, 1911, d. July 14, 2010, m. (July 19,
   1936) Mary Kathryn "Kay" Coolidge (b. September 7, 1911, d.
   May 29, 2002)
Alice Catherine Raub, b. November 25, 1914, d. June 2, 1997, m.
   (April 21, 1943) James S. Goddard (b. July 28, 1911, d. April 1975)

Emma Arabella Allwein died on November 6, 1954.[98] Her husband, George Albert Raub died several years later on February 25, 1971. They are buried in Cedar Lawn Cemetery (CE) on South Queen Street in the city of Lancaster, Pennsylvania.

Joseph Ignatious Allwein (1887-1959)
Borough of Lebanon, Pennsylvania

Joseph I. Allwein (M06-0405-0301-05), third son of Joseph B. and Angeline (Eisenhauer) Allwein, was born May 21, 1887 in Lebanon, Pennsylvania. The line of descent connecting Joseph Ignatious Allwein to Johannes Jacob and Catharina Allwein, progenitors of the Allwein family in colonial Pennsylvania, is as follows:

Generation 1: Johannes Jacob and Catharina Allwein—Berks County, Pa.
Generation 2: Conrad and Catharine (Weibel) Allwein—Dauphin County, Pa.
Generation 3: Philip and Barbara (Frantz) Allwein—Lebanon County, Pa.
Generation 4: Joseph Allwein and Anne Beber—Lebanon County, Pa.
Generation 5: Joseph B. and Angeline (Eisenhauer) Allwein—Lebanon County, Pa.
Generation 6: Joseph Ignatious and Anna (Reifsnyder) Allwein—Lebanon
   County, Pa.

---

[97]   Obituary for Charles Albert Raub, see United States Obituary Collection. Ancestry.com. Also, see obituary for Kathryn Raub, *Nashua Telegraph*, Nashua, New Hampshire, May 30, 2002; for Frieda Wright Raub, *The Pilot*, Southern Pines, North Carolina, Friday, December 5, 2003.
[98]   See the Pennsylvania Department of Health: http://www.health.state. pa.us.

Exhibit 11.8 Gravestone for Emma A. and George Albert Raub (and their son Archie M. Raub)—Cedar Lawn Cemetery, Lancaster, Pennsylvania

Joseph I. Allwein lived in Lebanon with his parents during his early adulthood.[99] In the 1910 Federal Census report he is listed as a "baker" working in a bakery. In the 1920 Federal Census report, his occupation is given as "waiter in a restaurant." He was a veteran of the First World War, serving in the Army with the 337th Quartermaster Detachment from September 19, 1917 to June 12, 1919.[100] He married Anna Houtz, widow of Henry E Houtz, and the daughter of Ezra and Margeret (Rehm) Reifsnyder, on April 12, 1920 at St. Mary's Catholic Church in Lebanon. The ceremony was performed by Rev. W.E. Martin.

Joseph I. and Anna (Houtz) Allwein eventually moved to Elizabeth, New Jersey. They can be located there in the 1930 Federal Census, where he was working in a dellicatesan.[101] Anna Houtz Allwein died in 1936 and is buried in Mt. Lebanon Cemetery (ML). The 1940 Federal Census enumerations of New Jersey list Joseph Allwein (age 54, widowed) in Elizabeth, Union County, where he was working as a "handy man in an oil refinery."[102] In 1942, Joseph Allwein registered for the draft for the Second World War at the age of 55, but he was not called for military service. His draft registration card indicates he was still living in Elizabeth, New Jersey.[103] He died on March 15, 1959 and is buried near his wife in Mt. Lebanon Cemetery (ML) in Lebanon, Pennsylvania.

---

[99]   *Twelfth Census of the United States* (1900), *Inhabitants of the 5*[th] *Ward, Lebanon City, Lebanon County, Pennsylvania*, E.D. No. 129, page 284A; *Thirteenth Census of the United States* (1910), *Inhabitants of the 5*[th] *Ward, Lebanon City, Lebanon County, Pennsylvania*, E.D. No. 155, page 220A; *Fourteenth Census of the United States* (1920), *Inhabitants of the 5*[th] *Ward, Lebanon City, Lebanon County, Pennsylvania*, E.D. No. 174, page 253B.
[100]   Pennsylvania Veterans Burial Cards, 1777-1999. Ancestry.com.
[101]   *Fifteenth Census of the United States* (1930), *Inhabitants of City of Elizabeth, Union County, New Jersey*, E.D. No. 20-20, page 12B.
[102]   *Sixteenth Census of the United States* (1940), *Inhabitants of City of Elizabeth, Union County, New Jersey*, E.D. No. 23-06, page 314B.
[103]   U.S. World War II Draft Registration Cards, 1942. Ancestry.com.

Exhibit 11.9 Gravestone for Joseph I. Allwein—Mount Lebanon Cemetery, Lebanon, Pennsylvania

Mary M. Allwein Wentling (1890-1954)
North Lebanon Township

Mary M. Allwein (F06-0405-0301-06), daughter of Joseph B. and Angeline (Eisenhauer) Allwein, was born July 9, 1890 in Lebanon, Pennsylvania. The line of descent connecting Mary M. Allwein to Johannes Jacob and Catharina Allwein, progenitors of the Allwein family in colonial Pennsylvania, is as follows:

Generation 1: Johannes Jacob and Catharina Allwein—Berks County, Pa.
Generation 2: Conrad and Catharine (Weibel) Allwein—Dauphin County, Pa.
Generation 3: Philip and Barbara (Frantz) Allwein—Lebanon County, Pa.
Generation 4: Joseph Allwein and Anne Beber—Lebanon County, Pa.
Generation 5: Joseph B. and Angeline (Eisenhauer) Allwein—Lebanon County, Pa.
Generation 6: Mary M. Allwein and William Peter Wentling—Lebanon
    County, Pa.

She married William Peter Wentling, son of John and Annie R. Wentling on January 20, 1910 in Lebanon. They lived in Lebanon, in 1920 in a household adjacent to Joseph B. and Angeline Allwein, and eventually in North Lebanon Township of Lebanon County.[104] He worked as a tinsmith for the railroad.

Based on Census reports and other archival materials, the information available on the four children born to them is as follows:[105]

---

[104] *Fourteenth Census of the United States* (1920), *Inhabitants of Lebanon Ward 5, Lebanon County, Pennsylvania*, E.D. No. 174, page 253B; *Fifteenth Census of the United States* (1930), *Inhabitants of North Lebanon Township, Lebanon County, Pennsylvania*, E.D. No. 38-35, page 276B; *Sixteenth Census of the United States* (1940), *Inhabitants of North Lebanon, Lebanon County, Pennsylvania*, E.D. No. 38-43, page 761A.

[105] Information on these children was obtained from the following sources: United States Obituary Collection. Social Security Death Index. Pennsylvania Veterans Burial Cards, 1977-1999. Ancestry.com. Information on some of these children and their spouses was obtained from obituaries published in the *Lebanon Daily News*, Lebanon, Pennsylvania, as follows: Wednesday, April 15, 2009; Friday, March 26, 2010.

Christina Elizabeth Wentling, b. January 18, 1911, d. April 12, 2009 (HC), unmarried

Charles D. Wentling, b. October 20, 1913, d. January 24, 1993, m. (November 24, 1934) Kathryn "Kit" M. Strouphar (b. August 24, 1916, d. October 23, 2009)

William A. Wentling, b. June 24, 1917, d. January 1, 1981 (HV), m. (November 29, 1947) Lena M. Tonini (b. August 5, 1923, d. March 25, 2010)

Mary Agnes Wentling, b. December 26, 1919, d. unknown, m. Francis Gerald Dennison (b. July 26, 1917, d. December 29, 1994)

Mary M. (Allwein) Wentling died December 29, 1954, and William Wentling died a few years later on September 19, 1959.[106] They are buried together at Holy Cross Cemetery (HC) in Lebanon, Pennsylvania.

Christina Maria Allwein Gress (1894-1984)
Lebanon and Reading, Pennsylvania

Christina Maria Allwein (F06-0405-0301-08), youngest daughter of Joseph B. and Angeline (Eisenhauer) Allwein, was born December 16, 1894. The line of descent connecting Christina Maria Allwein to Johannes Jacob and Catharina Allwein, progenitors of the Allwein family in colonial Pennsylvania, is as follows:

Generation 1: Johannes Jacob and Catharina Allwein—Berks County, Pa.
Generation 2: Conrad and Catharine (Weibel) Allwein—Dauphin County, Pa.
Generation 3: Philip and Barbara (Frantz) Allwein—Lebanon County, Pa.
Generation 4: Joseph Allwein and Anne Beber—Lebanon County, Pa.
Generation 5: Joseph B. and Angeline (Eisenhauer) Allwein—Lebanon County, Pa.
Generation 6: Christina Maria Allwein and Stephen Benedict Gress—Lebanon and Berks Counties, Pa.

---

[106] Obituaries, *Lebanon Daily News*, Lebanon, Pennsylvania, Wednesday Evening, December 29, 1954, and Saturday Evening, September 19, 1959. See also the Pennsylvania Department of Health: http://www.health.state. pa.us.

Exhibit 11.10 Gravestone for Mary M. and William Wentling—Holy Cross Catholic Cemetery, Lebanon, Pennsylvania

Christina Maria Allwein married Stephen Benedict Gress, son of John and Teresa (Kramer) Gress, on September 9, 1913 at St. Mary's Catholic Church in Lebanon, Pennsylvania. The ceremony was conducted by Rev. A. Christ. The Gress family emigrated from Czechoslovakia.

Stephen and Christina (Allwein) Gress lived in Lebanon in 1920, as registered in the Federal Census of that year, where he worked as a butcher in a butcher shop, but soon thereafter they moved to Reading.[107] A 1950 *Boyd's City Directory for Reading, Pennsylvania* lists him there working in a meat market.[108] They are buried at St. Mary's Catholic Cemetery (SM) in Lebanon, Pennsylvania. We return to a discussion of this family in Chapter 13, where we cover Allwein families living in the Reading area of Berks County.

Elizabeth Allwein Glick (1808-1850)
Bethel Township, Lebanon County

Elizabeth Allwein (F04-0405-02), the oldest daughter of Philip Allwein and Barbara Frantz, was born June 5, 1808 in Lebanon Township, Dauphin County and died December 20, 1851 in Mount Zion, Bethel Township, Lebanon County. The line of descent linking Elizabeth Allwein to the Johannes Jacob and Catharina Allwein, progenitors of the Allwein family in colonial Pennsylvania, is as follows:

Generation 1: Johannes Jacob and Catharina Allwein—Berks County, Pa.
Generation 2: Conrad and Catharine (Weibel) Allwein—Dauphin County, Pa.
Generation 3: Philip and Barbara (Frantz) Allwein—Lebanon County, Pa.
Generation 4: Elizabeth Allwein and Peter Glick—Lebanon County, Pa.

Elizabeth Allwein married Peter Glick (also spelled Klick in some record sources) and they lived in Mount Zion, Lebanon County for the remainder of their lives. The interested reader is referred to Chapter 7 of Volume 1 of *Familie Allwein* (see pages 376-379), where I summarized what we know about the lives of Peter Glick

---

[107] *Fourteenth Census of the United States* (1920), *Inhabitants of Ward 5, Lebanon City, Lebanon County, Pennsylvania*, E.D. No. 173, page 218B.
[108] U.S. City Directories. Boyd's Reading City Directory 1950. Ancestry. com.

and Elizabeth Allwein, and do not review that or follow any of these families here.

John Allwein (1811-1879)
Lebanon, Pennsylvania

John Allwein (M04-0405-04), the second son of Philip and Barbara (Frantz) Allwein, spent his entire life in the Lebanon area. The lineage for John Allwein, connecting him to Johannes Jacob and Catharina Allwein, progenitors of the Allwein family in colonial Pennsylvania, is as follows:

Generation 1: Johannes Jacob and Catharina Allwein—Berks County, Pa.
Generation 2: Conrad and Catharine (Weibel) Allwein—Dauphin County, Pa.
Generation 3: Philip and Barbara (Frantz) Allwein—Lebanon County, Pa.
Generation 4: John and Julia Ann (Howarter) Allwein—Lebanon County, Pa.

He married Julia Howarter and they raised a family in Lebanon County. In Chapter 7 of Volume 1 of *Familie Allwein* (see pages 383-387), I summarized what we know about the lives of John and Julia Ann (Howarter) Allwein, and briefly review this here, but the main focus of this section is on their descendants.

John Allwein learned the trade of coach making, and first operated a carriage-building and repair shop at Annville, Pennsylvania, west of the Borough of Lebanon. In 1866 he sold his business in Annville to his son Augustus P. Allwein and John Saylor, and then moved to Lebanon, where he continued the business on a smaller scale at 9th and Mifflin Streets. The existence of his carriage shop there is recorded in an 1875 *Atlas of Lebanon County* (see below). About 1870 he purchased a farm of about 80 acres in Bethel Township, Lebanon County, adjoining that of his brother Edward, which he rented out "for half."[109]

The locations of the property owned by John Allwein are documented in the 1875 *County Atlas of Lebanon*, which lists the residence of "J. Allwein, Sr." and carriage shop at 9th and Mifflin

---

[109] Jerome Allwein, *Genealogy of the Allwein-Arnold Families*, Philadelphia, Pa., 1902, pages 27. The phrase "for half" means that the rent he charged was equal to one-half of the profits from the sale of grain, livestock, and other goods produced by the renter from farming this land.

(see upper righthand corner of the extract from a Lebanon map in Exhibit 11.11 below) within the Borough of Lebanon. He also owned a farm near his brother Edward's farm in Bethel Township (see Exhibit 11.70 below).[110] John must have been a wealthy man. His "real estate" assets in the 1870 Census report are listed as $25,000, a considerable value for that historical period.[111]

Federal Census records place John and Julia Ann Allwein in the Lebanon area for more than forty years, from 1840 through 1870: in Annville Township in 1840, Millerstown, North Annville Township in 1850, in South Annville, South Annville Township in 1860, and in the Borough of Lebanon in 1870, where they lived for the rest of their lives. In the 1860 Federal Census, their household listing is as follows: John Allwein (age 48), Julia (age 50), Augustus P. (age 24), John W. (20)—both listed as Coachmakers—Louisa (age 18), Vincent H. (age 17) listed as "student," Elizabeth (age 14) Aaron (age 12). Also in both 1850 and 1860 there is a list of additional household members, including several apprentice blacksmiths, an apprentice woodworker, an apprentice painter, and a seamstress. In the 1860 Census, John Allwein served as an Assistant Marshall, and is listed as Census enumerator for North Annville Twp and South Annville Twp.[112]

In 1870, they are recorded in the Borough of Lebanon as follows: John Allwein (age 59), wife Juliana Allwein (age 59), Aaron Allwein (age 22), Lizzie Allwein (age 23), and Mary Allwein (age 6). The "Mary Allwein" in this listing is their granddaughter—the daughter of John W. Allwein and wife Sarah Jane Sherk (who died September 15, 1864).

---

[110] F.W. Beers, *County Atlas of Lebanon Pennsylvania from Recent and Actual Surveys and Records*, Reading & Philadelphia: F.A. Davis, 1875, pages 21 and 41.

[111] *Ninth Census of the United States* (1870), *Inhabitants of Borough of Lebanon, Lebanon County, Pennsylvania*, page 337.

[112] *Sixth Census of the United States* (1840), *Inhabitants of Annville Township, Lebanon County, Pennsylvania*, page 53; *Seventh Census of the United States,* (1850), *Inhabitants of North Annville Township, Lebanon County, Pennsylvania*, page 266; *Eighth Census of the United States* (1860), *Inhabitants of South Annville Township, Lebanon County, Pennsylvania*, page 649; *Ninth Census of the United States* (1870), *Inhabitants of Borough of Lebanon, Lebanon County, Pennsylvania*, page 337.

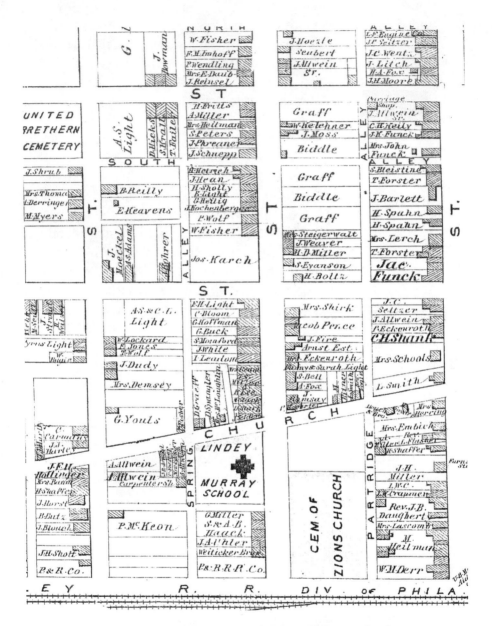

Exhibit 11.11 Extract of 1875 map of Lebanon Borough of area surrounding John Allwein's carriage shop at Ninth and Mifflin Streets, Lebanon, Pennsylvania (upper right)—and Adam Allwein's carpenter shop at Church Street and Spring Alley (lower left)

The children born to John and Julia Ann (Howarter) Allwein who survived to adulthood, and who we discuss in the following, are listed as follows:

Augustus "Gus" P Allwein (M05-0405-0401), b. August 1, 1836, d. June 15, 1907, m. Melinda Hershey (b. est. 1838, d. after 1910)

John W. Allwein (M05-0405-0402), b. September 13, 1839, d. October 3, 1882 (SM), m. (1) Sarah Jane Sherk (b. March 6, 1842, d. September 15, 1864, (2) Cecilia McConnel (b. unknown, d. September 1, 1889)

Louisa A. Allwein (F05-0405-0403), b. September 23, 1841, d. May 8, 1901 (MA), m. (1861) Oliver H. Henry (b. March 28, 1836, d. May 15, 1923)

Vincent H. Allwein (M05-0405-0404), b. September 5, 1843, d. October 10, 1895 (SM), m. (1868) Anna Margaret Ramsay (b. 1847, d. April 9, 1914)

Elizabeth Allwein (F05-0405-0405), b. September 29, 1845, d. February 13, 1900 (SM), m. Jacob Louser Rise (b. February 16, 1842, d. January 20, 1921 (ML))

Aaron D. Allwein (M05-0405-0406), b. July 7, 1847, d. October 31, 1917 (SM). m. (1870) Emma L. Eckenroth (b. March 1, 1852, d. September 30, 1932)

All of these children remained in the Lebanon area, and in the following set of narratives we review what is known about their lives.

Julia Ann Allwein died on August 20, 1873, and John Allwein followed her in death six years later on August 8, 1879. Both are buried in St. Mary's Catholic Cemetery (SM) in the Borough of Lebanon, Pennsylvania. Photos of their gravestones were printed in volume 1 of *Familie Allwein* and I do not reproduce them here (see *Familie Allwein*, volume 1, pages 383-387).

Augustus P. Allwein (1836-1907)
North Lebanon Township

Augustus "Gus" P. Allwein (M05-0405-0401), eldest son of John and Julia Ann (Howarter) Allwine, was born August 1, 1836 in Annville Township, Lebanon County, Pennsylvania. The lineage for Augustus P. Allwein, connecting him to Johannes Jacob and Catharina Allwein, progenitors of the Allwein family in colonial Pennsylvania, is as follows:

Generation 1: Johannes Jacob and Catharina Allwein—Berks County, Pa.
Generation 2: Conrad and Catharine (Weibel) Allwein—Dauphin County, Pa.
Generation 3: Philip and Barbara (Frantz) Allwein—Lebanon County, Pa.
Generation 4: John and Julia Ann (Howarter) Allwein—Lebanon County, Pa.
Generation 5: Augustus P. and Melinda (Hershey) Allwein—Lebanon County, Pa.

According to Jerome Allwein's *Genealogy*, Augustus . . .

. . . learned coachmaking in his father's establishment and about 1866 formed a partnership with John Saylor and purchased the business. Some years later he sold out his share to his partner who continued the business. He married Malinda Hershey and lived at Lebanon where he afterward conducted a wholesale liquor store for a time.[113]

Melinda Hershey was a descendant of the Hershey family that settled in the Lancaster countryside in the early 1700s—from whom the famous chocolate maker, Milton Snavely Hershey, also descended. She was the daughter of Christian and Anna Hershey, who were originally from Penn Township of Lancaster County, and ultimately Derry Township, Dauphin County, Pennsylvania.

Prior to his marriage, as a young man, Augustus P. Allwein served during the Civil War in the Pennsylvania Militia for a two-week period, from September 12 through September 24-25,

---

[113] Jerome Allwein, *Genealogy of the Allwein-Arnold Families*, Philadelphia, Pa., 1902, page 61.

1862.[114] Specifically, available sources indicate that Augustus Allwein served as a Sergeant with Captain John Ulrich in Company A of the 11th Regiment of the Militia of 1862. That regiment was organized September 11-13, 1862 and discharged September 23-25, 1862. It is certain that any man with knowledge of wagon-making and repair would have an invaluable role in such a militia. His uncle, John Henry Allwein, son of Philip and Elizabeth (Arentz) Allwein, who married Catherine Lenich, also served as a Private in the same company.

The designation of "militia" service in this context refers to emergency troops typically organized by local communities or provinces—what we would today probably refer to as the army reserves or the National Guard. This would explain why Augustus Allwein and John H. Allwein do not appear in the military records of the Union (or Federal) forces preserved at the National Archives, but do appear in Pennsylvania record sources.

Regarding the "Militia of 1862" the Samuel Bates' *History of Pennsylvania Volunteers* notes that after their triumph at the second Battle of Bull Run, the rebel army was moving northward, and in order to protect the southern border of Pennsylvania, local troops were mustered and assembled in the area of Harrisburg. After the Battle of Antietam in Northern Virginia (September 17, 1862), in which the Army of the Potomac under the command of General McClellan defeated Confederate forces, the emergency passed and militia troops were returned to Harrisburg and disbanded on the 24th of September, 1862. There are a number of sources that describe McClellan's victory over Lee at Antietam, but it is not clear what role the Pennsylvania militia played other than to provide backup support to the regular army troops who engaged Lee's troops.[115] In

---

[114] Samuel P. Bates, *History of Pennsylvania Volunteers 1861-65*, edited by Janet Hewett, Wilmington NC: Broadfoot Publishing Co., Volume 10, 1994, page 1173.
[115] Samuel P. Bates, *History of Pennsylvania Volunteers 1861-65*, edited by Janet Hewett, Wilmington NC: Broadfoot Publishing Co., Volume 10, 1994, page 1173.

other words, it is doubtful that Augustus P. and John H. Allwein actually fought in the Battle at Antietam and given their short-term membership in the militia they were probably not entitled to federal pension. Neither of them appears in the federal military and pension records.

In the 1860 Federal Census of Pennsylvania, Augustus P. Allwein is listed as a "coachmaker" (age 24) living in his father's household in Annville, Pennsylvania.[116] He evidently married soon thereafter, probably around 1865, as in the 1870 Federal Census he is living in the Borough of Lebanon with his wife Melinda and two children, Minnie (age 6) and Annie (age 3).[117] The existence of these children is confirmed in the Jerome Allwein *Genealogy*, which gives the following list of children born to Augustus Allwein and Melinda Hershey.[118]

Minnie Allwein (F06-0405-0401-01), b. January 20, 1866, d. unknown, m. unknown

Annie Allwein (F06-0405-0401-02), b. October 23, 1868, d. May 7, 1934 (ML), m. (November 6, 1890) George A. Bock (or Boch) (b. September 12, 1869, d. April 9, 1920)[119]

John C. Allwein (M06-0405-0401-03), b. October 16, 1874, d. unknown

The 1875 *County Atlas of Lebanon* lists the residence of "A.C. Allwein" on Jackson Street between 11th and 12th Streets in the

---

[116] *Eighth Census of the United States* (1860), *Inhabitants of South Annville Township, Lebanon County, Pennsylvania*, page 649.

[117] *Ninth Census of the United States* (1870), *Inhabitants of Lebanon Borough, Lebanon County, Pennsylvania*, page 322.

[118] Jerome Allwein, *Genealogy of the Allwein-Arnold Families*, Philadelphia, Pa., 1902, page 62.

[119] Obituary for Annie Allwein Bock in *Lebanon Daily News*, Lebanon, Pennsylvania, Tuesday Evening, May 8, 1934. Obituary for George A. Bock in *Lebanon Daily News*, Lebanon, Pennsylvania, Friday Evening, April 9, 1920.

Borough of Lebanon.[120] This is likely meant to be "A.P. Allwein" and if so, this would be the residence of Augustus P. Allwein.

There is a bit of a mystery surrounding what may have happened to this family, because in the 1880 Federal Census the family is not living together. Augustus Allwein (age 43) is living apart from his family and is listed in the census in the household of John J. Saylor as a "boarder" working as a "painter" in the carriage manufacturing business.[121] John J. Saylor was the man with whom the Jerome Allwein *Genealogy of the Allwein-Arnold Families* suggests he had gone into the carriage-making business. In that census document, his marital status is given as "married." In the 1880 Federal Census, all other family members—Melinda Allwein, Minnie Allwein, Annie Allwein, and John C. Allwein—are all living elsewhere (see below).

Thus, by the time of the 1880 Federal Census, Augustus Allwein was living in a non-family setting, apart from his children and his wife. One can only assume there was a marital separation or divorce between Augustus and Melinda Hershey Allwein. In the Federal Census of 1870, soon after the birth of their three children, they are listed as co-residing in the same dwelling, but by 1880, they were not living together, the separation therefore occurring after 1870 and prior to 1880. According to the 1880 Federal Census, Melinda Allwein was living separately with her daughter Minnie Allwein (age 15) in the Harrisburg area (Susquehanna Township) in the household of her brother Henry E. Hershey.[122] She would soon move farther west, because by 1882, Melinda Allwein was living in Kansas City, Missouri, where she operated a boarding house. She

---

[120] F.W. Beers, *County Atlas of Lebanon Pennsylvania from Recent and Actual Surveys and Records*, Reading & Philadelphia: F.A. Davis, 1875, page 41.
[121] *Tenth Census of the United States* (1880), *Inhabitants of South Annville Township, Lebanon County, Pennsylvania*, page 371.
[122] *Tenth Census of the United States* (1880), *Inhabitants of Susquehanna Township, Dauphin County, Pennsylvania*, page 130D.

later moved, with her brother Frank Hershey, to Buffalo County, in southcentral Nebraska, west of Grand Island (see below).

In the 1900 Federal Census, Augustus P. Allwein is located in North Lebanon Township, living with his daughter Annie (Allwein) Bock, wife of George A. Bock, on Maple Street. In the census document he is listed as "widowed."[123] Both Augustus and his wife must have claimed the other one was dead, for Melinda Allwein is also listed as a "widow" in city directories for Kansas City, Missouri in 1882 to 1888.[124] After that, in the 1900 and 1910 Censuses she is living with her brother Frank Hershey in Gibbon Township, Buffalo County, Nebraska, similarly stating that she was a widow.[125] In the 1882-1888 Kansas City, Missouri directories, she is listed as the "widow of Augustus P. Allwein" or "Mrs. Melinda Allwein." It is also relatively clear from these sources that in Kansas City, that she was an operator of a boarding house for several years, a profession she undoubtedly learned in part from her brother Henry E. Hershey.

Henry E. Hershey, the brother of Melinda Hershey Allwein, with whom she was living in 1880, was the proprietor of the Hershey House, Harrisburg, Pennsylvania.[126] The following is a narrative

---

[123] *Twelfth Census of the United States* (1900), *Inhabitants of North Lebanon Township, Lebanon County, Pennsylvania*, E.D. No. 138, page 154B.

[124] The sources of this information are *Hoye's Twelfth Volume Kansas City Directories, 1882*, page 37; *Hoye's City Directory of Kansas City, 1884*, page 55; *1886-1887 Hoye's City Directory of Kansas City, Missouri, including Kansas City, Kansas and Westport*, pages 69 and 881; *1887-1888 Hoye's City Directory of Kansas City, Missouri*, page 67.

[125] *Twelfth Census of the United States* (1900), *Inhabitants of Gibbon Township, Buffalo County, Nebraska*, E.D. No. 29, page 137A; *Thirteenth Census of the United States* (1910), *Inhabitants of Gibbon Township, Buffalo County, Nebraska*, E.D. No. 37, page 100B.

[126] For Henry E. Hershey, information is taken from the *Commemorative Biographical Encyclopedia of Dauphin County, Pennsylvania*, Chambersburg, Pennsylvania: J.M. Runk and Company, Publishers, 1896, page 614.

from the 1896 *Commemorative Biographical Encyclopedia of Dauphin County* about Henry E. Hershey.

> HERSHEY, HENRY E., proprietor of the Hershey House, Harrisburg, Pa., was born in Penn Township, Lancaster County, Pa., November 14, 1846. He is the son of Christian and Anna (Eresman) Hershey. Christian Hershey was born in Sporting Hill, Lancaster County, and resided in that county until 1861, when he removed to Dauphin County. Here he spent the remainder of his life, the latter part in West Hanover Township, where he died. The mother was also born in Lancaster County, and is still living and in good health at the age of eighty-three; she resides at Sporting Hill. Five of their six children are living: Maria; Melinda, widow of Augustus Alwine, of Kansas City, Mo.; Elizabeth; Frank, of Chicago, Ill.; and Henry E. (the subject).

> Henry E. Hershey spent his early life near Manheim, Lancaster County, where he received his first instruction in the public schools. At fourteen years of age he removed with his parents to Dauphin County, locating in Derry Township, six miles from Hummelstown. Here he finished his education, attending school in winter and doing home and farm work in the spring and summer. He was engaged in farming until 1873, when he decided to change his occupation, and began his career as landlord and hotel manager with the Park Hotel, at the fairgrounds, which he conducted successfully for two years. He next took charge of the Stockyard Hotel on the bank of the canal above the city limits, and managed it until 1881.His experience with these ventures was sufficient to develop his qualifications for the business, and to decide him to make it has life occupation. In 1881 he took the Hershey House, of which he has been proprietor and manager since that date. His house is widely and favorably known to the traveling public, and Mr. Hershey, after his career of twenty-three years, stands well in the honorable and popular class of hotel men.

> Henry E. Hershey was married, in Derry Township to Miss Mary A., daughter of Christian and Anna Wissler of Lancaster County,

both deceased. They have had nine children: Anna, Christian W., Daniel W., Elizabeth, George S., Melinda, Frank, Mabel, who died in infancy, and Helen. Mr. Hershey has served efficiently for two terms in select council, and during his last term was chairman of that body. He is not an active member of any secret organization. In political views he is Democratic. The family attended Zion English Lutheran church.

Except for the marriage of Annie Allwein to George Bock, as noted above, we have little further information about the children of Augustus P. Allwein and Melinda Hershey. As noted, in the 1880 Federal Census, Minnie Allwein is living with her mother Melinda Allwein in Susquehanna Township of Dauphin County, in the household of Henry E. Hershey. John C. Allwein can be located living in the household of Harvey Yundt, his cousin, along with their grandmother Annie Hershey.[127] Harvey Yundt was the son of one of Melinda Hershey's sisters (possibly Mary or Elizabeth Hershey), making him a first cousin to John C. Allwein, although the census document says he was a nephew. I can find no trace of John C. Allwein following the 1880 Federal Census.

Augustus P. Allwein died on June 15, 1907, as recorded in Pennsylvania Department of Health public death records.[128] As of this writing, we do not know where he is buried.

John W. Allwein (1839-1882)
Lebanon, Pennsylvania

John W. Allwein (M05-0405-0402), second son of John and Julia Ann (Howarter) Allwein, was born September 13, 1839 in Annville Township, Lebanon County, Pennsylvania. The lineage for John W. Allwein, connecting him to Johannes Jacob and Catharina Allwein, progenitors of the Allwein family in colonial Pennsylvania, is as follows:

---

[127] *Tenth Census of the United States* (1880), *Inhabitants of Derry Township, Dauphin County, Pennsylvania*, page 21.
[128] See the Pennsylvania Department of Health: http://www.health.state. pa.us

Generation 1: Johannes Jacob and Catharina Allwein—Berks County, Pa.
Generation 2: Conrad and Catharine (Weibel) Allwein—Dauphin County, Pa.
Generation 3: Philip and Barbara (Frantz) Allwein—Lebanon County, Pa.
Generation 4: John and Julia Ann (Howarter) Allwein—Lebanon County, Pa.
Generation 5: John W. and Sarah (Sherk) [and Cecilia (McConnel)] Allwein—
    Lebanon County, Pa.

Like his older brother Augustus, John W. Allwein followed his father into the carriage making business. Jerome Allwein's *Genealogy* gives the following information:

John W. Allwein was associated for some time with his father in business. He married Sarah Sherk—one daughter being born to this union (Mary, b. May 30, 1865, d., Sept. 21, 1891). After his wife died, he married to Cecilia O'Connor—one daughter being born to this union (Emma, b. unknown, d. unknown).

As noted above, in the 1860 Federal Census, John W. Allwein was living with his parents (see above).[129] He married soon thereafter to Sarah Jane Sherk, who died at a young age, possibly in connection with childbirth. She died September 15, 1864 (see Exhibit 11.13) and is buried in the Mount Lebanon Cemetery in Lebanon. John W. Allwein remarried to Cecilia "Lizzie" McConnel, daughter of Oliver McConnel and wife (the name is sometimes spelled McConnell, but this is how it appears on the family gravestones in Kimmerling's Cemetery).

In the 1870 Federal Census of the Borough of Lebanon, John W. Allwein (age 28) is living with wife Cecilia (age 22) and daughter Emma (age 2). His occupation is listed as "coachmaker," which converges with other information we have for him.[130] At that time, as we noted above, his daughter Mary Allwein (daughter with Sarah Jane Sherk) was living in the household of John W. Allwein's parents, John Allwein Sr., just a short distance away.[131] The

---

[129] *Eighth Census of the United States* (1860), *Inhabitants of South Annville Township, Lebanon County, Pennsylvania*, page 649.
[130] *Ninth Census of the United States* (1870), *Inhabitants of Borough of Lebanon, Lebanon County, Pennsylvania*, page 340.
[131] *Ninth Census of the United States* (1870), *Inhabitants of Borough of Lebanon, Lebanon County, Pennsylvania*, page 337.

residences of these families also recorded in the 1875 *County Atlas of Lebanon*, which lists the residence of "J. Allwein" (see map in Exhibit 11.11).[132]

To summarize, John W. Allwein's children were as follows:

Mary "Mame" Allwein (F06-0405-0402-01), b. May 30, 1865, d.
    September 21, 1891 (SM), m. John J. Shuler[133]
Emma Allwein (F06-0405-0402-02), b. est. 1868, d. unknown

In the 1880 Federal Census, John W. Allwein (age 39) is again listed in the Borough of Lebanon, with wife Cecilia (age 29) and daughter Mary (age 15).[134] In the 1880 Census his occupation is given as "painter." John W. Allwein died October 3, 1882 and is buried in St. Mary's Catholic Cemetery in Lebanon, Pennsylvania. Contrary to what Jerome Allwein's *Genealogy* states, John W. Allwein's second wife was actually, Cecilia McConnel (not Cecilia O'Connor), who is buried in Kimmerling's Cemetery (KR). She died September 1, 1889 about 7 years after John Allwein died on October 3, 1882.[135] Her gravestone is situated in Kimmerling's Cemetery with several other McConnel graves.

Mary "Mame" Allwein, the daughter of John W. and Sarah (Sherk) Allwein, married John J. Shuler, and she is buried in St. Mary's Cemetery in Lebanon.

---

[132] F.W. Beers, *County Atlas of Lebanon Pennsylvania from Recent and Actual Surveys and Records*, Reading & Philadelphia: F.A. Davis, 1875, page 48.
[133] There is an inconsistency between the date of death given on the gravestone of Mary Allwein's mother, Sarah Jane Sherk (d. September 15, 1864) and the date of birth given on the gravestone of daughter Mary Allwein (b. May 30, 1865). See Exhibits 11.13 and 11.15.
[134] *Tenth Census of the United States* (1880), *Inhabitants of Borough of Lebanon, Lebanon County, Pennsylvania*, page 345.
[135] *Lebanon Daily News*, Lebanon, Pennsylvania, Monday Evening, September 2, 1889.

Exhibit 11.12 Gravestone for John W. Allwein—St. Mary's Cemetery, Lebanon, Pennsylvania

Exhibit 11.13 Gravestone for Sarah Jane Sherk Allwein—Mount Lebanon Cemetery, Lebanon, Pennsylvania

Exhibit 11.14 Gravestone for Cecilia McConnel Allwein—
Kimmerling's Cemetery, North Lebanon Township, Lebanon Co,
Pennsylvania

Exhibit 11.15 Gravestone for Mary Allwein Shuler—St. Mary's Cemetery, Lebanon, Pennsylvania

Louisa A. Allwein Henry (1841-1901)
South Annville Township

Louisa A. Allwein (F05-0405-0403), the oldest daughter of John and Julia Ann (Howarter) Allwein was born September 23, 1841 in Annville Township, Lebanon County, Pennsylvania. The lineage for Louisa Allwein, connecting her to Johannes Jacob and Catharina Allwein, progenitors of the Allwein family in colonial Pennsylvania, is as follows:

Generation 1: Johannes Jacob and Catharina Allwein—Berks County, Pa.
Generation 2: Conrad and Catharine (Weibel) Allwein—Dauphin County, Pa.
Generation 3: Philip and Barbara (Frantz) Allwein—Lebanon County, Pa.
Generation 4: John and Julia Ann (Howarter) Allwein—Lebanon County, Pa.
Generation 5: Louisa A. Allwein and Oliver H. Henry—Lebanon County, Pa.

Louisa A. Allwein married Oliver H. Henry (b. March 28, 1836) in 1861. According to the Jerome Allwein *Genealogy*, Louisa A. Allwein . . .

> . . . married Oliver Henry (P). Mr. Henry was at one time a County Commissioner of Lebanon County, also Station agent at Annville, Pa. where they reside.[136]

There is an early genealogy of the Henry family, mentioned in William Henry Egle's *Notes and Queries*, which sometimes gets inserted into the family history of Oliver H. Henry.[137] This source indicates that Oliver H. Henry (b. March 28, 1836) was the first son of Andrew and Catharine (Rider) Henry. The original Henry (or Heinrich) family represented early settlers to the area. Egle's report on the Henry family begins as follows . . .

---

[136] Jerome Allwein, *Genealogy of the Allwein-Arnold Families*, Philadelphia, Pa., 1902, pages 62-63.

[137] William Henry Egle, *Notes and Queries: Historical, Biographical and Genealogical for Interior Pennsylvania*. Fourth Series, Volume 1. Baltimore, Maryland: Genealogical Publishing Company, 1970 [Originally published by Harrisburg Publishing Co., Harrisburg, Pennsylvania, 1893.], page 2.

George Heinrich or Henry, born April 22, 1722, in the Pfalz, Germany, emigrated to the Province of Pennsylvania, with his wife Elizabeth Balsbaugh, and her brother about the year 1752. He settled along the banks of Spring Creek about a mile north of the town of Palmyra, Lebanon County, where he purchased in 1754 about six hundred acres of land running from the Spring Creek to now near the center of Palmyra. On the banks of the creek he erected his home, while on the opposite side was afterwards built a meeting house (Dunkard), with a cemetery, the latter still known as the "Henry Graveyard." On this farm he lived and died, the latter occurring October 22, 1782. Nearly all this original tract of land is owned by his descendants.[138]

Oliver H. Henry and spouse of Louisa A. Allwein are listed in that source as descendants of George Henry, which is consistent with the place where they spent their entire lives, and where Oliver and Louisa (Allwein) Henry are consistently listed in the Federal Censuses from 1870 through 1900, living in South Annville Township.[139] Oliver Henry's occupation is given as "railroad ticket agent." According to his obituary in the *Lebanon Daily News* (see below) he spent over twenty years as station agent for the Philadelphia and Reading Railroad at Annville. The Henrys were members of the United Brethren Church in Annville. More biographical information on Oliver H. and Louisa (Allwein) Henry appears in an entry for Charles Vincent Henry, their son, in the *Biographical Annals of Lebanon County*, which is reproduced in its entirety here (see below).

---

[138] William Henry Egle, *Notes and Queries: Historical, Biographical and Genealogical for Interior Pennsylvania*. Fourth Series, Volume 1. Baltimore, Maryland: Genealogical Publishing Company, 1970 [Originally published by Harrisburg Publishing Co., Harrisburg, Pennsylvania, 1893.], page 2.

[139] *Ninth Census of the United States* (1870), *Inhabitants of Borough of Lebanon, Lebanon County, Pennsylvania*, page 371; *Tenth Census of the United States* (1880), *Inhabitants of Borough of Lebanon, Lebanon County, Pennsylvania*, page 364; *Twelfth Census of the United States* (1900), *Inhabitants of South Annville Township, Lebanon County, Pennsylvania*, E.D. No. 140, page 196A.

The children of Louisa A. Allwein and Oliver H. Henry are as follows:[140]

Elmer A. Henry, b. June 15, 1861, d. April 7, 1946, m. (1) (May 31, 1888) Lizzie M. Behm (b. December 19, 1865, d. January 6, 1903), (2) (April 26, 1906) Lottie F. Herr (b. August 21, 1878, d. November 15, 1962)
Charles Vincent Henry, b. May 23, 1865, d. December 8, 1957, m. (September 11, 1895) Josephine K. Kreider (b. March 16, 1873, d. June 16, 1947)

Louisa A. Allwein died May 8, 1901 and is buried, along with her husband, who died May 15, 1923, on the Henry family plot in Mount Annville Cemetery (MA), Palmyra, Pennsylvania.[141] Oliver Henry remarried to Kate E. Lambert (b. June 25, 1862, d. March 5, 1923), who is buried there as well.

Charles Vincent Henry, son of Louisa (Allwein) and Oliver Henry, was a lawyer and a prominent district attorney of Lebanon County. He attended Yale Law School in New Haven, Connecticut. There is an entry in the *Biographical Annals of Lebanon County* for Charles Vincent Henry, selections from which follow:[142]

Charles Vincent Henry attended the common schools in Annville until his fifteenth year, and then assisted his father in his duties at the Annville station for several years, subsequently entering the employ of the Cornwall & Lebanon Railway Company, of promotion, he was given the agency of the railroad at Mount Gretna,

---

[140] See Nancy Allwein Nebiker, "Descendants of Louisa A. Allwein," May 12, 2003. Also obituaries in *Lebanon Daily News*, Lebanon, Pennsylvania, Friday Evening, January 9, 1903; Tuesday Evening, June 17, 1947, and Friday Evening, November 16, 1962.
[141] Obituaries in *Lebanon Daily News*, Lebanon, Pennsylvania, Thursday Evening, May 9, 1901 and Wednesday Evening, May 16,1923.
[142] *Biographical Annals of Lebanon County, Pennsylvania, Containing Biographical Sketches of Prominent and Representative Citizens and of Many of the Early Settled Families*, J.H. Beers & Company, Chicago, 1904, page 635-636.

Exhibit 11.16 Gravestone for Louisa A. Allwein—Mount Annville Cemetery, Annville, Pennsylvania

and still later was advanced to the agency at Cornwall. Mr. Henry resigned this position in order to take charge of the private office of Robert H. Coleman, at Cornwall, where he remained from 1889 to 1893.

In the meantime Mr. Henry had decided to enter upon the serious study of the law, and in this resolve was encouraged by friends, who recognized his abilities. Consequently, in the fall of 1893, he entered Yale Law School, and was graduated from that institution in the class of 1895, making a brilliant record, taking honors in both years and graduating second in the large class. In the fall of 1895 he returned to Lebanon and took the necessary examinations, resulting in his admittance to the Bar July 29, 1895. In that city Mr. Henry has had much experience and many legal triumphs. His peculiar fitness for responsibility was recognized in 1901 by his election to the office of district attorney, for a term of three years.

In September, 1895, Mr. Henry was united in marriage with Miss Josephine Kreider, daughter of Joseph H. Kreider, of Annville, and two children have been born to this union: Vincent and Mary. Mr. Henry is interested in enterprises outside of his profession, and is one of the directors of the Annville National Bank.

Mr. Henry is an active member of various Masonic bodies and also of other fraternal organizations. The training which he has enjoyed enables him to give very efficient service in the honorable position he holds in Lebanon County, and it is reasonable to predict still higher honors offered for his acceptance in the future.

The mother of Mr. Henry was born in Annville, daughter of John Allwein, whose family also was one of the old and honorable ones of the locality. She passed out of life in the summer of 1900, in her fifty-eighth year. Oliver H. Henry, the father, for many years was the agent of the Philadelphia & Reading Railroad, serving at Annville from the date of the opening of the road until 1888. Subsequently he was the very efficient county commissioner for Lebanon county. The two children born to Oliver H. Henry and wife were both sons. Elmer A., the elder, is teller at the Annville National Bank, and for a number of years was the assistant railroad agent at that place.

Vincent H. Allwein (1843-1895)
Lebanon, Pennsylvania

Vincent H. Allwein (M05-0405-0404), the fourth child of John and Julia Ann (Howarter) Allwein, was born September 5, 1843 in Annville Township, Lebanon County, Pennsylvania. The lineage for Vincent H. Allwein, connecting him to Johannes Jacob and Catharina Allwein, progenitors of the Allwein family in colonial Pennsylvania, is as follows:

Generation 1: Johannes Jacob and Catharina Allwein—Berks County, Pa.
Generation 2: Conrad and Catharine (Weibel) Allwein—Dauphin County, Pa.
Generation 3: Philip and Barbara (Frantz) Allwein—Lebanon County, Pa.
Generation 4: John and Julia Ann (Howarter) Allwein—Lebanon County, Pa.
Generation 5: Vincent H. and Annie M. (Ramsay) Allwein—Lebanon County, Pa.

Vincent H. Allwein became an educator and a medical doctor. He was the only one of John and Julia Ann Allwein's sons that did not go into the carriage making business. From early on, he took his school studies very seriously, and excelled in all academic areas. He graduated from the University of Pennsylvania with a degree in Medicine (public commencement held on March 14, 1867).[143] Regarding his schooling, Jerome Allwein's *Genealogy*, provides a glimpse into the life of Vincent H. Allwein . . .

. . . attended the public schools, also Mount Saint Mary's College. He prepared for teaching at Millersville Normal School and taught in the public schools several years after which he studied Medicine with Dr. Cyrus Gloninger at Lebanon, Pa. He graduated at the Jefferson Medical College, Philadelphia in 1868, and started in the practice of medicine at Lebanon, Pa. and surrounding county with an office at his father's house at 9th and Mifflin Streets. Shortly after this he was married to Annie Ramsey (P). About four years after this he purchased a property on N. 9th Street and opened a Drug Store and carried on the Drug business in connection with his practice. Dr. Allwein was a noted physician and surgeon.

---

[143] *Catalogue of the Trustees, Officers and Students of the University of Pennsylvania*. One Hundred and Eighteenth Session, 1867-1868, page 43. Philadelphia, Pennsylvania.

He built up a large and lucrative practice and was looked upon as one of the leading men in the profession in his city. Under President Cleveland's first administration he served as examiner on the Pension Board. He was also a noted sporting man, taking frequent trips on fishing and gunning expeditions. He continued his profession until his death, October 10, 1895.[144]

The (P) in the above quote from Jerome Allwein's *Genealogy* indicates that Annie Ramsay, V.H. Allwein's wife, followed the Protestant faith tradition. In fact, while Vincent H. Allwein is buried in St. Mary's Catholic Cemetery in Lebanon, Annie Ramsay (spelling used on her gravestone—not RAMSEY) is buried in Mount Lebanon Cemetery, with her daughter Kora Magdalen Allwein, who married Oscar Klopp.

In the Federal Census of 1870, Vincent H. Allwein was living with his parents in the Borough of Lebanon.[145] He must have married soon thereafter, as he is listed in a local atlas for the Borough as having his own residence. The 1875 *County Atlas of Lebanon County* lists "V.H. Allwein" on 9th Street between Lehman and Mifflin Streets (see map in Exhibit 11.5).[146] This is where Vincent H. Allwein lived for many years and carried out his practice of medicine. In the 1880 Federal Census, he is similarly listed on 9th Street.[147]

Vincent H. Allwein and Annie Ramsay gave life to four children, three of whom survived to adulthood (one son, Carroll Allwein, died at the age of 13), as follows:

---

[144] Jerome Allwein, *Genealogy of the Allwein-Arnold Families*, Philadelphia, Pa., 1902, pages 62-63.
[145] *Ninth Census of the United States* (1870), *Inhabitants of Borough of Lebanon, Lebanon County, Pennsylvania*, page 337.
[146] F.W. Beers, *County Atlas of Lebanon Pennsylvania from Recent and Actual Surveys and Records*, Reading & Philadelphia: F.A. Davis, 1875, pages 41 and 48.
[147] *Tenth Census of the United States* (1880), *Inhabitants of Borough of Lebanon, Lebanon County, Pennsylvania*, page 334.

John Howard Allwein (M06-0405-0404-01), b. October 7, 1868, d. August 16, 1928, m. (January 1, 1919) Sarah "Sadie" E. Thomas (b. July 25, 1895, d. unknown)

Anna Cordelia "Delia" Allwein (F06-0405-0404-02), b. February 10, 1871, d. November 17, 1936 (SM), m. (December 10, 1895) Henry Woldmar Ruoff (b. November 3, 1867, d. July 2, 1935)[148]

T. Carroll "Carroll" Allwein (M06-0405-0404-03), b. 1873, d. December 15, 1886 (SM)

Kora Magdalen Allwein (F06-0405-0404-04), b. September 1875, d. October 14, 1953 (ML), m. (October 19, 1897) Oscar Gerhard Klopp (b. May 15, 1869, d. December 6, 1921)

Vincent H. Allwein's obituary, which appeared in the *Lebanon Daily News*, indicates that he was a beloved member of the community.[149] This obituary is reproduced here in its entirety:

Lebanon Semi-Weekly News Lebanon, Pennsylvania Thursday October 10, 1895

PROMINENT PHYSICIAN DIES

Dr. V. H. Allwein Succumbs After a Severe Illness

EMBOLISM THE CAUSE OF DEATH

As Physician and Citizen He Was Highly Esteemed—He Enjoyed the Respect and Confidence of This Community—A Successful Practitioner and Druggist.

Dr. Vincent H. Allwein peacefully yielded up his spirit in response to the summons of the dread angel of death at his home, on North

---

[148] Obituary for Cordelia Allwein Ruoff from the *Lebanon Semi-Weely Daily News*, Lebanon, Pennsylvania, Thursday Evening, November 19, 1936.

[149] Obituary from the *Lebanon Daily News*, Lebanon, Pennsylvania, Thursday October 10, 1895.

Ninth Street, about 8 o'clock this morning, surrounded by the grief stricken members of his family.

Dr. Allwein was stricken down in the North Lebanon house on October 1, while conversing with his brother and another relative, with a fainting spell, brought on, it is thought, from a heart affliction from which he had been suffering for several years. He was conveyed to his home, where under the treatment of Drs. W. M. Guilford and A. W. Schultz. He was brought to consciousness. The best was hoped for then and it was thought that he would entirely recover the attack, but to the great sorrow of his family and friends he soon commenced to sink until the end was expected to come daily. The immediate cause of death was embolism.

He is survived by his wife, Anna M. and three children, Dr. John Howard, A. Cordelia, and Cora Ann Allwein. Two brothers, August and Aaron E. Allwein, and two sisters, Mrs. O. H. Henry, of Annville, and Mrs. Jacob Rise, of this city, also survive.

Dr. Allwein was 52 years of age, having been born in Annville, September 5, 1843. He was the son of John Allwein, the coachmaker, and spent the days of his boyhood and youth in Annville. He received such education as was afforded by the common schools there, besides studiously applying himself in the study of branches not taught in school, in order to fit himself for his chosen profession. In 1862 his parents moved to Lebanon, and for many years his father conducted a flourishing coachmaking business at North and Mifflin streets.

A few years after coming to Lebanon deceased went to Philadelphia and commenced the study of medicine in the medical department of the University of Pennsylvania. He graduated from that institution as a medical doctor on March 14, 1867, and immediately came to Lebanon, where he soon built up a lucrative practice. Subsequently he also opened a drugstore and was very successful, as he attentive to business and esteemed by the people.

A year later, in 1868, Dr. Allwein married Miss Anna M. Ramsey. She was the daughter of Archibald and Margaret Ramsey, late of this city. They had four children, all of whom except a son survive. The deceased was an active member of St. Mary's Catholic church, and an active member of Catholic Benevolent Legion. In politics he was a Democrat, and was elected to council on his party's ticket while Lebanon was a borough and to select council after it became a city.

It is expected that the funeral will take place on Monday, due notice of which will be given.

Drs. Guilford and Schultz have had charge of the case since the first day of his illness, and they were ably assisted in the sick room by his son, Dr. J. Howard Allwein, and a number of other physicians who volunteered to act as nurses.

Dr. Allwein was a man well known and highly esteemed by the people of this community. He was liked by all who came in contact with him, on account of his excellent social qualities, and his presence in the sick room was like sunshine, his cheerfulness and geniality bringing fresh hope and buoyancy of spirit to the sufferers. His loss will be keenly felt by his many friends and particularly by his family, for he was a loving husband and kind and indulgent father. The sympathy of the entire community goes out to the afflicted ones in their hour of grief and despair. "After life's fitful fever he rests well."

Annie M. (Ramsay) Allwein died nineteen years later, on April 9, 1914, and is buried with her daughter Kora Magdalen Allwein, who married Oscar G. Klopp (see below), at Mount Lebanon Cemetery (ML) in Lebanon, Pennsylvania.[150]

---

[150] Obituary in the *Lebanon Daily News*, Lebanon, Pennsylvania, Thursday Evening, April 9, 1914.

Exhibit 11.17 Gravestone for V.H. Allwein and daughter Cordelia
Allwein Ruoff—St. Mary's Cemetery, Lebanon, Pennsylvania

John Howard Allwein (1868-1928)
Philadelphia, Pennsylvania

Vincent and Annie Allwein's son John Howard Allwein (M06-0405-0404-01) was born on October 7, 1868 in Lebanon, Pennsylvania.[151] He received a degree in Medicine from the University of Pennsylvania in 1892.[152] According to the Jerome Allwein *Genealogy*, after receiving his degree he returned to Lebanon, to work with his father for awhile. He was no doubt living in Lebanon at the time of his father's death, but soon thereafter he moved to Warren, Pennsylvania where he took a position on the Board of Physicians at the State Hospital for the Insane there, but eventually he moved to Philadelphia, and then to Scranton, where

---

[151] Record sources do not agree on the birth date of John Howard Allwein. Lafayette College records give August 7, 1868, which we use here. See the following (from Ancestry.com): *Biographical Catalogue of Lafayette College, 1832-1912*, compiled by John Franklin Stonecipher, Easton, Pennsylvania: Chemical Publishing Company, 1913, page 386; and *Men of Lafayette, 1826-1893*, compiled by Seldin J. Coffin, Easton, Pennsylvania: George W. West, 1891, page 280. Medical school records give: October 17, 1868. See the following (from Ancestry.com): *General Alumni Catalogue of the University of Pennsylvania*, compiled by W.J. Maxwell, Philadelphia, Pa: Alumni Association of the University of Pennsylvania, H.M. Lippincott, Secretary, 1922, page 588; and *The Directory of Deceased American Physicians, 1804-1929*, Arthur Wayne Hafner (editor), Chicago: American Medical Association, 1993. A third source is John Howard Allwein's application for a marriage license in Delaware County, Pennsylvania (date of application: December 31, 1918). This record gives October 17, 1869 as his date of birth.

[152] *General Alumni Catalogue of the University of Pennsylvania*. 1917. Alumni Association of the University, page 761. Philadelphia, Pennsylvania.

he died.[153] We discuss John Howard Allwein's life in more detail in Chapter 12, where we cover Allwein families in Philadelphia.

Anna Cordelia "Delia" Allwein Ruoff (1871-1936) Cambridge, Massachusetts

Anna Cordelia Allwein (F06-0405-0404-02), daughter of Vincent H. and Annie (Ramsay) Allwein, was born on February 10, 1871 in Lebanon, Pennsylvania. The line of descent for Anna Cordelia Allwein connecting her to Johannes Jacob and Catharina Allwein, progenitors of the Allwein family in colonial Pennsylvania, is as follows:

Generation 1: Johannes Jacob and Catharina Allwein—Berks County, Pa.
Generation 2: Conrad and Catharine (Weibel) Allwein—Dauphin County, Pa.
Generation 3: Philip and Barbara (Frantz) Allwein—Lebanon County, Pa.
Generation 4: John and Julia Ann (Howarter) Allwein—Lebanon County, Pa.
Generation 5: Vincent H. and Annie M. (Ramsay) Allwein—Lebanon County, Pa.
Generation 6: Anna Cordelia Allwein and Henry Woldmar Ruoff—Lebanon County and Cambridge, Massachusetts

She married Henry Woldmar Ruoff in Philadelphia on December 10, 1895. Their marriage announcement, appearing in the *Lebanon Daily News*, reads as follows:[154]

At 6 o'clock Tuesday evening at the home of his friend, the Rev. Dr. Furniss, in Philadelphia who also performed the ceremony.

---

[153] Jerome Allwein, *Genealogy of the Allwein-Arnold Families*, Philadelphia, Pa., 1902, pages 108; see the entry for "State Hospital for the Insane, Warren, Pa." in Henry M. Hurd (Ed.), *The Institutional Care of the Insane in the United States and Canada*, Volume 3, Baltimore, Maryland: Johns Hopkins University Press, 1916, page 476, and *Twelfth Census of the United States* (1900), *Inhabitants of Conewango Township, Warren County, Pennsylvania*, E.D. No. 132, page 81A; *Thirteenth Census of the United States* (1910), *Inhabitants of Scranton Ward 9, Lackawana County, Pennsylvania*, E.D. No. 35, page 28B. Obituary in the *Lebanon Semi-Weekly News*, Lebanon, Pennsylvania, Monday Evening, August 20, 1928.
[154] Marriage announcement from the *Lebanon Semi-Weekly News*, Lebanon, Pennsylvania, Thursday Evening, December 12, 1895.

Prof. Henry W. Ruoff, of Philadelphia was married to Miss Anna Cordelia Allwein, the eldest daughter of the late Dr. V. H. Allwein, of 430 North Ninth street, this city, in the presence of only a few of the most intimate relatives and friends of the contracting parties. The marriage was very quiet owing to the bride being in mourning for her father, who died in October. The bride wore a gown of white silk and carried a bouquet of white chrysanthemums and was attended by her sister, Miss Cora Allwein, who gowned in a dress of white swiss. The groom was attended by one of his friends. After the ceremony a wedding dinner was served at the Lafayette hotel and afterwords the young couple left on a wedding trip embracing all the principal eastern cities. They will return within the month and will spend the winter in Reading and Philadelphia, where the groom has business interests. Prof. Ruoff formerly held the chair of ethics at the State College, but is now extensively engaged in the publishing business.

Mr. Ruoff was a world-renowned author, editor and publisher. He was reportedly for a time a Professor of Ethics at Penn State University (then called the "State College"). He was born in Austria and immigrated to this country at the age of 12. He attended Harvard and George Washington Universities, and did post-graduate studies at Oxford University in England and a number of other places. Mr. Ruoff's obituary, reproduced in its entirety in the following, summarizes his career.[155]

Atlanta, Ga. July 2 (AP)—Dr. Henry W. Ruoff, author and publisher, formerly of Concord, Mass., was found dead in his room at a hotel here today. Physicians said death apparently was due to natural causes. He was in his seventieth year. He was president of the Standard Publication Company and had written a number of books. At one time he served as associate editor of The American Spectator. Dr. Ruoff was born in Austria and was a descendant of Heinrich Ruoff, Margrave of Moravia. His father

---

[155] Obituary from the *New York Times,* New York, New York, July 3, 1935.

was killed in the Austro-Prussian War and he was brought to this country at the age of 12. He attended Harvard and George Washington Universities, from which he later received degrees. He also pursued post-graduate studies at Oxford University, the University of Berlin and the Ecole des Sciences Politiques in Paris. From 1904 to 1906 he was associate editor of The American Spectator and later of a number of magazines in the United States. He taught at a number of institutions and was the author of a number of publications, including "Home and State," "Woman in the Middle Ages," "Century Book of Facts," "Leaders of Men," "The Circle of Knowledge," "Book of the War" and "The Standard Dictionary of facts."

Anna Cordelia "Delia" Allwein and Henry W. Ruoff were mainly located in Cambridge, Massachusetts, as recorded in the 1920 and 1930 Federal Censuses.[156] The 1910 Federal Census of Lebanon, Pennsylvania finds "Cordelia A. Ruoff" living in a Hotel, owned and operated by her aunt and uncle—Henry C. and Catherine S. Borgner, in Lebanon. There is a daughter, Helen I. Ruoff (age 13), living with her there, who is also mentioned in Cordelia Allwein Ruoff's obituary (as Mrs. W.C. Hitchcock). During that Federal Census, Henry W. Ruoff was living in Evanston, Illlinois.[157] Anna Cordelia (Allwein) Ruoff died on November 19, 1936 in Harrisburg, Pennsylvania.[158] She had been a resident of Waltham, Massachusetts. She is buried at St. Mary's Catholic Cemetery in Lebanon, with her father, Vincent H. Allwein, M.D., and brother, Carroll Allwein (see gravestone photo in Exhibit 11.17 above).

---

[156] *Fourteenth Census of the United States* (1920), *Inhabitants of Cambridge Ward 5, Middlesex County, Massachusetts*, E.D. No. 53, page 144A; *Fifteenth Census of the United States* (1930), *Inhabitants of Cambridge, Middlesex County, Massachusetts*, E.D. No. 9-66, page 83B.

[157] *Thirteenth Census of the United States* (1910), *Inhabitants of Lebanon Ward 2, Lebanon County, Pennsylvania*, E.D. No. 148, page 116A; *Thirteenth Census of the United States* (1910), *Inhabitants of Evanston Ward 1, Cook County, Illinois*, E.D. No. 98, page 30A.

[158] Obituary for Cordelia Allwein Ruoff from the *Lebanon Semi-Weely Daily News*, Lebanon, Pennsylvania, Thursday Evening, November 19, 1936.

Kora Magdalen Allwein Klopp (1875-1953)
Lebanon and Harrisburg, Pennsylvania

Kora Magdalen Allwein (F06-0405-0404-04), youngest daughter of Vincent H. and Annie (Ramsay) Allwein, was born in September 1875. The line of descent for Kora Magdalen Allwein, connecting her to Johannes Jacob and Catharina Allwein, progenitors of the Allwein family in colonial Pennsylvania, is as follows:

Generation 1: Johannes Jacob and Catharina Allwein—Berks County, Pa.
Generation 2: Conrad and Catharine (Weibel) Allwein—Dauphin County, Pa.
Generation 3: Philip and Barbara (Frantz) Allwein—Lebanon County, Pa.
Generation 4: John and Julia Ann (Howarter) Allwein—Lebanon County, Pa.
Generation 5: Vincent H. and Annie M. (Ramsay) Allwein—Lebanon County, Pa.
Generation 6: Kora Magdalen Allwein and Oscar Gerhard Klopp—Lebanon and
    Dauphin Counties, Pa.

Kora Magdalen Allwein married Oscar Gerhard Klopp on October 19, 1897, and there were two daughters born to this union, as follows:

Josephine Adele Klopp, b. July 13, 1900, d. October 1, 1981 (ML),
    m. (February 23, 1921) Leon (Lee) Daniel Metzger (b. April 23,
    1891, d. April 14, 1984)
Emilie G. Klopp, b. July 3, 1903, d. December 24, 1994 (ML),
    unmarried

In the 1900 and 1910 Federal Censuses, Oscar and Kora (Allwein) Klopp were residing in Lebanon, where he operated a retail coal business.[159] By 1920, Oscar and Kora (Allwein) Klopp had moved to Harrisburg, Pennsylvania, where he was employed as a bookkeeper in the State Treasury. At that time, their daughter, Josephine, was also employed as a bookkeeper in the State Treasury. Oscar G. Klopp died on December 6, 1921, at a relatively young age

---

[159] *Twelfth Census of the United States* (1900), *Inhabitants of Lebanon Ward 1, Lebanon County, Pennsylvania*, E.D. No. 123, page 173A; *Thirteenth Census of the United States* (1910), *Inhabitants of Lebanon Ward 4, Lebanon, County, Pennsylvania*, E.D. No. 152, page 155B.

Exhibit 11.18 Gravestone for Kora Allwein Klopp and others—Mount Lebanon Cemetery, Lebanon, Pennsylvania

of 52.[160] Kora (Allwein) Klopp continued to reside in Harrisburg, where she worked as a clerk at the State Capital.[161] Polk's 1940 City Directory for Harrisburg, Pennsylvania also lists her there.[162] She died on October 14, 1953. She is buried with her husband, and both of their daughters at Mount Lebanon Cemetery (ML) in Lebanon, Pennsylvania.

Elizabeth Allwein Rise (1845-1900)
Borough of Lebanon

Elizabeth Allwein (F05-0405-0405) was the youngest daughter of John and Julia Ann (Howarter) Allwein, born September 29, 1845. The line of descent for Elizabeth Allwein, connecting her to Johannes Jacob and Catharina Allwein, progenitors of the Allwein family in colonial Pennsylvania, is as follows:

Generation 1: Johannes Jacob and Catharina Allwein—Berks County, Pa.
Generation 2: Conrad and Catharine (Weibel) Allwein—Dauphin County, Pa.
Generation 3: Philip and Barbara (Frantz) Allwein—Lebanon County, Pa.
Generation 4: John and Julia Ann (Howarter) Allwein—Lebanon County, Pa.
Generation 5: Elizabeth Allwein and Jacob Louser Rise—Lebanon County, Pa.

In the 1870 Federal Census of Lebanon Borough, she is listed still living in the household of her parents.[163] She married Jacob L. Rise, son of Adam Rise and Rebecca Louser of Lebanon, Pennsylvania.[164] Jerome Allwein gives the name as "Rice" whereas

---

[160] Obituary from the *Lebanon Daily News*, Lebanon, Pennsylvania, Wednesday Evening, December 7, 1921.

[161] *Fourteenth Census of the United States* (1920), *Inhabitants of Harrisburg Ward 4, Dauphin County, Pennsylvania*, E.D. No. 69, page 20B; *Fifteenth Census of the United States* (1930), *Inhabitants of Harrisburg, Dauphin County, Pennsylvania*, E.D. No. 22-21, page 16B.

[162] Polk's 1940 City Directory for Harrisburg (Dauphin County), Pennsylvania. Ancestry.com.

[163] *Ninth Census of the United States* (1870), *Inhabitants of Borough of Lebanon, Lebanon County, Pennsylvania*, page 337.

[164] Entry for "Adam Rise," *Biographical Annals of Lebanon County, Pennsylvania, Containing Biographical Sketches of Prominent and Representative Citizens and of Many of the Early Settled Families*, J.H. Beers & Company, Chicago, 1904, pages 32-33.

her gravestone gives "Rise" (see Exhibit 11.19) as does the *Biographical Annals of Lebanon County*.

The Jerome Allwein *Genealogy* has this to say about Jacob Rise (Rice):

> Mr. Rice carried on the hat business at Lebanon Pa. with his father under the fine name of Adam Rice & Son.[165]

The *Biographical Annals of Lebanon County* states the following about Jacob Rise:

> Jacob L. Rise, active member of the firm of A. Rise & Son, possesses many traits characteristic of his father, and seems to be quite as successful in business, a large share of the progress made by the firm in recent years having been due to his wise management. As a young man he served valiantly in the Civil war for a full term of enlistment, as a member of Company E, One Hundred and Twenty-seventh Pennsylvania Volunteers Infantry, and was in the battles of Fredericksburg and Chancellorsville; he was discharged in May, 1863. He married Lizzie Alwine, of Lebanon, who died leaving three daughters, Julia, Rebecca and Catherine. Mr. Rise, like his father, is a Democrat. Fraternally he is a Mason in good standing. As a business man he is generous and honorable in all his dealings, and he has a host of warm friends.[166]

The marriage to Jacob L. Rise must have occurred after 1880, as he was still living in the household of his parents in the 1880 Federal Census.[167] There is no trace of the Elizabeth Allwein in the 1880 Federal Census—both her parents having died—it is unclear where she was living.

---

[165] Jerome Allwein, *Genealogy of the Allwein-Arnold Families*, Philadelphia, Pa., 1902, pages 63.

[166] *Biographical Annals of Lebanon County, Pennsylvania, Containing Biographical Sketches of Prominent and Representative Citizens and of Many of the Early Settled Families*, J.H. Beers & Company, Chicago, 1904, page 33.

[167] *Tenth Census of the United States* (1880), *Inhabitants of Borough of Lebanon, Lebanon County, Pennsylvania*, page 285B.

Based on the above sources, along with Federal Census information, three daughters were known to have been born to Elizabeth Allwein and Jacob L. Rise:[168]

Julia M. Rise, b. September 17, 1884, d. November 26, 1968 (ML), m. (September 16, 1919) Frank Hollinger Lehman (b. June 28, 1875, d. October 17, 1944)

Rebecca E. Rise, b. September 28, 1885, d. November 26, 1968 (ML), unmarried

Catherine Ethel Rise, b. July 2, 1889, d. December 26, 1956 (ML), m. (1) (November 17, 1908) John M. McDonald (b. est. 1882, d. unknown) (divorced), (2) (September 22, 1916) Howard Mansfield Eldridge, Jr. (b. unknown, d. unknown)

Elizabeth Allwein Rise died on February 13, 1900, prior to the 1900 Federal Census. In that census, her husband is listed with their three daughters—Julia M. Rise (age 15), Rebecca E. Rise (age 14) and Catherine E. Rise (age 11).[169] Elizabeth Allwein Rise is buried in St. Mary's Catholic Cemetery in Lebanon. Jacob L. Rise lived until January 20, 1921.[170] He is buried at Mount Lebanon Cemetery in Lebanon, Pennsylvania, with his family.

Aaron D. Allwein (1847-1917)
Lebanon, Pennsylvania

Aaron D. Allwein (M05-0405-0406) was the fourth son of John and Julia Ann (Howarter) Allwein, born July 7, 1847 in Lebanon County. The line of descent for Aaron D. Allwein, connecting him

---

[168] Information on some of these children was obtained from the *Lebanon Daily News*, Lebanon, Pennsylvania, Thursday Evening, October 19, 1944; Friday Evening, October 20, 1944; Tuesday, November 26, 1968; Wednesday, November 27, 1968.

[169] *Twelfth Census of the United States* (1900), *Inhabitants of Borough of Lebanon, Lebanon County, Pennsylvania*, E.D. No. 123, page 173A.

[170] Obituary from the *Lebanon Daily News*, Lebanon, Pennsylvania, Thursday Evening, January 20, 1921.

Exhibit 11.19 Gravestone for Elizabeth Allwein Rise—St. Mary's Cemetery, Lebanon, Pennsylvania

to Johannes Jacob and Catharina Allwein, progenitors of the Allwein family in colonial Pennsylvania, is as follows:

Generation 1: Johannes Jacob and Catharina Allwein—Berks County, Pa.
Generation 2: Conrad and Catharine (Weibel) Allwein—Dauphin County, Pa.
Generation 3: Philip and Barbara (Frantz) Allwein—Lebanon County, Pa.
Generation 4: John and Julia Ann (Howarter) Allwein—Lebanon County, Pa.
Generation 5: Aaron D. and Emma L. (Eckenroth) Allwein—Lebanon County, Pa.

Like his older brothers he followed his father into the coach-making business. He is mentioned in Jerome Allwein's *Genealogy*, but little information was available. He married Emma L. Eckenroth in 1870 and they had one child who died in infancy.[171]

In the 1870 Federal Census, Aaron D. Allwein was living with his parents in the Borough of Lebanon, listed as a "coachmaker".[172] He is similarly listed in the 1880 and 1900 Federal Censuses of Lebanon Borough.[173] In the 1910 Census he is listed as a "workman in a scrapyard".[174]

Aaron D. Allwein died on October 31, 1917.[175] Emma L. Allwein died September 30, 1932. Aaron Allwein and Emma L (Eckenroth) Allwein are buried together in St. Mary's Catholic Cemetery (SM) in Lebanon.

---

[171] Jerome Allwein, *Genealogy of the Allwein-Arnold Families*, Philadelphia, Pa., 1902, page 63.
[172] *Ninth Census of the United States* (1870), *Inhabitants of Borough of Lebanon, Lebanon County, Pennsylvania*, page 337.
[173] *Tenth Census of the United States* (1880), *Inhabitants of Borough of Lebanon, Lebanon County, Pennsylvania*, page 349; *Twelfth Census of the United States* (1900), *Inhabitants of Borough of Lebanon, Lebanon County, Pennsylvania*, E.D. No. 131, page 20A.
[174] *Thirteenth Census of the United States* (1910), *Inhabitants of Lebanon Ward 3, Lebanon County, Pennsylvania*, E.D. No. 151, page 144B.
[175] Obituary from the *Lebanon Daily News*, Lebanon, Pennsylvania, Wednesday Evening, October 31, 1917. Note that the Pennsylvania Department of Health Records gives October 30, 1917 as the recorded date of death. See: http://www.health.state.pa.us

Exhibit 11.20 Gravestone for Aaron D. Allwein and Emma L. Eckenroth Allwein—St. Mary's Cemetery, Lebanon, Pennsylvania

William Allwein (1813-1888)
North Lebanon, Pennsylvania

William Allwein (M04-0405-05), son of Philip and Barbara (Frantz) Allwein, was born June 8, 1813 and died October 18, 1888 in Lebanon, Pennsylvania.[176] We summarized what is known about the life of William Allwein in Chapter 7 of *Familie Allwein* Volume 1 (see pages 388-391), and briefly review this here. One new artifact that has come to light is shown in Exhibit 11.21, which is a "Taufscheine" (a birth and baptismal certificate) for William Allwein. This is an example of Fractur Art, which is something unique to Pennsylvania Germans—it is a style of folkart that involves artistic lettering and drawing to commemorate events.[177] The drawings were made in ink and/or watercolors, and the use of Fractur for birth and baptismal certificates was common, as the one shown in Exhibit 11.21. Common artistic motifs were drawings of birds, flowers and hearts, as well as blockletter and italic calligraphy. The text of the calligraphy in this Fractur drawing commemorating the birth and baptism of William Allwein roughly states the following:[178]

William Allwein was born on July 30, 1813 in Lebanon in Lebanon County. The parents are Philip Allwein and his wife Barbara Frantz. His parents are married and Catholic. His baptism was on September 26, 1813 by Reverend Barus. The sponsors were Johannes Arnold and his wife, who gave him the name of William.

---

[176] Birth and baptismal information for William Allwein were obtained from the baptismal records of St. Mary's Roman Catholic Church, Lancaster, Pennsylvania (1805-1841) (see *Familie Allwein*, appendix to Chapter 6, page 348).

[177] See Donald Shelly, *The Fractur Writings or Illuminated Manuscripts of the Pennsylvania Germans*, Allentown, Pennsylvania: Pennsylvania German Folklore Society, 1961.

[178] This text is written in the German dialect known as Pennsylvania Deutsch, commonly referred to as "Pennsylvania Dutch." It was translated with the help of Abigail Alwin and Jan Wolfrum.

Exhibit 11.21 Taufscheine (birth and baptismal certificate) as Fractur art for William Allwein, son of Philip Allwein and Barbara Frantz (contributed by Madeline Moyer)

This document simply confirms the information cited above which was recorded by the St. Mary's priests from Lancaster who visited Lebanon for the purpose of ministering to the Lebanon Catholic community and performing the sacraments (see pages 344-352 of *Familie Allwein*, volume 1).

In his adult years, William Allwein worked as a plasterer, a trade he plied for several years, in addition to working a small 20-acre farm near Kimmerling's Church in North Lebanon Township. William Allwein was married to Mary (Polly) Mars about 1835. Theirs was an inter-religious marriage, as Mary was a Protestant and William Allwein had been baptized Roman Catholic and raised in that faith. From all indications their children were raised in the Catholic faith, since many are buried in the Catholic cemeteries of the region, and according to Jerome Allwein's *Genealogy of the Allwein-Arnold Families* Mary Mars Allwein "was received into the Catholic Church" after his death. Both are buried in St. Mary's Cemetery in the Borough of Lebanon (see Chapter 7, *Familie Allwein*, volume 1, page 391).

We know from Mary's gravestone that she was born March 22, 1814 and died March 5, 1901, but we know little about her family of origin. There is even some dispute about how her family name was spelled. Her gravestone clearly bears the spelling "MARS," but some genealogists use the spelling "MAIRS."[179]

According to the Jerome Allwein *Genealogy*, William Allwein "purchased a farm of about twenty acres on the road between Kimmerling's Church and Mount Zion." In the 1850 Federal Census enumeration we find William Allwein (age 37) and wife "Maria" (age 35) in North Lebanon Township, presumably living on that farm, along with six of their children: Henry (age 14), Maria (age 13), Anthony (Frank) (age 11), Isaac (age 9), Amelia (age 5), and

---

[179] Jerome Allwein, *Genealogy of the Allwein-Arnold Families*, Philadelphia, Pa., 1902, page 28.

Nathaniel (age 1).[180] The 1860 Federal Census for North Lebanon Township places William and Mary in the same location, with ten children, as follows: Henry (age 23), Mary (age 22), Franklin (age 20), Isaac (age 18), Emeline (Amelia) (age 14), Nathaniel (age 12), John (age 9), Polly (age 7), Aaron (age 5), and Jerome (6 months).[181] All of these children, except Jerome, would live to adulthood (see below).

An 1875 *County Atlas of Lebanon* indicates where William Allwein's farm was located (see Exhibit 11.22).[182] This extract of the 1875 map shows the location of four Allwein farms (spelled ALLWINE on the map) in the vicinity of Kimmerling's Church and Cemetery (referred to as the German Reformed Church and Cemetery on the map).[183] In addition to the farm of William Allwein, this map shows the location of the farm of his son Isaac Allwein, the farm of his son Frank Allwein, as well as the farm of the widow of Philip Allwein (M04-0405-07), Catharine Arnold Allwein (indicated on the map as the farm of "Mrs. Allwine"). As I noted in Chapter 7 of Volume 1 (pages 402-404), Philip Allwein (son of Philip Allwein, Sr.) died at a relatively young age, on October 7, 1856, and his widow remained for some time on the family farm. Note also the farm of John Zweier on the map shown in Exhibit 11.22—who married Agnes Catharine Allwein (F05-0405-1103), daughter of Edward and Elizabeth (Arnold) Allwein (see below).

---

[180] *Seventh Census of the United States* (1850), *Inhabitants of North Lebanon Township, Lebanon County, Pennsylvania*, page 153.

[181] *Eighth Census of the United States* (1860), *Inhabitants of North Lebanon Township, Lebanon County, Pennsylvania*, page 454.

[182] F.W. Beers, *County Atlas of Lebanon Pennsylvania from Recent and Actual Surveys and Records*, Reading & Philadelphia: F.A. Davis, 1875, page 61.

[183] Whoever made the map of the North Lebanon territory used the ALLWINE spelling of the name. As far as we know, all of these families used the ALLWEIN spelling. Interestingly, with one or two exceptions, all other appearances in the *County Atlas of Lebanon* of the family name use the ALLWEIN spelling.

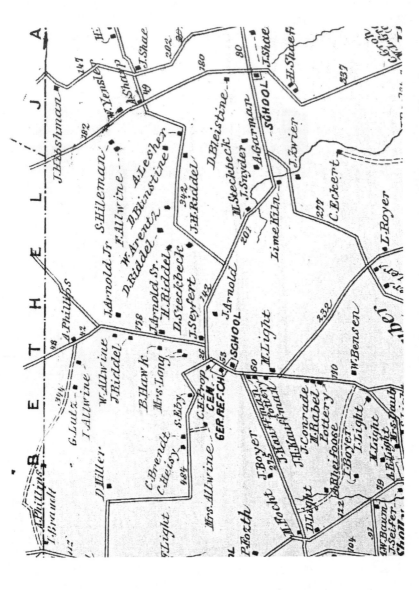

Exhibit 11.22 Extract of 1875 map of the east side of North Lebanon Township of an area including the location of several Allwein farms

William Allwein remained in this area until his death on October 18, 1888, as indicated by his presence in the 1870 and 1880 Federal Census enumerations.[184] William and Mary (Mars) Allwein had eleven children, nine of whom survived to adulthood, as follows (all children are listed in Chapter 7, volume 1, page 389):

Henry Mars Allwein (M05-0405-0501), b. September 25, 1836, d. July 18, 1894 (SM), m. (September 13, 1860) Annie E. McGinley (b. March 2, 1837, d. February 26, 1890)

Anna Maria Allwein (F05-0405-0502), b. November 19, 1837, d. September 18, 1874 (SM), m. John H. Schaeffer (b. June 30, 1840, d. November 30, 1917)

Frank Mars Allwein (M05-0405-0503), b. March 1, 1840, d. November 17, 1914 (HC), m. (1865) Rebecca Arentz (b. February 27, 1842, d. April 3, 1913)

Isaac Mars Allwein (M05-0405-0504), b. May 7, 1842, d. February 21, 1918 (SM), m. (November 14, 1867) Fianna "Anna" B. Gerhart (b. August 17, 1845, d. February 21, 1910)

Amelia Allwein (F05-0405-0506), b. June 27, 1846, d. January 4, 1929 (SM), m. (November 7, 1909) Cyrus W. Miller (b. January 26, 1847, d. February 4, 1932)

Nathaniel (Nathan) Mars Allwein (M05-0405-0507), b. January 1, 1848, d. February 25, 1923 (GS), m. (June 8, 1871) Clara J. Schaum (b. 1853, d. May 10, 1930)

John Mars Allwein (M05-0405-0508), b. December 15, 1850, d. November 11, 1929 (HC), m. (May 13, 1880) Mary Arnold Steckbeck (b. April 29, 1855, d. May 10, 1939)

Mary "Polly" M. Allwein (F05-0405-0509), b. January 11, 1853, d. May 7, 1924 (ML), m. (1874) Aaron H. Whitmer (b. November 4, 1849, d. January 22, 1919)

Aaron Mars Allwein (M05-0405-0510), b. April 24, 1855, d. July 17, 1916 (SM), unmarried

---

[184] *Ninth Census of the United States* (1870), *Inhabitants of North Lebanon Township, Lebanon County, Pennsylvania*, page 236; *Tenth Census of the United States* (1880), *Inhabitants of North Lebanon Township, Lebanon County, Pennsylvania*, page 234.

Notice from this list that all of the male children of William
and Mary Allwein have the middle name of Mars, Mary's maiden
name. The majority of the sons of William and Mary would become
teachers and teach in the common schools of the County. In the
following sections, I discuss what is known about each of William
and Mary (Mars) Allwein's children.

Henry Mars Allwein (1836-1894)
Lebanon, Pennsylvania

Henry Mars Allwein (M05-0405-0501), eldest son of William
and Mary (Mars) Allwein was born September 25, 1836 in North
Lebanon Township. He grew to adulthood on his father's farm and
spent his entire life in the Lebanon area. The lineage connecting
Henry Mars Allwein to Johannes Jacob and Catharina Allwein,
progenitors of the Allwein family in colonial Pennsylvania, is as
follows:

Generation 1: Johannes Jacob and Catharina Allwein—Berks County, Pa.
Generation 2: Conrad and Catharine (Weibel) Allwein—Dauphin County, Pa.
Generation 3: Philip and Barbara (Frantz) Allwein—Lebanon County, Pa.
Generation 4: William and Mary (Mars) Allwein—Lebanon County, Pa.
Generation 5: Henry Mars and Annie (McGinley) Allwein—Lebanon County, Pa.

According to the Jerome Allwein *Genealogy*, Henry Mars
Allwein "attended the public schools until he was about sixteen
years old after which he attended the Annville Academy for one
or two years preparatory to teaching. He taught four or five terms
in North Lebanon Township and afterwards moved to Lebanon
and taught the Parochial School attached to St. Mary's Church for
an equal length of time."[185] He taught there around 1865-67. John
Foster's account of the history of the Assumption of Blessed Virgin
Mary Church in Lebanon mentions that Henry Allwein was "held
in high esteem by the first pupils of St. Mary's School."[186] Among

---

[185] Jerome Allwein, *Genealogy of the Allwein-Arnold Families*,
Philadelphia, Pa., 1902, page 64.
[186] See John J. Foster, *The Story of Assumption of Blessed Virgin Mary
Church, Lebanon, Pennsylvania.* Lebanon, Pennsylvania: Sowers Printing
Company, 1951, page 39.

his pupils at that time were his cousins Ambrose Allwein, Henry Allwein and Mary G. Allwein (children of Samuel and Elizabeth Eisenhauer Allwein).

The genealogist's account of Henry Allwein continues as follows:

On September 13, 1860 Henry Allwein married Annie E. McGinley (b. March 2, 1837). They lived on North Eighth Street Lebanon and he worked at the trade as plasterer for part of the time. He also kept a stock of Catholic books being the only Catholic book store in Lebanon at this time. He was elected water superintendent for the city of Lebanon in the year 1889 and filled the office for three years. He died on July 18, 1894 and was buried at Lebanon.[187]

An 1875 *County Atlas of Lebanon* lists the residence of "H.A. Allwein" at 415 North Eighth Street between Lehman and Monument streets, across the street to the west from the Soldier's Monument Park (see map in Exhibit 11.5).[188] This is across the park from where his cousin Joseph B. Allwein lived for many years, as documented above. The 1888 map gives this same location for "H.M. Allwein," so I assume the 1875 map was in error regarding which Allwein family member lived in this location (see Exhibit 11.23). Note that the potential confusion here is with John Henry Allwein (who went by H.A. Allwein), whose address in 1870 was 823 Mifflin Street, near the corner of Ninth and Mifflin Streets.[189]

---

[187] Jerome Allwein, *Genealogy of the Allwein-Arnold Families*, Philadelphia, Pa., 1902, page 64.

[188] F.W. Beers, *County Atlas of Lebanon Pennsylvania from Recent and Actual Surveys and Records*, Reading & Philadelphia: F.A. Davis, 1875, page 48.

[189] Jerome Allwein, *Genealogy of the Allwein-Arnold Families*, 1902, pages 36-37. *Ninth Census of the United States* (1870), *Inhabitants of Lebanon Borough, Lebanon County, Pennsylvania*, page 323; *Tenth Census of the United States* (1880), *Inhabitants of Bethel Township, Lebanon County, Pennsylvania*, page 333; *Twelfth Census of the United States* (1900), *Inhabitants of Lebanon Ward 5, Lebanon County, Pennsylvania*, E.D. No. 129, page 270A; *Thirteenth Census of the United States* (1910), *Inhabitants of Lebanon Ward 5, Lebanon County, Pennsylvania*, E.D. No. 155, page 212A

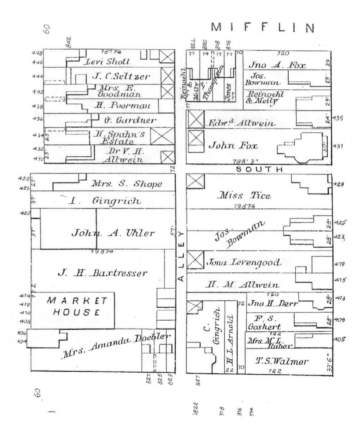

Exhibit 11.23 Extract from 1888 map for Soldier's

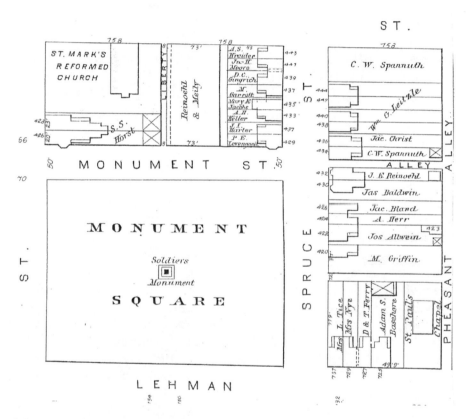

Monument Park showing Allwein households in the area

The 1875 *County Atlas of Lebanon, Pennsylvania* lists "H.A. Allwein" as owning property in the Borough of Lebanon near Ninth Street and Mifflin (see Exhibit 11.5 at the beginning of this chapter).

Henry Mars and Annie (McGinley) Allwein are listed in the 1870 and 1880 Federal Censuses living in the Borough of Lebanon at 415 North Eighth Street.[190] In both of these enumerations his occupation is given as "plasterer." There were seven children born to this union, as follows:[191]

Mary G. Allwein (F06-0405-0501-01), b. June 23, 1861, d. February 14, 1927 (SM), unmarried[192]

Frances C. Allwein (F06-0405-0501-02), b. June 3, 1863, d. July 15, 1937 (HC), unmarried[193]

---

[190]   *Ninth Census of the United States* (1870), *Inhabitants of Lebanon Borough, Lebanon County, Pennsylvania*, page 326; *Tenth Census of the United States* (1880), *Inhabitants of Lebanon Borough, Lebanon County, Pennsylvania*, page 331.

[191]   Jerome Allwein, *Genealogy of the Allwein-Arnold Families*, Philadelphia, Pa., 1902, page 64. Death dates for several of these children were obtained from the *Lebanon Daily News* as follows: Mary G. Allwein [Obituary, *Lebanon Daily News*, Lebanon, Pennsylvania, Thursday Evening, February 17, 1927], Frances C. Allwein [Obituary, *Lebanon Semi-weekly News*, Lebanon, Pennsylvania, Thursday Evening, July 15, 1937], Margaret L. Allwein [Funeral Notice, *Lebanon Daily News*, Lebanon, Pennsylvania, Friday Evening, October 28, 1932], Anna L. Allwein, Agnes Fitzgibbon/Reilly Allwein [Funeral Notice, *Lebanon Daily News*, Lebanon, Pennsylvania, Monday Evening, February 2, 1953], Anna L. Allwein [Obituary for Joseph A. Ganster, *Lebanon Daily News*, Lebanon, Pennsylvania, Wednesday, August 25, 1965], and Lewis A. Allwein [Funeral Notice, *Lebanon Daily News*, Lebanon, Pennsylvania, Thursday Evening, March 4, 1937].

[192]   Obituary and funeral notice for Mary G. Allwein from the *Lebanon Semi-Weekly News*, Lebanon, Pennsylvania, Thursday Evening, February 17, 1927.

[193]   Obituary for Frances C. Allwein, *Lebanon Semi-Weekly News*, Lebanon, Pennsylvania, Thursday Evening, July 15, 1937; Funeral notice, *Lebanon Semi-Weekly News*, Lebanon, Pennsylvania, Thursday Evening, July 19, 1937.

Margaret L. Allwein (F06-0405-0501-03), b. June 9, 1865, d. October 26, 1932 (HC), m. (July 2, 1901) Clifford Rhodes (b. December 1856, d. October 4, 1928)[194]

Anna L. Allwein (F06-0405-0501-04), b. February 17, 1871, d. February 12, 1934, m. (June 15, 1899) Joseph A. Ganster (b. May 14, 1877; d. August 23, 1965)

John William Allwein (M06-0405-0501-05), b. March 12, 1874, d. May 27, 1940 (HC), m. (1) Ethel Day (b. 1876, d. July 24, 1920) (2) (November 27, 1923) Agnes C. Fitzgibbon (nee Reilly) (b. 1878, d. February 1, 1953)

Lewis (Louis) A. Allwein (M06-0405-0501-06), b. August 18, 1876, d. March 4, 1937 (HC), unmarried[195]

Martha R. Allwein (F06-0405-0501-07), b. October 30, 1878, d. January 7, 1938 (HC), unmarried

Henry and Annie (McGinley) Allwein are buried in St. Mary's Cemetery (SM) in the Borough of Lebanon. Henry died July 18, 1894. Annie (McGinley) Allwein died February 26, 1890.

The children of Henry M. and Annie (McGinley) Allwein retained their parents' house at 415 North Eighth Street in Lebanon's 5th Ward, across the street from Monument Park, for most of their lives. In all years of the Federal Census from 1900 to 1930, some subset of these children were living there. For example, in the 1900 Federal Census, all of these children, except for Anna L. Allwein, who had married Joseph A. Ganster by that time (and had moved to Philadelphia), were living there—Mary G. Allwein, Frances C. Allwein, Margaret L. Allwein, John W. Allwein, Lewis A. Allwein and Martha R. Allwein.[196] Daughters Mary G. Allwein (F06-0405-0501-01) and Frances C. Allwein (F06-0405-0501-02)

---

[194] Funeral notices for Clifford and Margaret L. Rhodes from the *Lebanon Daily News*, Lebanon, Pennsylvania, Friday Evening, October 5, 1928; Friday Evening, October 28, 1932. See also the Pennsylvania Department of Health: http://www.health.state.pa.us.

[195] Obituary and funeral notice from the *Lebanon Daily News*, Lebanon, Pennsylvania, Thursday Evening, March 4, 1937; Monday Evening, March 8, 1937.

[196] *Twelfth Census of the United States* (1900), *Inhabitants of Lebanon Ward 5, Lebanon County, Pennsylvania*, E.D. No. 129, page 273A.

Exhibit 11.24 Gravestone for Henry Mars Allwein—St. Mary's Cemetery, Lebanon, Pennsylvania

Exhibit 11.25 Gravestone for Annie (McGinley) Allwein—St. Mary's Cemetery, Lebanon, Pennsylvania

and son Lewis A. Allwein (M06-0405-0501-06) never married. In the following paragraphs we cover what is known about all of these children, although we do not provide separate entries for Mary G. Allwein and Frances C. Allwein.

Margaret L. Allwein Rhodes (1865-1932)
Lebanon, Pennsylvania

Margaret L. Allwein (F06-0405-0501-03), daughter of Henry Mars and Annie (McGinley) Allwein, was born June 9, 1865. The lineage connecting Margaret L. Allwein to Johannes Jacob and Catharina Allwein, progenitors of the Allwein family in colonial Pennsylvania, is as follows:

Generation 1: Johannes Jacob and Catharina Allwein—Berks County, Pa.
Generation 2: Conrad and Catharine (Weibel) Allwein—Dauphin County, Pa.
Generation 3: Philip and Barbara (Frantz) Allwein—Lebanon County, Pa.
Generation 4: William and Mary (Mars) Allwein—Lebanon County, Pa.
Generation 5: Henry Mars and Annie (McGinley) Allwein—Lebanon County, Pa.
Generation 6: Margaret L. Allwein and Clifford Rhodes—Lebanon County, Pa.

On July 2, 1901, Margaret L. Allwein married Clifford Rhodes in Lebanon. By 1910, she and her husband were residing in Lebanon at the Allwein residence at 415 North Eighth, with Margaret's disabled sister, Martha R. Allwein. Clifford Rhodes operated a tailoring business from the home.[197] By 1920, Clifford Rhodes had moved to Philadelphia, where he was working as a guard at a steel plant, and Margaret remained in Lebanon at the residence, with Martha R. Allwein, their older sister Mary G. Allwein, and their niece Ethel F. Allwein, daughter of John W. Allwein (see below).[198] Clifford Rhodes died on October 4, 1928 and is buried in Greencastle, Franklin County, Pennsylvania. Margaret L. (Allwein)

---

[197] *Thirteenth Census of the United States* (1910), *Inhabitants of Lebanon Ward 5, Lebanon, County, Pennsylvania*, E.D. No. 155, page 215B.
[198] *Fourteenth Census of the United States* (1920), *Inhabitants of Lebanon Ward 5, Lebanon County, Pennsylvania*, E.D. No. 174, page 248A; *Fifteenth Census of the United States* (1930), *Inhabitants of Philadelphia Ward 38, Philadelphia County, Pennsylvania*, E.D. 1325, page 171A.

Rhodes died on October 26, 1932 and is buried in Lebanon at Holy Cross Cemetery (HC), along with several of her siblings.[199]

Anna L. Allwein Ganster (1871-1934)
Philadelphia, Pennsylvania

Annie L. Allwein (F06-0405-0501-04), daughter of Henry Mars and Annie (McGinley) Allwein, was born February 17, 1871. She married Joseph A. Ganster on June 15, 1899 and they remained in the Lebanon area for a few years. They lived at 441 North 8th Street, as recorded in the 1900 Federal Census. In the 1900 census report, Joseph Ganster's occupation was listed as "machinist." By 1910, they had moved to Philadelphia, where they were listed in the 1910 and 1920 Federal Census enumerations, and in 1930 they were living in the Borough of Yeadon, Delaware County, Pennsylvania (in suburban Philadelphia).[200] We return to a discussion of this family in Chapter 12, where we cover Allwein families in Philadelphia County.

John William Allwein (1874-1940)
Lebanon, Pennsylvania

John William Allwein (M06-0405-0501-05), oldest son of Henry Mars and Annie (McGinley) Allwein, was born March 12, 1874. The lineage connecting John W. Allwein to Johannes Jacob and

---

[199] Funeral notices for Clifford and Margaret L. Rhodes from the *Lebanon Daily News*, Lebanon, Pennsylvania, Friday Evening, October 5, 1928; Friday Evening, October 28, 1932. See also the Pennsylvania Department of Health: http://www.health.state.pa.us.

[200] *Twelfth Census of the United States* (1900), *Inhabitants of Lebanon Ward 5, Lebanon County, Pennsylvania*, E.D. No. 129, page 272B; *Thirteenth Census of the United States* (1910), *Inhabitants of Philadelphia Ward 24, Philadelphia County, Pennsylvania*, E.D. No. 501, page 262B; *Fourteenth Census of the United States* (1920), *Inhabitants of Philadelphia Ward 34, Philadelphia County, Pennsylvania*, E.D. No. 1173, page 235A; *Fifteenth Census of the United States* (1930), *Inhabitants of Borough of Yeadon, Delaware County, Pennsylvania*, E.D. 23-179, page 248A.

Catharina Allwein, progenitors of the Allwein family in colonial Pennsylvania, is as follows:

Generation 1: Johannes Jacob and Catharina Allwein—Berks County, Pa.
Generation 2: Conrad and Catharine (Weibel) Allwein—Dauphin County, Pa.
Generation 3: Philip and Barbara (Frantz) Allwein—Lebanon County, Pa.
Generation 4: William and Mary (Mars) Allwein—Lebanon County, Pa.
Generation 5: Henry Mars and Annie (McGinley) Allwein—Lebanon County, Pa.
Generation 6: John William and Ethel (Day) [and Agnes (Fitzgibbons)]
    Allwein—Lebanon County, Pa.

As noted above, at the time of the 1900 Federal Census, John William Allwein was living with his siblings at the parental residence at 415 North Eighth. Sometime around 1905, John William Allwein married Ethel Day, although as of this writing we have not found the marriage certificate. Based on information on their children from the 1910 and 1920 Federal Census enumerations, Ethel Day and John William Allwein gave birth to the following children:[201]

Alberta Allwein (F07-0405-0501-0401), b. 1904, d. March 10, 1914 (SM)[202]

Pauline M. Allwein (F07-0405-0501-0402), b. est. 1907, d. unknown m. Roy Shurr, Jr. (b. unknown, d. unknown)

John D. Allwein (M07-0405-0501-0403), b. July 1, 1908, d. March 11, 1969 (HC), m. (April 18, 1936) Marie C. Snyder (b. November 7, 1917, d. April 21, 1988)

Dorothy M. Allwein (F07-0405-0501-0404), b. January 10, 1913, d. March 15, 2004 (HC), m. Leon L. Reed (b. November 16, 1915, d. May 13, 1999)[203]

Ethel Frances Allwein (F07-0405-0501-0405), b. September 21, 1915, d. unknown, m. (1) (May 23, 1936) George Atkinson Hill

---

[201] *Thirteenth Census of the United States* (1910), *Inhabitants of Lebanon Ward 7, Lebanon, County, Pennsylvania*, E.D. No. 155, page 263B; *Fourteenth Census of the United States* (1920), *Inhabitants of Knox Township, Jefferson County, Ohio*, E.D. No. 189, page 92A.

[202] Obituary from the *Lebanon Daily News*, Lebanon, Pennsylvania, Wednesday Evening, March 11, 1914.

[203] Obituary for Dorothy M. Allwein Reed, *Lebanon Daily News*, Lebanon, Pennsylvania, Tuesday, March 16, 2004; obituary for Leon L. Reed, *Patriot News*, Harrisburg, Pennsylvania, May 14, 1999.

(b. August 6, 1915, d. June 20, 1953), (2) (October 28, 1971) Earl James Trollinger (b. October 19, 1918, d. unknown)

At the time of the 1910 Federal Census report they were living at 1123 Lehman Street in Lebanon. By 1920 they had moved to Knox Township in Jefferson County, Ohio, in the area of Steubenville, which borders the western counties of Pennsylvania. There John W. Allwein worked as a "pumper in a waterworks." Tragically, while living in Ohio, Ethel D. Allwein died on July 24, 1920 at the young age of 45.[204] She is buried in Toronto (Jefferson County), Ohio at the Toronto Union Cemetery (TU).

After Ethel Day Allwein died, John W. Allwein and his four children moved back to Lebanon, Pennsylvania, and on November 27, 1923 he remarried to Agnes C. Fitzgibbon, daughter of Bernard and Elizabeth (Youtz) Reilly. John W. and Agnes C. Allwein are listed in the 1930 and 1940 Federal Census enumerations for Lebanon, where he is listed as a "watchman for the railroad."[205] The following is the 1930 Federal Census listing for this household:

John W. Allwein (head, age 56, watchman for the railroad)
Agnes C. Allwein (spouse, age 52)
Pauline M. Allwein (daughter, age 22, trained nurse)
John P. Allwein (son, age 21, telegraph operator for the railroad)
Dorothy M. Allwein (daughter, age 17)
Elizabeth Fitzgibbon (age 13)

Daughter, Ethel F. Allwein, was living in the household of her aunts and uncles at the time of the 1930 Federal Census, which census listing is as follows:[206]

---

[204] State of Ohio Death Index—1908-1932. Ancestry.com.
[205] *Fifteenth Census of the United States* (1930), *Inhabitants of Lebanon, Lebanon County, Pennsylvania*, E.D. No. 38-21, page 157B; *Sixteenth Census of the United States* (1940), *Inhabitants of Lebanon, Lebanon County, Pennsylvania*, E.D. No. 38-28, page 461A.
[206] *Fifteenth Census of the United States* (1930), *Inhabitants of Lebanon, Lebanon County, Pennsylvania*, E.D. No. 38-22, page 186B.

Frances C. Allwein (head, age 68)
Margaret L. Rhodes (sister, age 64)
Lewis A. Allwein (brother, age 53, laborer in steel foundry)
Martha R. Allwein (sister, age 51)
Ethel F. Allwein (niece, age 14)

This appears to have been a close-knit family, consistently sharing the residence of their parental family, although this may have been due to socioeconomic circumstances. In addition, with a disabled sister (Martha R. Allwein became blind—see below), they were able to support one another's needs.

John W. Allwein died on May 27, 1940 and Agnes C. Allwein on February 1, 1953.[207] They are buried in Holy Cross Cemetery (HC) in Lebanon, Pennsylvania.

Lewis A. Allwein (1876-1937)
Philadelphia and Lebanon, Pennsylvania

Lewis A. Allwein (M06-0405-0501-06), son of Henry Mars and Annie (McGinley) Allwein, was born August 18, 1876 in Lebanon, Pennsylvania. The line of descent connecting Lewis A. Allwein to Johannes Jacob and Catharina Allwein, progenitors of the Allwein family in colonial Pennsylvania, is as follows:

Generation 1: Johannes Jacob and Catharina Allwein—Berks County, Pa.
Generation 2: Conrad and Catharine (Weibel) Allwein—Dauphin County, Pa.
Generation 3: Philip and Barbara (Frantz) Allwein—Lebanon County, Pa.
Generation 4: William and Mary (Mars) Allwein—Lebanon County, Pa.
Generation 5: Henry Mars and Annie (McGinley) Allwein—Lebanon County, Pa.
Generation 6: Lewis A. Allwein—Lebanon and Philadelphia Counties, Pa.

---

[207] Obituary for John W. Allwein from *Lebanon Daily News*, Lebanon, Pennsylvania, Monday Evening, May 27, 1940 and funeral notices for Agnes C. Reilly Fitzgibbon Allwein, *Lebanon Daily News*, Lebanon, Pennsylvania, Monday Evening, February 2, 1953; Wednesday Evening, February 4, 1953. See the Pennsylvania Department of Health: http://www. health.state.pa.us

Exhibit 11.26 Gravestones for John W. Allwein and Agnes C. Allwein—Holy Cross Cemetery, Lebanon, Pennsylvania

Lewis A. Allwein was unmarried. He spent most of his adult living in the households of his siblings. In 1900, they were almost all living together at the parental residence, at 415 North Eighth. In 1910, Lewis A. Allwein was living with his sister, Anna L. Allwein, and her husband, Joseph A. Ganster. In the 1920 census year, Lewis was living in a boarding house in Philadelphia, and in 1930 he was back in Lebanon, again at the family homestead.[208]

Lewis A. Allwein died on March 4 1937.[209] He is buried in Holy Cross Cemetery (HC) in Lebanon, Pennsylvania, near his parents, several of his sisters and his brother John W. Allwein.

Martha R. Allwein (1878-1938)
Lebanon, Pennsylvania

Martha R. Allwein (F06-0405-0501-07), youngest daughter of Henry Mars and Annie (McGinley) Allwein, was born October 30, 1878 and lived her entire life in Lebanon, except for a period of nearly four years when she served in the Army Nurse Corps in San Francisco and the Philippine Islands. In fact, my first introduction to this family was when I discovered a military pension record for Martha R. Allwein at the National Archives and Records Administration (NARA). The lineage connecting Martha R. Allwein to Johannes Jacob and Catharina Allwein, progenitors of the Allwein family in colonial Pennsylvania, is as follows:

---

[208] *Twelfth Census of the United States* (1900), *Inhabitants of Lebanon Ward 5, Lebanon County, Pennsylvania*, E.D. No. 129, page 273A; *Thirteenth Census of the United States* (1910), *Inhabitants of Philadelphia Ward 24, Philadelphia County, Pennsylvania*, E.D. No. 501, page 262B; *Fourteenth Census of the United States* (1920), *Inhabitants of Philadelphia Ward 44, Philadelphia County, Pennsylvania*, E.D. No. 1643, page 78A; *Fifteenth Census of the United States* (1930), *Inhabitants of Lebanon, Lebanon County, Pennsylvania*, E.D. 38-22, page 186B.
[209] See the Pennsylvania Department of Health: http://www.health.state. pa.us.

Generation 1: Johannes Jacob and Catharina Allwein—Berks County, Pa.
Generation 2: Conrad and Catharine (Weibel) Allwein—Dauphin County, Pa.
Generation 3: Philip and Barbara (Frantz) Allwein—Lebanon County, Pa.
Generation 4: William and Mary (Mars) Allwein—Lebanon County, Pa.
Generation 5: Henry Mars and Annie (McGinley) Allwein—Lebanon County, Pa.
Generation 6: Martha R. Allwein—Lebanon County, Pa.

Martha R. Allwein did not marry. As a young woman, she became a nurse, and on November 22, 1904, she enrolled in the Army Nurse Corps. She served in the Philippine Islands, but before going to Manila, she served nearly one year in the Presidio General Hospital on the military base at San Francisco. She worked in the Philippine Islands until April 14, 1908. She was discharged at San Francisco, California, and returned home to Lebanon at that time.[210] As a result of the tropical glare, she suffered total blindness and received pension support from the War Department.[211] In all Federal Census years from 1900 to 1930, she was living with her siblings in the house of her parents at 415 North Eighth Street in Lebanon, Pennsylvania.[212]

Martha R. Allwein died January 7, 1938 and is buried at Holy Cross Cemetery (HC), Lebanon, Pennsylvania, near several of her siblings.[213]

---

[210] Pension records for Martha R. Allwein, National Archive and Records Administration, Washington D.C.; see also the *Lebanon Daily News*, Lebanon, Pennsylvania, Tuesday Evening, April 14, 1908.

[211] Pension records for Martha R. Allwein, National Archive and Records Administration, Washington D.C.

[212] *Twelfth Census of the United States* (1900), *Inhabitants of Lebanon Ward 5, Lebanon County, Pennsylvania*, E.D. No. 129, page 273A; *Thirteenth Census of the United States* (1910), *Inhabitants of Lebanon Ward 5, Lebanon, County, Pennsylvania*, E.D. No. 155, page 215B; *Fourteenth Census of the United States* (1920), *Inhabitants of Lebanon Ward 5, Lebanon County, Pennsylvania*, E.D. No. 174, page 248A; *Fifteenth Census of the United States* (1930), *Inhabitants of Lebanon, Lebanon County, Pennsylvania*, E.D. 38-22, page 186B.

[213] See the Pennsylvania Department of Health: http://www.health.state.pa.us.

Exhibit 11.27 Gravestones for Margaret Rhodes, Lewis A. Allwein, Frances C. Allwein and Martha R. Allwein—Holy Cross Cemetery, Lebanon, Pennsylvania

Anna Maria Allwein Schaeffer (1837-1874)
Lebanon, Pennsylvania

Anna Maria Allwein (F05-0405-0502), oldest daughter of William and Mary (Mars) Allwein was born November 19, 1837 and died September 18, 1874 at a relatively young age. The lineage connecting Anna Maria Allwein to Johannes Jacob and Catharina Allwein, progenitors of the Allwein family in colonial Pennsylvania, is as follows:

Generation 1: Johannes Jacob and Catharina Allwein—Berks County, Pa.
Generation 2: Conrad and Catharine (Weibel) Allwein—Dauphin County, Pa.
Generation 3: Philip and Barbara (Frantz) Allwein—Lebanon County, Pa.
Generation 4: William and Mary (Mars) Allwein—Lebanon County, Pa.
Generation 5: Anna Maria Allwein and John H. Schaeffer—Lebanon County, Pa.

Anna Maria Allwein married John H. Schaeffer, and they gave birth to several children as follows:[214]

Jerome Schaeffer, b. August 7, 1863, d. January 19, 1936 (HC), m. (November 27, 1889) Maclata Smith (b. August 20, 1867, d. May 29, 1948)
Elizabeth Schaeffer, b. December 1864, d. January 30, 1957 (HC), m. Joseph J. Bowman (b. December 20, 1865, d. March 17, 1942)
Katie P. Schaeffer, b. March 22, 1866, d. April 1, 1866
Emma Schaeffer, b. March 27, 1867, d. January 4, 1953 (HC), m. (September 3, 1891) David Tice (b. May 8, 1868, d. May 18, 1932)
Amelia Schaeffer, b. November 23, 1868, d. November 16, 1955 (HC), m. (November 23, 1902) Clement Royer (b. February 7, 1878, d. December 11, 1934)
Mary A. Schaeffer, b. May 1872, d. 1908 (SM), m. (May 19, 1896) Joseph A. Seubert (b. March 1866, d. 1927)

After Anna Maria Allwein's death, John H. Schaeffer married Emma J. Swanger. Anna Maria Allwein Schaeffer, her husband, and his second wife are buried together in St. Mary's Cemetery (SM) in the Borough of Lebanon.

---

[214] Jerome Allwein, *Genealogy of the Allwein-Arnold Families*, Philadelphia, Pa., 1902, page 69, pages 110-111.

Exhibit 11.28 Gravestone for Anna Maria Allwein Schaeffer, wife of
John H. Schaeffer—St. Mary's Cemetery, Lebanon, Pennsylvania

Frank Mars Allwein (1840-1914)
Lebanon, Pennsylvania

Frank Mars Allwein (M05-0405-0503), second son of William and Mary (Mars) Allwein was born March 1, 1840 on his parents' farm in North Lebanon Township, Lebanon County, Pennsylvania. He lived his entire life in Lebanon, except for the brief time he was stationed away from home during the Civil War. The lineage connecting Frank Mars Allwein to Johannes Jacob and Catharina Allwein, progenitors of the Allwein family in colonial Pennsylvania, is as follows:

Generation 1: Johannes Jacob and Catharina Allwein—Berks County, Pa.
Generation 2: Conrad and Catharine (Weibel) Allwein—Dauphin County, Pa.
Generation 3: Philip and Barbara (Frantz) Allwein—Lebanon County, Pa.
Generation 4: William and Mary (Mars) Allwein—Lebanon County, Pa.
Generation 5: Frank Mars and Rebecca (Arentz) Allwein—Lebanon County, Pa.

The Jerome Allwein *Genealogy* records the following about Frank Mars Allwein:

> He attended the public schools and commenced to teach in 1859 continuing for seven successive terms. In 1863 he enlisted to serve with the home guard and was stationed at Reading and part of the time at Scranton, Pa., but after seven weeks of soldiering he was mustered out. He learned the trade of plastering. In 1865 he was married to Rebecca daughter of George and Sarah Arentz. Mr. Allwein continued at his trade and become the most prominent in his business at Lebanon being very successful and doing a large amount of work. Among some of the prominent buildings he plastered is the Lebanon Academy of Music. He lives with his family at 6th and Lehman streets, Lebanon, Pa.[215]

Frank M. Allwein served for a six-week term with Company F of the 48th Pennsylvania Emergency Militia of 1863 with his younger brother Isaac Mars Allwein, where he held the rank of Corporal,

---

[215] Jerome Allwein, *Genealogy of the Allwein-Arnold Families*, Philadelphia, Pa., 1902, pages 64-65.

from July 2 to August 26, 1863.[216] Regarding the "Militia of 1863"
the Samuel Bates' *History of Pennsylvania Volunteers* notes that
after the Confederate forces were successful at Fredericksburg in
December of 1862 and at Chancellorsville in early May of 1863, there
were rumors that the rebel army might be planning an invasion of
the North, and there was apprehension concerning the safety of the
border states. As a precautionary measure, the War Department acted
to established two new military units, one headquartered in Pittsburgh
in the Monongahela Valley, and one at Harrisburg in the Susquehanna
Valley. These new military departments issued orders calling upon the
people of the Commonwealth of Pennsylvania to volunteer, and under
this call, twenty-eight regiments of infantry were organized. The
48th regiment was mustered in at Reading. Although details of their
participation is lacking, most of these units were spared major combat,
owing to the defeat of the rebel army on July 3, 1863 at Gettysburg,
and the northern campaign of the Confederate forces was at an end.[217]
After his short term with the militia forces, Frank M. Allwein, did not
re-enlist with the regular army, as did his younger brother Isaac.

After the War ended, in 1865, Frank M. Allwein married
Rebecca Arentz, and they had the following seven children, five of
whom lived to adulthood:

Jerome H. Allwein (M06-0405-0503-01), b. 1866, d. 1868
George William Allwein (M06-0405-0503-02), b. October 13, 1867,
    d. March 15, 1870
Sarah "Sallie" M. Allwein (F06-0405-0503-03), b. July 20, 1869,
    d. August 16, 1945 (HC), m. (May 18, 1893), Philip A. Bleistein
    (b. 1867, d. April 8, 1942)
Mary E. Allwein (F06-0405-0503-04), b. April 28, 1872, d. August
    31, 1961 (CH), became a nun (Sister M. Genevieve / Mother
    Sister M. Genevieve)

---

[216] Samuel P. Bates, *History of Pennsylvania Volunteers 1861-65*, edited
by Janet Hewett, Wilmington NC: Broadfoot Publishing Co., Volume 10,
1994, page 1287.
[217] Samuel P. Bates, *History of Pennsylvania Volunteers 1861-65*, edited
by Janet Hewett, Wilmington NC: Broadfoot Publishing Co., Volume 10,
1994, pages 1222-1231.

Lucy C. Allwein (F06-0405-0503-05), b. August 11, 1876, d. September 8, 1956 (HC), unmarried

Francis Andrew Allwein (M06-0405-0503-06), b. March 1, 1879, d. August 30, 1919 (SM), m. (January 12, 1905) Agnes A. Aurentz (b. August 1877, d. July 5, 1937)

Cecilia A. Allwein (F06-0405-0503-07), b. June 5, 1881, d. January 16, 1955 (HC), unmarried

The Federal Censuses of 1870 through 1910 list Frank Allwein as living in the 5th Ward of the Borough of Lebanon on Lehman Street and list his occupation consistently as "plasterer" (except in 1910 when no occupation was given).[218]

An 1875 *County Atlas of Lebanon* indicates that Frank M. Allwein was living in the Borough of Lebanon on Lehman Street.[219] He is also shown living in the Borough of Lebanon in the 1888 *County Atlas* map (not shown).

Of the children born to Frank Mars and Rebecca (Arentz) Allwein, four daughters and one son, with one exception, all lived their entire lives in the Lebanon area. Two daughters, Lucy C. Allwein (F06-0405-0503-05) and Cecilia Allwein (F06-0405-0503-07) did not marry. These two daughters are both buried at Holy Cross Cemetery (HC) in Lebanon along with their parents and siblings. They are not discussed further here.

---

[218] *Ninth Census of the United States* (1870), *Inhabitants of Lebanon Borough, Lebanon County, Pennsylvania*, page 331; *Tenth Census of the United States* (1880), *Inhabitants of Lebanon Borough, Lebanon County, Pennsylvania*, page 325; *Twelfth Census of the United States* (1900), *Inhabitants of Lebanon Borough, Lebanon County, Pennsylvania*, E.D. No. 128, page 252B; *Thirteenth Census of the United States* (1910), *Inhabitants of Lebanon Borough, Lebanon County, Pennsylvania*, E.D. No. 154, page 186B.

[219] F.W. Beers, *County Atlas of Lebanon Pennsylvania from Recent and Actual Surveys and Records*, Reading & Philadelphia: F.A. Davis, 1875, page 61.

Exhibit 11.29 Gravestone for Frank Mars and Rebecca Arentz Allwein—Holy Cross Cemetery, Lebanon, Pennsylvania

Rebecca (Arentz) Allwein died April 3, 1913. Frank M. Allwein died one year and seven months later, on November 17, 1914. They are buried together, near some of their children, at Holy Cross Cemetery (HC) in Lebanon, Pennsylvania.

Daughter Mary E. Allwein (F06-0405-0503-04), born April 28, 1872, became a nun. She entered the Convent of Sisters of Saint Joseph at McSherrystown, Pennsylvania and was confirmed Sister M. Genevieve. She became Mother Superior in a convent, Oak Lane, near Philadelphia, on April 3, 1913. A member of the Order of St. Joseph for 70 years, she taught in the parochial schools of Philadelphia for many years. Prior to her assignments in Philadelphia, she was a teacher at the Hanover and McSherrystown parochial schools. She died August 31, 1961 and is buried at the Chestnut Hill Convent cemetery (CH) in Philadelphia.[220]

Sarah "Sallie" M. Allwein Bleistein (1869-1945)
Lebanon, Pennsylvania

Sarah M. Allwein (F06-0405-0503-03), eldest daughter of Frank Mars and Rebecca (Arentz) Allwein, was born July 20, 1869 in Lebanon. The lineage for Sarah M. Allwein, connecting her to Johannes Jacob and Catharina Allwein, progenitors of the Allwein family in colonial Pennsylvania, is as follows:

Generation 1: Johannes Jacob and Catharina Allwein—Berks County, Pa.
Generation 2: Conrad and Catharine (Weibel) Allwein—Dauphin County, Pa.
Generation 3: Philip and Barbara (Frantz) Allwein—Lebanon County, Pa.
Generation 4: William and Mary (Mars) Allwein—Lebanon County, Pa.
Generation 5: Frank Mars and Rebecca (Arentz) Allwein—Lebanon County, Pa.
Generation 6: Sarah M. Allwein and Philip A. Bleistein—Lebanon County, Pa.

Sarah M. Allwein married Philip A. Bleistein on May 18, 1893 at St. Mary's Church in Lebanon—he was the son of John H. and Elizabeth Bleistein, who emigrated from Berlin, Germany. Jerome Allwein's *Genealogy* says this about Philip A. Bleistein:[221]

---

[220] Jerome Allwein, *Genealogy of the Allwein-Arnold Families*, Philadelphia, Pa., 1902, page 110. Obituary in the *Lebanon Daily News*, Lebanon, Pennsylvania, Friday, September 1, 1961. See also the Pennsylvania Department of Health: http://www.health.state.pa.us.
[221] Jerome Allwein, *Genealogy of the Allwein-Arnold Families*, Philadelphia, Pa., 1902, page 109. See also obituary in *Lebanon Daily News*, Lebanon, Pennsylvania, Wednesday Evening, April 8, 1942.

Mr. Bleistein is a telegraph operator and for many years had charge of the Chestnut Street Station of the Cornwall and Lebanon Railroad, Lebanon, Pa.

Federal Census reports bear this out. They resided at 1026 Church Street through the 1910 census enumeration and by 1920 they were living at 529 Lehman Street, where they were in the 1930 and 1940 Federal Census enumerations.[222] In the 1930 Federal Census report Philip A. Bleistein's occupation was given as "hostler in railroad roundhouse."[223] In the 1940 report, his occupation is given as "telegraph operator for steam railroad."

Based on Federal Census reports, there were two children born to this union:

---

[222] *Twelfth Census of the United States* (1900), *Inhabitants of Lebanon Ward 6, Lebanon County, Pennsylvania*, E.D. No. 130, page 16A; *Thirteenth Census of the United States* (1910), *Inhabitants of Lebanon Ward 6, Lebanon, County, Pennsylvania*, E.D. No. 156, page 236B; *Fourteenth Census of the United States* (1920), *Inhabitants of Lebanon Ward 5, Lebanon County, Pennsylvania*, E.D. No. 173, page 202B; *Fifteenth Census of the United States* (1930), *Inhabitants of Lebanon, Lebanon County, Pennsylvania*, E.D. 38-20, page 150A; *Sixteenth Census of the United States* (1940), *Inhabitants of Lebanon, Lebanon County, Pennsylvania*, E.D. No. 38-25, page 418A.

[223] HOSTLER (r.r. trans.)—drives electric, diesel-electric, steam, or gas-turbine-electric locomotive to designated stations in railroad roundhouse to be cleaned, serviced, or repaired: Receives locomotive from LOCOMOTIVE ENGINEER (r.r. trans.) at termination of run. Observes oil, air, and steam pressure gauges and water level to ensure that locomotive is operating efficiently. Pushes or pulls levers to control movement of locomotive. Drives locomotive to various stations in roundhouse to be repaired, cleaned, or supplied with coal, fuel oil, water, lubricating oil, and sand, following instructions from ENGINE DISPATCHER (r.r.trans.). Drives locomotive from roundhouse to switching area and delivers serviced locomotive to engine crew. *Dictionary of Occupation Titles* Code: 910.683.010.

Exhibit 11.30 Gravestones for Sarah M. and Philip A. Bleistein—
Holy Cross Cemetery, Lebanon, Pennsylvania

Marie G. Bleistein, b. May 3, 1894, d. December 1978 (HC), m.
(February 10, 1916) Lemuel John Houck (b. July 9, 1892, d.
March 1, 1973)
Rita E. Bleistein, b. 1901, d. August 25, 1931 (HC), unmarried[224]

Sarah M. Allwein Bleistein died on August 16, 1945.[225] She is
buried with her husband and two daughters at Holy Cross Cemetery
(HC) in Lebanon.

Francis Andrew Allwein (1879-1919)
Lebanon, Pennsylvania

Francis Andrew Allwein (M06-0405-0503-06), the only surviving
son of Frank Mars Allwein and Rebecca Arentz, was born March
1, 1879 in Lebanon. The lineage for Francis Andrew Allwein,
connecting him to Johannes Jacob and Catharina Allwein,
progenitors of the Allwein family in colonial Pennsylvania, is as
follows:

Generation 1: Johannes Jacob and Catharina Allwein—Berks County, Pa.
Generation 2: Conrad and Catharine (Weibel) Allwein—Dauphin County, Pa.
Generation 3: Philip and Barbara (Frantz) Allwein—Lebanon County, Pa.
Generation 4: William and Mary (Mars) Allwein—Lebanon County, Pa.
Generation 5: Frank Mars and Rebecca (Arentz) Allwein—Lebanon County, Pa.
Generation 6: Francis Andrew and Agnes A. (Aurentz) Allwein—Lebanon
    County, Pa.

Francis Andrew Allwein married Agnes Aurentz on January 12,
1905.[226] She was the daughter of Aaron and Rebecca Aurentz. As

---

[224] Obituary from the *Lebanon Daily News*, Lebanon, Pennsylvania,
Tuesday Evening, August 25, 1931.
[225] See the Pennsylvania Department of Health: http://www.health.state.
pa.us.
[226] *Thirteenth Census of the United States* (1910), *Inhabitants of Lebanon
Ward 6, Lebanon, County, Pennsylvania*, E.D. No. 156, page 236B;
Fourteenth Census of the United States (1920), *Inhabitants of Lebanon
Ward 5, Lebanon County, Pennsylvania*, E.D. No. 173, page 202B;
Fifteenth Census of the United States (1930), *Inhabitants of Lebanon,
Lebanon County, Pennsylvania*, E.D. No. 38-20, page 150A.

far as I know, there were no children issuing from this union. There is one Federal Census report for Francis Andrew Allwein, in 1910, where they are listed with Aaron and Rebecca Aurentz. In that report Francis Allwein's occupation is given as "plasterer." Francis Andrew Allwein died on August 30, 1919 at the young age of 40. His wife, Agnes (Aurentz) Allwein died several years later on July 5, 1937. They are buried together in St. Mary's Cemetery (SM) in Lebanon.

Isaac Mars Allwein (1842-1918)
Lebanon, Pennsylvania

Isaac M. Allwein (M05-0405-0504), son of William and Mary (Mars) Allwein, was born May 7, 1842 on his parents' farm in North Lebanon Township in Lebanon County, Pennsylvania. Isaac Allwein grew up on his parents' farm and was educated in the public schools.[227] The lineage connecting Isaac Mars Allwein to Johannes Jacob and Catharina Allwein, progenitors of the Allwein family in colonial Pennsylvania, is as follows:

Generation 1: Johannes Jacob and Catharina Allwein—Berks County, Pa.
Generation 2: Conrad and Catharine (Weibel) Allwein—Dauphin County, Pa.
Generation 3: Philip and Barbara (Frantz) Allwein—Lebanon County, Pa.
Generation 4: William and Mary (Mars) Allwein—Lebanon County, Pa.
Generation 5: Isaac Mars and Fianna "Anna" (Gerhart) Allwein—Lebanon County, Pa.

According to Jerome Allwein's *Genealogy*, Isaac Mars Allwein "learned his father's trade of plastering but . . . commenced teaching in the public schools taking several sessions at a normal class in Lebanon, Pa." He and his five brothers—Henry, Frank, Nathaniel, John and Aaron—were all teachers at one time or another in the parochial and/or public schools of Lebanon and adjacent counties. Isaac began teaching while still in his teens and completed 19 terms altogether.

---

[227] Two main sources of information on Isaac Mars Allwein are available: (1) Civil War pension records for Isaac M. Allwein, the National Archives and Records Administration, Washington D.C. and (2) Jerome Allwein, *Genealogy of the Allwein-Arnold Families*, 1902, pages 65-67.

Exhibit 11.31 Gravestones for Francis A. and Agnes Aurentz
Allwein—St. Mary's Cemetery, Lebanon, Pennsylvania

Isaac Mars Allwein served with the Pennsylvania Volunteers during the Civil War. He first served for a six-week term with Company F of the 48th Pennsylvania Emergency Militia of 1863, from July 2 to August 26, 1863, with his older brother Frank Mars Allwein (see above).[228] Then in February 26, 1864 he enlisted for a 3-year term with the 93rd regiment, which was recruited from Lebanon. The 93rd regiment originated in Lebanon September 12, 1861 and its men served valiantly during the early years of the war. In early February, 1864 a large portion of the regiment returned home to Lebanon on a veteran furlough. The entire community celebrated their courage and endurance, and it was after these festivities that Isaac enlisted.[229] Among other things, his regiment participated in the Battle of the Wilderness in May 5-6, 1864. He was discharged June 27, 1865 after the defense of Washington, D.C.

Jerome Allwein's *Genealogy* has this to say about Isaac Mars Allwein's Civil War service:

> He served under Generals Grant, Meade, Hancock, Sheridan and others, was in action in the Battle of the Wilderness, Pennsylvania, Cold Harbor, Petersburg, Weldon, Winchester, Fisher's Hill, Cedar Creek and other minor engagements. He was never wounded in battle except a slight scratch on his right cheek, but his gun had three bullet marks received while fighting. He was honorably discharged at the close of the War June 27th, 1865 at the defenses of Washington.

After the War, Isaac Allwein returned to Lebanon and resumed teaching in the public schools. He married Fianna "Anna" B. Gerhart on November 14, 1867 at St. Mary's Catholic Church in

---

[228] Samuel P. Bates, *History of Pennsylvania Volunteers 1861-65*, edited by Janet Hewett, Wilmington NC: Broadfoot Publishing Co., 1994, Volume 10, page 1287.
[229] Samuel P. Bates, *History of Pennsylvania Volunteers 1861-65*, edited by Janet Hewett, Wilmington NC: Broadfoot Publishing Co., 1994, Volume 5, page 316.

Lebanon, the ceremony being performed by the Reverend Father Boetzkis.[230]

There were eight children born to this union, as follows:[231]

Harry P. Allwein (M06-0405-0504-01), b. November 21, 1868, d. April 22, 1957 (HC), unmarried

Ella (Ellen) Mary Allwein (F06-0405-0504-02), b. January 15, 1870, d. January 23, 1946 (HC), m. (June 24, 1895) Herman "Harry" Joseph Zweier (b. July 16, 1867, d. March 22, 1948)[232]

Catherine "Kate" S. Allwein (F06-0405-0504-03), b. August 5, 1871, December 15, 1954 (CA), m. (October 3, 1893) Henry "Harry" J. Becker (b. November 1868, d. May 23, 1946)

William Henry (Howard) Allwein (M06-0405-0504-04), b. May 23, 1873, d. December 11, 1936 (HC), m. (September 27, 1894) Emma R. Fernsler (b. November 1872, d. August 28, 1940)

John Franklin Allwein (M06-0405-0504-05), b. July 20, 1875, d. February 15, 1956 (HC), m. (June 9, 1903) Margaret I. Harter (b. November 5, 1876, d. October 30, 1960)

Nora Agnes Allwein (F06-0405-0504-06), b. April 22, 1879, d. February 10, 1964 (HC), unmarried

---

[230] Civil War pension records for Isaac M. Allwein, the National Archives and Records Administration, Washington D.C.

[231] Civil War pension records for Isaac M. Allwein, the National Archives and Records Administration, Washington D.C. This information was reported April 5, 1889 and again March 30, 1915 by Isaac Allwein to the Bureau of Pensions. The main discrepancy between the two sets of reports was the day of November in which Harry P. was born, inasmuch as the later report states it was November 21. Jerome Allwein's 1902 *Genealogy of the Allwein-Arnold Families* lists the name Henry P. Allwein for Harry P Allwein. The dates of birth given here for Isaac and Fianna's children agree with those reported in the *Genealogy*, except the latter gives 1886 as Clarence Allwein's birthyear.

[232] I relied on the document "Ancestors of Herman "Harry" Joseph Zweier" by Nancy Allwein Nebiker for this family. There is some inconsistency about his birthdate, as this document gives July 19, 1867, whereas the gravestone (see below) gives July 16, 1867.

Anna Mary (aka Anne B.) Allwein (F06-0405-0504-07), b. September 30, 1880, d. April 29, 1971 (HC), unmarried[233]
Clarence Philip Allwein (M06-0405-0504-08), b. October 9, 1888, d. August 2, 1951 (HC), unmarried

According to the Jerome Allwein *Genealogy*, after their marriage, Isaac and Fianna Allwein moved to Lebanon . . .

. . . and engaged in the Dry Goods business in partnership with Peter A. Glick under the firm name of Allwein & Glick at 745 Cumberland Street. The business not being very successful he sold out his interest after one year's trial in April 1869 to his partner Mr. Glick. He remained living in Lebanon another year, after which he purchased a property in North Lebanon Township of about five acres of Benjamin Swanger and moved with his family to this place in the Spring of 1870. He continued teaching in the public schools in the Winter time and in the Summer worked with neighboring farmers at harvesting. Altogether he taught nineteen terms, all in Lebanon County with the exception of one term in Schuylkill County and one term in Berks County, however, the last term which he taught at Glicks school near Mount Zion he was unable to finish on account of a severe attack of Rheumatism. In the spring of 1883 he sold his country property to Theodore H. Allwein and purchased a lot in Lebanon (5th and Lehman Sts.) upon which he erected a house and moved with his family on June 23rd the same year into the property and opened a Grocery store. He carried on the Grocery business also at the same time plastering and made a success in both. His son Harry taking care of the store trade while he worked at his trade of plastering. He continued in business successfully until the spring of 1890 when he sold out to his son Harry and son-in-law Harry Zweier after which he retired and moved to one of his properties on North Fifth Street.[234]

---

[233] Obituary and funeral notice in the *Lebanon Daily News,* Lebanon, Pennsylvania, Friday, April 30, 1971 and Monday, May 3, 1971.
[234] Jerome Allwein, *Genealogy of the Allwein-Arnold Families*, 1902, pages 65-67.

In the 1870 and 1880 Federal Censuses, Isaac Allwein is listed in North Lebanon Township on a farm adjacent to that of his father, William Allwein. The 1870 enumeration lists his occupation as "plasterer," and in the 1880 enumeration he is listed in North Lebanon Township as a "teacher."[235] Also the *Lebanon County Atlas* of 1875 indicates his residence in North Lebanon Township (see the name "I. Allwine" in Exhibit 11.22 above).[236] Consistent with the Jerome Allwein report, by 1900 he had moved into the Borough of Lebanon, where in the 1900 and 1910 Federal Censuses he is living in the 5th Ward at 345 Fifth Street.[237] The 1900 Federal Census listing gives the following information on Isaac Allwein's family:

Isaac Allwein (head, age 58, plasterer)
Fianna Allwein (spouse, age 54)
Harry P. Allwein (son age 32, grocer)
John Allwein (son, age 24, plasterer)
Nora Allwein (daughter, age 21, apprentice tailor)
Anna Allwein (age 19, at school)
Clarence Allwein (age 11, at school)

By 1900, son William H. Allwein and daughters Ella Mary Allwein and Catherine S. Allwein were married and living independently. At the time of the 1910 Census, Isaac's wife Fianna had recently died. He is listed as a widower and is living with several of his adult children: Harry Allwein (age 41, grocer), Nora

---

[235] *Ninth Census of the United States* (1870), *Inhabitants of North Lebanon Township, Lebanon County, Pennsylvania*, page 236; *Tenth Census of the United States* (1880), *Inhabitants of North Lebanon Township, Lebanon County, Pennsylvania*, page 236C.
[236] F.W. Beers, *County Atlas of Lebanon Pennsylvania from Recent and Actual Surveys and Records*, Reading & Philadelphia: F.A. Davis, 1875, page 61.
[237] *Twelfth Census of the United States* (1900), *Inhabitants of Lebanon Borough Ward 5, Lebanon County, Pennsylvania*, E.D. No. 128, page 250A; *Thirteenth Census of the United States* (1910), *Inhabitants of Lebanon Borough Ward 5, Lebanon County, Pennsylvania*, E.D. No. 154, page 205B.

Allwein (age 32, seamstress), Annie Allwein (age 29), and Clarence Allwein (age 21, telegraph operator for the railroad).

As indicated by the Jerome Allwein *Genealogy,* following his many years of public school teaching, Isaac Allwein later operated a grocery store and also pursued the trade of plastering in Lebanon. The grocery business was operated into the 1940s under the name "I.M. Allwein & Sons" for many years by his children and grandchildren, until about 1940 (see the city directories for Lebanon).

Isaac Allwein first filed for pension support in February of 1880 at the age of 37, claiming to suffer from chronic rheumatism originating during his war service. Lacking evidence that the condition was in fact stimulated by his war experience, the original application was denied. After a decade of bringing further evidence to bear on his claim, his declaration was finally accepted and he began receiving support on July 23, 1890 at the age of 48.[238] This support continued until his death on February 21, 1918 in Lebanon, Pennsylvania. His wife Fianna died in 1910.[239] They are buried side by side in St. Mary's Cemetery in Lebanon, Pennsylvania. Their children, by contrast, are (with one exception) all buried in the Holy Cross Cemetery in North Lebanon.

Harry P. Allwein (1868-1957), Nora Agnes Allwein (1879-1964), and Anna Mary Allwein (1880-1971) Lebanon, Pennsylvania

Harry P. Allwein (M06-0405-0504-01), eldest son of Isaac Mars and Fianna (Gerhart) Allwein, was born November 21, 1868 on his parents' farm in North Lebanon Township. His sisters, Nora Agnes Allwein (F06-0405-0504-06) and Anna Mary Allwein (F06-0405-0504-07), were born there too, on April 22, 1879 and

---

[238] Civil War pension records for Isaac M. Allwein, the National Archives and Records Administration, Washington D.C.
[239] Obituary from *Lebanon Daily News*, Lebanon, Pennsylvania, Tuesday, February 22, 1910.

Exhibit 11.32 Gravestones for Isaac M. Allwein and Fianna Gerhart Allwein—St. Mary's Cemetery, Lebanon, Pennsylvania

September 30, 1880, respectively. The line of descent connecting these children to Johannes Jacob and Catharina Allwein, progenitors of the Allwein family in colonial Pennsylvania, is as follows:

Generation 1: Johannes Jacob and Catharina Allwein—Berks County, Pa.
Generation 2: Conrad and Catharine (Weibel) Allwein—Dauphin County, Pa.
Generation 3: Philip and Barbara (Frantz) Allwein—Lebanon County, Pa.
Generation 4: William and Mary (Mars) Allwein—Lebanon County, Pa.
Generation 5: Isaac Mars and Fianna (Gerhart) Allwein—Lebanon County, Pa.
Generation 6: Harry P. Allwein, Nora Agnes Allwein and Anna Mary Allwein—
    Lebanon, Pa.

None of these three children married, and in 1910, as recorded in the 1910 Federal Census, they resided together with their father in the parental home at 345 Fifth Street (see above). After Isaac Mars Allwein's death in 1918, they continued to live there, and as far as I can tell, through the remainder of their lives. They are recorded as residing there in the 1920, 1930 and 1940 Federal Censuses.[240] Harry P. Allwein and his sisters Nora and Anna are also listed there in a 1940 City Directory for Lebanon.[241]

Harry P. Allwein operated a grocery store at the same address as their residence in Lebanon, taking over this business from his father. The grocery business was called "I.M. Alwein Sons." His sister Anna Mary Allwein worked there as a saleslady, and their sister, Nora Allwein, managed the household (see the Census reports mentioned above). Harry P. Allwein died in 1957, Nora Allwein in 1964, and Ann Mary (aka Anne B.) Allwein on April 29, 1971.[242] These children are buried in Holy Cross Cemetery (HC) in Lebanon.

---

[240] *Fourteenth Census of the United States* (1920), *Inhabitants of Lebanon Ward 5, Lebanon County, Pennsylvania*, E.D. No. 173, page 202B; *Fifteenth Census of the United States* (1930), *Inhabitants of Lebanon, Lebanon County, Pennsylvania*, E.D. 38-20, page 150A; *Sixteenth Census of the United States* (1940), Inhabitants of Lebanon, Lebanon County, Pennsylvania, E.D. 38-28, page 461A.

[241] *Polk's 1940 Lebanon City Directory*. Ancestry.com.

[242] See obituaries for Harry P. Allwein, Nora P. Allwein, and Anne B. Allwein in the *Lebanon Daily News*, Lebanon, Pennsylvania, Monday Evening, April 22, 1957; Tuesday Evening, February 11, 1964; Friday, April 30, 1971.

Exhibit 11.33 Gravestones for Harry P. Allwein and Nora A. Allwein—Holy Cross Cemetery, Lebanon, Pennsylvania

Exhibit 11.34 Gravestone for Anne B. Allwein   Holy Cross Cemetery, Lebanon, Pennsylvania

Ella (Ellen) Mary Allwein Zweier (1870-1946) Lebanon, Pennsylvania

Ella (Ellen) Mary Allwein (F06-0405-0504-02), eldest daughter of Isaac Mars and Fianna (Gerhart) Allwein was born on her parents' farm in North Lebanon Township, Lebanon County on January 15, 1870. The lineage connecting her to Johannes Jacob and Catharina Allwein, progenitors of the Allwein family in colonial Pennsylvania, is as follows:

Generation 1: Johannes Jacob and Catharina Allwein—Berks County, Pa.
Generation 2: Conrad and Catharine (Weibel) Allwein—Dauphin County, Pa.
Generation 3: Philip and Barbara (Frantz) Allwein—Lebanon County, Pa.
Generation 4: William and Mary (Mars) Allwein—Lebanon County, Pa.
Generation 5: Isaac Mars and Fianna (Gerhart) Allwein—Lebanon County, Pa.
Generation 6: Ella (Ellen) Mary Allwein and Herman "Harry" Joseph
    Zweier—Lebanon County, Pa.

Ella Allwein married Harry J. Zweier, son of George and Catharine Mary (Arnold) Zweier, on June 24, 1895 in Lebanon, and they settled there for the remainder of their lives. Harry Zweier established himself in the grocery business in Lebanon at 543 Cumberland Street, where they appear in Federal Censuses from 1910 to 1930.[243]

Three children were born to Ella Mary Allwein and Herman Joseph Zweier, as follows:[244]

Hilda M. Zweier, b. December 11, 1899, d. February 14, 1989, m. (July 19, 1928) Norman W. Boyd (b. January 22, 1900, d. October 1989)

Richard J. Zweier, Sr., b. February 19, 1902, d. December 6, 1971 (HC), m. (January 2, 1950) Verna Ruth Leedy (b. September 17, 1913, d. August 11, 2003)

Curtis J. Zweier, b. August 22, 1903, d. January 17, 1965 (HC), m. (September 12, 1934) Marie E. Horner (May 28, 1912, d. May 23, 1995)

Ella (Allwein) Zweier died on January 23, 1946. Harry J. Zweier died a few years later on March 22, 1948.[245] They are buried in Holy Cross Cemetery (HC) in Lebanon. Pennsylvania.

---

[243] *Twelfth Census of the United States* (1900), *Inhabitants of Lebanon Ward 5, Lebanon County, Pennsylvania*, E.D. No. 128, page 244B; *Thirteenth Census of the United States* (1910), *Inhabitants of Lebanon Ward 4, Lebanon County, Pennsylvania*, E.D. No. 153, page 166A; *Fourteenth Census of the United States* (1920), *Inhabitants of Lebanon Ward 4, Lebanon County, Pennsylvania*, E.D. No. 172, page 188B; *Fifteenth Census of the United States* (1930), *Inhabitants of Lebanon, Lebanon County, Pennsylvania*, E.D. No. 38-19, page 107A.

[244] Information on some of these children and their spouses was obtained from obituaries in the *Lebanon Daily News*, Lebanon, Pennsylvania, as follows: Monday Evening, January 18, 1965; Monday Evening, December 6, 1971; Wednesday, May 24, 1995; Tuesday, August 12, 2003.

[245] Obituaries for Ella and Harry J. Zweier from the *Lebanon Daily News*, Lebanon, Pennsylvania, Wednesday Evening, January 23, 1946; Monday Evening, March 22, 1948. See the Pennsylvania Department of Health: http://www.health.state.pa.us.

Exhibit 11.35 Gravestone for Ella and Harry J. Zweier—Holy Cross Cemetery, Lebanon, Pennsylvania

Catherine Suzanne Allwein Becker (1871-1954)
Altoona, Pennsylvania

Catherine Suzanne Allwein (F06-0405-0504-03), second daughter of Isaac Mars and Fianna (Gerhart) Allwein, was born on her parents' farm in North Lebanon Township, Lebanon County on August 5, 1871. She married Henry (Harry) J. Becker, son of Bernhard and Augusta (Shenck) Becker, on October 3, 1893 in Lebanon. They lived initially in Scranton, Pennsylvania, where Henry worked as a molder in a foundry, but they eventually settled in the Altoona (Blair County) area, where they lived for the remainder of their lives. Henry Becker worked for the Pennsylvania Railroad in Altoona. We cover what is known about this family in Chapter 16, where we discuss the Allwein families that settled in Blair County.

William Henry (Howard) Allwein (1873-1936)
Lebanon, Pennsylvania

William Henry (Howard) Allwein (M06-0405-0504-04), son of Isaac Mars and Fianna (Gerhart) Allwein was born on his parents' farm in North Lebanon Township, Lebanon County on May 23, 1873.[246] William Henry Allwein also went by the name of "Howard" Allwein. The line of descent connecting him to Johannes Jacob and Catharina Allwein, progenitors of the Allwein family in colonial Pennsylvania, is as follows:

Generation 1: Johannes Jacob and Catharina Allwein—Berks County, Pa.
Generation 2: Conrad and Catharine (Weibel) Allwein—Dauphin County, Pa.
Generation 3: Philip and Barbara (Frantz) Allwein—Lebanon County, Pa.
Generation 4: William and Mary (Mars) Allwein—Lebanon County, Pa.
Generation 5: Isaac Mars and Fianna (Gerhart) Allwein—Lebanon County, Pa.
Generation 6: William Henry (Howard) and Emma R. (Fernsler)
    Allwein—Lebanon County, Pa.

William Henry (Howard) Allwein married Emma R. Fernsler on September 27, 1894 in Lebanon, Pennsylvania. They settled

---

[246] Some sources give "Henry" as the middle name for William H. Allwein; however, in his World War I draft registration card, he signed it William Howard Allwein. World War I draft registration files. Ancestry. com.

in Ward 5 of Lebanon, where they remained for the rest of their lives.[247] According to the 1900 Federal Census enumeration, his first occupation was that of a "machine molder" in a foundry, but eventually he established himself in the grocery business at 325 Weidman in Lebanon, which he pursued for the remainder of his life. This grocery business went by the name "I.M. Allwein & Sons" and was operated as such after his death by his children (see the city directories for Lebanon).

Based on Federal Census reports for 1900 and 1910 and other information, we know that William (Howard) and Emma (Fernsler) Allwein had several children, as follows:[248]

Herbert I. Allwein (M07-0405-0504-0401), b. March 13, 1895, d. August 5, 1960 (HC), m. (1) (October 7, 1919) Bertha B. Bleistein (b. November 17, 1894, d. February 6, 1947), (2) (June 12, 1948) Margaret A. Burke (b. December 28, 1907, d. August 24, 1993)

Russell Cyril Allwein (M07-0405-0504-0402), b. March 10, 1897, d. April 9, 1982 (HC), m. (June 26, 1923) Florence M. Sullivan (b. February 1898, d. October 3, 1966)

William H. Allwein, Jr. (M07-0405-0504-0403), b. March 1899, d. May 17, 1937 (HC), m. Ruth Snow Snell (b. June 12, 1897, d. February 18, 1983)

Aloysius "Allen" Bernard Allwein (M07-0405-0504-0404), b. November 7, 1903, d. December 18, 1958, m. (1) (August 18,

---

[247] *Twelfth Census of the United States* (1900), *Inhabitants of Lebanon Ward 5, Lebanon County, Pennsylvania*, E.D. No. 128, page 246B; *Thirteenth Census of the United States* (1910), *Inhabitants of Lebanon Ward 5, Lebanon County, Pennsylvania*, E.D. No. 154, page 198B; *Fourteenth Census of the United States* (1920), *Inhabitants of Lebanon Ward 5, Lebanon County, Pennsylvania*, E.D. No. 173, page 210B; *Fifteenth Census of the United States* (1930), *Inhabitants of Lebanon, Lebanon County, Pennsylvania*, E.D. 38-20, page 159A.

[248] Information presented here comes in part from obituaries in the *Lebanon Semi-Weekly News* or *Lebanon Daily News*, Lebanon, Pennsylvania, as follows: Thursday Evening, May 20, 1937; Thursday Evening, February 6, 1947; Saturday, December 20, 1958; Friday, August 5, 1960; Monday Evening, October 3, 1966; Saturday, February 19, 1983.

1925) Lenore T. Isola (b. est. 1907, d. unknown), (2) Patricia
Unknown (b. unknown, d. unknown)
Catherine A. Allwein (F07-0405-0504-0405), b. July 4, 1909, d.
August 20, 1991, m. (November 25, 1931) Richard Edgar Heisey
(b. January 21, 1908, d. October 23, 1991)[249]

William Henry Allwein (Sr.) died in December 11, 1936. His
wife Emma R. Allwein died a few years later on August 28, 1940.[250]
They are buried at Holy Cross Cemetery (HC) in Lebanon.

John Franklin Allwein (1875-1956)
Lebanon, Pennsylvania

John Franklin Allwein (M06-0405-0504-05), son of Isaac Mars and
Fianna (Gerhart) Allwein, was born July 20, 1875 on his parents' farm
in North Lebanon Township, Lebanon County. The line of descent
connecting him to Johannes Jacob and Catharina Allwein, progenitors
of the Allwein family in colonial Pennsylvania, is as follows:

Generation 1: Johannes Jacob and Catharina Allwein—Berks County, Pa.
Generation 2: Conrad and Catharine (Weibel) Allwein—Dauphin County, Pa.
Generation 3: Philip and Barbara (Frantz) Allwein—Lebanon County, Pa.
Generation 4: William and Mary (Mars) Allwein—Lebanon County, Pa.
Generation 5: Isaac Mars and Fianna (Gerhart) Allwein—Lebanon County, Pa.
Generation 6: John Franklin and Margaret I (Harter) Allwein—Lebanon
    County, Pa.

John Franklin Allwein volunteered to serve in the Spanish
American War—enlisting on June 17, 1898 and mustering out on
November 16, 1898.[251] In the 1900 Federal Census, John Franklin

---

[249] Information on marriage date from Indiana Marriages, 1780-1992.
Ancestry.com.
[250] Funeral notice from the *Lebanon Semi-Weekly News*, Lebanon,
Pennsylvania, Thursday Evening, December 17, 1956. See also the
Pennsylvania Department of Health: http://www.health.state.pa.us
[251] <http://www.paspanishamericanwar.com/rosters.html>   See   PA
Volunteers of the Spanish American War 1898-1899 at this website, under
"Fourth Regiment."

Exhibit 11.36 Gravestone for William H. and Emma R. Allwein—Holy Cross Cemetery, Lebanon, Pennsylvania

Allwein had returned to live at home with his parents at 345 North Fifth Street in the 5th Ward of Lebanon. He took up the trade of his father, working as a "plasterer" (see above). He married Margaret I. Harter on June 9, 1903 at St. Mary's Church in Lebanon. They settled in Lebanon, where they remained through the 1910-1940 Federal Censuses.[252] With the invention and later mass production of the automobile, John Franklin Allwein became interested in the maintenance and repair of these motorized vehicles. In the 1910 Federal Census he is listed as the "proprietor of a garage," in 1920 as the "proprietor of an accessory shop," in 1930 as a "merchant in auto supplies." He is also listed in the 1940 Polk's Lebanon City Directory.

John Franklin Allwein and Margaret I. Harter had two children, as follows:

June E. Allwein (F07-0405-0504-0501), b. June 1, 1904, d. September 8, 1979 (ML), m. Enoch C. Byron (b. March 10, 1913, d. February 13, 1994)

Homer J. Allwein (M07-0405-0504-0502), b. March 30, 1906, d. May 30, 1989 (NM), m. (July 9, 1942) Marion N. Bowman (b. December 3, 1905, d. February 26, 1994)[253]

John Franklin Allwein died February 15, 1956 and is buried in Holy Cross Cemetery (HC) in Lebanon, Pennsylvania.[254] Margaret Harter Allwein died October 30, 1960 and is buried at Mount Lebanon Cemetery (ML) in Lebanon with her sister Gertrude (Harter) Mann and near her daughter.

---

[252] *Thirteenth Census of the United States* (1910), *Inhabitants of Lebanon Ward 5, Lebanon County, Pennsylvania*, E.D. No. 155, page 228B; *Fourteenth Census of the United States* (1920), *Inhabitants of Lebanon Ward 4, Lebanon County, Pennsylvania*, E.D. No. 172, page 186B; *Fifteenth Census of the United States* (1930), *Inhabitants of Lebanon, Lebanon County, Pennsylvania*, E.D. 38-19, page 124A; *Sixteenth Census of the United States* (1940), *Inhabitants of Lebanon, Lebanon County, Pennsylvania*, E.D. 38-23A, page 375B.

[253] Obituary for Homer Allwein from the *Patriot-News*, Harrisburg, Pennsylvania, May 31, 1989.

[254] Obituary for John F. Allwein from *Lebanon Daily News*, Lebanon, Pennsylvania, Thursday, February 16, 1956.

Exhibit 11.37 Gravestone for John F. Allwein—Holy Cross Cemetery, Lebanon, Pennsylvania

Clarence Philip Allwein (1888-1951)
Lebanon, Pennsylvania

Clarence Philip Allwein (M06-0405-0504-08), the youngest son of
Isaac Mars and Fianna (Gerhart) Allwein, was born October 9, 1888
on his parents' farm in North Lebanon, Pennsylvania. The line of
descent connecting him to Johannes Jacob and Catharina Allwein,
progenitors of the Allwein family in colonial Pennsylvania, is as
follows:

Generation 1: Johannes Jacob and Catharina Allwein—Berks County, Pa.
Generation 2: Conrad and Catharine (Weibel) Allwein—Dauphin County, Pa.
Generation 3: Philip and Barbara (Frantz) Allwein—Lebanon County, Pa.
Generation 4: William and Mary (Mars) Allwein—Lebanon County, Pa.
Generation 5: Isaac Mars and Fianna (Gerhart) Allwein—Lebanon County, Pa.
Generation 6: Clarence Philip Allwein—Lebanon County, Pa.

As noted above, as a young adult Clarence Philip Allwein was
a telegraph operator for the railroad. According to his obituary in
the *Lebanon Daily News*, he was a veteran of World War I, having
served with the Army Signal Corps. He was a retired sailor and
served, as a radio operator with the Merchant Marine from 1922
to 1932.[255] Seven times he traveled around the world during World
War I. He experienced a number of bombings and on one occasion
his ship was destroyed. He was a member of St. Mary's Catholic
Church and The Holy Name Society.

Clarence Philip Allwein died on August 2, 1951 at the age of
62.[256] He is buried in Holy Cross Cemetery (HC), near his brothers
and sisters.

---

[255] See New York Passenger Lists, 1820-1957. Ancestry.com.
[256] Obituary from the *Lebanon Daily News*, Lebanon, Pennsylvania,
Thursday August 2, 1951.

Exhibit 11.38 Gravestone for Clarence P. Allwein—Holy Cross Cemetery, Lebanon, Pennsylvania

Amelia Allwein Miller (1846-1929)
Lebanon, Pennsylvania

Amelia Allwein (F05-0405-0506), daughter of William and Mary (Mars) Allwein was born June 27, 1846 on her parents' farm in North Lebanon Township in Lebanon County, Pennsylvania. The lineage connecting Amelia Allwein to Johannes Jacob and Catharina Allwein, progenitors of the Allwein family in colonial Pennsylvania, is as follows:

Generation 1: Johannes Jacob and Catharina Allwein—Berks County, Pa.
Generation 2: Conrad and Catharine (Weibel) Allwein—Dauphin County, Pa.
Generation 3: Philip and Barbara (Frantz) Allwein—Lebanon County, Pa.
Generation 4: William and Mary (Mars) Allwein—Lebanon County, Pa.
Generation 5: Amelia Allwein and Cyrus Miller—Lebanon County, Pa.

Amelia Allwein married Cyrus Miller, but this did not occur until later in her life. At age 52, Amelia was still living with her mother Mary (Mars) Allwein and brother Aaron Mars Allwein in North Lebanon Township, as indicated in the 1900 Federal Census records. In the 1910 Census she is listed as married to Cyrus Miller, living in the Borough of Lebanon Ward 5 with her husband, in the household of her brother Aaron Mars Allwein. Her brother Aaron died on July 17, 1916, and she and her husband continued to live in the Borough of Lebanon. The 1920 Federal Census enumeration indicates they were still living in Lebanon Ward 5. She and her husband Cyrus Miller were in their early 70s, and he was working as a watchman in a lumber yard.[257] She died on January 4, 1929 and is buried at the St. Mary's Cemetery in Lebanon. Her husband is presumably buried elsewhere, suggesting that he may not have worshiped in the Catholic faith.

---

[257] *Twelfth Census of the United States* (1900), *Inhabitants of North Lebanon Township, East Election District, Lebanon County, Pennsylvania*, E.D. No. 137, page 133B; *Thirteenth Census of the United States* (1910), *Inhabitants of Lebanon Borough Ward 5, Lebanon County, Pennsylvania*, E.D. No. 154, page 202A; *Fourteenth Census of the United States* (1920), *Inhabitants of Lebanon Borough Ward 5, Lebanon County, Pennsylvania*, E.D. No. 173, page 210A.

Exhibit 11.39 Gravestone for Amelia Allwein, wife of Cyrus Miller—St. Mary's Cemetery, Lebanon, Pennsylvania

Nathaniel M. Allwein (1848-1923)
North Lebanon Township

Nathaniel Mars Allwein (M05-0405-0507), son of William and Mary (Mars) Allwein, was born January 1, 1848 on his parents' farm in North Lebanon Township. He grew up there and was educated in the public schools. The lineage connecting Nathaniel Mars Allwein to Johannes Jacob and Catharina Allwein, progenitors of the Allwein family in colonial Pennsylvania, is as follows:

Generation 1: Johannes Jacob and Catharina Allwein—Berks County, Pa.
Generation 2: Conrad and Catharine (Weibel) Allwein—Dauphin County, Pa.
Generation 3: Philip and Barbara (Frantz) Allwein—Lebanon County, Pa.
Generation 4: William and Mary (Mars) Allwein—Lebanon County, Pa.
Generation 5: Nathaniel Mars and Clara J. (Schaum) Allwein—Lebanon County, Pa.

Jerome Allwein's *Genealogy of the Allwein-Arnold Families* records the following about his life:[258]

Nathaniel M. Allwein, son of William and Mary (Mars) Allwein was born January 1, 1848 on his father's farm in Lebanon County, Pa. He attended the public schools; learned the trade of plastering with his father. He attended the Lebanon Normal School preparatory to teaching. At age of 20 he commenced teaching in the public schools and taught for eleven terms, part of the time in North Lebanon Township and part in Bethel Township. He was married on June 8th, 1871 to Clara, daughter of Jacob Shaun [Schaum] (P = protestant). Lived at Mount Zion until year 1878 when he built some houses on North 5th street, Lebanon and moved with his family to that city. He continued working at trade of plastering in Lebanon. He was also a musician of some note and while living at Mount Zion he was the leader of the Mount Zion Band after his brother John had resigned from the leadership.

---

[258] Jerome Allwein, *Genealogy of the Allwein-Arnold Families*, 1902, pages 67-68.

As noted in the above, on June 8, 1871 he married Clara J. Schaum, daughter of Jacob and Mary Schaum, and they had the following children:

Daisy Mary Allwein (F06-0405-0507-01), b. December 9, 1872, d. April 14, 1908 (SM), m. (September 21, 1907) Charles H. Swanger (b. June 30, 1877, d. 1945 (KR))

Victor Jacob Allwein (M06-0405-0507-02), b. December 15, 1877, d. January 29, 1932 (HC) m. Lucy Henrietta Allwein (b. July 12, 1890, d. December 19, 1949)

Arthur William Allwein (M06-0405-0507-03), b. January 19, 1881, d. April 29, 1940 (ML), m. (January 24, 1905) Marie Edith Ross (b. December 1882, d. August 29, 1942)

Irene Gertrude Allwein (F06-0405-0507-04), b. March 11, 1892, d. July 18, 1925 (ML), m. (August 14, 1919) Charles H. Grossman (b. March 1892, d. September 30, 1957)

In the 1880 Federal Census Nathaniel M. Allwein is listed as residing in the 5th Ward in the Borough of Lebanon.[259] Addresses were not provided in the 1880 Federal Census, but presumably when they moved from North Lebanon Township, they moved to 449 North Fifth Street, which is the address given for Nathaniel and Clara (Schaum) Allwein in the 1900, 1910 and 1920 Federal Censuses.[260]

The 1900 Federal Census listing recorded the household composition as follows:

Nathaniel Allwein (head, age 52, plasterer)

---

[259] *Tenth Census of the United States* (1880), *Inhabitants of Borough of Lebanon, Lebanon County, Pennsylvania*, page 321D. His name is erroneously recorded as "Daniel Allwein."

[260] *Twelfth Census of the United States* (1900), *Inhabitants of Lebanon Ward 5, Lebanon County, Pennsylvania*, E.D. No. 128, page 256B; *Thirteenth Census of the United States* (1910), *Inhabitants of Lebanon Borough, Lebanon County, Pennsylvania*, E.D. No. 154, page 188B; *Fourteenth Census of the United States* (1920), *Inhabitants of Lebanon Ward 5, Lebanon County, Pennsylvania*, ED No. 173, page 209A.

Clara Allwein (spouse, age 46)
Daisy Allwein (daughter, age 25, school teacher)
Victor Allwein (son, age 22, telegraph operator)
Arthur Allwein (son, age 19, telegraph operator)
Irene Allwein (daughter, age 8, in school)

Consistently over this time, Nathaniel gives his occupation as "house plasterer" in these Census reports.

Nathaniel Mars Allwein died in on February 25, 1923, Clara J (Schaum) Allwein on May 10, 1930.[261] They are buried in Goshert's Cemetery (GS) in Mt. Zion, north of Lebanon, Pennsylvania.

Daisy Mary Allwein Swanger (1872-1908)
Lebanon, Pennsylvania

Daisy M. Allwein (F06-0405-0507-01), oldest daughter of Nathaniel Mars and Clara (Schaum) Allwein, was born December 9, 1872 in Mt. Zion, Lebanon County, Pennsylvania. The lineage connecting Daisy Mary Allwein to Johannes Jacob and Catharina Allwein, progenitors of the Allwein family in colonial Pennsylvania, is as follows:

Generation 1: Johannes Jacob and Catharina Allwein—Berks County, Pa.
Generation 2: Conrad and Catharine (Weibel) Allwein—Dauphin County, Pa.
Generation 3: Philip and Barbara (Frantz) Allwein—Lebanon County, Pa.
Generation 4: William and Mary (Mars) Allwein—Lebanon County, Pa.
Generation 5: Nathaniel Mars and Clara J. (Schaum) Allwein—Lebanon County, Pa.
Generation 6: Daisy Mary Allwein and Charles H. Swanger—Lebanon County, Pa.

---

[261] See the Pennsylvania Department of Health: http://www.health. state.pa.us. See also the obituary for Clara Allwein from the *Lebanon Daily News*, Lebanon, Pennsylvania, Monday Evening, May 12, 1930, and the funeral notice for Nathaniel Allwein in the *Lebanon Daily News*, Wednesday Evening, February 28, 1923.

Exhibit 11.40 Gravestone for Nathaniel and Clara Schaum Allwein—Goshert's Cemetery, Mount Zion, Pennsylvania

Daisy M. Allwein was living with her parents at 449 North 5th Street in Lebanon at the time of the 1900 Federal Census, listed as a school teacher (see above). She married Charles H. Swanger, son of John and Annie Swanger of North Lebanon, on September 21, 1907 at Philadelphia, Pennsylvania. Daisy M. Allwein died at a very young age—35 years of age—on April 14, 1908.[262] She is buried at St. Mary's Catholic Cemetery (SM) in Lebanon.

Victor Jacob Allwein (1877-1932)
Lebanon, Pennsylvania

Victor Jacob Allwein (M06-0405-0507-02), oldest son of Nathaniel Mars and Clara (Schaum) Allwein, was born December 15, 1877 in Mt. Zion, Lebanon County, Pennsylvania. The lineage connecting Victor Jacob Allwein to Johannes Jacob and Catharina Allwein, progenitors of the Allwein family in colonial Pennsylvania, is as follows:

Generation 1: Johannes Jacob and Catharina Allwein—Berks County, Pa.
Generation 2: Conrad and Catharine (Weibel) Allwein—Dauphin County, Pa.
Generation 3: Philip and Barbara (Frantz) Allwein—Lebanon County, Pa.
Generation 4: William and Mary (Mars) Allwein—Lebanon County, Pa.
Generation 5: Nathaniel Mars and Clara J. (Schaum) Allwein—Lebanon
     County, Pa.
Generation 6: Victor Jacob and Lucy Henrietta (Allwein) Allwein—Lebanon
     County, Pa.

Census reports indicate that Victor Jacob Allwein lived with his parents at the time of the 1900, 1910 and 1920 Federal Censuses at 449 Fifth Street in Lebanon. Throughout his life, he worked as a telegraph operator for the railroad. Some time around 1925, he married Lucy Henrietta, daughter of Theodore and Catherine

---

[262] Obituary for Daisy Allwein Swanger from the *Lebanon Daily News*, Lebanon, Pennsylvania, Wednesday Evening, April 15, 1908.

Exhibit 11.41 Gravestone for Daisy Allwein Swanger—St. Mary's Cemetery, Lebanon, Pennsylvania

(McCann) Allwein, his second cousin. After his father's death, he and his family continued to reside with his mother on Fifth Street.[263]

Census information for 1930 indicates that Victor Jacob Allwein and Lucy Henrietta Allwein gave birth to a son:

Victor Edward Allwein (Jr.) (M07-0405-0507-0201), b. June 25, 1926, d. January 11, 1996 (HC), m. (May 29, 1948) Teresa May Arnold (b. May 8, 1928, d. July 4, 2005)[264]

Victor Jacob Allwein died on January 29, 1932.[265] His wife and son continued to live at the residence on Fifth Street, and are listed in the 1940 Polk's City Directory for Lebanon and enumerated in the 1940 Federal Census—Lucy Allwein (household head, age 49) and Victor Allwein (son, age 13).[266] Lucy H. Allwein died December 19, 1949.[267] They are buried at Holy Cross Cemetery (HC) in Lebanon, Pennsylvania.

---

[263] *Twelfth Census of the United States* (1900), *Lebanon Ward 5, Lebanon County, Pennsylvania*, E.D. No. 128, page 256B; *Thirteenth Census of the United States* (1910), *Inhabitants of Lebanon Borough, Lebanon County, Pennsylvania*, E.D. No. 154, page 188B; *Fourteenth Census of the United States* (1920), *Inhabitants of Lebanon Ward 5, Lebanon County, Pennsylvania*, ED No. 173, page 209A; *Fifteenth Census of the United States* (1930), *Inhabitants of Lebanon, Lebanon County, Pennsylvania*, E.D. No. 38-20, pages 146A & B.

[264] Obituaries from the *Lebanon Daily News*, Lebanon, Pennsylvania, Friday, January 12, 1996; Wednesday, July 6, 2005.

[265] See the Pennsylvania Department of Health: http://www.health.state. pa.us.

[266] *Sixteenth Census of the United States* (1940), *Inhabitants of Lebanon, Lebanon County, Pennsylvania*, E.D. No. 38-25, page 413A.

[267] Obituary for Lucy H. Allwein from the *Lebanon Daily News*, Lebanon, Pennsylvania, December 20, 1949.

Exhibit 11.42 Gravestone for Victor Jacob and Lucy Henrietta Allwein—Holy Cross Cemetery, Lebanon, Pennsylvania

Arthur William Allwein (1881-1940)
Lebanon, Pennsylvania

Arthur William Allwein (M06-0405-0507-03), youngest son of Nathaniel and Clara (Schaum) Allwein, was born January 19, 1881 in Lebanon. The line of descent connecting Arthur William Allwein to Johannes Jacob and Catharina Allwein, progenitors of the Allwein family in colonial Pennsylvania, is as follows:

Generation 1: Johannes Jacob and Catharina Allwein—Berks County, Pa.
Generation 2: Conrad and Catharine (Weibel) Allwein—Dauphin County, Pa.
Generation 3: Philip and Barbara (Frantz) Allwein—Lebanon County, Pa.
Generation 4: William and Mary (Mars) Allwein—Lebanon County, Pa.
Generation 5: Nathaniel Mars and Clara J. (Schaum) Allwein—Lebanon
     County, Pa.
Generation 6: Arthur William and Marie (Ross) Allwein—Lebanon County, Pa.

Arthur William Allwein was living with his parents in 1900 and working as a telegraph operator. He married Marie Edith Ross on January 24, 1905. She was the daughter of Herman J. Ross. They lived in Lebanon, where he worked for the Reading Company at various jobs, as reported in the Federal Censuses, beginning in 1910 as a telegraph operator, then as a clerk in 1920 and yardmaster in 1930 and 1940.[268] There were no children born to them.

Arthur William Allwein died April 29, 1940.[269] His wife Marie Edith (Ross) died in a tragic accident a few years later in Mt. Gretna

---

[268] *Twelfth Census of the United States* (1900), *Lebanon Ward 5, Lebanon County, Pennsylvania*, E.D. No. 128, page 256B; *Thirteenth Census of the United States* (1910), *Inhabitants of Lebanon Borough, Lebanon County, Pennsylvania*, E.D. No. 154, page 188B; *Fourteenth Census of the United States* (1920), *Inhabitants of Lebanon Ward 5, Lebanon County, Pennsylvania,* E.D. No. 173, page 209A; *Fifteenth Census of the United States* (1930), *Inhabitants of Lebanon, Lebanon County, Pennsylvania*, E.D. No. 38-20, pages 146A & B; *Sixteenth Census of the United States* (1940), *Inhabitants of Lebanon, Lebanon County, Pennsylvania*, E.D. No. 38-14A, page 202B.
[269] See the Pennsylvania Department of Health: http://www.health.state. pa.us.

Exhibit 11.43 Gravestones for Arthur W. Allwein and Marie R. Allwein—Mount Lebanon Cemetery, Lebanon, Pennsylvania

in which she fell from a high porch at her summer home in the Chautauqua Borough Reservation.[270] They are buried together in Mount Lebanon Cemetery (ML) in Lebanon, Pennsylvania.

Irene Gertrude Allwein Grossman (1892-1925)
Lebanon, Pennsylvania

Irene Gertrude Allwein (F06-0405-0507-04), the youngest child of Nathaniel and Clara (Schaum) Allwein, was born March 11, 1892 in Lebanon. The line of descent connecting Arthur William Allwein to Johannes Jacob and Catharina Allwein, progenitors of the Allwein family in colonial Pennsylvania, is as follows:

Generation 1: Johannes Jacob and Catharina Allwein—Berks County, Pa.
Generation 2: Conrad and Catharine (Weibel) Allwein—Dauphin County, Pa.
Generation 3: Philip and Barbara (Frantz) Allwein—Lebanon County, Pa.
Generation 4: William and Mary (Mars) Allwein—Lebanon County, Pa.
Generation 5: Nathaniel Mars and Clara J. (Schaum) Allwein—Lebanon
    County, Pa.
Generation 6: Irene Gertrude Allwein and Charles Grossman—Lebanon
    County, Pa.

She lived with her parents at 449 North Fifth Street up until her marriage. She married Charles Grossman, son of John and Barbara (Stump) Grossman, on August 14, 1919 in Reading, Berks County. They can be located in the 1920 Federal Census report for Lebanon.[271]

Irene Gertrude (Allwein) Grossman died on July 18, 1925. Charles H. Grossman died some thirty years later, on September 30, 1957.[272] They are buried at Mount Lebanon Cemetery in Lebanon, Pennsylvania.

---

[270] Obituary appeared in the *Lebanon Daily News*, Lebanon, Pennsylvania, Monday Evening, August 31, 1942. See also the Pennsylvania Department of Health: http://www.health.state.pa.us.

[271] *Fourteenth Census of the United States* (1920), *Inhabitants of Lebanon Ward 5, Lebanon County*, E.D. No. 174, page 259B.

[272] Obituaries from the *Lebanon Daily News*, Lebanon, Pennsylvania, Monday Evening, July 20, 1925; Thursday Evening, October 1, 1957. See also the Pennsylvania Department of Health: http://www.health.state.pa.us.

Exhibit 11.44 Gravestones for Irene Gertrude and Charles H. Grossman—Mount Lebanon Cemetery, Lebanon, Pennsylvania

John Mars Allwein (1850-1929)
Lebanon, Pennsylvania

John Mars Allwein (M05-0405-0508), son of William and Mary (Mars) Allwein, was born December 15, 1850 on his parents' farm in North Lebanon Township in Lebanon County, Pennsylvania. The lineage linking John Mars Allwein to Johannes Jacob and Catharina Allwein, progenitors of the Allwein family in colonial Pennsylvania, is as follows:

Generation 1: Johannes Jacob and Catharina Allwein—Berks County, Pa.
Generation 2: Conrad and Catharine (Weibel) Allwein—Dauphin County, Pa.
Generation 3: Philip and Barbara (Frantz) Allwein—Lebanon County, Pa.
Generation 4: William and Mary (Mars) Allwein—Lebanon County, Pa.
Generation 5: John Mars and Mary Arnold (Steckbeck) Allwein—Lebanon
    County, Pa.

The following narrative about John Mars Allwein is reproduced from the Jerome Allwein *Genealogy*:[273]

John M. Allwein, son of William and Mary (Mars) Allwein was born December 15, 1850 and was educated in the public schools until he was 17 years old after which he went to the Lebanon High School for a short time. Commenced to teach school at Mount Zion (Glicks School) in the Fall of 1870. He taught at this place for three successive terms after which he went to the Millersville Normal School, after taking the course at Millersville he returned and taught in the public schools of North Lebanon Township for seven successive terms, after which he discontinued teaching and entered the employ of the Miller Organ Co. at Lebanon. Soon after he was appointed a Census enumerator, in the Fall of 1880 he again entered teaching and taught one term after which he entered DeHuff and Mitchell's book store at Lebanon. Late in the fall of 1881 he accepted an offer to teach an unexpired term of the Webster-Grammer School, Independent District, Lebanon County, this ended his career as a teacher. He was engaged in the shoe business in Lebanon for several years and since has been

---

[273] Jerome Allwein, *Genealogy of the Allwein-Arnold Families*, Philadelphia, Pa., 1902, pages 68-69.

sell furniture for the American School Furniture Co., New York City making a decided success. On May 13, 1880 he was married to Mary, Daughter of David and Mary Steckbeck. They lived in Independent District, Lebanon, Pa., until the Spring of 1902 after which they moved in their new residence on North 8th street Lebanon, Pa.

There is also an entry in *Biographical Annals of Lebanon County* for John M. Allwein, and because of the valuable information it contains, it is reproduced here in its entirety:[274]

JOHN M. ALLWEIN, traveling salesman for the American School Furniture Company, of New York, and a resident of Lebanon, was born in North Lebanon Township, December 15, 1850, a son of William and Mary (Mars) Allwein, of German and English descent, respectively. William Allwein was a plasterer by trade, and was born in June, 1813, his death occurring in 1888. His father, Philip, devoted his active life to farming and blacksmithing, and reared a large family of whom Edward, Elijah, Henry, Adam, Sarah, Isabella and Rebecca are living; while John, Samuel, Joseph, William, Elizabeth, Polly, Catherine and Mary are deceased. Philip Allwein was one of the very early settlers of Lebanon County, and his little blacksmith shop was one of the busiest centers for miles around.

William Allwein was a farmer as well as a plasterer, and his property was always under a high state of cultivation, and yielded profitable harvests. He was a life-long Democrat, and a member of the Catholic Church. As his name implies, he was of German descent, and inherited the personal characteristics which have enabled Germany to impress itself upon the map of the world. To himself and wife, Mary, were born eleven children, of whom the following attained maturity: Henry, deceased; Maria, also deceased, Frank M., as plasterer of Lebanon; Isaac, a resident of

---

[274] *Biographical Annals of Lebanon County, Pennsylvania, Containing Biographical Sketches of Prominent and Representative Citizens and of Many of the Early Settled Families*, J.H. Beers & Company, Chicago, 1904, page 635-636.

Lebanon and a grocer by occupation; Amelia, living on the home farm in North Lebanon township; Nathaniel, also a plasterer by trade; John M.; Polly, the wife of Aaron Witmer, of Lebanon city; and Aaron, living on the home place. Mrs. Allwein was born in 1814 in the city of Lancaster and died March 4, 1901.

Although a farmer lad, and compelled at times to labor long and faithfully, John M. Allwein managed to secure a fair education, finishing in the State normal schools at Lebanon and Millersville, Pa. For twelve years he was engaged in teaching in the schools of Lebanon County, after which he came to Lebanon city in 1880, and clerked for some time. As a traveling salesman he was first identified with the Keystone Furniture Company, of Philadelphia, and afterward with the United States School Furniture Company of Chicago. In 1891 he became connected with the American School Furniture Company of New York City, for which he is still traveling. In the meantime he has established a reputation for executive and business ability of a high order, which has been duly recognized by his fellow townsmen on various occasions, and in various ways. His business interests are centered in some of the most important commercial concerns of the town, including the Lebanon County Trust Company, of which he is secretary, and a stock holder; he is a stockholder in both the Lebanon National and the Farmers National banks; a stock holder in the Mutual Benefit Building & Loan Association; and a director in the Mechanics Building and Loan Association. Mr. Allwein is a Democrat in politics, and a member of the Catholic Church.

On May 13, 1880, Mr. Allwein married Mary A. Steckbeck, born in Lebanon county April 29, 1855, a daughter of David and Mary (Arnold) Steckbeck, parents also of three other children: Priscilla, the wife of Henry Arnold, of Lebanon city; Moses, a resident of Avon; and Aaron, a farmer of North Lebanon Township. The father of Mrs. Allwein was one of the best and most prominent farmers of Lebanon County, and came from an old and honored family.

As noted in the above, John Mars Allwein married Mary Arnold Steckbeck on May 13, 1880. There were no children born to this union.

Exhibit 11.45 Gravestone for John M. Allwein—Holy Cross Cemetery, Lebanon, Pennsylvania

John M. Allwein is found in the listings of the Federal Census enumerations of Lebanon County from 1880 onward. In the 1880 Federal Census his occupation is given as "teacher." From the 1900 Federal Census onward he is listed as a "school furniture agent" and from that time on through to the 1920 Federal Census.[275] At the age of 70, he was still working as a travelling salesman for the American School Furniture Company.

John M. Allwein died November 11, 1929 and Mary Arnold (Steckbeck) Allwein on May 10, 1939.[276] They are buried at the Holy Cross Cemetery (HC), Lebanon.

---

[275] *Twelfth Census of the United States* (1900), *Inhabitants of North Lebanon Township, Lebanon County, Pennsylvania*, E.D. No. 138, page 152A; *Thirteenth Census of the United States* (1910), *Inhabitants of Lebanon Ward 5, Lebanon County, Pennsylvania*, E.D. No. 155, page 218B; *Fourteenth Census of the United States* (1920), *Inhabitants of Lebanon Ward 5, Lebanon County, Pennsylvania*, E.D. No. 174, page 251B.

[276] Obituaries from the *Lebanon Daily News*, Lebanon, Pennsylvania, Monday Evening, November 11, 1929; Wednesday Evening, May 10, 1939. See also the Pennsylvania Department of Health: http://www.health. state.pa.us.

Mary "Polly" M. Allwein Whitmer (1853-1924) Lebanon County, Pennsylvania

Mary "Polly" M. Allwein (F05-0405-0509), youngest daughter of William and Mary (Mars) Allwein, was born January 11, 1853 on her parents' farm in North Lebanon Township in Lebanon County, Pennsylvania. The line of descent linking Mary M. Allwein to Johannes Jacob and Catharina Allwein, progenitors of the Allwein family in colonial Pennsylvania, is as follows:

Generation 1: Johannes Jacob and Catharina Allwein—Berks County, Pa.
Generation 2: Conrad and Catharine (Weibel) Allwein—Dauphin County, Pa.
Generation 3: Philip and Barbara (Frantz) Allwein—Lebanon County, Pa.
Generation 4: William and Mary (Mars) Allwein—Lebanon County, Pa.
Generation 5: Mary M. Allwein and Aaron H. Whitmer—Lebanon County, Pa.

Mary M. Allwein married Aaron H. Whitmer about 1874, and in the 1880 Federal Census, they were living in Elizabeth Township of Lancaster County.[277] His occupation was given as "carpenter" in that report. By 1900 they had moved back to Lebanon, where they resided at 421 Weidman Street. Mr. Whitmer was working as a "building contractor," which continued through the 1910 Federal Census.[278]

Based on Federal Census reports and cemetery records, there were four children born to them:

Mary Ida Whitmer, b. November 21, 1872, d. November 13, 1882 (ML)
Harvey Whitmer, b. September 1, 1875, d. September 12, 1877 (ML)
Cora A. Whitmer, b. October 7, 1877, d. February 14, 1966 (HE), m. (February 21, 1907) Paris Nissley Hershey (b. July 27, 1883, d. December 30, 1956)[279]

---

[277] *Tenth Census of the United States* (1880), *Inhabitants of Elizabeth Township, Lancaster County, Pennsylvania*, page 349.

[278] *Twelfth Census of the United States* (1900), *Inhabitants of Lebanon Ward 5, Lebanon County, Pennsylvania*, E.D. No. 128, page 248B; *Thirteenth Census of the United States* (1910), *Inhabitants of Lebanon Ward 5, Lebanon County, Pennsylvania*, E.D. No. 155, page 218B.

[279] Obituary from the *Lebanon Daily News*, Lebanon, Pennsylvania, Monday Evening, December 31, 1956.

Sadie Elmira Whitmer, b. June 5, 1881, d. October 29, 1925 (ML), m. (June 24, 1912) Elam Siegrist (b. October 18, 1875, d. October 13, 1937)

Sadie Whitmer was a public school teacher. Cora Whitmer married Paris Nissley Hershey, who with his four brothers established the Hershey Creamery, which produced the famous Hershey's Ice Cream (not to be confused with the other Hershey, Milton Snavely Hershey, who established the Hershey Chocolate Company—a distant cousin to Paris N. Hershey). According to his obituary, Paris Nissley Hershey was a pioneer dairy products manufacturer and a leader in industry. He was a former teacher and civic leader in the Lebanon area. He taught in the public schools of Lancaster County. He attended the Kansas Agricultural College in Manhattan, Kansas, and was creamery operator of the Lebanon Creamery Company from 1905 to 1912. Beginning in 1912, he became a director of the milk division of the Hershey Chocolate Corporation and (from 1928) the agricultural manager of the Hershey Estates and a director of the Hershey Chocolate Corporation. He was a business leader in the Lebanon community—president of the Hershey National Bank, a director of the Fidelity Building and Loan Association of Lebanon, the Hershey Trust Company and the Hershey Foundation. He had also been president of the Lebanon School Board and school director for 25 years. Paris Nissley Hershey died on December 30, 1956; his wife Cora A. Whitmer died ten years later on February 14, 1966.[280]

Mary Allwein Whitmer died May 7, 1924. Her husband Aaron H. Whitmer died several years earlier on January 22, 1919.[281] They are buried at Mount Lebanon Cemetery (ML), Lebanon, Pennsylvania. Daughter, Sadie Whitmer Siegrist, and her husband are buried at Mount Lebanon as well. Cora (Whitmer) Hershey and her husband, Paris Nissley Hershey, are buried at the Hershey Cemetery (HE) in Hershey, Pennsylvania.

---

[280] Obituaries from the *Lebanon Daily News*, Lebanon, Pennsylvania, Monday Evening, December 31, 1956; *Lebanon Daily News*, Lebanon, Pennsylvania, Tuesday Evening, February 15, 1966.

[281] Obituaries, *Lebanon Daily News*, Lebanon, Pennsylvania, Wednesday Evening, January 22, 1919; Wednesday Evening, May 7, 1924. See the Pennsylvania Department of Health: http://www.health.state.pa.us.

Exhibit 11.46 Gravestones for Mary M. and Aaron H.
Whitmer—Mount Lebanon Cemetery, Lebanon, Pennsylvania

Aaron Mars Allwein (1855-1916)
Lebanon, Pennsylvania

Aaron Mars Allwein (M05-0405-0510), youngest son of William and Mary (Mars) Allwein was born April 24, 1855 on his parents' farm in North Lebanon Township in Lebanon County, Pennsylvania. The line of descent connecting Aaron Mars Allwein to Johannes Jacob and Catharina Allwein, progenitors of the Allwein family in colonial Pennsylvania, is as follows:

Generation 1: Johannes Jacob and Catharina Allwein—Berks County, Pa.
Generation 2: Conrad and Catharine (Weibel) Allwein—Dauphin County, Pa.
Generation 3: Philip and Barbara (Frantz) Allwein—Lebanon County, Pa.
Generation 4: William and Mary (Mars) Allwein—Lebanon County, Pa.
Generation 5: Aaron Mars Allwein—Lebanon County, Pa.

There is no record of his biography in the Jerome Allwein *Genealogy*. What we know about him comes primarily from census reports from which it is apparent that he never married. In the 1870 and 1880 Federal Census reports he is listed as living in his parents' household in North Lebanon Township.[282]

In the 1880 enumeration Aaron M. Allwein's occupation is listed as "teacher," so it is apparent that he, like his brothers taught in the public schools of the county. In the 1900 Federal Census, he is listed as the head of household in North Lebanon Township, living with his mother (age 86) and sister Amelia (age 52), and then in the 1910 Federal Census he is listed as the head of household living with sister and her husband Cyrus Miller in the Borough of Lebanon.[283] The 1900 listing for North Lebanon Township gives

---

[282] *Ninth Census of the United States* (1870), *Inhabitants of North Lebanon Township, Lebanon County, Pennsylvania*, page 236; *Tenth Census of the United States* (1880), *Inhabitants of North Lebanon Township, Lebanon County, Pennsylvania*, page 234.

[283] *Twelfth Census of the United States* (1900), *Inhabitants of North Lebanon Township, East Election District, Lebanon County, Pennsylvania*, E.D. No. 137, page 133B; *Thirteenth Census of the United States* (1910), *Inhabitants of Lebanon Borough Ward 5, Lebanon County, Pennsylvania*, E.D. No. 154, page 202A.

his occupation as "farmer," and the 1910 census listing indicates he was a "salesman in grocery store." This suggests that in 1900 they were still living on the family farm in North Lebanon Township and that subsequently, after his mother died on March 5, 1901, he and his sister Amelia moved into the Borough of Lebanon. Aaron M. Allwein died July 17, 1916, at the age of sixty-six.[284] He is buried in St. Mary's Cemetery (SM) in the Borough of Lebanon.

Samuel Allwein (1817-1885)
Lebanon County, Pennsylvania

Several of the inhabitants of Lebanon County in the late 19th and early 20th centuries were descendants of Samuel Allwein (M04-0405-06) and Elizabeth Eisenhauer. Samuel was one of ten children born to Philip and Barbara (Frantz) Allwein and one of eight—three daughters and five sons—who survived to adulthood. Although Samuel and Elizabeth Allwein had nine children, only four of them remained in the Lebanon area: Mary Ann Allwein (who married Moses Bowman), Jared Allwein (who married Sarah Bowman and later Alice Stanley), Elizabeth Allwein (who married George Francis), and Hiram Allwein (who married Sarah Bross). Only one, Hiram J. Allwein, helped perpetuate the Allwein name in the area. In Chapter 7 of *Familie Allwein*, Volume 1 (see pages 392-396), I summarized what we know about the lives of Samuel and Elizabeth (Eisenhauer) Allwein, and I do not repeat that material here, except to list their children, as follows.

Mary Ann Allwein (F05-0405-0601), b. April 2, 1843, d. November 21, 1899 (SM), m. Moses Bowman (b. June 4, 1833, d. June 10, 1912)

Franklin Philip Allwein (M05-0405-0602), b. March 26, 1844, d. June 3, 1919 (CL), m. Lydia Atchison (b. April 14, 1844, d. October 18, 1908)

---

284   See the Pennsylvania Department of Health: http://www.health.state. pa.us.

Exhibit 11.47 Gravestone of Aaron M. Allwein—St. Mary's
Cemetery, Lebanon, Pennsylvania

Hiram J. Allwein (M05-0405-0603), b. March 20, 1847, d.
November 14, 1921 (SM), m. Sarah Bross (b. September 16,
1849, d. January 2, 1923)

Jonathan Allwein (M05-0405-0604), b. January 11, 1849, d.
February 3, 1865 (NC)

Jared J. Allwein (M05-0405-0605), b. February 12, 1851, d.
November 3, 1893 (SM), m. (1) (est. 1875) Sarah Bowman (b.
August 6, 1854, d. April 27, 1886), (2) (June 13, 1889) Alice
Stanley (b. July 11, 1852, d. January 24, 1890)

Elizabeth Allwein (F05-0405-0606), b. June 6, 1853, d. 1913 (RM),
m. (January 2, 1892) George W. Francis (or Frances) (b. July
1839, d. unknown)

Samuel J. Allwein (M05-0405-0607), b. November 3, 1854, d.
December 6, 1923 (SH), m. (December 15, 1875) Catharine
Dennis (b. 1853, d. February 15, 1936)

Ambrose (Harry) Allwein (M05-0405-0608), b. December 11,
1857, d. December 3, 1935 (OZ), m. (October 19, 1880) Ida M.
Wood (b. est. 1862, d. before 1930)

Henry E. Allwein (M05-0405-0609), b. February 12, 1859, d.
October 3, 1926 (OL), m. (June 18, 1885) Mary Payne (b.
August 14, 1859, d. March 12, 1938)

As noted in the earlier narrative, due to Samuel Allwein's
desertion of Elizabeth and the children prior to 1860, in the 1860
Federal Census listings, most of the children were found living with
other families. With the exception of Jonathan, whose life was cut
short by an enemy artillery shell at the Battle of Petersburg in the
Civil War, all of their children grew to adulthood. Some of Samuel
and Elizabeth Allwein's children moved elsewhere. Samuel and
Henry moved to Ohio, and Franklin and Ambrose (Harry) moved
to Indiana. In the following I discuss what is known about each
of Samuel and Elizabeth Allweins' children who remained in the
Lebanon area and refer the reader to later chapters for those who
migrated elsewhere.

Mary Ann Allwein Bowman (1843-1899)
Lebanon, Pennsylvania

As noted above, Mary Ann Allwein (F05-0405-0601), oldest child of Samuel and Elizabeth (Eisenhauer) Allwein, was born April 2, 1843 and died November 21, 1899. The line of descent connecting her to Johannes Jacob and Catharina Allwein, progenitors of the Allwein family in colonial Pennsylvania, is as follows:

Generation 1: Johannes Jacob and Catharina Allwein—Berks County, Pa.
Generation 2: Conrad and Catharine (Weibel) Allwein—Dauphin County, Pa.
Generation 3: Philip and Barbara (Frantz) Allwein—Lebanon County, Pa.
Generation 4: Samuel and Elizabeth (Eisenhauer) Allwein—Lebanon County, Pa.
Generation 5: Mary Ann Allwein and Moses Bowman—Lebanon County, Pa.

Mary Ann Allwein married Moses Bowman on October 27, 1859 when she was 17 years of age.[285] Moses Bowman was born June 4, 1833 and died June 10, 1912. He was the son of John and Sarah Anna (Seifert) Bowman, whose origins were in Berks County, Pennsylvania.[286] He was a carpenter/cabinet maker by trade.[287]

By most accounts, ten children were born to Moses and Mary Ann (Allwein) Bowman, as follows:[288]

---

[285] This information was obtained from Jerome Allwein's *Genealogy of the Allwein-Arnold Families*, Philadelphia, Pa., 1902, page 70.

[286] What this information reveals is that Moses Bowman was a second cousin to Samuel Allwein, Mary Ann's father, since Moses and Samuel both had the same great grandparents, viz. Johann Jacob and Catharina Allweins (see previous chapters). Thus, Mary Ann was a second cousin, once removed, to her husband Moses Bowman.

[287] This information was obtained from Jerome Allwein's *Genealogy of the Allwein-Arnold Families*, Philadelphia, Pa., 1902, page 70, and confirmed by Federal Census materials.

[288] Most of the information on Mary Ann Allwein and Moses Bowman's children was obtained from Jerome Allwein's *Genealogy of the Allwein-Arnold Families*, page 70, supplemented and/or confirmed by Census materials. Some information was obtained from obituaries in the *Lebanon Daily News*, Lebanon, Pennsylvania, as follows: Monday Evening, October, 14, 1901; Monday Evening, January 11, 1909; Thursday Evening, February 24, 1916; Thursday Evening, February 23, 1950; Thursday Evening, January 11, 1951.

Exhibit 11.48 Family portrait (left half) of Elizabeth (Eisenhauer) Allwein family (circa 1896)—Lebanon, Pennsylvania [contributed by Nancy Allwein Nebiker]. Top row (from left to right): Elizabeth Allwein Francis, John A. Allwein, unknown, unknown, Andrew Aloysius Allwein, unknown, unknown; Middle row (seated, left to right): unknown, unknown, Franklin P. Allwein; Middle row—girls in sailor dresses, possibly Ellen "Ella" C. Allwein Coil and Catherine "Kate" M. Allwein Bender Guare; Front row—on floor (left to right) Martha M. Allwein Frazier, unknown.

Exhibit 11.49 Family portrait (right half) of Elizabeth (Eisenhauer) Allwein family—Lebanon, Pennsylvania [contributed by Nancy Allwein Nebiker]. Top row (from left to right): unknown, unknown, Hiram J. Allwein, Sarah A. (Bross) Allwein, unknown, unknown; Middle row—standing (left to right): unknown, Raymond H. "Cottie" Allwein; Middle row—seated (left to right): Elizabeth Eisenhauer Allwein, Harry (Ambrose) Allwein, Gayle Delbert Allwein; Front row—on floor (left to right): Sarah E. Allwein Rudy, unknown.

Elizabeth Bowman, b. November 29, 1861, d. July 30, 1902 m.
   (October 27, 1885) John Henry Hecker (aka Henry J. Hecker)
   (b. April 28, 1857, d. unknown)
Agnes L. Bowman, b. August 4, 1866, d. November 1931 (HC),
   unmarried
Harry H. Bowman, b. May 11, 1868, d. 1929, m. (May 30, 1901)
   Annie Zweier (b. July 14, 1877, d. unknown)
Selim Bowman, b. April, 1870, died young
Bernard Andrew Bowman, b. October 5, 1872, d. February 22,
   1950 (buried in Hammond, In.), m. (September 10, 1902) Sarah
   "Sadie" A. Dugan (b. April 1874, d. unknown)
John J. Bowman, b. August 21, 1874, d. October 12, 1901 (SM),
   unmarried
Charles Borromes Bowman, b. December 22, 1876, d. January 10,
   1951 (HC), m. (May 7, 1903) Margaret Viola Yeingst (b. July
   1876, d. April 19, 1946)
Gertrude S. Bowman, b. October 3, 1878, d. February 23, 1916
   (SM), m. (May 10, 1909) Herman Hershberger (b. 1886, d.
   March 9, 1939)
Sarah A. Bowman, b. April 17, 1881, d. February 6, 1946 (HC), m.
   (June 25, 1907) John Adam Flocken (b. June 16, 1877, d. April
   27, 1944)
Adam A. Bowman, b. October 26, 1882, d. January 10, 1909 (SM),
   unmarried

In the 1870 and 1880 Federal Censuses Moses and Mary
Ann Bowman were living in the Borough of Lebanon, where
they presumably lived the remainder of their lives.[289] They are
both buried in St. Mary's Cemetery in the Borough of Lebanon,
Pennsylvania.

---

[289] *Ninth Census of the United States* (1870), *Inhabitants of Borough of
Lebanon, Lebanon County, Pennsylvania*, page 344, and *Tenth Census of
the United States* (1880), *Inhabitants of Borough of Lebanon, Lebanon
County, Pennsylvania*, page 352.

Exhibit 11.50 Gravestone for Mary A. Allwein—St. Mary's
Cemetery, Lebanon, Pennsylvania

Franklin Philip Allwein (1844-1919)
Whitley County, Indiana

Franklin Philip Allwein (M05-0405-0602), the eldest son of Samuel and Elizabeth Allwein, was born March 26, 1844 in Lebanon, Pennsylvania. He became independent at an early age. By the age of 15 he was an apprentice coach smith, learning the trade from Joseph Arnold. Soon after the outbreak of the Civil War, "he enlisted in Company G, 5th Pennsylvania Volunteer Infantry, and, after his term expired, he re-enlisted in the 127th Pennsylvania Volunteer Infantry as 4th Sergeant, where he continued until the regiment was mustered out of service."[290] This second term began August 13, 1862 and ended May 29, 1863, during which time his regiment "saw active service in the battles of Fredericksburg, Chancellorsville, besides many raids, skirmishes, etc." He enrolled for yet a third term of service "when he re-enlisted again in Company F, 48th Regiment, and remained with them as First Lieutenant for three months, when he went to Washington, acting as First Lieutenant in the Quartermaster's Department, where he continued until February, 1866, when he was finally discharged."[291] After his discharge from the military he moved to Indiana, settling in the area of Fort Wayne (Allen County), Indiana, where on December 6, 1866 he was married to Lydia Atchison (b. April 14, 1844), daughter of Silas P. and Anne Atchison. They were married in nearby Whitley County

---

[290] Information in this section is drawn from a biographical sketch provided by Weston A. Goodspeed and Charles Blanchard, Editors, *Counties of Whitley and Noble, Indiana—Historical and Biographical*, Chicago: F.A. Battey & Co., Publishers, 1882, page 238. I have provided quotation marks to denote the material taken from this source.

[291] Only the first term of Franklin Allwein's service is documented in Samuel P. Bates, *History of Pennsylvania Volunteers 1861-65*, edited by Janet Hewett, Wilmington NC: Broadfoot Publishing Co., 1994, Volume 7, page 156. We can verify that the first two terms of service are on record with the National Archives and Records Administration in Washington, D.C., but I cannot find any record of the third, however we have no reason to doubt this report of this third term of Civil War service.

by Rev. James Atchison, the bride's uncle.[292] More information regarding Franklin P. Allwein is presented in Chapter 21 of volume 3, which deals with those families that migrated to Indiana.

Hiram J. Allwein (1847-1921)
Lebanon, Pennsylvania

Hiram J. Allwein (M05-0405-0603), the second son of Samuel and Elizabeth Allwein, was born March 20, 1847 in Lebanon, Pennsylvania. He is mentioned in the Jerome Allwein *Genealogy*, but there is very little information provided there.[293] Now we know much more. His connection to Johannes Jacob and Catharina Allwein, progenitors of the Allwein family in colonial Pennsylvania, is as follows:

Generation 1: Johannes Jacob and Catharina Allwein—Berks County, Pa.
Generation 2: Conrad and Catharine (Weibel) Allwein—Dauphin County, Pa.
Generation 3: Philip and Barbara (Frantz) Allwein—Lebanon County, Pa.
Generation 4: Samuel and Elizabeth (Eisenhauer) Allwein—Lebanon County, Pa.
Generation 5: Hiram J. and Sarah (Bross) Allwein—Lebanon County, Pa.

Hiram J. Allwein was baptized March 26, 1847 at St. Mary's Assumption Church, Lebanon.[294] At the age of 13 he went to live with Edmund Kimmel, a tailor, and his wife Barbara, where he became an apprentice tailor.[295] It was a vocation that suited him, as this was the occupation he pursued for the remainder of his life.

During the Civil War, once he came of age, Hiram J. Allwein enlisted with Company I, 83rd Regiment of the Pennsylvania Infantry. He served from February 1, 1865 through to the end of the War. His unit joined the Siege of Petersburg (Virginia) in June of

---

[292] Nellie M. Raber, *Marriage Records of Whitley County, Indiana 1860-1884*. Fort Wayne Public Library, 1973.
[293] Jerome Allwein, *Genealogy of the Allwein-Arnold Families*, Philadelphia, Pa., 1902, page 71.
[294] Pension records for Hiram Allwein, the National Archives and Records Administration (NARA), Washington, D.C.
[295] *Eighth Census of the United States* (1860), *Inhabitants of North Lebanon Borough, Lebanon County, Pennsylvania*, page 406.

1865, where his brother Jonathan was killed, and he was mustered out with his company on June 28, 1865.[296]

After his discharge from the army, he returned to Lebanon to resume his tailoring business. He married Sarah Bross on November 12, 1868 at St. Mary's Church. The marriage was performed by Rev. J.W. Boetzkes.[297] From this marriage there were 12 children born, as follows:[298]

Jeremiah Allwein (M06-0405-0603-01), b. March 26, 1869, d. in childhood
Andrew Aloysius Allwein (M06-0405-0603-02), b. November 1, 1871, d. June 8, 1930 (HC), m. (October 26, 1899), Margaret "Maggie" Mary Guare (b. July 28, 1872, d. February 21, 1939)
Carol Allwein (F06-0405-0603-03), b. April 6, 1872, d. in childhood
George Irvin Allwein (M06-0405-0603-04), b. March 11, 1874, d. September 25, 1897 (SM), unmarried
John Aloysius Allwein (M06-0405-0603-05), b. March 30, 1877, d. November 12, 1957 (ML), m. (October 31, 1899) Mabel Elizabeth Dennis (b. est. January 23, 1879, d. May 8, 1948)
Catherine M. Allwein (F06-0405-0603-06), b. April 10, 1879, d. March 4, 1942 (HC), m. (1) (September 4, 1901), John Francis Bender (b. December 17, 1875, d. June 2, 1920), (2) (January 27, 1925) John Patrick Guare (b. January 12, 1879, d. February 4, 1925)
Agnes C. Allwein (F06-0405-0603-07), b. September 8, 1881, d. May 27, 1901
Ellen "Ella" C. Allwein (F06-0405-0603-08), b. May 25, 1883, d. May 8, 1937 (ML), m. (December 20, 1915) George Washington Coil (b. December 11, 1882, d. February 27, 1963)

---

[296] Samuel P. Bates, *History of Pennsylvania Volunteers 1861-65*, edited by Janet Hewett, Wilmington NC: Broadfoot Publishing Co., 1994, Volume 4, page 1299.

[297] Pension records for Hiram Allwein and Sarah Allwein, NARA, Washington, D.C.

[298] Birth information for these children is taken from Hiram Allwein's own report to the Pension Office, although in that source he omits information about Carol. Other information is derived from various other sources, including tombstone inscriptions from St. Mary's and Holy Cross Cemeteries, Lebanon, Pennsylvania, and information from Nancy Allwein Nebiker, great granddaughter of Hiram Allwein.

Raymond "Cottie" Hiram Allwein (M06-0405-0603-09), b. August 16, 1885, d. March 7, 1929 (SM), unmarried

Martha M. Allwein (F06-0405-0603-10), b. February 9, 1887, d. July 19, 1961 (HC), m. (December 29, 1907), William Maurice Frazier (b. September 24, 1885, d. August 18, 1962)

Henry Alfred Allwein (F06-0405-0603-11), b. November 28, 1889, d. May 19, 1894 (SM)

Sarah Elizabeth Allwein (F06-0405-0603-12), b. January 19, 1893, d. February 8, 1966 (SM), m. (May 18, 1912), Horace Monroe Rudy (b. March 14, 1891, d. April 22, 1948)

Several of these children died in childhood (Jeremiah Allwein, Carol Allwein, and Henry Alfred Allwein) or in young adulthood (George Irvin Allwein and Agnes C. Allwein). These five children are not discussed further in this volume. We cover the remaining children seven children: Andrew Aloysius Allwein (M06-0405-0603-02), John Aloysius Allwein (M06-0405-0603-05), Catherine M. Allwein (F06-0405-0603-06), Ellen "Ella" C. Allwein (F06-0405-0603-08), Raymond Hiram Allwein (M06-0405-0603-09), Martha M. Allwein (F06-0405-0603-10), and Sarah Elizabeth Allwein (F06-0405-0603-12) in the following sections.

Hiram and Sarah (Bross) Allwein spent their entire lives in the environs of Lebanon, Pennsylvania. The Federal Census enumeration for 1870 locates them in the Borough of Lebanon, the 1880 Census places them in South Lebanon Township, and the 1900 and 1910 Censuses record their address as 610 Locust Street in the first ward of the Borough of Lebanon, where they lived until Hiram's death.[299] At the end of her life Sarah lived in the household

---

[299] *Ninth Census of the United States* (1870), *Inhabitants of Borough of Lebanon, Lebanon County, Pennsylvania,* page 326; *Tenth Census of the United States* (1880), *Inhabitants of South Lebanon Township, Lebanon County, Pennsylvania,* page 389C; *Twelfth Census of the United States* (1900), *Inhabitants of the Borough of Lebanon, Lebanon County, Pennsylvania,* E.D. No. 123, page 167A; *Thirteenth Census of the United States* (1910), *Inhabitants of the Borough of Lebanon, Lebanon County, Pennsylvania,* E.D. 147, page 6B.

of her daughter, Catherine (Allwein) Bender (then a widow) at 334 North 11th Street.[300]

The household listing for the 1900 Federal Census is informative because all of the Hiram and Sarah Allwein children were still present at home:

Hiram Allwein (head, age 63, tailor)
Sarah A. Allwein (spouse, age 50)
Andrew A. Allwein (son, age 29, tapper in a steel mill)
John A. Allwein (son, age 22, day laborer)
Catherine (daughter, age 21)
Agnes C. Allwein (daughter, age 18)
Ellen Allwein (daughter, age 17, machine works)
Raymond H. Allwein (son, age 14, at school)
Martha M. Allwein (daughter, age 13, at school)
Sarah E. Allwein (daughter, age 7)

In just 10 short years, virtually all of these children would leave the parental home. In the 1910 Federal Census, only three remained—Ella C. Allwein (age 26, hemstitcher), Raymond H. Allwein (age 24, no occupation), and Sarah E. Allwein (age 17, hemstitcher). By 1920, Raymond Allwein (age 34, laborer in steel mill) was the only one who remained in the parental household.[301]

Hiram received a pension for his military service during the Civil War, beginning around 1900. He died on November 14, 1921 at the age of 74. After his death, his wife Sarah qualified for a widow's pension, which she received until her death on January 2, 1923.[302]

---

[300] Civil War pension records for Sarah Allwein, the National Archives and Records Administration, Washington D.C.
[301] *Thirteenth Census of the United States* (1910), *Inhabitants of Lebanon Ward 7, Lebanon County, Pennsylvania*, E.D. No. 147, page 92B & 93A; *Fourteenth Census of the United States* (1920), *Inhabitants of Lebanon Ward 1, Lebanon County, Pennsylvania*, E.D. No. 168, page 112B.
[302] Civil War pension records for Hiram Allwein and Sarah Allwein, the National Archives and Records Administration, Washington D.C.

Exhibit 11.51 Gravestone for Hiram Allwein, St. Mary's Cemetery, Lebanon, Pennsylvania

Hiram Allwein's obituary indicated that "he was a respected citizen and a member of St. Mary's Catholic Church."[303]

Hiram Allwein's tombstone inscription in St. Mary's Cemetery in the Borough of Lebanon spells his surname as "ALWEIN," which suggests that this family may have used a somewhat different spelling than others in the Lebanon area (see below). With a few exceptions, all of his correspondence with the Pension Office also uses this spelling, and I conclude therefore that this was clearly his preference. None of the gravestones of his children that I could locate perpetuate this spelling, however, all using "ALLWEIN" instead. Both Hiram and Sarah Allwein are buried in St. Mary's Cemetery in the Borough of Lebanon, in a location near some of their children.[304]

Andrew Aloysius Allwein (1871-1930)
Lebanon, Pennsylvania

Andrew Aloysius Allwein (M06-0405-0603-01), eldest son of Hiram and Sarah (Bross) Allwein, was born November 1, 1871 in Lebanon, Pennsylvania. The line of descent connecting Andrew Aloysius Allwein to Johannes Jacob and Catharina Allwein, progenitors of the Allwein family in colonial Pennsylvania, is as follows:

Generation 1: Johannes Jacob and Catharina Allwein—Berks County, Pa.
Generation 2: Conrad and Catharine (Weibel) Allwein—Dauphin County, Pa.
Generation 3: Philip and Barbara (Frantz) Allwein—Lebanon County, Pa.
Generation 4: Samuel and Elizabeth (Eisenhauer) Allwein—Lebanon County, Pa.
Generation 5: Hiram J. and Sarah (Bross) Allwein—Lebanon County, Pa.
Generation 6: Andrew Aloysius and Margaret (Guare) Allwein—Lebanon
      County, Pa.

---

[303] Hiram Allwein's obituary appeared in the *Lebanon Daily News*, November 14, 1921. The obituary of Sarah Allwein, his widow, is in the *Lebanon Daily News*, Tuesday Evening, January 2, 1923. See the Pennsylvania Department of Health: http://www.health.state.pa.us.
[304] Hiram Allwein's tombstone in St. Mary's Cemetery is well preserved and easy to find, but the whereabouts of Sarah Allwein's grave is unknown to this author. The presence of Sarah Allwein's grave in the St. Mary's Cemetery is indicated by correspondence between their daughter Catherine Bender and the Commissioner of Pensions on file with Sarah Allwein's pension records.

Andrew Aloysius married Margaret Guare on October 26, 1899 at St. Mary's Catholic Church. She was the daughter of Patrick and Anne (Connell) Guare. The ceremony was performed by Rev. A. Christ.

Federal Census enumerations for Lebanon indicate Andrew Aloysius and Margaret (Guare) Allwein resided in Lebanon for the remainder of their lives. Information on Andrew's occupation indicates he was a laborer in a bolt manufacturing company.[305] The 1890-91 *Shaffer Lebanon City Directory* lists him as a "boltmaker."

Available information indicates that eight children were born to this union, but several of them died in childhood:

Anna Allwein (F07-0405-0603-0101), b. September 8, 1900, d. October 7, 1911 (SM)
Mary Allwein (F07-0405-0603-0102), b. February 8, 1902, d. March 10, 1902 (SM)
Sara Ellen Allwein (F07-0405-0603-0103), b. March 21, 1903, d. September 20, 1948 (HC), m. (December 29, 1925) Joseph John Michaels, Sr. (b. May 25, 1902, d. August 26, 1975, buried in Springfield MA)
Margaret Allwein (F07-0405-0603-0104), b. June 26, 1905, d. March 19, 1910 (SM)
Catharine Allwein (F07-0405-0603-0105), b. August 10, 1907, d. March 20, 1910 (SM)
Elizabeth "Betty" Mary Allwein (F07-0405-0603-0106), b. March 30, 1910, d. January 7, 1996 (HC), m. (November 27, 1946) Lloyd Gingrich (b. April 5, 1918, d. June 23, 1992)
Marie Allwein (F07-0405-0603-0107), b. 1911, d. January 2, 1914 (SM)

---

[305] *Thirteenth Census of the United States* (1910), *Inhabitants of Lebanon Ward 7, Lebanon County, Pennsylvania*, E.D. No. 157, page 252B; *Fourteenth Census of the United States* (1920), *Inhabitants of Lebanon Ward 1, Lebanon County, Pennsylvania*, E.D. No. 168, page 124A; *Fifteenth Census of the United States* (1930), *Inhabitants of Lebanon, Lebanon County, Pennsylvania*, E.D. No. 38-23, page 206A.

Andrew "Andy" James Allwein (M07-0405-0603-0108), b.
February 19, 1915, d. May 7, 1964 (HC), m. (August 31, 1940)
Ida Mary Rossi (b. June 9, 1920, d. January 20, 2013)

Andrew Aloysius Allwein died on June 8, 1930 in a boating
accident on the Susquehanna River, near Columbia, Pennsylvania.[306]
Margaret (Guare) Allwein died a few years later on February 21,
1939. They are buried together in Holy Cross Cemetery (HC) in
Lebanon, Pennsylvania.

Andrew James Allwein (1915-1964)[307]
Lebanon, Pennsylvania

Andrew "Andy" James Allwein (M07-0405-0603-0108), born on
February 19, 1915 in Lebanon, Pennsylvania, was the last child
(and the only boy) born to Andrew Aloysius and Margaret (Guare)
Allwein. After his father's (Andrew Aloysius Allwein—see above)
accidental death in June of 1930, Andrew James Allwein had to
support his mother and quit high school for a short time. Eventually
Andy returned to Lebanon High, where he excelled in sports. He
was athletically gifted in many sports and played all three years in
basketball and football. In 1934, his senior year, he was the captain
of the football team and played right end. In a news article by Leo
Prendergast, coach of Bethlehem High, it was stated that Andy
Allwein was one of the best scholastic wingmen that season. Andy
Allwein was one of the players selected for All-State honors in that
year. Andy also received several swimming medals during his youth.

After graduation from high school, Andy played for the famous
St. Mary's Indies, which are now memorialized in the Pennsylvania
Sports Hall of Fame. During the fall of 1935 he played for "Old
Reading Beer," a semi-pro football team. The Old Reading team
was the Lebanon-Berks-Dauphin County league champions. Andy
also played baseball for the "Boro and Brooks" team. His final
batting average while playing for the Brooks team was .348.

---

[306] See the Pennsylvania Department of Health: http://www.health.state.
pa.us.
[307] This narrative was contributed by Nancy Allwein Nebiker about her father.

Exhibit 11.52 Gravestone for Andrew Aloysius and Margaret M. (Guare) Allwein—Holy Cross Cemetery, Lebanon, Pennsylvania

On August 31, 1940, Andy Allwein married Ida Rossi, daughter of Frank and Rosa (Gherardini) Rossi, at St. Joan of Arc Church in Hershey, Dauphin County, Pennsylvania. They were married by Rev. John A. Maguire. The couple had a large family of six children, and lived in the city of Lebanon. In 1942, Andy joined the Lebanon City Police Force, and in 1948 he was promoted to the rank of Corporal. A year later, in 1949, he retired to become the proprietor of the Silver Dollar Grille located on North Ninth Street, in Lebanon. In 1954 Andy purchased another taproom establishment in Lebanon called the Lafayette Hotel located on 6th and Walnut Streets.

Andy Allwein enjoyed every minute of life. In the summers he and his family vacationed on the Delaware coast, at a location known as the "Indian River Inlet." The family returned year after year to the same place. The following narrative is excerpted from a story written by Nancy Allwein Nebiker about the family vacations they had at the Inlet:[308]

Indian River Inlet was a summer community that consisted of cottages, camper trailers, a trailer park, tents, a grocery store, two restaurants, a snack shop, a fishing gear store, a small boat rental and a fish cleaning stand. This area wasn't just for renting party boats for the day, but for people who came from near and far to get away from the hustle and bustle of home and work. Indian River Inlet was a favorite vacation spot for hundreds of people, including my family. My memories began in the summer of 1954 when the Andrew James Allwein, Sr. family from Lebanon, Pennsylvania spent their first summer at the cottage in Indian River Inlet. My father and a few men from Lebanon built a little cottage on rented land owned by John Marsh. My father named the cottage "The Gar," a name for a fish. The people who vacationed at the Inlet came primarily from Delaware or Pennsylvania.

---

[308]   These paragraphs are excerpted from an article contributed by Nancy Allwein Nebiker titled the "Indian River Inlet—Delaware's Forgotten Summer Resort," published in the *Kent & Sussex Crossroads, The News Journal*, Wilmington, Delaware, Saturday March 22, 2008.

Exhibit 11.53 Photograph of Andrew "Andy" James Allwein in his policeman uniform

The drive from Lebanon, Pennsylvania to the Inlet took approximately three hours. With some exceptions, most of the roads from Lebanon to the Inlet were two-lane highways. When we drove past the big iron bridge at Barker's Landing, south of the Dover Air Force Base, I could smell the marsh, and I knew it was only a few miles to the Inlet.

In the early years, my parents made this trek with six children crammed in a Pontiac station wagon, along with food, drinks, boxes of clothing packed in liquor boxes. It was not unusual to fit an extra childhood friend, or relative into our already cramped cozy car. During those early years, I was too young to visualize how full this station wagon felt to me.

Each spring, my father made repairs or additions to the buildings. I still can hear the sounds of the saw, and the smell of paint and turpentine. The original size of the cottage was one large room. The kitchen was divided by a curtain at night in those first couple of years. Eventually a permanent room divider was added to the kitchen room and living room/sleeping area. An enclosed porch, boat garage, large outhouse, and a large bedroom that included two sets of bunk beds and a single bed, were eventually added. When visitors stayed with our family, we had quite a supply of cots to sleep on. My father bought the small trailer behind the cottage for guests to stay while vacationing with us. Our family always invited many friends and relatives to stay with us during the summer months.

When our family arrived at the cottage, shoes and socks were off the feet, because the ground was sandy. My mother had a hard time keeping the sand out of the house, because as kids we always brought sand into the house, and into our beds. Air conditioning was unnecessary at the inlet; there was always a cool breeze from the strong cool ocean waters flowing into the bay. In fact, on some summer evenings the house shutters were closed.

The cottage did not have running water, but we did have electricity in the house. We got water from the neighbor's well using a hand pump. Every so many years, the outhouse would need to be moved, and the boardwalk path from the cottage to the outhouse had to be changed to fit the new direction.

Since my father had two taverns in Lebanon, he would take his beer kegs to the Rehoboth Ice Plant, and fill those kegs with water. There was an enclosed storage room in the rear of the cottage that housed a pump. The pump was connected to a hose that ran into the kitchen. My mother heated the water over the stove for washing dishes, and heated water in a basin, so we could take baths and wash our hair.

Since this was a fishing community, my father had a small, old mahogany boat. He used this boat for claming at Sea Gull Island, and Burton Island areas and for fishing for flounder in the bay. I would walk to the fishing docks where the men were cleaning fish, and I'd get a bucket of fresh cut fish heads for crabbing. Our family crabbed along the Rehoboth Bay coast line, near Cotton Patch. Some of the crabs were used to catch minnows, which were needed for fishing.

Our small cottage was located across the street from the bay. I loved to walk along the edge of the water to see if anything had changed, or to just listen to the sounds of the waves hitting the beach. During the full moon in June, I was able to see many horseshoe crabs along the water line. Pea size horseshoe crabs eggs were often discovered in the sand. That always fascinated me! The shore line has changed over the years. At one time there was a very large sandbar that extended from the coast line past the coast guard station, and out into the bay. I used to walk on this sandbar to look for shells or just explore the sand. When the low tide was out, and the sand bar was exposed, it trapped many blue claw crabs. One day my oldest brother used a crab net to scoop them up. My mother steamed the crabs, and my father drove back to Lebanon in his pick-up truck, and sold the crabs to his friend Mr. Kugler, who owned Kugler's Fish store.

The Inlet's shore line had a very nice clean sandy beach. It was safe for families to take their small children into the clear shallow water, with very little waves. It was convenient for my father to anchor his small fishing boat on shore, and get a quick lunch at the cottage. As I walked along the water-way to an area called the Point, the soil turned from sand to clay. The water was rough at this area because it was the entrance for boats to dock.

My father died in May of 1964, and two years later my mother re-married. Our new family continued visiting Indian Inlet and the cottage, but its days were numbered. Labor Day, 1971 would be the last time I would see the cottage, because the state bought the land from Mr. Marsh, and the land was to be used for a state park.

I visited the area again during the summer of 1982, and walked with my husband across the new landscape of what is now Indian River Inlet State Park. We walked along the shore line, guessing where the cottage was located. To my surprise I found a long, wide, thick piece of wood, the kind of wood that was used as a base for our front porch. Walking in the dunes I found what we called pressed wood with a Pennsylvania Dutch hex sign, old plaster painted pink, and a small piece of green linoleum. The hex sign was from our outside shutters, the pink plaster was from the bedroom, and the green linoleum was from the kitchen. I collected the linoleum and hex sign for keepsake, to remember my family's summer cottage, "The Gar."

A lot of roads have changed over time, especially after the March storm. The State of Delaware placed large rocks on the perimeter of the shore line, to eliminate more sand from washing into the bay. The state park currently issues boat dock rentals, charter boat services, tackle and bait sales, fish cleaning, fresh seafood sales, and a few cottage rentals.

Today, on a winter day, when the marsh isn't high or green, I can still view that old wooden bridge along the sandy banks of the Rehoboth Bay, located north of the Inlet.

Andy Allwein passed away on May 7, 1964 at the young age of 49 years. A large array of floral baskets and Mass Cards were received from many who knew him. People lined up down the block at the Thompson Funeral Home to say their last good-byes to a man who enjoyed being with people. His wife, Ida Mary Rossi, remarried to John Pentony on June 13, 1966. She died on January 20, 2013. They are buried together at Holy Cross Cemetery (HC) in Lebanon, Pennsylvania.

Exhibit 11.54 Grave marker for Andrew "Andy" James Allwein and Ida Rossi Allwein Pentony—Holy Cross Cemetery, Lebanon, Pennsylvania

John Aloysius Allwein (1877-1957)
Lebanon, Pennsylvania

John Aloysius Allwein (M06-0405-0603-05), the second son of Hiram and Sarah (Bross) Allwein, was born March 30, 1877 in Lebanon, Pennsylvania. The line of descent connecting John Aloysius Allwein to Johannes Jacob and Catharina Allwein, progenitors of the Allwein family in colonial Pennsylvania, is as follows:

Generation 1: Johannes Jacob and Catharina Allwein—Berks County, Pa.
Generation 2: Conrad and Catharine (Weibel) Allwein—Dauphin County, Pa.
Generation 3: Philip and Barbara (Frantz) Allwein—Lebanon County, Pa.
Generation 4: Samuel and Elizabeth (Eisenhauer) Allwein—Lebanon County, Pa.
Generation 5: Hiram J. and Sarah (Bross) Allwein—Lebanon County, Pa.
Generation 6: John Aloysius and Mabel (Dennis) Allwein—Lebanon County, Pa.

John Aloysius Allwein married Mabel Elizabeth Dennis, daughter of Ira and Margaretta Dennis, on October 31, 1899 at St. Mary's Catholic Church in Lebanon. The ceremony was performed by Rev. A. Christ.

Federal Census enumerations of Lebanon County indicate that John and Mabel Allwein were living there for the remainder of their lives.[309] His occupation in 1910 is given as "tapper in steel works," in 1920 "machine operator in steel works," and in the 1930 and 1940 Federal Census reports he was listed as an "inspector in steel mill."

---

[309] *Thirteenth Census of the United States* (1910), *Inhabitants of Lebanon Ward 1, Lebanon County, Pennsylvania*, E.D. No. 147, page 90A; *Fourteenth Census of the United States* (1920), *Inhabitants of Lebanon Ward 1, Lebanon County, Pennsylvania,* E.D. No. 167, page 87B; *Fifteenth Census of the United States* (1930), *Inhabitants of Lebanon, Lebanon County, Pennsylvania*, E.D. No. 38-15, page 46A; *Sixteenth Census of the United States* (1940), *Inhabitants of Lebanon, Lebanon County, Pennsylvania*, E.D. No. 38-15, page 244B.

Based on Federal Census reports, and other available records, we have the following information on the children of John Aloysius and Mabel (Dennis) Allwein:[310]

Florence E. Allwein, (F07-0405-0603-0501), b. April 4, 1900, d. August, 13, 1985 (ML), unmarried

Ira Joseph Allwein, (M07-0405-0603-0502), b. July 24, 1903, d. July 28, 1973 (ML), m. (March 22, 1923) Helen E. Eldridge (b. February 13, 1901, d. June 17, 1987)[311]

Both of these children are listed in Polk's 1940 Lebanon City Directory. Mabel Allwein died on May 8, 1948 and John Aloysius Allwein died November 12, 1957.[312] They are buried in Mount Lebanon Cemetery (ML) in Lebanon, Pennsylvania. Both of their children are buried there as well.

Catherine M. Allwein Bender Guare (1879-1942)
Lebanon, Pennsylvania

Catherine M. Allwein (F06-0405-0603-06), daughter of Hiram and Sarah (Bross) Allwein, was born April 10, 1879 in Lebanon. The line of descent connecting Catherine M. Allwein to Johannes Jacob and Catharina Allwein, progenitors of the Allwein family in colonial Pennsylvania, is as follows:

Generation 1: Johannes Jacob and Catharina Allwein—Berks County, Pa.
Generation 2: Conrad and Catharine (Weibel) Allwein—Dauphin County, Pa.
Generation 3: Philip and Barbara (Frantz) Allwein—Lebanon County, Pa.
Generation 4: Samuel and Elizabeth (Eisenhauer) Allwein—Lebanon County, Pa.
Generation 5: Hiram J. and Sarah (Bross) Allwein—Lebanon County, Pa.
Generation 6: Catherine M. Allwein and John F. Bender—Lebanon County, Pa.

---

[310] Death dates for these children were obtained from obituaries from the *Lebanon Daily News*, Lebanon, Pennsylvania, Saturday, July 28, 1973; Tuesday, August 13, 1985. See also the Pennsylvania Department of Health: http://www.health.state.pa.us.

[311] Obituaries for Ira J. Allwein and Helen (Eldridge) Allwein from the *Lebanon Daily News*, Lebanon, Pennsylvania, Saturday, July 28, 1973 and June 19, 1987.

[312] Obituary for Mabel (Dennis) Allwein, *Lebanon Daily News*, Lebanon, Pennsylvania, Saturday Evening, May 8, 1948.

Exhibit 11.55 Gravestone of John Aloysius and Mabel (Dennis) Allwein—Mount Lebanon Cemetery, Lebanon, Pennsylvania

Catherine M. Allwein married John Francis Bender, son of John and Pauline Bender, on September 4, 1901 at St. Mary's Catholic Church. The ceremony was performed by Rev. A. Christ. Following their marriage, they settled in Lebanon, where John Bender worked as a bricklayer.[313]

Based on Census reports and additional information, the following were the children born to Catherine M. and John F. Bender:[314]

John Hiram Bender, b. June 12, 1901, d. January 28, 1969 (HC), m. (June 20, 1922) Anna R. Horn (b. June 15, 1905, d. November 1983)

Raymond J. Bender, b. March 13, 1904, d. May 8, 1972 (HC), m. (August 8, 1936) Josephine C. Daubert (b. March 16, 1916, d. March 4, 2011)

Joseph A. Bender, b. September 24, 1905, d. September 10, 1989 (HC), m. (1) (August 30, 1927) Josephine LaSalle (September 17, 1908, d. unknown), (2) (January 19, 1936) Ellen M. Helm (b. March 11, 1915, d. August 10, 2006)

Pauline E. Bender, b. February 1, 1907, d. October 16, 1992 (GE), m. (July 15, 1933) Adam J. Maurer, Jr. (b. July 2, 1906, d. March 13, 1996)

---

[313] *Twelfth Census of the United States* (1900), *Inhabitants of Lebanon Ward 5, Lebanon County, Pennsylvania*, E.D. No. 123, page 167B; *Thirteenth Census of the United States* (1910), *Inhabitants of Lebanon Ward 7, Lebanon County, Pennsylvania*, E.D. No. 158, page 267B; *Fourteenth Census of the United States* (1920), *Inhabitants of Lebanon Ward 5, Lebanon County, Pennsylvania,* E.D. No. 176, page 299B.

[314] Obituaries from the *Lebanon Daily News*, Lebanon, Pennsylvania, Saturday Evening, April 4, 1964; Wednesday, January 10, 1968; Thursday Evening, January 28, 1969; Tuesday, May 9, 1972; Monday, September 16, 1974; Monday, September 11, 1989; Wednesday, March 13, 1996; Tuesday, April 8, 2003; Saturday, December 23, 2005; Saturday, August 12, 2006; Sunday, March 6, 2011; and the *Sunday Patriot News*, Harrisburg, Pennsylvania, October 18, 1992.

Richard Herbert Bender, b. August 6, 1908, d. April 4 1964 (HC),
   m. (January 22, 1939), Catherine "Katie" Eulalia Vancho (b.
   November 16, 1912, d. April 7, 2003)
Guy J. Bender, b. December 11, 1910, d. September 14, 1974 (HC),
   m. (December 19, 1936) Louise E. Miller (b. August 5, 1918, d.
   January 9, 1968)
M. Florence Bender, b. July 29, 1917, d. December 23, 2005, m. (June
   3, 1939) Joseph A. Smetana (b. November 10, 1910, d. July 1980)

   John F. Bender died June 2, 1920. Catherine remarried to John
Patrick Guare on January 27, 1925 and he died soon thereafter, on
February 4, 1925. There was one son, James Patrick Guare (b. May
19, 1925, d. May 18, 2006), born to them. In the 1930 and 1940
Federal Census enumerations, Catherine M. (Allwein) Bender is
listed as "Catherine M. Guare," a widow.[315] Catherine M. Allwein
died on March 4, 1942.[316] She is buried at Holy Cross Cemetery,
Lebanon, Pennsylvania with her two husbands.

Ellen "Ella" C. Allwein Coil (1883-1937)
Lebanon, Pennsylvania

Ellen C. Allwein (F06-0405-0603-08), daughter of Hiram and Sarah
(Bross) Allwein, was born May 24, 1883 in Lebanon. The line of descent
connecting Ellen C. Allwein to Johannes Jacob and Catharina Allwein,
progenitors of the Allwein family in colonial Pennsylvania, is as follows:

Generation 1: Johannes Jacob and Catharina Allwein—Berks County, Pa.
Generation 2: Conrad and Catharine (Weibel) Allwein—Dauphin County, Pa.
Generation 3: Philip and Barbara (Frantz) Allwein—Lebanon County, Pa.
Generation 4: Samuel and Elizabeth (Eisenhauer) Allwein—Lebanon County, Pa.
Generation 5: Hiram J. and Sarah (Bross) Allwein—Lebanon County, Pa.
Generation 6: Ellen C. Allwein and George Washington Coil—Lebanon
   County, Pa.

---

[315] *Fifteenth Census of the United States* (1930), *Inhabitants of Lebanon,
Lebanon County, Pennsylvania*, E.D. No. 38-23, page 202A; *Sixteenth
Census of the United States* (1940), *Inhabitants of Lebanon, Lebanon
County, Pennsylvania*, E.D. No. 39-28, page 489A.
[316] Obituary *Lebanon Daily News*, Lebanon, Pennsylvania, Thursday
Evening, March 5, 1942. See also the Pennsylvania Department of Health:
http://www.health.state.pa.us.

Exhibit 11.56 Gravestone for Catherine M. Allwein, John Francis Bender, and John Patrick Guare—Holy Cross Cemetery, Lebanon, Pennsylvania

Ellen C. Allwein married George Washington Coil, son of George Coil Sr. and wife Louise, on December 20, 1915 in Lebanon. They settled in the Fifth Ward of Lebanon Borough, where George Coil worked as a "die setter" in the iron and steel industry.[317]

Federal Census information for 1920 and 1930 indicate there was one child born to them, as follows:[318]

George James Coil, b. March 5, 1919, d. May 31, 1972 (ML), unmarried

Ellen C. (Allwein) Coil died on May 8, 1937.[319] George W. Coil died February 27, 1963.[320] They are buried at Mount Lebanon Cemetery, Lebanon, Pennsylvania.

Raymond Hiram "Cottie" Allwein (1885-1929)
Lebanon, Pennsylvania

Raymond Hiram Allwein (M06-0405-0603-09), the youngest son of Hiram and Sarah (Bross) Allwein, was born August 16, 1885 in Lebanon. His nickname was "Cottie." The line of descent connecting Raymond Hiram Allwein to Johannes Jacob and Catharina Allwein, progenitors of the Allwein family in colonial Pennsylvania, is as follows:

Generation 1: Johannes Jacob and Catharina Allwein—Berks County, Pa.
Generation 2: Conrad and Catharine (Weibel) Allwein—Dauphin County, Pa.
Generation 3: Philip and Barbara (Frantz) Allwein—Lebanon County, Pa.
Generation 4: Samuel and Elizabeth (Eisenhauer) Allwein—Lebanon County, Pa.
Generation 5: Hiram J. and Sarah (Bross) Allwein—Lebanon County, Pa.
Generation 6: Raymond Hiram Allwein—Lebanon County, Pa.

---

[317] *Fourteenth Census of the United States* (1920), *Inhabitants of Lebanon Ward 5, Lebanon County, Pennsylvania,* E.D. No. 173, page 221B; *Fifteenth Census of the United States* (1930), *Inhabitants of Lebanon, Lebanon County, Pennsylvania*, E.D. No. 38-27, page 160A.
[318] Obituary for George James Coil in *Lebanon Daily News*, Lebanon, Pennsylvania, Thursday Evening, June 1, 1972.
[319] See the Pennsylvania Department of Health: http://www.health.state.pa.us.
[320] Obituaries from the *Lebanon Daily News*, Lebanon, Pennsylvania, Monday Evening, May 10, 1937; Friday Evening, March 1, 1963.

Exhibit 11.57 Gravestone for Ella C. and George W. Coil—Mount Lebanon Cemetery, Lebanon, Pennsylvania

Raymond Hiram Allwein never married, and spent most of his life in the parental home at 610 Locust Street. He was a veteran of the First World War. He served as a private in the Army from October 15 1917 to January 9, 1918 in Company I, 61st Infantry Regiment. In the 1920 Federal Census, Raymond Allwein (age 34) is listed in his parents' household, working as a "laborer in steel mill."[321] He died on March 7, 1929 and is buried in St. Mary's Cemetery (SM) in Lebanon.

Martha M. Allwein Frazier (1887-1961)
Lebanon, Pennsylvania

Martha M. Allwein (F06-0405-0603-10), daughter of Hiram and Sarah (Bross) Allwein, was born February 9, 1887 in Lebanon, Pennsylvania. The line of descent connecting Martha M. Allwein to Johannes Jacob and Catharina Allwein, progenitors of the Allwein family in colonial Pennsylvania, is as follows:

Generation 1: Johannes Jacob and Catharina Allwein—Berks County, Pa.
Generation 2: Conrad and Catharine (Weibel) Allwein—Dauphin County, Pa.
Generation 3: Philip and Barbara (Frantz) Allwein—Lebanon County, Pa.
Generation 4: Samuel and Elizabeth (Eisenhauer) Allwein—Lebanon County, Pa.
Generation 5: Hiram J. and Sarah (Bross) Allwein—Lebanon County, Pa.
Generation 6: Martha M. Allwein and William Maurice Frazier—Lebanon
    County, Pa.

Martha M. Allwein married William Maurice Frazier, son of John and Katherine Frazier, on December 29, 1907 in Lebanon. They lived with William Frazier's parents in the Fifth Ward at 314 Lehman Street for most of their adult lives. They were listed at this address in all Federal Censuses from 1900 to 1940. William Frazier

---

[321] *Fourteenth Census of the United States* (1920), *Inhabitants of Lebanon Ward 1, Lebanon County, Pennsylvania*, E.D. No. 168, page 112B.

Exhibit 11.58 Gravestone for Raymond Hiram Allwein—St. Mary's Cemetery, Lebanon, Pennsylvania

worked in the iron and steel industry, and spent some time as a clerk for a local hotel.[322]

Available records on this family indicate that there were eight children born to Martha M. Allwein and William Maurice Frazier, as follows:[323]

George W. Frazier, b. June 5, 1908, d. December 9, 1967 (HC), m. (November 26, 1931) Josephine M. Gogolak (b. April 14, 1909, d. October 4, 1994)

James M. Frazier, b. September 12, 1910, d. August 21, 1973 (HC), m. (December 27, 1932) Agnes M. Kline (b. January 14, 1911, d. July 31, 2000)

Elizabeth M. Frazier, b. March 11, 1914, d. August 28, 2006 (HC), m. (June 12, 1937) Russell E. Kaley (b. July 7, 1917, d. October 5, 1984)

Charles J. Frazier, b. November 17, 1916, d. May 7, 1994 (IG), m. (June 14, 1941) Eleanor Black (b. unknown, d. unknown)

William M. Frazier, b. October 23, 1918, d. August 24, 2000, m. (March 19, 1942) Josephine Margaret Kissinger (b. June 22, 1919, d. unknown)

---

[322] *Twelfth Census of the United States* (1900), *Inhabitants of Lebanon Ward 5, Lebanon County, Pennsylvania*, E.D. No. 128, page 247A; *Thirteenth Census of the United States* (1910), *Inhabitants of Lebanon Ward 5, Lebanon County, Pennsylvania*, E.D. No. 154 page 199B; *Fourteenth Census of the United States* (1920), *Inhabitants of Lebanon Ward 5, Lebanon County, Pennsylvania,* E.D. No. 173, page 217B; *Fifteenth Census of the United States* (1930), *Inhabitants of Lebanon, Lebanon County, Pennsylvania,* E.D. No. 38-21, page 162A; *Sixteenth Census of the United States* (1940), *Inhabitants of Lebanon, Lebanon County, Pennsylvania*, E.D. No. 38-28, page 468B.

[323] Information on dates of death were obtained from obituaries in the *Lebanon Daily News*, Lebanon, Pennsylvania, Saturday, December 9, 1967; Tuesday, Auguest 21, 1973; Saturday, October 6, 1984; Monday May 9, 1994; Wednesday, October 5, 1994; Wednesday, August 2, 2000; Friday, August 25, 2000; Tuesday, August 29, 2006; Wednesday, November 26, 2008; and *The Evening News*, Harrisburg, Pennsylvania, January 19, 1995.

Patrick Hiram Frazier, b. August 12, 1921, d. June 4, 2008 (in Cheboygan, Michigan), m. Margaret Pachaco (b. unknown, d. unknown)

Marion C. Frazier, b. August 11, 1923, d. January 17, 1995 (HC), m. (June 28, 1947) Carl "Clark" James Gable (b. September 29, 1923, d. February 27, 1999)

Edward Frazier, b. May 30, 1926, d. November 24, 2008 (IG), m. (October 11, 1947) Mary Louise Mellinger (b. September 1926, d. unknown)

Martha M. Allwein Frazier died July 19, 1961. William Maurice Frazier died August 18, 1962.[324] They are buried at Holy Cross Cemetery, Lebanon, Pennsylvania.

Sarah E. Allwein Rudy (1893-1966)
Lebanon, Pennsylvania

Sarah E. Allwein (F06-0405-0603-10), youngest daughter of Hiram and Sarah (Bross) Allwein, was born January 19, 1893 in Lebanon, Pennsylvania. The line of descent connecting Sarah E. Allwein to Johannes Jacob and Catharina Allwein, progenitors of the Allwein family in colonial Pennsylvania, is as follows:

Generation 1: Johannes Jacob and Catharina Allwein—Berks County, Pa.
Generation 2: Conrad and Catharine (Weibel) Allwein—Dauphin County, Pa.
Generation 3: Philip and Barbara (Frantz) Allwein—Lebanon County, Pa.
Generation 4: Samuel and Elizabeth (Eisenhauer) Allwein—Lebanon County, Pa.
Generation 5: Hiram J. and Sarah (Bross) Allwein—Lebanon County, Pa.
Generation 6: Sarah E. Allwein and Horace M. Rudy—Lebanon County, Pa.

Sarah E. Allwein married Horace Monroe Rudy, son of Jacob B. and Ellen Rudy of Cornwall, on May 18, 1912 in Lebanon. The ceremony was conducted by Rev. H.B. Strickland.

---

[324] Obituaries from the *Lebanon Daily News*, Lebanon, Pennsylvania, Monday August 10, 1962. See also the Pennsylvania Department of Health: http://www.health.state.pa.us.

Exhibit 11.59 Gravestone for Martha M. and William M. Frazier—Holy Cross Cemetery, Lebanon, Pennsylvania

The couple settled in Lebanon. In the 1930 Federal Census, Horace Rudy's occupation was given as "salesman for an oil company," and in the 1940 returns, he was listed as a "printer at a printing press."[325]

Based on Census reports, Sarah E. Allwein and Horace M. Rudy raised the following children:[326]

Margaret Rudy, b. 1912, d. November 25, 1914 (SM)

Christine Rudy, b. March 25, 1914, d. March 29, 1996 (HC), m. (August 11, 1934) Harry E. Shay (b. January 16, 1911, d. August 1, 1990)

Alma Rudy, b. August 3, 1915, d. July 15, 1965 (HC), m. (August 27, 1942) Joshua (James) Lee Griffin, Jr. (b. September 4, 1916, d. July 7, 2006 (MZ))

Gladys Rudy, b. June 2, 1917, d. May 1, 1976 (GP), m. Wilson W. Englehart (b. November 26, 1912, d. December 22, 1988)

Marvin Richard Rudy, b. August 1918, d. February 10, 1926 (HC)

Marie Sara Rudy, b. October 7, 1919, d. March 5, 2007 (HC), m. (October 7. 1939) Robert Edward Berkheiser (b. September 7, 1915, d. November 14, 2002)

Bertha C. Rudy, b. January 6, 1923, d. March 1, 1984 (GP), m. William R. McKinney (b. June 1, 1922, d. October 19, 1994)

Louise S. Rudy, b. August 1924, d. June 7, 1931

---

[325] *Fifteenth Census of the United States* (1930), *Inhabitants of Lebanon, Lebanon County, Pennsylvania*, E.D. No. 38-17, page 77A; *Sixteenth Census of the United States* (1940), *Inhabitants of Lebanon, Lebanon County, Pennsylvania*, E.D. No. 38-15, page 226A.

[326] Information on dates of death for these children were obtained from obituaries in the *Lebanon Daily News*, Lebanon, Pennsylvania, Friday Evening, November 27, 1914; Thursday Evening, February 11, 1926; Monday Evening, June 8, 1931; Thursday, July 15, 1965; Monday Evening, May 3, 1976; Friday, March 2, 1984; Thursday, August 2, 1990; Friday, November 15, 2002; Wednesday, March 7, 2007; and *The Harrisburg Patriot*, Friday, October 21, 1994; Saturday, March 30, 1996.

Horace Rudy died April 22, 1948. Sarah E. Allwein died several years later on February 8, 1966.[327] They are buried at Holy Cross Cemetery, Lebanon, Pennsylvania.

Jonathan Allwein (1849-1865)
Lebanon, Pennsylvania

The third son of Samuel and Elizabeth (Eisenhauer) Allwein, Jonathan Allwein (M05-0405-0604) was born January 11, 1849. Due to his mother's circumstances, at the age of eleven he went to live with Moses Arnold, a farmer, and his wife Sarah, where he is listed in the 1860 Federal Census report.[328] At fifteen he joined the army and enrolled on the 25th day of February 1864 at Reading Pa. in Company E, 50th Regiment of Pennsylvania Volunteers to serve three years and mustered into service as a Private. He was reported killed in action at the Siege of Petersburg on February 3, 1965.[329] The details of his death were reported in Chapter 7 of Volume 1 of *Familie Allwein*, where we discuss his role in supporting his deserted mother, Elizabeth Eisenhauer Allwein (pages 396-399).

Jared J. Allwein (1851-1893)
Lebanon, Pennsylvania

The fourth son of Samuel and Elizabeth (Eisenhauer) Allwein, Jared J. Allwein (M05-0405-0605) was born on February 12, 1851. The line of descent connecting Jared J. Allwein to Johannes Jacob and Catharina Allwein, progenitors of the Allwein family in colonial Pennsylvania, is as follows:

---

[327] Obituaries *Lebanon Daily News*, Lebanon, Pennsylvania, Thursday Evening, April 22, 1948;Tuesday Evening, February 8, 1966.
[328] Jonathan's father was a second cousin to Moses Arnold, as they both had the same great grandparents, Johannes Jacob and Catharina Allwein.
[329] Samuel P. Bates, *History of Pennsylvania Volunteers 1861-65*, edited by Janet Hewett, Wilmington NC: Broadfoot Publishing Co., 1994, Volume II, Page 1297, and Volume IV, page 1338.

Exhibit 11.60 Gravestones for Sarah E. and Horace Rudy—Holy Cross Cemetery, Lebanon, Pennsylvania

Generation 1: Johannes Jacob and Catharina Allwein—Berks County, Pa.
Generation 2: Conrad and Catharine (Weibel) Allwein—Dauphin County, Pa.
Generation 3: Philip and Barbara (Frantz) Allwein—Lebanon County, Pa.
Generation 4: Samuel and Elizabeth (Eisenhauer) Allwein—Lebanon County, Pa.
Generation 5: Jared J. and Sarah (Bowman) Allwein—Lebanon County, Pa.

Due to the disruption of his parent's marriage, at the age of 9 he moved to the household of Peter Arnold, coachmaker, and his wife Sarah. He learned blacksmithing from his uncle John W. Allwein (brother to Samuel Allwein), the coachmaker, in whose home he was living in the 1870 Federal Census.[330] In that Census Jared's occupation is given as "coachsmith"—note that reference to the trades of coachsmith and blacksmith were often interchanged due to the fact that they both involved forging objects from iron.

About 1875 Jared Allwein married Sarah Bowman, the only daughter of Joseph and Mary Ann (Arnold) Bowman, and his third cousin.[331] According to Jerome Allwein's *Genealogy*, he then became employed by Mr. Bowman, who was a well-known cabinetmaker in the town. The 1880 Federal Census enumeration for the Borough of Lebanon indicates that Jared and Sarah Allwein were living in the same household with Joseph Bowman and wife Mary Ann.[332] According to the genealogist . . .

His business qualities impressed Mr. Bowman favorably, who took him in partnership under firm name of Bowman & Co. After

---

[330] See Jerome Allwein, *Genealogy of the Allwein-Arnold Families*. Philadelphia, Pa., 1902, page 71 and *Ninth Census of the United States* (1870), *Inhabitants of Borough of Lebanon, Lebanon County, Pennsylvania*, page 340.

[331] Joseph and Moses Bowman were brothers—sons of John and Sarah Anna (Seifert) Bowman. Sarah Anna Seifert was the daughter of Joseph S. and Catherine (Allwein) Seifert. Catherine Allwein was the daughter of Hans Jacob and Catharina Allwein. Thus, Sarah Bowman and Jared Allwein were third cousins.

[332] *Tenth Census of the United States* (1880), *Inhabitants of Borough of Lebanon, Lebanon County, Pennsylvania*, page 350C.

Mr. Bowman's death James F. McGovern entered the firm trading as McGovern & Allwein. They continued about one year when he withdrew and formed a copartnership with Pierce H. Thompson trading as Allwein & Thompson. This business continued only a short time when he died.[333]

It is noteworthy that the 1880 Federal Census record referred to above lists Pierce H. Thompson as a cabinetmaker's apprentice also living in the Joseph Bowman household. It appears, then, that toward the later part of his work life Jared Allwein changed occupations. Pierce Thompson would go on to become a funeral director and embalmer, specializing in fine "estate furniture." Pierce Thompson married Elizabeth Allwein, daughter of Henry and Elizabeth (Dentzler) Allwein of Lancaster County (see below).[334]

After Sarah (Bowman) Allwein died on April 27, 1886, Jared remarried. His second marriage was to Alice Stanley (b. July 11, 1852). She died a few years thereafter on January 24, 1890, and Jared soon after that on November 3, 1893. They all three died at a relatively young age. They are buried in St. Mary's Cemetery in the Borough of Lebanon.

There were no children issuing from either of these marriages, although there was one child with Sarah Bowman who died in infancy.[335]

---

[333] Jerome Allwein, *Genealogy of the Allwein-Arnold Families.* Philadelphia, Pa., 1902, page 71.
[334] Jerome Allwein, *Genealogy of the Allwein-Arnold Families.* Philadelphia, Pa., 1902, page 57.
[335] Jerome Allwein, *Genealogy of the Allwein-Arnold Families.* Philadelphia, Pa., 1902, page 71.

Exhibit 11.61 Gravestone for Jared Allwein, St. Mary's Cemetery, Lebanon County, Pennsylvania

Exhibit 11.62 Gravestone for Alice Stanley Allwein, St. Mary's Cemetery, Lebanon County, Pennsylvania

Elizabeth Allwein Francis (1853-1913)
Lebanon, Pennsylvania

Little is known about Elizabeth Allwein (F05-0405-0606), the youngest daughter of Samuel and Elizabeth (Eisenhauer) Allwein. She was born on June 6, 1853 and that at the age of 7 she went to live in the household of Joseph Arnold, a farmer, and his wife Sarah. The line of descent connecting Elizabeth Allwein to Johannes Jacob and Catharina Allwein, progenitors of the Allwein family in colonial Pennsylvania, is as follows:

Generation 1: Johannes Jacob and Catharina Allwein—Berks County, Pa.
Generation 2: Conrad and Catharine (Weibel) Allwein—Dauphin County, Pa.
Generation 3: Philip and Barbara (Frantz) Allwein—Lebanon County, Pa.
Generation 4: Samuel and Elizabeth (Eisenhauer) Allwein—Lebanon County, Pa.
Generation 5: Hiram J. and Sarah (Bross) Allwein—Lebanon County, Pa.
Generation 6: Elizabeth Allwein and George W. Francis—Morris County,
    New Jersey

She married George Francis, son of Elias and Sarah R. (Smith) Francis, on January 2, 1892 in Manhattan, New York.[336] They are listed in the 1900 and 1910 Federal Census reports for the city of Rockaway in Morris County, New Jersey.[337] In the 1900 report, George W. Francis is listed as a "hotel keeper" (age 60). That record indicates that there were no children born to them.

Elizabeth Allwein Francis died in 1913 and is buried at the Rockaway Valley United Methodist Church Cemetery (RM) in Boonton, New Jersey. Her gravestone records the spelling of George's family name as FRANCES, whereas virtually all other records sources use FRANCIS.

---

[336] Information contributed by Nancy Allwein Nebiker, February 12, 2012. See also Jerome Allwein, *Genealogy of the Allwein-Arnold Families*. Philadelphia, Pa., 1902, page 72.
[337] *Twelfth Census of the United States* (1900), *Inhabitants of Rockaway, Morris County, New Jersey*, E.D. No. 79, page 166B; *Thirteenth Census of the United States* (1910), *Inhabitants of Rockaway Township, Morris County, New Jersey*, E.D. No. 41, page 102B.

Exhibit 11.63 Gravestone for Elizabeth Allwein Frances—
Rockaway Valley United Methodist Church Cemetery, Boonton,
New Jersey (gravestone photo obtained from Find-A-Grave).

Samuel J. Allwein (1854-1923)
Morrow County, Ohio

The fifth son of Samuel and Elizabeth (Eisenhauer) Allwein, Samuel J. Allwein (M05-0405-0607) was born November 3, 1854. He moved to Morrow County, Ohio some time prior to 1875, when he married Catharine Dennis on September 15, 1875.[338] Except for the information presented in Chapter 7 of Volume 1 (pages 394-395), we have little knowledge of his whereabouts up until his move to Ohio. We present more information on Samuel J. Allwein in Chapter 20 (volume 3), where we deal with Allwein families that migrated to Ohio.

Ambrose (Harry) Allwein (1857-1935)
Grant County, Indiana

The sixth son of Samuel and Elizabeth (Eisenhauer) Allwein, Ambrose (Harry) Allwein (M05-0405-0608) was born December 11, 1857. He was 2 years old when his family was disrupted due to his father's desertion. He remained in the care of his mother until adolescence, when at the age of 12 he went to live with Cyrus Smith, a farmer, and his wife Lizzie. In the 1870 Federal Census Ambrose was living in the Smith household working as a "farm laborer."[339]

Ambrose and his brother Henry E. Allwein (see below) attended the first Catholic school in Lebanon and are listed as pupils of St. Mary's School for the years 1865 to 1867.[340] We know little else about his years in Lebanon, Pennsylvania. We know, however that by 1880 he had moved to the state of Indiana, where he lived for a while with his oldest brother Franklin—in the Federal Census of that year Ambrose (Harry) was living with Franklin's household.[341]

---

[338] Marriage records, Morrow County Historical Library, Mt. Gilead, Ohio.

[339] *Ninth Census of the United States* (1870), *Inhabitants of Cornwall Township, Lebanon County, Pennsylvania*, page 56.

[340] See John J. Foster, *The Story of Assumption of Blessed Virgin Mary Church, Lebanon, Pennsylvania.* Lebanon, Pennsylvania: Sowers Printing Company, 1951.

[341] *Tenth Census of the United States* (1880), *Inhabitants of Richland Township, Whitley County, Indiana*, page 418.

We present more information on this life in Indiana in Chapter 21 (volume 3) of *Familie Allwein*.

Henry E. Allwein (1859-1926)
Richland County, Ohio

The youngest son of Samuel and Elizabeth (Eisenhauer) Allwein, Henry E. Allwein (M05-0405-0609) was born February 12, 1859 in Lebanon, Pennsylvania.[342] He was raised by his mother following the breakup of his parents' household. He moved to Richland County, Ohio when he was a young man. Henry's older brother Samuel Allwein had moved to Ohio some years earlier, living in adjacent Morrow County (see above).

Henry E. Allwein attended the first Catholic school in Lebanon; he and his brother Ambrose are listed as pupils of St. Mary's School for the years 1865 to 1867.[343] From all indications he did not adhere to the Catholic faith during his adult years.

By the early 1880s Henry E. Allwein had moved to Shelby, Ohio, in the same general vicinity as his brother Samuel, who lived in Morrow County to the southwest. We present more information on Henry E. Allwein in Chapter 20 (volume 3), along with his brother Samuel, where we deal with Allwein families that migrated to Ohio.

Philip Allwein (1819-1856)
Lebanon County, Pennsylvania

Philip Allwein (M04-0405-07), son of Philip and Barbara (Frantz) Allwein, was born May 6, 1819 on his parents' farm in Lebanon Township of Lebanon County, Pennsylvania. The line of descent

---

[342] Jerome Allwein's *Genealogy* gives 1860 as the year of birth. Both the tombstone inscription and Henry Allwein's obituary in the Richland, Ohio newspaper give 1859.

[343] See John J. Foster, *The Story of Assumption of Blessed Virgin Mary Church, Lebanon, Pennsylvania.* Lebanon, Pennsylvania: Sowers Printing Company, 1951.

connecting Philip Allwein to Johannes Jacob and Catharina Allwein, progenitors of the Allwein family in colonial Pennsylvania, is as follows:

Generation 1: Johannes Jacob and Catharina Allwein—Berks County, Pa.
Generation 2: Conrad and Catharine (Weibel) Allwein—Dauphin County, Pa.
Generation 3: Philip and Barbara (Frantz) Allwein—Lebanon County, Pa.
Generation 4: Philip and Catherine (Arnold) Allwein—Lebanon County, Pa.

He married Catherine Arnold (b. January 16, 1819, d. April 27, 1896), daughter of Peter and Margaret Arnold. In addition to farming, Philip Allwein was a butcher, a trade he followed throughout his life.[344] More about Philip Allwein can be found in *Familie Allwein*, volume 1 (pages 402-405).

Philip and Catharine (Arnold) Allwein had four children that survived to adulthood:

Mary Allwein (F05-0405-0701), b. March 7, 1841, d. December 7, 1909 (SM), m. (May 1859) Jonathan Levengood (b. January 17, 1833, d. July 17, 1917)
Jared P. Allwein (M05-0405-0702), b. July 12, 1847, d. September 20, 1864 (SM), unmarried
Sarah Allwein (F05-0405-0703), b. December 29, 1848, d. November 27, 1919 (SM), m. (November 25, 1869) William J. Harter (b. June 16, 1848, d. June 21, 1925)
Rebecca Allwein (F05-0405-0704), b. September 1852, d. December 27, 1936, m. (1875) Martin Griffin (b November 1850, d. November 15, 1923)

As I indicated in *Famillie Allwein*, volume 1, Philip and Catharine Allwein took into their home Philip's nephew—Joseph B. Allwein—who lived with them a short time (see the discussion of Joseph B. Allwein at the beginning of this chapter). Joseph B. Allwein was the son of Philip's older brother Joseph Allwein. Philip appears in one Federal Census, for the year 1850, where he is located in North Lebanon Township of Lebanon County. This was

---

[344] Jerome Allwein, *Genealogy of the Allwein-Arnold Families*. Philadelphia, Pa., 1902, page 29.

his last appearance in the Federal Census records because Philip Allwein died October 7, 1856 in Lebanon, Pennsylvania, a relatively young man. At the time of his death, he and Catharine were living on the farm in North Lebanon Township. She remained there for several years, after which time she moved in to Lebanon where she lived for the remainder of her life.

An 1875 *County Atlas of Lebanon* lists a "Mrs. Allwine" in North Lebanon Township near Kimmerling's (German Reformed) Church (see Exhibit 11.22 above).[345] Her son Jared Allwein died at the young age of 17 in 1864, leaving Catharine with the support of her three daughters. In her later years she lived with her daughter Rebecca Allwein Griffin on Spruce Street in Lebanon (see Exhibit 11.23 above). Catharine Allwein died April 27, 1896, and she is buried together with Philip Allwein in St. Mary's Cemetery in Lebanon. Their gravestones are shown in volume 1 of *Familie Allwein* (page 405).

Mary Allwein Levengood (1841-1909)
Lebanon, Pennsylvania

Mary Allwein (F05-0405-0701), oldest daughter of Philip and Catherine (Arnold) Allwein, was born March 7, 1841 on her parents' farm in North Lebanon Township, Lebanon County, Pennsylvania. The line of descent connecting Mary Allwein to Johannes Jacob and Catharina Allwein, progenitors of the Allwein family in colonial Pennsylvania, is as follows:

Generation 1: Johannes Jacob and Catharina Allwein—Berks County, Pa.
Generation 2: Conrad and Catharine (Weibel) Allwein—Dauphin County, Pa.
Generation 3: Philip and Barbara (Frantz) Allwein—Lebanon County, Pa.
Generation 4: Philip and Catherine (Arnold) Allwein—Lebanon County, Pa.
Generation 5: Mary Allwein and Jonathan Levengood—Lebanon County, Pa.

Mary Allwein married Jonathan Levengood in May 1859 and they lived in Lebanon. One can see the location of their residence at

---

[345] F.W. Beers, *County Atlas of Lebanon Pennsylvania from Recent and Actual Surveys and Records*, Reading & Philadelphia: F.A. Davis, 1875, page 61.

Exhibit 11.64 Gravestone for Jared P. Allwein—St. Mary's Cemetery, Lebanon, Pennsylvania

419 North 8th Street, across from Monument Park, in the extract of an 1875 map of Lebanon (see Exhibit 11.5 above). In the 1880 and 1900 Federal Censuses of Lebanon, they are listed at this address and Jonathan's occupation is given as "pattern maker," presumably working in the steel industry.[346]

The children of Mary and Jonathan Levengood, listed in Jerome Allwein's *Genealogy*, are as follows:[347]

Helena Mary Levengood, b. February 21, 1860, d. May 6, 1943, m.
    (1885) Charles V. Arnold (b. April 4, 1857, December 24, 1934)
Philip E. Levengood, b. June 23, 1861, d. February 8, 1937 (HC), m.
    (1880) Caroline Feit (b. December 1861, d. September 4, 1933)
Gabriel Levengood, b. April 11, 1863, d. August 23, 1863
Ellen C. Levengood, b. May 17, 1864, d. January 2, 1893 (HC), m.
    (May 26, 1887) Stephen F. Arnold (b. November 10, 1861, d.
    Auguest 21, 1959)
Elizabeth Levengood, b. January 7, 1868, d. June 3, 1869

Mary Allwein Levengood died on December 7, 1909 and Jonathan Levengood on July 17, 1917.[348] They are buried in St. Mary's Cemetery (SM) in Lebanon.

---

[346] *Tenth Census of the United States* (1880), *Inhabitants of Lebanon Borough, Lebanon County, Pennsylvania*, page 331C; *Twelfth Census of the United States* (1900), *Inhabitants of Lebanon Ward 5, Lebanon County, Pennsylvania*, E.D. No. 129, 273A.
[347] Jerome Allwein, *Genealogy of the Allwein-Arnold Families*. Philadelphia, Pa., 1902, pages 73, 112. Information on these children was obtained from obituaries in the *Lebanon Daily News*, Lebanon, Pennsylvania, as follows: Monday Evening, December 24, 1934; Tuesday Evening, February 9, 1937; Thursday Evening, May 6, 1943; Friday Evening, August 21, 1959.
[348] Obituaries appeared in the *Lebanon Daily News*, Lebanon, Pennsylvania, Wednesday Evening, July 18, 1917; Tuesday, December 7, 1909. See also the Pennsylvania Department of Health: http://www.health.state.pa.us.

Exhibit 11.65 Gravestone for Mary Allwein Levengood—St. Mary's Cemetery, Lebanon, Pennsylvania

Exhibit 11.66 Gravestone for Jonathan Levengood—St. Mary's
Cemetery, Lebanon, Pennsylvania

Sarah Allwein Harter (1848-1919)
Lebanon, Pennsylvania

Sarah Allwein (F05-0405-0703), daughter of Philip and Catherine (Arnold) Allwein, was born December 29, 1848 in North Lebanon Township, Lebanon County, Pennsylvania. The line of descent connecting Sarah Allwein to Johannes Jacob and Catharina Allwein, progenitors of the Allwein family in colonial Pennsylvania, is as follows:

Generation 1: Johannes Jacob and Catharina Allwein—Berks County, Pa.
Generation 2: Conrad and Catharine (Weibel) Allwein—Dauphin County, Pa.
Generation 3: Philip and Barbara (Frantz) Allwein—Lebanon County, Pa.
Generation 4: Philip and Catherine (Arnold) Allwein—Lebanon County, Pa.
Generation 5: Sarah Allwein and William Harter—Lebanon County, Pa.

Sarah Allwein married William J. Harter on November 25, 1869 in Lebanon and they settled there. William Harter worked in the slate roofing business for many years, as consistently indicated in the Federal Censuses from 1880 through 1910. In the 1920 Federal Census, he is listed as a widower, living with his son Charles and his family at 417 North 12th Street in Lebanon.[349]

There were several children born to Sarah Allwein and William Harter, listed in Jerome Allwein's *Genealogy*, as follows:[350]

---

[349] *Tenth Census of the United States* (1880), *Inhabitants of Lebanon Borough, Lebanon County, Pennsylvania*, page 325C; *Twelfth Census of the United States* (1900), *Inhabitants of Lebanon Ward 5, Lebanon County, Pennsylvania*, E.D. No. 129, 274A; *Thirteenth Census of the United States* (1910), *Inhabitants of Lebanon Ward 7, Lebanon County, Pennsylvania*, E.D. No. 158, page 263B; *Fourteenth Census of the United States* (1920), *Inhabitants of Lebanon Ward 7, Lebanon County, Pennsylvania*, E.D. No. 176, page 299B.

[350] The list of children was obtained from Jerome Allwein, *Genealogy of the Allwein-Arnold Families*. Philadelphia, Pa., 1902, pages 73, 112, 113. Information on these children was obtained from obituaries in the *Lebanon Daily News*, Lebanon, Pennsylvania, as follows: Monday Evening, March 20, 1899; Tuesday Evening, March 24, 1936; Wednesday, September 2, 1936; Saturday Evening, August 16, 1941; Friday Evening, February 22, 1946; Thursday Evening, July 8, 1948; Thursday Evening, September 16, 1954; Friday Evening, August 12, 1955; Friday Evening, October 12, 1956; Wednesday Evening, February 3, 1960; Tuesday Evening, March 23, 1965; Friday Evening, September 24, 1965; Thursday Evening, August 4, 1966; Friday Evening, December 2, 1966; and the *Lebanon Semi-Weekly News*, Thursday Evening, August 11, 1932.

Irvin Harter, b. August 26, 1870, d. March 10, 1871

Genevieve "Jennie" M. Harter, b. August 27, 1871, d. July 5, 1948 (HC), m. (November 19, 1891) J. Frank Jones (b. est. 1867, d. August 31, 1936)

Anthony P. Harter, b. October 14, 1873, d. September 30, 1874

Catherine "Katie" C. Harter, b. January 1, 1875, d. March 23, 1965 (HC), m. (November 3, 1898) J. William Yake (b. August 13, 1870, d. August 11, 1955)

Mary "Mame" G. Harter, b. March 17, 1876, d. June 10, 1957, m. (October 17, 1900) Charles Aloysius Seubert (b. September 23, 1876, d. June 3, 1958)

Annie H. Harter, b. August 5, 1877, d. September 15, 1954 (HC), m. (November 19, 1918) Daniel E. Dore (b. February 1869, d. August 9, 1932)

John S. Harter, b. December 20, 1878, d. September 24, 1965 (HC), m. (October 29, 1905) Anna Scheib (b. February 15, 1883, d. October 18, 1954)

Charles Vincent Harter, b. July 9, 1880, d. December 2, 1966 (HC), m. (May 15, 1906) Anna B. Werth (b. 1882, d. 1962)

William Francis Harter, b. December 23, 1881, d. October 11, 1956, m. (January 30, 1906) Sarah "Sadie" A. Leitz (b. April 8, 1883, d. February 22, 1946)

Sarah A. Harter, b. June 22, 1883, d. March 23, 1936 (HC), m. Aloysius Francis Ganster (b. October 5, 1882, d. August 3, 1966)

Ella A. Harter, b. January 7, 1885, d. March 18, 1899

Raphael George Harter, b. August 11, 1886, d. February 2, 1960 (SM), m. unknown

Estelle "Stella" C. Harter, b. February 7, 1888, d. August 1973, m. unmarried

Carroll A. Harter, b. April 19, 1892, d. December 25, 1892

Raymond M. Harter, b. September 12, 1893, d. August 16, 1941 (SM), m. (February 10, 1912) Mabel E. Wagner (b. May 8, 1895, d. unknown)

Sarah Allwein Harter died on November 27, 1919 and William J. Harter died a few years later, on June 21, 1925.[351] They are buried at St. Mary's Cemetery (SM) in Lebanon, Pennsylvania, along with several of their children.

---

[351] Obituary for William J. Harter from the *Lebanon Semi-Weekly News*, Lebanon, Pennsylvania, Thursday Evening, June 25, 1925. See also the Pennsylvania Department of Health: http://www.health.state.pa.us.

Exhibit 11.67 Gravestone for Sarah and William Harter—St. Mary's Cemetery, Lebanon, Pennsylvania

Rebecca Allwein Griffin (1852-1936)
Lebanon, Pennsylvania

Rebecca Allwein (F05-0405-0704), youngest daughter of Philip and Catherine (Arnold) Allwein, was born in September of 1852 in North Lebanon Township, Lebanon County, Pennsylvania. The line of descent connecting Rebecca Allwein to Johannes Jacob and Catharina Allwein, progenitors of the Allwein family in colonial Pennsylvania, is as follows:

Generation 1: Johannes Jacob and Catharina Allwein—Berks County, Pa.
Generation 2: Conrad and Catharine (Weibel) Allwein—Dauphin County, Pa.
Generation 3: Philip and Barbara (Frantz) Allwein—Lebanon County, Pa.
Generation 4: Philip and Catherine (Arnold) Allwein—Lebanon County, Pa.
Generation 5: Rebecca Allwein and Martin Griffin—Lebanon County, Pa.

Rebecca Allwein married Martin Griffin, who carried out the grocery business in Lebanon for many years. They are recorded in the available Federal Censuses from1880 through to 1920, initially on Spruce Street, and later at various other addresses. These censuses consistently list Martin Griffin as a grocer.[352] There were no children born to this union. In the 1900 and 1910 Federal Censuses, Rebecca Allwein's nephew, Raphael G. Harter, is also living with them, helping with the grocery business.

Martin Griffin died November 15, 1923 and Rebecca Allwein Griffin several years later on December 27, 1936.[353] They are buried at St. Mary's Cemetery, Lebanon, Pennsylvania.

---

[352] *Tenth Census of the United States* (1880), *Inhabitants of Lebanon Borough, Lebanon County, Pennsylvania*, page 328A; *Twelfth Census of the United States* (1900), *Inhabitants of Lebanon Ward 7, Lebanon County, Pennsylvania*, E.D. No. 131, page 37B; *Thirteenth Census of the United States* (1910), *Inhabitants of Lebanon Ward 6, Lebanon County, Pennsylvania*, E.D. No. 156, page 244A; *Fourteenth Census of the United States* (1920), *Inhabitants of Lebanon Ward 6, Lebanon County, Pennsylvania*, E.D. No. 175, page 274A.
[353] Obituaries appeared in the *Lebanon Daily News*, Lebanon, Pennsylvania, Monday Evening, November 19, 1923; Tuesday Evening, December 29, 1936. See also the Pennsylvania Department of Health: http://www.health.state.pa.us.

Exhibit 11.68 Gravestones for Rebecca and Martin Griffin—St. Mary's Cemetery, Lebanon, Pennsylvania

Mary (Polly) Allwein Miller (1822-1900)
Lebanon, Pennsylvania

Mary (Polly) Allwein (F04-0405-08), daughter of Philip and Barbara (Frantz) Allwein, was born January 17, 1822 on her parents' farm in Lebanon Township of Lebanon County, and died October 26, 1900. She married David L. Miller, and they had two daughters, Angeline Miller (b. August 14, 1844, d. March 30, 1910) and Mary Ann Miller (b. April 3, 1849, d. 1926). More about Mary (Polly) Allwein can be found in *Familie Allwein*, volume 1 (pages 406-407).

Sarah (Sallie) Allwein Arnold (1824-1902)
Lebanon, Pennsylvania

Sarah (Sallie) Allwein (F04-0405-09), daughter of Philip and Barbara (Frantz) Allwein, was born February 12, 1824 on her parents' farm in Lebanon Township of Lebanon County, and died October 24, 1902. She married Joseph Arnold, a son of Peter Arnold, and they lived in Lebanon, Pennsylvania. More about Sarah (Sallie) Allwein can be found in *Familie Allwein,* volume 1 (pages 407-410).

John Edward Allwein (1828-1909)
Lebanon County, Pennsylvania

John Edward Allwein (M04-0405-11), eldest son of Philip and Elizabeth (Arentz) Allwein, was born April 27, 1828 on his parents' farm in Bethel Township of Lebanon County, Pennsylvania. He went by the name of "Edward" or "J. Edward" Allwein. The line of descent connecting Edward Allwein to Johannes Jacob and Catharina Allwein, progenitors of the Allwein family in colonial Pennsylvania, is as follows:

Generation 1: Johannes Jacob and Catharina Allwein—Berks County, Pa.
Generation 2: Conrad and Catharine (Weibel) Allwein—Dauphin County, Pa.
Generation 3: Philip and Elizabeth (Arentz) Allwein—Lebanon County, Pa.
Generation 4: Edward and Elizabeth (Arnold) [and Catharine (Zweier)]
      Allwein—Lebanon County, Pa.

In Chapter 7 of *Familie Allwein*, volume 1 (see pages 411-419), I summarized what we know about the early life of Edward Allwein, and briefly review this here, but the main focus of this section is on his descendants.

Federal Census records for 1850 indicate that Edward Allwein is still living on the farm with his parents in 1850.[354] Soon after the census enumeration, on September 3, 1850, he married Elizabeth Arnold, daughter of Herman and Elizabeth (Smith or Schmidt) Arnold at St. Mary's Church in Lebanon. Upon his father's retirement in 1851, Edward rented the family farm and pursued a life of farming. His father's will allowed him the right to purchase the property (see *Familie Allwein*, volume 1 pages 462-463). He eventually purchased the farm from the estate and the land was deeded to him in 1857. Federal Census records for 1860 through 1880 locate Edward and his family in Bethel Township.[355] The 1875 *County Atlas of Lebanon, Pennsylvania* shows the location of the farm in Bethel Township.[356] An extract of this map is given in Exhibit 11.70 below. This map also shows the farm of John Allwein, the older brother of Edward Allwein.

To locate this area today, one drives north of Lebanon on Mount Zion Road, bearing left on Morrisey Road, after passing Kimmerling's Church and Cemetery; then upon entering Bethel Township, make a left on Heffelfinger Road. Progressing down that road a few hundred feet, the Edward Allwein farm is the first farmstead on the rightside (or northside) of the road. Recall that this was once Philip Allwein's farm, which he gave his son Edward the option to purchase, which Edward did. Edward kept the farm, until he moved into the Borough of Lebanon. At that time, he rented it for awhile to his son Theodore Henry Allwein.

---

[354] *Seventh Census of the United States* (1850), *Inhabitants of Bethel Township, Lebanon County, Pennsylvania*, page 207.
[355] *Eighth Census of the United States* (1860), *Inhabitants of Bethel Township, Lebanon County, Pennsylvania*, page 10; *Ninth Census of the United States* (1870), *Inhabitants of Bethel Township, Lebanon County, Pennsylvania*, page 13; *Tenth Census of the United States* (1880), *Inhabitants of Bethel Township, Lebanon County, Pennsylvania*, page 16.
[356] F.W. Beers, *County Atlas of Lebanon Pennsylvania from Recent and Actual Surveys and Records*, Reading & Philadelphia: F.A. Davis, 1875, page 21.

Exhibit 11.69 Reproduction of photograph of Edward Allwein in 1850 at the age of 22 years (contributed by Madeline Moyer)

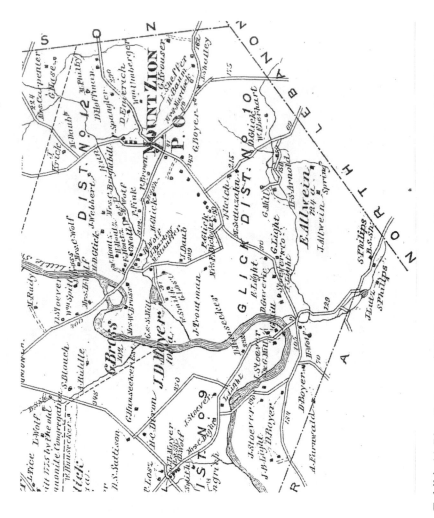

Exhibit 11.70—Extract of 1875 map of the eastside of Bethel Township, Lebanon County, showing the location of the Allwein farms

Nine children were born to Edward and Elizabeth (Arnold) Allwein on this farm, eight of whom survived into adulthood, as follows:

Emma Mary Allwein (F05-0405-1101), b. February 10, 1852, d. July 21, 1919 (SM), unmarried

Theodore Henry Allwein (M05-0405-1102), b. January 22, 1854, d. December 23, 1920 (SM), m. (1) (November 27, 1878) Sarah Arnold (b. May 18, 1856, d. January 21, 1882 (SM)), (2) (February 1, 1883) Catharine McCann (b. May 4, 1857, d. May 27, 1943 (SM)

Agnes Catharine Allwein (F05-0405-1103), b. March 17, 1856, d. July 22, 1919 (SM), m. (September 12, 1876) John Zweier (b. April 24, 1854, d. October 8, 1899)

Mary Jane Allwein (F05-0405-1105), b. May 16, 1859, d. August 19, 1880 (SM), m. (November 1879) Jacob Seifert (b. March 21, 1858, d. July 22, 1880)

Elizabeth Regina Allwein (F05-0405-1106), b. February 28, 1862, d. August 18, 1916 (SM), m. (February 16, 1887) Andrew Jackson Lewis (b. May 22, 1857, d. December 21, 1928)

Anna Mary Appolonia Allwein (F05-0405-1107), b. July 26, 1864, d. April 15, 1945 in Kentucky, [Sister Luigi, August 15, 1887]

Jerome Adam Allwein (M05-0405-1108), b. February 23, 1867, d. July 19, 1931 (NW), m. (May 9, 1894) Sophia M. Schaefer (b. March 21, 1867, d. February 14, 1954)

Catharine Magdaline Allwein (F05-0405-1109), b. August 4, 1869, d. January 7, 1893 (SM), unmarried

One of Edward Allwein's daughters, Catharine Magdaline Allwein (F05-0405-1109) died at a young age on January 7, 1893. We do not discuss her further here. In the following pages we cover what is known about her brothers and sisters.

Exhibit 11.71 Reproduction of a photograph of the Children of Edward and Elizabeth (Arnold) Allwein (contributed by Madeline Paine Moyer)

On September 27, 1880, Elizabeth (Arnold) Allwein died of typhoid fever. She is buried in St. Mary's Cemetery, Lebanon. At this time, their daughter, Emma Allwein, who never married, took over the responsibilities of managing the household for her father and helped tend to the needs of her younger siblings. About five years later, on February 10, 1885 Edward Allwein remarried—to Catharine Zweier, daughter of Anthony and Elizabeth Zweier, and widow of J. Jeremiah Eck. There were no children resulting from this union.[357]

Of Edward Allwein's later years, the Jerome Allwein *Genealogy* states that "in 1886 he purchased a lot on North Eighth Street, Lebanon, Pa. and erected a brick dwelling house. The following spring, he retired from the farm and rented same to his son Theodore. On August 11, 1887 he moved with his family to his new home at Lebanon, Pa. . . ."[358] The Federal Census for 1900 confirms his presence at 435 North Eighth Street in the Borough of Lebanon, living with his wife Catharine ("Kate") and daughter, Emma.[359] This dwelling is also indicated as belonging to Edward Allwein on the 1888 *Atlas of Lebanon County* (see the extract of the map in Exhibit 11.23 above).[360]

Catharine (Zweier / Eck) Allwein died several years after moving into the Borough of Lebanon—on September 7, 1902. Edward Allwein died a few years later on September 27, 1909 in Lebanon of a heart ailment.[361] He preceded his brother, George

---

[357] Jerome Allwein, *Genealogy of the Allwein-Arnold Families*. Philadelphia, Pa., 1902, pages 32 and 74.

[358] Jerome Allwein, *Genealogy of the Allwein-Arnold Families*. Philadelphia, Pa., 1902, pages 32-33.

[359] *Twelfth Census of the United States* (1900), *Inhabitants of Lebanon Ward 5, Lebanon County, Pennsylvania*, E.D. No. 129, page 5A.

[360] Frederick B. Roe, *Atlas of the City of Lebanon, Lebanon County, Pennsylvania / Compiled, drawn and published from official plans and actual surveys*. Philadelphia: F.B. Roe, 1888.

[361] Obituary, *Lebanon Daily News*, Lebanon, Pennsylvania, Tuesday Evening, September 28, 1909.

Elijah Allwein (see below), in death by a few days. He is buried in the Allwein family plot in St. Mary's Cemetery, Lebanon, along with his first wife Elizabeth (Arnold) Allwein, many of their children, and his second wife, Catharine (Zweier or Swoyer) Allwein. [Photographs of the graves of Edward Allwein and his two wives were reproduced in *Familie Allwein*, volume 1, pages 417 and 419.]

Emma Mary Allwein (1852-1919)
Lebanon, Pennsylvania

Emma Mary Allwein (F05-0405-1101), oldest daughter of Edward and Elizabeth (Arnold) Allwein, was born February 10, 1852 on her parents' farm in Bethel Township, Lebanon County, Pennsylvania. The line of descent connecting Emma Mary Allwein to Johannes Jacob and Catharina Allwein, progenitors of the Allwein family in colonial Pennsylvania, is as follows:

Generation 1: Johannes Jacob and Catharina Allwein—Berks County, Pa.
Generation 2: Conrad and Catharine (Weibel) Allwein—Dauphin County, Pa.
Generation 3: Philip and Elizabeth (Arentz) Allwein—Lebanon County, Pa.
Generation 4: Edward and Elizabeth (Arnold) Allwein—Lebanon County, Pa.
Generation 5: Emma Mary Allwein—Lebanon County, Pa.

Emma Mary Allwein did not marry. After her mother died in 1880, Emma took over the responsibilities of managing the household for her father and helped tend to the needs of her younger siblings. She remained with her father after her father's remarriage to Catharine Zweier in 1885. The Federal Census for 1900 confirms her presence in the Borough of Lebanon, living with her father and Catharine ("Kate").[362]

Jerome Allwein's *Genealogy* has this to say about Emma Allwein:[363]

---

[362] *Twelfth Census of the United States* (1900), *Inhabitants of Lebanon Ward 5, Lebanon County, Pennsylvania*, E.D. No. 129, page 5A.
[363] Jerome Allwein, *Genealogy of the Allwein-Arnold Families.* Philadelphia, Pa., 1902, page 74.

Exhibit 11.72 Reproduction of a photograph of Frank Schaefer with some of his grandchildren about 1907—bottom row, left to right: Mary Magdalene Allwein, Cecilia Emma Allwein; middle row left to right: Aloysius Francis Allwein, Agnes Zweier, Sophia (Schaefer) Allwein (his daughter) and Charles Leo Allwein; center back: Frank Schaefer (Contributed by Edward Allwein)

Exhibit 11.73 Reproduction of a photograph of Edward Allwein in 1909 at the age of 81

Emma was, from her youth, a great help to her mother. She did most of the sewing for the family, nursed them when ill and was ever ready to make any sacrifice in order to comfort her parents, brothers, or sisters. She nursed both her mother and sister Jane in their last illnesses. The welfare of her sister Jane's baby boy, Jacob Vincent, was confided to her which trust she held as sacred. After her mother's death the management of the household duties devolved upon her which she performed until her father's second marriage. For a period of about one year, she acted as housekeeper for Father McMonigle at the little Cornwall Church attending to his personal wants until his death December 16, 1893, after which she again returned home.

In the 1910 Federal Census of Lebanon, Emma is listed at the 435 North Eighth address, as the head of household, along with her sister Agnes Allwein Zweier and George Zweier, her nephew.[364] Emma Mary died on July 21, 1919 and is buried in St. Mary's Cemetery (SM) in Lebanon, Pennsylvania.[365]

Theodore Henry Allwein (1854-1920)
Bethel Township, Lebanon County, Pennsylvania

Theodore Henry Allwein (M05-0405-1102), eldest son of Edward and Elizabeth (Arnold) Allwein, was born January 22, 1854 on his parents' farm in Bethel Township, Lebanon County, Pennsylvania. The line of descent connecting Theodore Henry Allwein to Johannes Jacob and Catharina Allwein, progenitors of the Allwein family in colonial Pennsylvania, is as follows:

Generation 1: Johannes Jacob and Catharina Allwein—Berks County, Pa.
Generation 2: Conrad and Catharine (Weibel) Allwein—Dauphin County, Pa.
Generation 3: Philip and Elizabeth (Arentz) Allwein—Lebanon County, Pa.
Generation 4: Edward and Elizabeth (Arnold) Allwein—Lebanon County, Pa.
Generation 5: Theodore Henry and Sarah (Arnold) [and Catherine (McCann)]
    Allwein—Lebanon County, Pa.

---

[364] *Thirteenth Census of the United States* (1910), *Inhabitants of Lebanon Ward 5, Lebanon County, Pennsylvania*, E.D. No. 155, page 214B.
[365] See the Pennsylvania Department of Health: http://www.health.state. pa.us.

Exhibit 11.74 Gravestone for Emma Mary Allwein—St. Mary's
Cemetery, Lebanon, Pennsylvania

The Jerome Allwein *Genealogy* had this to say about Theodore H. Allwein:[366]

> . . . he lived with his parents, working on the farm until he was about 24 years of age. He married November 27, 1878 in St. Mary's Roman Catholic Church Sarah, daughter of Philip and Rebecca Arnold. They moved on his grand-mother's farm near Kimmerling's Church and farmed this land for several years after which he moved to a larger farm adjoining this owned by a Mr. Riefus and lived there for one year when his wife Sarah died. He sold his stock and farming implements moving to Lebanon, Pa. and did laboring work for several years. On February 1, 1883 he married Catherine, daughter of George and Mary McCann of Middletown, Pa., after which he purchased a property and about five acres of ground from Isaac M. Allwein and moved on this property which was situated on the south of his father's farm. He engaged with his father and worked on the farm until his father retired in 1887 when he moved on the old homestead farming same until the Spring of 1898 when he made public sale disposing of part of his stock and implements and removing the balance to a farm of about 33 acres about two miles south of Jonestown which he purchased. (This farm was known as the Heisy farm.)

The children born to Theodore Allwein and Sarah Arnold were as follows:

William Aloysius Allwein (M06-0405-1102-01), b. May 13, 1879, d. March 23, 1918 (SM), m. (September 19, 1901) Mary A. Bleistein (b. August 15, 1880, d. February 16, 1961)
Francis "Frank" Xavier Allwein (M06-0405-1102-02), b. August 13, 1880, d. April 24, 1901, m. unknown
Pierce Allwein (M06-0405-1102-03), b. January 19, 1882, d. January 21, 1882

With his second wife, Catharine McCann, there were the following children:

---

[366] Jerome Allwein, *Genealogy of the Allwein-Arnold Families.* Philadelphia, Pa., 1902, page 75.

Charles Theodore Allwein (M06-0405-1102-04), b. December 18, 1883, d. December 17, 1956 (HC), m. (January 30, 1913) Catherine S. (nee Treist) Spangler (b. July 3, 1885, d. October 7, 1955)

Estella "Stella" Catharine Allwein (F06-0405-1102-05), b. March 16, 1886, d. December 20, 1964 (GP), m. (October 14, 1911) George W. Shaud (b. January 16, 1885, d. April 11, 1952)

Edward George Allwein (M06-0405-1102-06), b. November 7, 1888, d. April 18, 1949 (HC), m. (February 5, 1914) Mary E. Seifert (b. May 6, 1892, d. April 27, 1959)

Lucy (Louisa) Henrietta Allwein (F06-0405-1102-07), b. July 12, 1890, d. December 19, 1949 (HC), m. Victor Jacob Allwein (b. December 15, 1877, d. January 29, 1932)

The 1880 Federal Census registers the presence of Theodore H. Allwein in North Lebanon Township, with his spouse Sarah and son William, as it was indicated in the genealogist's narrative above.[367] Given the timing of the death of the infant Pierce Allwein (see above), it is likely that Theodore's wife Sarah Arnold may have died due to complications of childbirth.

We do not have census information for this family until 1900, when they were living in Swatara Township, on the "Heisy farm" south of Jonestown. It is possible to find the location of this farm on the 1875 map of Swatara Township in the *County Atlas of Lebanon*—referred to there as the property of J.E. Heisey.[368] The household listing for Theodore H. Allwein from the 1900 Federal Census is as follows:[369]

Theodore H. Allwein (head, age 46, farmer)
Catharine Allwein (spouse, age 43)
Frank X. Allwein (son, age 18, day laborer)
Charles Allwein (son, age 16, day laborer)

---

[367] *Tenth Census of the United States* (1880), *Inhabitants of North Lebanon Township, Lebanon County, Pennsylvania*, page 249.

[368] F.W. Beers, *County Atlas of Lebanon Pennsylvania from Recent and Actual Surveys and Records*, Reading & Philadelphia: F.A. Davis, 1875, page 63.

[369] *Twelfth Census of the United States* (1900), *Inhabitants of Swatara Township, Lebanon County, Pennsylvania*, E.D. No. 144, page 247B.

Stella Allwein (daughter, age 14)
Edward A. Allwein (son, age 11, farm laborer)
Louisa Allwein (daughter, age 9)

Francis "Frank" Allwein, son of Theodore and Sarah (Arnold) Allwein, would die about a year following this census, at a very young age. His death was due to a tragic accident at the Colebrook Furnaces, where he was employed. In brief, he was working on a section of track belonging to the furnace railway, when he was struck from behind by a railroad car moved by a shifting engine on the track. An inquest was conducted by the Lebanon County Coroner. The coroner's jury concluded that "death was due to an accident caused by carelessness and misunderstanding of orders of company employees."[370] He was buried at St. Mary's Cemetery (SM) in Lebanon. The remaining children would survive into adulthood.

Theodore Henry Allwein would remain on the farm in Swatara Township until his death on December 23, 1920.[371] He is buried, along with his first wife Sarah at St. Mary's Cemetery in Lebanon. Catharine Ann McCann is also buried at St. Mary's Cemetery.[372]

William Aloysius Allwein (1879-1918)
Lebanon, Pennsylvania

William Aloysius Allwein (M06-0405-1102-01), oldest son of Theodore Henry and Sarah (Arnold) Allwein, was born on May 13, 1879 on his parents' farm in Bethel Township, Lebanon County, Pennsylvania. This is presumably the old Allwein homestead, in that William's father had taken over farming this land, prior to the death of William's mother

---

[370] This accident was covered by several stories appearing in the *Lebanon Daily News*, Lebanon, Pennsylvania, dated Wednesday, April 24, 1901, Thursday, April 25, 1901, and Friday, April 26, 1901.

[371] *Thirteenth Census of the United States* (1910), *Inhabitants of Swatara Township, Lebanon County, Pennsylvania*, E.D. No. 170, page 235A; *Fourteenth Census of the United States* (1920), *Inhabitants of Swatara Township, Lebanon County, Pennsylvania*, E.D. No. 197, page 301B.

[372] Obituaries from the *Lebanon Daily News*, Lebanon, Pennsylvania, Friday, December 24, 1920 and Thursday, May 27, 1943. Pennsylvania Health Department records give December 24, 1920 as the date of death. See the Pennsylvania Department of Health: http://www.health.state.pa.us.

Exhibit 11.75 Gravestone for Francis X. Allwein—St. Mary's Cemetery, Lebanon, Pennsylvania

Exhibit 11.76 Gravestone for Theodore Henry Allwein—St. Mary's Cemetery, Lebanon, Pennsylvania

Exhibit 11.77 Gravestone for Sarah (Arnold) Allwein—St. Mary's
Cemetery, Lebanon, Pennsylvania

Sarah Arnold.[373] The line of descent connecting William Aloysius Allwein to Johannes Jacob and Catharina Allwein, progenitors of the Allwein family in colonial Pennsylvania, is as follows:

Generation 1: Johannes Jacob and Catharina Allwein—Berks County, Pa.
Generation 2: Conrad and Catharine (Weibel) Allwein—Dauphin County, Pa.
Generation 3: Philip and Elizabeth (Arentz) Allwein—Lebanon County, Pa.
Generation 4: Edward and Elizabeth (Arnold) Allwein—Lebanon County, Pa.
Generation 5: Theodore Henry and Sarah (Arnold) Allwein—Lebanon County, Pa.
Generation 6: William Aloysius and Mary A. (Bleistein) Allwein—Lebanon County, Pa.

William Aloysius Allwein married Mary A. Bleistein, daughter of Levi and Lizzie Bleistein, at St. Mary's Church in Lebanon on September 19, 1901. They appear in the Federal Census enumeration of Lebanon for 1910, living in Swatara Township, Lebanon County, not far from his parents' farm. William's occupation is given as "laborer in a bolt works."[374]

Based on Census materials and other materials, we find the following eight children were born to William A. and Mary (Bleistein) Allwein:

Mary Allwein (F07-0405-1102-0101), b. May 8, 1902, d. May 8, 1902
Andrew Allwein (M07-0405-1102-0102), b. September 20, 1903, d. January 23, 2000, m. (May 19, 1928) Florence J. Eisenhauer (b. January 8, 1904, d. September 14, 1998)
Sarah Allwein (F07-0405-1102-0103), b. July 18, 1905, d. May 28, 1907
Eva I. Allwein (F07-0405-1102-0104), b. December 16, 1906, d. February 27, 1937 (HC), m. (1) Joseph Dilger (b. December 1, 1903, d. December 4, 1975 (HC)), (2) (November 16, 1935) Raymond Leroy Schroff (CG) (b. 1905, d. November 10, 1958)

---

[373] Jerome Allwein, *Genealogy of the Allwein-Arnold Families.* Philadelphia, Pa., 1902, page 75.
[374] *Eleventh Census of the United States* (1910), *Inhabitants of Swatara Township, Lebanon County, Pennsylvania*, E.D. No. 170, page 238A.

Margaret H. Allwein (F07-0405-1102-0105), b. April 19, 1909, d. September 24, 1959 (HC), m. (May 29, 1937) Henry Wilson Sherer, Jr. (b. May 23, 1909, d. June 20, 1988)[375]

Catharine Allwein (F07-0405-1102-0106), b. November 26, 1910, d. September 11, 1911

Theodore W. Allwein (M07-0405-1102-0107), b. November 29, 1913, d. April 17, 2001 (MU), m. (March 2, 1941) Elizabeth "Betty" J. Manderbach (b. February 2, 1925, d. July 25, 1993)[376]

Raphael "Ray" E. Allwein (M07-0405-1102-0108), b. October 31, 1917, d. April 6, 1999 (HC), m. (1) (January 6, 1934) Sara M. Carpenter (b. March 15, 1915, d. February 13, 1990) (remarried to Herman R. Livering), (2) (October 26, 1948 at Wilmington DE) Anna May Snyder (nee Mohr) (b. May 6, 1904, d. May 21, 1991) (3) Mary J. Burd (nee Ferry) (b. July 15, 1921, d. January 23, 2006)[377]

William Aloysius Allwein died on March 23, 1918, before the age of 40. Mary Bleistein Allwein remained a widow for another forty-three years, raising several children on her own. She moved from Swatara Township into the Borough of Lebanon, residing at 220 Guilford Street. She is listed there in the 1920 and 1930 Federal Census enumerations for Lebanon, living with several of her children.[378] Mary A. (Bleistein) Allwein died February 16, 1961.[379] Both she and William Allwein are buried in St. Mary's Cemetery in Lebanon, Pennsylvania.

---

[375] Obituary for Margaret H. Allwein appeared in the *Lebanon Daily News*, Lebanon, Pennsylvania, Saturday, September 26, 1959.

[376] Obituaries in *Lebanon Daily News*, Lebanon, Pennsylvania, July 25, 1993; Sunday, April 22, 2001.

[377] Obituaries in *Lebanon Daily News*, Lebanon, Pennsylvania, February 14, 1990; Wednesday, May 22, 1991; and *The Patriot News*, Harrisburg, Pennsylvania, April 7, 1999; January 25, 2006.

[378] *Fourteenth Census of the United States* (1920), *Inhabitants of Lebanon Ward 5, Lebanon County, Pennsylvania*, E.D. No. 173, page 222B; *Fifteenth Census of the United States* (1930) *Inhabitants of Lebanon, Lebanon County, Pennsylvania*, E.D. No. 38-22, page 138A.

[379] Although the gravestone indicates she died on February 12, 1961, the obituary for Mary A. (Bleistein) Allwein from the *Lebanon Daily News*, Lebanon, Pennsylvania, Thursday Evening, February 16, 1961, indicates that it was February 16, 1961. See also the Pennsylvania Department of Health: http://www.health.state.pa.us.

Exhibit 11.78 Gravestone for William Aloysius and Mary (Bleistein) Allwein—St. Mary's Cemetery, Lebanon, Pennsylvania

Charles Theodore Allwein (1883-1956)
Lebanon, Pennsylvania

Charles Theodore Allwein (M06-0405-1102-04), first son of Theodore Henry and Catharine (McCann) Allwein, was born on December 13, 1883 in Bethel Township, Lebanon County, Pennsylvania. The line of descent connecting Charles Theodore Allwein to Johannes Jacob and Catharina Allwein, progenitors of the Allwein family in colonial Pennsylvania, is as follows:

Generation 1: Johannes Jacob and Catharina Allwein—Berks County, Pa.
Generation 2: Conrad and Catharine (Weibel) Allwein—Dauphin County, Pa.
Generation 3: Philip and Elizabeth (Arentz) Allwein—Lebanon County, Pa.
Generation 4: Edward and Elizabeth (Arnold) Allwein—Lebanon County, Pa.
Generation 5: Theodore Henry and Catherine (McCann) Allwein—Lebanon County, Pa.
Generation 6: Charles Theodore and Catherine (Spangler) Allwein—Lebanon County, Pa.

Charles Theodore Allwein married Catherine Spangler, daughter of Reuben and Amanda Treist, on January 30, 1913 at Lebanon. Spangler was her married name from a previous marriage, her former husband having died. In the Federal Census enumerations from 1910 to 1930, Charles and Catherine Allwein are listed in Lebanon County, initially in Swatara Township, but by 1930 they were living in North Annville Township.[380] Charles T. Allwein was a farmer.

Charles Theodore Allwein gained three step-children from Catherine Spangler's previous marriage—Irene, Catherine and Edith Spangler—who appear in the Federal Census reports, but are not listed here. There were four children issuing from the marriage between Charles Theodore and Catherine Allwein, as follows:

---

[380] *Thirteenth Census of the United States* (1910), *Inhabitants of Swatara Township, Lebanon County, Pennsylvania*, E.D. No. 170, page 235A; *Fourteenth Census of the United States* (1920), *Inhabitants of Swatara Township, Lebanon County, Pennsylvania*, E.D. No. 197, page 301B; *Fifteenth Census of the United States* (1930) *Inhabitants of North Annville Township, Lebanon County, Pennsylvania*, E.D. No. 38-32, page 224A.

Esther M. Allwein (F07-0405-1102-0401), b. August 25, 1913, d. January 11, 1998 (HC), unmarried

Mabel G. Allwein (F07-0405-1102-0402), b. September 3, 1915, d. August 1, 1978 (HC), unmarried

Charles Richard Allwein (M07-0405-1102-0403), b. September 15, 1917, d. November 25, 1968 (HC), m. (November 24, 1937) Margaret Minerva Schauer (b. March 6, 1921, d. November 21, 2012) (remarried to Harold Charles Darcas)[381]

Mark Theodore Allwein (M07-0405-1102-0404), b. September 15, 1919, d. unknown (GP), m. (September 28, 1940) Helen H. Frantz (b. January 28, 1919, d. May 29, 1996)

Charles Theodore Allwein died on December 17, 1956 and Catharine (Treist) Spangler Allwein died on October 7, 1955.[382] They are buried at Holy Cross Cemetery (HC) in Lebanon, Pennsylvania.

Estella "Stella" Catharine Allwein Shaud (1886-1964) Lebanon, Pennsylvania

Estella "Stella" Catharine Allwein (F06-0405-1102-05), daughter of Theodore and Catharine (McCann) Allwein was born March 16, 1886 on her parents' farm in Bethel Township, Lebanon County, Pennsylvania. The line of descent connecting Estella Catharine Allwein to Johannes Jacob and Catharina Allwein, progenitors of the Allwein family in colonial Pennsylvania, is as follows:

Generation 1: Johannes Jacob and Catharina Allwein—Berks County, Pa.
Generation 2: Conrad and Catharine (Weibel) Allwein—Dauphin County, Pa.
Generation 3: Philip and Elizabeth (Arentz) Allwein—Lebanon County, Pa.
Generation 4: Edward and Elizabeth (Arnold) Allwein—Lebanon County, Pa.
Generation 5: Theodore Henry and Catherine (McCann) Allwein—Lebanon County, Pa.
Generation 6: Estella Catharine Allwein and George W. Shaud—Lebanon County, Pa.

---

[381] Obituaries for Charles R. Allwein and Margaret Allwein Darcas from the *Lebanon Daily News*, Lebanon, Pennsylvania, Monday, November 25, 1968 and Sunday, November 25, 2012.

[382] Obituary from *Lebanon Daily News*, Lebanon, Pennsylvania, Saturday, October 8, 1955.

Exhibit 11.79 Gravestone for Charles Theodore and Catharine
Spangler Allwein—Holy Cross Cemetery, Lebanon, Pennsylvania

Estella Catharine Allwein married George W. Shaud on October 14, 1911 at Hebron in Lebanon County, Pennsylvania. George W. Shaud worked as a laborer, in the 1920 Federal Census report for the Lebanon Valley Iron Company, in the 1930 Federal Census report for the gas company, and the 1940 report for the WPA / public roads.[383] The 1930 Federal Census listings indicate that at the time, they were living very near her older brother Charles Theodore Allwein.

Based on Census reports and other materials, the following children were born to Stella Allwein and George Shaud:[384]

Arthur W. Shaud, b. February 8, 1912, d. December 14, 1970 (GP), m. (July 3, 1934) Lucy Rebecca Bedleyoung (b. January 28, 1917, d. November 28, 1994)

Viola M. Shaud, b. March 27, 1916, d. February 18, 1974 (AU), m. (April 8, 1933) Paul H. Diamond (b. June 8, 1906, d. April 11, 1978)

Catherine A. Shaud, b. October 30, 1919, d. February 23, 2004 (GP), m. (February 20, 1937) Anthony C. Gerstner, Sr. (b. November 12, 1911, d. April 8, 1988)

Bessie Elizabeth Shaud, b. January 13, 1922, d. January 29, 2007, m. (November 9, 1957) William R. Heilman, Sr. (b. December 9, 1906, d. May 8, 1987)

---

[383] *Fourteenth Census of the United States* (1920), *Inhabitants of Lebanon Ward 4, Lebanon County, Pennsylvania*, E.D. No. 172, page 190B; *Fifteenth Census of the United States* (1930) *Inhabitants of North Annville Township, Lebanon County, Pennsylvania*, E.D. No. 38-32, page 228B; *Sixteenth Census of the United States* (1940), *Inhabitants of North Annville Township, Lebanon County, Pennsylvania*, E.D. No. 38-40, page 701B.

[384] See obituaries in the *Lebanon Daily News*, Lebanon, Pennsylvania: Tuesday Evening, December 15, 1970; Tuesday, September 12, 1972; Tuesday Evening, February 19, 1974; Thursday, April 13, 1978; Friday, May 8, 1987; Saturday, April 9, 1988; Saturday, March 25, 2000; Tuesday, February 24, 2004; Tuesday, January 30, 2007; Wednesday, November 25, 2009; Friday, August 6, 2010.

Stella I. Shaud, b. December 2, 1923, d. March 24, 2000 (GP), m.
    Steward E. George (b. May 31, 1921, d. September 11, 1972)
Esther M. Shaud, b. December 29, 1925, d. August 5, 2010 (GP), m.
    (January 17, 1942) Paul K.Westhafer (b. September 2, 1914, d.
    September 9, 1989)
Mabel G. Shaud, b. February 11, 1928, d. November 23, 2009 (GP),
    m. Dale E. Bicksler (b. September 21, 1930, d. January 3, 1999)

George W. Shaud died on April 11, 1952. Estella Allwein Shaud
lived until December 20, 1964. George Shaud is buried at Evergreen
Cemetery (EA) Annville, Pennsylvania. Stella Shaud is buried at
Grandview Memorial Park (GP).[385]

Edward George Allwein (1888-1949)
Lebanon, Pennsylvania

The youngest child of Theodore and Catharine (McCann) Allwein,
Edward George Allwein (M06-0405-1102-06) was born November
7, 1888 on his parents' farm in Bethel Township, Lebanon County,
Pennsylvania. The line of descent connecting Edward George
Allwein to Johannes Jacob and Catharina Allwein, progenitors of
the Allwein family in colonial Pennsylvania, is as follows:

Generation 1: Johannes Jacob and Catharina Allwein—Berks County, Pa.
Generation 2: Conrad and Catharine (Weibel) Allwein—Dauphin County, Pa.
Generation 3: Philip and Elizabeth (Arentz) Allwein—Lebanon County, Pa.
Generation 4: Edward and Elizabeth (Arnold) Allwein—Lebanon County, Pa.
Generation 5: Theodore Henry and Catherine (McCann) Allwein—Lebanon
    County, Pa.
Generation 6: Edward George and Mary E. (Seifert) Allwein—Lebanon
    County, Pa.

Edward G. Allwein married Mary E. Seifert (or Seyfert),
daughter of Benjamin and Elizabeth (Eagle) Seifert, on February 5,
1914 at St. Mary's Church in Lebanon. The wedding was performed

---

[385] Obituaries from the *Lebanon Daily News*, Lebanon, Pennsylvania,
Friday Evening, April 11, 1952; Wednesday Evening, December 23, 1964.

by Rev. A. Christ. They remained in the Lebanon area, appearing in the 1920, 1930 and 1940 Federal Censuses. They lived in North Lebanon Township on Kimmerling's Road. Edward G. Allwein was engaged in farming.[386] His WWII draft registration card also places them there in April 1942 as well.[387]

According to census reports, there were two sons born to this union, as follows:[388]

Francis Aloysius Allwein (M07-0405-1102-0601), b. January 3, 1915, d. March 30, 1975 (ML), m. (1) (November 24, 1938) Margaret Cecilia Arnold (July 3, 1917, d. July 6, 1972), (2) Anna E. Gettie (b. October 6, 1920, d. April 29, 2002)

George A. Allwein (M07-0405-1102-0602), b. October 28, 1917, d. March 29, 1987 (Colorado Springs, Co.), m. (August 27, 1938) Eleanor C. Grodensky (b. July 31, 1921, d. August 24, 1989)

Edward George Allwein died on April 18, 1949 in Lebanon. Mary E Seifert Allwein died ten years later on April 27, 1959.[389] They are buried in Holy Cross Cemetery, Lebanon, Pennsylvania.

---

[386] *Fourteenth Census of the United States* (1920), *Inhabitants of North Lebanon Township, Lebanon County, Pennsylvania*, E.D. No. 186, page 167B; *Fifteenth Census of the United States* (1930) *Inhabitants of North Lebanon Township, Lebanon County, Pennsylvania*, E.D. No. 38-34, page 265B; *Sixteenth Census of the United States* (1940), *Inhabitants of North Lebanon Township, Lebanon County, Pennsylvania*, E.D. No. 38-42, page 738B.

[387] World War II Draft Registration Cards. Ancestry.com.

[388] This information largely came from obituaries in the *Lebanon Daily News*, Lebanon, Pennsylvania, Monday Evening, March 31, 1975; Friday, July 7, 1972; Tuesday, April 30, 2002; Friday, May 8, 1987; and the *Colorado Springs Gazette*, Sunday, August 27, 1989.

[389] Obituary in *Lebanon Daily News*, Lebanon, Pennsylvania, Tuesday Evening, April 28, 1959. See also the Pennsylvania Department of Health: http://www.health.state.pa.us.

Exhibit 11.80 Gravestone for Edward G. and Mary E. Allwein—Holy Cross Cemetery, Lebanon, Pennsylvania

Lucy (Louisa) Henrietta Allwein (1890-1949)
Lebanon, Pennsylvania

Lucy (Louisa) Henrietta Allwein (F06-0405-1102-07), youngest daughter of Theodore Henry and Catharine (McCann) Allwein, was born July 12, 1890 on her parents' farm in Swatara Township, Lebanon County, Pennsylvania. The line of descent connecting Lucy Henrietta Allwein to Johannes Jacob and Catharina Allwein, progenitors of the Allwein family in colonial Pennsylvania, is as follows:

Generation 1: Johannes Jacob and Catharina Allwein—Berks County, Pa.
Generation 2: Conrad and Catharine (Weibel) Allwein—Dauphin County, Pa.
Generation 3: Philip and Elizabeth (Arentz) Allwein—Lebanon County, Pa.
Generation 4: Edward and Elizabeth (Arnold) Allwein—Lebanon County, Pa.
Generation 5: Theodore Henry and Catherine (McCann) Allwein—Lebanon County, Pa.
Generation 6: Lucy Henrietta Allwein and Victor Jacob Allwein—Lebanon County, Pa.

Lucy (Louisa) Allwein married Victor J. Allwein (M06-0405-0507-02), the son of Nathaniel Mars and Clara (Schraum) Allwein, her second cousin. They were second cousins because they both had the same great grandfather—Philip Allwein—and their fathers were first cousins. I discuss Lucy Henrietta and Victor J. Allwein in the above section, where I consider descendants of William Allwein (M04-0405-05), and I will not duplicate that discussion here.

Agnes Catherine Allwein Zweir (1856-1919)
Lebanon, Pennsylvania

Agnes Catharine Allwein (F05-0405-1103), daughter of Edward and Elizabeth (Arnold) Allwein, was born March 17, 1856 on her parents' farm in Bethel Township, Lebanon County, Pennsylvania. The line of descent connecting Agnes Catherine Allwein to Johannes Jacob and Catharina Allwein, progenitors of the Allwein family in colonial Pennsylvania, is as follows:

Generation 1: Johannes Jacob and Catharina Allwein—Berks County, Pa.
Generation 2: Conrad and Catharine (Weibel) Allwein—Dauphin County, Pa.

Generation 3: Philip and Elizabeth (Arentz) Allwein—Lebanon County, Pa.
Generation 4: Edward and Elizabeth (Arnold) Allwein—Lebanon County, Pa.
Generation 5: Agnes Catherine Allwein and John Zweier—Lebanon County, Pa.

Agnes Catharine Allwein married John Zweier, son of Joseph and Elizabeth Zweier, on September 12, 1876. The Jerome Allwein *Genealogy* had this to say about the fate of this family:[390]

> Mr. Zweier lived on his father's farm near Prescott and cultivated this until after his father's death when he purchased the farm. Through some misfortune several years after the purchase, Mr. Zweier was forced to sell after which he moved with his family to Lebanon, Pa. and did laboring work in the Rolling mills of East Lebanon. Early in the year 1899 he was taken sick. Medical aid availed not and after lingering about seven months he died.

Federal Census reports for 1880 establish that their residence in that year was actually in North Lebanon Township (although near Prescott station which is in South Lebanon Township). The 1875 *County Atlas of Lebanon Pennsylvania* also verifies the existence of the "J. Zwier" farm in the southeast part of North Lebanon Townshp (see Exhibit 11.22 above).[391]

The following children were born to Agnes Catharine Allwein and John Zweier:

Annie Elisabeth Zweier, b. July 14, 1877, d. unknown (in Rhode Island), m. (May 30, 1901) Harry H. Bowman (b. May 11, 1868, d. 1929)
Jacob Zweier, b. July 23, 1878, d. August 1, 1878 (SM)
Francis Aloysius Zweier, b. July 23, 1879, d. unknown, m. unknown
Mary Jane Zweier, b. February 21, 1882, d. March 12, 1949 (HC), m. (May 5, 1904) Daniel Bartholomew Sullivan (b. June 24, 1875, d. April 24, 1959)

---

[390] Jerome Allwein, *Genealogy of the Allwein-Arnold Families.* Philadelphia, Pa., 1902, page 76.
[391] F.W. Beers, *County Atlas of Lebanon Pennsylvania from Recent and Actual Surveys and Records*, Reading & Philadelphia: F.A. Davis, 1875, page 61.

John Adam Zweier, b. August 6, 1884, d. May 23, 1949 (HC), m. (April 26, 1907) Elizabeth Minerva Snyder (b. October 2, 1888, d. May 19, 1974)

Jacob Daniel Zweier, b. February 26, 1886, d. March 3, 1886 (SM)

Stephen Joseph Zweier, b. February 8, 1888, d. November 8, 1973, m. Isabel McElaney (b. June 2, 1887, d. September 22, 1940)

Agnes Cecelia Zweier, b. December 25, 1890, d. after March 12, 1949, became a nun (Sister Benedict de Francois, Little Sisters of the Poor, Scranton, Pennsylvania)

George Henry Zweier, b. October 21, 1893, d. November 1976, m. Margaret Ragan (b. unknown, d. unknown)

Frederick James Zweier, b. August 25, 1896, d. July 27, 1898 (SM)

John Zweier died on October 8, 1899 at the relatively young age of 45.[392] The Federal Census report for 1900 lists Agnes Catharine Zweier at 324 Lehman Street in Lebanon's Fifth Ward, with her seven children. Except for the three youngest children, who were in school, the older children were working to help support the family. Agnes Catharine Zweier supported herself by doing laundry in her home, as indicated in the 1910 Federal Census, at which time she was living with her sister Emma Allwein at 435 North Eighth Street, which was the house built by their father.[393] By this time, her daughter Agnes Cecelia Zweier was living with her brother Jerome Allwein in Philadelphia (see Chapter 13).

As noted above, John Zweier died in 1899. Agnes Catherine Zweier died some twenty years later on July 22, 1919.[394] They are buried in St. Mary's Cemetery (SM) in Lebanon, Pennsylvania.

---

[392] Obituary from the *Lebanon Daily News*, Lebanon, Pennsylvania, Monday, October 9, 1899.

[393] *Tenth Census of the United States* (1900), *Inhabitants of Lebanon Ward 5, Lebanon County, Pennsylvania*, E.D. No. 128, page 248A; *Eleventh Census of the United States* (1910), *Inhabitants of Lebanon Ward 5, Lebanon County, Pennsylvania*, E.D. No. 155, page 214B.

[394] Obituary from the *Lebanon Daily News*, Lebanon, Pennsylvania, Wednesday Evening, July 23, 1919; Funeral Notice, *Lebanon Daily News*, Lebanon, Pennsylvania, Friday, July 25, 1919. See also the Pennsylvania Department of Health: http://www.health.state.pa.us.

Exhibit 11.81 Gravestone for John and Agnes Catherine Zweier—
St. Mary's Cemetery, Lebanon, Pennsylvania

Mary Jane Allwein Seifert (1859-1880)
Lebanon, Pennsylvania

Mary Jane Allwein (F05-0405-1105), daughter of Edward and Elizabeth (Arnold) Allwein, was born May 16, 1859 on her parents' farm in Bethel Township, Lebanon County, Pennsylvania. The line of descent connecting Mary Jane Allwein to Johannes Jacob and Catharina Allwein, progenitors of the Allwein family in colonial Pennsylvania, is as follows:

Generation 1: Johannes Jacob and Catharina Allwein—Berks County, Pa.
Generation 2: Conrad and Catharine (Weibel) Allwein—Dauphin County, Pa.
Generation 3: Philip and Elizabeth (Arentz) Allwein—Lebanon County, Pa.
Generation 4: Edward and Elizabeth (Arnold) Allwein—Lebanon County, Pa.
Generation 5: Mary Jane Allwein and Jacob V. Seifert—Lebanon County, Pa.

Jerome Allwein's *Genealogy* provides the following narrative on Mary Jane Allwein:

Mary Jane Allwein, daughter of Edward and Elizabeth (Arnold) Allwein married Jacob V., son of Jacob and Sarah Seifert, November 1879. Mr. Seifert was a blacksmith by trade, lived with his father on the farm and had a small shop where he was doing his work. About seven months after his marriage he took sick with Typhoid fever being nursed during his sickness by his wife Jane at his father's house until he died. After his death his widow returned to her parent's home, living but a short time afterward.

The 1880 Federal Census enumeration of Edward Allwein's household (dated June 15, 1880) lists Jane M Seifert as a member of the household, obviously pregnant and being cared for by her family.[395] Jacob V. Seifert died on July 22, 1880 and Mary Jane's death followed shortly thereafter on August 19, 1880. They are buried in St. Mary's Cemetery (SM) in Lebanon, Pennsylvania. The birth of their child, Jacob Vincent Seifert (b. August 16, 1880), likely prompted Mary Jane's death.

---

[395] *Tenth Census of the United States* (1880), *Inhabitants of Bethel Township, Lebanon County, Pennsylvania*, page 16.

Jacob Vincent Seifert, Jr., b. August 16, 1880, d. October 1972, m. (May 16, 1906) Elizabeth C. Bechtel (b. October 18, 1881, d. September 21, 1953)[396]

After his mother's tragic death, when he was still an infant, he was taken care of and raised by his Aunt Emma Mary Allwein in the household of his grandfather, Edward Allwein.[397] At the time of the 1900 Federal Census, when he was 19 years of age, he was living with his uncle Jerome Allwein and his family in Philadelphia.[398] We discuss him briefly in the next chapter where we consider Allwein families living in Philadelphia.

Elizabeth Regina Allwein Lewis (1862-1916) Lebanon, Pennsylvania

Elizabeth Regina Allwein (F05-0405-1106), daughter of Edward and Elizabeth (Arnold) Allwein, was born February 28, 1862 on her parents' farm in Bethel Township, Lebanon County, Pennsylvania. The line of descent connecting Elizabeth Regina Allwein to Johannes Jacob and Catharina Allwein, progenitors of the Allwein family in colonial Pennsylvania, is as follows:

Generation 1: Johannes Jacob and Catharina Allwein—Berks County, Pa.
Generation 2: Conrad and Catharine (Weibel) Allwein—Dauphin County, Pa.
Generation 3: Philip and Elizabeth (Arentz) Allwein—Lebanon County, Pa.
Generation 4: Edward and Elizabeth (Arnold) Allwein—Lebanon County, Pa.
Generation 5: Elizabeth Regina Allwein and Andrew Jackson Lewis—Lebanon County, Pa.

---

[396] The Jerome Allwein *Genealogy of the Allwein-Arnold Families* gives his name as "Jacob Vincent Seifert," as do his World War I and II draft registration cards. Some record sources give the middle initial as B, but this is likely an error. Marriage information was obtained from the Philadelphia County Orphan's Court, Philadelphia, Pennsylvania and death information for Elizabeth Seifert from the Pennsylvania Department of Health: http://www.health.state.pa.us.
[397] Jerome Allwein *Genealogy of the Allwein-Arnold Families*, 1902, page 74, states regarding Emma Mary Allwein: "The welfare of her sister Jane's baby boy, Jacob Vincent, was confided to her, which trust she held as sacred."
[398] *Twelfth Census of the United States* (1900), *Inhabitants of Philadelphia Ward 31, Philadelphia County, Pennsylvania*, E.D. No. 780, pages 154B and 155A.

Exhibit 11.82 Reproduction of a photograph of Jacob Seifert at a young age (contributed by Madeline Moyer)

The Jerome Allwein *Genealogy* wrote this about Elizabeth Regina Allwein:[399]

Elizabeth, daughter of Edward and Elizabeth (Arnold) Allwein, was educated in the public school and at St. Mary's parochial school. She studied music under the instruction of Sister M. Gabriel taking the Silver Medal at the Commencement. After she left school she kept house for her grandmother Arnold for some years from which place she was married February 16, 1887 to Andrew Jackson Lewis, son of Andrew and Maria (Bruce) Lewis.

The genealogist also provides narrative about Elizabeth Regina's husband, Andrew Jackson Lewis, which is summarized here:[400]

He was born in Ebensburg, Pa. May 22, 1857, lived with his parents, and attending school until he was 16 years of age. . . . he came to Lebanon July 14, 1873 to learn the trade of stonemason with John G. Nepps, contractor who was working at this time at building the Perkiomen R.R. at East Greenville, Pa. . . . After this, he returned to Lebanon and worked at his trade about town during years of 1875-76 and 77, part of this time he was working on the foundation of St. Mary's Catholic Church. . . . (He travelled) to Kansas to visit his uncle William Bruce), and then went to Leavenworth, Kansas and secured a position as clerk in the Washington Hotel which position he held until June 1879 . . . (he then went) to Atchison, Kansas in search of employment at his trade. . . . (Soon thereafter he went to Chicago, Illinois where) he worked in a lumber yard until December 6, 1879 when he left for his home at Lebanon, Pa. Here he secured employment at his trade

---

[399] Jerome Allwein, *Genealogy of the Allwein-Arnold Families.* Philadelphia, Pa., 1902, page 77.
[400] Jerome Allwein, *Genealogy of the Allwein-Arnold Families.* Philadelphia, Pa., 1902, page 77-78.

Exhibit 11.83 Reproduction of a photograph of Elizabeth Regina Allwein Lewis (contributed by Madeline Moyer)

and worked at same since. The greater part of the time he worked at the Lebanon Furnaces.

The children born to Elizabeth Regina Allwein and Andrew Jackson Lewis are as follows:[401]

Martha Grace Lewis, b. December 3, 1887, d. September 27, 1970 (HC), m. (April 22, 1915) Edward Aloysius Emerich (b. December 22, 1885, d. May 2, 1964)

Agnes Augusta Lewis, b. February 23, 1889, d. January 27, 1975 (SM), unmarried

Andrew Joseph Lewis, b. May 12, 1891, d. August 24, 1894 (SM)

Edward Bernard Lewis, b. August 19, 1893, d. July 14, 1981 (SM), m. (June 20, 1928) Dorothy Louise Rogers (b. August 19, 1901, d. September 10, 1966)

Mary Catharine Lewis, b. October 16, 1896, d. June 4, 1979 (HC), m. (June 23, 1921) Robert Treat Paine (b. November 25, 1899, d. February 23, 1971)

Anna Maria Lewis, b. August 19, 1899, d. August 31, 1901 (SM)

Katharine Elizabeth Lewis, b. November 25, 1902, d. October 10, 1995 (SM), unmarried

Elizabeth Regina Allwein Lewis died on August 18, 1916, and Andrew J. Lewis died some years later on December 21, 1928.[402] They are buried, along with several of their children in St. Mary's Cemetery (SM), Lebanon, Pennsylvania.

---

[401] Jerome Allwein, *Genealogy of the Allwein-Arnold Families*. Philadelphia, Pa., 1902, page 78. See also the obituaries in the *Lebanon Daily News*, Lebanon, Pennsylvania: Monday Evening, September 2, 1901; Monday, September 12, 1966; Saturday, February 27, 1971; Tuesday, June 5, 1979; Wednesday, July 15, 1981.

[402] Obituary for Andrew J. Lewis, *Lebanon Daily News*, Lebanon, Pennsylvania, Friday Evening, December 21, 1928. See also the Pennsylvania Department of Health: http://www.health.state.pa.us.

Exhibit 11.84 Monument for Lewis family—St. Mary's Cemetery, Lebanon, Pennsylvania

Anna Mary Appolonia Allwein (Sister Luigi) (1864-1945) Sisters of Charity

Anna Mary Appolonia Allwein (F05-0405-1107), daughter of Edward and Elizabeth (Arnold) Allwein, was born July 26, 1864 on her parents' farm in Bethel Township, Lebanon County, Pennsylvania. The line of descent connecting Anna Mary Appolonia Allwein to Johannes Jacob and Catharina Allwein, progenitors of the Allwein family in colonial Pennsylvania, is as follows:

Generation 1: Johannes Jacob and Catharina Allwein—Berks County, Pa.
Generation 2: Conrad and Catharine (Weibel) Allwein—Dauphin County, Pa.
Generation 3: Philip and Elizabeth (Arentz) Allwein—Lebanon County, Pa.
Generation 4: Edward and Elizabeth (Arnold) Allwein—Lebanon County, Pa.
Generation 5: Anna Mary Appolonia Allwein—Sisters of Charity

Anna Mary Appolonia Allwein became a nun. She entered the Novitiate under Sisters of Charity at Nazareth, Kentucky, on February 15, 1887. Her name under the Habit was Sister Luigi [Aloysius]. She made her profession at Nazareth Kentucky, August 15, 1888. She worked as a teacher in several locations including Frankfurt, Kentucky, Circleville, Ohio, and Hyde Park, Massachusetts. In Massachusetts she also worked in orphanages in Dorchester and Newburyport, Massachusetts.[403] She died on April 15, 1945. At this writing, I do not know where she is buried.

Jerome Adam Allwein (1867-1931) Philadelphia, Pennsylvania

Jerome Adam Allwein (M05-0405-1108), youngest son of Edward and Elizabeth (Arnold) Allwein, was born February 23, 1867 on his parents' farm in Bethel Township, Lebanon County, Pennsylvania. Jerome Allwein was the author of one of the most important genealogies of the Allwein family in Lebanon County, Pennsylvania and its environs—the *Genealogy of the Allwein-Arnold Family*— published in 1902. After growing up in the Lebanon County area,

---

[403] Jerome Allwein, *Genealogy of the Allwein-Arnold Families*. Philadelphia, Pa., 1902, page 79. See also Kentucky Death Records, 1852-1953. Ancestry.com.

he moved to Philadelphia, where he lived the remainder of his life. We cover this family in Chapter 12, where we review the Allwein families who settled in the Philadelphia area.

Rebecca Allwein Arnold (1830-1890)
Lebanon, Pennsylvania

Rebecca Allwein (F04-0405-12), the eldest daughter of Philip and Elizabeth (Arentz) Allwein, was born January 6, 1830 on her parents' farm in Bethel Township of Lebanon County, Pennsylvania. Rebecca Allwein married Philip Arnold, son of Herman and Elizabeth (Smith) Arnold. She died October 11, 1890. We cover this family in Chapter 7 of *Familie Allwein*, volume 1 (pages 420-422), and we do not discuss them here.

Mary Ann Allwein Bixler (1831-1878)
Lebanon, Pennsylvania

Mary Ann Allwein (F04-0405-13), daughter of Philip and Elizabeth (Arentz) Allwein, was born December 31, 1831 on her parents' farm in Bethel Township of Lebanon County Pennsylvania. She married Jonathan Bixler (Bicksler) and they raised several children. She died May 1, 1878. We cover this family in Chapter 7 of *Familie Allwein*, volume 1 (pages 423-425), and we do not discuss them further here.

George Elijah Allwein (1833-1909)
Lebanon County, Pennsylvania

George Elijah Allwein (M04-0405-14), son of Philip and Elizabeth (Arentz) Allwein, was born November 3, 1833 on his parents' farm in Bethel Township of Lebanon County, Pennsylvania. He was known as "Elijah" Allwein and almost all record sources list him this way. He died on October 2, 1909—his gravestone in St. Mary's Cemetery in Lebanon (see chapter 7 of *Familie Allwein*, volume 1, page 430) bears the name Elijah, and that is how we refer to him here. The line of descent connecting Elijah Allwein to Johannes Jacob and Catharina Allwein, the progenitors of the Allwein family in colonial Pennsylvania, is as follows:

Generation 1: Johannes Jacob and Catharina Allwein—Berks County, Pa.
Generation 2: Conrad and Catharine (Weibel) Allwein—Dauphin County, Pa.
Generation 3: Philip and Elizabeth (Arentz) Allwein—Lebanon County, Pa.
Generation 4: Elijah and Angeline (Arentz) [and Mary (Snyder)] Allwein—
     Lebanon County, Pa.

We covered Elijah Allwein's early life in Chapter 7 of *Familie Allwein*, volume 1 (pages 426-430), and we will not repeat that material here, except to review his adult life. The following is what the Jerome Allwein *Genealogy* had to say about this:[404]

Elijah Allwein, son of Philip and Elizabeth (Arentz) Allwein was born on his father's farm in Lebanon County, Pa. Nov. 3, 1833. After leaving school he learned the trade of cabinetmaker. On October 27, 1856 he married Angeline, daughter of Jacob and Hannah Arentz and moved to Lebanon, Pa. where he did hauling for Philip Arnold for a short period. Soon after, he purchased a farm of about forty acres in North Lebanon Township about five miles Northeast of Lebanon. He moved on the premises, working at the Lebanon car shops in connection with farming for some years. July 14, 1875 his wife Angeline died. In 1876 he married Mary, daughter of Joseph and Elizabeth Snyder. About 1895, he erected a new house on (the) farm and three years later retired and moved with family, in April, to Sweet Home, Lebanon, Pa. In 1899 he opened a retail grocery store and carried on the Grocery and Provision business. After leaving farming, (he) sold same to E. Eberhart. He now owns a number of properties along the turnpike where he lives.

According to the above narrative, Elijah Allwein learned the trade of cabinetmaker, but as we see from the available Federal Census reports, he mainly worked as a teamster, a farmer, and eventually a grocer. He married Angeline Arentz (b. December 3, 1836), daughter of Jacob and Hannah Arentz, on October 27, 1856. Angeline and Elijah had ten children (see below), and soon after the tenth was born, on July 14, 1875, Angeline (Arentz) Allwein died. Soon thereafter, Elijah remarried to Mary Snyder, daughter of

---

[404] Jerome Allwein, *Genealogy of the Allwein-Arnold Families*. Philadelphia, Pa., 1902, page 24.

Joseph and Elizabeth Snyder. Elijah was more than 15 years Mary's senior, as she was born March 29, 1850.

Eight of the ten children born to Elijah and Angeline (Arentz) Allwein survived to adulthood, and are as follows:[405]

Charles M. Allwein (M05-0405-1401), b. January 6, 1858, d. February 1, 1929, m. (1881) Margaret "Maggie" S. Callahan (b. July 1859, d. November 1, 1919)

Pierce William Allwein (M05-0405-1402), b. June 2, 1859, d. June 19, 1926 (SM), m. (1882) Agnes E. Arnold (est. July 1859, d. December 13, 1928)

Philip James Allwein (M05-0405-1403), b. October 3, 1861, d. September 4, 1953 (HC), m. (April 8, 1892) Elizabeth "Lizzie" E. Blouch (b. August 10, 1869, d. September 28, 1946)

Catharine Allwein (F05-0405-1404), b. July 10, 1864, d. September 4, 1925 (SM), unmarried

Margaret "Maggie" Allwein (F05-0405-1405), b. October 1, 1865, d. April 17, 1929 (SM), unmarried

Elizabeth "Lizzie" Rebecca Allwein (F05-0405-1406), b. July 17, 1868, d. July 24, 1951 (SM), m. (November 21, 1895) Jerome Steckbeck Arnold (b. September 24, 1863, d. October 20, 1960)

Mary A. Allwein (F05-0405-1409), b. January 2, 1873, d. July 19, 1937 (HC), unmarried

Sara A. Allwein (F05-0405-1410), b. July 10, 1875, d. January 9, 1957 (HC), entered convent, December 7, 1901[406]

---

[405] Date of death information for some of these children was obtained from obituaries in the *Lebanon Daily News*, Lebanon, Pennsylvania, as follows: Friday Evening, September 4, 1925; Saturday Evening, June 19, 1926; Thursday Evening, April 18, 1929; Friday Evening, June 21, 1946; Saturday, September 28, 1946; Wednesday Evening, July 25, 1951; Friday, September 4, 1953; Thursday Evening, October 20, 1960; and *Lebanon Semi-Weekly News*, Lebanon, Pennsylvania, Monday Evening, July 19, 1937.

[406] Convent of Sisters of Saint Joseph at Mount Saint Mary's Academy, Chestnut Hill, Philadelphia. Jerome Allwein, *Genealogy of the Allwein-Arnold Families*. Philadelphia, Pa., 1902, page 85.

There were four children born to Elijah and Mary (Snyder) Allwein, as follows:[407]

Jennie A. Allwein (F05-0405-1411), b. October 23, 1877, d. March 19, 1949 (HC), unmarried

Emma Gertrude Allwein (F05-0405-1412), b. April 11, 1879, d. January 18, 1909 (SM), unmarried

William J. Allwein (M05-0405-1413), b. October 7, 1880, d. November 26, 1899 (SM), unmarried

Stephen Adam Allwein (M05-0405-1414), b. April 23, 1885, d. October 24, 1918 (HC), m. (May 12, 1910) Cora E. Steckbeck (b. November 25, 1884, d. June 30, 1942)

Federal Census enumerations for 1860 through 1900 locate Elijah Allwein and his family in the Lebanon area. After his first marriage, he settled in Lebanon Borough, where he can be found in 1860, working as a teamster. Sometime prior to 1870 he had purchased a small farm in North Lebanon Township, and was located there in the 1870 Federal Census. By 1880 he had moved to another farm in Bethel Township. After several years on the farm, Elijah retired and moved with the family to North Lebanon Township, presumably closer to the Borough of Lebanon, where he opened a retail grocery business.[408]

---

[407] Date of death information for some of these children was obtained from obituaries in the *Lebanon Daily News*, Lebanon, Pennsylvania, as follows: Monday Evening, November 27, 1899; Monday Evening, January 18, 1909; Thursday Evening, October 24, 1918; Tuesday Evening, June 30, 1942; Monday Evening, March 21, 1949.

[408] *Eighth Census of the United States* (1860), *Inhabitants of Lebanon Borough, Lebanon County, Pennsylvania*, page 395; *Ninth Census of the United States* (1870), *Inhabitants of North Lebanon Township, Lebanon County, Pennsylvania*, page 234B; *Tenth Census of the United States* (1880), *Inhabitants of Bethel Township, Lebanon County, Pennsylvania*, page 16D; *Twelfth Census of the United States* (1900), *Inhabitants of North Lebanon Township, Lebanon County, Pennsylvania*, E.D. No. 137, page 123B.

Elijah Allwein's second wife, Mary (Snyder) Allwein, died April 21, 1906, and he died a few years later, on October 2, 1909.[409] He died within a few days of his brother, Edward Allwein (see the following text of his obituary). Elijah Allwein is buried in St. Mary's Cemetery, Lebanon, along with his two wives and several of their children (see photo of gravestones, *Familie Allwein*, volume 1, page 430).

This is the text of the obituary for Elijah Allwein that appeared in the *Lebanon Daily News* on October 2, 1909:

> Elijah Allwein, a retired farmer, of No. 41 East Cumberland Street, died early this morning after a lingering illness of a complication of ailments, aged 76 years and eleven months. His wife died many years ago. He is survived by the following children, ten in number: Charles, of Reading, Pierce, Philip, Katharine, Margaret, Mrs. Jerome Arnold, Mary, Sarah, Jennie and Stephan, the latter proprietor of a grocery store at No. 41 East Cumberland Street.
>
> Adam Allwein, of Lancaster, and Henry Allwein, of Lebanon, are brothers and Mrs. Joseph Gouldin, wife of congressman from the Eleventh Congressional District of New York, is a sister. Another brother Edward, died this week and was interred only on Friday. The deceased was a member of St. Mary's Catholic Church.

Children of Elijah Allwein

There were twelve children of Elijah Allwein (M04-0405-14), mentioned above, and although it is the plan of the book to discuss each 5th and 6th generation Allwein descendant separately, we here depart from that rule in order to discuss seven of Elijah Allwein's children as a group—Catharine Allwein (F05-0405-1404), Margaret Allwein (F05-0405-1405), Mary A. Allwein (F05-0405-1409), Sara A. Allwein (F05-0405-1410), Jennie A. Allwein (F05-0405-1411), Emma Gertrude Allwein (F05-0405-1412), and William J.

---

[409] Obituaries for Mary Allwein and Elijah Allwein from the *Lebanon Daily News*, Lebanon, Pennsylvania, Saturday, April 21, 1906 and Saturday, October 2, 1909.

Allwein (M05-0405-1413). The other five—Charles M. Allwein (M05-0405-1401), Pierce William Allwein (M05-0405-1402), Philip James Allwein (M05-0405-1403), Elizabeth Rebecca Allwein (F05-0405-1406), and Stephen Adam Allwein (M05-0405-1414)—we discuss separately.

A good place to begin when discussing these children is the 1900 Federal Census enumeration of Lebanon County, Pennsylvania, in which the household listing for Elijah and Mary Allwein in the east part of North Lebanon Township is as follows:[410]

Elijah Allwein (head, age 66, grocer)
Mary Allwein (spouse, age 50)
Jennie Allwein (daughter, age 22)
Emma Allwein (daughter, age 21)
Stephen Allwein (son, age 15, in school)
Kate (Catherine) Allwein (daughter, age 37)

There were no occupations given for the three daughters—Jennie, Emma, and Catherine Allwein—but presumably they were helping out with the grocery business. The narrative supplied in the Jerome Allwein *Genealogy* mentions the location of this household was in "Sweet Home" Lebanon County, but to date we have been unable to determine where this place was.

At the time of the 1900 Federal Census, the four older children (discussed separately below) were already living on their own—Charles M. Allwein in Reading, and the others in Lebanon. Son William J Allwein (M05-0405-1413) had already passed away, Sara A. Allwein (F05-0405-1410) had entered a convent in Philadelphia, and Mary Allwein (F05-0405-1409) was living in the household of Pierce Arnold in Lebanon's Fifth Ward, at 506 North 8th Street, working as his housekeeper.[411] We have been unable to locate daughter Margaret Allwein in the 1900 Census.

---

[410]   *Twelfth Census of the United States* (1900), *Inhabitants of North Lebanon Township, Lebanon County, Pennsylvania,* E.D. No. 137, page 123B.
[411]   *Twelfth Census of the United States* (1900), *Inhabitants of Lebanon Ward 5, Lebanon County, Pennsylvania,* E.D. No. 129, page 289A.

By the time of the 1910 Federal Census, both Elijah and Mary (Snyder) Allwein had died, and five of their children remained in North Lebanon Township, presumably at the same residential location, although we do not know this for sure. The household was headed by daughter Catherine Allwein, and four of her siblings— Margaret Allwein, Mary A Allwein, Jennie A. Allwein, and Stephen Adam Allwein—were also living there.[412] It appears that they were still operating the grocery business, as the two youngest children are listed as salespersons in a grocery store. By 1910, daughter Emma had passed away.

In the 1920 Federal Census, three daughters—Catherine, Margaret and Jennie A. Allwein—were living at 41 Hoffman Street in Lebanon's Ninth Ward. Catherine Allwein was working as a seamstress in a factory, Margaret Allwein was working as a housekeeper for a private family, and Jennie Allwein was working as a clerk in a store.[413]

By 1920, Mary A. Allwein had entered the state mental hospital in Susquehanna Township, Dauphin County, near Harrisburg, where she was also living at the time of the 1930 Federal Census.[414] Founded in 1845 "as the Pennsylvania State Lunatic Hospital by Dorothea Dix, a New England schoolteacher-writer-philanthropist who was also largely responsible for the early support of the hospital, its name was changed to the Harrisburg State Hospital in 1921, reflecting then-changing attitudes toward the treatment of the mentally ill."[415]

---

[412] *Thirteenth Census of the United States* (1910), *Inhabitants of North Lebanon Township, Lebanon County, Pennsylvania,* E.D. No. 163, page 78A.

[413] *Fourteenth Census of the United States* (1920), *Inhabitants of Lebanon Ward 9, Lebanon County, Pennsylvania,* E.D. No. 178, page 310B.

[414] *Fourteenth Census of the United States* (1920), *Inhabitants of the Pennsylvania State Lunatic Hospital, Susquehanna Township, Dauphin County, Pennsylvania,* E.D. No. 144, page 236A; *Fifteenth Census of the United States* (1930), *Inhabitants of the Pennsylvania State Lunatic Hospital, Susquehanna Township, Dauphin County, Pennsylvania,* E.D. No. 22-102, page 66A.

[415] From: http://www.rootsweb.ancestry.com/~asylums/.

By 1910, Sara A. Allwein was no longer living in a convent, but was working as a servant in the household of Henry Deitz in Philadelphia, where she can also be located in the 1920 Federal Census.[416] And, by 1930, she had returned to Lebanon, where in the 1930 and 1940 Federal Censuses she is living with her sister Jennie Allwein. They operated a grocery business.[417]

Several of these children are buried in St. Mary's Cemetery (SM) in Lebanon—Catherine Allwein (died 1925), Margaret (died 1929), Emma Gertrude (died 1909), and William J. Allwein (died 1899). Three others—Mary A. Allwein (died 1937), Jennie A. Allwein (died 1949), and Sara A. Allwein (died 1957)—are buried in Holy Cross Cemetery (HC).

Charles M. Allwein (1858-1929)
Lebanon and Reading, Pennsylvania

Charles M. Allwein (M05-0405-1401), first child of George Elijah and Angeline (Arentz) Allwein, was born January 6, 1858 in the Borough of Lebanon. He married Margaret Callahan in 1881. They lived for awhile in Lebanon where they maintained his father's grocery business. Charles also worked for some years at the Miller Organ Company in Lebanon.[418] By 1895 they had moved to Reading, Berks County, Pennsylvania—he appears in *Boyd's City Directory* for that year, listed as a laborer living at 1212 Fidelity Street.[419] We present what is known about this family in Chapter 13, where we cover those Allwein family members who lived in Berks County.

---

[416] *Thirteenth Census of the United States* (1910), *Inhabitants of Philadelphia Ward 47, Philadelphia County, Pennsylvania,* E.D. No. 1201, page 50A; *Fourteenth Census of the United States* (1920), *Inhabitants of Philadelphia Ward 47, Philadelphia County, Pennsylvania,* E.D. No. 1784, page 242A.

[417] *Fifteenth Census of the United States* (1930), *Inhabitants of Lebanon, Lebanon County, Pennsylvania,* E.D. No. 38-26, page 265A; *Sixteenth Census of the United States* (1940), *Inhabitants of Lebanon, Lebanon County, Pennsylvania,* E.D. No. 38-34, page 578B.

[418] Jerome Allwein, *Genealogy of the Allwein-Arnold Families.* Philadelphia, Pa., 1902, page 83.

[419] Boyd's Reading City Directories 1895-97 and 1898-1901. Ancestry.com.

Exhibit 11.85 Gravestones for Emma Gertrude Allwein and William J. Allwein—St. Mary's Cemetery, Lebanon, Pennsylvania

Exhibit 11.86 Gravestones for Margaret Allwein and Catherine Allwein—St. Mary's Cemetery, Lebanon, Pennsylvania

Exhibit 11.87 Gravestone for Jennie A. Allwein, Sara A. Allwein, and Mary A. Allwein—Holy Cross Cemetery, Lebanon, Pennsylvania

Pierce William Allwein (1859-1926)
Lebanon, Pennsylvania

Pierce William Allwein (M05-0405-1402), second child of George Elijah and Angeline (Arentz) Allwein, was born June 2, 1859 in the Borough of Lebanon and he spent his entire life there. The line of descent connecting Pierce William Allwein to Johannes Jacob and Catharina Allwein, the progenitors of the Allwein family in colonial Pennsylvania, is as follows:

Generation 1: Johannes Jacob and Catharina Allwein—Berks County, Pa.
Generation 2: Conrad and Catharine (Weibel) Allwein—Dauphin County, Pa.
Generation 3: Philip and Elizabeth (Arentz) Allwein—Lebanon County, Pa.
Generation 4: Elijah and Angeline (Arentz) Allwein—Lebanon County, Pa.
Generation 5: Pierce William and Agnes E. (Arnold) Allwein—Lebanon County, Pa.

Pierce William Allwein married Agnes E. Arnold, daughter of Ambrose and Catherine Arnold, in 1882 and they had the following children:[420]

Charles Harry Allwein (M06-0405-1402-01), b. February 6, 1883, d. November 28, 1940 (HC), m. (June 25, 1907) Ellen "Ella" Matilda Yocum (b. 1882, d. April 13, 1930)
Raymond V. Allwein (M06-0405-1402-02), b. August 27, 1884, d. July 11, 1885 (SM)
Paul Aloysius Allwein (M06-0405-1402-03), b. December 29, 1885, d. August 28, 1950 (HC), m. (November 24, 1914) Annie L. Shay (b. January 1887, d. March 4, 1968)
Catharine E. Allwein (F06-0405-1402-04), b. May 15, 1887, d. January 27, 1958, m. (June 30, 1917) Harry William Swope (b. October 8, 1884, d. unknown)

---

[420] Jerome Allwein, *Genealogy of the Allwein-Arnold Families*. Philadelphia, Pa., 1902, page 84. Information on dates of death for some of these children were obtained from the *Lebanon Daily News*, Lebanon, Pennsylvania, as follows: Tuesday Evening, February 4, 1919; Thursday Evening, March 22, 1923; Friday Evening, November 29, 1940; Thursday Evening, August 31, 1950; Wednesday, January 29, 1958; Monday, March 4, 1968.

Sarah "Sadie" R. Allwein (F06-0405-1402-05), b. August 21, 1889, d. February 3, 1919 (SM), unmarried

Gertrude C. Allwein (F06-0405-1402-06), b. September 4, 1890, d. August 19, 1891 (SM)

James Herman Allwein (M06-0405-1402-07), b. July 25, 1892, d. March 21, 1923 (SM), unmarried

E. Herman Allwein (M06-0405-1402-08), b. June 6, 1894, d. August 7, 1894 (SM)

C. Margaret Allwein (F06-0405-1402-09), b. April 2, 1896, d. July 17, 1896 (SM)

Federal Census enumerations for 1900 and 1910 place them in North Lebanon Township, where he worked in a steel plant. In their later years, they moved to the Borough of Lebanon, in Ward 9.[421]

Pierce William Allwein died June 19, 1926 and Agnes (Arnold) Allwein died a few years later on December 13, 1928.[422] They are buried in St. Mary's Cemetery (SM) in Lebanon, Pennsylvania, amongst many of their children.

Charles Harry Allwein (1883-1940)
Lebanon, Pennsylvania

Charles Harry Allwein (M06-0405-1402-01), oldest son of Pierce William and Agnes E. (Arnold) Allwein, was born February 6, 1883 in North Lebanon Township, Lebanon County. The line of descent connecting Charles H. Allwein to Johannes Jacob and Catharina Allwein, the progenitors of the Allwein family in colonial Pennsylvania, is as follows:

---

[421] *Twelfth Census of the United States* (1900), *Inhabitants of North Lebanon Township, Lebanon County, Pennsylvania*, E.D. No. 137, page 120B; *Thirteenth Census of the United States* (1910), *Inhabitants of North Lebanon Township, Lebanon County, Pennsylvania*, E.D. No. 163, page 75A; *Fourteenth Census of the United States* (1920), *Inhabitants of Lebanon Ward 9, Lebanon County, Pennsylvania*, E.D. No. 178, page 313A.

[422] See the Pennsylvania Department of Health: http://www.health.state.pa.us.

Exhibit 11.88 Gravestones for Pierce William Allwein and Agnes E. (Arnold) Allwein—St. Mary's Cemetery, Lebanon, Pennsylvania

Generation 1: Johannes Jacob and Catharina Allwein—Berks County, Pa.
Generation 2: Conrad and Catharine (Weibel) Allwein—Dauphin County, Pa.
Generation 3: Philip and Elizabeth (Arentz) Allwein—Lebanon County, Pa.
Generation 4: Elijah and Angeline (Arentz) Allwein—Lebanon County, Pa.
Generation 5: Pierce William and Agnes E. (Arnold) Allwein—Lebanon
    County, Pa.
Generation 6: Charles H. and Ellen M. (Yocum) Allwein—Lebanon County, Pa.

Charles Harry Allwein married Ellen M. Yocum, daughter of John and Mary Yocum, on June 25, 1907 at St. Mary's Catholic Church in Lebanon. Rev. A. Christ performed the services. They settled in Lebanon, residing at 410 Weidman Street in the Fifth Ward, and later on, at 401 East Cumberland Street. Charles H. Allwein worked as a machinist in the iron and steel industry in Lebanon.[423]

Based on census materials, the record indicates that Charles Harry and Ellen M. (Yocum) Allwein had three sons, as follows:[424]

Cyril J. Allwein (M07-0405-1402-0101), b. September 8, 1910, d. January 8, 1957 (HC), became a priest

Richard P. Allwein (M07-0405-1402-0102), b. December 3, 1912, d. March 24, 1987 (HC), m. (1) (August 31, 1935) Mary E. O'Donnell (b. August 23, 1916, d. May 23, 1965), (2) (September 30, 1971) Eleanor Mae Barbini (nee Mease) (b. January 29, 1914, d. March 14, 1989 (GP))

Robert A. Allwein (M07-0405-1402-0103), b. July 12, 1916, d. October 8, 1917 (SM)

---

[423] *Thirteenth Census of the United States* (1910), *Inhabitants of Lebanon Ward 5, Lebanon County, Pennsylvania*, E.D. No. 154, page 202B; *Fourteenth Census of the United States* (1920), *Inhabitants of Lebanon Ward 5, Lebanon County, Pennsylvania*, E.D. No. 173, page 211A; *Fifteenth Census of the United States* (1930), *Inhabitants of Lebanon, Lebanon County, Pennsylvania*, E.D. No. 38-26, page 266B.

[424] Information on dates of death for some of these children are from obituaries in the *Lebanon Daily News*, Lebanon, Pennsylvania, as follows: Monday Evening, October 8, 1917; Wednesday Evening, May 24, 1965; Thursday, March 16, 1989; and the *Gettysburg Times*, Gettysburg, Pennsylvania, Tuesday Evening, January 8, 1957.

Mary Ellen Allwein (F07-0405-1402-0104), b. 1920, d. October 14, 1921 (SM)

Their son Cyril J. Allwein attended St. Vincent College and Seminary at Latrobe, Pennsylvania. He was ordained into the priesthood on June 15, 1935, after which he served as assistant pastor of Our Lady of Mount Carmel Catholic Church in Mount Carmel, and St. Mary's Catholic Church, Harrisburg. Later he attended Catholic University in Washington DC, where he studied school administration. He was a former principal of Delone Catholic High School in McSherrystown, and then became priest at St. Andrews Catholic Church in Waynesboro, prior to serving as rector of Villa Vianney, a retirement village for priests located in Trenton, New Jersey.[425]

Charles Allwein died on November 28, 1940. His wife, who died April 13, 1930, had preceded him in death by some 10 years.[426] They are buried in Holy Cross Cemetery (HC) in Lebanon. Their sons are buried there as well. In fact, there is a monument to Cyril J. Allwein among the dozen or so priests whose graves are located at the entrance to the Holy Cross Cemetery in Lebanon.

Paul Aloysius Allwein (1885-1950)
Lebanon, Pennsylvania

Paul Aloysius Allwein (M06-0405-1402-03), son of Pierce William and Agnes E. (Arnold) Allwein, was born December 29, 1885 in North Lebanon Township, Lebanon County, Pennsylvania. The line of descent connecting Paul Aloysius Allwein to Johannes Jacob and Catharina Allwein, the progenitors of the Allwein family in colonial Pennsylvania, is as follows:

---

[425] Obituary from the *Gettysburg Times*, Gettysburg, Pennsylvania, Tuesday Evening, January 8, 1957.
[426] Obituary from the *Lebanon Daily News*, Lebanon, Pennsylvania, Friday Evening, November 29, 1940. See also the Pennsylvania Department of Health: http://www.health.state.pa.us.

Exhibit 11.89 Gravestone for Charles H. and Ellen M. (Yocum) Allwein—Holy Cross Cemetery, Lebanon, Pennsylvania

REV. CYRIL J. ALLWEIN
SEPT. 8, 1910
JAN. 8, 1957
RECTOR OF VILLA VIANNEY
LEBANON
ORDAINED JUNE 15, 1935

Exhibit 11.90 Gravestone for Rev. Cyril J. Allwein—Holy Cross
Cemetery, Lebanon, Pennsylvania

Exhibit 11.91 Gravestone for Richard P. and Mary E. (O'Donnell) Allwein—Holy Cross Cemetery, Lebanon, Pennsylvania

Generation 1: Johannes Jacob and Catharina Allwein—Berks County, Pa.
Generation 2: Conrad and Catharine (Weibel) Allwein—Dauphin County, Pa.
Generation 3: Philip and Elizabeth (Arentz) Allwein—Lebanon County, Pa.
Generation 4: Elijah and Angeline (Arentz) Allwein—Lebanon County, Pa.
Generation 5: Pierce William and Agnes E. (Arnold) Allwein—Lebanon
    County, Pa.
Generation 6: Paul Aloysius and Annie L. (Shay) Allwein—Lebanon County, Pa.

Paul Aloysius Allwein married Annie L. Shay, daughter of John Clinton and Aquilla (Light) Shay, at St. Mary's Church in Lebanon. The marriage was performed by Rev. A. Christ on November 24, 1914. They settled in Lebanon, residing at 426 North Sixth Street. He worked as a machinist for the Bethlehem Steel Company.[427]

Based on Census reports and other materials, we know that Paul A. and Annie L. Allwein gave life to the following children (all of these children are listed in the 1940 Federal Census report):[428]

Helen A. Allwein (F07-0405-1402-0301), b. est. February 1915, d. February 12, 1999, became a nun (Sister Mary Esdras, Sisters of St. Joseph, Flourtown, Montgomery County, Pennsylvania)[429]

---

[427] *Fourteenth Census of the United States* (1920), *Inhabitants of Lebanon Ward 6, Lebanon County, Pennsylvania*, E.D. No. 175, page 265B; *Fifteenth Census of the United States* (1930), *Inhabitants of Lebanon, Lebanon County, Pennsylvania*, E.D. No. 38-20, page 150B; *Sixteenth Census of the United States* (1940), *Inhabitants of Lebanon, Lebanon County, Pennsylvania*, E.D. No. 38-28, page 417A.

[428] Information on dates of death for many of these children were obtained from obituaries in the *Lebanon Daily News*, Lebanon, Pennsylvania, as follows: Saturday, May 28, 1983; Monday, June 2, 1997; Wednesday March 17, 1998; Monday March 22, 1999; August 8, 2000; Thursday, August 3, 2006; Wednesday, October 6, 2010; Tuesday, April 5, 2011; Tuesday, June 7, 2011; February 6, 2013; and *The Harrisburg Evening News*, Thursday, June 23, 1994.

[429] Obituary for Helen Allwein (Sister Mary Esdras) in the *Allentown Morning Call*, Monday, February 15, 1999.

Paul "Bud" John Allwein (M07-0405-1402-0302), b. May 30, 1916, d. July 27, 2006 (QH), m. (August 18, 1951) Mary A. Lazorick (b. September 3, 1920, d. March 31, 2011)[430]

Herman Mark Allwein (M07-0405-1402-0303), b. July 23, 1917, d. March 14, 1999 (OA), m. (September 27, 1947) Mildred J. Stroh (b. July 27, 1918, d. unknown)

James E. Allwein (M07-0405-1402-0304), b. September 23, 1918, d. March 15, 1998 (IG), m. (April 19, 1947) Anita F. Sullivan (b.October 4, 1923, d. June 22, 1994)

Joseph L. Allwein (M07-0405-1402-0305), b. April 19, 1920, d. June 5, 2011 (HC), unmarried

Robert A. Allwein (M07-0405-1402-0306), b. January 22, 1922, m. (1) (November 19, 1949) Margaret E. Kane (b. 1920, d. October 10, 1960), (2) (February 16, 1963) Elizabeth Mary Foster (b. December 5, 1923, d. July 25, 2013)

Anne Louise Allwein (F07-0405-1402-0307)), b. est. 1923, d. January 26, 2013, became a nun (Sister Leonard Therese, entered the community of the Adorers of the Blood of Christ at Saint Joseph's Convent, Columbia, Pennsylvania, 1946)[431]

John Henry Allwein (M07-0405-1402-0308), b. October 1, 1924, d. May 27, 1997 (Watertown, Connecticut), m. (September 15, 1951) Mary Louise Shay (b. June 6, 1925, d. unknown)

Mary Elizabeth Allwein (F07-0405-1402-0309), b. January 3, 1927, d. February 3, 2013 (IG), m. (October 7, 1961) Paul Raymond Sattazahn (b. April 16, 1936, d. October 4, 2010)

Pierce "Peter" Charles Allwein (M07-0405-1402-0310), b. July 9, 1928, d. June 1, 1997 (GE), m. (October 30, 1965) Dorothy Irene Kreiser (b. August 20, 1930, d. August 6, 2000)

Clare M. Allwein (F07-0405-1402-0311), b. July 1, 1931, m. (October 5, 1949) Harold David Barbini (b. May 17, 1932, unknown)

---

[430] Obituary for Mary A. Lazorick Allwein, Amigone Funeral Home, Clarence, New York, March 31, 2011. Ancestry.com.

[431] Obituary for Sister Ann L. Allwein, *Lebanon Daily News*, Lebanon, Pennsylvania, Tuesday, January 29, 2013.

Paul A. Allwein died on August 28, 1950 and Annie (Shay) Allwein in March 4, 1968.[432] They are buried at Holy Cross Cemetery in Lebanon, Pennsylvania.

Catharine E. Allwein Swope (1887-1958)
Lebanon, Pennsylvania

Catherine E. Allwein (F06-0405-1402-04), daughter of Pierce William and Agnes E. (Arnold) Allwein, was born May 15, 1887 in North Lebanon Township, Lebanon County, Pennsylvania. The line of descent connecting Catherine E. Allwein to Johannes Jacob and Catharina Allwein, the progenitors of the Allwein family in colonial Pennsylvania, is as follows:

Generation 1: Johannes Jacob and Catharina Allwein—Berks County, Pa.
Generation 2: Conrad and Catharine (Weibel) Allwein—Dauphin County, Pa.
Generation 3: Philip and Elizabeth (Arentz) Allwein—Lebanon County, Pa.
Generation 4: Elijah and Angeline (Arentz) Allwein—Lebanon County, Pa.
Generation 5: Pierce William and Agnes E. (Arnold) Allwein—Lebanon
     County, Pa.
Generation 6: Catharine E. Allwein and Harry W. Swope—Lebanon County, Pa.

Catharine E. Allwein married Harry William Swope, son of Charles D and Clara (Eberhart) Swope, on June 30, 1917 at St. Mary's Catholic Church in Lebanon. The marriage was performed by Rev. W.E. Martin. They settled in Lebanon, listed in the 1920 Federal Census, living in the household of Pierce and Agnes Allwein at 401 Cumberland Street, and in the 1930 Federal Census listing at 405 East Cumberland, next door to Catherine's brother Charles Allwein.[433] Harry Swope worked as a carpenter. By 1940, they had

---

[432] Obituary and funeral notice for Paul Allwein in *Lebanon Daily News*, Lebanon, Pennsylvania, Tuesday Evening, August 29, 1950 and Friday Evening, September 1, 1950. See also the Pennsylvania Department of Health: http://www.health.state.pa.us.

[433] *Fourteenth Census of the United States* (1920), *Inhabitants of Lebanon Ward 6, Lebanon County, Pennsylvania*, E.D. No. 178, page 313A; *Fifteenth Census of the United States* (1930), *Inhabitants of Lebanon, Lebanon County, Pennsylvania*, E.D. No. 38-26, page 266B; *Sixteenth Census of the United States* (1940), *Inhabitants of Hanover, York County, Pennsylvania*, E.D. No. 67-39, page 502A.

Exhibit 11.92 Gravestone for Paul A. and Annie L. (Shay) Allwein—Holy Cross Cemetery, Lebanon, Pennsylvania

moved to Hanover, York County, Pennsylvania, where he pursued the same line of work. His World War II draft registration indicated that in 1942 he was working for the York Housing Corporation.[434] There were no children born to this union.

Catherine E (Allwein) Swope died on January 27, 1958.[435] As of this writing, we do not have information regarding Harry Swope's death or where they are buried.

Sarah "Sadie" R. Allwein (1889-1919)
Lebanon, Pennsylvania

Sarah "Sadie" R. Allwein (F06-0405-1402-05), daughter of Pierce William and Agnes E. (Arnold) Allwein, was born August 21, 1889 in North Lebanon Township, Lebanon County, Pennsylvania. The line of descent connecting Sarah R. Allwein to Johannes Jacob and Catharina Allwein, the progenitors of the Allwein family in colonial Pennsylvania, is as follows:

Generation 1: Johannes Jacob and Catharina Allwein—Berks County, Pa.
Generation 2: Conrad and Catharine (Weibel) Allwein—Dauphin County, Pa.
Generation 3: Philip and Elizabeth (Arentz) Allwein—Lebanon County, Pa.
Generation 4: Elijah and Angeline (Arentz) Allwein—Lebanon County, Pa.
Generation 5: Pierce William and Agnes E. (Arnold) Allwein—Lebanon County, Pa.
Generation 6: Sarah "Sadie" R. Allwein—Lebanon County, Pa.

Sarah R. Allwein was living with her parents when she was in her early twenties, as indicated by the 1910 Federal Census enumeration of her parents' household (see above). She is listed as working as a stenographer in an office. She never married and died in her late twenties of unknown causes, on February 3, 1919.[436] She

---

[434] World War II Draft Registration Cards. Ancestry.com.
[435] See the Pennsylvania Department of Health: http://www.health.state.pa.us.
[436] See the Pennsylvania Department of Health: http://www.health.state.pa.us.

is buried, along with her parents and many of her siblings, in St. Mary's Cemetery in Lebanon (see below).

James Herman Allwein (1892-1923)
Lebanon, Pennsylvania

James Herman Allwein (M06-0405-1402-07), son of Pierce William and Agnes (Arnold) Allwein, was born July 25, 1892 in North Lebanon Township, Lebanon County, Pennsylvania. The lineage connecting James Herman Allwein to Johannes Jacob and Catharina Allwein, the progenitors of the Allwein family in colonial Pennsylvania, is as follows:

Generation 1: Johannes Jacob and Catharina Allwein—Berks County, Pa.
Generation 2: Conrad and Catharine (Weibel) Allwein—Dauphin County, Pa.
Generation 3: Philip and Elizabeth (Arentz) Allwein—Lebanon County, Pa.
Generation 4: Elijah and Angeline (Arentz) Allwein—Lebanon County, Pa.
Generation 5: Pierce William and Agnes E. (Arnold) Allwein—Lebanon
    County, Pa.
Generation 6: James Herman Allwein—Lebanon County, Pa.

James Herman Allwein never married. He was a veteran of the First World War, serving from February 19, 1919 in Battery E, 34th Artillery Regiment of the U.S. Army until the end of the War. He was living with his parents at 401 Cumberland Street in the Borough of Lebanon at the time of the 1920 Federal Census.[437] He worked as a machinist in the steel industry.

James Herman Allwein died on March 21 1923 at a young age.[438] He is buried in St. Mary's Cemetery (SM), Lebanon, Pennsylvania.

---

[437] *Fourteenth Census of the United States* (1920), *Inhabitants of Lebanon Ward 9, Lebanon County, Pennsylvania*, E.D. No. 178, page 313A.
[438] See the Pennsylvania Department of Health: http://www.health.state.pa.us.

Exhibit 11.93 Gravestones for Sarah H. Allwein and James H. Allwein—St. Mary's Cemetery, Lebanon, Pennsylvania

Philip James Allwein (1861-1953)
Lebanon, Pennsylvania

Philip James Allwein (M05-0405-1403), son of Elijah and Angeline (Arentz) Allwein, was born October 3, 1861 in Lebanon, Pennsylvania. He grew to maturity in Lebanon and lived his entire life there. The line of descent connecting Philip James Allwein to Johannes Jacob and Catharina Allwein, progenitors of the Allwein family in colonial Pennsylvania, is as follows:

Generation 1: Johannes Jacob and Catharina Allwein—Berks County, Pa.
Generation 2: Conrad and Catharine (Weibel) Allwein—Dauphin County, Pa.
Generation 3: Philip and Elizabeth (Arentz) Allwein—Lebanon County, Pa.
Generation 4: George Elijah and Angeline (Arentz) Allwein—Lebanon
    County, Pa.
Generation 5: Philip James and Elizabeth "Lizzie" (Blouch) Allwein—Lebanon
    County, Pa.

According to the Jerome Allwein *Genealogy* he "worked at the Butcher business for some time, later was engaged in the Laundry business" but little else was known.[439] He married Elizabeth "Lizzie" Blouch on April 8, 1892 in Lebanon and they settled there.[440]

They lived in a number of different places within the Borough of Lebanon, and he worked at a variety of different jobs. The 1900 Federal Census enumeration of Lebanon places Philip and Lizzie Allwein in the Sixth Ward, residing at 1027 West Church Street.

---

[439] Jerome Allwein, *Genealogy of the Allwein-Arnold Families.* Philadelphia, Pa., 1902, page 84.

[440] *Twelfth Census of the United States* (1900), *Inhabitants of Ward 6 Lebanon, Lebanon County, Pennsylvania,* E.D. No. 130, 203B; *Thirteenth Census of the United States* (1910), *Inhabitants of Ward 5 Lebanon, Lebanon County, Pennsylvania,* E.D. No. 154, page 201B; *Fourteenth Census of the United States* (1920), *Inhabitants of Ward 9 Lebanon, Lebanon County, Pennsylvania,* E.D. No. 178, page 312B; *Fifteenth Census of the United States* (1930) *Inhabitants of Lebanon, Lebanon County, Pennsylvania,* E.D. No. 38-26, page 266B; *Sixteenth Census of the United States* (1940), *Inhabitants of Lebanon, Lebanon County, Pennsylvania,* E.D. No. 38-34, page 576A.

There he is listed as operating a laundry. In the 1910 Federal Census, they were living in the East Precinct of neighboring Fifth Ward, at 425 Scull Street. His occupation is given as "nut packer in an iron works," and then in 1920 they were living in the Ninth Ward at 309 East Cumberland Street, when he was working as a "laborer in mill." In the 1930 and 1940 Federal Censuses they were still listed as living on East Cumberland Street, and in the 1930 report, he was working as a "laborer in a steel mill."

There were eight children born to Philip James and Elizabeth (Blouch) Allwein, as follows:[441]

Mary Louella Allwein (F06-0405-1403-01), b. June 27, 1893, d. January 21, 1969 (HC), m. (June 20, 1916) John Raymond Embich (b. May 29, 1889, July 26, 1973)

Bertha Agnes Allwein (F06-0405-1403-02), b. January 1, 1895, d. May 19, 1989, m. (November 25, 1920) Thomas F. Barry (b. April 29, 1896, d. November 15, 1969)

Helen Virginia Allwein (F06-0405-1403-03), b. July 4, 1896, d. August 12, 1986 (HC), unmarried

Elmer Aloysius Allwein (M06-0405-1403-04), b. February 16, 1898, d. February 14, 1970 (FC), m. (July 20, 1920) Naomi Graffious (b. February 28, 1902, d. August 5, 1988)

Leroy Arthur Allwein (M06-0405-1403-05), b. May 16, 1899, d. August 17, 1969 (AK), m. (August 14, 1923) Clara M. Knapp (b. October 26, 1902, d. September 30, 1980)

Margaret S. Allwein (F06-0405-1403-06), b. April 21, 1902, d. September 6, 1996 (HC), unmarried

---

[441] This list of children comes from Jerome Allwein, *Genealogy of the Allwein-Arnold Families*. Philadelphia, Pa., 1902, page 84, supplemented by additional information from the Social Security Death Index, and obituaries from the *Lebanon Daily News*, as follows: Friday, November 23, 1962; Wednesday, January 22, 1969; Wednesday, August 20, 1969; Monday Evening, November 17, 1969; Thursday Evening, July 26, 1973; Wednesday Evening, August 13, 1986; Saturday, May 20, 1989; the *Harrisburg Patriot*, Harrisburg, Pennsylvania, September 7, 1996; Monday, December 18, 2000; and Ohio Deaths, 1958-2000. Ancestry.com.

Herman Joseph Allwein (M06-0405-1403-07), b. August 9, 1903,
d. November 21, 1962 (HC), m. (July 28, 1927) Mary Catherine
Arnold (b. April 20, 1905, d. December 16, 2000)

Raphael Joseph Allwein (M06-0405-1403-08), b. March 27, 1909,
d. October 23, 1988 (HC), m. (April 14, 1928) Frances Bowers
(b. November 12, 1908, d. February 22, 1979) (remarried to Earl
H. Spangler)

Philip James Allwein died September 4, 1953; his wife,
Elizabeth (Blouch) Allwein, on September 28, 1946.[442] They are
buried at Holy Cross Cemetery (HC) in Lebanon.

Mary Louella Allwein Embich (1893-1969)
Lebanon, Pennsylvania

Mary Louella Allwein (F06-0405-1403-01), daughter of Philip
James and Elizabeth (Blouch) Allwein, was born in Lebanon,
Pennsylvania on June 27, 1893. The line of descent connecting
Mary Luella Allwein to Johannes Jacob and Catharina Allwein, the
progenitors of the Allwein family in colonial Pennsylvania, is as
follows:

Generation 1: Johannes Jacob and Catharina Allwein—Berks County, Pa.
Generation 2: Conrad and Catharine (Weibel) Allwein—Dauphin County, Pa.
Generation 3: Philip and Elizabeth (Arentz) Allwein—Lebanon County, Pa.
Generation 4: George Elijah and Angeline (Arentz) Allwein—Lebanon County, Pa.
Generation 5: Philip James and Elizabeth (Blouch) Allwein—Lebanon County, Pa.
Generation 6: Mary Louella Allwein and John R. Embich—Lebanon County, Pa.

Mary Louella Allwein married John Raymond Embich (b. May
29, 1889, d. July, 1973), son of Elmer E. and Clara A. (Walmer)
Embich, at St. Mary's Catholic Church in Lebanon, Pennsylvania
on June 20, 1916. The marriage was performed by Rev. William E.
Martin. They settled in Lebanon, eventually residing at 124 South

---

[442] See the Pennsylvania Department of Health: http://www.health.state.
pa.us.

Exhibit 11.94 Gravestone for Philip J. and Elizabeth E. (Blouch) Allwein—Holy Cross Cemetery, Lebanon, Pennsylvania

Second Street.[443] John Embich was a machinist for the Bethlehem Steel Company.[444]

Based on Federal Census records and other materials, we conclude that Mary Louella and John R. Embich gave birth to the following children:[445]

Richard K. Embich, b. April 27, 1917, d. March 21, 2002, m. (January 31, 1942) Gladys C. Gloss (b. December 27, 1919, d. February 26, 2000)

Mary Elizabeth Embich, b. October 13 1918, unknown, m. (July 21, 1945) Neil Eugene Fleischer (b. May 1, 1919, d. June 30, 1962)

Nancy J. Embich, b. July 16, 1924, d. July 7, 2011 (IG), m. Edward J. Walls (b. November 3, 1919, d. October 22, 1991)[446]

John Allwein Embich, b. August 18, 1928, d. November 24, 2013 (HC), m. (September 28, 1950) Justine L. Youtz (b. December 31, 1930, d. February 26, 2006)

Patricia Embich, b. November 19, 1932, d.unknown, m. (June 4, 1955) Donald Paul Barry (b. October 29, 1928)

Mary Louella (Allwein) Embich died on January 21, 1969 and John Raymond Embich died July 26, 1973. They are buried at Holy Cross Cemetery, Lebanon, Pennsylvania.

---

[443] *Fourteenth Census of the United States* (1920), *Inhabitants of Lebanon Ward 8, Lebanon County, Pennsylvania*, E.D. No. 177, page 306A; *Fifteenth Census of the United States* (1930) *Inhabitants of Lebanon, Lebanon County, Pennsylvania*, E.D. No. 38-14, page 4B; *Sixteenth Census of the United States* (1940), *Inhabitants of Lebanon, Lebanon County, Pennsylvania*, E.D. No. 38-14A, page 206B.

[444] World War II Draft Registration Cards. Polk's 1938 Lebanon City Directory. Ancestry.com.

[445] Obituaries from the *Lebanon Daily News*, Lebanon, Pennsylvania, as follows: Monday Evening, July 2, 1962; Friday, March 22, 2002; Tuesday, February 28, 2006.

[446] Obituary for Nancy E. Embich Walls from the *Lebanon Daily News*, Lebanon, Pennsylvania, Saturday, July 9, 2011.

Exhibit 11.95 Gravestone for Mary Louella (Allwein) Embich—Holy Cross Cemetery, Lebanon, Pennsylvania

Bertha Agnes Allwein Barry (1895-1989)
Lebanon, Pennsylvania

Bertha A. Allwein (F06-0405-1403-02), daughter of Philip James and Elizabeth (Blouch) Allwein, was born in Lebanon, Pennsylvania on January 1, 1895. The line of descent connecting Bertha A. Allwein to Johannes Jacob and Catharina Allwein, the progenitors of the Allwein family in colonial Pennsylvania, is as follows:

Generation 1: Johannes Jacob and Catharina Allwein—Berks County, Pa.
Generation 2: Conrad and Catharine (Weibel) Allwein—Dauphin County, Pa.
Generation 3: Philip and Elizabeth (Arentz) Allwein—Lebanon County, Pa.
Generation 4: George Elijah and Angeline (Arentz) Allwein—Lebanon County, Pa.
Generation 5: Philip James and Elizabeth (Blouch) Allwein—Lebanon County, Pa.
Generation 6: Bertha A. Allwein and Thomas F. Barry—Lebanon County, Pa.

Bertha A. Allwein married Thomas F. Barry on November 25, 1920 at St. Mary's Catholic Church in Lebanon. The marriage was performed by Rev. W.E. Martin. He was the son of Thomas and Delia (O'Dey) Barry. After they married, they settled in North Cornwall Township of Lebanon County.[447]

Based on census records, the following children are recorded for this family:[448]

Robert Commodore Barry, b. August 25, 1921, d. September 9, 1997, m. (August 29, 1942) Anna Stella Maika (b. July 2, 1921)
Elizabeth Ann Barry, b. June 10, 1923, d. unknown, m. (August 18, 1947) Paul J. Murray (b. unknown, d. unknown)
Kathleen Theresa Barry, b. August 3, 1925, d. 1972, m. (July 16, 1947) Carl William Rudegeair (b. August 27, 1924, d. November 28, 2001)
Marguerite Helen Barry, b. July 10, 1929, d. unknown, m. unknown

Bertha A. (Allwein) Barry died May 19, 1989 in Lebanon. Thomas F. Barry died on November 15, 1969. They are buried at Holy Cross Cemetery, Lebanon, Pennsylvania.

---

[447] *Fifteenth Census of the United States* (1930) *Inhabitants of North Cornwall Township, Lebanon County, Pennsylvania*, E.D. No. 38-33, page 249B.
[448] Obituaries from the *Lebanon Daily News*, Lebanon, Pennsylvania, as follows: Wednesday, September 10, 1997.

Exhibit 11.96 Gravestone for Thomas and Bertha Barry—Holy Cross Cemetery, Lebanon, Pennsylvania

Helen Virginia Allwein (1896-1986)
Harrisburg, Pennsylvania

Helen Virginia Allwein (F06-0405-1403-03), daughter of Philip James and Elizabeth (Blouch) Allwein, was born in Lebanon, Pennsylvania on July 4, 1896. She died August 12, 1986. Helen Virginia Allwein moved to Harrisburg, and we cover her in Chapter 14, where we deal with Allwein families in Dauphin County.

Elmer Aloysius Allwein (1898-1970)[449]
Lebanon and Beaver County, Pennsylvania

Elmer Aloysius Allwein (M06-0405-1403-04), son of Philip James and Elizabeth (Blouch) Allwein, was born in Lebanon, Pennsylvania on February 16, 1898. The line of descent connecting Elmer Aloysius Allwein to Johannes Jacob and Catharina Allwein, the progenitors of the Allwein family in colonial Pennsylvania, is as follows:

Generation 1: Johannes Jacob and Catharina Allwein—Berks County, Pa.
Generation 2: Conrad and Catharine (Weibel) Allwein—Dauphin County, Pa.
Generation 3: Philip and Elizabeth (Arentz) Allwein—Lebanon County, Pa.
Generation 4: George Elijah and Angeline (Arentz) Allwein—Lebanon County, Pa.
Generation 5: Philip James and Elizabeth (Blouch) Allwein—Lebanon County, Pa.
Generation 6: Elmer Aloysius and Naomi (Graffious) Allwein—Beaver County,
    Pa. and Flint, Michigan

Elmer A. Allwein is listed in his parents' household in the 1910 and 1920 Federal Censuses of Lebanon.[450] He married Naomi Graffious on July 20, 1920 in Lebanon. Naomi was the daughter of Billy and Anna (Krieger) Graffious. By 1930, Elmer and Naomi Allwein had moved to Beaver County, where they were listed in

---

[449] In writing this section, I was assisted by Mary Simoni, a granddaughter of Elmer and Naomi Allwein.
[450] *Thirteenth Census of the United State* (1910), *Inhabitants of Lebanon Borough Ward 5, Lebanon County, Pennsylvania*, E.D. No. 154, page 201B; *Fourteenth Census of the United States* (1920), *Inhabitants of Lebanon Borough Ward 9, Lebanon County, Pennsylvania*, E.D. No. 178, page 312B.

the 1930 and 1940 Federal Censuses for Aliquippa, Beaver County, Pennsylvania, where he was a foreman in a steel mill.[451] Later on, in their retirement years, they moved to Flint, Michigan. I provide a discussion of Elmer and Naomi (Graffious) Allwein in Chapter 17, where we discuss Allwein families in Beaver and Butler Counties in Pennsylvania and also provide a brief mention of them in Chapter 22, where I cover Allwein families in Michigan.

Leroy Arthur Allwein (1899-1969)
Lebanon and Summit County, Ohio

Leroy Arthur Allwein (M06-0405-1403-05), son of Philip James and Elizabeth (Blouch) Allwein, was born in Lebanon, Pennsylvania on May 16, 1899. The line of descent connecting Leroy Allwein to Johannes Jacob and Catharina Allwein, the progenitors of the Allwein family in colonial Pennsylvania, is as follows:

Generation 1: Johannes Jacob and Catharina Allwein—Berks County, Pa.
Generation 2: Conrad and Catharine (Weibel) Allwein—Dauphin County, Pa.
Generation 3: Philip and Elizabeth (Arentz) Allwein—Lebanon County, Pa.
Generation 4: George Elijah and Angeline (Arentz) Allwein—Lebanon County, Pa.
Generation 5: Philip James and Elizabeth (Blouch) Allwein—Lebanon County, Pa.
Generation 6: Leroy A. and Clara M. (Knapp) Allwein—Summit County, Ohio

Leroy Arthur Allwein apparently had a child born out of wedlock (Leroy Arthur Allwein, Jr.) who died in infancy. The mother was Mamie Garrett, daughter of Harrie and Maggie Garrett.[452]

Leroy Arthur Allwein, Jr. (M07-0405-1403-0501), b. June 23, 1921, d. February 27, 1922 (ML)

---

[451] *Fifteenth Census of the United States* (1930), *Inhabitants of Aliquippa, Beaver County, Pennsylvania*, E.D. No. 4-11, page 216B; *Sixteenth Census of the United States* (1940), *Inhabitants of Aliquippa, Beaver County, Pennsylvania*, E.D. No. 4-11, page 216A.
[452] Obituary for Leroy Arthur Allwein, Jr., from the *Lebanon Daily News*, Lebanon, Pennsylvania, Tuesday Evening, February 28, 1922.

Leroy Arthur Allwein married Clara M. Knapp, daughter of Elmer and Perla (Swartz) Knapp, in Lebanon on August 14, 1923. By 1930, they had moved to Akron, Ohio, as they are listed in the city of Akron in the 1930 and 1940 Federal Census enumerations.[453] He worked as a machinist in a mold manufacturing plant. Leroy A. Allwein is also listed in the 1931 through 1949 city directories for Akron and surrounding areas.[454] The 1948-1949 directory indicates that he was a machinist for the Akron Equipment Company, living at 825 Ravenswood Street. As of this writing, we have no way of knowing whether there were children born to them, but there is little indication that this was the case.

Available records indicate Leroy Arthur and Clara M. Allwein remained in the Akron area for the remainder of their lives. Leroy died there on August 17, 1969, and Clara on September 30, 1980.[455] They buried at the East Akron Cemetery (AK) in Akron, Ohio. I visited the graves of Leroy Arthur Allwein and Clara M. Allwein in the spring of 2012. Marked by a flat stone, when I visited this grave, the marker was overgrown with sod and difficult to read.

Margaret S. Allwein (1902-1996)
Lebanon, Pennsylvania

Margaret S. Allwein (F06-0405-1403-06), daughter of Philip James and Elizabeth (Blouch) Allwein, was born in Lebanon, Pennsylvania on April 21, 1902. The line of descent connecting Margaret S. Allwein to Johannes Jacob and Catharina Allwein, the progenitors of the Allwein family in colonial Pennsylvania, is as follows:

---

[453] *Fifteenth Census of the United States* (1930), *Inhabitants of Akron, Summit County, Ohio*, E.D. No. 77-47, page 127A; *Sixteenth Census of the United States* (1940), *Inhabitants of Akron, Summit County, Ohio*, E.D. No. 89-109, page 1532B.

[454] 1931 Akron, Barberton and Cuyahoga Falls Official City Directory; 1948-1949 Akron, Tallmadge, Portage Lakes, Barberton and Cuyahoga Falls Official City Directory. Ancestry.com.

[455] Obituary for Leroy A. Allwein from the *Lebanon Daily News*, Lebanon, Pennsylvania, Wednesday, August 20, 1969. The death date for Clara Allwein was obtained from the Ohio Death Records, Ancestry.com.

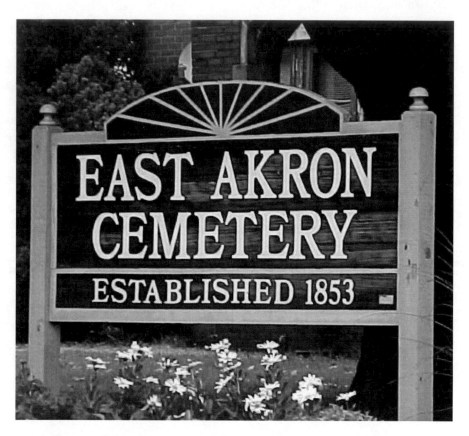

Exhibit 11.97 Location of burial of Leroy Arthur and Clara
Allwein—East Akron Cemetery, Akron, Ohio

Generation 1: Johannes Jacob and Catharina Allwein—Berks County, Pa.
Generation 2: Conrad and Catharine (Weibel) Allwein—Dauphin County, Pa.
Generation 3: Philip and Elizabeth (Arentz) Allwein—Lebanon County, Pa.
Generation 4: George Elijah and Angeline (Arentz) Allwein—Lebanon County, Pa.
Generation 5: Philip James and Elizabeth (Blouch) Allwein—Lebanon County, Pa.
Generation 6: Margaret S. Allwein—Lebanon County, Pa.

Margaret S. Allwein never married. In the 1930 and 1940 Federal Census she was living in her parents' household at 309 East Cumberland in Lebanon.[456] She was still living at that residence in 1940, as indicated by the 1940 Polk's city directory for Lebanon.[457] In both records she is listed as working as a "saleslady in a clothing store."

Margaret S. Allwein died September 6, 1996 in Lebanon. She is buried in Holy Cross Cemetery (HC), Lebanon, Pennsylvania, beside her sister Helen V. Allwein (see above and Chapter 14).

Herman Joseph Allwein (1903-1962)
Lebanon, Pennsylvania

Herman Joseph Allwein (M06-0405-1403-07), son of Philip James and Elizabeth (Blouch) Allwein, was born in Lebanon, Pennsylvania on August 9, 1903. The line of descent connecting Herman Joseph Allwein to Johannes Jacob and Catharina Allwein, the progenitors of the Allwein family in colonial Pennsylvania, is as follows:

Generation 1: Johannes Jacob and Catharina Allwein—Berks County, Pa.
Generation 2: Conrad and Catharine (Weibel) Allwein—Dauphin County, Pa.
Generation 3: Philip and Elizabeth (Arentz) Allwein—Lebanon County, Pa.
Generation 4: George Elijah and Angeline (Arentz) Allwein—Lebanon County, Pa.
Generation 5: Philip James and Elizabeth (Blouch) Allwein—Lebanon County, Pa.
Generation 6: Herman Joseph and Mary Catherine (Arnold) Allwein—Lebanon County, Pa.

---

[456] *Fifteenth Census of the United States* (1930) *Inhabitants of Lebanon, Lebanon County, Pennsylvania*, E.D. No. 38-26, page 266B; *Sixteenth Census of the United States* (1940), *Inhabitants of Lebanon, Lebanon County, Pennsylvania*, E.D. No. 38-34, page 576A.
[457] *1940 Polk's Lebanon City Directory*, Lebanon County, Pennsylvania. Ancestry.com.

Exhibit 11.98 Gravestone for Margaret S. Allwein and Helen V. Allwein—Holy Cross Cemetery, Lebanon, Pennsylvania

Herman Joseph Allwein married Mary Catherine Arnold (b. April 20, 1905), daughter of William and Susan (Light) Arnold at St. Mary's Catholic Church on July 28, 1927 in Lebanon. The wedding ceremony was performed by Rev. H.B. Strickland. They settled in Lebanon. Herman Joseph Allwein was an electrician working for the steel foundry in North Lebanon Township. The 1930 Federal Census enumerations, plus Polk's City Directories for Lebanon place them in North Lebanon Township at 529 Hill Street.[458]

Based on available record sources, we have the following information on the children born to Herman Joseph and Mary C (Arnold) Allwein, as follows:[459]

Herman Joseph Allwein (Jr.) (M07-0405-1403-0701), b. February 21, 1928, January 22, 1983 (HC), m. (December 20, 1952) Mary Laverne Ritchey (b. July 12, 1916, d. June 24, 1965)[460]

William P. Allwein (M07-0405-1403-0702), b. November 4, 1930, d. January 18, 2013 (HC)[461]

Donald Edward Allwein (M07-0405-1403-0703), b. January 16, 1933, d. January 17, 1984 (LM), m. (1) (August 27, 1955) Mary Theresa Greish (b. January 16, 1935, d. unknown), (2) (October 8, 1962) Shirley Rhea (b. March 2, 1933, d. unknown)[462]

Two sons (Edward J. Allwein and Thomas A. Allwein) are still living.[463] Herman Joseph Allwein died on November 21, 1962 and Mary Catherine (Arnold) Allwein in on December 16, 2000. They are buried in Holy Cross Cemetery (HC) in Lebanon, Pennsylvania.

---

[458] *Fifteenth Census of the United States* (1930), *Inhabitants of North Lebanon Township, Lebanon County, Pennsylvania*, E.D. No. 38-34, page 256B.

[459] Some information for the following children was obtained from obituaries in the *Lebanon Daily News*, Lebanon, Pennsylvania, January 22, 1983 and January 17, 1984.

[460] Obituaries from the *Lebanon Daily News*, Lebanon, Pennsylvania and the *Daily News*, Huntingdon, Pennsylvania.

[461] Obituary for William P. Allwein from the *Lebanon Daily News*, Lebanon, Pennsylvania, Sunday, January 20, 2013.

[462] Obituary for Donald Edward Allwein from the *Capital*, Annapolis, Maryland, Wednesday, January 18, 1984.

[463] See the obituary for William P. Allwein from the *Lebanon Daily News*, Lebanon, Pennsylvania, Sunday, January 20, 2013.

Exhibit 11.99 Gravestone for Herman J. and Mary C. Allwein—Holy Cross Cemetery, Lebanon, Pennsylvania

Raphael Joseph Allwein (1909-1988)
Lebanon, Pennsylvania

Raphael Joseph Allwein (M06-0405-1403-08), son of Philip James and Elizabeth (Blouch) Allwein, was born in Lebanon, Pennsylvania on March 27, 1909. The line of descent connecting Raphael Joseph Allwein to Johannes Jacob and Catharina Allwein, the progenitors of the Allwein family in colonial Pennsylvania, is as follows:

Generation 1: Johannes Jacob and Catharina Allwein—Berks County, Pa.
Generation 2: Conrad and Catharine (Weibel) Allwein—Dauphin County, Pa.
Generation 3: Philip and Elizabeth (Arentz) Allwein—Lebanon County, Pa.
Generation 4: George Elijah and Angeline (Arentz) Allwein—Lebanon County, Pa.
Generation 5: Philip James and Elizabeth (Blouch) Allwein—Lebanon County, Pa.
Generation 6: Raphael Joseph and Frances (Bowers) Allwein—Lebanon
County, Pa.

Raphael Joseph Allwein married Frances K. Bowers on April 14, 1928 in Lebanon. She was the daughter of Reuben Bowers and Mary Wilhelm Bowers. Following their marriage, they settled in Lebanon residing in the household of Frances' Bowers parents. In the 1930 Federal Census, they are listed in this household, and Raphael is listed as working in a steel foundary.[464]

Based on available record sources, we have the following information on the children born to Raphael Joseph and Frances (Bowers) Allwein: (see the census materials cited above):

James Joseph Allwein (M07-0405-1403-0801), b. December 8, 1928, d. January 31, 1992, m. (1) (June 26, 1954) Patricia Ann Allwein (b. June 6, 1935, May 14, 1983), (2) (December 31, 1984) Carol Fay Cofran (Brosey) (b. July 8, 1933, d. January 10, 1992)[465]

---

[464] *Fifteenth Census of the United States* (1930), *Inhabitants of Lebanon, Lebanon County, Pennsylvania*, E.D. No. 38-23, page 210A.

[465] Obituaries from the *Lebanon Daily News* Lebanon, Pennsylvania, as follows: Monday, May 16, 1983; the *Palm Beach Post*, January 12, 1992; and the *Sun-Sentinel*, Broward and Palm Beach Counties, Florida, February 3, 1992. See also Florida Marriage Records, 1927-2001. Ancestry.com.

Rita Jean Allwein (F07-0405-1403-0802), b. March 10, 1930, d.
January 7, 2001, m. (July 24, 1948) Edward Philip Miller (b.
November 24, 1929, d. September 5, 2000)
Helen V. Allwein (F07-0405-1403-0803), b. est. 1932, d. unknown,
m. Richard M. Conner (b. April 20, 1928, d. November 1982)

This marriage did not work out for some unknown reason.
Frances K. (Bowers) Allwein remarried to Earl H. Spangler, and
the above children, along with "Frances K. Spangler" are listed in
that household in the 1940 Federal Census enumeration, the 1940
Palmyra City Directory and the 1945-1946 Lebanon County City
Directory.[466]

Raphael Joseph Allwein moved to the Harrisburg area in the
late 1930s. He is listed in Polk's city directories for Harrisburg
from 1936 to 1949. He worked at various occupations, including
die maker and airplane mechanic.[467] He remarried to Pearl E (family
name unknown) around 1942.

Raphael Joseph Allwein died on October 23, 1988 and is buried
in Holy Cross Cemetery (HC) in Lebanon, Pennsylvania.

Elizabeth Rebecca Allwein Arnold (1868-1951) Lebanon, Pennsylvania

Elizabeth Rebecca Allwein (F05-0405-1406), daughter of Elijah and
Angeline (Arentz) Allwein, was born July 17, 1868 on her parents'
farm in North Lebanon Township. Her mother died when she was a
child, and her father remarried soon thereafter. The line of descent
connecting Elizabeth Rebecca Allwein to Johannes Jacob and
Catharina Allwein, the progenitors of the Allwein family in colonial
Pennsylvania, is as follows:

---

[466] *Sixteenth Census of the United States* (1940), *Inhabitants of Lebanon,
Lebanon County, Pennsylvania*, E.D. No. 38-45, page 793A.
[467] *1936-1949 Polk's City Directory for Harrisburg, Pennsylvania.*
Ancestry.com.

Exhibit 11.100 Gravestone for Raphael Joseph Allwein—Holy
Cross Cemetery, Lebanon, Pennsylvania

Generation 1: Johannes Jacob and Catharina Allwein—Berks County, Pa.
Generation 2: Conrad and Catharine (Weibel) Allwein—Dauphin County, Pa.
Generation 3: Philip and Elizabeth (Arentz) Allwein—Lebanon County, Pa.
Generation 4: Elijah and Angeline (Arentz) Allwein—Lebanon County, Pa.
Generation 5: Elizabeth Rebecca Allwein and Jerome S. Arnold—Lebanon
    County, Pa.

Elizabeth Rebecca Allwein married Jerome S. Arnold, son of Henry and Priscilla Anna (Steckbeck) Arnold, on November 21, 1895 at St. Mary's Catholic Church in Lebanon, Pennsylvania. The marriage ceremony was performed by Rev. A. Christ. They settled in Bethel Township, where Jerome Arnold pursued a life of farming the land. They are listed in Federal Censuses for Bethel Township in all census years from 1900 to 1940.[468]

Based on Arnold family genealogical information, we have the following information on the children of Elizabeth Rebecca (Allwein) and Jerome Arnold:[469]

Clarence Aloysius Arnold, b. September 12, 1896, d. November 20, 1962 (HC), m. (June 21, 1919) Edith Sybilia Spotts (b. April 29, 1898, d. November 9, 1973)

---

[468] *Twelfth Census of the United States* (1900), *Inhabitants of Mt. Zion, Bethel Township, Lebanon County, Pennsylvania*, E.D. No. 113, 23B; *Thirteenth Census of the United States* (1910), *Inhabitants of Bethel Township, Lebanon County, Pennsylvania*, E.D. No. 137, page 234A; *Fourteenth Census of the United States* (1920), *Inhabitants of Bethel Township, Lebanon County, Pennsylvania*, E.D. No. 157, page 43A; *Fifteenth Census of the United States* (1930) *Inhabitants of Bethel Township, Lebanon County, Pennsylvania*, E.D. No. 38-5, page 45A; *Sixteenth Census of the United States* (1940), *Inhabitants of Bethel Township, Lebanon County, Pennsylvania*, E.D. No. 38-4, page 69B.
[469] "Modified Register for Arnoldt," obtained from Nancy Allwein Nebiker. Information was also obtained from obituaries in the *Lebanon Daily News*, Lebanon, Pennsylvania, as follows: Monday, March 14, 1955; Tuesday Evening, November 20, 1962; Saturday Evening, December 4, 1965; Friday Evening, November 9, 1973; Sunday, February 1, 1987; Friday, September 22, 1989; Friday, May 4, 1990; Tuesday, February 20, 1996; Monday, January 17, 2000; Thursday, August 30, 2001; and the *Harrisburg Patriot News*, Tuesday, April 15, 1997.

Howard Henry Arnold, b. July 15, 1898, d. February 19, 1996 (HC), m. (1) Mabel Ellen Allwein (b. February 23, 1900, d. March 12, 1955), (2) Viola L. Zimmerman (b. May 14, 1909, d. August 28, 2001)

Caroline "Carrie" Rebecca Arnold, b. December 1, 1899, d. July 1978, m. (June 15, 1929) Charles Grover Miller (b. November 16, 1892, d. August 4, 1963)

Henry Jerome Arnold, b. July 16, 1901, d. September 22, 1989 (HC), m. Mary E. Heisey (b. June 8, 1905, d. June 7, 1977)

Stephen J. Arnold, b. September 4, 1903, d. April 13, 1997 (HC), m. (April 2, 1939) Miriam E. Miller (b. October 24, 1905, d. February 1978)

Kathryn P. Arnold, b. August 16, 1905, d. January 31,1987 (HC), m. (June 16, 1927) Clarence J. Arnold (b. September 9, 1905, d. December 4, 1965)

Elijah Herman Arnold, b. March 15, 1907, d. May 3, 1990 (HC), m. (August 28, 1928) Cora Ellen Spitler (b. September 9, 1909, d. January 16, 2000)

Charles R. Arnold, b. January 31, 1909, d. March 29, 1909 (SM)

David A. Arnold, b. December 4, 1909, d. December 12, 1909 (SM)

Marie A. Arnold, b. April 30, 1910, d. January 28, 1952, m. (June 27, 1935) Leo Cyril Rudegeair (b. December 9, 1895, d. May 8, 1954)

Elizabeth Rebecca Allwein died July 24, 1951 and Jerome S. Arnold on October 20, 1960.[470] They are buried in St. Mary's Cemetery (SM) in Lebanon.

Stephen Adam Allwein (1885-1918)
Lebanon, Pennsylvania

Stephen Adam Allwein (M05-0405-1414), youngest son of Elijah and Mary (Snyder) Allwein, was born April 23, 1885 on his parents' farm in Bethel Township of Lebanon County, Pennsylvania. The line of descent connecting Stephen Adam Allwein to Johannes Jacob and Catharina Allwein, the progenitors of the Allwein family in colonial Pennsylvania, is as follows:

---

[470] See the Pennsylvania Department of Health: http://www.health.state. pa.us.

Exhibit 11.101 Gravestones for Elizabeth Rebecca Allwein and
Jerome S. Arnold—St. Mary's Cemetery, Lebanon, Pennsylvania

Generation 1: Johannes Jacob and Catharina Allwein—Berks County, Pa.
Generation 2: Conrad and Catharine (Weibel) Allwein—Dauphin County, Pa.
Generation 3: Philip and Elizabeth (Arentz) Allwein—Lebanon County, Pa.
Generation 4: Elijah and Mary (Snyder) Allwein—Lebanon County, Pa.
Generation 5: Stephen Adam and Cora E. (Steckbeck) Allwein—Lebanon
   County, Pa.

Stephen Adam Allwein married Cora E. Steckbeck daughter of Aaron and Mary (Schaeffer) Steckbeck, on May 12, 1910 at St. Mary's Catholic Church in Lebanon. The wedding service was performed by Rev. A. Christ. Stephen A. Allwein is listed in the 1910 Federal Census of North Lebanon Township living with four of his sisters in what was formerly his parents' house.[471] His occupation in that report is given as "salesman in a commercial enterprise," which I assume referred to his job in the family grocery business.

There were two children born to this marriage, as follows:

Beatrice Allwein (F06-0405-1414-01), b. July 23, 1911, d. February 22, 2013, m. (November 9, 1940) Herbert J. Benninghoff (b. May 15, 1907, d. November 1978)[472]
Elizabeth Mary Allwein (F06-0405-1414-02), b. July 3, 1915, m. (September 3, 1942) John Joseph McDonnell (b. December 21, 1902)

Stephen Adam Allwein died on October 24, 1918 at the young age of 33.[473] Holy Cross Cemetery was opened in 1917 and his was the first burial there.[474] Stephen Allwein's widow, Cora E. (Steckbeck) Allwein, continued to run the grocery business and

---

[471] *Thirteenth Census of the United States* (1910), *Inhabitants of North Lebanon, Lebanon County, Pennsylvania*, E.D. No. 163, page 78A.
[472] Obituary for Beatrice A. Benninghoff from the *Lebanon Daily News*, Lebanon, Pennsylvania, Sunday, February 24, 2013.
[473] See the Pennsylvania Department of Health: http://www.health.state. pa.us.
[474] John J. Foster, *The Story of Assumption of Blessed Virgin Mary Church, Lebanon, Pennsylvania.* Lebanon, Pennsylvania: Sowers Printing Company, 1951, page 85.

Exhibit 11.102 Gravestones for Stephen Adam Allwein and Cora
(Steckbeck) Allwein Reilly—Holy Cross Cemetery, Lebanon,
Pennsylvania

appears as "grocery store merchant" in the 1920 Federal Census.[475] She remarried to James F. Reilly, son of James F. (Sr.) and Mary Reilly, on June 1, 1926 at Lebanon. Stephen Adam Allwein and Cora (Steckbeck) Allwein Reilly are buried together at Holy Cross Cemetery (HC) in Lebanon.

John Henry Allwein (1837-1919)[476]
Lebanon County, Pennsylvania

John Henry Allwein (M04-0405-16), son of Philip and Elizabeth (Arentz) Allwein, was born August 9, 1837 on his parents' farm in Bethel Township of Lebanon County, Pennsylvania, one of many children. He was known as "Henry A. Allwein" and almost all record sources list him this way, including his gravestone. We do not know precisely what the middle initial "A" stood for, but some have speculated that it was Aloysius. The line of descent connecting Henry A. Allwein to Johannes Jacob and Catharina Allwein, the progenitors of the Allwein family in colonial Pennsylvania, is as follows:

Generation 1: Johannes Jacob and Catharina Allwein—Berks County, Pa.
Generation 2: Conrad and Catharine (Weibel) Allwein—Dauphin County, Pa.
Generation 3: Philip and Elizabeth (Arentz) Allwein—Lebanon County, Pa.
Generation 4: Henry A. and Catharine Ann (Lenich) Allwein—Lebanon County, Pa.

We covered Henry Allwein's early life in Chapter 7 of *Familie Allwein*, volume 1 (pages 432-436), and we refer the reader to that source. We will not repeat that material here, except to review his adult life.

Regarding Henry Allwein's adult life, we must piece together information from several sources. We know that he was a carpenter by trade and that he spent most of his life in Lebanon plying this trade in one way or another. According to Jerome Allwein's *Genealogy of the Allwein-Arnold Family*, he learned cabinet making

---

[475] *Thirteenth Census of the United States* (1920), *Inhabitants of Lebanon Ward 8, Lebanon County, Pennsylvania*, E.D. No. 177, page 304A.
[476] The author gratefully acknowledges the contributions of Patti Keefer Billow for the information presented in this section of the chapter.

by apprenticing himself to Joseph Bowman in Lebanon, and later
"started a furniture business at Lebanon, but sold out after five
months trial and started to work at the North Lebanon Furnaces as
a carpenter." In the 1860 Federal Census (return dated July 1860)
he is listed living in a hotel in North Lebanon Township as a single
man, working as a carpenter.[477]

On November 20, 1860, Henry Allwein married Catharine Ann
Lenich, daughter of Jonathan and Mary Lenich of Lebanon, at St.
Mary's Catholic Church in Lebanon. The marriage was performed
by Rev. A.M. Grundtner. Henry Allwein pursued the carpenter's
trade throughout his life, as confirmed by the several sources
mentioned here, but in the months and years following his marriage,
he appears to have focused on furniture making.

His furniture business may well have lasted more than 5
months—from what is known, I suggest it may have been more like
5 years—but in fact we do not know when he made the transition
from a self-employed furniture maker to working as a carpenter for
the furnaces. It was probably not until about 1870 that he made this
transition. Henry's "day book" for November of 1863 to January
of 1865, lists several major woodworking projects—a range of
projects, including tables, chairs, chests, bedsteads, bureaus, rocking
chairs, wash stands, and other types of household furniture.[478] The
last order listed in the available day book was one (for Louisa
Seifert) dated as ordered April 8, 1868 and completed on March 11,
1869. The photograph in Exhibit 11.104 (see below) reflects the fine
craftsmanship of Henry Allwein's work.

We surmise that by about 1870 he was probably working as a
carpenter / pattern maker for the furnaces in Lebanon. Unfortunately,
while the early Federal Censuses recorded the "occupation" a
person followed, they did not specify the industry in the Census

---

[477] *Eighth Census of the United States* (1860), *Inhabitants of North
Lebanon Township, Lebanon County, Pennsylvania*, page 419.

[478] This particular day book is in the possession of Patti Keefer Billow,
and there may be others. He appears to have opened this book on
November 20, 1864, there are several entries dated prior to that time.

Exhibit 11.103 Reproduction of photograph of John Henry "Henry A." Allwein as a young man—in the late 1850s (contributed by Patti Keefer Billow)

enumerations until 1910. As noted above, the 1860, 1870, 1880, and 1900 Federal Censuses list Henry Allwein as a carpenter, and Lebanon city directories from 1889 to 1899 confirm that during this period he is listed as either a carpenter or patternmaker. We suspect that in addition to his employment with the furnaces, he pursued furniture making throughout his life, but that in his early life, this was his main vocation. It may be true, as well, that he again returned to furniture making after he stopped working in the factories. In the 1910 Federal Census report he is listed (at age 72) as "cabinet maker" in the "cabinet" industry, suggesting that he no longer worked as a carpenter at the furnaces, but as a self-employed furniture maker.[479]

Once Henry and Catharine settled in Lebanon Borough, they lived in one location most of their adult lives, at 823 Mifflin Street, near the corner of Ninth and Mifflin Streets.[480] The 1875 *County Atlas of Lebanon, Pennsylvania* lists Henry A. Allwein as owning property in the Borough of Lebanon near Ninth Street and Mifflin (see Exhibit 11.5 at the beginning of this chapter).[481]

---

[479] *Directory of Lebanon City and County, The Lebanon Directory Company*, 1889-90; *Boyd's Directory of Lebanon City, Names of the Citizens*, 1891-1893; *Boyd's Directory of Lebanon City, Names of the Citizens*, 1895-1896; *Shaffer and Company's Complete Directory of Lebanon City and Suburbs*. Compiled and Published by Chas. C. Shaffer & Co, 1897; *Shaffer's Directory of Lebanon City and Suburbs*. Compiled and Published by Chas. C. Shaffer & Co, 1899.

[480] Jerome Allwein, *Genealogy of the Allwein-Arnold Families*, 1902, pages 36-37. *Ninth Census of the United States* (1870), *Inhabitants of Lebanon Borough, Lebanon County, Pennsylvania*, page 323; *Tenth Census of the United States* (1880), *Inhabitants of Bethel Township, Lebanon County, Pennsylvania*, page 333; *Twelfth Census of the United States* (1900), *Inhabitants of Lebanon Borough, Lebanon County, Pennsylvania*, E.D. No. 129, page 270A; *Thirteenth Census of the United States* (1910), *Inhabitants of Lebanon Ward 5, Lebanon County, Pennsylvania*, E.D. No. 155, page 212A

[481] F.W. Beers, *County Atlas of Lebanon Pennsylvania from Recent and Actual Surveys and Records*, Reading & Philadelphia: F.A. Davis, 1875, page 48.

Exhibit 11.104 Reproduction of a photograph of rolltop desk made by Henry Allwein (contributed by Patti Keefer Billow)

There were eleven children born to Catharine (Lenich) and
Henry Allwein, eight of whom *survived to adulthood*, as follows:[482]

Mary Elizabeth Allwein (F05-0405-1601), b. September 29, 1861,
  d. May 24, 1918, c. Sister Christopher, August 23, 1894
Francis Ervin (Aloysius) Allwein (M05-0405-1604), b. May 6,
  1867, d. January 2, 1953 (HC), m. (June 9, 1892) Amanda
  Elizabeth Beamesderfer (b. April 23, 1873, d. November 11, 1940)
Alice Rebecca Allwein (F05-0405-1605), b. February 19, 1869,
  d. January 7, 1950 (HC), m. (December 27, 1894) William E.
  Lenich (b. April 4, 1871, d. March 6, 1941)
Agnes Cecilia Allwein (F05-0405-1606), b. October 20, 1870, d.
  October 4, 1960 (SM), unmarried
Andrew Philip Allwein (M05-0405-1607), b. January 21, 1873, d.
  May 26, 1916 (SM), m. (April 17, 1901) Catharine A. Dunn (b.
  April 2, 1873, d. unknown)
Lucy Anna Allwein (F05-0405-1608), b. January 3, 1875, d. July
  11, 1943, c. Sister Mary Jeannette, August 21, 1902
Clara Regina Allwein (F05-0405-1609), b. September 23, 1876, d.
  August 21, 1953 (SM), unmarried
Regina Ellen Allwein (F05-0405-1611), b. November 8, 1882, d.
  July 1, 1966 (SM), unmarried

Two of Henry and Catharine (Lenich) Allwein's daughters
became nuns and joined convents—Mary Elizabeth Allwein (Sister
Christopher) and Lucy Anna Allwein (Sister Jeannette). Mary
Elizabeth Allwein entered the Convent of Sisters of Saint Francis
at Glen Riddle on April 9, 1892. She received her final vows two
years later in August of 1894 and ministered (1894-1911) at Mount
Saint Mary College and Seminary, Emmitsburg, Maryland, and
(1911-1918) at St. Joseph Hospital, Baltimore, Maryland.[483] She
died May 24, 1918 in Baltimore, and is buried at the Most Holy
Redeemer Cemetery (RB), Baltimore, Maryland.

---

[482] The information on births and deaths presented here was contributed
by Patti Keefer and was obtained from the Henry A. Allwein family bible.
The children who died in childhood are listed in volume 1 of *Familie
Allwein* (page 435).
[483] Information obtained from Jerome Allwein, *Genealogy of the
Allwein-Arnold Families*, 1902, pages 85-86, supplemented with information
provided by Patti Keefer Billow, correspondence dated October 12, 2011.

Exhibit 11.105 Reproduction of Photograph of Henry and Catharine Allwein family—seated (left to right) in the front row: Lucy (Sister Jeannette), Henry, Regina, Catharine and Clara—standing (left to right) in the back row: Agnes, Francis, Mary (Sister Christopher), Andrew and Alice Allwein (contributed by Patti Keefer Billow)

Lucy Anna Allwein (Sister Mary Jeannette) entered St. Agnes Hospital in Philadelphia on January 21, 1900 as a postulant for Sisters of Saint Francis, and also eventually moved to the Convent at Glen Riddle.[484] She entered the field of education, holding teaching positions in Wilmington, Delaware and Baltimore, Maryland from 1902 to 1943. She died on July 11, 1943 at St. Agnes Hospital, Philadelphia, Pennsylvania and is buried at the Cathedral Cemetery (CD), Wilmington, Delaware.

In addition, three other daughters did not marry—Agnes Cecilia Allwein (F05-0405-1606), Clara Regina Allwein (F05-0405-1609), and Regina Ellen Allwein (F05-0405-1611)—and they remained in their parents' residence in Lebanon. Agnes Allwein worked at the Bon Ton department store in the Borough of Lebanon for many years (see the Lebanon city directories for this period). She began as a sales lady and moved up to become head of the women's department, then later was head of sportswear. She also made several trips as a buyer for the store. Clara Allwein also worked as a sales lady for the Bon Ton (see the city directories for Lebanon). Regina Ellen Allwein kept house for her parents and her sisters.

The 1900 and 1910 Federal Censuses list Henry and Catharine Allwein at 823 Mifflin Street in Lebanon's 5th Ward.[485] Henry Allwein died on November 30, 1919 and Catharine (Lenich) Allwein died several years later on February 19, 1926.[486] After Henry Allwein died, the three sisters—Agnes, Clara and Regina Ellen Allwein—remained with their mother, Catharine (Lenich) Allwein. And after their mother died, the three daughters remained in their

---

[484] *Twelfth Census of the United States* (1900), *Inhabitants of Philadelphia Ward 26, Philadelphia County, Pennsylvania*, E.D. No. 639, page 2B; Jerome Allwein, *Genealogy of the Allwein-Arnold Families*, 1902, pages 85-86.

[485] *Twelfth Census of the United States* (1900), *Inhabitants of Lebanon Ward 5, Lebanon County, Pennsylvania*, E.D. No. 129, 270A; *Thirteenth Census of the United States* (1910), *Inhabitants of Lebanon Ward 5, Lebanon County, Pennsylvania*, E.D. No. 155, page 212A.

[486] See the Pennsylvania Department of Health: http://www.health.state.pa.us.

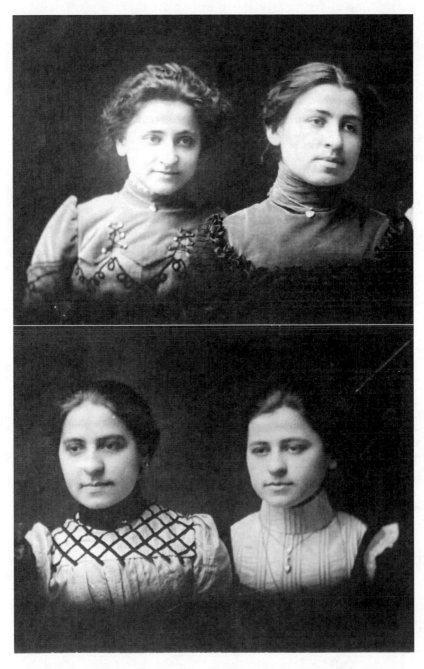

Exhibit 11.106 Reproduction of Photographs of Allwein sisters—
top: Clara and Agnes, bottom: Lucy Anna and Regina Allwein—
circa 1897 (contributed by Patti Keefer Billow)

parents' home, for nearly the duration of their lives.[487] Clara died in 1953 and Agnes and Regina stayed on at the family residence. Shortly after Agnes death in 1960, Regina moved to the Villa St. Elizabeth Home in Reading, Pennsylvania. Wayne Allwein, son of Francis Allwein (see below), purchased the house after Regina left and he converted it into two apartments. It remains that way today. These three daughters, and their brother Andrew Philip Allwein, are buried with their parents on the family plot in St. Mary's Catholic Cemetery (SM) in Lebanon.

In the following pages, I discuss what is known of the remaining children of Henry and Catharine (Lenich) Allwein—Francis Aloysius Allwein (M05-0405-1604), Alice Rebecca Allwein (F05-0405-1605), and Andrew Philip Allwein (M05-0405-1607)—and their descendants.

Francis Ervin (Aloysius) Allwein (1867-1953) Lebanon, Pennsylvania

Francis Ervin (Aloysius) Allwein (M05-0405-1604), oldest son of Henry and Catharine (Lenich) Allwein, was born May 6, 1867 in Lebanon, Pennsylvania. Although he was baptized Francis Ervin Allwein, his middle name was changed to Aloysius at some point and the name Ervin was dropped. The line of descent connecting Francis Aloysius Allwein to Johannes Jacob and Catharina Allwein, the progenitors of the Allwein family in colonial Pennsylvania, is as follows:

Generation 1: Johannes Jacob and Catharina Allwein—Berks County, Pa.
Generation 2: Conrad and Catharine (Weibel) Allwein—Dauphin County, Pa.
Generation 3: Philip and Elizabeth (Arentz) Allwein—Lebanon County, Pa.
Generation 4: Henry A. and Catharine (Lenich) Allwein—Lebanon County, Pa.
Generation 5: Francis Aloysius and Amanda Elizabeth (Beamesderfer) Allwein—
    Lebanon County, Pa.

---

[487] *Fourteenth Census of the United States* (1920), *Inhabitants of Lebanon Ward 5, Lebanon County, Pennsylvania*, E.D. No. 174, page 253A; *Fifteenth Census of the United States* (1930) *Inhabitants of Lebanon, Lebanon County, Pennsylvania*, E.D. No. 38-22, page 190A; *Sixteenth Census of the United States* (1940), *Inhabitants of Lebanon, Lebanon County, Pennsylvania*, E.D. 38-26, page 434A.

Exhibit 11.107 Reproduction of photograph of Allwein family, circa 1938—back row (left to right): Alice Lenich, Francis Allwein, Agnes Allwein; front row (left to right): Clara Allwein, Sister Jeannette, Regina Allwein (contributed by Patti Keefer Billow)

Francis Aloysius Allwein married Amanda Elizabeth Beamesderfer (b. April 23, 1873, d. November 11, 1940), daughter of Adam and Elizabeth Beamesderfer, at St. Mary's Catholic Church in Lebanon on June 9, 1892. The wedding ceremony was conducted by Rev. James A Huber. Francis and Amanda (Beamesderfer) Allwein settled in the city of Lebanon, and with the exception of a short time when Francis moved to Philadelphia with his brother Andrew to find work, they lived there for the remainder of their lives. Francis Allwein went to live and work in Philadelphia with his brother around 1895 and is listed there in the 1895 Philadelphia city directory.[488] Although his brother remained in Philadelphia, Francis returned after a short while to Lebanon, where he remained for the rest of his life.

In the 1900 Federal Census, Francis and Amanda Allwein are listed at 815 Mifflin Street in Lebanon, and thereafter (in the 1910 through 1940 Censuses) they lived at 909 Maple Street.[489] They purchased this property in October of 1915 and lived there throughout their lives.[490] Francis A. Allwein's occupation is consistently given as "pattern maker" in a steel mill or foundry. A *pattern maker* in a foundry "lays out, mills, drills, turns, grinds, fits, and assembles castings and parts to make metal foundry patterns, core boxes, and match plates, using handtools and machine tools, and analyzing

---

[488] *Gopsill's Philadelphia City Directory for 1895*, Philadelphia: James Gopsill's Sons.

[489] *Twelfth Census of the United States* (1900), *Inhabitants of Lebanon Ward 5, Lebanon County, Pennsylvania*, E.D. No. 129, 286B; *Thirteenth Census of the United States* (1910), *Inhabitants of North Lebanon, Lebanon County, Pennsylvania*, E.D. No. 164, page 133A; *Fourteenth Census of the United States* (1920), *Inhabitants of Lebanon Ward 7, Lebanon County, Pennsylvania*, E.D. No. 176, page 283A; *Fifteenth Census of the United States* (1930) *Inhabitants of Lebanon, Lebanon County, Pennsylvania*, E.D. No. 38-24, page 236A; *Sixteenth Census of the United States* (1940), *Inhabitants of Lebanon, Lebanon County, Pennsylvania*, E.D. 38-30, page 519A.

[490] See also Polk's 1940 City Directory, Lebanon, Pennsylvania. Ancestry.com.

Exhibit 11.108 Reproduction of wedding photograph of Francis
Aloysius Allwein (seated) and Amanda Beamesderfer—Lebanon,
Pennsylvania, June 9, 1892 (wedding party: Charles Hemerly and
Alice Allwein) (contributed by Patti Keefer Billow)

specifications, according to knowledge of patternmaking methods: Studies blueprint of part to be cast, computes dimensions, and plans sequence of operations." [*Dictionary of Occupational Titles*, DOT code: 600.280.050.]

There were fourteen children born to this union, as follows (three of these children died in childhood):[491]

James "Jim" Adam Allwein (M06-0405-1604-01), b. November 4, 1892, d. January 23, 1945 (CW) m. (April 26, 1913) Julietta "Julia" Elizabeth Lombardy (b. May 28, 1894, d. December 23, 1961)

Clement "Clem" Henry Allwein (M06-0405-1604-02), b. March 15, 1895, d. June 16, 1969 (HC), m. (November 25, 1916) Grace Odelia Bright (b. March 25, 1896, d. December 3, 1981)

Carroll Francis (Robert) Allwein (M06-0405-1604-03), b. January 23, 1897, d. November 28, 1986 (GE), m. (January 1, 1920) (1) Emma E. Oliver (b. December 26, 1897, d. November 4, 1948 (BK)), (2) (November 24, 1949) Mary A. Ferrocco (nee Katala) (b. August 10, 1907, d. July 24, 1960 (GE))

Wayne Christopher Allwein (M06-0405-1604-04), b. December 29, 1898, d. August 20, 1973 (HC), m. (February 18, 1922) Eva May Miller (b. October 12, 1903, d. October 23, 1993)

Thomas "Tom" Lucian Allwein (M06-0405-1604-05), b. June 29, 1900, d. January 25, 2002 (HC), m. (1) (August 27, 1920) Bessie Miller (b. August 20, 1902, d. October 16, 1985, (2) (December 15, 1934) Lillian Irene Frederick (b. April 14, 1911, d. December 26, 2002)

Bernard "Bern" William Allwein (M06-0405-1604-06), b. October 15, 1901, d. December 27, 1994 (HC), m. (1) (June 18, 1925) Hilda E. Arnold (b. June 27, 1902, d. October 6, 1961), (2) (April 27, 1963) Margaret Mary Snyder (b.April 21, 1902, d. September 6, 1996)

---

[491] For most cases birth and death dates verified by the Social Security Death Index. Ancestry.com.

Exhibit 11.109 Reproduction of a photograph of the residence of Francis Aloysius and Amanda Allwein at 909 Maple Street, Lebanon, Pennsylvania—photo taken in 1923 (contributed by Patti Keefer Billow)

Mark Joseph Allwein (M06-0405-1604-07), b. June 30, 1903, d. May 18, 1990 (FR), m. (December 13, 1922) Elizabeth V. Smith (b. December 9, 1903, d. December 7, 1988)

Frederick "Fritz" George Allwein (M06-0405-1604-08), b. June 13, 1905, d. March 28, 1998 (HC), m. (May 16, 1927) Clara Marie Stasko (b. September 2, 1904, d. August 7, 1990)

Catherine "Caty" Elizabeth Allwein (F06-0405-1604-09), b. December 3, 1906, d. October 11, 1991 (HC), m. (June 22, 1935) Frank L. Cincel (b. February 19, 1905, d. March 1, 1996)

Francis Stephen Allwein (M06-0405-1604-10), b. December 26, 1908, d. July 9, 1909 (SM)

Josephine "Jo" Harriet Allwein (F06-0405-1604-11), March 22, 1910, d. December 5, 2004 (HC), m. (November 22, 1944) Francis James Bunch, Sr. (b. April 20, 1913, d. March 18, 1979)

Jeannette "Net" Mary Allwein (F06-0405-1604-12), b. March 17, 1911, d. May 29, 2009 (HC), m. (November 17, 1934) Donald Daniel Keefer (b. April 17, 1903, d. March 15, 1985)

Richard Paul Allwein (M06-0405-1604-13), b. July 27, 1912, d. July 21, 1913 (SM)

Edward Francis Allwein (M06-0405-1604-14), b. June 21, 1914, d. May 23, 1916 (SM)

Amanda Beamesderfer Allwein died on November 11, 1940 at the age of 67, and Francis Allwein died several years later on January 2, 1953.[492] Francis' obituary notes that he was prominent for many years in the activities of the St. Mary's of the Assumption parish in Lebanon, including membership in the St. Mary's Holy Name Society, the Saint Patrick's Society and the Lebanon lodge of the Knights of Columbus. Francis and Amanda Allwein are buried at Holy Cross Catholic Cemetery (HC) in Lebanon, Pennsylvania.

---

[492] Obituaries in the *Lebanon Daily News,* Lebanon, Pennsylvania, November 11, 1940, and January 3, 1953.

Exhibit 11.110 Reproduction of a photograph of the Francis and Amanda (Beamesderfer) Allwein family—Lebanon, Pennsylvania, circa 1916: front row (left to right): Bernard, Catherine, Amanda, Jeannette, Francis, Josephine and Frederick Allwein; back row (left to right) Carroll, Mark, Wayne, Thomas, James, and Clement Allwein (contributed by Patti Keefer Billow)

Exhibit 11.111 Reproduction of a photograph of Francis and Amanda Allwein, circa late 1920s (contributed by Patti Keefer Billow)

Exhibit 11.112 Gravestone for Francis A. and Amanda E. Allwein—Holy Cross Cemetery, Lebanon, Pennsylvania

James "Jim" Adam Allwein (1892-1945)
Lebanon, Pennsylvania

James "Jim" Adam Allwein (M06-0405-1604-01), oldest son of Francis Aloysius Allwein and Amanda Beamesderfer, was born November 4, 1892 in Lebanon, Pennsylvania. The line of descent connecting James Adam Allwein to Johannes Jacob and Catharina Allwein, the progenitors of the Allwein family in colonial Pennsylvania, is as follows:

Generation 1: Johannes Jacob and Catharina Allwein—Berks County, Pa.
Generation 2: Conrad and Catharine (Weibel) Allwein—Dauphin County, Pa.
Generation 3: Philip and Elizabeth (Arentz) Allwein—Lebanon County, Pa.
Generation 4: Henry A. and Catharine (Lenich) Allwein—Lebanon County, Pa.
Generation 5: Francis Aloysius and Amanda (Beamesderfer)Allwein—Lebanon County, Pa.
Generation 6: James "Jim" Adam and Julietta "Julia" Elizabeth (Lombardy) Allwein—Lebanon County, Pa.

James Adam Allwein married Julia Elizabeth Lombardy (b. May 28, 1894, d. December 23, 1961), daughter of Michael and Mary Bertha Lombardy, on April 26, 1913 at St. Mary's Catholic Church in Lebanon. The marriage was performed by Rev. H.B. Strickland. They settled in Cornwall Township, Lebanon County, where they are listed in the 1920 through 1940 Federal Census enumerations.[493] James Allwein was employed as a foreman carpenter at the Cornwall iron ore mines.

Based on census records and addition information, we know there were two children born to this union, as follows:

Margaret Marie Allwein (F07-0405-1604-0101), b. December 2, 1913, d. December 11, 1913)

---

[493] *Fourteenth Census of the United States* (1920), *Inhabitants of Cornwall Township, Lebanon County, Pennsylvania*, E.D. No. 160, page 69A; *Fifteenth Census of the United States* (1930), *Inhabitants of Cornwall Township, Lebanon County, Pennsylvania*, E.D. No. 38-7, page 78B; *Sixteenth Census of the United States* (1940), *Inhabitants of Cornwall, Lebanon County, Pennsylvania*, E.D. 38-7, page 93A.

Exhibit 11.113 Reproductions of photographs of Jim and Julia Allwein, 1922 (contributed by Patti Keefer Billow)

Kenneth James Allwein (M07-0405-1604-0102), b. July 29, 1916, d. June 15, 1958 (CW), m. (September 5, 1938) Sally Ellen Kreider (b. July 26, 1916, d. June 20, 2000)

James Adam Allwein had been an employee of the Bethlehem Steel Company for thirty-eight years. He was a member of the Cornwall Methodist Church and he was engaged as a janitor for the church for several years. He was interested in civilian defense and was involved in Boy Scouts. He died January 23, 1945, and Julia (Lombardy) Allwein died December 23, 1961.[494] They are buried, along with their son Kenneth and his wife, in Cornwall Cemetery (CW) Lebanon County, Pennsylvania.

Clement "Clem" Henry Allwein (1895-1969)
Lebanon, Pennsylvania

Clement "Clem" Henry Allwein (M06-0405-1604-02), son of Francis Aloysius Allwein and Amanda Beamesderfer, was born March 15, 1895 in Lebanon, Pennsylvania. The line of descent connecting Clement Henry Allwein to Johannes Jacob and Catharina Allwein, the progenitors of the Allwein family in colonial Pennsylvania, is as follows:

Generation 1: Johannes Jacob and Catharina Allwein—Berks County, Pa.
Generation 2: Conrad and Catharine (Weibel) Allwein—Dauphin County, Pa.
Generation 3: Philip and Elizabeth (Arentz) Allwein—Lebanon County, Pa.
Generation 4: Henry A. and Catharine (Lenich) Allwein—Lebanon County, Pa.
Generation 5: Francis Aloysius and Amanda (Beamesderfer)Allwein—Lebanon County, Pa.
Generation 6: Clement "Clem" Henry and Grace Odelia (Bright) Allwein—Lebanon County, Pa.

Clement Henry Allwein married Grace O. Bright, daughter of Morris and Joanna (Lengle) Bright, on November 25, 1916 at St. Mary's Catholic Church in Lebanon. The marriage was performed by Rev. William E. Martin. They settled in the city of Lebanon,

---

[494] See the Pennsylvania Department of Health: http://www.health. state.pa.us. Obituary for James Allwein from the *Lebanon Daily News*, Lebanon, Pennsylvania, Wednesday, January 24, 1945, page 8.

Exhibit 11.114 Gravestone for James Adam and Julia (Lombardy) Allwein—Cornwall Cemetery, Cornwall, Pennsylvania

Exhibit 11.115 Reproduction of photograph of Clem and Grace
Allwein, circa 1922 (contributed by Patti Keefer Billow)

where they are listed in the 1920 through 1940 Federal Census
enumerations of Lebanon.[495] In the 1920 Census report his
occupation is given as "shipping clerk" for a blast furnace, the 1930
Census report lists his occupation as a "truck driver for an express
company," and in his World War II draft registration (dated April 27,
1942) he indicates he was working for a railway express agency at
Reading Station.[496]

---

[495] *Fourteenth Census of the United States* (1920), *Inhabitants of
Lebanon Ward 7, Lebanon County, Pennsylvania*, E.D. No. 176, page
283A; *Fifteenth Census of the United States* (1930), *Inhabitants of
Lebanon, Lebanon County, Pennsylvania*, E.D. No. 38-27, page 164B;
Sixteenth Census of the United States (1940), *Inhabitants of Lebanon,
Lebanon County, Pennsylvania*, E.D. 38-24, page 393A.
[496] U.S. World War II Draft Registration Cards, 1942. Ancestry.com.

Exhibit 11.116 Reproduction of photograph of Clem Allwein, May 1955 (contributed by Patti Keefer Billow)

Based on census records and addition information, we know the following children were born to Clement and Grace Allwein:

Richard Paul Allwein (M07-0405-1604-0201), b. May 13, 1917, d. September 2, 1917

Jeannette A. Allwein (F07-0405-1604-0202), b. August 20, 1918, d. October 19, 2013, m. (November 25, 1941) Robert C. Tribley (b. May 24, 1918, d. April 29, 1988)

Marjorie Ann Allwein (F07-0405-1604-0203), b. September 22, 1920, d. November 23, 2009 (GE), m. (1) (January 27, 1940) Henry F. Falk (b. January 29, 1921, d. July 21, 1982). (2) Francis J. Agresta (b. November 25, 1918, d. March 4, 2000)

Mary Elizabeth Allwein (F07-0405-1604-0204), b. September 20, 1922, m. (December 18, 1943) James W. Calhoun (b. October 30, 1921, d. February 1, 2005)

James Francis Allwein (M07-0405-1604-0205), b. March 21,1925, d. June 2, 1925

William Edward Allwein (M07-0405-1604-0206), b. January 30, 1926, d. January 29, 1995 (IG), m. (June 18, 1946) Kathryn J. Shirk (b. est. 1925)

Clement Henry Allwein was a member of the St. Gregory Catholic Church, the Holy Name Society, of which he was a past president, and the Railway Brotherhood. He died on June 16, 1969.[497] Grace Bright Allwein died several years later on December 3, 1981. They are buried at Holy Cross Catholic Cemetery (HC), Lebanon, Pennsylvania.

Carroll Robert Allwein (1897-1986)
Lebanon, Pennsylvania

Carroll Robert Allwein (M06-0405-1604-03), son of Francis Aloysius Allwein and Amanda Beamesderfer, was born January 23, 1897 in Lebanon, Pennsylvania. According to family history, Carroll Allwein was baptized Carroll Francis Allwein, and this name appears in some early record sources. Sometime after 1910 and prior

---

[497] Obituary in *Lebanon Daily News*, Lebanon, Pennsylvania, Monday, June 16, 1969.

Exhibit 11.117 Gravestone for Clement Henry and Grace O. Allwein—Holy Cross Cemetery, Lebanon, Pennsylvania

to World War I, he started using Robert as his middle name.[498] The
line of descent connecting Carroll Robert Allwein to Johannes Jacob
and Catharina Allwein, the progenitors of the Allwein family in
colonial Pennsylvania, is as follows:

Generation 1: Johannes Jacob and Catharina Allwein—Berks County, Pa.
Generation 2: Conrad and Catharine (Weibel) Allwein—Dauphin County, Pa.
Generation 3: Philip and Elizabeth (Arentz) Allwein—Lebanon County, Pa.
Generation 4: Henry A. and Catharine (Lenich) Allwein—Lebanon County, Pa.
Generation 5: Francis Aloysius and Amanda (Beamesderfer)Allwein—Lebanon
    County, Pa.
Generation 6: Carroll Robert and Emma E. (Oliver) [and Mary A. Ferrocco (nee
    Katala)] Allwein—Lebanon and Dauphin Counties, Pa.

After his discharge from the Army, on May 6, 1919 Carroll
Robert Allwein returned to Lebanon. A few months later, he married
Emma E. Oliver, daughter of Hayes and Kathryn McMinn Oliver
of Lebanon. They eloped—and were married in Philadelphia on
January 1, 1920.[499] They settled thereafter in Lebanon. 1930 Federal
Census listings place them in Lebanon as does the 1940 Polk's city
directory for Lebanon.[500] Emma (Oliver) Allwein died on November
4, 1948 and is buried at Bismarck Cemetery in Quentin, Lebanon
County. Carroll R. Allwein later married Mary A. Ferrocco (nee
Katala) on November 24, 1949.[501]

---

[498] As is true of most other information in this section, this information
comes from Patti Keefer Billow, who suggests that Robert may have
been his confirmation name, and like his father, he began using this as his
middle name. Federal Censuses for 1900 and 1910 list him as "Carroll F."
See *Twelfth Census of the United States* (1900), *Inhabitants of Lebanon
Ward 5, Lebanon County, Pennsylvania*, E.D. No. 129, 286B; *Thirteenth
Census of the United States* (1910), *Inhabitants of North Lebanon,
Lebanon County, Pennsylvania*, E.D. No. 164, page 133A;
[499] The report in the newspaper [*Lebanon Semi-Weekly News*, Lebanon,
Pennsylvania, Thursday Evening, January 15, 1920] gives December 31,
1919 as the marriage date. The actual return of the marriage certificate
from Delaware County gives January 1, 1920.
[500] *Fifteenth Census of the United States* (1930), *Inhabitants of Lebanon,
Lebanon County, Pennsylvania*, E.D. No. 38-25, page 244B.
[501] *Lebanon Daily News*, Lebanon, Pennsylvania, Friday Evening,
November 25, 1949.

Exhibit 11.118 Reproduction of photograph of Carroll Robert Allwein in his World War I Army uniform (contributed by Patti Keefer Billow)

Exhibit 11.119 Reproduction of photograph of Carroll and Emma
Allwein—date unknown (contributed by Patti Keefer Billow)

Carroll Robert Allwein held a number of jobs throughout his lifetime, including working in clerical positions for Bethlehem Steel in Lebanon as a young man, clerical and management positions at the Pennsylvania Liquor Control Board in Harrisburg for several years, and in his later years as a postman in Lebanon.[502] His wedding announcement, referred to above, states that at the time of his marriage he was "employed by the Bethlehem Steel Company as a car tracer and a demurrage clerk at the North Lebanon furnaces." He is listed in the Harrisburg city directories for several years from 1936 through 1943, which refer to his job with the Liquor Control Board located in Harrisburg. His World War II draft registration card (dated April 29, 1942) gives this as his occupation at the time. Following this, about 1943 he took a job as a letter carrier with the U.S. Postal Service in Lebanon. He retired from his job with the post office, after nearly 22 years, on December 30, 1964.[503]

He was a member of St. Gertrude's Catholic Church in Lebanon and was an active Boy Scout troop leader. He was awarded the Silver Beaver Award in 1956 for nearly 20 years of service in leadership roles with the Boy Scouts, and in 1973, he was awarded the St. George Medal, the highest honor in Catholic scouting. He was a volunteer fireman and a lifetime member of the Lebanon First Aid and Safety Patrol, as well as a lifetime member of the VFW.[504]

From his first marriage there was one child born to Carroll Robert Allwein and Emma E. Oliver, as follows:

Robert Charles Allwein (M07-0405-1604-0301), b. October 28, 1920, m. (July 25, 1942) Violet M. Witmyer (b. October 22, 1920, d. July 19, 2008)

---

[502] *Fourteenth Census of the United States* (1920), *Inhabitants of Lebanon Ward 7, Lebanon County, Pennsylvania*, E.D. No. 176, page 283A; *Fifteenth Census of the United States* (1930), *Inhabitants of Lebanon, Lebanon County, Pennsylvania*, E.D. No. 38-25, page 244B; *Sixteenth Census of the United States* (1940), *Inhabitants of Lebanon, Lebanon County, Pennsylvania*, E.D. 38-20, page 326B.
[503] *Lebanon Daily News*, Lebanon, Pennsylvania, Wednesday, December 23, 1964.
[504] Obituary in *Lebanon Daily News*, Lebanon, Pennsylvania, Saturday, November 29, 1986.

Twice a widower, Carroll Robert Allwein's second wife, Mary A. Ferrocco (nee Katala), died on July 24, 1960. He died twenty-six years later, on November 28, 1986. They are buried together at Saint Gertrude's Cemetery (GE), on the northeast side of Lebanon, Pennsylvania.

Wayne Christopher Allwein (1898-1973)
Lebanon, Pennsylvania

Wayne Christopher Allwein (M06-0405-1604-04), son of Francis Aloysius Allwein and Amanda Beamesderfer, was born December 29, 1898 in Lebanon, Pennsylvania. The line of descent connecting Wayne Christopher Allwein to Johannes Jacob and Catharina Allwein, the progenitors of the Allwein family in colonial Pennsylvania, is as follows:

Generation 1: Johannes Jacob and Catharina Allwein—Berks County, Pa.
Generation 2: Conrad and Catharine (Weibel) Allwein—Dauphin County, Pa.
Generation 3: Philip and Elizabeth (Arentz) Allwein—Lebanon County, Pa.
Generation 4: Henry A. and Catharine (Lenich) Allwein—Lebanon County, Pa.
Generation 5: Francis Aloysius and Amanda (Beamesderfer) Allwein—Lebanon County, Pa.
Generation 6: Wayne Christopher and Eva May (Miller) Allwein—Lebanon County, Pa.

Wayne Christopher Allwein was a veteran of World War I, having served in France and Germany. He enlisted on July 22, 1917 through August 7, 1919 and served with Company B, 58th Infantry Brigade, 4th Division, U.S. Army. He was on a British ship, the S.S. Moldavia, when it was sunk by a German submarine in 1918. According to some stories, he was initially reported to his family as one of the casualties, but he survived the disaster.[505]

Wayne Christopher Allwein married Eva May Miller (b. October 12, 1903), daughter of Isaac and Eliza (Zimmerman) Miller, on February 18, 1922 in Lebanon. The marriage was performed by Rev. A.L. Topper. They settled in Lebanon. In the 1930 Federal Census

---

[505] See stories in the *Lebanon Daily News*, Lebanon, Pennsylvania, Saturday Evening, May 25, 1918; Saturday Evening, June 8, 1918; *Lebanon Semi-Weekly News*, Monday Evening, August 11, 1919.

Exhibit 11.120 Gravestone for Carroll Robert and Mary A. Allwein—St. Gertrude's Cemetery, Lebanon, Pennsylvania

enumerations of Lebanon County, Wayne Allwein is listed at 911
Maple Street next door to the household of his parents, Francis A.
and Amanda E. Allwein.[506] They are also listed in the Lebanon city
directories from 1936 through the early 1940s. The 1930 Federal
Census gave his occupation as a "laborer in a steel plant," later
city directories and the 1940 Federal Census give his occupation
as "policeman."[507] According to his obituary in the *Lebanon Daily
News* he retired from the Lebanon police force in 1955 after 20
years of service.[508]

Based on census records and other resources, we have this
information on the children of Wayne Christopher Allwein and Eva
May Miller:[509]

Joseph R. Allwein (M07-0405-1604-0401), b. March 19, 1923, d.
December 21, 1944 (killed in action in Belgium) (HC)[510]
Mary Louise Allwein (F07-0405-1604-0402), b. June 15, 1925,
d. August 1, 2005 (IG), m. (December 4, 1942) Edward W.
Koehler (b. March 11, 1922, d. January 22, 1986)
Nancy J. Allwein (F07-0405-1604-0403), b. September 28, 1927,
d. November 12, 2008, m. (1) (November 2, 1946) Glenn G.
DeTurk (b. May 22, 1928, d. 1989), (2) (est. 1958) Bernard S.
Bretherick (b. February 18, 1934)
Theresa Regina Allwein (F07-0405-1604-0404), b. March 9, 1929,
m. (August 21, 1948) Anthony J. Dooley, Jr. (b. July 21, 1927)
Wayne Christopher Allwein (Jr.) (M07-0405-1604-0405), b.
February 28, 1931, d. September 5, 2007 (HC), m. (May 16,
1949) Sarah L. Williams (b. est. 1931)

---

[506] *Fifteenth Census of the United States* (1930), *Inhabitants of Lebanon,
Lebanon County, Pennsylvania*, E.D. No. 38-24, page 236A.
[507] *Sixteenth Census of the United States* (1940), *Inhabitants of Lebanon,
Lebanon County, Pennsylvania*, E.D. 38-30, page 519A.
[508] Obituary from the *Lebanon Daily News*, Lebanon, Pennsylvania,
Tuesday, August 21, 1973.
[509] Obituaries from the *Lebanon Daily News*, Lebanon, Pennsylvania,
Monday, December 6, 1948; Wednesday, January 22, 1982; Tuesday, August
2, 2005; Friday, September 7, 2007; Sunday, November 16, 2008; and the
Morning Call, Allentown, Pennsylvania, Thursday, February 23, 2006.
[510] Veterans Burial Cards, Pennsylvania, 1977-1999. Ancestry.com.

Exhibit 11.121 Reproductions of photographs of Wayne Allwein (1922) and Eva May Allwein (date unknown) in her Liberty Fire Company Ladies Auxiliary uniform

Exhibit 11.122 Reproduction of photograph of Wayne and Eva
Allwein, Woods Creek Park, 1959

Exhibit 11.123 Gravestones for Wayne Christopher and Eva May Allwein—Holy Cross Cemetery, Lebanon, Pennsylvania

Barbara Ann Allwein (F07-0405-1604-0406), b. November 25, 1932, m. (October 27, 1956) Donald Lloyd Speck (b. October 8, 1934)

David John Allwein (M07-0405-1604-0407), b. December 18, 1936, d. July 6, 2011 (LW), m. (1) (June 25, 1955) Shirley Ann McAllister (b. September 13, 1938), (2) (September 9, 1995) Betty Jane Walters (b. December 24, 1938, d. February 21, 2006)[511]

Wayne Christopher Allwein died August 20, 1973.[512] His obituary indicates that he was an active adult leader in the Boy Scouts, a member of the St. Mary's Catholic Church, its Holy Name Society, the Knights of Columbus, as well as a number of other civic and fraternal organizations. His wife, Eva May (Miller) Allwein died several years later on October 23, 1993. They are buried at Holy Cross Cemetery (HC), Lebanon, Pennsylvania.

Thomas Lucian Allwein (1900-2002)
Lebanon, Pennsylvania

Thomas Lucian Allwein (M06-0405-1604-05), son of Francis Aloysius Allwein and Amanda Beamesderfer, was born on June 29, 1900 in Lebanon, Pennsylvania. The line of descent connecting Thomas Lucian Allwein to Johannes Jacob and Catharina Allwein, the progenitors of the Allwein family in colonial Pennsylvania, is as follows:

Generation 1: Johannes Jacob and Catharina Allwein—Berks County, Pa.
Generation 2: Conrad and Catharine (Weibel) Allwein—Dauphin County, Pa.
Generation 3: Philip and Elizabeth (Arentz) Allwein—Lebanon County, Pa.
Generation 4: Henry A. and Catharine (Lenich) Allwein—Lebanon County, Pa.
Generation 5: Francis Aloysius and Amanda (Beamesderfer)Allwein—Lebanon County, Pa.
Generation 6: Thomas Lucian and Bessie (Miller) [and Lillian I. (Frederick)] Allwein—Lebanon County, Pa.

Thomas Lucian Allwein married Bessie Miller, daughter of Philip and Rebecca (Batdorf) Miller at St. Mary's Catholic Church in Lebanon on August 27, 1920. The marriage was performed by

---

[511] Obituary for David John Allwein appeared in the *Lebanon Daily News*, Lebanon, Pennsylvania, July 8, 2011.

[512] Obituary for Wayne Christopher Allwein from the *Lebanon Daily News*, Lebanon, Pennsylvania, Tuesday, August 21, 1973.

Exhibit 11.124 Reproduction of a photograph of Thomas, Bessie and Pauline Allwein—1922 (contributed by Patti Keefer Billow)

Rev. W.E. Martin. In the 1930 Federal Census enumerations of Lebanon County Thomas Allwein is listed in the household of his parents, Francis A. and Amanda E. Allwein.[513] His marital status is given as married, but his wife is not listed there with him. At the time of the 1930 Federal Census, his wife, Bessie Allwein and his daughter Pauline Allwein, were living in the household of her mother Rebecca Miller.[514] In this household listing, Bessie Allwein's marital status is given as "widowed." In fact, the marriage did not work out, and it ended in divorce on November 29, 1933.

Based on census reports and other resources, we know that there was as least one child born to Thomas Lucian Allwein and Bessie Miller, as follows:

Pauline R. Allwein (F07-0405-1604-0501), b. April 15, 1921, m. (1) (June 4, 1938) Thomas Woodrow Spitler (b. April 18, 1918, d. October 8, 1989) [divorced October 21, 1944], (2) (November 9, 1944) Frank Lloyd Stonecypher (b. April 24, 1918, d. October 15, 1997)

Thomas L Allwein remarried soon thereafter, to Lillian Frederick, daughter of Daniel Monroe Frederick and Louise May Putt of North Cornwall, on December 15, 1934, in West Chester (Chester County), Pennsylvania. Thomas and Lillian Allwein are listed in the 1940 Federal Census, living on Quentin Road in Lebanon.[515] In that report, Thomas's occupation is given as "shoe cutter" in a shoe factory. Lillian was working as a "sewing machine operator" in a blouse factory.

Thomas Lucian Allwein died January 25, 2002 and Lillian Allwein died on December 26, 2002.[516] They are buried in Holy Cross Cemetery (HC) in Lebanon, Pennsylvania.

---

[513] *Fifteenth Census of the United States* (1930), *Inhabitants of Lebanon, Lebanon County, Pennsylvania*, E.D. No. 38-26, page 264A.

[514] *Fifteenth Census of the United States* (1930), *Inhabitants of Lebanon, Lebanon County, Pennsylvania*, E.D. No. 38-24, page 236A.

[515] *Sixteenth Census of the United States* (1940), *Inhabitants of Lebanon, Lebanon County, Pennsylvania*, E.D. 38-20, page 327A.

[516] Obituaries for Thomas Lucian Allwein and Lillian (Frederick) Allwein from the *Lebanon Daily News*, Lebanon, Pennsylvania, January 26, 2002 and December 27, 2002.

Exhibit 11.125 Reproduction of a photograph of Tom and Lillian
Allwein (contributed by Patti Keefer Billow)

Exhibit 11.126 Gravestone for Thomas L. and Lillian Allwein—Holy Cross Cemetery, Lebanon, Pennsylvania

Bernard William Allwein (1901-1994)
Lebanon, Pennsylvania

Bernard "Bern" William Allwein (M06-0405-1604-06), son of Francis Aloysius Allwein and Amanda Beamesderfer, was born October 15, 1901 in Lebanon, Pennsylvania. The line of descent connecting Bernard William Allwein to Johannes Jacob and Catharina Allwein, the progenitors of the Allwein family in colonial Pennsylvania, is as follows:

Generation 1: Johannes Jacob and Catharina Allwein—Berks County, Pa.
Generation 2: Conrad and Catharine (Weibel) Allwein—Dauphin County, Pa.
Generation 3: Philip and Elizabeth (Arentz) Allwein—Lebanon County, Pa.
Generation 4: Henry A. and Catharine (Lenich) Allwein—Lebanon County, Pa.
Generation 5: Francis Aloysius and Amanda (Beamesderfer)Allwein—Lebanon County, Pa.
Generation 6: Bernard William and Margaret (Snyder Keim) [and Hilda E. (Arnold)] Allwein—Lebanon County, Pa.

Bernard William Allwein married Hilda E. Arnold, daughter of William J. and Elizabeth (Steckbeck) Arnold on June 18, 1925 in Lebanon. The marriage was performed by Rev. John C. McGovern. They settled in Lebanon, where they are listed in the 1930 and 1940 Federal Census enumerations.[517] In 1930 Bernard Allwein's occupation was given as machinist in the steel mill; in 1940 it was given as "loom fixer" in a silk cloth factory. In the 1940 report, Hilda Allwein's occupation was given as "substitute school teacher" in the public schools. Bernard Allwein is listed in Lebanon city directories beginning in 1936.

According to Bernard Allwein's obituary, he was retired from the former Lebanon Steel Foundry where he worked as a core maker. He was a member of the Retired Steelworkers Club, the Knights of Columbus and its Fourth Degree Assembly, and was named Knight of the Year in 1991. He was a member of the Pennsylvania Catholic Beneficial League, a charter member of the Friendship Fire Co., the Senior Citizens Center, Verbena Club, Holy Name Society and was a member of St. Gregory the Great Church.[518]

---

[517] *Fifteenth Census of the United States* (1930), *Inhabitants of Lebanon, Lebanon County, Pennsylvania*, E.D. No. 38-25, page 243B.
[518] Obituary for Bernard W. Allwein from the *Lebanon Daily News*, Lebanon, Pennsylvania, Tuesday, December 27, 1994.

Exhibit 11.127 Reproduction of photograph of Bernard Allwein—
circa 1923 (contributed by Patti Keefer Billow)

Exhibit 11.128 Reproduction of the wedding photograph of
Bernard Allwein and Hilda Arnold, with attendants Leroy Arnold
and Catherine Allwein, 1925 (contributed by Patti Keefer Billow)

Based on information from the family, 1940 Federal Census records, and Lebanon County marriage records, we know Bernard W. Allwein and Hilda E. Arnold gave birth to the following five children:

William Francis Allwein (M07-0405-1604-0601), b. July 30, 1926, m. (1) (November 15, 1947) Serafina (Sarah) Christine Vancho (b. July 25, 1928, d. August 8, 1992),[519] (2) (October 19, 1996) Kathleen Mae Krissinger (nee Wolf) (b. August 4, 1941)

Patricia Ann Allwein (F07-0405-1604-0602), b. January 28, 1930, d. May 17, 1989, m. (1) (October 8, 1949) Donald Hershour (b. December 23, 1927, d. November 20, 2012), (2) Paul J. Rittle (b. January 31, 1917, d. May 28, 2007)[520]

Louise E. Allwein (F07-0405-1604-0603), b. February 17, 1933, m. Anthony S. Pugliese (b. November 20, 1930, d. June 18, 1979)

Charles "Chuck" Bernard Allwein (M07-0405-1604-0604), b. September 21, 1936, m. (April 4, 1959) Charlotte Elsie Ditzler (b. November 7, 1938)

Mary Agnes Allwein (F07-0405-1604-0605), b. February 18, 1942, m. (1) Gordon E. Patton (October 26, 1963), (2) (October 22, 1966) Edward Duffy

Hilda Arnold Allwein died on October 6, 1961.[521] A few years after Hilda's death, on April 27, 1963, Bernard William Allwein married Margaret Mary Keim (nee Snyder). She was the daughter of William J. Snyder and Anna E. Seyfert and the widow of Harry T. Keim. Bernard William Allwein died many years later on December 27, 1994. Bernard's second wife, Margaret Snyder (nee Keim) Allwein died September 6, 1996. Bernard and Hilda (Arnold) Allwein are buried together at Holy Cross Cemetery (HC) in Lebanon, Pennsylvania.

---

[519] Obituary for Sarah C. Allwein from the *Patriot News*, Harrisburg, Pennsylvania, Sunday, August 9, 1992.

[520] Obituary for Paul J. Rittle from the *Intelligencer Journal*, Lancaster, Pennsylvania, May 30, 2007.

[521] See the Pennsylvania Department of Health: http://www.health.state.pa.us.

Exhibit 11.129 Reproduction of a photograph of Bernard and
Hilda Allwein, 1959 (contributed by Patti Keefer Billow)

Exhibit 11.130 Gravestone for Bernard William and Hilda Allwein—Holy Cross Cemetery, Lebanon, Pennsylvania

Mark Joseph Allwein (1903-1990)
Lebanon, Pennsylvania

Mark Joseph Allwein (M06-0405-1604-07), son of Francis Aloysius Allwein and Amanda Beamesderfer, was born June 30, 1903 in Lebanon, Pennsylvania. The line of descent connecting Mark Joseph Allwein to Johannes Jacob and Catharina Allwein, the progenitors of the Allwein family in colonial Pennsylvania, is as follows:

Generation 1: Johannes Jacob and Catharina Allwein—Berks County, Pa.
Generation 2: Conrad and Catharine (Weibel) Allwein—Dauphin County, Pa.
Generation 3: Philip and Elizabeth (Arentz) Allwein—Lebanon County, Pa.
Generation 4: Henry A. and Catharine (Lenich) Allwein—Lebanon County, Pa.
Generation 5: Francis Aloysius and Amanda (Beamesderfer)Allwein—Lebanon County, Pa.
Generation 6: Mark Joseph and Elizabeth V. (Smith) Allwein—Lebanon County, Pa.

Mark Joseph Allwein married Elizabeth V. Smith, daughter of Wesley and Gertrude (Cramp) Smith, at St. Mary's Catholic Church in Lebanon on December 13, 1922. The marriage ceremony was performed by Rev. H.B. Strickland. Prior to his marriage, Mark Joseph Allwein was listed in the 1920 Federal Census in Lebanon, living in his parents' household. In the 1930 Federal Census, Mark and Elizabeth Allwein were living in North Cornwall Township.[522] His occupation in 1930 was given as "weighmaster" in a steel mill. By 1935, they had moved into the Borough of Lebanon, as indicated in the 1940 Federal Census enumerations for Lebanon.[523] His occupation was given as "steel worker in a steel mill." According to his obituary, he was later employed at the Hershey Chocolate Factory in Hershey. He was a member of St. Mary's Catholic Church in Lebanon.

---

[522] *Fourteenth Census of the United States* (1920), *Inhabitants of Lebanon Ward 7, Lebanon County, Pennsylvania*, E.D. No. 176, page 283A; *Fifteenth Census of the United States* (1930), *Inhabitants of North Cornwall, Lebanon County, Pennsylvania*, E.D. No. 38-33, page 241A.
[523] *Sixteenth Census of the United States* (1940), *Inhabitants of Lebanon, Lebanon County, Pennsylvania*, E.D. 38-23A, page 374A.

Exhibit 11.131 Reproduction of a photograph of Mark Joseph and
Elizabeth Allwein in 1922 (contributed by Patti Keefer Billow)

Mark Joseph Allwein served in World War II, but held a civil
occupation, meaning that he was enlisted in the military, but worked
in manufacturing jobs related to the war effort rather than a military
assignment. His enlistment was from May 18, 1920 to October 2,
1921.[524]

Based on census reports and information from family members,
we know the following for the four children born to Mark Joseph
Allwein and Elizabeth V. (Smith) Allwein:

Ermine "Minie" Elizabeth Allwein (F07-0405-1604-0701), b.
December 31, 1924, d. January 27, 2005, m. (September 13, 1947)
Robert James Piarote (b. October 12, 1922, d. February 4, 1989)[525]

---

[524] World War II Army Enlistment Records, 1938-1946. Ancestry.com.
[525] Obituary for Erimine E. Piarote from the *Lebanon Daily News*,
Lebanon, Pennsylvania, Saturday, January 29, 2005.

Christine "Teen" Eleanor Allwein (F07-0405-1604-0702), b. January 29, 1926, d. October 17, 2013, m. (October 4, 1947) Cecil Wade Rhoads, Jr. (b. January 21, 1924, d.July 8, 2010)[526]

Jean Marie Allwein (F07-0405-1604-0703), b. September 29, 1928, m. (October 25, 1947) Victor W. Smith, Jr. (b. March 17, 1926, d. October 11, 1992)[527]

Dale Frederick Allwein (M07-0405-1604-0704), b. August 22, 1930, m. (April 10, 1954) Dorothy Anne Fasick (b. January 3, 1934)

Mark Joseph Allwein died on May 18, 1990. Elizabeth (Smith) Allwein died a few years earlier on December 7, 1988.[528] They are both buried at Fairland Cemetery (FR), Cleona, Pennsylvania.

Frederick "Fritz" George Allwein (1905-1998)
Lebanon, Pennsylvania

Frederick "Fritz" George Allwein (M06-0405-1604-08), son of Francis Aloysius Allwein and Amanda Beamesderfer, was born June 13, 1905 in Lebanon, Pennsylvania. The line of descent connecting Frederick George Allwein to Johannes Jacob and Catharina Allwein, the progenitors of the Allwein family in colonial Pennsylvania, is as follows:

Generation 1: Johannes Jacob and Catharina Allwein—Berks County, Pa.
Generation 2: Conrad and Catharine (Weibel) Allwein—Dauphin County, Pa.
Generation 3: Philip and Elizabeth (Arentz) Allwein—Lebanon County, Pa.
Generation 4: Henry A. and Catharine (Lenich) Allwein—Lebanon County, Pa.
Generation 5: Francis Aloysius and Amanda (Beamesderfer)Allwein—Lebanon County, Pa.
Generation 6: Frederick George and Clara Marie (Stasko) Allwein—Lebanon County, Pa.

---

[526] Obituary for Cecil W Rhoads, Jr. in the *Lebanon Daily News*, Lebanon, Pennsylvania, Saturday, July 10, 2010.

[527] Obituary for Victor W. Smith, Jr. in the *Evening News*, Harrisburg, Pennsylvania, Wednesday, October 14, 1992.

[528] Obituary for Mark Joseph Allwein from the *Lebanon Daily News*, Lebanon, Pennsylvania, Saturday, May 19, 1990.

Exhibit 11.132 Gravestone for Mark J. and Elizabeth Allwein—Fairland Cemetery, Cleona, Pennsylvania

Frederick George Allwein married Clara Marie Stasko, daughter of John and Anna (Ockay) Stasko at St. Mary's Catholic Church in Lebanon on May 16, 1927. The marriage ceremony was performed by Rev. H. B. Strickland. Before his marriage, Frederick Allwein can be found in the 1920 Federal Census in his parents' household. After he married, he and his wife settled in Lebanon, living in the household of her parents at 1216 Brandywine Street in Lebanon, where they remained until they moved to Campbelltown in their later years.[529] Frederick George Allwein was a machine operator and later became an electrician. He worked for Peiffer's Electric in Lebanon and eventually was self-employed.

One son was born to them, as follows:

Frederick John Allwein (M07-0405-1604-0801), b. October 3, 1936, d. July 7, 2003 (IG), m. (April 12, 1969) Thelma Almeda Sweigert (b. February 24, 1949)[530]

Frederick George Allwein died March 28, 1998.[531] Clara M. Allwein died several years earlier. They are buried together at Holy Cross Cemetery (HC) in Lebanon, Pennsylvania.

---

[529] *Fourteenth Census of the United States* (1920), *Inhabitants of Lebanon Ward 7, Lebanon County, Pennsylvania*, E.D. No. 176, page 283A; *Fifteenth Census of the United States* (1930), *Inhabitants of Lebanon, Lebanon County, Pennsylvania*, E.D. No. 38-23, page 207A; *Sixteenth Census of the United States* (1940), *Inhabitants of Lebanon, Lebanon County, Pennsylvania*, E.D. No. 38-29, page 495A.

[530] Obituary for Frederick J. Allwein, *Lebanon Daily News*, Lebanon, Pennsylvania, July 9, 2003.

[531] Obituary for Frederick G. Allwein, *Lebanon Daily News*, Lebanon, Pennsylvania, March 30, 1998. The obituary states that he died on Saturday, March 28th. The Social Security Death Index gives March 26th, which may be an error.

Exhibit 11.133 Reproduction of photograph of Fred Allwein in 1922

Exhibit 11.134 Reproduction of photograph of Clara and Freddie Allwein in 1937

Exhibit 11.135 Gravestone for Frederick George and Clara Marie
Allwein—Holy Cross Cemetery, Lebanon, Pennsylvania

Catherine "Caty" Elizabeth Allwein Cincel (1906-1991) Lebanon, Pennsylvania

Catherine "Caty" Elizabeth Allwein (F06-0405-1604-09), daughter
of Francis A. and Amanda (Beamesderfer) Allwein, was born
December 3, 1906 in Lebanon. The line of descent connecting
Catherine Elizabeth Allwein to Johannes Jacob and Catharina
Allwein, the progenitors of the Allwein family in colonial
Pennsylvania, is as follows:

Generation 1: Johannes Jacob and Catharina Allwein—Berks County, Pa.
Generation 2: Conrad and Catharine (Weibel) Allwein—Dauphin County, Pa.
Generation 3: Philip and Elizabeth (Arentz) Allwein—Lebanon County, Pa.
Generation 4: Henry A. and Catharine (Lenich) Allwein—Lebanon County, Pa.
Generation 5: Francis Aloysius and Amanda (Beamesderfer)Allwein—Lebanon
    County, Pa.
Generation 6: Catherine Elizabeth Allwein and Frank L. Cincel—Lebanon
    County, Pa.

There were three Allwein sisters—Catherine Elizabeth, Josephine Harriet and Jeannette Mary (see below)—who were the youngest surviving children of Francis and Amanda Allwein. They were very close and all enjoyed many of the same activities. Patti Keefer Billow (granddaughter of Jeannette Allwein Keefer) contributed the following story about them:

> Catherine (Caty), Josephine (Jo), and Jeannette (Net) were all very active in different groups within St. Mary's Church and in the Lebanon Flower Club. As children, we used to go with them to the Lebanon Flower Shows and a few times we even got to enter a flower we grew or a terrarium we created. Since the three of them lived so close together, they spent a lot of time with each other at these and other social functions.

> In 1960 they also started a business together called The Costume Shop where they rented costumes for Halloween and other functions. They operated out of the basement of 909 Maple Street for ten years and made many of the costumes themselves. As a child, I remember that we had the best costumes! One year I was half of an elephant and another year I was a Lebanon Bologna. I'm not sure where I carried my candy.

> In 1970, Caty and Jo retired from the business and my Aunt Joan O'Hara took over the business with my grandmother. They moved the shop down the street to my Aunt's garage at 831 Maple Street. They sold the shop to another owner in 1977.

Catherine Elizabeth Allwein married Frank L. Cincel, son of Louis and Catherine (Yurschik) Cincel, at St. Mary's Catholic Church in Lebanon on June 22, 1935. The marriage ceremony was performed by Rev. John J. Lawley. Frank Cincel was born in Passaic, New Jersey and grew up in Bethlehem, Pennsylvania. He attended Temple University and received professional training in pharmacy there. They settled initially in Bethlehem, but eventually relocated to Lebanon. He was employed as a pharmacist in Lebanon for more than 50 years, as indicated by the city directories for Lebanon. According to a newspaper story in the *Lebanon Daily News*, he initially managed the Lebanon store of the Whelan Drug

Exhibit 11.136 Reproduction of a photograph of the Allwein
sisters—Catherine, Jeannette and Josephine—circa mid-1930s
(contributed by Patti Keefer Billow)

Company, and joined Saylor's Pharmacy in 1937. He retired in 1972, after which time he worked part time for Loehle's Pharmacy in Lebanon.[532]

According to her obituary, Catherine E. Cincel was a homemaker, and as noted above, was active in St. Mary's Church and other community activities. Catherine Elizabeth Allwein and Frank L. Cincel gave life to two daughters, as follows:

Mary Jo Cincel, b. December 31, 1936, m. (1) (September 12, 1959) Joseph McFerren Steiner (b. March 4, 1938, d. January 15, 1992, (2) (February 1998) Leo I. Sprankle (b. July 9, 1936)
Catherine Frances Cincel, b. June 12, 1941, d. June 28, 2007, unmarried

Catherine Elizabeth Allwein Cincel died October 11, 1991.[533] Frank L. Cincel died on March 1, 1996. Both are buried in Holy Cross Cemetery (HC) in Lebanon, Pennsylvania.

Josephine Harriet Allwein Bunch (1910-2004)
Lebanon, Pennsylvania

Josephine "Jo" Harriet Allwein (F06-0405-1604-10), daughter of Francis A. and Amanda (Beamesderfer) Allwein, was born March 22, 1910 in Lebanon. The line of descent connecting Josephine Harriet Allwein to Johannes Jacob and Catharina Allwein, the progenitors of the Allwein family in colonial Pennsylvania, is as follows:

Generation 1: Johannes Jacob and Catharina Allwein—Berks County, Pa.
Generation 2: Conrad and Catharine (Weibel) Allwein—Dauphin County, Pa.
Generation 3: Philip and Elizabeth (Arentz) Allwein—Lebanon County, Pa.
Generation 4: Henry A. and Catharine (Lenich) Allwein—Lebanon County, Pa.
Generation 5: Francis Aloysius and Amanda (Beamesderfer)Allwein—Lebanon County, Pa.
Generation 6: Josephine Harriet Allwein and Francis James Bunch, Sr.—Lebanon County, Pa.

---

[532] Story about Frank Cincel from the *Lebanon Daily News*, Lebanon, Pennsylvania, Wednesday, May 25, 1988 on the occasion of his selection as Knight of the Year by the Lebanon Council of the Knights of Columbus.
[533] Obituary for Catherine E. Cincel from the *Lebanon Daily News*, Lebanon, Pennsylvania, Friday, October 11, 1991.

Exhibit 11.137 Reproduction of a photograph of the Cincel family, 1941 (contributed by Patti Keefer Billow)

Exhibit 11.138 Gravestone for Catherine Elizabeth Allwein and Frank L. Cincel—Holy Cross Cemetery, Lebanon, Pennsylvania

Josephine Harriet Allwein attended St. Agnes Hospital in Philadelphia and became a registered nurse.[534] At the time of the 1940 Federal Census, she was living with her parents in Lebanon, working as a "registered nurse."[535] She worked for Dr. John F. Loehle in Lebanon.

Josephine Harriet Allwein married Francis James Bunch, Sr., son of Charles A. Bunch and Mary Soblesky, on November 22, 1944, and they settled in Lebanon. They were married by Rev. John J. Lawley at St. Mary's Catholic Church. Francis James Bunch was a Seaman 2nd class in the United States Navy at the time. He enlisted in the Navy during World War II from December 27, 1943 to December 23, 1945. He was stationed at Okinawa at the end of the war. After the War, Francis served as a Pennsylvania State Police Officer for 23 years. Following his retirement from the State Police, he worked for the Alcoa Company in Lebanon.

Josephine Harriet Allwein and Francis James Bunch, Sr. had the following children:

Mary Elizabeth Bunch, b. November 1, 1945, m. Joseph T. Hinks, Jr. (b. February 8, 1940)

Francis James Bunch, Jr., b. December 15, 1946, m. (1) (June 5, 1971) Donna Rae Langdon (b. November 23, 1948), (2) Cathy Boger (b. April 16, 1949)

Thomas Charles Bunch, b. November 22, 1947, m. (1) (September 19, 1970) Cheryl Elizabeth Luxford, (2) (April 29, 1989) Nancy Ellen Springborn (nee Schott) (b. August 24, 1954), (3) Elizabeth M. Hockenberry (b. August 9, 1953)

Josephine Allwein Bunch was a member of St. Mary's Church and the Parish Council of Catholic Women, Verbena and Flower Clubs, Senior Center and Lebanon's Good Samaritan Hospital

---

[534] *Fifteenth Census of the United States* (1930), *Inhabitants of Philadelphia, Philadelphia County, Pennsylvania*, E.D. No. 51-85, page 159A.

[535] *Sixteenth Census of the United States* (1940), *Inhabitants of Lebanon, Lebanon County, Pennsylvania*, E.D. 38-30, page 519A.

Exhibit 11.139 Reproduction of photograph of Josephine Allwein, circa 1930 (contributed by Patti Keefer Billow)

Exhibit 11.140 Reproduction of photograph of Francis and
Josephine Bunch, with Joel Keefer, circa 1949 (contributed by
Patti Keefer Billow)

Exhibit 11.141 Reproduction of a photograph of the Allwein sisters—Catherine Cincel, Jeannette Keefer, and Josephine Bunch, circa mid-1960s (contributed by Patti Keefer Billow)

Auxiliary. After her father died in 1953, Josephine Bunch and her family lived at the family homestead at 909 Maple Street, where she lived until her later years.

Josephine Harriet Allwein died on December 5, 2004 at the age of 94.[536] Her husband, Francis James Bunch, Sr., died several years earlier on March 18, 1979. She and her husband are buried at Holy Cross Cemetery (HC) in Lebanon, Pennsylvania.

---

[536] Obituary for Josephine Allwein Bunch, *Lebanon Daily News*, Lebanon, Pennsylvania, Tuesday, December 7, 2004.

Exhibit 11.142 Gravestone for Josephine H. Allwein and Francis J. Bunch—Holy Cross Cemetery, Lebanon, Pennsylvania

Jeannette Mary Allwein Keefer (1911-2009)
Lebanon, Pennsylvania

Jeannette "Net" Mary Allwein (F06-0405-1604-11), youngest daughter of Francis A. and Amanda (Beamesderfer) Allwein, was born March 17, 1911 in Lebanon. The line of descent connecting Jeannette Mary Allwein to Johannes Jacob and Catharina Allwein, the progenitors of the Allwein family in colonial Pennsylvania, is as follows:

Generation 1: Johannes Jacob and Catharina Allwein—Berks County, Pa.
Generation 2: Conrad and Catharine (Weibel) Allwein—Dauphin County, Pa.
Generation 3: Philip and Elizabeth (Arentz) Allwein—Lebanon County, Pa.
Generation 4: Henry A. and Catharine (Lenich) Allwein—Lebanon County, Pa.
Generation 5: Francis Aloysius and Amanda (Beamesderfer)Allwein—Lebanon County, Pa.
Generation 6: Jeannette Mary Allwein and Donald D. Keefer—Lebanon County, Pa.

Jeannette Mary Allwein married Donald Daniel Keefer, son of Milton and Carrie (Yiengst) Keefer, on November 17, 1934 at Quarryville, Pennsylvania by Samuel G. Gall, justice of the peace. They are listed in Lebanon city directories beginning in 1936 through the early 1940s, and are listed in the 1940 Federal Census living at 431 Canal Street in Lebanon.[537]

---

[537] *Sixteenth Census of the United States* (1940), *Inhabitants of Lebanon, Lebanon County, Pennsylvania*, E.D. 38-35, page 589A.

Exhibit 11.143 Jeannette and Donald Keefer around the time of their marriage in 1934 (contributed by Patti Keefer Billow)

Jeannette Mary Allwein and Donald D. Keefer had three children, as follows:

Robert Adrian Keefer, b. May 13, 1935, m. (May 12, 1956) Virginia
    Marie Heckman (b. December 25, 1935, d. January 21, 2006)
Joan Elizabeth Keefer, b. May 20, 1942, m. (May 16, 1964) James
    Patrick O'Hara (b. August 26, 1921, d. September 17, 1996)
Joel David Keefer, b. July 14, 1949, m. (September 4, 1977) Jolene
    Schaefer (b. November 7, 1946)

Donald Keefer worked in the cold bolt department of Bethlehem Steel Company in Lebanon. The Keefers lived with her parents Francis and Amanda Allwein at 909 Maple Street for awhile, prior to purchasing a home at 810 Water Street in the late 1940s, where they lived until their later years.

Jeannette M. (Allwein) Keefer died May 29, 2009. Donald D. Keefer died several years earlier on March 15, 1985 (the date on the gravestone below is incorrect). They are buried at the Holy Cross Cemetery (HC) in Lebanon, Pennsylvania.[538]

The descendants of Francis and Amanda Allwein have been holding family reunions regularly for at least 60 years. A story in the *Lebanon Daily News*, which appeared on June 16, 1952 recorded an early observance of such a reunion.[539] The story in the *News* indicated that the reunion was held at Coleman Memorial Park and that ninety family members were in attendance. The author attended the reunion of this branch of the family in September 2012.

---

[538] Obituary for Jeannette M. Keefer from the *Lebanon Daily News*, Lebanon, Pennsylvania, May 31, 2009.
[539] "Ninety Descendants Attend Reunion of F.A. Allwein Family," *Lebanon Daily News,* Lebanon, Pennsylvania, June 16, 1952.

Exhibit 11.144 Jeannette and Donald Keefer, circa 1980s
(contributed by Patti Keefer Billow)

Exhibit 11.145 Gravestone for Jeannette and Donald D. Keefer—Holy Cross Cemetery, Lebanon, Pennsylvania

Exhibit 11.146 Reproduction of a photograph of Allwein brothers and sisters at Woods Creek Park, 1959—front row (left to right) Bernard, Catherine, Jeannette, Josephine and Frederick; standing (left to right) Clement, Carroll, Tom and Wayne (contributed by Patti Keefer Billow)

Alice Rebecca Allwein Lenich (1869-1950)
Lebanon, Pennsylvania

Alice Rebecca Allwein (F05-0405-1605), daughter of Henry and Catharine (Lenich) Allwein, was born February 19, 1869 in Lebanon. The line of descent connecting Alice Rebecca Allwein to Johannes Jacob and Catharina Allwein, the progenitors of the Allwein family in colonial Pennsylvania, is as follows:

Generation 1: Johannes Jacob and Catharina Allwein—Berks County, Pa.
Generation 2: Conrad and Catharine (Weibel) Allwein—Dauphin County, Pa.
Generation 3: Philip and Elizabeth (Arentz) Allwein—Lebanon County, Pa.
Generation 4: Henry A. and Catharine (Lenich) Allwein—Lebanon County, Pa.
Generation 5: Alice Rebecca Allwein and William Lenich—Lebanon County, Pa.

Alice Rebecca Allwein married William E. Lenich, son of John H. Lenich and wife, at St. Mary's Catholic Church in Lebanon on December 27, 1894. The wedding ceremony was conducted by Rev. A. Christ. They settled in Lebanon, where they lived at 416 North Ninth Street for most of their adult lives.[540] He was a printer. Two children are recorded in Census records:

Christine Lenich, b. November 15, 1897, d. May 14, 1954 (HC), m. (May 17, 1921) Lloyd R. Wolf (b. December 1897, d. June 15, 1934)[541]

---

[540] *Twelfth Census of the United States* (1900), *Inhabitants of Lebanon Ward 5, Lebanon County, Pennsylvania*, E.D. No. 129, page 287A; *Thirteenth Census of the United States* (1910), *Inhabitants of Ward 5 Lebanon, Lebanon County, Pennsylvania*, E.D. No. 155, page 210B; *Fourteenth Census of the United States* (1920), *Inhabitants of Ward 5 Lebanon, Lebanon County, Pennsylvania*, E.D. No. 174, page 242B; *Fifteenth Census of the United States* (1930) *Inhabitants of Lebanon, Lebanon County, Pennsylvania*, E.D. No. 38-22, page 191B; *Sixteenth Census of the United States* (1940), *Inhabitants of Lebanon, Lebanon County, Pennsylvania*, E.D. 38-27, page 444A.
[541] See obituary/funeral notices for Christine Lenich Wolf in *Lebanon Daily News*, Lebanon, Pennsylvania, Saturday Evening, May 15, 1954. Obituary for Lloyd R. Wolf, *Lebanon Daily News*, Lebanon, Pennsylvania, Tuesday Evening, June 19, 1934. See also the death records of the Pennsylvania Department of Health: http://www.health.state.pa.us.

Robert Edward Lenich, b. February 13, 1900, d. September 20, 1962 (HC), m. unknown[542]

These children were living in their parents' household in the 1900-1920 Federal Censuses. In 1920 their occupations are both listed as "bookkeeper," Christine working in the Post Office, and Robert in the office of the steel mill.

Robert Lenich's WWI draft registration indicates he was working as a clerk for the Bethlehem Steel Company, and living with his parents at 416 North Ninth Street in Lebanon on November 12, 1911.[543] He remained in his parents' household until their deaths, as indicated by the 1930 and 1940 Federal Census enumerations.[544] In those listings, his occupation is given as "core maker in a foundry" in 1930 and 1940. His obituary mentions a son, Robert Lee Lenich, although as of this writing, we do not have any information on whether and to whom he was married.

Christine Lenich Wolf's obituary states that she was widely known in Lebanon County in the activities of the Democratic Party. She had been employed in the state of Pennsylvania Auditor's office and at the Bureau of the Census in Washington D.C. The 1940 Federal Census lists her in Washington D.C. working as a file clerk at the Census Bureau.[545]

---

[542] See obituary/funeral notices for Robert Lenich in *Lebanon Daily News*, Lebanon, Pennsylvania, Friday, September 21, 1962, and Tuesday, September 25, 1962.

[543] WWI Draft Registration Cards, 1917-1918. Ancestry.com. See also obituary in the *Lebanon Daily News*, Lebanon, Pennsylvania, Friday Evening, September 21, 1962.

[544] *Fifteenth Census of the United States* (1930) *Inhabitants of Lebanon, Lebanon County, Pennsylvania*, E.D. No. 38-22, page 191B; *Sixteenth Census of the United States* (1940), *Inhabitants of Lebanon, Lebanon County, Pennsylvania*, E.D. No. 38-27, page 444A.

[545] *Sixteenth Census of the United States* (1940), *Washington, District of Columbia*, E.D. No. 1-339, page 587A.

Exhibit 11.147 Reproduction of a photograph of Christine Lenich Wolf, Lebanon, Pennsylvania, circa 1917 (contributed by Patti Keefer Billow)

William Lenich died on March 6, 1941; Alice Rebecca (Allwein) Lenich died on January 7, 1950.[546] They are buried, along side their children, at Holy Cross Cemetery (HC) at Lebanon, Pennsylvania.

Andrew Philip Allwein (1873-1916)
Lebanon and Philadelphia, Pennsylvania

Andrew Philip Allwein (M05-0405-1607), the second son of Henry and Catharine (Lenich) Allwein, was born January 21, 1873 in Lebanon, Pennsylvania. The line of descent connecting Andrew Philip Allwein to Johannes Jacob and Catharina Allwein, the progenitors of the Allwein family in colonial Pennsylvania, is as follows:

Generation 1: Johannes Jacob and Catharina Allwein—Berks County, Pa.
Generation 2: Conrad and Catharine (Weibel) Allwein—Dauphin County, Pa.
Generation 3: Philip and Elizabeth (Arentz) Allwein—Lebanon County, Pa.
Generation 4: Henry A. and Catharine (Lenich) Allwein—Lebanon County, Pa.
Generation 5: Andrew Philip and Catharine A. (Dunn) Allwein—Philadelphia
    County, Pa.

The Jerome Allwein *Genealogy* notes that he "attended the parochial school in Lebanon and after he left school he clerked in a grocery store for a short time after which he learned pattern making. Soon after he was done serving his apprenticeship he went to Philadelphia to work at his trade."[547] Andrew P. Allwein married Catharine A. Dunn, daughter of William J. Dunn, in Philadelphia on April 17, 1901. There were no children born to this union.

---

[546] The gravestone indicates she died in1949, but all other sources indicate it was 1950, including the Pennsylvania Health Department death records. See also obituary for Alice Allwein Lenich in the *Lebanon Daily News*, Lebanon, Pennsylvania, January 7 and January 10, 1950. The obituary and funeral notice for William E. Lenich appeared in the *Lebanon Daily News*, Lebanon, Pennsylvania, March 7 and March 10, 1941.

[547] Jerome Allwein, *Genealogy of the Allwein-Arnold Families*, 1902, page 86.

Exhibit 11.148 Gravestone for Alice Rebecca and William Lenich—Holy Cross Cemetery, Lebanon, Pennsylvania

In the 1895-96 Polk's City Directory for Lebanon, Andrew P. Allwein is listed living at 833 Guilford Street in Lebanon.[548] Consistent with other records, his occupation given there is "patternmaker."

Philadelphia city directories for the period 1895 to 1915 list Andrew P. Allwein as "pattern maker" living in the city of Philadelphia.[549] The 1910 Federal Census lists Andrew P. Allwein and wife "Catherine A. Allwein," living on 51st Street in Philadelphia, where his occupation is given as "pattern maker in woodworking industry."[550] We discuss more about Andrew Philip Allwein in chapter 13, where we cover Allwein families living in Philadelphia.

Andrew P. Allwein died at a relatively young age, on May 26, 1916, of acute myocarditis.[551] He is buried with his parents and several of his sisters on the family plot in St. Mary's Catholic Cemetery (SM) in Lebanon. As of this writing we do not know the whereabouts of his wife Catherine A. (Dunn) Allwein after this time.

John Adam Allwein (1839-1918)
Lebanon and Lancaster Counties

John Adam Allwein (M04-0405-17), son of Philip and Elizabeth (Arentz) Allwein, was born July 28, 1839 on his parents' farm in Bethel Township, Lebanon County, Pennsylvania, and died December 28, 1918 in Lebanon, Pennsylvania. He was baptized

---

[548] Polk's 1895-96 City Directory, Lebanon, Pennsylvania. Ancestry.com.
[549] *Gopsill's Philadelphia City Directory for 1895*, Philadelphia: James Gopsill's Sons; *Gopsill's Philadelphia City Directory for 1900*, Philadelphia: James Gopsill's Sons; *Gopsill's Philadelphia City Directory for 1905*, Philadelphia: James Gopsill's Sons; *Boyd's City Directory of Philadelphia 1910*, Philadelphia: C.E. Howe Company; and *Boyd's City Directory of Philadelphia 1915*, Philadelphia: C.E. Howe Company.
[550] *Thirteenth Census of the United States* (1910), *Inhabitants of Philadelphia Ward 44, Philadelphia County, Pennsylvania*, E.D. No. 11-42, page 20A.
[551] Obituary and Death Notice, *Lebanon Daily News*, Lebanon, Pennsylvania, May 27, 1916 and May 29, 1916.

Exhibit 11.149 Gravestone for Andrew P. Allwein—St. Mary's Cemetery, Lebanon, Pennsylvania

into the Roman Catholic faith September 29, 1839 at St. Mary's Assumption Church in Lebanon.[552] He was the youngest of Philip and Elizabeth Allwein's sons to survive to adulthood. He went by "Adam" and is listed in most record sources under this name. The line of descent connecting Adam Allwein to Johannes Jacob and Catharina Allwein, the progenitors of the Allwein family in colonial Pennsylvania, is as follows:

Generation 1: Johannes Jacob and Catharina Allwein—Berks County, Pa.
Generation 2: Conrad and Catharine (Weibel) Allwein—Dauphin County, Pa.
Generation 3: Philip and Elizabeth (Arentz) Allwein—Lebanon County, Pa.
Generation 4: Adam and Margaret (Foster) Allwein—Lebanon and Lancaster Counties, Pa.

We covered most of what we know about John Adam Allwein's early life in Chapter 7 of *Familie Allwein* (pages 437 to 446), and there is no need to repeat that here. Also we briefly mention Adam Allwein later (Chapter 14 of *Familie Allwein*, volume 2), where we cover the families in Lancaster and Dauphin Counties that descended from him. In this section we cover his marriage and family, as well as the location of his carpentry shops in Lebanon's Sixth Ward.

Adam Allwein married Margaret Foster (b. May 4, 1838), in Lebanon on May 22, 1866 at St. Mary's Catholic Church. She was the daughter of James and Catherine Foster of the Lebanon/ Lancaster area.[553] Following their marriage, Adam and Margaret Allwein settled in Lebanon and raised a family there. Federal Census reports for 1870 and 1880 list them in the Borough of

---

[552] Unless otherwise noted, most of the factual information provided in this section was obtained from the Civil War pension records for John Adam Allwein deposited at the National Archives and Records Administration (NARA), Washington D.C.

[553] *Seventh Census of the United States* (1850), *Inhabitants of South Lebanon Township, Lebanon County, Pennsylvania,* page 104; *Eighth Census of the United States* (1860), *Inhabitants of Elizabeth Township, Lancaster County, Pennsylvania,* page 376.

Lebanon.[554] Adam's mother was living with them at the time of the 1880 Census.

Margaret and Adam Allwein gave life to eight children, five of whom survived to adulthood, as follows:[555]

Caroline Isabella Allwein (F05-0405-1701), b. April 13, 1867, d. January 5, 1936 (SM), unmarried

George Franklin Allwein (M05-0405-1703), b. October 29, 1870, d. December 11, 1901 (SM), m. (June 15, 1899) Alice B. Hummel (b. January 1873, d. unknown) [remarried to William T. Best in 1910]

Emma Gertrude "Gertie" Allwein (F05-0405-1704), b. December 28, 1872, d. February 2, 1952 (SM), unmarried

Mary Deborah Allwein (F05-0404-1705), b. January 27, 1874, d. January 25, 1946 (LC), m. (September 22, 1904) Jacob Hill Byrne (b. October 24, 1874, d. June 27, 1940)

Robert Adam Allwein (M05-0405-1707), b. November 14, 1878, d. October 15, 1950 (SA), m. (February 10, 1903) Mary Elizabeth Steinwandel (b. September 21, 1881, d. January 25, 1956)

We cover the family histories of these children and their descendants later (Chapter 14), where we discuss families living in Dauphin and Lancaster Counties.

Throughout his life Adam Allwein was a "builder and contractor," focusing on the construction of residential and

---

[554] *Ninth Census of the United States* (1870), *Inhabitants of Lebanon Borough, Lebanon County, Pennsylvania*, page 335; *Tenth Census of the United States* (1880), *Inhabitants of Lebanon Borough, Lebanon County, Pennsylvania*, page 338C.

[555] Information on Adam and Margaret's children came from Adam Allwein's pension file on record at the National Archives and Records Administration, Washington, D.C., supplemented with information from the Jerome Allwein *Genealogy*. The three children who died in childhood are listed in volume 1 of *Familie Allwein* (page 442).

commercial buildings. The Jerome Allwein *Genealogy* indicated that in Lebanon he ultimately located his residence and shop on Church Street near Tenth.[556] This is confirmed by the 1875 *County Atlas of Lebanon, Pennsylvania*, which lists his residence and carpentry shop at 1020 Church Street (see Exhibit 11.11 above).[557]

By 1888, he had moved to a location a few blocks to the west and north. In Exhibit 11.150 is shown an extract of an 1888 map of the 6th Ward of Lebanon, showing the location of Adam Allwein's residence and carpentry shops—at the corner of North 13th and Brandywine Streets, just two blocks north of Church Street. At the time of the 1888 *Atlas Map*, Adam Allwein was in the construction business with Mr. Bowman. Soon thereafter, around 1895, after all of their children had grown, Adam and Margaret (Foster) Allwein moved to Lancaster (see Chapter 14).[558]

Although they relocated to Lancaster at the turn of the century, Adam and Margaret (Foster) Allwein maintained close ties to the Lebanon community. Both Adam and Margaret Allwein are buried at St. Mary's Catholic Cemetery in the Borough of Lebanon, Pennsylvania. Both died in 1918, Margaret on January 23 and Adam on December 28. The three children who died in childhood—James Foster Allwein (b. 1868, d. 1875), Margaret Sarah Allwein (b. 1876, d. 1886), and James Philip Allwein (b. 1881, d. 1882)—are buried there as well. In addition, three of their children who lived to adulthood—Caroline "Carrie" Isabella (b. 1867, d. 1936), George Franklin (b. 1870, d. 1901), and Emma Gertrude "Gertie" (b. 1872, d. 1952)—are also buried at St. Mary's Cemetery in Lebanon (see Chapter 14).

---

[556] Jerome Allwein, *Genealogy of the Allwein-Arnold Families*, Philadelphia, 1902, page 38.
[557] F.W. Beers, *County Atlas of Lebanon Pennsylvania From Recent and Actual Surveys and Records*, Reading & Philadelphia: F.A. Davis, 1875.
[558] Jerome Al¹wein, *Genealogy of the Allwein-Arnold Families*, Philadelphia, 1902, page 38.

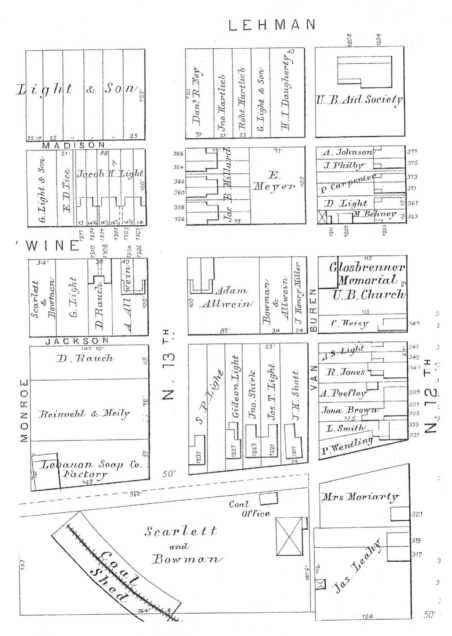

Exhibit 11.150 Extract of an 1888 map of the 6th Ward of Lebanon, Pennsylvania showing the location of Adam Allwein's residence and carpentry shops

Catharine Anna Allwein Thompson (1841-1864)
Lebanon, Pennsylvania

Catharine Anna Allwein (F04-0405-18), daughter of Philip and Elizabeth (Arentz) Allwein, was born July 7, 1841 on her parents' farm in Bethel Township of Lebanon County, Pennsylvania. Catharine (Kate) was about fourteen years old when her father died, and she lived with her mother on the family farm until her marriage to Daniel Thompson. She and Daniel Thompson were married shortly thereafter and they had two daughters. Catharine Allwein Thompson died on March 20, 1864 during child birth. The baby died a few weeks later. Both are buried in St. Mary's Cemetery, Lebanon. Her namesake, Catharine Thompson (b. June 10, 1862, d. June 4, 1944), survived childhood but never married. I cover this family fully in volume 1 of *Familie Allwein*, and do not discuss them further here.

Isabella Allwein Goulden (1847-1927)
Pittsburgh, Pennsylvania and New York City

Isabella Allwein (F04-0405-21), youngest daughter of Philip and Elizabeth (Arentz) Allwein, was born August 31, 1849 on her parents' farm in Bethel Township of Lebanon County, Pennsylvania. Isabella Allwein married Joseph A. Goulden on December 26, 1867 at St. Mary's Church in Lebanon. He was the eldest son of William and Mary (Wivell) Goulden of Taneytown, Carroll County, Maryland. Joseph Goulden was a veteran of the Civil War and eventually served several terms as a member of the U.S. Congress from New York. Prior to his service as a congressman, he worked for several years in the newspaper business in Pittsburgh, Pennsylvania. Joseph Goulden collapsed and died at the Broad Street Station of the Pennsylvania Railroad in Philadelphia, Pennsylvania, on May 3, 1915. She died some years later, in 1927, and is buried with her husband in St. Joseph Roman Catholic Church Cemetery, Taneytown, Carroll County, Maryland. I cover this family in detail in volume 1 of *Familie Allwein*, and do not discuss them further here.

Samuel Allwine (1813-1887)
Swatara Township, Lebanon County

Samuel Allwine (M04-0404-05), son of John and Elizabeth (Felix) Allwine, was born March 18, 1813 on his parents' farm in Dauphin County, Pennsylvania (see Chapter 14, this volume). The name on the tombstone reads SAMUEL ALWINE—most other records suggest he used ALLWINE, and some of his children used ALLWEIN. His birth and baptism are recorded in the baptismal records kept by the St. Mary's priests from Lancaster who visited the Catholic congregation in Elizabethtown, where his parents worshiped and observed the holy sacraments.[559]

The line of descent connecting Samuel Allwine to Johannes Jacob and Catharina Allwein, the progenitors of the Allwein family in colonial Pennsylvania, is as follows:

Generation 1: Johannes Jacob and Catharina Allwein—Berks County, Pa.
Generation 2: Conrad and Catharine (Weibel) Allwein—Dauphin County, Pa.
Generation 3: John and Elizabeth (Felix) Allwine—Dauphin County, Pa.
Generation 4: Samuel and Elizabeth (Kreiser) Allwine—Lebanon County, Pa.

---

[559] The biographical information presented here comes largely from chapter 6 of *Familie Allwein*, Volume 1, pages 276-280, obtained from the Lancaster St. Mary's parish records. There is some disagreement concerning his date of birth. The Jonestown Lutheran Church records [*Zion Evangelical Lutheran Church, Parish Register* (Book II)] indicate he was "born May 1, 1811 and died February 20, 1887." Further, while the date of birth on his tombstone inscription in the Jonestown Lutheran Cemetery is essentially unreadable (see below), I can understand how a visual inspection of the gravestone might support either claim. My preference is to accept the information provided by the St. Mary's priests because (a) the original parish documents that exist on microfilm in the Diocese of Harrisburg are highly readable, and (b) it occurs in a chronological series of baptismal events, and there is no "Samuel Allwine" anywhere near the date of May 1, 1811. Moreover, his sister Elizabeth Allwine was born November 3, 1811 (see *Familie Allwein*, volume 1, page 272) which renders the May 1, 1811 date a virtual impossibility. Anyone wishing to see copies of the original documents should contact the author.

Samuel Allwine was the youngest of John and Elizabeth Allwine's children and he was just a few years old when his mother died. His father remarried within a few years, and as a result, Samuel had many younger siblings. Interestingly, although his name is listed in Jerome Allwein's *Genealogy of the Allwein-Arnold Families,* no information is given about him in that source.[560] I rely on the information presented in *Familie Allwein* Volume 1 to develop the history of this family, in addition to newer findings. I use the ALLWINE spelling for this family, unless it is clear that they chose another form (e.g., some used ALLWEIN).

Although raised in Dauphin County, in his early adulthood Samuel Allwine moved north and east into Swatara Township in the environs of Jonestown, Pennsylvania, an area north of Lebanon in Lebanon County. From this time, he appears to have been a lifelong resident of the northern townships of Lebanon County, as he is listed in Union or Swatara Townships in the area of Jonestown, Pennsylvania in the Federal Censuses of 1850 through 1880.[561] He and some of his descendants also appear in the records of the Jonestown Lutheran Church in Jonestown, Pennsylvania.[562] The latter records report that he married Elizabeth Kreiser (b. January 8, 1807, d. November 23, 1888) sometime prior to 1840 and that they had several children. This source also indicates that Samuel Allwine

---

[560] Jerome Allwein, *Genealogy of the Allwein-Arnold Families,* Philadelphia, Pa., 1902, page 10.

[561] *Sixth Census of the United States* (1840), *Inhabitants of Swatara Township, Lebanon County, Pennsylvania,* page 27; *Seventh Census of the United States* (1850), *Inhabitants of Swatara Township, Lebanon County, Pennsylvania,* page 189; *Eighth Census of the United States* (1860), *Inhabitants of Union Township, Lebanon County, Pennsylvania,* page 798; *Ninth Census of the United States* (1870), *Inhabitants of Swatara Township, Lebanon County, Pennsylvania,* page 407; *Tenth Census of the United States* (1880), *Inhabitants of Swatara Township, Lebanon County, Pennsylvania,* page 404.

[562] *Zion Evangelical Lutheran Church, Parish Register.* Book II. Jonestown, Lebanon County, Pennsylvania. This source is available at the Lebanon County Historical Society, 924 Cumberland Street, Lebanon, Pennsylvania 17042.

died on February 20, 1887 and is buried in the Zion Lutheran Cemetery in Jonestown, along with Elizabeth, who died a few years later on November 23, 1888.

By all accounts, Samuel and Elizabeth (Kreiser) Allwine had at least six children. The following is the list of children given in volume 1 of *Familie Allwein* for Samuel and Elizabeth Allwine, updated on the basis of a more detailed examination of census materials, church records and newspaper death notices. These children were given as follows:[563]

Moses Allwine (M05-0404-0501), b. October 5, 1835, d. February 10, 1858, unmarried

Lydi Ann (Lydian or Lydia) Allwine (F05-0404-0502), b. January 29, 1839, d. April 4, 1878 (ZJ), m. (1859) William Bedger (b. November 18, 1837, d. September 1, 1902)

Lucetta Allwine (F05-0404-0503), b. October 24, 1840, d. September 30, 1873, m. Nathaniel Hartline (b. est. 1838, d. May 30, 1894) [remarried Amanda Hoch (b. December 4, 1840, d. August 22, 1902)]

Peter Allwein (M05-0404-0504) b. June 24, 1843, d. July 18, 1908 (KR), m. Elizabeth Reifine (b. est. 1849, d. May 19, 1902)

---

[563] The information on Samuel and Elizabeth (Kreiser's) Allwine's children has been updated to reflect what is available in more current sources and supercedes what was provided in Volume 1 of *Familie Allwein*. To date, we have found no birth records for Samuel Allwine's children, so it is necessary to rely on other sources. The information given for Moses Allwine is from a death notice appearing in the *Lebanon Courier*, February 12, 1885. Information for Peter Allwine is from an obituary appearing in the *Lebanon Daily News*, Lebanon, Pennsylvania, Monday Evening, July 20, 1908. In addition, some information on Lydi Ann "Lydian" (Allwine) Bedger, Lucetta (Allwine) Hartlein, Jeremiah Allwine, and John Henry Allwine is provided by the *Zion Evangelical Lutheran Church, Parish Register.* Book II, Jonestown, Lebanon County, Pennsylvania. These resources are available at the Lebanon County Historical Society, 924 Cumberland Street, Lebanon, Pennsylvania 17042..

Jeremiah Allwine (M05-0404-0505), b. March 26, 1846, d. September 27, 1862, unmarried

John Henry Allwine (M05-0404-0506), b. September 6, 1851, d. December 24, 1890 (ZJ), m. Elizabeth "Lizzie" Daub (b. June 1857, d. March 26, 1930) [remarried (May 13, 1893) Francis C. Gratz (b. August 1847, d. January 23, 1913) and (1904) Frank E. Ford (b. April 1973, d. July 29, 1948)]

Samuel Allwine and his wife Elizabeth (Kreiser) Allwine outlived all but one of their children—Peter Allwein. The oldest child of Samuel and Elizabeth Allwine—Moses Allwine died at a young age of 23 (b. 1835, d. 1858) and is therefore not present at the time of the 1860 Federal Census. Two of Samuel and Elizabeth's daughters and another son died at an early age as well. The daughters—Lydi Ann Allwine and Lucetta Allwine—died in their thirties. They had likely both married by the time of the 1860 Census, although I cannot find them listed there. Both appear with their husbands in the 1870 Federal Census—Lydi Ann married William Bedger and Lucetta Allwine married Nathaniel Hartline (or Hartlein).[564] Both Lydi Ann and Lucetta Allwine died before the 1880 Federal Census—Lucetta at the age of 33 and Lydi Ann at the age of 38—so there is no known record of them beyond what is reported here. I cannot locate Peter Allwein or Jeremiah Allwine in the 1860 Federal Census enumerations, although both appear to be living at that time. Jonestown Lutheran Church records indicate that Jeremiah Allwine died as a child in 1862.[565] Peter Allwein (he was the only one of this family that spelled the name ALLWEIN), who I discuss further below, is listed in the 1870, 1880, and 1900 Federal Censuses, and eventually established himself as a resident of Lebanon County.

---

[564] *Ninth Census of the United States* (1870), *Inhabitants of Swatara Township, Lebanon County, Pennsylvania*, pages 399 and 408.
[565] *Zion Evangelical Lutheran Church, Parish Register.* Book II. Jonestown, Lebanon County, Pennsylvania This source is available at the Lebanon County Historical Society, 924 Cumberland Street, Lebanon, Pennsylvania 17042.

Exhibit 11.151 Gravestone for Samuel and Elizabeth (nee Kreiser) Allwine—Jonestown Lutheran Cemetery, Jonestown, Pennsylvania

As I noted before, Samuel Allwine died on February 20, 1887 and is buried in the Zion Evangelical Lutheran Cemetery in Jonestown, along with Elizabeth (nee Kreiser) Allwein, who died a few years later on November 23, 1888, and several of their descendants.

In the "Zion's Evangelical Lutheran Cemetery" (aka the Jonestown Lutheran Cemetery) (ZJ) in Jonestown, Pennsylvania there is a monument for the Samuel Alwine family, "erected by Adam A. Bedger and wife" (see below). On one side of the monument is given the names of Samuel and his wife Elizabeth (nee Kreiser) along with their dates of birth and of death (see Exhibit 11.151). On the opposite side are the names and similarly birth and death information for Lydian Alwine Bedger and her brother John Henry Alwine. On the eastside there is a list of Bedger children who died in childhood—Lizzie, Thomas, Annie, Henry "children of William and Lydian Bedger."

In the remainder of this section, I report additional information concerning what is known about the descendants of Samuel and Elizabeth Allwine Specifically, I discuss the following fifth generation Allwein descendants: Lydi Ann Allwine (who married William Bedger), Lucetta Allwine (who married Nathaniel Hartline), Peter Allwein and John Henry Allwine.

Lydi Ann (Lydian) Allwine Bedger (1839-1878) Jonestown, Pennsylvania

Lydi Ann (or Lydian) Allwine (F05-0404-0502) was born January 29, 1839, the second child of Samuel and Elizabeth Kreiser Allwine. Her name also appears as "Lydia Ann" in some records, but more often than not it is given as "Lydi Ann" or "Lydian." She married William Bedger—they had several children, but sadly most of them died in childhood.[566]

---

[566] The records of the Zion Lutheran Church in Jonestown, Pennsylvania mention four children who died in childhood. Lydi Ann Allwine's gravestone in Zion Lutheran Cemetery in Jonestown, Pennsylvania gives January 29, 1832 as the date of birth. See *Zion Evangelical Lutheran Church, Parish Register.* Book II. Jonestown, Lebanon County, Pennsylvania

The line of descent connecting Lydi Ann Allwine and her descendants to Johannes Jacob and Catharina Allwein, the progenitors of the Allwein family in colonial Pennsylvania, is as follows:

Generation 1: Johannes Jacob and Catharina Allwein—Berks County, Pa.
Generation 2: Conrad and Catharine (Weibel) Allwein—Dauphin County, Pa.
Generation 3: John and Elizabeth (Felix) Allwine—Dauphin County, Pa.
Generation 4: Samuel and Elizabeth (Kreiser) Allwine—Lebanon County, Pa.
Generation 5: Lydia Ann Allwine and William Bedger—Lebanon County, Pa.

In the 1860 Federal Census Lydi Ann Allwine is listed in the household of her parents along with her son Adam Bedger. In the 1870 Federal Censuses, the William Bedger household is listed adjacent to the Samuel Allwine (recorded as ALLWEIN) household, with the following household composition from 1870:[567]

Allwein, Samuel (laborer, age 59)
Allwein, Elizabeth (spouse, age 49)
Allwein, Henry (son, age 19)

Bedger, William (laborer, age 31)
Bedger, Lydi Ann (spouse, age 28),
Bedger, Adam (son, age 9)
Bedger, Ellen (daughter, age 5)

In the 1880 Federal Census, the two grandchildren—Adam and Ellen Bedger (ages 22 and 17, respectively)—were living in the household of Samuel and Elizabeth Allwine. We have information indicating that Lydi Ann Bedger died April 4, 1878—we assume their father was unable to care for them. A story in the *Lebanon Daily News* in 1902 announcing the accidental death of William Bedger provides some insight into his whereabouts. According to this news story, about 1879 he migrated west, accumulated some wealth, and returned to Jonestown in 1902 with the intention of purchasing a small tract of land to start truck farming. His life, however, was cut short by a tragic accident in which he was

---

[567] *Ninth Census of the United States* (1870), *Inhabitants of Swatara Township, Lebanon County, Pennsylvania*, pages 408.

knocked from and crushed by a wagon he was operating containing a heavy load of shingles.[568] The 1900 Federal Census lists a William Bedger, who was born in Pennsylvania, listed in the enumeration of Portage Township (in the city of South Bend) of St. Joseph County, Indiana.[569] His occupation is given as teamster.

William and Lydi Ann Bedger gave birth to the following seven children, five of whom died in childhood (marked in *italics*):[570]

Adam A. Bedger, April 6, 1858, d. September 15, 1937 (US), m.
    Sallie A. Loser (b. January 19, 1854, d. September 2, 1924)
Emma Catherine Bedger, b. August 28, 1860, d. May 29, 1865 (ZJ)
Ellen Bedger, b. October 3, 1862, d. January 5, 1943 (US), m. Adam
    Eisenhower (b. March 25, 1861, November 20, 1924)
Elizabeth Bedger, b. October 13, 1864, d. September 3, 1865 (ZJ)
Thomas Bedger, b. April 11, 1866, d. January 23, 1867 (ZJ)
Anna Bedger, b. June 17, 1867, died young (ZJ)
John Henry Bedger, b. January 2, 1871, d. April 9, 1873 (ZJ)

As noted above, Lydi Ann (Allwine) Bedger died April 4, 1878 at a relatively young age—age 38—and is buried in the Jonestown Zion Lutheran Cemetery (ZJ) with her parents. As noted, it appears that Adam Bedger and Ellen Bedger are the only children of Lydi Ann Allwine to survive to adulthood. They both outlived their parents and siblings. As noted above, Adam Bedger and his wife erected a monument to the Samuel Alwine family in the Jonestown Zion Lutheran Cemetery. William Bedger died, as noted above, on September 1, 1902. He is buried with his son, Adam Bedger, at the United-Salem Evangelical Congregational Cemetery (US) in Lickdale, Lebanon County, Pennsylvania.

---

[568] *Lebanon Daily News*, Lebanon, Pennsylvania, Tuesday Evening, September 2, 1902.

[569] *Twelfth Census of the United States* (1900), *Inhabitants of Portage Township, St. Joseph County, Indiana,* E.D. No. 121, page 312B.

[570] These records were obtained from the *Zion Evangelical Lutheran Church, Parish Register.* Book II. Jonestown, Lebanon County, Pennsylvania. This source is available at the Lebanon County Historical Society, 924 Cumberland Street, Lebanon, Pennsylvania 17042.

Exhibit 11.152 Inscriptions for Lydian Alwine Bedger and John Henry Alwine on the Samuel Alwine gravestone—Jonestown Evangelical Lutheran Cemetery, Jonestown, Pennsylvania

Exhibit 11.153 Gravestone for William Bedger and Lydia A. Alwine
Bedger—Union-Salem Evangelical Congregational Cemetery,
Lickdale, Lebanon County, Pennsylvania

Although Lydi Ann (Allwine) is buried with her parents in Jonestown, she is commemorated on the gravestone for William Bedger at the United-Salem Cemetery in Lickdale, where her name is given as "Lydia A. Alwine." Ellen Bedger and her husband, Adam Eisenhower, are also buried at the United-Salem Evangelical Congregational Cemetery in Lickdale.

Lucetta Allwine Hartline (1840-1873)
Swatara Township, Lebanon County

Lucetta Allwine (F05-0404-0503), the third child of Samuel and Elizabeth (Kreiser) Allwine, was born October 24, 1840 in her parents' farm in northern Lebanon County. She married Nathaniel Hartline and they had two children. She, like her older sister Lydi Ann (Allwine) Bedger, also died at a very young age, on Sept. 30, 1873, at the young age of 33.

The line of descent connecting Lucetta Allwine and her descendants to Johannes Jacob and Catharina Allwein, the progenitors of the Allwein family in colonial Pennsylvania, is as follows:

Generation 1: Johannes Jacob and Catharina Allwein—Berks County, Pa.
Generation 2: Conrad and Catharine (Weibel) Allwein—Dauphin County, Pa.
Generation 3: John and Elizabeth (Felix) Allwine—Dauphin County, Pa.
Generation 4: Samuel and Elizabeth (Kreiser) Allwine—Lebanon County, Pa.
Generation 5: Lucetta (Allwine) and Nathaniel Hartline—Lebanon County, Pa.

In the 1870 Federal Census, Lucetta and Nathaniel Hartline were residing in the same dwelling as Peter Allwein and his family in Swatara Township. The basic information from the two-family listing in the 1870 Federal Census is as follows:[571]

Hartline, Nathaniel (engineer, age 40)
Hartline, Lucetta (spouse, age 29)
Hartline, Thomas (son, age 11)

---

[571] *Ninth Census of the United States* (1870), *Inhabitants of Swatara Township, Lebanon County, Pennsylvania*, page 399.

Allwein, Peter (farmer, age 25)
Allwein, Elizabeth (spouse, age 25)
Allwein, Agnes (daughter, age 5)
Allwein, Amos (son, age 3)
Allwein, Sarah (daughter, age 9/12)

As far as we know, there were two children born to Lucetta and Nathaniel Hartline:

Thomas A. Hartline, b. March 19, 1860, d. February 9. 1928 (CG), m.
    Catharine Elizabeth Maus (b. March 30, 1859, d. October 23, 1936)
Henry Hartline, b. February 24, 1865, d. April 27, 1866

Lucetta's death on September 30, 1873 is recorded in the parish registers of the Jonestown Zion Lutheran Church.[572] It is not clear where she is buried, but we assume she was buried at the Zion Evangelical Lutheran Cemetery in Jonestown. After her death, Nathaniel Hartline married Amanda Hoch (on October 22, 1876). He died on May 30, 1894 and is buried at the Zion Evangelical Lutheran Cemetery in Jonestown. The only surviving son, Thomas A. Hartline, is listed in the 1880 Federal Census living in Middle Paxton Township of Dauphin County, and in the 1900 Federal Census, living in the environs of Lebanon.[573] He and his wife are buried at the Covenant Greenwood Cemetery (CG) in Ebenezer, Lebanon County, Pennsylvania.

Peter Allwein (1843-1908)
North Lebanon Township

Peter Allwein (M05-0404-0504), fourth child of Samuel and Elizabeth (Kreiser) Allwine, was born June 24, 1843 on his parents' farm in the northern region of Lebanon County. This family used the

---

[572] *Zion Evangelical Lutheran Church, Parish Register.* Book II. Jonestown, Lebanon County, Pennsylvania, page 103.
[573] *Tenth Census of the United States* (1880), *Inhabitants of Middle Paxton Township, Dauphin County, Pennsylvania*, page 71B; *Twelfth Census of the United States* (1900), *Inhabitants of West Lebanon Township, Lebanon County, Pennsylvania*, E.D. No. 146, page 273B.

ALLWEIN spelling of the family name. As noted above, in the 1870 Federal Census listings (given above), Peter Allwein and his family were living in the same dwelling as his sister, Lucetta (Allwine) Hartline. Peter Allwein married Elizabeth Reifine.

The line of descent connecting Peter Allwein to Johannes Jacob and Catharina Allwein, the progenitors of the Allwein family in colonial Pennsylvania, is as follows:

Generation 1: Johannes Jacob and Catharina Allwein—Berks County, Pa.
Generation 2: Conrad and Catharine (Weibel) Allwein—Dauphin County, Pa.
Generation 3: John and Elizabeth (Felix) Allwine—Dauphin County, Pa.
Generation 4: Samuel and Elizabeth (Kreiser) Allwine—Lebanon County, Pa.
Generation 5: Peter and Elizabeth (Reifine) Allwein—Lebanon County, Pa.

As a young man, Peter Allwein served during the Civil War in the Pennsylvania Militia for a two-week period. He served as a Private in Company B under Captain George F. Meily in the 11th Regiment of the Militia of 1862. That regiment was organized Sept. 11-13, 1862 and discharged Sept. 23-25, 1862.[574]

As noted earlier in the chapter, the designation of "militia" service in this context refers to emergency troops typically organized by local communities or provinces—what we would today probably refer to as the army reserves or the national guard. This would explain why Peter Allwein does not appear in the military records of the Union (or federal) forces preserved at the National Archives, but does appear in Pennsylvania record sources.

Regarding the "Militia of 1862," the Samuel Bates' *History of Pennsylvania Volunteers* notes that after their triumph at the second Battle of Bull Run, the rebel army was moving northward, and in order to protect the southern border of Pennsylvania, local troops were mustered and assembled in the area of Harrisburg. After the Battle of Antietam in Northern Virginia (Sept. 17, 1862), in which the Army of the Potomac under the command of General McClellan

---

[574] Samuel P. Bates, *History of Pennsylvania Volunteers 1861*-65, edited by Janet Hewett, Wilmington NC: Broadfoot Publishing Co., Volume 10, 1994, pages 1172-1173.

defeated Confederate forces, the emergency passed and militia troops were returned to Harrisburg and disbanded on the 24th of September, 1862. There are a number of sources that describe McClellan's victory over Lee at Antietam, but it is not clear what role the Pennsylvania militia played other than to provide backup support to the regular army troops who engaged Lee's troops.[575]

In the 1870 Federal Census, Peter Allwein and his family were residing in the same dwelling as (Lucetta Allwine) and her husband Nathaniel Hartline in Swatara Township of Lebanon County.[576] By 1880, Peter Allwein had resettled to Upper Rapho Township in Lancaster County, along with his younger brother John Henry Allwine. There they lived in adjacent households, and they were both working as teamsters, according to the Census enumeration. The 1880 Census listing for the two households (spelled as ALLWINE) is as follows:[577]

Allwine, John H. Allwine (teamster, age 29)
Allwine, Lizzie (spouse, age 21)
Allwine, Carrie N. (daughter, age 3)
Allwine, Peter (teamster, age 37)
Allwine, Elizabeth (spouse, age 35)
Allwine, Agnes (daughter, age 15)
Allwine, Amos (son, age 11)
Allwine, Sarah (daughter, age 10)
Allwine, Lizzie (daughter, age 1 mo)

Based on the above census listing and other Federal Census enumerations, marriage records, and other sources, it can be established that Peter and Elizabeth Allwein gave life to the following children:

---

[575] Samuel P. Bates, *History of Pennsylvania Volunteers 1861-65*, edited by Janet Hewett, Wilmington NC: Broadfoot Publishing Co., Volume 10, 1994, page 1173.

[576] *Ninth Census of the United States* (1870), *Inhabitants of Swatara Township, Lebanon County, Pennsylvania*, page 399.

[577] *Tenth Census of the United States* (1880), *Inhabitants of Upper Rapho Township, Lancaster County, Pennsylvania*, pages 195C and 195D.

Agnes "Aggie" Allwein (F06-0404-0504-01), b. December 10, 1865, d. June 26, 1913 (EL), m. (May 24, 1888) William Jennings Yorty (b. July 23, 1863, d. April 9, 1937)

Amos R. Allwein (M06-0404-0504-02), b. April, 1871, d. September 23, 1934 (EM), m. (June 27, 1891) Anna S. Boughter (b. January 1872, d. September 12, 1936)

Sarah "Sallie" Allwein (F06-0404-0504-03), b. October 1872, d. July 9, 1937 (KR), m. (July 2, 1892) Ephraim C. Weirich (b. May 1871, d. July 14, 1934)

Elizabeth "Lizzie" Allwein (F06-0404-0504-04), b. April 20, 1880, d. November 5, 1922 (CG), m. (December 6, 1898) Martin D. Moyer (b. November 11, 1874, d. September 8, 1942)

William Augusta Allwein (M06-0404-0504-05), b. August 6, 1885, d. August 8, 1958, m. unknown

It is not clear how long Peter Allwein remained in the Lancaster County area, where we found him in the 1880 Federal Census (see above), as he eventually resettled in North Lebanon Township of Lebanon County where he is listed in the 1900 Federal Census.[578] The 1900 Census reports that he was working as a teamster for a brewery at the time—it was the New Lebanon Brewery (see the obituary included below), and his son William was living at home. Their son Amos had also established residence in North Lebanon Township, not far from the location of his parents' household.[579] Eventually, Peter and his sons moved into the Borough of Lebanon. Indeed, we expect that Amos and William, along with their parents, had moved into the Borough of Lebanon well before 1910. In any event, this is where they were located in the 1910 Federal Census.[580]

---

[578] *Twelfth Census of the United States* (1900), *Inhabitants of North Lebanon Township, West Precinct, Lebanon County, Pennsylvania*, E.D. No. 138, page 156A.

[579] *Twelfth Census of the United States* (1900), *Inhabitants of North Lebanon Township, West Precinct, Lebanon County, Pennsylvania*, E.D. No. 138, page 153A.

[580] *Thirteenth Census of the United States* (1910), *Inhabitants of Lebanon Ward 6, Lebanon County, Pennsylvania*, E.D. No. 156, page 233A.

Peter Allwein died on July 18, 1908, at the age of 65. A narrative of the circumstances of his death is provided in his obituary in the Lebanon newspapers, which I reproduce verbatim in the following:[581]

WATCHMAN DIES WHILE AT WORK

PETER ALLWEIN EXPIRES AT LEBANON HAT FACTORY

Death Was Due to Heart Disease—Deceased Was a Native of Swatara Township

Peter Allwein, of 612 Maple Street, died suddenly on Saturday evening at 8:30 o'clock from heart failure. Mr. Allwein was employed as a watchman at the Lebanon hat factory, at corner of Spruce and Lehman streets, and had begun his new duties for the first time on Saturday evening, starting at 6 o'clock.

At half past eight the manager of the factory went into the establishment to instruct him as to certain points and to see how he was getting along. He was greatly shocked to see the new watchman lying on the floor with a hose grasped in his hand. Examination showed that he had suffered heart failure while engaged in cleaning some of the machinery.

Deputy Coroner T. J. Kohr was notified and when he arrived on the scene sent for McGovern's ambulance and removed the dead man to the morgue. Dr. John Walter had also been summoned in the meanwhile and pronounced death due to heart failure.

Peter Allwein had been employed for many years as a driver for the New Lebanon brewing company and had only recently vacated that position on account of his inability to do heavy work.

---

[581] Information for Peter Allwein is from an obituary appearing in *The Lebanon Daily News*, Lebanon, Pennsylvania, Monday Evening, July 20, 1908, page 1. There were a number of additional newspaper accounts of his death. These resources are available at the Lebanon County Historical Society, 924 Cumberland Street, Lebanon, Pennsylvania 17042.

The body now reposes at the home of daughter, Mrs. Martin Moyer, of 607 Hill Street, from whence burial will occur on Wednesday.

Peter Allwein was born on June 24, 1843, in Swatara township, Lebanon county. He married Miss Elizabeth Reifine (or Rifine), who preceded him in death six years.

The deceased was well known throughout the city and county and his sudden death is caused for regret to numerous friends who join in offering sympathy to the grief-stricken children.

The survivors are three daughters, Mrs. Martin Moyer, of 607 Hill street, Mrs. Ephraim Weirick, of Eustontown, Mrs. William Yorty, of East Hanover township, two sons, Amos Allwein, of 543 Maple street, and William Allwein, of 612 Maple street, with whom he resided.

Peter Allwein's wife had preceded him in death six years earlier—on May 19, 1902.[582] The obituary of Peter Allwein mentions that three daughters and two sons survived him; however, there is no mention of his children in his will, set forth a few months before his death on January 15, 1908. Peter Allwein left his estate to his housekeeper, Elizabeth Seiders Peiffer, who he named as sole executor and beneficiary of his last will and testament.[583] This is not explained in any of the available records. The newspaper stories about Peter Allwein indicate that interment will be at Kimmerling's Cemetery. To date, however, I have been unable to find a gravestone for him there.

---

[582] Obituary from *Lebanon Daily News*, Lebanon, Pennsylvania, Tuesday Evening, May 20, 1902.
[583] Lebanon County Estate Records. Clerk of Courts, Lebanon, Pennsylvania. Available from the Pennsylvania State Archives, Harrisburg, Pennsylvania.

Agnes "Aggie" Allwein Yorty (1865-1913)
East Hanover Township

Peter and Elizabeth Allwein's oldest child, daughter Agnes "Aggie" Allwein (F06-0404-0504-01), was born December 10, 1865. The line of descent connecting Agnes Allwein to Johannes Jacob and Catharina Allwein, the progenitors of the Allwein family in colonial Pennsylvania, is as follows:

Generation 1: Johannes Jacob and Catharina Allwein—Berks County, Pa.
Generation 2: Conrad and Catharine (Weibel) Allwein—Dauphin County, Pa.
Generation 3: John and Elizabeth (Felix) Allwine—Dauphin County, Pa.
Generation 4: Samuel and Elizabeth (Kreiser) Allwine—Lebanon County, Pa.
Generation 5: Peter and Elizabeth (Reifine) Allwein—Lebanon County, Pa.
Generation 6: Agnes Allwein and William Jennings Yorty—Lebanon County, Pa.

Agnes Allwein married William Jennings Yorty on May 24, 1888 in Lebanon. They lived in East Hanover Township of Lebanon County, and raised several children there—Harry R. Yorty, Lizzie F. Yorty, Esther R. Yorty and Agnes L. Yorty.[584] William Yorty worked as a farm laborer, and continued to be listed in the 1920 and 1930 Federal Censuses. He can be located in Union Township, Lebanon County in 1920 and Derry Township of Dauphin County in 1930 In the latter year, he is listed in the household of his son, Harry Yorty.[585] Agnes Allwein Yorty died June 26, 1913 is therefore not listed in the 1920 and 1930 censuses with her husband, who outlived her by several years. William J. Yorty died on April 9, 1937.[586] They are buried in the Zion Lutheran and Reformed Cemetery (EL) in East Hanover Township of Lebanon County. This cemetery is located on the old Jonestown Road near the present-day border of Dauphin and Lebanon Counties.

---

[584] *Twelfth Census of the United States* (1900), *Inhabitants of East Hanover Township, Lebanon County, Pennsylvania*, E.D. No. 116, page 73B; *Thirteenth Census of the United States* (1910), *Inhabitants of East Hanover Township, Lebanon County*, E.D. 140, page 276B.
[585] *Fourteenth Census of the United States* (1920), *Inhabitants of Union Township, Lebanon County*, E.D. No. 159, page 63B; *Fifteenth Census of the United States* (1930), *Inhabitants of Derry Township, Dauphin County, Pennsylvania,* E.D. No. 22-6, page 238A.
[586] See the Pennsylvania Department of Health: http://www.health.state.pa.us.

Exhibit 11.154 Gravestone of Agnes and William Yorty—Zion
Lutheran and Reformed Cemetery, East Hanover Township,
Pennsylvania

Amos R. Allwein (1869-1934)
Lebanon, Pennsylvania

Peter and Elizabeth Allwein's son Amos R. Allwein (M06-0404-0504-02) was born in 1869 and was raised in the northern territories of Lebanon County. The line of descent connecting Amos R. Allwein to Johannes Jacob and Catharina Allwein, the progenitors of the Allwein family in colonial Pennsylvania, is as follows:

Generation 1: Johannes Jacob and Catharina Allwein—Berks County, Pa.
Generation 2: Conrad and Catharine (Weibel) Allwein—Dauphin County, Pa.
Generation 3: John and Elizabeth (Felix) Allwine—Dauphin County, Pa.
Generation 4: Samuel and Elizabeth (Kreiser) Allwine—Lebanon County, Pa.
Generation 5: Peter and Elizabeth (Reifine) Allwein—Lebanon County, Pa.
Generation 6: Amos R. and Annie S. (Boughter) Allwein—Lebanon County, Pa.

Amos R. Allwein married Anna S. Boughter on June 27, 1891 at Lebanon. At the time of the 1900 Federal Census, they were living in North Lebanon Township near his parents' residence. Eventually Amos and Anna Allwein moved into the Borough of Lebanon where they can be located in the 1910 Federal Census living on Church Street and in 1920 and 1930 in Ward 7 of Lebanon on North 11th Street.[587] Amos R. Allwein died in on September 23, 1934. His wife died September 12, 1936.[588] There were no children born to Amos and Anna (Boughter) Allwein. They are buried in the East Petersburg Mennonite Cemetery (EM) in East Petersburg, Lancaster County, Pennsylvania.

---

[587] *Twelfth Census of the United States* (1900), *Inhabitants of North Lebanon Township, West Precinct, Lebanon County, Pennsylvania*, E.D. No. 138, page 153A; *Thirteenth Census of the United States* (1910), *Inhabitants of Lebanon Ward 6, Lebanon County, Pennsylvania*, E.D. No. 156, page 233A; *Fourteenth Census of the United States* (1920), *Inhabitants of Ward 7 Lebanon City*, E.D. No. 176, page 296B; *Fifteenth Census of the United States* (1930), *Inhabitants of Ward 7 Lebanon City, Lebanon County, Pennsylvania,* E.D. No. 38-24, page 217B.

[588] See the Pennsylvania Department of Health: http://www.health.state. pa.us. Note that the year of death on the gravestone—1935—disagrees with the Pennsylvania death records.

Exhibit 11.155 Gravestone of Amos R. and Anna S. Allwein, East
Petersburg Mennonite Cemetery, East Petersburg, Pennsylvania

Sarah "Sallie" Allwein Weirich (1874-1937)
North Lebanon Township

Peter and Elizabeth Allwein's daughter Sarah "Sallie" Allwein (F06-0404-0504-03) was born in 1874. The line of descent connecting Sarah Allwein to Johannes Jacob and Catharina Allwein, the progenitors of the Allwein family in colonial Pennsylvania, is as follows:

Generation 1: Johannes Jacob and Catharina Allwein—Berks County, Pa.
Generation 2: Conrad and Catharine (Weibel) Allwein—Dauphin County, Pa.
Generation 3: John and Elizabeth (Felix) Allwine—Dauphin County, Pa.
Generation 4: Samuel and Elizabeth (Kreiser) Allwine—Lebanon County, Pa.
Generation 5: Peter and Elizabeth (Reifine) Allwein—Lebanon County, Pa.
Generation 6: Sarah "Sallie" Allwein and Ephraim C. Weirich—Lebanon County, Pa.

Sarah Allwein married Ephraim C. Weirich on July 2, 1892 at Lebanon. Several Federal Censuses—1900, 1910 and 1920—record their presence in the western precincts of North Lebanon Township where Ephraim Weirich worked as a furnace laborer in the 1910 Census.[589] Ephraim and Sarah (Allwein) Weirich appear to have raised several children—Peter Weirich, William Weirich, Elsie Weirich, Della Weirich, and Mary Weirich—all raised in North Lebanon Township. Sarah Allwein Weirich died on July 9, 1937; Ephraim Weirich a few years earlier on July 14, 1934.[590] They are buried in Kimmerling's Reformed Cemetery (KR) in North Lebanon Township of Lebanon County.[591]

---

[589] *Twelfth Census of the United States* (1900), *Inhabitants of North Lebanon Township, Lebanon County, Pennsylvania*, E.D. No. 137, page 129A; *Thirteenth Census of the United States* (1910), *Inhabitants of North Lebanon Township, Lebanon County*, E.D. 163, page 101A; *Fourteenth Census of the United States* (1920), *Inhabitants of North Lebanon Township West Precinct, Lebanon County, Pennsylvania*, E.D. No. 187, page 176B.
[590] See the Pennsylvania Department of Health: http://www.health. state.pa.us. See also obituary in the *Lebanon Daily News*, Lebanon, Pennsylvania, Monday Evening, July 16, 1934.
[591] *Kimmerling's Cemetery, North Lebanon Twp., Lebanon Co., PA*, compiled by Kenneth Long. This source is available at the Lebanon County Historical Society, 924 Cumberland Street, Lebanon, Pennsylvania 17042. Obituaries in *Lebanon Daily News*, Lebanon, Pennsylvania, Monday Evening, July 16, 1934 and Monday Evening, July 12, 1937.

Exhibit 11.156 Gravestones of Sarah and Ephraim Weirich—
Kimmerling's Cemetery, North Lebanon Township, Pennsylvania

Elizabeth "Lizzie" Allwein Moyer (1880-1922)
North Lebanon Township

Peter and Elizabeth Allwein's daughter Elizabeth "Lizzie" Allwein (F06-0404-0504-04) was born April 20, 1880. The line of descent connecting Elizabeth Allwein to Johannes Jacob and Catharina Allwein, the progenitors of the Allwein family in colonial Pennsylvania, is as follows:

Generation 1: Johannes Jacob and Catharina Allwein—Berks County, Pa.
Generation 2: Conrad and Catharine (Weibel) Allwein—Dauphin County, Pa.
Generation 3: John and Elizabeth (Felix) Allwine—Dauphin County, Pa.
Generation 4: Samuel and Elizabeth (Kreiser) Allwine—Lebanon County, Pa.
Generation 5: Peter and Elizabeth (Reifine) Allwein—Lebanon County, Pa.
Generation 6: Elizabeth Allwein and Martin D. Moyer—Lebanon County, Pa.

She married Martin D. Moyer on December 6, 1898. On the marriage application, he is listed as "M.D. Moyer" with the occupation of "cigar-maker." This was also the occupation listed in the 1910 Federal Census.[592] Elizabeth "Lizzie" Allwein died November 6, 1922, and Martin D. Moyer died many years later on September 8, 1942.[593] They are buried at Covenant Greenwood Cemetery (CG) in Ebenezer, North Lebanon Township, Lebanon County.

William Augusta Allwein (1885-1958)
Reading, Pennsylvania

William Augusta Allwein (M06-0404-0504-05), the youngest son of Peter and Elizabeth Allwein, was born in Lebanon County on August 6, 1885.[594] He was living at home with his parents at the time of the

---

[592] *Thirteenth Census of the United States* (1910), *Inhabitants of North Lebanon Township, Lebanon County*, E.D. 157, page 253B.

[593] *Lebanon Daily News*, Lebanon, Pennsylvania, Monday Evening, November 6, 1922; Tuesday Evening, September 8, 1942. See the Pennsylvania Department of Health: http://www.health.state.pa.us.

[594] Birth information for William Augusta Allwein was obtained from his draft registration cards, obtained from Ancestry.com. Both WWI and WWII registration cards give the same date of birth, August 6, 1885.

Exhibit 11.157 Gravestone for Elizabeth Allwine and Martin D. Moyer—Covenant Greenwood Cemetery, Ebenezer, North Lebanon Township, Pennsylvania

1900 Federal Census, and as far as we know, he moved to Reading soon thereafter.[595] We cover what is known about him in Chapter 13.

John Henry Allwine (1851-1890)
Jonestown, Pennsylvania

John Henry Allwine (M05-0404-0506), the youngest child of Samuel and Elizabeth (Kreiser) Allwine, was born Sept. 6, 1851 on his parents' farm in Swatara Township of Lebanon County. Despite the presence of other spellings, I believe John Henry used the ALLWINE spelling of the family name and that is the practice I follow for him here. The line of descent connecting John Henry Allwine to Johannes Jacob and Catharina Allwein, the progenitors of the Allwein family in colonial Pennsylvania, is as follows:

Generation 1: Johannes Jacob and Catharina Allwein—Berks County, Pa.
Generation 2: Conrad and Catharine (Weibel) Allwein—Dauphin County, Pa.
Generation 3: John and Elizabeth (Felix) Allwine—Dauphin County, Pa.
Generation 4: Samuel and Elizabeth (Kreiser) Allwine—Lebanon County, Pa.
Generation 5: John Henry and Elizabeth "Lizzie" (Daub) Allwine—Lebanon
     County, Pa.

There is not much known about John Henry Allwine. We surmise that he was married to Elizabeth "Lizzie" Daub (see below). By 1880, John Henry Allwine was no longer living with his parents, but as noted above, he was working as a teamster in Lancaster County, Upper Rapho Township. He lived there in a dwelling unit adjacent to his brother, Peter Allwein. He died on December 24, 1890 at the relatively young age of 39 and there is a monument bearing his name in the Jonestown Zion Evangelical Lutheran Cemetery (ZJ).[596]

John Henry Allwine's widow, Lizzie Allwine, remarried to Francis C. Gratz on May 13, 1893 at Lebanon, Pennsylvania.

---

[595] *Twelfth Census of the United States* (1900), *Inhabitants of North Lebanon Township, West Precinct, Lebanon County, Pennsylvania*, E.D. No. 138, page 153A.
[596] *Zion Evangelical Lutheran Church, Parish Register.* Book II. Jonestown, Lebanon County, Pennsylvania, page 223.

Francis C. Gratz was a Civil War veteran, and on May 12, 1898 he was admitted to the Southern Branch of the U.S. National Homes for Disabled Volunteer Soldiers in Hampton, Virginia.[597] In the 1900 Federal Census, she was listed as "Elizabeth Allwine," and was operating a boarding house in Harrisburg, Pennsylvania. The Federal Census of 1900 gives the following children of John Henry and Elizabeth Allwine:[598]

Catherine (Carrie) Madora Allwine (F06-0404-0506-01), b. March 1877, d. July 13, 1932, m. (1) (October 14, 1896) David C. Devlin (b. 1877, d. June 18, 1949) [Divorced February 1900], (2) (March 12, 1901) Charles Wesley Haupt (b. November 22, 1872, d. April 26, 1921), (3) (April 22, 1924) Frank Michael Adams (b. est. 1885, d. May 30, 1945)[599]

Ida M. Allwine (F06-0404-0506-02), b. August 1880, d. June 23, 1943, m. (March 29, 1903) Forse W. Knaub (b. July 2, 1881, d. January 9, 1946 (DC)

Howard H. Allwine (M06-0404-0506-03), b. March 1883, d. January 13, 1930 (EN), m. unknown

John Adam Allwine (M06-0404-0506-04), b. October 6, 1884, d. August 11, 1949 (LI), m. Mary Unknown (b. February 2, 1888, d. March 5, 1973)

Margaret G. Allwine (F06-0404-0506-05), b. August 1888, d. unknown, m. unknown

Elizabeth Allwine (nee Daub) later moved to Philadelphia and apparently married a third time, about 1904, to Frank Ford.[600] She

---

[597] U.S. National Homes for Disabled Volunteer Soldiers, 1866-1938. Ancestry.com.

[598] *Twelfth Census of the United States* (1900), *Inhabitants of Harrisburg, Ward 5, Dauphin County, Pennsylvania*, E.D. No. 56, pages 2B and 3A.

[599] For the death dates given in this entry, see the Pennsylvania Department of Health: http://www.health.state.pa.us. Obituary for Frank M. Adams from the *Gettysburg Compiler*, Gettysburg, Pennsylvania, June 2, 1945, page 3.

[600] See *Thirteenth Census of the United States* (1910), *Inhabitants of Ward 24 Philadelphia, Philadelphia County, Pennsylvania*, E.D. No. 490, page 36A; *Fourteenth Census of the United States* (1920), *Inhabitants of Ward 44, Philadelphia, Pennsylvania*, E.D. No. 1679, page 155B.

died in East Pennsboro Township in Cumberland County on March 26, 1930.[601] Little more is known about this family, although there is one further piece of information, which I discuss in the following.

Kate Daub's Will

In the above narrative I indicated that John Henry Allwein married Lizzie Daub. This claim is based on the following. In James Beidler's chapter on "Genealogy" in the recent and definitive *History of the Commonwealth*, he reproduces the will of Kate Daub, in part to inform, but to entertain as well.[602] It reads as follows:

> I, Kate Daub, widow, residing at 344 N. 12th Street, in the city of Lebanon, Pa., do make and publish my last will and testament, as follows:
>
> To my youngest child, Mary, wife of Levi Keller, I give nothing, because she never tried to please me and was not obedient to my wishes. To my oldest son, Rolandus, I give nothing, because, some years ago, I have good reason to believe he made an unsuccessful attempt to kill me. Jere Gamber is to have his home in my house as long as he lives, rent free, and in case he needs help. Adam Bombergers is hereby directed and ordered to give him cash whenever necessary and charge the same against my estate. At the death of said Jere Gamber it is my wish that my two other children, Lizzie and Harry, shall give him a decent burial. All my just debts are to be paid, and the remainder of my whole estate, real and personal, I give, devise and bequeath until my two children Lizzie and Harry, executors of this my last will and testament. I give unto my grandchild, Carrie Allwein, my white

---

[601] See the Pennsylvania Department of Health: http://www.health.state. pa.us.
[602] From James M. Beidler, "Genealogy," in Randall M. Miller and William Pencak (Eds.), *Pennsylvania: A History of the Commonwealth* (pp. 481-500) University Park, Pa.: Pennsylvania State University Press, 2002, page 487.

sewing machine. In testimony whereof, I have hereunto set my hand and seal, this tenth day of March A.D. 1902. Kate Daub

Witnesses:
Aaron Sattezahn
Robt. L. Miller

Apart from whatever intention James Beidler had in publishing Kate Daub's will, the reference to Carrie Allwein in this will suggests a linkage to the Allwein family. According to the will, Carrie Allwein's mother was "Lizzie," Kate Daub's daughter. This, along with the following listing in the 1880 Federal Census, strongly suggests that Lizzie Allwein, whose daughter was Carrie Allwein, was one and the same person as the Lizzie Daub, daughter of Kate Daub, referred to in the will. The 1880 Census listing for the John Henry Allwine household (spelled as ALLWINE) is as follows:[603]

Allwine, John H. (teamster, age 29)
Allwine, Lizzie (spouse, age 21)
Allwine, Carrie N. (daughter, age 3)

We can find only one "Carrie Allwine" in the vicinity of Lebanon County Pennsylvania, and so we conclude that there is a connection to John H. Allwine. There may be other possible conclusions, and this claim needs to be corroborated by other information, but this provides circumstantial evidence for my claim that John Henry Allwine married Elizabeth "Lizzie" Daub. There were no county marriage records at that time, and it has not been possible to nail down this possibility. As noted earlier, John Henry Allwine died on December 24, 1890 at the relatively young age of 39. Consequently, the 1880 Federal Census is essentially the last public record we have for him at this time. John Henry Allwine is buried in the Jonestown Lutheran Cemetery (see Exhibit 11.152 above).

---

[603] *Tenth Census of the United States* (1880), *Inhabitants of Upper Rapho Township, Lancaster County, Pennsylvania*, pages 195C and 195D.

Philip Stephen Allwein (1835-1897)
North Lebanon, Lebanon County[604]

Philip Stephen Allwein (M04-0404-15), son of John and Mary M. (Eckenroth) Allwine, was born June 21, 1835 in Londonderry Township of Dauphin County, Pennsylvania. His birth and baptism are recorded in the baptismal records kept by the St. Mary's priests from Lancaster who visited the Catholic congregation in Elizabethtown, where his parents worshiped and observed the sacraments. Like his older brother, Henry E. Allwein, Philip spelled the name ALLWEIN. Although reared in the Elizabethtown area, where the name was spelled ALLWINE, Philip Allwine settled in North Lebanon as a young man, where he was perhaps influenced by the predominant way the name was spelled there. He worked primarily as a teamster throughout his adult life.

The line of descent connecting Philip Stephen Allwein to Johannes Jacob and Catharina Allwein, the progenitors of the Allwein family in colonial Pennsylvania, is as follows:

Generation 1: Johannes Jacob and Catharina Allwein—Berks County, Pa.
Generation 2: Conrad and Catharine (Weibel) Allwein—Dauphin County, Pa.
Generation 3: John and Mary M. (Eckenroth) Allwine—Dauphin County, Pa.
Generation 4: Philip Stephen and Cecilia (Arnold) [and Sarah (Arnold)]
      Allwein—Lebanon County, Pa.

We covered the early life of Philip S. Allwein in Volume 1 of *Familie Allwein* (Chapter 6, pages 333-337) and do not repeat that here, except to note his marriages and children. He married Cecilia Arnold, the daughter of Herman and Elizabeth Arnold, prior to 1860, and settled in Lebanon, Pennsylvania. Cecilia died a few years later—on October 14, 1862—and she is buried in St. Mary's Catholic Cemetery in Lebanon. After Philip S. Allwein's

---

[604] The biographical information here comes from chapter 6 of *Familie Allwein*, Volume 1, pages 333-336. This presentation was also assisted by a "Register Report for Philip Stephen Allwein" provided by Nancy Nebiker, March 24, 2009.

first wife died, he remarried to Sarah Arnold, daughter of Peter and Margaret Arnold.[605] Sarah Arnold had also been widowed—she was married to Daniel Thompson and was the mother of Pierce Henry Thompson, making the latter a step-child of Philip S. Allwein. We return to a discussion of Pierce Thompson below.

According to all accounts, five children are known to have been born to Sarah Arnold and Philip S. Allwein, as follows:

John Peter Allwein (M05-0404-1501), b. October 4, 1863, d. February 12, 1928 (ML), m. (1) (October 26, 1886) Mary L. Hollinger (b. est. 1866, d. unknown), (2) (December 30, 1905) Lucreta C. Conner (b. abt 1868, d. December 6, 1929)

George Henry Allwein (M05-0404-1502), b. July 18, 1866, d. April 6, 1942 (ML), unmarried

William Allwein (M05-0404-1503), b. March 6, 1868, d. October 22, 1943 (SM), m. (April 23, 1891) Alice Sattazahn (b. 1870, d. August 12, 1944)

Mary Rebecca Allwein (F05-0404-1504), b. December 16, 1869, d. February 12, 1951 (HC), m. (February 4, 1897) Augustus P. Arnold (b. October 31, 1858, d. July 19, 1941)

Philip Joseph Allwein (M05-0404-1505), b. March 8, 1875, d. January 25, 1922 (SD), m. (1900 in Iowa) Jennie L. Safelsberg (b. est. 1869, d. after 1932)

The 1870 and 1880 Federal Censuses verify this information; the 1880 census listing is recorded as follows:[606]

Philip Allwein (farmer, age 44)
Sarah A. Allwein (spouse, age 40)

---

[605] Jerome Allwein, *Genealogy of the Allwein-Arnold Families*, 1902, page 25.

[606] *Ninth Census of the United States* (1870), *Inhabitants of North Lebanon Township, Lebanon County, Pennsylvania*, page 242; *Tenth Census of the United States* (1880), *Inhabitants of North Lebanon Township, Lebanon County, Pennsylvania*, page 240.

John P. Allwein (son, age 15)
George Allwein (son, age 13)
Willie Allwein (son, age 12)
Beckie Allwein (daughter, age 10)
Philip J. Allwein (son, age 5)

As noted above, there was also a step-child, Pierce Henry Thompson (b. August 12, 1859, d. May 10, 1922), son of Sarah (Arnold) and Daniel Thompson, but in the 1880 Federal Census, Pierce Thompson was living in the household of Joseph Bowman (cabinet maker), working as an apprentice cabinet maker.[607]

Philip S. Allwein died August 12, 1897 and Sarah (Arnold) Allwein some years later, on August 19, 1922.[608] They are buried together in St. Mary's Catholic Cemetery (SM), Lebanon, Pennsylvania.[609] A photo of their gravestone marker is reproduced in volume 1 of *Familie Allwein* (page 337).

Jerome Allwein's *Genealogy of the Allwein-Arnold Families* mentions more about three of these children—John Peter Allwein (M05-0404-1501), Rebecca Allwein (F05-0404-1504), and William Allwein (M05-0404-1503)—but very little was known about them or the other two children at that time.[610] Now we know much more, and in the following we discuss what we now know about the other children—George Henry Allwein (M05-0404-1502) and Philip Joseph Allwein (M05-0404-1505)—as well.

---

[607] *Tenth Census of the United States* (1880), *Inhabitants of North Lebanon Township, Lebanon County, Pennsylvania*, page 350.
[608] See the Pennsylvania Department of Health: http://www.health.state. pa.us.
[609] See Funeral announcements, *Lebanon Daily News*, Lebanon, Pennsylvania, Aug. 16, 1897, and *Lebanon Daily News*, Lebanon, Pennsylvania, Saturday Evening, August 19, 1922
[610] Jerome Allwein, *Genealogy of the Allwein-Arnold Families*, 1902, page 57.

John Peter Allwein (1863-1928)
Lebanon, Pennsylvania

John Peter Allwein (M05-0404-1501), the eldest son of Philip S. and Sarah (Arnold) Allwein, was born October 4, 1863 in Lebanon County. He lived his entire life in the area of the Borough of Lebanon.[611] The line of descent connecting John Peter Allwein to Johannes Jacob and Catharina Allwein, the progenitors of the Allwein family in colonial Pennsylvania, is as follows:

Generation 1: Johannes Jacob and Catharina Allwein—Berks County, Pa.
Generation 2: Conrad and Catharine (Weibel) Allwein—Dauphin County, Pa.
Generation 3: John and Mary M. (Eckenroth) Allwine—Dauphin County, Pa.
Generation 4: Philip Stephen and Sarah A. (Arnold) Allwein—Lebanon County, Pa.
Generation 5: John Peter and Mary (Hollinger) [and Lucreta (Conner)] Allwein—
    Lebanon County, Pa.

At the age of 22, John Peter Allwein married Mary L. Hollinger on October 26, 1886. They had one (adopted) child, Annie Allwein (born about 1894). Mary Hollinger Allwein died in 1902. John Peter Allwein remarried to Lucreta C. Conner on December 30, 1905, who had a child, Ruth Burt, from a previous marriage. There were no children born to these two unions.

In the 1900 Federal Census John Peter and Mary (Hollinger) Allwein were living in the East Precinct of the 5th Ward of Lebanon Borough on North Fifth Street. He was working as a "heater" in a "mill" (a furnace operator in a iron/steel mill) [Dictionary of Occupational Titles: 619.682-022; 542.362-010; or 613.362-010]. In the 1910 Federal Census he and his wife, Lucreta (Conner) Allwein, were living in South Lebanon Township, where he was again

---

[611] *Twelfth Census of the United States* (1900), *Inhabitants of Lebanon Ward 5, Lebanon County, Pennsylvania*, E.D. No. 128, page 244A; *Thirteenth Census of the United States* (1910), *Inhabitants of South Lebanon Township, Lebanon County, Pennsylvania*, E.D. No. 167 page 183A; *Fourteenth Census of the United States* (1920), *Inhabitants of East Precinct, Lebanon Ward 5, Lebanon County, Pennsylvania*, E.D. No. 173, page 226A.

working as a "heater in an iron works." In the 1920 Federal Census, they were living in Lebanon's Fifth ward, where he worked for the Bethlehem Steel Company as a patrolman (see Census citations above).

John Peter Allwein died of heart problems on February 12, 1928 at the relatively young age of 62.[612] He is buried in Mount Lebanon Cemetery (ML) in Lebanon.[613] As of this writing, we do not know exactly where his wives are buried.

George Henry Allwein (1866-1942)
Lebanon, Pennsylvania

George Henry Allwein (M05-0404-1502), second son of Philip S. and Sarah (Arnold) Allwein, was born July 18, 1866 in Lebanon County. He lived his entire life in and around the Borough of Lebanon. The line of descent connecting George Henry Allwein to Johannes Jacob and Catharina Allwein, the progenitors of the Allwein family in colonial Pennsylvania, is as follows:

Generation 1: Johannes Jacob and Catharina Allwein—Berks County, Pa.
Generation 2: Conrad and Catharine (Weibel) Allwein—Dauphin County, Pa.
Generation 3: John and Mary M. (Eckenroth) Allwine—Dauphin County, Pa.
Generation 4: Philip Stephen and Sarah A. (Arnold) Allwein—Lebanon County, Pa.
Generation 5: George Henry Allwein—Lebanon County, Pa.

George Henry Allwein did not marry. He lived in a boarding house his entire adult life in the 2nd and 3rd wards of Lebanon. His principle occupation was that of teamster, primarily working for a

---

[612] See the Pennsylvania Department of Health: http://www.health.state. pa.us.
[613] News item, "J. P. ALLWEIN FELL OVER DEAD WHILE ON DUTY: As Policeman at the Bethlehem Steel Co. Plant," *Lebanon Semi-Weekly News*, Lebanon, Pennsylvania Monday Evening, February 13, 1928; Funeral announcement, *Lebanon Semi-Weekly News*, Lebanon, Pennsylvania, Thursday Evening February 16, 1928.

Exhibit 11.158 Gravestone for John Peter Allwein—Mt. Lebanon Cemetery, Lebanon, Pennsylvania

furniture store.[614] In the 1930 Federal Census his occupation is given as "laborer in electric truck factory."

George Allwein's obituary noted that at the time of his death he "was retired for some years and was a member of the Union Fire Company, where he was very active in his earlier years and served as a driver for the company."

George Henry Allwein died April 6, 1942.[615] He is buried in Mount Lebanon Cemetery (ML), Lebanon, Pennsylvania.[616]

William Allwein (1868-1943)
Lebanon and Reading, Pennsylvania

William Allwein (M05-0404-1503), third son of Philip S. and Sarah (Arnold) Allwein, was born March 6, 1868 in Lebanon County. He married Alice Sattazahn on April 23, 1891 in Lebanon, and by 1900 they had moved to Reading, Pennsylvania, where they appear in Federal Censuses from that time onward. We cover what is known about them in Chapter 13, where we deal with Allwein families who lived in Berks County, Pennsylvania.

---

[614] *Twelfth Census of the United States* (1900), *Inhabitants of Lebanon Ward 2, Lebanon County, Pennsylvania*, E.D. No. 125, 203B; *Thirteenth Census of the United States* (1910), *Inhabitants of Ward 2 Lebanon Borough, Lebanon County, Pennsylvania*, E.D. No. 148, page 117B; *Fourteenth Census of the United States* (1920), *Inhabitants of East Precinct, Borough of Lebanon, Lebanon County, Pennsylvania*, E.D. No. 169, page 137B; *Fifteenth Census of the United States* (1930) *Inhabitants of Lebanon Ward 2, Lebanon County, Pennsylvania*, E.D. No. 38-16, page 56A; *Sixteenth Census of the United States* (1940), *Inhabitants of Lebanon, Lebanon County, Pennsylvania*, E.D. No. 38-18, page 292B.
[615] See the Pennsylvania Department of Health: http://www.health.state.pa.us.
[616] Funeral announcement, *Lebanon Daily News*, Lebanon, Pennsylvania, Tuesday Evening, April 7, 1942.

Exhibit 11.159 Gravestone for George Henry Allwein—Mt. Lebanon Cemetery, Lebanon, Pennsylvania

Mary Rebecca Allwein Arnold (1869-1951)
Lebanon, Pennsylvania

Mary Rebecca Allwein (F05-0404-1504), the only daughter of
Philip S. and Sarah (Arnold) Allwein, was born December 16, 1869,
The line of descent connecting Mary Rebecca Allwein to Johannes
Jacob and Catharina Allwein, the progenitors of the Allwein family
in colonial Pennsylvania, is as follows:

Generation 1: Johannes Jacob and Catharina Allwein—Berks County, Pa.
Generation 2: Conrad and Catharine (Weibel) Allwein—Dauphin County, Pa.
Generation 3: John and Mary M. (Eckenroth) Allwine—Dauphin County, Pa.
Generation 4: Philip Stephen and Sarah A. (Arnold) Allwein—Lebanon
     County, Pa.
Generation 5: Mary Rebecca Allwein and Augustus P. Arnold—Lebanon
     County, Pa.

Mary Rebecca Allwein married Augustus P. Arnold on February.
4, 1897, and they settled in Lebanon, where he pursued the trade
of cabinet-making. Available Federal Census reports from 1900
through 1940 indicate their presence there.[617]

Mary Rebecca Allwein and Augustus P. Arnold had three
children, as follows:

Sarah Rebecca Arnold, b. April 26, 1897, d. November 1954 (in
     Norman, Oklahoma),[618] m. (November 11, 1919) Richard M.
     Cavanaugh, Sr. (b. August 21, 1892, d. March 1981)

---

[617] *Twelfth Census of the United States* (1900), *Inhabitants of North
Lebanon Township, Lebanon County, Pennsylvania*, E.D. No. 137, page
121A; *Thirteenth Census of the United States* (1910), *Inhabitants of
North Lebanon Township, Lebanon County, Pennsylvania*, E.D. No. 163,
page 75B; *Fourteenth Census of the United States* (1920), *Inhabitants
of Lebanon, Lebanon County, Pennsylvania*, E.D. No. 178, page 312B;
Fifteenth Census of the United States (1930) *Inhabitants of Lebanon,
Lebanon County, Pennsylvania*, E.D. No. 38-26, page 266B; *Sixteenth
Census of the United States* (1940), *Inhabitants of Lebanon, Lebanon
County, Pennsylvania*, E.D. No. 38-15, page 241A.
[618] See announcement in the *Lebanon Daily News*, Lebanon,
Pennsylvania, Friday, December 3, 1954.

Catharine E. Arnold, b. August 6, 1898, d. January 1987 (in
   Oklahoma), m. (September 26, 1922) Edward C. Fagan (b. July
   21, 1896, d. March 1986)
Anna Mary Magdalena Arnold, b. April 17, 1901, d. January 25,
   1981 (HC), m. (February 12, 1922) Henry William Bleistein (b.
   January 1, 1895, d. March 14, 1958)

The 1904 *Biographic Annals of Lebanon County* included an
entry for Augustus Arnold, which reads as follows:

Augustus P. Arnold was born in South Lebanon Township,
October 31, 1858, he being the fourth child in the order of
birth in the family of Moses Arnold. He was educated in the
public schools, and at the age of seventeen went to learn the
cabinetmaking trade with Joseph Bowman, which calling he has
followed in the leading cities of Pennsylvania, and in the West as
far as Kansas City, Mo. Later he took up farming in conjunction
with his trade, but being a thorough mechanic, he prefers to spend
the greater portion of his time along the line of his calling, and
he keeps in touch with advanced ideas. On February 4, 1897, he
was married to Rebecca Allwine, daughter of Philip and Sarah
Allwine. Three children have been born to this union: Sarah,
Catherine and Annie. Both Mr. Arnold and his wife are connected
with St. Mary's Catholic Church. They reside in East Lebanon, on
Cumberland Street, where they have a beautiful home and extend
a kindly hospitality to their many friends.[619]

Mary Rebecca (Allwein) Arnold died on February 12, 1951
(HC); Augustus Arnold died July 19, 1941.[620] They are buried in
Holy Cross Cemetery (HC) in Lebanon, Pennsylvania.

---

[619] *Biographic Annals of Lebanon County* 1904, page 765.
[620] Funeral announcement, *Lebanon Daily News*, Lebanon,
Pennsylvania, Wednesday Evening, February 14, 1951, *Lebanon Daily
News*, Lebanon, Pennsylvania, Thursday Evening, February 15, 1951.
See also the Pennsylvania Department of Health: http://www.health.
state.pa.us.

Exhibit 11.160 Gravestone for Mary Rebecca and Augustus Arnold—Holy Cross Cemetery, Lebanon, Pennsylvania

Philip Joseph "P. J." Allwein (1875-1922)
West Burlington, Iowa

Philip Joseph Allwein (M05-0404-1505), son of Philip Stephen and Sarah A. (Arnold) Allwein, was born in Lebanon, Pennsylvania on March 8, 1875. He was the youngest of five children. The line of descent connecting Philip Joseph Allwein to Johannes Jacob and Catharina Allwein, the progenitors of the Allwein family in colonial Pennsylvania, is as follows:

Generation 1: Johannes Jacob and Catharina Allwein—Berks County, Pa.
Generation 2: Conrad and Catharine (Weibel) Allwein—Dauphin County, Pa.
Generation 3: John and Mary M. (Eckenroth) Allwine—Dauphin County, Pa.
Generation 4: Philip Stephen and Sarah A. (Arnold) Allwein—Lebanon County, Pa.
Generation 5: Philip Joseph and Jennie (Safelsberg) Allwein—Des Moines
    County, Ia.

In the 1880 Federal Census, Philip Joseph Allwein (age 5) was listed in the household of his parents residing in North Lebanon Township.[621] They lived for a number of years on the Kline farm at the old Union Canal and Front Street, in North Lebanon Township.[622] He grew to adulthood in the environs of Lebanon, and in 1898 moved to the vicinity of Burlington, Des Moines County, Iowa. We cover more about Philip Joseph Allwein in Chapter 22 (volume 3), where we consider Allwein descendants who moved to Iowa.

Pierce Henry Thompson (1859-1922)
Lebanon, Pennsylvania

Pierce Henry Thompson, son of Sarah Arnold and Daniel Thompson, was born in Lebanon on August 12, 1859. After Pierce Thompson's father died in 1861, his mother remarried to Philip S. Allwein, making Pierce Thompson a step-son of Philip S. Allwein.

---

[621] *Tenth Census of the United States* (1880), *Inhabitants of North Lebanon Township, Lebanon County, Pennsylvania*, page 240.
[622] Jerome Allwein, *Genealogy of the Allwein-Arnold Families*, 1902, page 25.

The *Biographical Annals of Lebanon County* states the following about Pierce Henry Thompson:[623]

Pierce Henry Thompson, one of the well-known citizens of the Second ward, of Lebanon, is a leading furniture dealer and undertaker, with commodious places of business located at Nos. 124-126 South Ninth Street. Mr. Thompson was born August 12, 1859, in Lebanon, son of Daniel E. and Sarah A. (Arnold) Thompson, the former of whom was born in Berks county, and died in 1881 [should be 1861], in his forty-third year. The mother was born in Lebanon township Lebanon County, February 22, 1840, a daughter of Peter Arnold, a native of Lebanon County.

Pierce Henry Thompson, the only child born to his parents, was reared on the farm from his fourth to his eighteenth year. His mother subsequently married Philip Allwein, and had a family of five children, but has now passed out of life also. Mr. Thompson obtained his education in the common schools of North Lebanon township, and when eighteen years old, began, on November 12, 1877, an apprenticeship at the furniture trade and undertaking, with Joseph Bowman, on North Ninth street, with whom he continued until May 30, 1890. At this date Mr. Thompson embarked in the business for himself in the Louser building on South Ninth street. In 1893 he erected his large business place, and in December of the same year established himself in it. The building is 47 x 19, with three floors, and his handsome residence, also three stories high, is 33 x 150 feet. Mr. Thompson is thoroughly equipped with all kinds of modern improvements in his undertaking business, and he took a course in embalming in the Oriental Embalming College at Harrisburg, and received his diploma on June 24, 1892.

On May 10, 1881, Mr. Thompson was married to Mary Hartman, daughter of E. Hartman, who died October 1, 1886, leaving one son and one daughter: (1) Charles H., born March 15, 1882, was

---

[623] *Biographical Annals of Lebanon County, Pennsylvania, Containing Biographical Sketches of Prominent and Representative Citizens and of Many of the Early Settled Families*, J.H. Beers & Company, Chicago, 1904, pages 624-625.

educated in the parochial school of Lebanon, graduating June 18, 1896, later attending the Lebanon Business College and graduating April 5, 1897. He then took a course at the Champion College of Embalming at Philadelphia, in August, 1900, and in August, 1901, he took a finishing course at the Renouard Training School for Embalming, in New York City. This talented and thoroughly educated young man is associated with his father in business. (2) Miss Emma C., was born December 18, 1884.

Mr. Thompson was married (second) November 20, 1888 to Emma E. Hain, born in Lebanon county, daughter of Peter Hain. She died July 17, 1898. The children of this marriage were: Lucy R., Paul, Herman F., Andrew P, Robert A. and Helen (who died when eight weeks old). Mr. Thompson was married (third) October 17, 1899 to Elizabeth Allwein, who was born in Dauphin county. The religious connection of the family is with St. Mary's Catholic Church.

Pierce Thompson married Elizabeth Allwein, daughter of Henry E. and Elizabeth (Dentzler) Allwein on October 19, 1899 (see above). As noted in the above narrative, Pierce Thompson would go on to become a well-known funeral director and embalmer in the Lebanon area. They can be found in the Borough of Lebanon in Federal Censuses from 1900 through 1920.[624] In the 1910 and 1920 Censuses Pierce's mother, Sarah (Arnold/Thompson) Allwein is living with them. She died on August 19, 1922.

The Thompson Funeral Home is still operated by this family in Lebanon. The fourth generation of the Thompson family currently operates the business. The following narrative can be found on website of the Thompson Funeral Home:[625]

---

[624] *Twelfth Census of the United States* (1900), *Inhabitants of Lebanon Ward 2, Lebanon County, Pennsylvania*, E.D. No. 125, page 204A; *Thirteenth Census of the United States* (1910), *Inhabitants of Lebanon Ward 2, Lebanon County, Pennsylvania,* E.D. No. 148, page 105A; *Fourteenth Census of the United States* (1920), *Inhabitants of Lebanon Ward 2, Lebanon County, Pennsylvania,* E.D. No. 169, page 139A.

[625] See http://www.thompsonfuneralhomelebanon.com/?page=history.

Exhibit 11.161 Reproduction of a photograph of Pierce Henry Thompson, Lebanon, Pennsylvania

"Started in business June 19, 1890 in Louser building," Pierce H. Thompson wrote on the first page of his ledger. He kept meticulous notes on his business. On that first page, he also noted when he bought his new hearse, March 22, 1892, and when he took delivery on a new ambulance in 1894.

On September 27, 1904, he bought a new horse from Harry Light. "His name will be George," he wrote. Thompson operated both a funeral home and a furniture store, a common combination in those days. The main reason for this is because the cabinet makers also made wooden caskets.

Pierce died at his home above the business in 1922. Pierces' sons continued the business, and in 1924, Andrew P. Thompson, became licensed as an undertaker. He died in 1959. John P. Thompson, son of Andrew, began working with his father and uncles in 1956. After completing a business degree and completion of embalming school, John became a licensed funeral director in 1957. He purchased the business in 1975 from his Uncle Herman's estate.

Stephen P. Thompson, John's son and current owner, became licensed as a funeral director in August of 1985 and became owner in 2006. He is the 4th generation of Thompson's to continue the ownership of the family funeral home.

As noted in the above narrative, Pierce Thompson died on May 10, 1922. His wife Elizabeth died on September 8, 1925.[626] They are buried in St. Mary's Cemetery (SM) in Lebanon.

Elizabeth Allwein Thompson (1852-1925)
Lebanon, Pennsylvania

Elizabeth Allwein (F05-0404-0806), daughter of Henry E. and Elizabeth (Dentzler) Allwein (see Chapter 14), was born December 14, 1852 on her parents' farm in Londonderry Township of Lebanon County. The line of descent for Elizabeth Allwein, connecting her to

---

[626] See the Pennsylvania Department of Health: http://www.health.state. pa.us.

Exhibit 11.162 Reproduction of a photograph of Elizabeth Allwein, daughter of Henry E. and Elizabeth Dentzler Allwein and wife of Pierce Henry Thompson (contributed by Tommy Sims)

Johannes Jacob and Catharina Allwein, progenitors of the Allwein family in colonial Pennsylvania, is as follows:

Generation 1: Johannes Jacob and Catharina Allwein—Berks County, Pa.
Generation 2: Conrad and Catharine (Weibel) Allwein—Dauphin County, Pa.
Generation 3: John and Mary M. (Eckenroth) Allwine—Dauphin County, Pa.
Generation 4: Henry and Elizabeth (Dentzler) Allwine—Dauphin and Lebanon
    Counties, Pa.
Generation 5: Elizabeth Allwein and Pierce Henry Thompson—Dauphin and
    Lebanon Counties, Pa.

Elizabeth Allwein moved to the Borough of Lebanon with her parents around 1880, where she appears in the household listing in the 1880 Federal Census for her parents' household.[627] As noted above, she married Pierce Henry Thompson (see above) in Lebanon on October 19, 1899 and they remained in Lebanon until their deaths in 1922 and 1925, respectively.

William Allwein (1845-1912)
North Lebanon Township

William Allwein (M05-0404-0802), eldest son of Henry and Elizabeth (Dentzler) Allwein (see Chapter 14), was born on his parents' farm in Londonderry Township of Lebanon County on February 28, 1845.[628] The line of descent connecting William Allwein to Johannes Jacob and Catharina Allwein, the progenitors of the Allwein family in colonial Pennsylvania, is as follows:

Generation 1: Johannes Jacob and Catharina Allwein—Berks County, Pa.
Generation 2: Conrad and Catharine (Weibel) Allwein—Dauphin County, Pa.
Generation 3: John and Mary M. (Eckenroth) Allwine—Dauphin County, Pa.
Generation 4: Henry and Elizabeth (Dentzler) Allwein—Lebanon County, Pa.
Generation 5: William and Malinda E. (Koons) Allwein—Lebanon County, Pa.

---

[627] *Tenth Census of the United States* (1880), *Inhabitants of Ward 1 Lebanon, Lebanon County, Pennsylvania*, page 265.

[628] William Allwein was baptized in Elizabethtown May 25, 1845. The biographical information here comes from chapter 6 of *Familie Allwein*, Volume 1, pages 276-280. The date of birth comes from St. Peter's baptismal records from Elizabethtown. The birthdate given on his tombstone agrees with the baptismal records.

Exhibit 11.163 Gravestones for Elizabeth Allwein Thompson and
Pierce Henry Thompson—St. Mary's Cemetery, Lebanon, Pa.

William Allwein married Malinda E. Koons (b. June 2, 1843, d. May 18, 1900), daughter of Joseph and Lydia Koons. Interestingly, except for his date of birth, there is no information provided in Jerome Allwein's *Genealogy* pertaining to William Allwein, despite his clear presence in Lebanon County during the period covered by that *Genealogy*.

William Allwein was a lifelong resident of Lebanon County, although according to the Federal decennial censuses he lived in several different places—in the 1870 census he was living on the eastern side of the county in South Lebanon Township, in 1880 he was living in Londonderry Township in the west of the county, and then in the 1900 and 1910 Censuses living again of the east side in North Lebanon Township.[629] He and many in his family are buried in the cemeteries in the eastern side of North Lebanon Township—Goshert's Cemetery (GS) and Zoar Lutheran Cemetery (ZL), both in Mt. Zion, north of Lebanon in Bethel Township, and Kimmerling's Cemetery (KR), originally a German Reformed Church cemetery on the road to Mt. Zion. According to his obituary, which appeared in the *Lebanon Daily News*, he was a member of the Reformed congregation, and worshiped at Kimmerling's Reformed Church in North Lebanon Township.[630]

Based on census information, tombstone inscriptions, and other sources, the following is a list of the children of William Allwein and Malinda Koons:

---

[629] *Ninth Census of the United States* (1870), *Inhabitants of South Lebanon Township, Lebanon County, Pennsylvania*, page 407; *Tenth Census of the United States* (1880), *Inhabitants of Londonderry Township, Lebanon County, Pennsylvania*, page 404; *Twelfth Census of the United States* (1900), *Inhabitants of North Lebanon Township, Lebanon County, Pennsylvania*, E.D. No. 137, page 127B; *Thirteenth Census of the United States* (1910), *Inhabitants of North Lebanon Township, Lebanon County*, E.D. 163, page 106A.

[630] *Lebanon Daily News*, Lebanon, Pennsylvania, Wednesday Evening, June 12, 1912.

Allen H.J. Allwein (M06-0404-0802-01), b. July 23, 1867, d. January 26, 1935 (KR), unmarried

George W.P. Allwein (M06-0404-0802-02), b. November 17, 1869, d. March 6, 1870 (KR)

Amelia R. Allwein (F06-0404-0802-03), b. October 7, 1870, d. October 14, 1870 (KR)

Mary Magdalena Allwein (F06-0404-0802-04), b. October 14, 1871, d. February 16, 1916 (KR), unmarried

Aaron Philip Allwein (M06-0404-0802-05), b. June 16, 1873, d. August 16, 1904 (KR), m. (January 26, 1895) Kate M. Kreider (b. December 22, 1873, d. April 29, 1907)

Adam James Allwein (M06-0404-0802-06), b. June 28, 1875, d. December 28, 1954 (ZL), m. (December 24, 1903) Kate Lydia Spannuth (b. December 28, 1883, d. July 8, 1941)

Augustus Christian Allwein (M06-0404-0802-07), b. January 16, 1881, d. December 3, 1944, unmarried

Christian "Christ" Augustus Allwein (M06-0404-0802-08), b. January 16, 1881, d. August 12, 1961 (MM), m. (1) (June 7, 1902) Kate Umbenhocker (b. August 10, 1886, d. August 2, 1926), (2) (December 19, 1934) Martha Kline (b. April 14, 1907, d. June 9, 1977)

Amos Allwein (M06-0404-0802-09), b. December 8, 1885, d. January 14, 1937 (GS), m. (November 3, 1906) Ella N. Guldin (b. August 6, 1888, d. June 2, 1961)

Malinda (Koons) Allwein died May 18, 1900. William Allwein died June 12, 1912.[631] They are buried at Kimmerling's Cemetery (KR), on the eastside, near the church, amidst most of their children.[632]

---

[631] See the Pennsylvania Department of Health: http://www.health.state. pa.us.

[632] *Kimmerling's Cemetery, North Lebanon Twp., Lebanon Co.,* PA, compiled by Kenneth Long. I spell their names as they appear on the tombstone inscriptions. This source is available at the Lebanon County Historical Society, 924 Cumberland Street, Lebanon, Pennsylvania 17042.

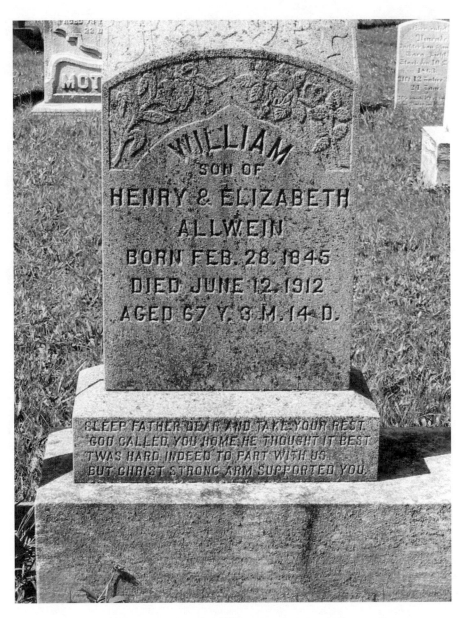

Exhibit 11.164 Gravestone for William Allwein—Kimmerling's Cemetery, North Lebanon Township, Lebanon County, Pennsylvania

Exhibit 11.165 Gravestone for Malinda Allwein—Kimmerling's
Cemetery, North Lebanon Township, Lebanon County,
Pennsylvania

Allen H.J. Allwein (1867-1935)
North Lebanon, Lebanon County

Allen H.J. Allwein (M06-0404-0802-01), oldest son of William and Malinda (Koons) Allwein, was born on July 23, 1867 on his parents' farm near Campbelltown in Londonderry Township, Lebanan County, Pennsylvania. His parents moved to North Lebanon Township sometime before 1900 and he lived the remainder of his entire life in North Lebanon Township, remaining on his parents' farm for most of his life. The line of descent connecting Allen H.J. Allwein to Johannes Jacob and Catharina Allwein, the progenitors of the Allwein family in colonial Pennsylvania, is as follows:

Generation 1: Johannes Jacob and Catharina Allwein—Berks County, Pa.
Generation 2: Conrad and Catharine (Weibel) Allwein—Dauphin County, Pa.
Generation 3: John and Mary M. (Eckenroth) Allwine—Dauphin County, Pa.
Generation 4: Henry and Elizabeth (Dentzler) Allwein—Lebanon County, Pa.
Generation 5: William and Malinda E. (Koons) Allwein—Lebanon County, Pa.
Generation 6: Allen H.J. Allwein—Lebanon County, Pa.

Allen H.J. Allwein did not marry. He worked as a laborer most of his life. In the 1900 and 1910 Federal Census enumerations of North Lebanon Township, he is listed in the household of his father. In these reports his occupation is given as "laborer in a rolling mill." After his father died, he lived in the household of his younger brother, Amos Allwein, where he is listed in the 1920 and 1930 Federal Census reports.[633] In the 1920 report his occupation is given as "laborer in steel works" and in 1930, he is working as a laborer on his brother's farm.

Allen H.J. Allwein died on January 26, 1935.[634] He is buried, along with his parents and several siblings at Kimmerling's Cemetery (KR) in North Lebanon Township, Lebanon County.

---

[633] *Twelfth Census of the United States* (1900), *Inhabitants of North Lebanon Township, Lebanon County, Pennsylvania*, E.D. No. 137, page 127B; *Thirteenth Census of the United States* (1910), *Inhabitants of North Lebanon Township, Lebanon County*, E.D. 163, page 106A; *Fourteenth Census of the United States* (1920), *Inhabitants of North Lebanon Township West Precinct, Lebanon County, Pennsylvania*, E.D. No. 186, page 168A; *Fifteenth Census of the United States* (1930), *Inhabitants of North Lebanon Township, Lebanon County, Pennsylvania*, E.D. No. 38-34, page 256B.

[634] See the Pennsylvania Department of Health: http://www.health.state.pa.us.

Exhibit 11.166 Gravestone for Allen H.J. Allwein in Kimmerling's Cemetery, North Lebanon, Lebanon County, Pennsylvania

Mary Magdalena Allwein (1871-1916)
North Lebanon, Lebanon County

Mary Magdalena Allwein (F06-0404-0802-04), oldest daughter of William and Malinda (Koons) Allwein, was born October 14, 1871 on her parents' farm near Campbelltown in Londonderry Township, Lebanan County, Pennsylvania. The line of descent connecting Mary Magdalena Allwein to Johannes Jacob and Catharina Allwein, the progenitors of the Allwein family in colonial Pennsylvania, is as follows:

Generation 1: Johannes Jacob and Catharina Allwein—Berks County, Pa.
Generation 2: Conrad and Catharine (Weibel) Allwein—Dauphin County, Pa.
Generation 3: John and Mary M. (Eckenroth) Allwine—Dauphin County, Pa.
Generation 4: Henry and Elizabeth (Dentzler) Allwein—Lebanon County, Pa.
Generation 5: William and Malinda E. (Koons) Allwein—Lebanon County, Pa.
Generation 6: Mary Magdalena Allwein—Lebanon County, Pa.

Mary Magdalena Allwein did not marry. She continued to live in her father's household after her mother died.[635] Mary M. Allwein died on February 16, 1916.[636] She is buried, along with her parents and several siblings at Kimmerling's Cemetery (KR) in North Lebanon Township, Lebanon County.

Aaron Philip Allwein (1873-1904)
North Lebanon, Lebanon County

Aaron Philip Allwein (M06-0404-0802-05), son of William and Malinda (Koons) Allwein, was born in June 16, 1873 on his parents' farm near Campbelltown in Londonderry Township, Lebanan County, Pennsylvania. The line of descent connecting Aaron Philip Allwein to Johannes Jacob and Catharina Allwein, the progenitors of the Allwein family in colonial Pennsylvania, is as follows:

---

[635] *Twelfth Census of the United States* (1900), *Inhabitants of North Lebanon Township, Lebanon County, Pennsylvania*, E.D. No. 137, page 127B; *Thirteenth Census of the United States* (1910), *Inhabitants of North Lebanon Township, Lebanon County*, E.D. 163, page 106A.
[636] See the Pennsylvania Department of Health: http://www.health.state.pa.us.

Exhibit 11.167 Gravestone for Mary Magdalena Allwein in Kimmerling's Cemetery, North Lebanon, Lebanon County, Pennsylvania

Generation 1: Johannes Jacob and Catharina Allwein—Berks County, Pa.
Generation 2: Conrad and Catharine (Weibel) Allwein—Dauphin County, Pa.
Generation 3: John and Mary M. (Eckenroth) Allwine—Dauphin County, Pa.
Generation 4: Henry and Elizabeth (Dentzler) Allwein—Lebanon County, Pa.
Generation 5: William and Malinda E. (Koons) Allwein—Lebanon County, Pa.
Generation 6: Aaron Philip and Kate (Kreider) Allwein—Lebanon County, Pa.

Aaron Philip Allwein married Kate M. Kreider (or Krider), daughter of Josiah and Mariah Kreider, on January 26, 1895 at Lebanon. They settled in South Lebanon Township of Lebanon County. In the 1900 Federal Census, they are listed in the enumeration of South Lebanon Township, and his occupation is given as "laborer in a rolling mill."[637]

Based on the 1900 Federal Census enumeration, cemetery enumerations and other information, there were five daughters born to Aaron Philip and Kate (Kreider) Allwein, as follows:[638]

Kate M. "Mary" Allwein (F07-0404-0802-0501), b. February 12, 1896, d. July 22, 1953 (KR), m. (November 11, 1916) John H. Troutman (b. February 12, 1892, d. November 30, 1956)

Leah M. Allwein (F07-0404-0802-0502), b. May 26, 1898, d. January 8, 1961 (KR), m. (December 18, 1920) Paul W. Troutman (b. December 4, 1895, d. July 17, 1962)

Mabel Ellen Allwein (F07-0404-0802-0503), b. February 23, 1900, d. March 12, 1955 (HC), m. (May 28, 1917) Howard Henry Arnold (b. July 15, 1898, d. February 19, 1996)

Mary E. Allwein (F07-0404-0802-0504), b. September 14, 1902, d. September 28, 1993 (KR), m. (January 1, 1921) Paul Cyrus Muth (b. May 29, 1898, d. May 14, 1968)

Clara A. Allwein (F07-0404-0802-0505), b. December 21, 1904, d. December 1979 (KR), m. (June 17, 1922) Oscar C. Thomas Klick (b. January 3, 1900, d. March 25, 1954)

---

[637] *Twelfth Census of the United States* (1900), *Inhabitants of South Lebanon Township, Lebanon County, Pennsylvania*, E.D. No. 141, page 218B.

[638] Some information for these children and their spouses were obtained from obituaries in the *Lebanon Daily News*, Lebanon, Pennsylvania, Thursday Evening, July 23, 1953; Friday Evening, March 26, 1954; Monday, March 14, 1955; Monday Evening, December 3, 1956; Wednesday Evening, July 18, 1962; Wednesday Evening, May 15, 1968; Tuesday, February 20, 1996.

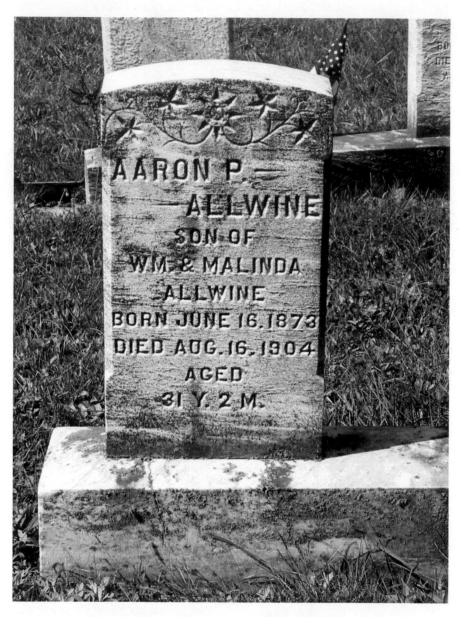

Exhibit 11.168 Gravestone for Aaron Philip Allwein in Kimmerling's Cemetery, North Lebanon, Lebanon County, Pennsylvania

Aaron and his wife both died at a young age—Aaron died at age 31 and Kate at age 33. Some of the children were living with their grandfather in the 1910 and 1920 Federal Censuses of North Lebanon Township (see above). Aaron died August 16, 1904 and Kate (Kreider) Allwein on April 29, 1907, and they are buried, along with his parents and several siblings at Kimmerling's Cemetery (KR) in North Lebanon Township, Lebanon County.

Adam James Allwein (1875-1954)
North Lebanon, Lebanon County

Adam James Allwein (M06-0404-0802-06), son of William and Malinda (Koons) Allwein, was born June 28, 1875 on his parents' farm near Campbelltown in Londonderry Township, Lebanan County, Pennsylvania. His parents moved to North Lebanon Township sometime before 1900 and he lived the remainder of his life there. The line of descent connecting Adam James Allwein to Johannes Jacob and Catharina Allwein, the progenitors of the Allwein family in colonial Pennsylvania, is as follows:

Generation 1: Johannes Jacob and Catharina Allwein—Berks County, Pa.
Generation 2: Conrad and Catharine (Weibel) Allwein—Dauphin County, Pa.
Generation 3: John and Mary M. (Eckenroth) Allwine—Dauphin County, Pa.
Generation 4: Henry and Elizabeth (Dentzler) Allwein—Lebanon County, Pa.
Generation 5: William and Malinda E. (Koons) Allwein—Lebanon County, Pa.
Generation 6: Adam James and Kate L. (Spannuth) Allwein—Lebanon County, Pa.

Adam James Allwein married Kate L. Spannuth, daughter of George and Emma Spannuth, on December 24, 1903 at Jonestown, Pennsylvania. They settled in North Lebanon Township of Lebanon County, where they can be located in Federal Census enumerations from 1910 to 1940.[639] He worked as a house painter most of his life.

---

[639] *Thirteenth Census of the United States* (1910), *Inhabitants of North Lebanon Township, Lebanon County*, E.D. 163, page 86A; *Fourteenth Census of the United States* (1920), *Inhabitants of North Lebanon Township, Lebanon County, Pennsylvania*, E.D. No. 188, page 184A; *Fifteenth Census of the United States* (1930), *Inhabitants of North Lebanon Township, Lebanon County, Pennsylvania*, E.D. No. 38-34, page 262A; *Sixteenth Census of the United States* (1940), *Inhabitants of North Lebanon Township, Lebanon County, Pennsylvania*, E.D. No. 38-42, page 742B.

Exhibit 11.169 Gravestone for Kate Kreider Allwein in Kimmerling's Cemetery, North Lebanon, Lebanon County, Pennsylvania

In the 1940 Federal Census his occupation is given as "proprietor, roofing contractor."

Based on census enumerations and other information, the following is a list of the children born to Adam James and Kate L. (Spannuth) Allwein:[640]

Emma Margaret Allwein (F07-0404-0802-0601), b. July 26, 1904, d. January 28, 1945 (KC), m. (April 22, 1937) John Henry Mease (b. February 26, 1884, d. December 1, 1955)

George W. Allwein (M07-0404-0802-0602), b. November 18, 1905, d. October 25, 1995, m. (June 2, 1928) Alice C. Wagner (b. July 17, 1909, d. July 1991)

Marian Maria Allwein (F07-0404-0802-0603), b. February 8, 1907, d. September 1983 (ZL), m. (November 24, 1923) Levi V. Sonnon, Jr. (b. February 14, 1903, d. August 30, 1970)

Leo H. Allwein (M07-0404-0802-0604), b. June 6, 1909, d. March 22, 1970 (ZL), unmarried

Paul A. Allwein (M07-0404-0802-0605), b. est. 1911, d. April 1, 1939, m. (February 26, 1938) Carrie Marie Mengel (b. December 22, 1912, d. November 13, 2001) [remarried (April 10, 1948) Harold Angstadt (b. January 28, 1916, d. December 19, 1994 (FH))]

Helen E. "Sus" Allwein (F07-0404-0802-0606), b. August 24, 1912, d. October 10, 1998 (ZL), unmarried[641]

Mary Alice Allwein (F07-0404-0802-0607), b. December 13, 1913, d. January 21, 1998 (GW), m. (April 11, 1936) Harry Joseph Sheffy (b. March 21, 1913, d. August 4, 2004)

James Edwin Allwein (M07-0404-0802-0608), b. October 16, 1915, d. June 29, 1969 (ZL),

Charles Allwein (M07-0404-0802-0609), b. November 29, 1917, d. November 29, 1917 (ZL)

---

[640] Some information for these children and their spouses was obtained from obituaries in the *Lebanon Daily News*, Lebanon, Pennsylvania: Monday, January 29, 1945; Friday Evening, December 2, 1955.

[641] Death notice for Helen E. Allwein from the *Patriot News*, Harrisburg, Pennsylvania.

Raymond L. Allwein (M07-0404-0802-0610), b. March 12, 1920, d. November 14, 1992 (in Florida), m. (June 8, 1945) Bernice J. Biever (b. April 28, 1921, d. unknown)

Adam James Allwein died on December 28, 1954, and Kate L. (Spannuth) Allwein on July 8, 1941.[642] They are buried in Zoar Lutheran Cemetery (ZL) in Mt. Zion, Lebanon County, Pennsylvania.

Augustus Christian Allwein (1881-1944)
North Lebanon, Lebanon County

Augustus Christian Allwein (M06-0404-0802-07), son of William and Malinda (Koons) Allwein and twin brother to Christian Augustus Allwein, was born January 16, 1881 on his parents' farm near Campbelltown in Londonderry Township, Lebanan County, Pennsylvania. His parents moved to North Lebanon Township, Lebanan County, some time prior to 1900, and he lived the remainder of this life there. The line of descent connecting Augustus Christian Allwein to Johannes Jacob and Catharina Allwein, the progenitors of the Allwein family in colonial Pennsylvania, is as follows:

Generation 1: Johannes Jacob and Catharina Allwein—Berks County, Pa.
Generation 2: Conrad and Catharine (Weibel) Allwein—Dauphin County, Pa.
Generation 3: John and Mary M. (Eckenroth) Allwine—Dauphin County, Pa.
Generation 4: Henry and Elizabeth (Dentzler) Allwein—Lebanon County, Pa.
Generation 5: William and Malinda E. (Koons) Allwein—Lebanon County, Pa.
Generation 6: Augustus Christian Allwein—Lebanon County, Pa.

As far as we know, Augustus Christian Allwein did not marry. He lived in the household of his father throughout his early adulthood, as indicated by the 1900 and 1910 Federal Censuses.[643] Then, following the death of his father, he lived in the household

---

[642] See the Pennsylvania Department of Health: http://www.health.state. pa.us.

[643] *Twelfth Census of the United States* (1900), *Inhabitants of North Lebanon Township, Lebanon County, Pennsylvania*, E.D. No. 137, page 127B; *Thirteenth Census of the United States* (1910), *Inhabitants of North Lebanon Township, Lebanon County*, E.D. 163, page 106A.

Exhibit 11.170 Gravestone for Adam J. and Kate L. Allwein—Zoar Lutheran Cemetery, Mt. Zion, Pennsylvania

of his brother, Amos Allwein, in North Lebanon Township (see below).[644] In the 1940 Federal Census he is listed living by himself in South Lebanon Township.[645]

[It is important to note some potential confusion here. There is a second "Augustus C. Allwein" (Augustus Claude Allwein, son of Augustus D. Allwein) which can be confused with the present Augustus Christian Allwein. Augustus Claude Allwein married Cora A. Douple, daughter of Jesse and Amanda (Getz) Douple, on December 22, 1914 at Lebanon. In the 1920 Federal Census, Augustus and Cora Allwein were living in the Borough of Lebanon, in the first Ward, where he was working as a drayman. At the time of the 1920 census, Amanda Douple, Augustus's mother-in-law, was also noted in the census listings. By 1930, they had moved to North Cornwall Township, where Augustus is listed as working as a "collector for an insurance company."[646] From the 1930 census listings, we find the union between Augustus C. Allwein and Cora A. (Douple) produced one daughter: Elizabeth Allwein (F07-0404-0802-0701), born about 1922. We cover this family in Chapter 14, where we discuss the Allwein families originating in Dauphin County.]

Augustus Christian Allwein died December 3, 1944, after contracting pneumonia.[647] He is buried with his family at Kimmerling's Cemetery, North Lebanon Township.

---

[644] *Fourteenth Census of the United States* (1920), *Inhabitants of North Lebanon Township West Precinct, Lebanon County, Pennsylvania*, E.D. No. 167, page 89A; *Fifteenth Census of the United States* (1930), *Inhabitants of North Lebanon Township, Lebanon County, Pennsylvania*, E.D. No. 38-34, page 256B.

[645] *Sixteenth Census of the United States* (1940), *Inhabitants of South Lebanon Township, Lebanon County, Pennsylvania*, E.D. No. 38-51, page 889B.

[646] *Fourteenth Census of the United States* (1920), *Inhabitants of North Lebanon Township West Precinct, Lebanon County, Pennsylvania*, E.D. No. 167, page 89A; *Fifteenth Census of the United States* (1930), *Inhabitants of North Cornwall Township, Lebanon County, Pennsylvania*, E.D. No. 38-33, page 249A.

[647] Obituary in *Lebanon Daily News*, Lebanon, Pennsylvania, Monday Evening, December 4, 1944. See also the Pennsylvania Department of Health: http://www.health.state.pa.us.

Exhibit 11.171 Gravestone for Augustus Christian Allwein—Kimmerling's Cemetery, North Lebanon Township, Lebanon County, Pennsylvania

Christian "Christ" Augustus Allwein (1881-1961)
North Lebanon, Lebanon County

Christian "Christ" Augustus Allwein (M06-0404-0802-08), son of William and Malinda (Koons) Allwein and twin brother to Augustus Christian Allwein, was born January 16, 1881 on his parents' farm near Campbelltown in Londonderry Township, Lebanan County, Pennsylvania. His parents moved to North Lebanon Township, Lebanon County, at some time prior to 1900, and he began his adult life there. The line of descent connecting Christian Augustus Allwein to Johannes Jacob and Catharina Allwein, the progenitors of the Allwein family in colonial Pennsylvania, is as follows:

Generation 1: Johannes Jacob and Catharina Allwein—Berks County, Pa.
Generation 2: Conrad and Catharine (Weibel) Allwein—Dauphin County, Pa.
Generation 3: John and Mary M. (Eckenroth) Allwine—Dauphin County, Pa.
Generation 4: Henry and Elizabeth (Dentzler) Allwein—Lebanon County, Pa.
Generation 5: William and Malinda E. (Koons) Allwein—Lebanon County, Pa.
Generation 6: Christian "Christ" Augustus and Kate (Umbenhocker) [Martha
    (Kline)] Allwein—Lebanon County, Pa.

Christian Augustus Allwein married Kate Umbenhocker, daughter of Jeranuis and Mary Umbenhocker, on June 7, 1902 at Lebanon. They settled initially in North Lebanon Township where Christian Augustus worked as a "puddler in a puddle mill."[648] Eventually, they ended up in Jackson Township of Lebanon County, as indicated in the 1910 through 1930 Federal Census listings, where they remained until they moved to Lebanon, where they are

---

[648] See *Dictionary of Occupational Titles*. Mixes and dumps raw materials, such as silicas or clays, into mixers: Obtains materials from storage area, using shovel, wheelbarrow, or towmotor, and transports material to batching area. Measures specified quantities of materials according to batch cards, using scales or measuring box. Dumps material from sacks onto conveyor leading to mixer or empties bulk material from wheelbarrow into mixer. DOT code: 570.687-010.

recorded in the 1940 Federal Census.[649] In the 1920 Census report, Christian Allwein was a laborer in a stone quarry, and in the 1930 Census report, a few years after Kate Umbenhocker Allwein had died (August 2, 1926), Christian Augustus was living in a boarding house in Jackson Township, not employed.

Based on census reports and other materials, we have the following information about the children of Christian Augustus Allwein and Kate Umbenhocker:

Nora M. Allwein (F07-0404-0802-0801), b. September 12, 1905, d. March 23, 1947 (KR), m. (February 27, 1932), Paul W. Good, Sr. (b. October 14, 1909, d. July 17, 1990 (HA))

Lizzie M. Allwein (F06-0404-0802-0802), b. May 20, 1906, d. August 20, 1908 (KR)

Lillian "Lillie" M. Allwein (F07-0404-0802-0803), b. March 16, 1908, d. September 1975, m. (February 1, 1932) James C. Good (b. October 6, 1910, d. February 21, 1990 (HF))

Kate Umbenhocker died on August 2, 1926.[650] She is buried with her daughter Nora M. Allwein at Kimmerling's Cemetery in North Lebanon.

---

[649] *Thirteenth Census of the United States* (1910), *Inhabitants of North Lebanon Township*, E.D. No. 163, page 86A; *Fourteenth Census of the United States* (1920), *Inhabitants of Jackson Township, Lebanon County, Pennsylvania*, E.D. No. 165, page 49A; *Fifteenth Census of the United States* (1930), *Inhabitants of Jackson Township, Lebanon County, Pennsylvania*, E.D. No. 38-11, page 119A; *Sixteenth Census of the United States* (1940), *Inhabitants of Lebanon, Lebanon County, Pennsylvania*, E.D. No. 38-17, page 269A.

[650] Funeral notice for Kate Allwein in the *Lebanon Daily News* and *Lebanon Semi-Weekly News*, Lebanon, Pennsylvania, Thursday, August 12, 1926. The funeral notice does not clarify the date of Kate Allwein's death— this was obtained from Christian's marriage application at the time of his marriage to Martha Kline. See also the Pennsylvania Department of Health: http://www.health.state.pa.us. The date of death given on her gravestone at Kimmerling's Cemetery is August 8, 1928, which we believe is in error.

Exhibit 11.172 Gravestones for Katie (Umbenhocker) Allwein and Nora M. (Allwein) Good—Kimmerling's Cemetery, North Lebanon Township, Lebanon County, Pennsylvania

Several years after the death of his first wife, Christian Augustus Allwein married Martha Kline, daughter of Amos and Catherine (Wolfersberger) Kline, in Lebanon on December 19, 1934. According to available information they had two children:

Catherine Ann Allwein (F07-0404-0802-0804), b. May 20, 1927, d. December 19, 2012 (MM), m. (July 14, 1950) Aaron H. Dowhower (b. September 30, 1928, d. August 1978)

Amos Allen Allwein (M07-0404-0802-0805), b. July 28, 1932, d. January 5, 1997 (FV), m. unknown

For some period of time, Christ Allwein apparently practiced folk magic or faith healing. In times past, these practitioners were called "hex doctors" or "pow wow doctors." These practices were prominent among Pennsylvania Germans, especially in Amish, Mennonite and Dunker communities, but also among the Lutheran and German Reformed groups.[651] Such practitioners used spells, incantations, and prayers to heal people afflicted with sickness and distress, and they often had a significant following in most all communities. The tradition of "hex signs" (or pentagrams) painted on Pennsylvania barns in some areas were originally part of this tradition and were thought to have talismanic properties. Today these hex signs are simply considered decorative, and the tradition has generally fallen out of favor.

Local laws were enacted to discourage these practices, and Christ Allwein found himself in trouble for practicing these rituals. A story appearing the *The Gettysburg Times* in September of 1934 read as follows:[652]

HOLD TWO MEN IN HEX CASE—CHARGES WITH PRETENDING TO EFFECT PURPOSES BY CHARMS AND SPELLS

Lebanon, Pa. Sept. 15—Another "hex" case in Lebanon came to light Friday afternoon in the arrest of Henry H. Becker, of South

---

[651] See the following URLs: http://www.berkshistory.org/articles/pow-wow.html and http://www.esoteric.msu.edu/VolumeIV/Powwow.htm
[652] *The Gettysburg Times*, Gettysburg, Pennsylvania, September 15, 1934.

Lebanon township, and Christian Allwein, of North Lebanon township, on charges of "pretending to effect purpose by spells, charms and incantations." Both furnished bail for hearings next week before Alderman Nathan Sundel in this city. David C. Donmoyer, of North Cornwall township, the Commonwealth's principal witness, is in a Lebanon hospital recovering from an operation made necessary by neglect of an ulcerated leg which he charges both Becker and Allwein promised to heal and for the treatment of which he paid both in cash. After the affected leg failed to show improvement as the result of Allwein's incantations, Donmoyer said he paid Becker several fees to break Allwein's so-called spell. Counsel for the prosecution announced Friday afternoon possession of a list of prominent Lebanon people whom Becker claims to have treated.

He apparently continued to engage in these practices, for in the application for marriage of Catherine Ann Allwein and Aaron H. Dowhower, dated July 14, 1950, Catherine listed her father's occupation as "pow wow doctor."

Christian "Christ" Augustus Allwein died on August 12, 1961 and his wife, Martha (Kline) Allwein, died on June 9, 1977.[653] He is buried at the Mount Hope Cemetery (MM) in Myerstown, Lebanon County, Pennsylvania. His gravestone is located a few feet from the graves of Martha's parents Amos and Catherine Kline, but it is unclear where she is buried.

Amos Allwein (1885-1937)
North Lebanon, Lebanon County

Amos Allwein (M06-0404-0802-09), youngest son of William and Malinda (Koons) Allwein, was born December 8, 1885 on his parents' farm near Campbelltown in Londonderry Township, Lebanan County, Pennsylvania. His parents moved to North

---

[653] Obituaries for Christian Augustus Allwein and Martha Kline Allwein from the *Lebanon Daily News*, Lebanon, Pennsylvania, Monday, August 14, 1961; Friday Evening, June 10, 1977. See the Pennsylvania Department of Health: http://www.health.state.pa.us.

Exhibit 11.173 Gravestone for Christ A. and Martha Allwein—Mount Hope Cemetery, Myerstown, Lebanon County, Pennsylvania

Lebanon Township when he was young, and there he began his adult life. The line of descent connecting Amos Allwein to Johannes Jacob and Catharina Allwein, the progenitors of the Allwein family in colonial Pennsylvania, is as follows:

Generation 1: Johannes Jacob and Catharina Allwein—Berks County, Pa.
Generation 2: Conrad and Catharine (Weibel) Allwein—Dauphin County, Pa.
Generation 3: John and Mary M. (Eckenroth) Allwine—Dauphin County, Pa.
Generation 4: Henry and Elizabeth (Dentzler) Allwein—Lebanon County, Pa.
Generation 5: William and Malinda E. (Koons) Allwein—Lebanon County, Pa.
Generation 6: Amos and Ella N. (Guldin) Allwein—Lebanon County, Pa.

Amos Allwein married Ella N. Guldin, daughter of Calvin and Kate Guldin, on November 3, 1906 at Lebanon. They settled initially in South Lebanon Township, where Amos was employed as a "puddler in an iron works," after which time they returned to North Lebanon Township, and Amos farmed the land.[654]

Based on census reports and other materials, Amos Allwein and Ella N. Guldin had the following children:[655]

Infant twin boys (M07-0404-0802-0901), b. March 17, 1907, d. March 17, 1907 (GS)

---

[654] *Thirteenth Census of the United States* (1910), *Inhabitants of South Lebanon Township, Lebanon County*, E.D. No. 167, page 190A; Fourteenth *Census of the United States* (1920), *Inhabitants of North Lebanon Township West Precinct, Lebanon County, Pennsylvania*, E.D. No. 167, page 89A; *Fifteenth Census of the United States* (1930), *Inhabitants of North Lebanon Township, Lebanon County, Pennsylvania*, E.D. No. 38-34, page 256B.

[655] Some information for these children and their spouses were obtained from obituaries in the *Lebanon Daily News*, Lebanon, Pennsylvania, Monday Evening, February 23, 1925; Friday Evening, January 22, 1943; Thursday Evening, November 14, 1963; Wednesday Evening, November 21, 1973; Sunday, October 16, 1983; Tuesday, January 3, 1995; Monday, April 26, 1999; Monday, May 4, 2005; Tuesday, April 18, 2006; and *The Evening News*, Harrisburg, Pennsylvania, Thursday, February 20, 1992.

Mary Catherine Allwein (F07-0404-0802-0902), b. March 1, 1908, d. April 30, 1908 (GS)

Ammon W. Allwein (M07-0404-0802-0903), b. est. 1909, d. November 20, 1973 (GP), m. (1) (March 15, 1930) Lillian Sonnon (b. 1912, d. November 13, 1963), (2) Mary E. Brandt (nee Hudson) (b. January 31, 1909, d. December 31, 1994)

Warren H. Allwein (M07-0404-0802-0904), b. December 16, 1910, d. February 22, 1925 (GS)

Henry W. Allwein (M07-0404-0802-0905), b. March 30, 1912, d. January 19, 1943 (GS) (enlisted World War II, December 14, 1942)[656]

Anna Mae Allwein (F07-0404-0802-0906), b. June 26, 1914, d. May 3, 2005 (GP), m. Irwin E. Keller, Sr. (b. March 20, 1908, d. February 18, 1992)

Wayne Leroy Allwein (M07-0404-0802-0907), b. October 26,1918, d. October 14, 1983 (GP) (enlisted World War II, October 17, 1942), m. Christena Leona Soule (b. June 26, 1922, d. April 17, 2006)

Irene Mildred Allwein (F07-0404-0802-0908), b. June 30, 1920, d. April 25, 1999 (HC), m. (September 5, 1942) James Vincent Di Scuillo (b. est. 1897, d. unknown)

Amos Allwein died on January 14, 1937, and Ella Guldin Allwein on June 2, 1961.[657] They are buried together at Goshert's Cemetery in Mt. Zion, Lebanon County, Pennsylvania.

---

[656] Henry W. Allwein died while in military service at Camp Crowder, Missouri. He died of cerebral hemorrhage. Prior to his induction into the military, he was employed as a laborer for the Bethlehem Steel Company. See the *Lebanon Daily News*, Lebanon, Pennsylvania, Friday Evening, January 22, 1943.

[657] See the Pennsylvania Department of Health: http://www.health.state. pa.us.

Exhibit 11.174 Gravestone for Amos and Ella Allwein—Goshert's Cemetery, Mt. Zion, Pennsylvania

Closing

This chapter has focused on the Allwein families that lived in Lebanon County, Pennsylvania in the latter part of the 19th century and the beginning of the 20th century. Specifically, we have chronicled what we know about the lives of Allwein families in the area of Lebanon County from about 1870 through 1940, using all available record sources, including census materials, city directories, county marriage records, local atlases and maps of the County, family genealogies, local histories, cemetery inscriptions, and other archival data to inform what we here call their "journeys in time and place."

In this chapter we extend the work begun in the earlier chapters of *Familie Allwein* devoted to the Allwein families that settled in the Lebanon area at the end of the 18th century. Virtually without exception, Allwein and Allwine residents of these areas of central Pennsylvania during that period were descendants of Conrad and Catharine Allwein (see Chapter 3 of *Familie Allwein*, volume 1). Two of their children specifically—sons Philip Allwein (M03-0405) and John Allwine (M03-0404) did much to establish the Allwein and Allwine families we find in the three-county area of Lebanon, Dauphin and Lancaster Counties in the late 19th century. Indeed, each of these men did much to help populate the area with the ALLWEIN, ALLWINE and/or ALWINE name in this three-county area. Philip and his two wives had 21 children who survived to adulthood—John Allwine and his two wives had 16 children who survived to adulthood. Chapter 14 focuses on several related Allwein and Allwine families of nearby Dauphin and Lancaster Counties.

The main focus of the present chapter has been on the *fourth*, *fifth* and *sixth* generation members of the Allwein families in Lebanon County. Where we have information on *seventh* generation family members, we make that available to the extent possible as well. Thus, we have arbitrarily gone no farther with 7th-generation families, except to list them, where they are known. These practices are applied throughout all chapters of this volume.

Many Allwein descendants can be found in the area today, and probably many more than is the case in other locales. A 1994 zip code search of addresses in Lebanon County, for example, turned up 3 ALWINE and 45 ALLWEIN households. Allwein family descendants in the area can be sure that the history of their families and the lives of their ancestors are recorded in this volume for future generations to reflect upon. More research is necessary, and hopefully this will provide a baseline for further study.

The next two chapters cover several Allwein families from the Lebanon area and elsewhere who settled in Philadelphia (Chapter 12) and Berks County (Chapter 13).

CHAPTER TWELVE

Allwein Families in Philadelphia County

Introduction

It was through the port of Philadelphia that Hans Jacob Allwein, our immigrant ancestor, came. He was part of an 18th century migration involving thousands of German-speaking people coming to the American colonies. He did not settle there, however, and soon after his arrival in 1741, he moved on to Bern Township of what would eventually become Berks County (see Chapter 13). In this chapter we focus on Allwein families that eventually came to settle in Philadelphia County in the late 19th and early 20th century. Many of these families, although by no means all of them, came from those Allwein families of Lebanon County discussed in the previous chapter.

Philadelphia County

Philadelphia was the name given to one of three original counties established by the Penn family in the Pennsylvania Colony—the others were Bucks and Chester. We do not know the exact date for the formation of the three original counties, nor is much known about the origins of the names, except that they were chosen by William Penn. One author had this to say about the original three counties:[658]

---

[658] A. Howry Espenshade, *Pennsylvania Place Names*, State College, Pennsylvania: The Pennsylvania State College, 1925 (Republished by Gale Research Company, Detroit: Book Tower, 1969), chapter 3, pages 29-40.

. . . shortly after his arrival, probably in November, 1682, he divided his province into the three counties of Philadelphia, Buckingham (which was later called Bucks), and Upland (which was soon changed to Chester); for in November of this year he appointed a sheriff for each county. These three counties were represented in the first provincial Assembly, which met at Upland December 4, 1682, and remained in session four days, ratifying the code of laws drawn up in England, and formally annexing the three counties of Delaware to Pennsylvania.

Philadelphia County included the new city of Philadelphia and the surrounding region. The original city of Philadelphia had been specified by Penn to be a spacious city located on the Delaware River covering 10,000 acres. Bucks County lay to the north, with the Delaware River forming its eastern boundary, but except for this and the boundary with New York colony on the north, Bucks County had no definite boundaries. Chester County lay to the south and extended westward from the city of Upland (or Chester), again without any certain boundaries. Philadelphia County would essentially retain much of its original boundaries, and due to their lack of any definite limits, Bucks and Chester Counties would form the basis for many further county divisions that would come later.

The city of Philadelphia was known as the "city of brotherly love," and although the exact origins of the name are uncertain, it is generally accepted that Penn made this choice based on the Biblical city of Philadelphia mentioned in the early Greek text of the New Testament, which was the seat of one of the seven early Christian churches. In this context, the Greek word *Philadelphia* is translated in several instances as "the city of brotherly love." This was, in any event, the sentiment that Penn wanted expressed in the name of his new city, and the name of Philadelphia appears in a land warrant executed July 10, 1682.[659]

---

[659] A. Howry Espenshade, *Pennsylvania Place Names*, State College, Pennsylvania: The Pennsylvania State College, 1925 (Republished by Gale Research Company, Detroit: Book Tower, 1969), chapter 3, page 31.

Allwine Families in Philadelphia

As I already noted, Hans Jacob Allwein entered the port of Philadelphia in 1741, arriving on October 2 on the ship St. Andrew, commanded by Charles Stedman. Soon after his arrival, he moved on to Bern Township of what would eventually become Berks County (see Chapter 13). Nonetheless, there were other Allwine families in Philadelphia from about 1785 onward. However, the connection of these earliest families to the Allwein family that is the subject of this book remains somewhat of a puzzle. A man by the name of Lawrence Allwine lived in the city of Philadelphia from about 1785 until 1809.[660] The earliest records concerning Lawrence Allwine indicate that he probably originated in Berks County and fought in the Revolutionary War. He lived in New York during much of the War, and in the years following the Revolution he settled in Philadelphia, where he was engaged in furniture making for almost 25 years. His residence and furniture manufactory were located just around the corner and a few blocks from the residence of Benjamin Franklin, among other famous patriots. Early newspaper accounts, census records, and city directories all establish the presence of Lawrence Allwine in Philadelphia, and there were also other Allwine families in Philadelphia and environs at that time.

Lawrence Allwine was a veteran of the Revolutionary War, having purportedly joined the "Flying Camp" (a mobile unit of soldiers) in Pennsylvania and probably fought in the first major battle of the War, the Battle of Brooklyn. While there is no record of his enlistment in the Pennsylvania forces, his name does appear— both as Lawrence Allwine and Lawrence Ohlwein—in the records of the New Jersey Continental Army.[661]

---

[660] See Duane F. Alwin, *A Soldier's Tale—A Biography of Lawrence Allwine, Philadelphia Chairmaker and Ohio Pioneer.* Unpublished monograph.

[661] William S. Stryker, *Official Register of the Officers and Men of New Jersey in the Revolutionary War*, published by William T. Nicholson & Co., Printers, Trenton NJ, 1872.

In the first Federal Census of the United States, taken in the year 1790, Lawrence Allwine was listed in the city of Philadelphia by the name "Lewis Alwine," living at "99 Front Street." His occupation is given as "chair maker."[662] In the 1800 Federal Census of Pennsylvania, he is listed again in Philadelphia, this time as "Lawrence Allwine."[663]

Lawrence Allwine's ancestral origins are not clear and it has not yet been determined whether and how he is related to Familie Allwein, that is, the descendants of Hans Jacob and Catharina Allwein, the progenitors of the Allwein family in America. Because of the spelling of his last name, many genealogists of the Allwein family have assumed he was a 2nd generation member of the ALLWEIN family.[664] In my view, this is based on speculation and not necessarily tied to the facts.[665] As more and more information has become available, I have learned that it was much more likely that he originated from another German immigrant family—the family OHLWEIN (OLEWINE or OLDWINE)—and that he changed his name. There is a strong suggestion that his brothers Charles and Barnard (Barney) used one or other of the OHLWEIN names. In fact, in his pension application files held at the National Archives, there is a suggestion, made by Lawrence Allwine himself,

---

[662] *Heads of Families at the First Census of the United States Taken in the Year 1790, Pennsylvania.* Washington, D.C.: Government Printing Office, 1908, page 235.

[663] *Second Census of the United States, Inhabitants of Walnut Ward, Philadelphia, Philadelphia County, Pennsylvania,* Page 76 (1800).

[664] I have challenged this argument in *Familie Allwein—Hans Jacob and Catharina Allwein and their Descendants.* Volume 1: *An Early History of the Allwein Family in America.* Bloomington, IN: Xlibris, 2009.

[665] The source of this information is from a book by Edmund Adams and Barbara Brady O'Keefe, *Catholic Trails West: The Founding Catholic Families of Pennsylvania,* volume 2, Baltimore MD: Gateway Press,1989, page 456. There is no documentation of the source of this information. I contacted the authors, and they could not tell me where they obtained this information. Their source may have been Msgr. Charles Leo Allwein, whose notes include reference to Lawrence Allwine.

that his origins were from the OLEWINE or OLDWINE family.[666] According to this theory, he would have later changed his name to ALLWINE, which is how the German pronunciation of the name "Ohlwein" may have sounded in English.

Nevertheless, it is important to document what we know about Lawrence Allwine, should later research reveal that he was in fact a member of the Allwein family. The first record we have of Lawrence Allwine in Philadelphia is the 1785 city directory, where he is listed as "Lawrence Alwine, New-Street." He is listed in the early city directories for Philadelphia in virtually every year records are available from 1785 through 1809, typically at the same address, 99 South Front Street, although the last name is variously spelled ALWEIN, ALWINE or ALLWAIN, but usually ALLWINE. During this period his occupation is consistently given as *Windsor chair maker*. He later changed the focus of his craft. Beginning in 1801 he is listed at several different addresses on South Front Street and North Second Street, a few blocks away, and during this later period his occupation was given as "oil and colour man."[667] This is compatible with our knowledge of the fact that he applied for and received a patent from the U.S. Patent Office in Philadelphia for a paint or varnish for coloring wood, and also established a paint and wood covering business, obtaining the first U.S. patent on a special decorative paint, referred to as "Allwine gloss."[668]

In the early 19th century, after a long and productive life in Philadelphia, Lawrence Allwine suffered several hardships, both personal and professional, and he migrated to Ohio around 1809. He established himself in Blue Rock Township, about ten miles south of the town of Zanesville, where he was an innkeeper and

---

[666] Revolutionary War Pension and Bounty-Land Warrant Application Files. National Archive and Records Administration. Washington DC.

[667] This information was obtained from city directories at the Historical Society of Pennsylvania, 1300 Locust Street, Philadelphia, Pennsylvania.

[668] See "List of All U.S. Patents and Patentees (1790-1829)," Kenneth W. Dobyns, *History of the United States Patent Office*, 1994. This can be found on the following website: http://www.myoutbox.net/poinvtrs.htm

was elected the first Justice of the Peace.[669] He and his children remained in the Zanesville area until his death on October 1, 1833 at the age of seventy-seven. There are remnants of his descendants in Muskingum, Guernsey, Noble and Perry Counties of east-central Ohio throughout the past two centuries, even today.

There is also someone who appears to be a relative of Lawrence Allwine living in the Philadelphia area during this period, and although Lawrence Allwine moved to Ohio, there may have been remnants of the family in Philadelphia. As recorded in the 1790 Federal Census of the North Liberties Township, to the north of the city of Philadelphia, there is a John Ohlwein [given as "John Olwein" in the 1790 Census—we use the OHLWEIN spelling here] who is likely a relative of Lawrence Allwine.[670] We do not yet know the relationship of these two men, but I assume they are members of the same family—John Ohlwein and Lawrence Allwine may have been brothers, or cousins, or one might have been an uncle of the other one. We know that John Ohlwein had two sons—John Ohlwein, Jr., and Peter Ohlwein—who were formally apprentices to Lawrence Allwine.[671] In the "apprentice indenture" documents, the names of John and Peter are explicitly given as "Peter Ohlwine or Peter Allwine, with the Consent of his father, John Ohlwine or Allwine," and similarly as "John Ohlwine or John Allwine, with the Consent of his father, John Ohlwine or Allwine." At the same time, it appears that Lawrence Allwine had a son named John Allwine, so some of the references to John Allwine may be ambiguous, because there were at least two men with identical names.

---

[669] The sources of this historical information are: J. Hope Sutor, *Past and Present of the City of Zanesville and Muskingum County, Ohio*, Chicago: Arke Publishing Co., 1905; and *Biographical and Historical Memoirs of Muskingum County, Ohio*, Chicago: The Goodspeed Publishing Co., 1892.
[670] *Heads of Families at the First Census of the United States Taken in the Year 1790: Pennsylvania*, Baltimore MD: Genealogical Publishing Company, Inc., 1977, page 206.
[671] Nancy Goyne Evans, *Windsor-Chair Making in America—From Craft Shop to Consumer*, Hanover, New Hampshire: University Press of New England, 2006, pages 7-9.

However, from the time Lawrence Allwine made his exit from Philadelphia—around 1809—there were hardly any Allwine family members appearing in the city directories of the city of Philadelphia. It was not until 1844 that Allwine or Alwine families reappear in the record of these directories. City directories beginning in 1844 record several Alwine families. In the following we discuss those Allwein family members living in Philadelphia, whose origins are known.

William B. Allwine (1837-1912)
Dauphin County and Philadelphia

William B. Allwine (M04-0404-16) was the youngest son of John and Mary (Eckenroth) Allwine of Dauphin County (see Chapter 14 for further discussion of this family). He was born January 31, 1837 on his parents' farm in Londonderry Township of Dauphin County, Pennsylvania. He grew to adulthood in Dauphin County and became employed by the railroad at an early age. His occupation gave him the opportunity to live in a number of different locations over his lifetime. One of those was Philadelphia.

I provided a detailed discussion of William B. Allwine's early life in volume 1 of *Familie Allwein* (Chapter 6, pages 338-341) and do not repeat that material here. Rather I focus on what is known about the twenty or so years he lived in Philadelphia. He had begun his life in Dauphin County, remaining close to his mother. After she died, he moved to Marietta in Lancaster County. There he was a "foreman" with the railroad. After his first wife died in Marietta, he shortly remarried and he moved his family to Philadelphia. The 1880 Federal Census of Philadelphia provides the following enumeration for William B. Allwine's household:[672]

> William B. Allwine (head, railroad foreman, age 39)
> Julia Allwine (spouse, age 49)
> Maggie Allwine (daughter, age 18)
> Frank Allwine (son, age 17)

---

[672] *Tenth Census of the United States* (1880), *Inhabitants of Philadelphia, Philadelphia County, Pennsylvania*, page 189.

William B. Allwine was also listed as a "foreman" in the Philadelphia city directories, but he was not so listed until 1900.[673] By that time he had already returned to Dauphin County, living in Harrisburg, where he was recorded in the 1900 Federal Census of Harrisburg. There he was working as a "railway contractor," and eventually went to work for the Pennsylvania Traction Company in Harrisburg.[674] In Chapter 14, we discuss his presence in Harrisburg from 1900 onward.

Jerome Adam Allwein (1867-1931)[675]
Lebanon and Philadelphia, Pennsylvania

Jerome Adam Allwein (M05-0405-1108), youngest son of Edward and Elizabeth (Arnold) Allwein, was born February 23, 1867 on his parents' farm in Bethel Township, Lebanon County, Pennsylvania. The line of descent connecting Jerome Adam Allwein to Johannes Jacob and Catharina Allwein, progenitors of the Allwein family in colonial Pennsylvania, is as follows:

Generation 1: Johannes Jacob and Catharina Allwein—Berks County, Pa.
Generation 2: Conrad and Catharine (Weibel) Allwein—Dauphin County, Pa.
Generation 3: Philip and Elizabeth (Arentz) Allwein—Lebanon County, Pa.
Generation 4: Edward and Elizabeth (Arnold) Allwein—Lebanon County, Pa.
Generation 5: Jerome Adam and Sophia M. (Schaefer) Allwein—Philadelphia, Pa.

Jerome Adam Allwein's mother died when he was thirteen years old. At this time, his older sister Emma Allwein, who never married, took over the responsibilities of managing the household for her father and helped tend to the needs of her younger siblings. Within a few years, Jerome Adam Allwein had left the parental home and

---

[673] *Gopsill's Philadelphia City Directory for 1900*, Philadelphia: James Gopsill's Sons.
[674] *Twelfth Census of the United States* (1900), *Inhabitants of City of Harrisburg, Dauphin County, Pennsylvania*, E.D. No. 77, page 9B.
[675] The author acknowledges the assistance of Madeline Paine Moyer, Edward Allwein and Nancy Allwein Nebiker in the development of this section on Jerome Allwein, and I am grateful for the photographs they provided.

would experience the opportunities and challenges of the outside world.

Jerome Adam Allwein was the author of one of the most important genealogies of the Allwein family in Lebanon County, Pennsylvania—the *Genealogy of the Allwein-Arnold Family*—written in 1902. This is what the genealogist said about himself:[676]

Jerome A. Allwein, the youngest son of Edward and Elizabeth (Arnold) Allwein was born and reared on his father's farm in Lebanon County, Pa. (He) attended the Public Schools until he was 16 years of age after which he attended Normal Class at Mount Nebo Normal School at Lock Haven, Pa. and a Normal Class at Annville. (He) started teaching Sep. 1885. (He) taught successfully for three terms in the Public Schools of Lebanon County. At the close of his third term as a teacher he entered the Eastman National Business College of Poughkeepsie, New York, April 3, 1888, where he took a course of business training graduating with honor July 24th following. In the Spring of 1889 he left Lebanon, went to Philadelphia in search of employment. After a week's hunt he found employment with the Knickerbocker Ice Co. and continued with this company for several years. In the Summer of 1892 the National Wall Paper Co. was organized and in August of that year he accepted a position with their principal Jobbing Branch in Philadelphia taking charge of the accounting department which position he held until dissolution August 1909, after which he filled like position with the succeeding firm, Carey Bros. & Crevemeyer. When the Order of the Knights of Columbus was introduced in Pennsylvania he was among the first to subscribe his name and take up the cause. (He) was elected Financial Secretary of the first Council November 1896 and unanimously re-elected each year, filling the office 9 years. On May 9, 1894 he was married to Sophia M. daughter of Frank and Mary Schaefer by Rev. Conrad Rephan, C. SS. R. at High Mass 9 A.M. (Wednesday) at St. Bonifacius Church, Philadelphia.

---

[676] Jerome Allwein, *Genealogy of the Allwein-Arnold Families.* Philadelphia, Pa., 1902, pages 80-81.

Exhibit 12.1 Reproduction of a photograph of Jerome Allwein
as a young man—taken in Poughkeepsie, New York in 1888
(contributed by Madeline Moyer)

As noted in the above narrative, Jerome Allwein and Sophia Marie Schaefer, daughter of Frank and Mary Schaefer, were married in Philadelphia on May 9, 1894. Beginning in 1890 and extending through 1930, Jerome Allwein is listed in the city directories of Philadelphia.[677] The 1900 through 1930 Federal Census enumerations confirm their presence there as well.[678] The 1900 Federal Census report for their household indicates there are several additional family members living with them, including Jacob Seifert (Jr.) (age 19) the orphan son of Jerome Allwein's sister, Mary Jane Allwein, who married Jacob Seifert (Sr.), as well as his father-in-law (Frank Schaefer, age 66) and brother-in-law (John Schaefer, age 21).

The 1910 Federal Census listing for the household of Jerome and Sophia Allwein is as follows:

Jerome Allwein (head, proprietor, age 43)
Sophia Allwein (spouse, age 43)

---

[677] *Gopsill's Philadelphia City Directory for 1890*, Philadelphia: James Gopsill's Sons; *Gopsill's Philadelphia City Directory for 1895*, Philadelphia: James Gopsill's Sons; *Gopsill's Philadelphia City Directory for 1900*, Philadelphia: James Gopsill's Sons; *Gopsill's Philadelphia City Directory for 1905*, Philadelphia: James Gopsill's Sons; *Boyd's City Directory of Philadelphia 1910*, Philadelphia: C.E. Howe Company; and *Boyd's City Directory of Philadelphia 1915*, Philadelphia: C.E. Howe Company; *Boyd's Combined City and Business Directory of Philadelphia 1919-1920*, Philadelphia: C.E. Howe Company; *Polk's Philadelphia Directory 1925*, Philadelphia: R.L. Polk & Company; *Polk's Philadelphia City Directory 1930*, Philadelphia: R.L. Polk & Company; *Polk's Philadelphia City Directory, 1935-36*, Philadelphia: R.L. Polk & Company.

[678] *Twelfth Census of the United States* (1900), *Inhabitants of Philadelphia Ward 31, Philadelphia County, Pennsylvania*, E.D. No. 780, pages 154B and 155A; *Thirteenth Census of the United States* (1910), *Inhabitants of Philadelphia Ward 23, Philadelphia County, Pennsylvania*, E.D. No. 462, page 255B; *Fourteenth Census of the United States* (1920), *Inhabitants of Philadelphia Ward 23, Philadelphia County, Pennsylvania*, E.D. No. 661, page 251A; *Fifteenth Census of the United States* (1930), *Inhabitants of Philadelphia City, Philadelphia County, Pennsylvania*, E.D. No. 878, page 26B.

Aloysius Allwein (son, age 15)
Mary Allwein (daughter, age 11)
Cecilia Allwein (daughter, age 8)
Charles Allwein (son, age 6)
Frank Schaefer (father-in-law, age 76)
Agnes Zweier (niece, housekeeper, age 19)

Agnes Zweier is the daughter of Agnes Catharine Allwein (F05-0405-1103) and John Zweier of Lebanon County (see Chapter 11 of this volume). She became a nun, Sister Benedict de Francois, Little Sisters of the Poor, Scranton, Pennsylvania.

Based on census and other records, there were four children born to Jerome Allwein and Sophia Schaefer, as follows:[679]

Aloysius Francis Allwein (M06-0405-1108-01), b. April 11, 1895, d. August 28, 1978, m. (June 22, 1929) Mary M. McCluskey (b. October 31, 1902, d. July 1994)

Mary Magdalene Allwein (F06-0405-1108-02), b. January 10, 1899, d. December 1, 1979, became a nun, Sister Clare Imelda

Cecilia Emma Allwein (F06-0405-1108-03), b. January 27, 1902, d. September 3, 1995, became a nun, Sister Maria Cecilia

Charles Leo Allwein (M06-0405-1108-04), b. July 3, 1903, d. February 4, 1995 (BB), became a priest, ordained September 21, 1929

With the exception of Aloysius Francis Allwein, these children appear in the photograph contained in Exhibit 12.2 below.

We know from the above narrative that Jerome Adam Allwein was an educated man. He had attended normal school and taught for several years in the public schools of Lebanon County, after which time he entered a course of business training in New York. He was also a religious man—active in the Knights of Columbus from the beginnings of the Philadelphia chapter. As we shall see, these were orientations he encouraged in his children as well. Son Aloysius

---

[679] See Jerome Allwein, *Genealogy of the Allwein-Arnold Families*, 1902, pages 80-81.

Exhibit 12.2 Reproduction of a photograph of members of Jerome Allwein family/household in 1910—Philadelphia, Pennsylvania. Left to right: Mary Allwein, Agnes Zweier, Charles Leo Allwein, Sophia (Schaefer) Allwein, Cecilia Allwein; center back: Mary Catherine Lewis (daughter of Elizabeth Regina Allwein Lewis) (contributed by Madeline Moyer)

Francis Allwein (also known as A. Francis Allwein) graduated from the University of Pennsylvania in 1916 with a degree in electrical engineering, and distinguished himself with a career in developmental engineering (see below). The two daughters, Mary Magdalen Allwein (Sister Clare Imelda) and Cecilia Emma Allwein (Sister Marie Cecilia) both became nuns and pursued the religious life. The youngest son, Charles L. Allwein entered the priesthood, becoming ordained on September 21, 1929. He was raised to the title of Monsignor and held important administrative duties in the Catholic Church. He was eventually appointed to posts in Berks County and is covered in the next chapter (Chapter 13).

The 1900 Federal Census lists Jerome Allwein's occupation as "bookkeeper," and this is consistent with the narrative he provided about himself in the *Genealogy of the Allwein-Arnold Families*. By 1910 he became the proprietor of a store dealing in "notions and novelties," and in the 1920 and 1930 Federal Censuses he was listed as "owner of a dry goods store" on Frankford Avenue. A photo of this store is provided in Exhibit 12.3. It was located at 4284-4286 Frankford Avenue, and family occupied the 2nd and 3rd floors of the building. All Federal Censuses beginning in 1910 through 1930 place them at this address. In the 1920 Census, the document uses the phrase "Frankford Town" in specifying the relevant division of the County inhabited by those enumerated households.

In the 1930 Federal Census Jerome Allwein's family were all living relatively close to home. Son A. Francis Allwein was living in Philadelphia; Charles L. Allwein is listed as a Catholic priest in the Borough of Lansdale, Montgomery County, living in the Catholic parish; daughter Mary M. Allwein (age 31) was living in the Convent of the Sisters of the Immaculate Heart of Mary in Philadelphia; and daughter Cecilia E. Allwein (age 28) was living with the parents, Jerome and Sophia Allwein, in Philadelphia.[680]

---

[680] *Fifteenth Census of the United States* (1930), *Inhabitants of Philadelphia City, Philadelphia County, Pennsylvania*, E.D. No. 625, page 19A; E.D. No. 878, page 26B; E.D. No. 351, page 1A; *Inhabitants of Borough of Lansdale, Montgomery County, Pennsylvania*, E.D. No. 53, page 15A.

Exhibit 12.3 Reproduction of a photograph of Jerome Allwein's Dry Goods Store at 4284-86 Frankford Avenue, Philadelphia, Pennsylvania (contributed by Edward F. Allwein)

Exhibit 12.4 Reproduction of a photograph of Jerome and Sophia Allwein in their later years (contributed by Edward F. Allwein)

Jerome Adam Allwein died on July 19, 1931 and Sophia (Schaefer) Allwein continued to reside at 4286 Frankford Avenue in Philadelphia, as recorded in the 1940 Federal Census enumeration.[681] Her niece, Catherine Lewis, was living with her. Sophia Allwein died more than twenty years later on February 14, 1954.[682] Prior to her death, Sophia Allwein was under the care of her son Msgr. Charles L. Allwein, as she died in Bally, where he was living at the time. Jerome and Sophia Allwein are buried at New Cathedral Cemetery (NW), North Front and Luzerne Streets, Philadelphia.

Aloysius Francis Allwein (1895-1978)
Philadelphia, Pennsylvania

Aloysius Francis Allwein (M06-0405-1108-01), son of Jerome Adam and Sophia (Schaeffer) Allwein, was born in Philadelphia on April 11, 1895. The line of descent connecting Aloysius Francis Allwein to Johannes Jacob and Catharina Allwein, progenitors of the Allwein family in colonial Pennsylvania, is as follows:

Generation 1: Johannes Jacob and Catharina Allwein—Berks County, Pa.
Generation 2: Conrad and Catharine (Weibel) Allwein—Lebanon County, Pa.
Generation 3: Philip and Elizabeth (Arentz) Allwein—Lebanon County, Pa.
Generation 4: Edward and Elizabeth (Arnold) Allwein—Lebanon County, Pa.
Generation 5: Jerome Adam and Sophia M. (Schaefer) Allwein—Philadelphia, Pa.
Generation 6: Aloysius Francis and Mary M. (McCluskey) Allwein—Philadelphia, Pa.

An entry for "A. Francis Allwein" in a 1939 *Who's Who in Pennsylvania* provided a summary of his educational and occupational career.[683] He attended Northeast High School in Philadelphia, graduating in 1912. He attended the University of Pennsylvania in Philadelphia, graduating with a BS in electrical engineering in 1916. He worked as a "test engineer" for the General

---

[681] *Sixteenth Census of the United States* (1940), *Inhabitants of Philadelphia City, Philadelphia County, Pennsylvania*, E.D. No. 51-623, page 7338A.

[682] See the Pennsylvania Department of Health records: http://www. health.state.pa.us.

[683] *Who's Who in Pennsylvania*, Volume 1, Chicago: The Albert Nelson Marquis Company, 1939, page 12.

Exhibit 12.5 Gravestone for Schaeffer and Allwein families—New Cathedral Cemetery, Philadelphia, Pennsylvania

Electric Company in Schnectady, New York from 1916-1919, and then returned to Philadelphia, where he taught mechanical engineering at the University of Pennsylvania from 1919 to 1926 and taught evening classes at the Drexel Institute from 1920-1931. He was employed as a developmental engineer by several firms in the Philadelphia area—Atwater Kent Manufacturing Company (1926-1930), Leeds & Northrup Company (1930-1931), H.A. DeVry Incorporated (1931-1935), and the Brown Instrument Company (1935-1939). He was a member of the American Institute of Electrical Engineers and the American Society for Metals.

Aloysius Francis Allwein married Mary M. McCluskey, daughter of David and Mary (Rice) McCluskey, in Philadelphia on October 31, 1929. They settled in Philadelphia and lived there for the remainder of their lives. Aloysius Francis Allwein is listed in the Philadelphia city directories from 1925 through 1935.[684] They are also listed in the 1930 Federal Census of Philadelphia, with one child.[685] This child—*Janet E. Allwein* (F07-0405-1108-0101)—born in 1930, died in infancy on August 5, 1930.[686] The 1940 Federal Census similarly lists them in Philadelphia, where Aloysius Francis Allwein's occupation is given as "development engineer, industrial instrument manufacturing."[687] A second child, a son, Edward F. Allwein (M07-0405-1108-0102), listed in the 1940 census reports, is still living, and in keeping with our practice, no further information is provided about him. Aloysius Francis Allwein died August 28, 1978. Mary M. (McCluskey) Allwein in July of 1994.[688]

---

[684] *Polk's Philadelphia Directory 1925*, Philadelphia: R.L. Polk & Company; *Polk's Philadelphia City Directory 1930*, Philadelphia: R.L. Polk & Company; *Polk's Philadelphia City Directory, 1935-36*, Philadelphia: R.L. Polk & Company.

[685] *Fifteenth Census of the United States* (1930), *Inhabitants of Philadelphia City, Philadelphia County, Pennsylvania*, E.D. No. 625, page 19A.

[686] See the Pennsylvania Department of Health records: http://www.health.state.pa.us.

[687] *Sixteenth Census of the United States* (1940), *Inhabitants of Philadelphia City, Philadelphia County, Pennsylvania*, E.D. No. 51-564, page 6612B.

[688] Further information regarding the descendants of this family may be obtained by contacting Edward F. Allwein, a descendant of Aloysius Francis Allwein.

Exhibit 12.6 Reproduction of a photograph of Aloysius Francis Allwein in middle age—circa 1950s (contributed by Edward F. Allwein)

Jacob Vincent Seifert, Jr. (1880-1972)
Philadelphia, Pennsylvania

Jacob Vincent Seifert, Jr. was the son of Mary Jane Allwein (F05-0405-1105) and Jacob V. Seifert, who was born on August 16, 1880. His parents died around the time of his birth and he was raised by his aunts and uncles. His father, Jacob V. Seifert, died on July 22, 1880 and his mother died August 19, 1880. The birth of Jacob, Jr., likely prompted Mary Jane's death. The line of descent connecting Jacob V. Seifert, Jr. to Johannes Jacob and Catharina Allwein, progenitors of the Allwein family in colonial Pennsylvania, is as follows:

Generation 1: Johannes Jacob and Catharina Allwein—Berks County, Pa.
Generation 2: Conrad and Catharine (Weibel) Allwein—Dauphin County, Pa.
Generation 3: Philip and Elizabeth (Arentz) Allwein—Lebanon County, Pa.
Generation 4: Edward and Elizabeth (Arnold) Allwein—Lebanon County, Pa.
Generation 5: Mary Jane Allwein and Jacob Vincent Seifert—Lebanon
    County, Pa.
Generation 6: Jacob Vincent Seifert and Elizabeth Bechtel—Philadelphia, Pa.

After his mother's tragic death, when he was still an infant, he was taken care of and raised by his Aunt Emma Mary Allwein (F05-0405-1101), in the household of his grandfather, Edward Allwein. At the time of the 1900 Federal Census, when he was 19 years of age, he was living with his uncle Jerome Allwein and his family in Philadelphia (see above).

Jacob Seifert married Elizabeth C Bechtel in Nesquehoning (Carbon County), Pennsylvania, and they settled in Philadelphia. His draft registration card for World War I, dated September 12, 1918, gives his occupation as "accountant," employed by the J.T. Kirkpatrick Company. It lists his wife as "Elizabeth C. Seifert" and their residence as 1720 North 62nd Street. They can be located at that residence in the 1920, 1930 and 1940 Federal Censuses of Philadelphia, where he is listed as a "private secretary" in the 1920 report, as a "manager of a rubber manufacturing company" in 1930, and in 1940 as working in the office of a leather manufacturing company.[689] His World War II draft registration card, dated April 27, 1947, again lists them at the same address on 62nd Street, and indicates he was working for the Middlebury Tanning Corporation in Philadelphia.[690] As far as we know, there were no children born to this union. Elizabeth Seifert died on September 21, 1953. Jacob Seifert died in October 1972 at the age of 92. As of this writing, we do not know where they are buried.

Andrew Philip Allwein (1873-1916) Philadelphia, Pennsylvania

Andrew Philip Allwein (M05-0405-1607), the second son of Henry and Catharine (Lenich) Allwein, was born January 21, 1873 in Lebanon, Pennsylvania. The line of descent connecting Andrew Philip Allwein to Johannes Jacob and Catharina Allwein, the progenitors of the Allwein family in colonial Pennsylvania, is as follows:

Generation 1: Johannes Jacob and Catharina Allwein—Berks County, Pa.
Generation 2: Conrad and Catharine (Weibel) Allwein—Dauphin County, Pa.
Generation 3: Philip and Elizabeth (Arentz) Allwein—Lebanon County, Pa.
Generation 4: Henry A. and Catharine (Lenich) Allwein—Lebanon County, Pa.
Generation 5: Andrew Philip and Catharine A. (Dunn) Allwein—Lebanon and
    Philadelphia Counties, Pa.

Andrew Philip Allwein and Jerome Adam Allwein were contemporaries and first cousins. The Jerome Allwein *Genealogy* notes that Andrew P. Allwein "attended the parochial school in Lebanon and after he left school he clerked in a grocery store for a short time after which he learned pattern making. Soon after he

---

[689] *Fourteenth Census of the United States* (1920), *Inhabitants of Philadelphia Ward 34, Philadelphia County, Pennsylvania*, E.D. No. 1217, page 232A; *Fifteenth Census of the United States* (1930), *Inhabitants of Philadelphia City, Philadelphia County, Pennsylvania*, E.D. No. 51-445, page 126B; *Sixteenth Census of the United States* (1940), *Inhabitants of Philadelphia, Philadelphia County, Pennsylvania*, E.D. No. 51-1136, page 13862A.
[690] World War I and World War II draft registration cards. Ancestry.com.

was done serving his apprenticeship he went to Philadelphia to work at his trade."[691] Andrew P. Allwein married Catharine A. Dunn (b. April 2, 1873, d. unknown) in Philadelphia on April 17, 1901. As far as we know, there were no children born to this union.

In the 1895-96 Polk's City Directory for Lebanon, Andrew P. Allwein is listed living at 833 Guilford in Lebanon.[692] His occupation given there is "patternmaker." Philadelphia city directories for the period 1895 to 1915 list Andrew P. Allwein as "pattern maker" living in the city of Philadelphia.[693] In the 1895 city directory his address was given as 5126 Warren, and his brother Francis A. Allwein (M05-0405-1604), also listed as a patternmaker, was living at the same address. Francis A. Allwein returned to Lebanon, and Andrew P. Allwein remained in Philadelphia. The 1910 Federal Census lists Andrew P. Allwein and wife "Catherine A. Allwein," living on 51st Street in Philadelphia, where his occupation is given as "pattern maker in woodworking industry."[694]

---

[691] Jerome Allwein, *Genealogy of the Allwein-Arnold Families*, 1902, page 86.

[692] Polk's 1895-96 City Directory, Lebanon, Pennsylvania. Ancestry.com.

[693] *Gopsill's Philadelphia City Directory for 1895*, Philadelphia: James Gopsill's Sons; *Gopsill's Philadelphia City Directory for 1900*, Philadelphia: James Gopsill's Sons; *Gopsill's Philadelphia City Directory for 1905*, Philadelphia: James Gopsill's Sons; *Boyd's City Directory of Philadelphia 1910*, Philadelphia: C.E. Howe Company; and *Boyd's City Directory of Philadelphia 1915*, Philadelphia: C.E. Howe Company.

[694] *Thirteenth Census of the United States* (1910), *Inhabitants of Philadelphia Ward 44, Philadelphia County, Pennsylvania*, E.D. No. 11-42, page 20A. A *pattern maker* in the furniture industry "sketches and constructs patterns from blueprints for use in manufacture of metal furniture parts: Draws outline of part on paper or traces it from blueprint. Transfers outline onto pattern materials, such as metal, plastic, or rubber by tracing over lines. Cuts out pattern with lathe or handtools and power tools, such as tin snips and power hacksaw. Assembles pattern sections, using handtools, such as hammer and screwdriver. Marks identifying number or symbol on pattern.." [*Dictionary of Occupational Titles*, DOT code: 709.381.034.]

Andrew P. Allwein died at a relatively young age, on May 26, 1916, of acute myocarditis.[695] His obituary reads: "Besides the parents, he is also survived by three sisters and a brother— Sister Christopher, in a Baltimore convent, Sister Jeanette, in a Wilmington convent, Mrs. William Lenich, Miss Agnes, Miss Regina, and Miss Cora, and brother Francis." Andrew P. Allwein is buried with his parents and several of his sisters on the family plot in St. Mary's Catholic Cemetery (SM) in Lebanon. As of this writing, we do not know what happened to his widow, Catherine (Dunn) Allwein, following his death.

Anna L. Allwein Ganster (1871-1934)
Philadelphia, Pennsylvania

Anna L. Allwein (F06-0405-0501-04), daughter of Henry Mars and Annie (McGinley) Allwein, was born February 17, 1871. The lineage connecting Annie L. Allwein to Johannes Jacob and Catharina Allwein, progenitors of the Allwein family in colonial Pennsylvania, is as follows:

Generation 1: Johannes Jacob and Catharina Allwein—Berks County, Pa.
Generation 2: Conrad and Catharine (Weibel) Allwein—Dauphin County, Pa.
Generation 3: Philip and Barbara (Frantz) Allwein—Lebanon County, Pa.
Generation 4: William and Mary (Mars) Allwein—Lebanon County, Pa.
Generation 5: Henry Mars and Annie (McGinley) Allwein—Lebanon County, Pa.
Generation 6: Anna L. Allwein and Joseph A. Ganster—Lebanon County, Pa.
    Philadelphia, Pa., and Delaware County, Pa.

Anna L. Allwein married Joseph A. Ganster on June 15, 1899 and they remained in the Lebanon area for a few years. They lived at 441 North 8th Street, as recorded in the 1900 Federal Census. In this report, Joseph Ganster's occupation was listed as "machinist." While in Lebanon, they began a family and had the following children:

Julia Ganster, b. July 2, 1900, d. February 1985, unmarried
Joseph Ganster (Jr.), b. July 31, 1903, d. February 1976, m. unknown
Louise Ganster, b. est. 1915, d. unknown, m. unknown

---

[695] Obituary and Death Notice, *Lebanon Daily News, Lebanon, Pennsylvania, May 27, 1916 and May 29, 1916.*

Exhibit 12.7 Gravestone for Andrew P. Allwein—St. Mary's Cemetery, Lebanon, Pennsylvania

By 1910, they had moved to Philadelphia, where they were listed in the 1910 and 1920 Federal Census enumerations, and in 1930 they were living in the Borough of Yeadon, Delaware County, Pennsylvania (in suburban Philadelphia).[696] The 1910 Federal Census report indicates that Anna's brother, Lewis Allwein, was living with them (see Chapter 11). In the 1910 report Joseph Ganster's occupation was "foreman in an iron works," in 1920 he was a "manager in manufacturing," and in 1930 he owned his own machinery business. The 1940 Federal Census report for Lower Merion Township in Montgomery County, Pennsylvania lists Joseph A. Ganster as widowed, and living with three of his children—Julia A. Ganster, Joseph A. Ganster and Louise Ganster.[697] Joseph A. Ganster's occupation is given as "mechanical engineer in a steel roller mill." That report also indicates that they had been living in Yeadon, Delaware County as of 1935. As of this writing we do not know where Anna L. Allwein Ganster and her family members are buried.

Lewis A. Allwein (1876-1937)
Lebanon and Philadelphia, Pennsylvania

Lewis A. Allwein (M06-0405-0501-06), son of Henry Mars and Annie (McGinley) Allwein, was born August 18, 1876 in Lebanon, Pennsylvania. Lewis A. Allwein was unmarried, and he spent most of his adult living in the households of his siblings. In 1910, Lewis A. Allwein was living with his sister, Anna L. Allwein, and her husband, Joseph A. Ganster in Philadelphia (see entry immediately

---

[696] *Twelfth Census of the United States* (1900), *Inhabitants of Lebanon Ward 5, Lebanon County, Pennsylvania*, E.D. No. 129, page 272B; *Thirteenth Census of the United States* (1910), *Inhabitants of Philadelphia Ward 24, Philadelphia County, Pennsylvania*, E.D. No. 501, page 262B; *Fourteenth Census of the United States* (1920), *Inhabitants of Philadelphia Ward 34, Philadelphia County, Pennsylvania*, E.D. No. 1173, page 235A; *Fifteenth Census of the United States* (1930), *Inhabitants of Borough of Yeadon, Delaware County, Pennsylvania*, E.D. 23-179, page 248A.
[697] *Sixteenth Census of the United States* (1940), *Inhabitants of Lower Merion Township, Montgomery County, Pennsylvania*, E.D. No. 46-86, page 1510A.

above), and in the 1920 census year, Lewis was living in a boarding house in Philadelphia. By 1930, he was back in Lebanon, again at the family homestead (see Chapter 11).[698]

John Howard Allwein (1868-1928)
Lebanon and Philadelphia, Pennsylvania

John Howard Allwein (M06-0405-0404-03), son of Vincent and Annie M. (Ramsay) Allwein, was born October 7, 1868 in Lebanon, Pennsylvania (see footnote 151 above). He grew to adulthood in Lebanon, but eventually moved to Philadelphia and then on to Scranton, where he died. The line of descent connecting him to Johannes Jacob and Catharina Allwein, progenitors of the Allwein family in colonial Pennsylvania, is as follows:

Generation 1: Johannes Jacob and Catharina Allwein—Berks County, Pa.
Generation 2: Conrad and Catharine (Weibel) Allwein—Dauphin County, Pa.
Generation 3: Philip and Barbara (Frantz) Allwein—Lebanon County, Pa.
Generation 4: John and Julia Ann (Howarter) Allwein—Lebanon County, Pa.
Generation 5: Vincent H. and Annie M. (Ramsay) Allwein—Lebanon County, Pa.
Generation 6: John Howard Allwein—Philadelphia, Pa.

Following in his father's footsteps, he received a degree in Medicine from the University of Pennsylvania in 1892.[699] Prior to attending Medical School, he graduated from Lafayette College in Easton, Pennsylvania.[700] According to the Jerome Allwein

---

[698] *Twelfth Census of the United States* (1900), *Inhabitants of Lebanon Ward 5, Lebanon County, Pennsylvania*, E.D. No. 129, page 273A; *Thirteenth Census of the United States* (1910), *Inhabitants of Philadelphia Ward 24, Philadelphia County, Pennsylvania*, E.D. No. 501, page 262B; *Fourteenth Census of the United States* (1920), *Inhabitants of Philadelphia Ward 44, Philadelphia County, Pennsylvania*, E.D. No. 1643, page 78A; *Fifteenth Census of the United States* (1930), *Inhabitants of Lebanon, Lebanon County, Pennsylvania*, E.D. No. 38-22, page 186B.

[699] *General Alumni Catalogue of the University of Pennsylvania.* 1917. Alumni Association of the University, page 761. Philadelphia, Pennsylvania.

[700] Selden J. Coffin, *The Men of Lafayette, 1826-1893—Lafayette College, Its History, Its Men & Their Record*, Easton, Pennsylvania: George W. West, 1891, page 280. Ancestry.com.

Genealogy, after receiving his medical degree he returned to Lebanon, to work with his father for awhile. He was living in Lebanon at the time of his father's death in 1895 (see the obituary for Vincent H. Allwein in Chapter 11), but soon thereafter he moved to Warren, Pennsylvania where he took a position on the Board of Physicians at the State Hospital for the Insane there.[701] Warren is located in Warren County, in northwest Pennsylvania, adjacent to Erie County.

As noted, eventually John Howard Allwein moved to Philadelphia, where he is listed in the 1905 and 1910 Philadelphia city directories as a physician, living at 3417 Walnut Street.[702] The 1910 Federal Census lists him in Scranton, Lackawana County, and again his occupation is given as physician.[703] He married Sarah "Sadie" E. Thomas, an immigrant from Wales, on January 1, 1919 in Philadelphia. She was a nurse. They are listed in the city directories for Scranton in the years 1920 through 1928.[704] He died August 16, 1928 in Scranton, Pennsylvania.[705]

---

[701] Jerome Allwein, *Genealogy of the Allwein-Arnold Families*, Philadelphia, Pa., 1902, pages 108; see the entry for "State Hospital for the Insane, Warren, Pa." in Henry M. Hurd (Ed.), *The Institutional Care of the Insane in the United States and Canada*, Volume 3, Baltimore, Maryland: Johns Hopkins University Press, 1916, page 476, and *Twelfth Census of the United States* (1900), *Inhabitants of Conewango Township, Warren County, Pennsylvania*, E.D. No. 132, page 81A.
[702] *Gopsill's Philadelphia City Directory for 1905*, Philadelphia: James Gopsill's Sons; *Boyd's City Directory of Philadelphia 1910*, Philadelphia: C.E. Howe Company.
[703] *Thirteenth Census of the United States* (1910), *Inhabitants of Scranton Ward 9, Lackawana County, Pennsylvania*, E.D. No. 35, page 28B.
[704] City directories for Scranton, Pennsylvania. Ancestry.com.
[705] Obituary in the *Lebanon Semi-Weekly News*, Lebanon, Pennsylvania, Monday Evening, August 20, 1928. The Pennsylvania Department of Health records give August 16, 1928 as the date of death. See: http://www. health.state.pa.us.

Samuel Alwine (1869-1942)
Butler County and Philadelphia, Pennsylvania

Samuel Alwine (M06-0406-0604-03) was born July 12, 1869 in Butler County, Pennsylvania, son of Francis and Mary (Hinchberger) Alwine. He grew to adulthood in Butler County and at the age of 30 he married Christianna Powers (b. April 6, 1872) in Philadelphia, Pennsylvania on November 29, 1899. She was a native of Philadelphia. They lived for a short while in Butler County, but eventually they moved back to Philadelphia.

The line of descent connecting Samuel Alwine to Johannes Jacob and Catharina Allwein, progenitors of the Allwein family in colonial Pennsylvania, is as follows:

Generation 1: Johannes Jacob and Catharina Allwein—Berks County, Pa.
Generation 2: Conrad and Catharine (Weibel) Allwein—Dauphin County, Pa.
Generation 3: Conrad and Susanna (Eckenrode) Alwine—Adams County, Pa.
Generation 4: John Adam and Catherine (Lawrence) Alwine—York and Butler Counties, Pa.
Generation 5: Francis and Mary (Hinchberger) Alwine—Butler County, Pa.
Generation 6: Samuel and Christianna (Powers) Alwine—Butler County and Philadelphia, Pa.

The 1900 Federal Census records them living in Jefferson Township of Butler County, presumably in the Saxonburg area (see Chapter 19).[706] The household included Samuel Alwine, his wife Christianna, and his brother Christopher Alwine. Soon thereafter—at least by 1905—Samuel and Christianna Alwine moved to Philadelphia, where they are listed in Federal Censuses from 1910 through 1930.[707] In the 1910 census his occupation is

---

[706] *Twelfth Census of the United States* (1900), *Inhabitants of Jefferson Township, Butler County, Pennsylvania*, E.D. No. 29, page 179B.

[707] *Thirteenth Census of the United States* (1910), *Inhabitants of Philadelphia Ward 5, Philadelphia County, Pennsylvania*, E.D. No. 67, page 28A; *Fourteenth Census of the United States* (1920), *Inhabitants of Philadelphia Ward 22, Philadelphia County, Pennsylvania*, E.D. No.614, page 98B; *Fifteenth Census of the United States* (1930), *Inhabitants of Germantown Township, Philadelphia County, Pennsylvania*, E.D. No. 628, page 207A.

given as "teamster," and in later censuses he is listed as a "landscape gardener." Philadelphia city directories, from 1905 to 1935 list Samuel Alwine as a resident of Philadelphia, in the later years in Germantown, a suburb to the north of the city, and similarly list his occupation as "gardener."[708] City directories over this period give a number of other occupations, including brickmaker, as well as gardener. The 1930 Federal Census of Philadelphia lists him as widowed, and living with his children, working as a "landscape gardener." The 1940 Federal Census of Philadelphia similarly lists him as widowed, and working as a "landscape gardener," operating is own business.[709] The 1940 household listing includes his daughter, Christiana Dobler (age 33), her husband, William A. Dobler (age 38), and their daughter Christiana Dobler (age 5).

Based on 1910 and 1920 Federal Census reports, marriage records and other information, we conclude that Samuel and Christiana had three children, as follows:

Samuel Powers Alwine (M07-0406-0604-0301), b. January 3, 1901, d. January 23, 1951, m. (October 31, 1923) Katherine L. Smith (b. March 28, 1903, d. unknown)

Catherine H. Alwine (F07-0406-0604-0302), b. October 13, 1904, d. May 13, 1912

Christiana H. Alwine (F07-0406-0604-0303), b. August 11, 1906, d. December 7, 1997, m. (September 16, 1933) William A. Dobler (b. October 31, 1901, d. March 1982)

---

[708] *Boyd's City Directory of Philadelphia 1915*, Philadelphia: C.E. Howe Company; *Boyd's Combined City and Business Directory of Philadelphia 1919-1920*, Philadelphia: C.E. Howe Company; *Polk's Philadelphia Directory 1925*, Philadelphia: R.L. Polk & Company; *Polk's Philadelphia City Directory 1930*, Philadelphia: R.L. Polk & Company; *Polk's Philadelphia City Directory, 1935-36*, Philadelphia: R.L. Polk & Company.

[709] *Sixteenth Census of the United States* (1940), *Inhabitants of Philadelphia, Philadelphia County, Pennsylvania*, E.D. No. 51-486, page 5644B.

As noted above, Christiana and William Dobler were living with her father Samuel Alwine, in Philadelphia at the time of the 1940 Federal Census. Eventually they resettled to Berks County. In the 1930 Federal Census listings, Samuel P. Alwine's occupation is given as manager of a "grocery warehouse." At the time of the 1940 Federal Census, Samuel P. Alwine was working as a "caretaker" in a private household in the city of Philadelphia. His wife and children (Samuel, age 14, and Edward, age 11) were living with her parents, Edward C. and Katherine Smith, a short distance away.[710]

Christianna (Powers) Alwine died in Philadelphia on September 1, 1923. Samuel Alwine died there on November 23, 1942.[711] As of this writing, we do not know where they are buried.

Niles Gaylord Alwine (1902-1964)
York County and Philadelphia

Niles Gaylord Alwine (M06-0410-0609-01), son of Edward Romanus and Elsie M. (Rutters) Alwine, was born November 22, 1902 in York County, Pennsylvania. His father, Edward Romanus Alwine (M05-0410-0609) was a son of Peter S. Alwine and Catherine Dahlhammer—Peter S. Alwine was the brickmaker from York County and a founder of the Alwine Brick Company (see Chapter 15). Niles Gaylord Alwine married Buelah E.M. Brown (b. April 6, 1906, d. January 1974), daughter of Noah and Frances (Wentz) Brown, on April 5, 1924 in York County and shortly thereafter they moved to Philadelphia. They lived in Philadelphia long enough to register a presence there in the early decades of the 20th century, but did not remain there for long. The 1930 Federal Census of Philadelphia lists Niles and Beulah Alwine, where his

---

[710] *Fifteenth Census of the United States* (1930), *Inhabitants of Germantown Township, Philadelphia County, Pennsylvania*, E.D. No. 628, page 207A; *Sixteenth Census of the United States* (1940), *Inhabitants of Philadelphia, 22nd Ward, Philadelphia County, Pennsylvania*, E.D. No. 51-462, page 5389A; E.D. No. 51-485, page 5628A.

[711] See the Pennsylvania Department of Health records: http://www.health.state.pa.us.

occupation is given as "machinist in a bakery."[712] The 1930 *Polk's City Directory* for Philadelphia also registers their presence there.[713] According to the 1940 Federal Census, Niles and Beulah Alwine moved back to York County by 1935 and that is where they are located in 1940.[714] Soon thereafter, they moved to California (see Chapter 24, volume 3).

Closing

Philadelphia was the port through which our immigrant ancestor, Hans Jacob Allwein, arrived in America in 1741, although he did not spend much time there. Instead he settled in Bern Township, some 80 miles inland, in what would a decade later become part of Berks County (see Chapter 13). Most of what we know about Hans Jacob Allwein and his wife Catharina is summarized in Chapter 1 of *Familie Allwein*, volume 1, and we have not covered any of that material here. To the extent there is new information on Hans Jacob and Catharina Allwein, this will be covered in *Familie Allwein*, volume 3, where I provide an "update" on the Allwein family in America.

There were members of the Allwein family who settled in Philadelphia County in the late 1800s and early 1900s, and this chapter has covered these families. Those who came from Lebanon County used the ALLWEIN spelling. These families are descendants of Philip Allwein. There were also several families in Philadelphia from 1844 through 1930 that used the ALWINE or ALLWINE spelling of the name. Some of these are perhaps descendants of another family that also used the ALWINE or ALLWINE spelling, but whose origins are in the Ohlwein families of the region. Others using these renderings of the family name are descendants of John

---

[712] *Fifteenth Census of the United States* (1930), *Inhabitants of Philadelphia, Philadelphia County, Pennsylvania*, E.D. No.51-848, page 157B.

[713] *Polk's Philadelphia City Directory 1930*, Philadelphia: R.L. Polk & Company.

[714] *Sixteenth Census of the United States* (1940), *Inhabitants of Jackson Township, York County, Pennsylvania*, E.D. No. 67-45, page 597A.

Allwine of Dauphin County, and some are descendants of Conrad Alwine and Samuel Allwine, who settled in the Adams and York County areas of Pennsylvania.

Some Allwein descendants can be found in Philadelphia County today. A 1994 zip code search of addresses in Philadelphia County revealed there were 6 ALWINE households (and no ALLWEIN or ALLWINE households) listed there, suggesting that those ALLWEIN families who migrated to Philadelphia around the turn of the 20th century had dispersed into adjacent counties and are no longer there in more recent times. The origins of those ALWINE families still remaining in contemporary Philadelphia are unclear.

CHAPTER THIRTEEN

Allwein Families in Berks County

Introduction

Berks County, Pennsylvania figures prominently in the early Allwein family history in America. Historical records indicate that Bern Township (now Upper Bern and Tilden Townships) was the location of the original settlement of our immigrant ancestors, Hans Jacob and Catharina Allwein. There are traces of the original family in the records kept by the Goshenhoppen mission priests, colonial government land records, Berks County tax lists, and a few cemetery records of the region. Although some of their progeny remained in Berks County, most moved to other locales. One daughter, Mary Elizabeth Allwein, married Philip Schmidt and they remained in Penn Township of Berks County. The other daughter, Catharine Allwein, married Joseph Seyfert, and they lived in Reading, Berks County (see volume 1). Hans Jacob and Catharina's oldest son, Johannes (John) Allwein, remained in Berks County, but his only surviving son moved to Somerset County (see Chapter 4 of *Familie Allwein*, volume 1 and Chapter 17 of volume 2). Their other son, Conrad Allwein, moved to Lebanon Township in Dauphin County (see Chapters 3 and 6 of *Familie Allwein*, volume 1). It was not until later that 5th and 6th generation members of this family line returned to the area. In this chapter, we review what is known about Allwein family members living in Berks County in the late 1800s and early 1900s.

In this chapter we begin by discussing the historical context of the settlement in Berks County by our immigrant ancestors, Hans Jacob and Catharina Allwein, and then I cover Allwein families who lived in Berks County at the end of the 1800s and into the early 1900s. The history of Berks County is important because this was the site of the Catholic mission at Goshenhoppen, where the itinerant priests of the Catholic Church were based, and where another more recent priest in our family, Rev. Msgr. Charles Leo Allwein, settled in the early 1900s.

Berks County

Berks County was formed from parts of Philadelphia, Chester and Lancaster Counties on March 11, 1752. Its boundaries were changed in 1772 and ultimately did not take its present form until 1811. In the early 1700s these were the "back woods," and still inhabited largely by First Nations people, and literally on the frontiers of European settlement.

The name Berks came from the County of Berkshire in England, where the Penn family had large estates.[715] The town of Reading, which would become the County Seat of Berks County, was laid out in several years before, and was located on land that had been the private property of William Penn's sons, Richard and Thomas Penn. It was named for the capital of Berkshire in England.[716]

Located to the northwest of Philadelphia, Berks County was one of the early areas settled by the immigrant Germans or Pennsylvania Dutch. Prior to the existence of Berks County, there were German settlements throughout the region, and as noted above, Berks County was the location of the settlement of Hans Jacob and Catharina

---

[715] Morton L. Montgomery, *Historical and Biographical Annals of Berks County Pennsylvania Embracing a Concise History of the County and a Genealogical and Biographical Record of Representative Families.* Volume I. Chicago: J.H. Beers & Co.

[716] A. Howry Espenshade, *Pennsylvania Place Names*, State College, Pennsylvania: The Pennsylvania State College, 1925 (Republished by Gale Research Company, Detroit: Book Tower, 1969), chapter 3, pages 46-47.

Allwein. They settled in Bern Township of what would eventually become Berks County. Bern Township actually existed prior to Berks County as part of Lancaster County. It became part of Berks County when the latter was formed from parts of Philadelphia, Chester and Lancaster Counties in 1752. In the northern part of Berks County, Bern Township contained all of the present-day townships of Bern, Upper Bern (formed in 1789), Penn (formed in 1841), Centre (formed in 1843) and Tilden (formed in 1887).

There were originally twenty townships that made up Berks County at the time of its formation—now there are forty-four. The map of present-day Berks County is given in Exhibit 13.1, showing the townships in existence today. This map can help orient the reader to the following presentation, in that references are often made to the townships in which family members lived and where certain events happened.

Familie Allwein in Berks County

Hans Jacob Allwein is listed among the "taxables" of Bern Township in 1754 soon after the formation of Berks County.[717] Tax records for all available years between 1767 and 1781 also list him in Bern Township.[718] In Chapter 1 of *Familie Allwein*, volume 1 (pages 24-31) I reviewed all of the available land warrant information that allowed us to pinpoint the location of Hans Jacob and Catharina's land.[719] Bern Township was later subdivided, and although their property was in

---

[717] Morton L. Montgomery, *Historical and Biographical Annals of Berks County Pennsylvania Embracing a Concise History of the County and a Genealogical and Biographical Record of Representative Families*. Volume I. Chicago: J.H. Beers & Co.

[718] This information was published in "Proprietary and State Tax Lists of the County of Berks, for the Years 1767, 1768, 1779, 1780, 1781, 1784, 1785," *Pennsylvania Archives*, Third Series, Volume 18, edited by William Henry Egle. Harrisburg PA: W.S. Ray, State Printer of Pennsylvania, 1898, pages 81, 108, 199, 318, and 446.

[719] Kenneth D. McCrea, *Pennsylvania Land Applications—Volume 1: East Side Applications, 1765-1769*, Strasburg, Pennsylvania: McCrea Research, Inc., 2002.

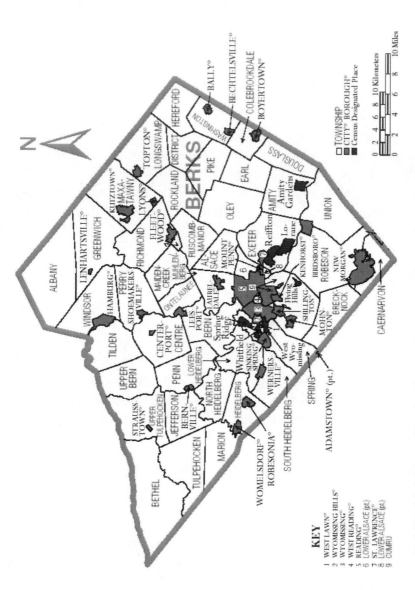

Exhibit 13.1 Map of Berks County, Pennsylvania with Municipal Labels showing Cities and Boroughs, Townships, and Census-designated places

Bern Township when they acquired it, the land warrant records indicate that according to more recent demarcations of townships they were located in Upper Bern and Tilden Townships.

The land where Hans Jacob and Catharina Allwein settled lies in the foothills of the Blue Mountains in northern Berks County. The Blue Mountain is a ridge that forms the eastern edge of the Appalachian mountain range in Pennsylvania, running about 150 miles from the New Jersey border in the northeast to the Big Gap west of Shippensburg at its southwestern terminus. What is today known as the Appalachian Trail follows this ridge along the border of Berks and Schuylkill Counties, and as mentioned above, Hans Jacob Allwein's land can be located amongst the fertile farmlands to the south of these mountains, a few miles due east of Shartlesville, Pennsylvania, a settlement named for the Shartle family who established an Inn at that location in 1765. The land to the north of the Allwein property, east of St. Michael's Church Road, was land held by the St. Michael's Lutheran congregation and is the present-day location of St. Michael's Lutheran Church and St. Michael's Union Cemetery (see Exhibit 13.4).

I have already thoroughly discussed what is known about Hans Jacob and Catharina Allwein's settlement in Pennsylvania in the first volume of *Familie Allwein* (see Chapter 1), and I will not repeat that material here, except to note three early connections to Berks County. The first is the connection of Allwein families to the Catholic mission at Goshenhoppen (now Bally). The second is the burial of Allwein family members in St. Michael's Union Cemetery, which I discuss further below. This again reinforces the location of these families in present-day Upper Bern and Tilden Townships. The third early connection to Berks County is the burial of Allwein family members in Deppen Cemetery, near Bernville in Penn Township, which I discussed in *Familie Allwein*, volume 1 (pages 93-98). This cemetery is where Mary Elizabeth Allwein, a daughter of Hans Jacob and Catharina Allwein, and her husband Philip Schmidt are buried.

Goshenhoppen[720]

Prior to the existence of Berks County, there were German settlements throughout the region, and as noted at the outset, one of these areas was known as "Goshenhoppen," which I briefly review here because of its significance, not only in terms of German colonial history, but also because of its importance to Allwein family history. There is no town or village called Goshenhoppen anymore, and as a "place name" its use has nearly faded from existence.

Most people agree that the earliest reference to Goshenhoppen was reported by historian William J. Hinke who found a petition to the governor of Pennsylvania dated May 10, 1728 requesting protection against a threatened Indian attack by people living in that area. Hinke identified Goshenhoppen (spelled 'Coshahopin') "as a region about ten miles long and five miles wide, which 'extends along the Perkiomen Creek, in the upper end of Montgomery County, Pennsylvania and covers also small strips of land in the adjacent counties of Berks, Lehigh and Bucks."[721] Of course, most of these counties were not in existence in the 1730s and 1740s. Berks County was not created until 1752, and its present-day boundaries were not set until 1811. Present-day Montgomery County (to the south) did not exist then either; it was formed out of part of Philadelphia County in 1784.

There is little consensus on the origins of the name *Goshenhoppen* or what it means, or even how it should be spelled. One theory is that it comes from the name "Shakahoppa," which

---

[720] This section is based on the author's article "On Sacred Ground: Exploring Goshenhoppen Churches," *Journal of the Berks County Genealogical Society*, vol. 21, no. 2, Winter, 2000, pages 14-19.

[721] Quoted by Charles Glatfelter in *Pastors and People: German Lutheran and Reformed Churches in the Pennsylvania Field, 1717-1793*. Volume I: Pastors and Congregations. Breinigsville, Pennsylvania: The Pennsylvania German Society, 1980, page 373.

is the name of a Lanape Indian chief who ruled the Perkiomen Creek area in the 1600s (see the URL: http: //www. luther95. net/ALCG-HPA). Others suggest that the name Goshenhoppen was an Indian word for "meeting place."[722] Yet another idea is that the name is an adaptation of the Old Testament reference to *Goshen*, in Hebrew tradition the fertile area in Egypt given to the Israelites, which meant "promised land" (see Genesis 45:10). One interpretation consistent with this is that it was a name for a community of origin in Germany, namely "Goshenhof," which sounds German, but I have not be able to verify the existence of such a place.[723] The word may have originated from one or some combination of all of these sources, but we do not know for sure. Whatever its origins and despite its relative disuse, there are many places in southeastern Pennsylvania that have borne the name Goshenhoppen in past centuries, and although there is little present-day use of the name for places, there are several historically-linked references to the churches of Goshenhoppen.

The name *Goshenhoppen* is also preserved today in the folklife community of southeastern Pennsylvania. As part of the revival of interest in preserving Pennsylvania German culture that emerged in the late 1950s and early 1960s, a group called the "Goschenhoppen Historians" was founded to collect, preserve and display the elements of history and folk culture of the Pennsylvania Dutch region of southeastern Pennsylvania. [Notice the unique spelling of Goshenhoppen used by this group.] They are one of several groups of people that help keep the German folkways alive today. Headquartered in Red Men's Hall in Green Lane, Pennsylvania, the Historians maintain a museum, library and folklife center, and they have for thirty-five years held the Goschenhoppen Folk Festival, an

---

[722] See Leo Gregory Fink (p. 7), *From Bally to Valley Forge: Historical Monograph of the Catholic Church in the Perkiomen Valley from 1741 to 1952.* N.p. 1953.

[723] This is the interpretation given by Donald F. Roan, in "The Goshenhoppen Historians: Preserving and Celebrating Pennsylvania German Folk Culture." *Pennsylvania Folklife Magazine*, Spring, 1996, page 114.

annual celebration that is a part of the German folklife festivals that are held in the region each year.[724]

There is a wealth of information about the dynamics of religion and church life in colonial Pennsylvania. Perhaps one of the best known parts of this history is the fact that 18th-century Pennsylvania was a refuge for radical Protestant pietistic sects escaping from religious tyranny in Europe. Indeed, many such German-speaking sects, including the Mennonites, the Amish, the Dunkards (German Brethren), Moravians, Schwenkfelders, and Waldensians immigrated to the American colony in the early 1700s, and among other places, many of these settled in the land of Goshenhoppen. The presence of Mennonites and Schwenkfelders as some of the earliest settlers to the area has been well documented. The Mennonites were undoubtedly there first, owing to their early arrival to the Pennsylvania colony. The Mennonites built a log church there in 1731, and it is a fair guess that the Mennonite history probably holds the key to the mysterious origins of the name of Goshenhoppen.[725]

By the middle of the 18th century, there were many religious groups present in the southeastern counties of Pennsylvania and a

---

[724] The Goschenhoppen Folk Festival is held on the second Saturday and Sunday of August in New Goschenhoppen Park in East Greenville, Pennsylvania. See Donald F. Roan, "The Goschenhoppen Historians: Preserving and Celebrating Pennsylvania German Folk Culture." *Pennsylvania Folklife Magazine*, Spring, 1996, pp. 114-125. Also, perhaps the best known German folklife festival is the Kutztown Pennsylvania German Festival held at the Kutztown, Pennsylvania Fairgrounds each July (URL: http://www.kutztownfestival.com). This celebration was the subject of a *National Geographic* article, "Pennsylvania's Old-Time Dutch Treat," written by Kent Britt, published in April, 1973.

[725] Alexander Waldenrath "Goshenhoppen (Bally), Early Center of Roman Catholicism in Berks County," *Historical Review of Berks County* (Summer, 1974, pp. 93-95, 111-115) makes reference to the building of the Mennonite Church in Goshenhoppen. Also, for an historical account of the early immigration of these pietist sects to Pennsylvania in the 18th century, see Aaron Fogelman (1996), *Hopeful Journeys: German Immigration, Settlement, and Political Culture in Colonial America, 1717-1775*. Philadelphia: University of Pennsylvania Press (pp. 100-107).

wide spectrum of churches established in the area of Goshenhoppen. Some of the religious (e.g. the Mennonites, Catholics and Schwenkfelders) came in groups and settled as communities. Most people, however, did not, and whatever religion people identified with was probably as much a function of what churches were available for meeting their spiritual needs. The vast majority of German-speaking immigrants were connected to the Lutheran and Reformed faiths, and with time, these churches provided clergy in numbers sufficient to minister to their needs.[726] The Lutheran and Reformed Germans began coming to Pennsylvania in large numbers after 1710. Indeed, the first Lutheran and Reformed churches were formed within a decade of the arrival of these immigrants, and Goshenhoppen was the early site of this activity. The first German Lutheran congregation was formed at New Hanover in upper Montgomery County by Anthony Jacob Henkel, who came to Pennsylvania from Germany in 1717. According to Charles Glatfelter, the earliest German Reformed congregations were formed soon thereafter, when John Philip Boehm, a schoolmaster who immigrated in 1720, began conducting Sunday services. Boehm ministered to early Reformed congregations in Falkner Swamp and Skippack in the Goshenhoppen area and White Marsh farther to the east.[727]

The name Goshenhoppen was also connected to an early Roman Catholic mission in Pennsylvania, the third in the state, founded by the Jesuit priest Reverend Theodore Schneider. This mission was located in what would later become Washington Township in lower Berks County and was also the site of the first Catholic school in the state. Reverend Schneider, who came from Germany in 1741, and his fellow Goshenhoppen priests ministered to Catholics throughout Berks County and the surrounding region. Historian William J. Hinke mentions there being 231 Catholics appearing

---

[726] Charles Glatfelter, *Pastors and People: German Lutheran and Reformed Churches in the Pennsylvania Field, 1717 to 1793*. Volume II: The History. Breinigsville, Pennsylvania: The Pennsylvania German Society, 1981.
[727] Charles Glatfelter, *Pastors and People: German Lutheran and Reformed Churches in the Pennsylvania Field, 1717 to 1793*. Volume I: Pastors and Congregations. Breinigsville, Pennsylvania: The Pennsylvania German Society, 1980, page 3.

on the Philadelphia Ship lists from 1727-1775, and many of these probably settled in Goshenhoppen.[728] The name of this town was later changed to Bally, after Augustin Bally, a Catholic priest who served the community for several years.[729]

Jerome Allwein (see Chapter 12), wrote in his 1902 *Genealogy of the Allwein-Arnold Families* that one of the first "authentic records of the Allwein family" is found in Father Schneider's marriage register at Goshenhoppen where is recorded the marriage of Conrad Allwein and Catharine Weibel on May 16, 1773. The record suggests that the Allwein and Weibel families were among the first Catholic families that were connected to Goshenhoppen and other early Catholic congregations. Conrad and Catharine Allwein were my 4th great grandparents. They were married at Christian Henrich's house at Sharp Mountain (also called Asperum Collem by the mission priests) in the vicinity of present-day town of Lenhartsville in Albany Township (see *Familie Allwein*, volume 1, pages 113-122). The marriage record, kept by Father de Ritter, indicates that *three* marriages occurred there that day, which was typical given the infrequency of the visits of the mission priests.[730]

It is important to understand that Conrad and Catharine (Weibel) did not reside at or near Goshenhoppen, but in the northern part of Berks County east of Shartlesville. By today's routes, they lived some 40 miles from the Catholic mission at Goshenhoppen. As noted, their marriage took place at Christian Henry's house in Albany Township, about 20 miles from where they actually lived.

---

[728] See the material published by Ralph Strassburger, and edited by William Hinke, in *Pennsylvania German Pioneers: A Publication of the Original Lists of Arrivals in the Port of Philadelphia From 1727 to 1808* (Baltimore, Genealogical Publishing Co., 1980); Alexander Waldenrath (1974, pp. 94-95) "Goshenhoppen (Bally), Early Center of Roman Catholicism in Berks County," *Historical Review of Berks County*, vol. 39, no. 3.

[729] William Bishop Schuyler, "Memoirs of the Rev. Augustin Bally, S.J.," *Records of the American Catholic Historical Society*, September, 1909, pp. 209-249.

[730] *The Goshenhoppen Registers, 1741-1819*, reprinted from *Records of the American Catholic Historical Society of Philadelphia*, Baltimore, Maryland: Clearfield Publishers, pages 105-106.

The Catholic mission at Goshenhoppen later became known as St. Paul's Chapel and eventually was renamed the Church of the Most Blessed Sacrament. The modern church building, erected in 1837 on the site of the original church, is a monument to the history of German Catholic settlement in the region. The original chapel is preserved in the apse of the present building, where the bodies of the earliest mission priests are buried.[731] One can see the original structure of St. Paul's Chapel from the rear of the present-day church building (barely visible at the extreme right in the photo of the church in Exhibit 13.2). The photo in Exhibit 13.3 shows the exterior remains of the original St. Paul's Chapel which was enclosed within the apse of the new building.

The Catholic Church at Bally is still a thriving religious community. It has played an important role in the development of Catholicism in the region, as a mission church spawning more than half a dozen other Catholic congregations in the Perkiomen valley and elsewhere. It was from here that the Jesuit missionaries served the needs of a dispersed Catholic community. The Church of the Most Blessed Sacrament, stands in one of the most serene settings imaginable, about one-fourth mile to the east of present-day Bally. It stands as a monument to the history of German Catholic immigration to America. The present church was erected on the site of the original chapel, St. Paul's Chapel, which is literally a memorial to Catholic history in southeastern Pennsylvania. The original chapel is preserved in the apse of the present building, where the bodies of the earliest mission priests are buried and where today it serves as a museum preserving the past. The school, founded in 1743, is the oldest Roman Catholic school in the original 13 colonies. The parish at Bally has a personal significance for the Allwein family, as Monsignor Charles L. Allwein, served as rector of the school there from 1952 to 1972. Our ancestors had contact with St. Paul's Chapel at Goshenhoppen, through its mission priests, from its earliest days, and Msgr. Allwein has done much to help discover and preserve our family's broader Catholic heritage (see below).

---

[731] Alexander Waldenrath, Goshenhoppen (Bally), Early Center of Roman Catholicism in Berks County, *Historical Review of Berks County*, Summer, 1974; and Leo Gregory Fink, *From Bally to Valley Forge: Historical Monograph of the Catholic Church in the Perkiomen Valley from 1741 to 1952*, no publisher given, 1953.

Exhibit 13.2 Most Blessed Sacrament Roman Catholic Church and former Parish School, Bally, Berks County, Pennsylvania

Exhibit 13.3 Remaining exterior of St. Paul's Chapel enclosed within the apse of the Church of the Most Blessed Sacrament, Bally, Pennsylvania

Exhibit 13.4 St. Michael's Union Church and Cemetery, Tilden Township, Berks County, Pennsylvania

St. Michael's Church and Cemetery

The St. Michael's Union Church and Cemetery (now St. Michael's Lutheran Church and St. Michael's Union Cemetery) were founded in 1766, and they were located on land adjacent to the property owned by Hans Jacob and Catharina Allwein. As is made clear by the Pennsylvania land warrant records, reviewed in volume 1 of *Familie Allwein* (pages 24-31), the land to the north of the Allwein property was "church land." Specifically, this was land held in trust for later use by the St. Michael's Lutheran congregation and is the present-day location of the church and cemetery. The new St. Michael's cemetery on the hill to the south of St. Michael's Lutheran Church may well be situated on land that belonged to the Allwein family. We do not know this for sure.

What we do know is that, in addition to Hans Jacob and Catharina Allwein, this was the area settled by their son, Johannes (John) Allwein, and the old St. Michael's Union Cemetery is the burial location for some Allwein family members (see *Familie Allwein*, Chapter 2, pages 85-88).[732] There are two graves in the old St. Michael's Union Cemetery we know for sure are Allwein family members—one for "Eva Christina Allweins" (see Exhibit 13.5), wife of Johannes (John) Allweins (the eldest son of Hans Jacob and Catharina Allwein) and one for "Johannes Alwein," a son of Johannes (John) Allweins and Eva Christina Allweins, who died in childhood (see Exhibit 13.6). The inscriptions on these gravestones read as follows (translating into English) [note also that the surname given for Eva Christina is ALLWEINS and the surname given for Johannes is ALLWEIN]:

> Eva Christina Allweins—born—1742—died June 22, 1797—55 years of age
> Johannes Allwein—born September 27, 1787—died February 8, 1794—6 years, 4 months, 11 days

In volume 1 of *Familie Allwein* (Chapter 2, page 86), I speculated that there were other unidentified gravestones that might be for other members of the Allwein family. Specifically,

---

[732] *Saint Michael's Church Record of Burials, 1766-2009.* Saint Michael's Cemetery Corporation. 529 Saint Michael's Road, Hamburg, Pennsylvania, March 2010.

I speculated that there may be a connection to the gravestones adjacent to those for these two members of the Allwein family. We have no way of knowing this without further information. In one case, the gravestone to the left of that for Eva Christina Allweins, we have been able to remove the basis for any such speculation. It was found to belong to a child of the Shartel/Shartle (also Sherdel) family that also settled in this area.[733]

The inscription for this child reads as follows (see Exhibit 13.7):

John Scherdel, son of Jacob Scherdel and Anna Maria—born May 27, 1813—died May 18, 1814

The father of this child, Jacob Scherdel/Shertle (b. November 25, 1780, d. December 10, 1839), was a son of Jacob Schertel (b. April 29, 1747, d. February 18, 1819), who was one of the early settlers in this part of Berks County. We do not know at this time whether there is a connection between the Allwein and Shartle (Scherdel/Shertle) families, aside from their geographic propinquity. Specifically, we have no clues about whether there is a family relationship, or whether the proximity of the gravestones is purely coincidental. Further research into the connections of persons buried in this old graveyard will be necessary to shed further light on this subject.

There is a fourth gravestone on this plot that appears to mark an Allwein grave (see Exhibit 13.8), which has the same design as the headstone for Johannes Allwein (Exhibit 13.6). The stone is seriously degraded and the inscription is presently unreadable. Earlier I speculated that this grave might contain the remains of Joseph Allwein, son of John and Eva Christina Allwein, who died in 1806 (see page 86 of *Familie Allwein*, volume 1). We must, however, accept the fact that we do not know whose grave this is, and any claim that it is an Allwein family member who is buried there is based on speculation.

---

[733] This information is based in part on a list of burials given in the Saint Michael's Union Church, Upper Bern Township, 1769-1847, Account Book. Research conducted November 10, 2009 at the Historical Society of Pennsylvania, 1300 Locust Street, Philadelphia, Pennsylvania. Documentation is available upon request.

Exhibit 13.5 Gravestone for Eva Christina Alweins—St. Michael's Union Cemetery, Tilden Township, Berks County, Pennsylvania

Exhibit 13.6 Gravestone for Johannes Allwein—St. Michael's
Union Cemetery, Tilden Township, Berks County, Pennsylvania

Exhibit 13.7 Gravestone for Johannes Scherdel—St. Michael's
Union Cemetery, Tilden Township, Berks County, Pennsylvania

Exhibit 13.8 Gravestone for Unknown Allwein—St. Michael's
Union Cemetery, Tilden Township, Berks County, Pennsylvania

Deppen Cemetery

Deppen Cemetery has its own interesting history, which is summarized on a plaque located on the cemetery wall today, which reads as follows:

> It was originally located near Mt. Pleasant in Berks County. Begun as a family burial ground, Deppen Cemetery was originally located a half-mile west of Mt. Pleasant, south of Pennsylvania Route 183. Known locally as "The Catholic Cemetery," it was moved to this spot by the Army Corps of Engineers' Philadelphia District during the summer of 1978 in connection with construction of Blue Marsh Lake on nearby Tulpehocken Creek. The first known burial took place in 1808, the last in 1915. An extensive search of the cemetery and vicinity revealed 68 graves, only 36 of which were identifiable. The others were unmarked and may have included the 20 to 30 Irish laborers who fell victim to "canal" or "swamp" fever while constructing the Union Canal during the 1820s.

What this does *not* say is that originally this was a family graveyard and the first person buried there was Philip Schmidt (Sr.). In 1784 he had purchased seventy four acres of land along the Tulpehocken Creek in Penn Township. It was at the corner of that property, behind the Schmidt house, that the cemetery was located. Philip Schmidt (Sr.) sold the house and the land to his son, Philip Schmidt (Jr.) prior to his death in 1808. Philip Schmidt (Jr.) is known to Allwein family historians because he married Mary Elizabeth Allwein, the daughter of Hans Jacob and Catharina Allwein. In 1814, Philip Schmidt (Jr.) passed away, stating in his will that the land was to be rented out until his eldest son, John Schmidt, reached the age of 21. John Schmidt, in 1822, died at the young age of twelve, and the homestead then became the property of his younger brother, Philip III. Due to his young age—at the time of his acquisition of the land, Philip Schmidt III was only seven years old—the Berks County Court appointed Dr. Daniel Deppen, the husband of Philip Schmidt III's elder sister, as guardian until he came of age. Upon reaching his maturity in 1836, Philip III sold the land to Dr. Deppen. As a result of this sale, the burial ground at the corner of the Schmidt property became known as the Deppen

Exhibit 13.9 Deppen Cemetery, located at the Berks County Heritage Center, Wyomissing, Pennsylvania, containing graves of Philip Schmidt (Jr.) and Mary Elizabeth Allwein, daughter of Hans Jacob and Catharina Allwein

Cemetery (see *Familie Allwein*, volume 1, pages 93-97). As noted above, when the Blue Marsh Lake on nearby Tulpehocken Creek was constructed by the Army Corps of Engineers, this cemetery was relocated to the Berks County Heritage Center, in Wyomising, Pennsylvania.

Charles M. Allwein (1858-1929)
Lebanon and Reading, Pennsylvania

Charles M. Allwein (M05-0405-1401), first child of George Elijah and Angeline (Arentz) Allwein, was born January 6, 1858 in the Borough of Lebanon. The line of descent connecting Charles M. Allwein to Johannes Jacob and Catharina Allwein, the progenitors of the Allwein family in colonial Pennsylvania, is as follows:

Generation 1: Johannes Jacob and Catharina Allwein—Berks County, Pa.
Generation 2: Conrad and Catharine (Weibel) Allwein—Dauphin County, Pa.
Generation 3: Philip and Elizabeth (Arentz) Allwein—Lebanon County, Pa.
Generation 4: Elijah and Angeline (Arentz) Allwein—Lebanon County, Pa.
Generation 5: Charles M. and Margaret S. (Callahan) Allwein—Lebanon and
    Berks Counties, Pa.

Charles M. Allwein married Margaret S. Callahan, daughter of Evan and Mary Callahan of Colebrook, Lebanon County, Pennsylvania, in 1881. They lived for awhile in Lebanon where they maintained his father's grocery business. Charles also worked for some years at the Miller Organ Company in Lebanon.[734] By 1895 they had moved to Reading, Berks County, Pennsylvania, where he appears in *Boyd's City Directory* for several years, where he was listed as a cabinetmaker living at 1212 Fidelity Street.[735] The 1900 Federal Census similarly places them at this address in Reading. By 1910, they had moved to 922 North Eleventh Street in the 13th Precinct of Reading, where they remained for the remainder of their lives, as confirmed by the 1910 and 1920 Federal Census listings. Throughout this period,

---

[734] Jerome Allwein, *Genealogy of the Allwein-Arnold Families*. Philadelphia, Pa., 1902, page 83.
[735] Boyd's Reading City Directory 1895-97, Boyd's Reading City Directory 1898-1909. Ancestry.com.

his occupation is consistently given as a carpenter working in the railway car shops.[736]

Based on census reports and other information, Charles M. Allwein and Margaret Callahan gave life to the following children, all born during their time in Lebanon:

Mary A. Allwein (F06-0405-1401-01), b. April 27, 1882, d. April 27, 1944, m. (February 1, 1906) Raymond Hesser Riffert (b. July 25, 1880, d. unknown)

Grace B. Allwein (F06-0405-1401-02), b. November 1883, d. October 15, 1950 (GT), m. (May 12, 1903) Henry (Harold) "Harry" J. Cassidy (b. September 1881, d. July 10, 1917)[737]

Charles Edward Allwein (M06-0405-1401-03), b. March 21, 1887, d. October 16, 1918 (GT),[738] m. (June 29, 1917) Anna Sarah Bertolet (b. November 3, 1897, d. October 1986) [remarried to (1) Harry L. Schafer (b. unknown, d. June 25, 1932) and (2) (September 4, 1934) William Seaman (b. unknown, d. unknown)]

Anne "Anna" P. Allwein (F06-0405-1401-04), b. July 1889, d. June 2, 1965 (GT), unmarried

Margaret (Callahan) Allwein died November 1, 1919. Her obituary indicates there were three surviving children—Anna, Mary and Grace. She was predeceased by their son Charles E. Allwein (M06-0405-1401-03), who died on October 16, 1918 at a young age. Charles M. Allwein died some ten years later, on February 1, 1929

---

[736] *Twelfth Census of the United States* (1900), *Inhabitants of Reading Ward 9, Berks County, Pennsylvania*, E.D. No. 77, page 246A; *Thirteenth Census of the United States* (1910), *Inhabitants of Reading Ward 13, Berks County, Pennsylvania*, E.D. No. 93, page 137A; *Fourteenth Census of the United States* (1920), *Inhabitants of Reading Ward 13, Berks County, Pennsylvania*, E.D. No. 103, page 116B.

[737] Obituary for Grace B. Allwein Cassidy from the *Lebanon Daily News*, Lebanon, Pennsylvania, Monday Evening, October 16, 1950. For death dates, see the Pennsylvania Department of Health: http://www.health.state. pa.us

[738] See the Pennsylvania Department of Health: http://www.health.state. pa.us

at Reading.[739] This family attended St. Joseph's Catholic Church in Reading. Charles and Margaret Allwein are buried in Gethsemane Catholic Cemetery in Laureldale, Pennsylvania, along with their son, Charles E. Allwein, and two of their daughters, Grace (Allwein) Cassidy and Anne P. Allwein. The oldest daughter Mary Allwein married Raymond H. Riffert and they moved to eastern Pennsylvania, first to Philadelphia, and later to Delaware County (see below).

Mary A. Allwein Riffert (1882-1944)
Delaware County, Pennsylvania

Mary A. Allwein (F06-0405-1401-01), oldest daughter of Charles M. and Margaret (Callahan) Allwein, was born on April 27, 1882 in Lebanon, Pennsylvania. The line of descent connecting Mary Allwein to Johannes Jacob and Catharina Allwein, the progenitors of the Allwein family in colonial Pennsylvania, is as follows:

Generation 1: Johannes Jacob and Catharina Allwein—Berks County, Pa.
Generation 2: Conrad and Catharine (Weibel) Allwein—Dauphin County, Pa.
Generation 3: Philip and Elizabeth (Arentz) Allwein—Lebanon County, Pa.
Generation 4: Elijah and Angeline (Arentz) Allwein—Lebanon County, Pa.
Generation 5: Charles M. and Margaret S. (Callahan) Allwein—Lebanon and
    Berks Counties, Pa.
Generation 6: Mary A. Allwein and Raymond H. Riffert—Delaware County, Pa.

Mary A. Allwein married Raymond Hesser Riffert on February 1, 1906 in Philadelphia. They settled there, as recorded in the 1910 and 1920 Federal Census enumerations of Philadelphia.[740] Prior to

---

[739] Obituaries in the *Lebanon Semi-Weekly News*, Lebanon, Pennsylvania, Monday Evening, November 3, 1919, the *Lebanon Daily News*, Lebanon, Pennsylvania, Monday Evening, February 4, 1929, and funeral notices in the *Reading Eagle*, Monday, November 3, 1919 and Sunday, February 3, 1929. See also the Pennsylvania Department of Health: http://www.health. state.pa.us

[740] *Thirteenth Census of the United States* (1910), *Inhabitants of Philadelphia Ward 42, Philadelphia County, Pennsylvania*, E.D. No. 1059, page 100A; *Fourteenth Census of the United States* (1920), *Inhabitants of Philadelphia Ward 38, Philadelphia County, Pennsylvania*, E.D. No. 1354, page 189A.

Exhibit 13.10 Gravestones for Margaret and Charles M. Allwein—
Gethsemane Cemetery, Laureldale, Pennsylvania

Exhibit 13.11 Gravestone for Charles E. Allwein—Gethsemane
Cemetery, Laureldale, Pennsylvania

1910 they lived for a time in Canton (Stark County), Ohio, where
their oldest child was born.[741] By 1930, they had moved to Upper
Darby Township in nearby Delaware County, where they remained
through the 1940 Federal Census.[742] In the 1940 census listings,
several of their children were living in their household—Raymond
H., Jr. (age 33), George (age 28), Mary S. (age 26), Frederick H.
(age 24), Theodore A. (age 23), Quentin E. (age 20), and Phyllis
(age 15). In addition, Mary Riffert's younger sister, Anna P. Allwein,
was living with them. Raymond Riffert was a salesman, working
for a number of different establishments. In the 1940 Census his
occupation was given as "salesman, utility company."

Based on census reports and other records, we have the
following information for the children born to Mary Allwein and
Raymond Riffert:

---

[741] See Ohio Births and Christenings Index, 1800-1962. Ancestry.com.

[742] *Fifteenth Census of the United States* (1930), *Inhabitants of Upper
Darby Township, Delaware County, Pennsylvania*, E.D. No. 23-170, page
247B; *Sixteenth Census of the United States* (1940), *Inhabitants of Upper
Darby Township, Delaware County, Pennsylvania*, E.D. No. 23-202, page
3621A.

Raymond Hesser Riffert, Jr., b. December 2, 1906, d. September 30, 2000 (AZ), m. (October 18, 1941) Beatrice E. Hoekstra (b. September 12, 1914, d. September 16, 1995)

Earl C. Riffert, b. December 6, 1910, d. June 1979, m. Virginia Bowers (b. est. 1913, d. unknown)

George M. Riffert, b. March 29, 1912, d. October 28, 2008, m. Gertrude B. Unknown (b. May 26, 1922, d. June 1, 2010)

Mary S. Riffert, b. est. 1914, d. August 16, 1959, unmarried

Frederick H. Riffert, b. July 14, 1915, d. October 8, 1988, m. unknown

Theodore A. Riffert, b. June 29, 1916, d. October 14, 1997, m. (October 4, 1947) Phyllis M. Tate (b. August 26, 1922, d. February 1, 2003)

Charles H. Riffert, b. November 29, 1917, d. May 26, 1987, m. Jean Unknown (b. September 17, 1918, d. May 1981)

Quentin E. Riffert, b. June 18, 1919, d. July 24, 2004, m. Ann M. Unknown (b. July 30, 1927, d. unknown)

Phyllis Riffert, b. December 22, 1924, d. October 29, 2007, m. (1) Unknown Dryden, (2) Unknown Hobbs, (3) Joseph Wizenick (b. June 28, 1908, d. December 1986)[743]

Mary (Allwein) Riffert died on April 27, 1944.[744] It is not known when Raymond H. Riffert, Sr. died, or where they are buried.

Grace B. Allwein Cassidy (1883-1950)
Reading, Pennsylvania

Grace B. Allwein (F06-0405-1401-02), daughter of Charles M. and Margaret (Callahan) Allwein, was born in November of 1883 in Lebanon, Pennsylvania. The line of descent connecting Grace B. Allwein to Johannes Jacob and Catharina Allwein, the progenitors of the Allwein family in colonial Pennsylvania, is as follows:

---

[743] Obituary for Phillis Riffert Wizenick from the *Lake Zurich Courier*, Lake Zurich, Illinois, November 1, 2007. Ancestry.com.

[744] Obituary for Mary Riffert from the *Lebanon Daily News*, Lebanon, Pennsylvania, Friday Evening, April 28, 1944. See also the death records at the Pennsylvania Department of Health: http://www.health.state.pa.us

Generation 1: Johannes Jacob and Catharina Allwein—Berks County, Pa.
Generation 2: Conrad and Catharine (Weibel) Allwein—Dauphin County, Pa.
Generation 3: Philip and Elizabeth (Arentz) Allwein—Lebanon County, Pa.
Generation 4: Elijah and Angeline (Arentz) Allwein—Lebanon County, Pa.
Generation 5: Charles M. and Margaret S. (Callahan) Allwein—Lebanon and
    Berks Counties, Pa.
Generation 6: Grace B. Allwein and Henry "Harry" J. Cassidy—Berks County, Pa.

Grace B. Allwein married Henry "Harry" J. Cassidy, son of Michael and Margaret Cassidy, on May 12, 1903 in Reading, Pennsylvania. The listing from the 1910 Federal Census of Berks County for the household of Charles M. Allwein (see above) is as follows:

Charles M. Allwein (head, age 50, carpenter, railway shop)
Margaret A. Allwein (spouse, age 50)
Grace B. Cassidy (daughter, age 26)
Charles E. Allwein (son, age 23, machinist, railway shop)
Anna Allwein (daughter, age 19, saleslady, dry goods store)
Mary Cassidy (granddaughter, age 5)
Helen Cassidy (granddaughter, age 3)
Henry Cassidy (grandson, age 3)
Beatrice Cassidy (granddaughter, 5 months)
Harry J. Cassidy (son-in-law, age 30)

As this listing indicates, Grace B. Allwein and her husband Henry "Harry" J. Cassidy, along with several of their children, were living with her parents at the time of this Census. Within the relatively short space of a few years, Grace Allwein would see several close family members pass away—her husband died on July 12, 1917, her brother, Charles E. Allwein died on October 16, 1918, and her mother, Margaret (Callahan) Allwein died on November 1, 1919. In addition, she lost three children—John C. Cassidy (died May 25, 1913), Michael Cassidy (died July 28, 1913), and Henry Cassidy (died November 26, 1920)—during this period.

Based on census listings, cemetery burial records and other information, we know that Grace Allwein and Harry Cassidy had the following children:

Mary E. Cassidy, b. est. 1906, d. unknown, m. (1) (September 29, 1926) Anthony C. Siegfried (b. unknown, d. unknown), (2) Allan Haus (b. unknown, d. unknown)

Helen M. Cassidy, b. est. 1908 (twin), d. unknown, m. (1) unknown (divorced July 5, 1927), (2) (March 17, 1928) William C. Allen, (3) Paul Kern (b. 1905, d. February 2, 1951)

Henry E. Cassidy, b. est. 1908 (twin), d. November 21, 1920

Beatrice Cassidy, b. November 7, 1909, d. April 1986, m. Harold Heckman (b. March 3, 1905, d. January 1985)

John C. Cassidy, b. unknown, d. May 25, 1913

Michael L. Cassidy, b. unknown, d. July 28, 1913

Rita Elizabeth Cassidy, b. March 19, 1918, d. November 1977, m. (September 14, 1940) Richard Henry Busby (b. June 28, 1918, d. March 8, 2003)

After their mother died, Grace (Allwein) Cassidy and Anne P. Allwein (F06-0405-1401-04) remained with their father at 922 North 11th Street, as indicated by the 1920 Federal Census listing:

Charles M. Allwein (head, age 60, carpenter, railway shop)
Anna P. Allwein (daughter, age 27)
Grace B. Cassidy (daughter, age 35)
Mary E. Cassidy (granddaughter, age 14)
Helen M Cassidy (granddaughter, age 12)
Henry Cassidy (grandson, age 12)
Beatrice M. Cassidy (granddaughter, age 10)
Rita E. Cassidy (granddaughter, age 1 & 9/12)

Following their father's death on February 1, 1929, Grace and Anna remained in this household with a number of Grace's surviving children, as indicated by the 1930 Federal Census report.[745] At the time of the 1930 census report, Anna Allwein was working as a clerk in an alderman's office. Grace Cassidy and Anna Allwein were

---

[745] *Fourteenth Census of the United States* (1920), *Inhabitants of Reading Ward 13, Berks County, Pennsylvania*, E.D. No. 103, page 116B; *Fifteenth Census of the United States* (1930), *Inhabitants of Reading, Berks County, Pennsylvania*, E.D. No. 6-45, page 264A.

Exhibit 13.12 Gravestone for Anne P. Allwein and Grace B. Cassidy—Gethsemane Cemetery, Laureldale, Pennsylvania

consistently listed in Reading city directories throughout this period. In the 1940 Federal Census report for Reading, Grace Cassidy was listed in the household of her daughter, Helen Kern and her family.[746] In addition to Grace, her daughters, Beatrice and Rita Cassidy were also living in the Kern household.

Grace B. (Allwein) Cassidy died on October 15, 1950.[747] Anne P. Allwein, who never married, died several years later, on June 2, 1965. They are buried together at the Gethsemane Catholic Cemetery in Laureldale, Pennsylvania, near the graves of their brother, the unmarked graves of Grace's husband and several children, and their parents Charles M. and Margaret (Callahan) Allwein.

William Allwein (1868-1943)
Lebanon, Pennsylvania

William Allwein (M05-0404-1503), third son of Philip S. and Sarah (Arnold) Allwein, was born March 6, 1868 in Lebanon County. The line of descent connecting William Allwein to Johannes Jacob and Catharina Allwein, the progenitors of the Allwein family in colonial Pennsylvania, is as follows:

Generation 1: Johannes Jacob and Catharina Allwein—Berks County, Pa.
Generation 2: Conrad and Catharine (Weibel) Allwein—Lebanon County, Pa.
Generation 3: John and Mary (Eckenroth) Allwine—Lebanon County, Pa.
Generation 4: Philip Stephen and Sarah A. (Arnold) Allwein—Lebanon County, Pa.
Generation 5: William and Alice (Sattazahn) Allwein—Lebanon County, Pa.

William Allwein married Alice Sattazahn on April 23, 1891 in Lebanon, and by 1900 they moved to Reading, Pennsylvania, where

---

[746] *Sixteenth Census of the United States* (1940), *Inhabitants of Reading, Berks County, Pennsylvania*, E.D. No. 70-106, page 1425A.
[747] Obituary for Grace B. (Allwein) Cassidy from the *Lebanon Daily News*, Lebanon, Pennsylvania, Monday Evening, October 16, 1950. For death dates, see the Pennsylvania Department of Health: http://www.health.state.pa.us

Exhibit 13.13 Gravestone for William and Alice Allwein—St. Mary's Cemetery, Lebanon, Pennsylvania

they appear in Federal Censuses from that time onward.[748] His occupation is typically given as "laborer." As far as we know, there were no children born to this union. William Allwein died October 22, 1943 and Alice (Sattazahn) Allwein died on August 12, 1944.[749] They are buried together in St. Mary's Cemetery (SM), Lebanon, Pennsylvania.[750]

William Augusta Allwein (1885-1958)
Reading, Pennsylvania

William Augusta Allwein (M06-0404-0504-05), the youngest son of Peter and Elizabeth Allwein, was born in Lebanon County on August 6, 1885 (see Chapter 11).[751] The line of descent connecting William Augusta Allwein to Johannes Jacob and Catharina Allwein, the progenitors of the Allwein family in colonial Pennsylvania, is as follows:

Generation 1: Johannes Jacob and Catharina Allwein—Berks County, Pa.
Generation 2: Conrad and Catharine (Weibel) Allwein—Dauphin County, Pa.
Generation 3: John and Elizabeth (Felix) Allwine—Dauphin County, Pa.
Generation 4: Samuel and Elizabeth (Kreiser) Allwine—Lebanon County, Pa.
Generation 5: Peter and Elizabeth (Reifine) Allwein—Lebanon County, Pa.
Generation 6: William Augusta Allwein—Lebanon and Berks Counties, Pa.

---

[748] *Twelfth Census of the United States* (1900), *Inhabitants of West Reading, Cumru Township, Berks County, Pennsylvania*, E.D. No. 13, 175B; *Fourteenth Census of the United States* (1920), *Inhabitants of West Reading, Berks County, Pennsylvania*, E.D. No. 149, page 260A; *Fifteenth Census of the United States* (1930) *Inhabitants of Reading, Berks County, Pennsylvania*, E.D. No. 6-11, page 40A.
[749] See the Pennsylvania Department of Health: http://www.health.state. pa.us.
[750] Funeral announcement, *Lebanon Daily News*, Lebanon, Pennsylvania, Friday Evening, October 22, 1943.
[751] Birth information for William Augusta Allwein was obtained from his draft registration cards. Ancestry.com. Both WWI and WWII registration cards give the same date of birth, August 6, 1885.

William Augusta Allwein was still living at home with his parents at the time of the 1900 Federal Census, but it is difficult to locate him in subsequent censuses.[752] With the exception of the 1930 Federal Census, we have not been able to locate him in later Federal Censuses. The 1930 Federal Census lists him as an inmate of the Berks County prison.[753] That census report also indicates that he had married at the age of 22, but we can find no marriage record in Lebanon, or any of the adjacent counties.

We have his World War I and World War II draft registration cards, dated September 11, 1918, and April 27, 1942, respectively. These documents tell an interesting story. In the 1918 document he listed his job as "cook" with the Lee Brothers Circus. This was a well-known circus travelling the cities and towns of Pennsylvania and other nearby locations—so he was for some time a person "without roots" in the sense that he did not establish a permanent residence for a period of time. And then, in the 1942 document he listed his place of residence as the Hope Rescue Mission, 16th North 2nd Street, Reading, Pennsylvania, and this place was also listed as the "name and address of person who will always know your address." His siblings had pretty much already passed away—Aggie died in 1913, Lizzie in 1922, Amos in 1935 and Sally in 1937, suggesting that he was not in contact with other family members (see Chapter 11). He appears to have been somewhat down on his luck. He was living at a rescue mission, and he was applying for military service at the age of 56. There is a William Alwine listed in the 1950 *Boyd's Reading City Directory* as a laborer.[754] In any event, at this writing, further information on the circumstances of his life is unavailable. He appears to have died on August 8, 1958.[755]

---

[752] *Twelfth Census of the United States* (1900), *Inhabitants of North Lebanon Township, West Precinct, Lebanon County, Pennsylvania*, E.D. No. 138, page 153A.

[753] *Fifteenth Census of the United States* (1930), *Inhabitants of Reading, Berks County, Pennsylvania*, E.D. No. 6-62, page 181A.

[754] Boyd's Reading (Berks County, Pennsylvania) City Directory, volume 86, 1950. Ancestry.com.

[755] See the Pennsylvania Department of Health: http://www.health.state.pa.us

Christina Maria Allwein Gress (1894-1984)
Reading, Berks County, Pennsylvania

Christina Maria Allwein (F06-0405-0301-08), youngest daughter of Joseph B. and Angeline (Eisenhauer) Allwein, was born December 16, 1894. The line of descent connecting Christina Maria Allwein to Johannes Jacob and Catharina Allwein, progenitors of the Allwein family in colonial Pennsylvania, is as follows:

Generation 1: Johannes Jacob and Catharina Allwein—Berks County, Pa.
Generation 2: Conrad and Catharine (Weibel) Allwein—Dauphin County, Pa.
Generation 3: Philip and Barbara (Frantz) Allwein—Lebanon County, Pa.
Generation 4: Joseph Allwein and Anne Beber—Lebanon County, Pa.
Generation 5: Joseph B. and Angeline (Eisenhauer) Allwein—Lebanon County, Pa.
Generation 6: Christina Maria Allwein and Stephen Benedict Gress—Lebanon
    County, Pa.

Christina Maria Allwein married Stephen Benedict Gress (b. August 31, 1895), son of John and Teresa (Kramer) Gress, on September 9, 1913 at St. Mary's Catholic Church in Lebanon, Pennsylvania. The ceremony was conducted by Rev. A. Christ. The Gress family emigrated from Czechoslovakia.

Stephen and Christina (Allwein) Gress lived in Lebanon in 1920, as registered in the Federal Census of that year, where he worked as a butcher in a butcher shop.[756] The 1937-1950 *Boyd's City Directories* for Reading, Pennsylvania, place them in Reading, where Stephen Gress is listed as working in the Keystone Meat Market.[757]

As far as we know, there were two children issuing from this union:

Christine Gress, b. unknown, d. unknown, m. Unknown Siegrist
Catharine T. Gress, b. March 21, 1914, d. July 19, 2010 (HC), m.
    (December 28, 1935) Joseph H. Hartman (b. July 21, 1909, d.
    May 17, 1993)[758]

---

[756] *Fourteenth Census of the United States* (1920), *Inhabitants of Ward 5, Lebanon City, Lebanon County, Pennsylvania*, E.D. 173, page 218B.
[757] Boyd's Reading City Directory, 1937-1950. Ancestry.com.
[758] Obituary in the *Lebanon Daily News*, Lebanon, Pennsylvania, Wednesday, July 19, 2010.

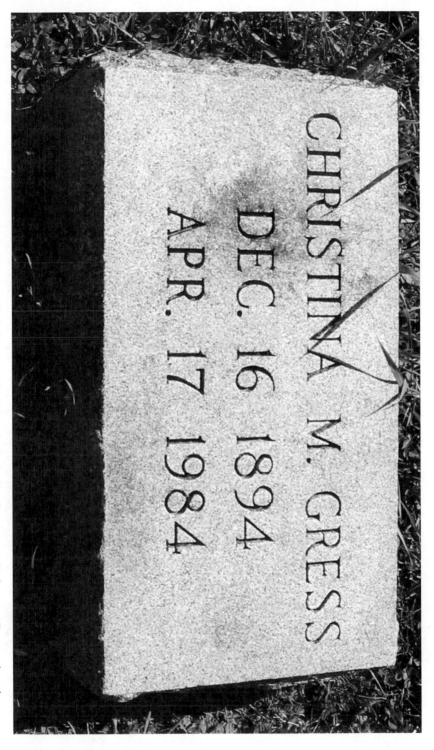

CHRISTINA M. GRESS
DEC. 16 1894
APR. 17 1984

Exhibit 13.14 Gravestone for Christina Maria Allwein—St. Mary's Catholic Cemetery, Lebanon, Pennsylvania

Christina Maria Allwein Gress died on April 17, 1984. Stephen B. Gress died February 13, 1957. They are buried at St. Mary's Catholic Cemetery in Lebanon

Charles Leo Allwein (1904-1995)[759]
Berks County, Pennsylvania

Charles Leo Allwein (M06-0405-1108-01), youngest son of Jerome Adam Allwein and Sophia M. (Schaefer) Allwein, was born July 3, 1904 in Philadelphia, Pennsylvania. His father was the son of John Edward Allwein and Elizabeth (Arnold) Allwein, descendants of two of the Catholic families that had settled in Lebanon, Pennsylvania in the early 1800s. His mother was the daughter of Frank and Mary (Nabbe) Schaefer. The line of descent connecting Charles Leo Allwein to Johannes Jacob and Catharina Allwein, the progenitors of the Allwein family in colonial Pennsylvania, is as follows:

Generation 1: Johannes Jacob and Catharina Allwein—Berks County, Pa
Generation 2: Conrad and Catharine (Weibel) Allwein—Dauphin County, Pa
Generation 3: Philip and Elizabeth (Arentz) Allwein—Lebanon County, Pa
Generation 4: John Edward and Elizabeth (Arnold) Allwein—Lebanon County, Pa
Generation 5: Jerome Adam and Sophia (Schaefer) Allwein—Philadelphia, Pa
Generation 6: Charles Leo Allwein—Berks County, Pa

Charles L. Allwein's father, Jerome Allwein (M04-0405-1108), was an educated man. He attended normal school and taught for several years in the public schools of Lebanon County, after which time he entered a course of business training in New York. He was also a religious man—active in the Knights of Columbus from the beginnings of the Philadelphia chapter (see Chapter 12). These were orientations he encouraged in his children as well.

Charles L. Allwein had one brother, Aloysius Francis Allwein (also known as A. Francis Allwein), and two sisters, Mary Magdalen Allwein and Cecilia Emma Allwein, whom we discussed in Chapter 12.

---

[759] This narrative on Charles Leo Allwein is based on the author's article "Msgr. Charles Leo Allwein (1904-1995)—Bally, Berks County, Pennsylvania." *Journal of the Berks County Genealogical Society*, Winter, 2009, pages 8-12.

Both sisters became nuns and pursued the religious life. His brother, Aloysius Francis Allwein, graduated from the University of Pennsylvania in 1916 with a degree in electrical engineering, and distinguished himself with a career in developmental engineering (see Chapter 12).

The father, Jerome A. Allwein, was the well-known genealogist who in 1902 published a definitive *Genealogy of the Allwein— Arnold Families*. Charles L. Allwein would one day, like his father, undertake an active interest in the genealogy of the Allwein family, and he was very much aware of his heritage. In the book about the history of the Most Blessed Sacrament Catholic Church in Bally, on which he collaborated with Edward Quinter, Charles L. Allwein writes: ". . . Philip Schmidt, whose house was used as a Catholic center, was a son of Philip Schmidt, Sr. an early Catholic settler . . . Philip Schmidt, Jr. married Elizabeth Allwein, widow of Joseph Obold, and daughter of Jacob Allwein, both Catholic pioneers of Bern Township."[760]

After the completion of his schooling, Charles L. Allwein entered the priesthood, becoming ordained on September 21, 1929. In the 1930 Federal Census Charles L. Allwein is listed as a Catholic priest in the Borough of Lansdale, Montgomery County, living in the Catholic parish.[761]

Later his work took him to Reading, Pennsylvania. In the 1940 Federal Census he is listed as a Catholic priest working as an assistant pastor in the Sisters of Charity convent.[762] During that year, he became the first principal of Reading Central Catholic High School, the first centralized Catholic High School in Berks County.[763]

---

[760] Edward H. Quinter, in collaboration with Charles L. Allwein, *Most Blessed Sacrament Church Bally, Pennsylvania, originally known as St. Paul's Chapel of Goshenhoppen, Berks County, Pennsylvania*, Publisher unknown, Page 60, 1976.

[761] *Fifteenth Census of the United States* (1930), *Inhabitants of Borough of Lansdale, Montgomery County, Pennsylvania*, E.D. No. 53, Page 15A.

[762] *Sixteenth Census of the United States* (1940), *Inhabitants of Reading, Berks County, Pennsylvania*, E.D. No. 70-35, Page 496A.

[763] See the following URL: < http://www.cchsbc.pvt.k12.pa.us/ >

Exhibit 13.15 Rev. Charles Leo Allwein and his sister, Cecilia Emma Allwein (Sister Maria Cecilia) (contributed by Madeline Moyer)

On May 22, 1952 he was appointed pastor of the Most Blessed Sacrament Church at Bally, Pennsylvania (see photo in Exhibit 13.2). He was no stranger to Bally and the Most Blessed Sacrament Church, as he had been officially appointed as Administrator of the rectory in 1930-31 during the illness of Father Scherf, the rector there at that time. As we noted earlier, this church, originally known as St. Paul's Chapel, was established in 1741 at a location known historically as Goshenhoppen. As noted earlier, originally a Mennonite settlement, Goshenhoppen was the site of Father Schneider's Jesuit mission church, which served the religious needs of Catholics scattered throughout Berks County and surrounding areas. St. Paul's Church played an important role in the development of Catholicism in the region and eventually spawned more than half a dozen other Catholic congregations in the Perkiomen valley and elsewhere.

One of Rev. Allwein's first projects at Bally was to build a new school, which was completed in 1953 (shown in Exhibit 13.2 on the extreme left).[764] The original school, founded in 1743 by Father Theodore Schneider, is the oldest Roman Catholic school in the original thirteen colonies. Now located in a modern building, it is called St. Francis Academy—it is a pre-kindergarten through 8th grade private school serving the area.

As noted earlier, the Catholic Church at Bally is still a thriving religious community, but the present church has the unusual distinction that it is literally a memorial to the German Catholic history of the region. The original Chapel, located directly behind the Main Altar and Sanctuary of the present Church, is preserved in its original state, and many of the original religious artifacts are still present. Soon after coming to Bally, Rev. Allwein decided to create a museum to preserve the records and relics of the Goshenhoppen mission that were of historical interest, and to use the old two-story brick building that sits immediately adjacent to the original Chapel for this purpose. The museum was created and opened to the public in August 1957, as the Bally Memorial Museum and Library, named for Father Augustin Bally, beloved pastor who served the Blessed Sacrament Church from

---

[764] Edward H. Quinter, in collaboration with Rev. Monsignor Charles L. Allwein, *Most Blessed Sacrament Church Bally, Pennsylvania, originally known as St. Paul's Chapel of Goshenhoppen, Berks County, Pennsylvania*, Publisher unknown, Page 81, 1976.

Exhibit 13.16 Entrance to the Monsignor Charles Allwein Museum, Bally, Berks County, Pennsylvania

Exhibit 13.17 Reproduction of a photograph (from left to right) of Rev. Charles L. Allwein, his sisters, Mary Magdalen Allwein (Sister Clare Imelda) and Cecilia Emma Allwein (Sister Maria Cecilia), and brother, Aloysius Francis Allwein (contributed by Edward Allwein)

1837-1881, and for whom the town is named.[765] After the Rev. Msgr. Allwein's death, owing to his important role in its development, the Museum was renamed the Monsignor Charles Allwein Museum (see the photo of the front entrance in Exhibit 13.16).

After 20 years of service as rector of the Bally Church and School, Monsignor Allwein retired from active service to the Diocese in 1972. His father, Jerome Allwein, had written a genealogy of the Allwein family, which has proven to be an extremely valuable source of information on what was known about Allwein families originating from Lebanon County, Pennsylvania at the turn of the 19th century. Msgr. Allwein picked up this work, supplemented with his own research, and continued the genealogical work of his father.

It is quite common to see references to Rev. Msgr. Charles L. Allwein in scholarly writings dealing with the Catholic history of southeastern Pennsylvania, including the monograph he collaborated on with Edward Quinter.[766] Msgr. Allwein worked tirelessly as priest, educator, historian, preservationist, and genealogist. He did much to help discover and preserve the broader heritage of his German Catholic forebears in the area. He was beloved by all who knew him. I reproduce one such tribute written by Bill Melcher in an appendix to this chapter.

In retirement Msgr. Allwein lived at the Holy Family Villa for Priests in Bethlehem, Pa. After a long and enduring life of service to God, his Church and family, Msgr. Allwein died February 4, 1995. He was buried February 8th in the Most Blessed Sacrament Church Cemetery across the road on the hillside to the southwest facing the Church.

---

[765] Edward H. Quinter, in collaboration with Rev. Monsignor Charles L. Allwein, *Most Blessed Sacrament Church Bally, Pennsylvania, originally known as St. Paul's Chapel of Goshenhoppen, Berks County, Pennsylvania*, Publisher unknown, Pages 108-125, 1976.
[766] See, e.g., Leo Gregory Fink, The First Catholics in Reading, *Historical Review of Berks County*, Summer, 1968; Leo Gregory Fink, *From Bally to Valley Forge: Historical Monograph of the Catholic Church in the Perkiomen Valley from 1741 to 1952*, no publisher given, 1953; Alexander Waldenrath, Goshenhoppen (Bally), Early Center of Roman Catholicism in Berks County, *Historical Review of Berks County*, Summer, 1974; and Edward H. Quinter, in collaboration with Rev. Monsignor Charles L. Allwein, *Most Blessed Sacrament Church Bally, Pennsylvania, originally known as St. Paul's Chapel of Goshenhoppen, Berks County, Pennsylvania*, Publisher unknown, 1976.

Exhibit 13.18 Gravestone for Monsignor Charles L. Allwein—
Most Blessed Sacrament Cemetery, Bally, Pennsylvania

Closing

In this chapter, we noted that Berks County, Pennsylvania figures prominently in the early Allwein family history in America, given this was the location of the original settlement of our immigrant ancestors, Hans Jacob and Catharina Allwein. The history of Berks County is also important because this was the site of the Catholic mission at Goshenhoppen, where the itinerant priests of the Catholic Church were based, and where another more recent priest in our family, Rev. Msgr. Charles Leo Allwein, settled in the early 1900s. After discussing the historical context of their settlement in Bern (later Upper Bern and Tilden) Township, and several historical remnants of the Allwein family in Berks County, I reviewed what is known about members of the later generations of Allwein families who settled in Berks County in the early 1900s. Marriage records for Berks County register a presence for Allwein families there. Still, few Allwein family members returned to Berks County, and there are few remnants of the Allwein family in Berks County today, when compared to other parts of Pennsylvania. A 1994 zip code search of addresses in Berks County revealed there were 4 ALLWEIN households (and no ALLWINE or ALWINE households) listed there.

Appendix to Chapter 13

MSGR. CHARLES L. ALLWEIN
PRE-EMINENT BALLY GENEALOGIST
AND CHURCHMAN

by Bill Melcher
(circa 1993)

When I first went to meet him, many years after we had begun corresponding through the mails, I paused in the hot sun for a moment and regarded the place where he was living. At once I felt a sense of awe. It was as if I was gazing upon a temple. This hallowed place was the repository of the records of the historic pastoral acts of Theo. Schneider, John B. deRitter, Peter Boniface Corvin, Paul Erntzen, Augustus Bally, and other Jesuits at Cussahoppen, missionaries who tended to the German Catholic congregation along the frontier since at least 1741, the land of my People. Indeed, this was a place where the very soul of genealogical and other forms of highly moral inquiry resided.

I was admitted to the place where he lives with other priests in retirement, one of whom had baptized me during the Great War, and remained standing in great wonder, awaiting the man with whom I had been faithfully yet facelessly corresponding for so very long.

I found him to be very much as I had always pictured him—a stern man of God, yet one who has with him a sense of natural kindness as well. The German word Gemutlichkeit expresses this much better—one feels immediately comfortable in his presence. He is learned and yet so very humble.

One could fill page after page with a listing of his works, fulfillments earned in his service to the Church and also by his many good acts toward the lay populace, be they members of his congregation or not.

He first came to pastoral service at Bally in 1930, but was soon thereafter called away to educational work. In 1940 he established the Catholic high school at Reading, converting the 44-room Luden Mansion for that purpose, later building upon it as its needs quickly grew. And years later he returned to Bally, again to serve at one of the oldest existing Catholic Church structures in the country, thrilled at being called again to tend to the historic congregation of Father Bally and to be able to contribute his work with the many historical records and artifacts that he had begun to organize some years before. He worked tirelessly toward that end, and effort that after many years was finally completed.

Monsignor Allwein—and I cannot speak of him without using his formal title, so great is my respect and admiration for him—has preserved for us the history of eastern Berks / western Montgomery Counties from their very earliest days. His exhaustive compilation, with the assistance of his devoted students at Reading Central Catholic High School, comprise most of the pastoral acts and critical records of the Catholic church at Goshenhoppen. He has thus far searched in vain for the marriage records covering the years between 1748 and 1758, and the baptism registers from 1747 through 1765 unfortunately remain only in fragments, critical years that would tell the story of the Indian depredations along the frontier during the French and Indian Wars, unwittingly wrought upon the peaceful German settlers who had come here only to farm and to escape violent political unrest in the Rhineland, a land so very similar in its unparalleled beauty to what they had found here.

One of the earliest recorded death entries reads as follows, written in a beautiful German hand:

> Magdalen Eck, daughter of John Eck, farmer in Rich Valley, had been aiding Mary Hartman during her illness and having contracted the same ailment during her labor of charity, died of the same and was buried September 2, 1765 in the graveyard used by the Lutherans near her father's house.

Records of this kind, crucial though they may be, have historically been ignored by the writers. The kind Schwenckfelders assisted him with much of the documentary research for his several publications which are modestly priced at the church office.

Through his efforts, if one has a Catholic background, one can easily trace his family history from the earliest immigrant, and I have done just that. With my Reformed and Lutheran lines he cannot help me much, but having learned his precise research techniques, I have all of these lines in order too. He has also urged brevity upon me, good advice but one thing I cannot seem to follow.

His personal lines are well-rooted in Pennsylvania German history, and represent Catholic as well as the great Protestant heritage upon which our Province was built. His lines include Allwein, Arnold, Arents, Smith, Weibel, Eck, Grett, Riffel, and German. It is through several of these lines that I am proud to say we connect.

I have no direct Amish or Mennonite lines but always attend their services when I am Home. This, of course, must never be made known to Msgr. Allwein—well, I think he secretly knows. Going now into his 89th year, he has given me boundless moral strength and a yearning to know the Universal God, the God of us all.

I am singularly honored to call him my very great friend and congratulate him on the very great honor that you have bestowed upon him. But know that he is not only an able researcher. He is also the original recorder and himself a pioneer.

He lived and helped shape the Berks County that we, in our comparative youth, can only read about. He will be long remembered as one of the great Pennsylvania German churchmen. In retirement now, he is much loved by his congregation. Which surely includes me. And, really, everyone who has ever been in his presence.

APPENDICES

APPENDIX A

Sources of Information

Not only is the present volume an update on the families covered in volume 1 of *Familie Allwein*, it also presents many new collections of facts. There are several major record sources that need to be consulted in an effort such as this. The present volume goes beyond the early land and estate records, to include marriage records, draft registration records, census records, atlases and local histories. Due to the modern computer and the availability of massive internet data bases, it is sometimes possible to search these record sources online. However, for the most part, *primary records* sources are typically not online—some are, but most are not.

According to James Beidler, former Executive Director of the Genealogical Society of Pennsylvania, major record sources differ according to the type of information they provide.[767] Information on birth, marriage, death, residence, military service and immigration are all important, but one cannot obtain access to all of these in one location, and in most cases each is helpful for a somewhat narrow range of genealogical material. Knowing the difference between "primary" and "secondary" sources, is what James Beidler

---

[767] James M. Beidler, "Genealogy." In Randall M. Miller and William Pencak (Eds.), *Pennsylvania: A History of the Commonwealth* (pages 481-500), University Park, Pennsylvania: Pennsylvania State University Press, 2002.

says is "critical in determining the believability of an individual's research."[768]

Primary vs. Secondary Sources[769]

According to James Beidler, a good genealogist never relies on a *secondary* source unless the *primary* source is unavailable. In his words,

> . . . the convenience of secondary sources often makes them a seductive substitute for primary sources in genealogists' eyes. But good genealogists never rely on that secondary source unless the primary data is literally no longer available (as opposed to merely difficult or inconvenient to access); instead, they use the secondary source as a gateway to finding the primary source, and then use the primary source as their evidence

The distinction between *primary* and *secondary* sources is as follows:

> Primary sources are documents or records created around the time of the event in question by or with the help of someone in the position to have participated in or observed the events and ideas

---

[768] James M. Beidler is the former Executive Director for the Genealogical Society of Pennsylvania. He writes "Roots & Branches," an award-winning weekly syndicated newspaper column, which appears in the *Patriot News* of Harrisburg, Pennsylvania. He is also an instructor for Family Tree University, a columnist for German Life magazine and is editor of Der Kurier, the quarterly journal of the Mid-Atlantic Germanic Society. He is the President of the International Society of Family History Writers and Editors as well as Second Vice President of the Pennsylvania Chapter, Palatines to America., and he served as national co-chairman for the 2008 Federation of Genealogical Societies conference in Philadelphia. In addition to writing on genealogical concerns, he sits on the State Historic Records Advisory Board.

[769] James M. Beidler, "Genealogy," in Randall M. Miller and William Pencak (Eds.), *Pennsylvania: A History of the Commonwealth*, University Park, Pa.: Pennsylvania State University Press, 2002, page 486.

in the document or record. The definition of secondary sources is easier. Secondary sources are any records or documents that are not primary. Examples, as usual, will help turn words into learning. The original will of an individual on file in a county courthouse is a primary source. A compilation of abstracts from that original will and others, possibly rearranged and usually indexed, is a secondary source.

Thus, in my own research the main elements of what I consider to be historical "evidence" come primarily from *primary* sources, such as ship lists, baptismal records, censuses, tax lists, court records, military and pension records, estate records, tombstone inscriptions, and other archival material. I also rely on what are essentially secondary sources including things such as genealogies, local histories, obituaries, and family stories. I rarely, if ever, use anything obtained from the *worldwide web*, unless it is a facsimile reproduction of a primary document, such as downloadable census enumerations, i.e. digital versions of actual census documents.[770]

There is a third category of information—farther from primary and secondary sources—which is potentially "fiction." This is third-hand information, usually in the form of family stories handed down, which cannot be verified. This is information that we should take with a grain of salt. One might argue that despite the inability to document any of these narratives, they may still be valuable to have. The problem is that they cannot be elevated beyond what they are—fictional accounts of what may have happened.

In the following paragraphs I summarize the major records sources I used for this research. This discussion follows the outline provided in Beidler's chapter on "Genealogy" mentioned above

---

[770] I share the results of my research through publication, rather than via the internet, and I expect others transcribe these results into GEDCOM files (often without giving proper credit as to the source of the information), I personally do not trust the quality of the information available there; and, of course, little there is adequately documented.

which appeared in the volume *Pennsylvania—A History of the Commonwealth*.[771]

Primary Data on Vital Events

So if one is serious about *separating facts from fiction*, where does one get the facts? In this section and the next, I discuss several standard sources that one can search for such relevant information. The key word here is "search," because one has to look for it and sometimes literally "dig it up." And, if it is not there, one cannot fabricate it to fill in the blanks. Sometimes one has to simply accept the fact that it is "missing" for now. Further, often we obtain information from people's private collections—it is always necessary to check out the facts that others provide, and every bit of information should be documented as to its source.

Although there is much more to family history than knowledge of the dates of *births*, *marriages* and *deaths*, these are important vital statistics. Not only do they anchor individual biographies in family and kinship arrangements, they also record the historical location of individual lives. These are what genealogists often refer to as the "big 3" with respect to the primary information necessary for developing pedigree charts and family trees.[772]

As is the case with most information about one's ancestry, you have to search for it. Prior to the availability of public records concerning births, marriages and deaths, the major source of information for many Allwein families are Christian registries. For the period covered by early immigrant histories, there are few if any public records concerning births, marriages and deaths. I have found that Protestant churches were less adept at keeping records of births and baptisms, compared to the Roman Catholic parishes. In the

---

[771] James M. Beidler, "Genealogy," in Randall M. Miller and William Pencak (Eds.), *Pennsylvania: A History of the Commonwealth*, University Park, Pa.: Pennsylvania State University Press, 2002, page 490.

[772] This discussion relies in part on James M. Beidler, "Genealogy," in Randall M. Miller and William Pencak (Eds.), *Pennsylvania: A History of the Commonwealth* (pp. 481-500), University Park, Pa.: Pennsylvania State University Press, 2002.

Catholic faith, after all, baptism is a sacrament, and therefore keeping a record of baptismal events was incumbent on the local parish priests, and the early records of many Roman Catholic parishes can play an important role in family history research. Similarly, if one's ancestors were Protestant, the records of these congregations, although much more sparse, are also an important source. The baptismal records in these sources typically provide the date of the baptism, the date of birth, the names of both parents, including in most cases the mother's family name, as well as the names of witnesses or sponsors. In volume 1 of *Familie Allwein*, we presented the available baptismal records for Lebanon and Lancaster Counties from the archives of the Diocese of Harrisburg (see Chapter 6, pages 344-352).

It was not until the late 19th and early 20th centuries that states began collecting information on births, marriages and deaths. Each state is somewhat different with respect to when they began collecting vital records information, but there are some similarities as well. In the Commonwealth of Pennsylvania, about which I have the most familiarity, until 1885 in the case of marriages and 1893 for births and deaths, the state made no continuing and consistent effort to keep such vital records. There was a law enacted in 1852 to require persons officiating at marriages, as well as physicians and others in authority, to maintain registers of vital statistics and to make reports of all marriages, births, and deaths to the office of the register of wills in each county. This law was generally ignored and later repealed due to its ineffectiveness.

In 1885, a law was enacted that required marriages to be licensed by the clerk of the orphan's court in each county and the person performing the marriage to make a return certifying that the marriage had taken place. Without these two conditions, persons could not legally be considered married. This law is still in force and marriage records are available from that time, and in some cases earlier, at the county level throughout the Commonwealth.

In 1893, a similar act required local assessors to report births and deaths occurring in their jurisdiction to the clerk of the orphan's court, but this law was superseded in 1905 by the present system requiring the registration of all births and deaths with the Division of Vital Statistics, Pennsylvania Department of Health, located in

New Castle, Pennsylvania. Birth records for the 20th century are very difficult to get access to, although with proper information, certified copies of birth and death records occurring from January 1, 1906 may be obtained from this source. Some counties still keep the birth and death records for the period 1893 to 1905, and in some cases I have relied on that material for the present volume.

Marriage records are different—these are almost universally public records and in most cases available for inspection. In virtually all counties in the United States, county court houses maintain marriage records. These are kept in various forms—some are digitized and available on the computers available in the court house, some are recorded on microfiche (or microfilm) and can be read using a microfiche (or microfilm) reader, and in other cases they exist in their original form as paper copies in those large legal binders used universally by clerks of court. I have visited dozens of county court houses and have encountered many different types of record forms, and (with one exception) I have never been denied access to marriage records.

Pennsylvania Death Records

There are a number of sources for death records, but these are not always easily obtainable from the state. In some cases they are available from death registers kept at the county level, but for the most part one needs to rely on estate records, church burial records, tombstones, cemetery listings, and newspaper obituaries, especially for the pre-1900 period.

In 1893, a law was enacted in the Commonwealth of Pennsylvania that required local (or county) assessors to report births and deaths occurring in their jurisdiction to the county clerk of the orphan's court. When the Pennsylvania Department of Health was established in 1905, this law was superseded by the present system requiring the registration of all births and deaths with the Division of Vital Statistics, Pennsylvania Department of Health, located in New Castle, Pennsylvania. Presently, the administration of vital records is governed by the Vital Statistics Law of 1953, which provides for applicants to obtain certified copies of birth and death records. However, only certain people can request birth and death certificates. In the case of birth records, one must be the person named on the birth certificate, his or her legal representative, his or her husband or wife, or specific immediate (or extended) family members. In the case of death records, one must be the legal representative of the decedent's estate, an immediate family member, an extended family member who indicates a direct relationship to the decedent, or someone who has power of attorney. With proper identification, applicants can obtain certified copies of birth and death records occurring from January 1, 1906.

This meant that birth and death records for the 20th century are difficult to get access to for genealogical research, but this changed on December 15, 2011, when Senate Bill 361 was approved, which amended the law in order to provide for public access to certain birth and death certificates after a fixed amount of time has passed. This legislation provided that such documents become public records 105 years after the date of birth or 50 years after the date of death. It is difficult to assess the quality of this information, but in my experience, with a few exceptions, dates of death in these state records generally agree with other available information. There are, however, some inconsistencies we have to live with.

One may also apply for a non-certified copy of a given death record. The state file number that is listed in these sources is necessary for making such an application, and these may be obtained at the Pennsylvania Department of Health website, which is as follows:

http://www.portal.state.pa.us/portal/server.pt/community/
public_records/20686

Social Security Death Records

For those persons who have died since the passage of the Social Security Act of 1935, and for whom there are Social Security records, the Social Security Administration makes public its master file containing over 88 million records of persons registered with the agency who have died. The file is created from internal SSA records of deceased persons possessing social security numbers and whose deaths were reported to the SSA. Often this was done in connection with filing for death benefits by a family member, an attorney, a mortuary, etc. These records contain information on the following: first and last name, social security number, state of issue, birth date, death date, and last known residence. These records are available online through Ancestry.com.[773]

Gravestone Inscriptions

Gravestones are a fool-proof source of information on dates of births and deaths. In the past, these were not easy to come by. Early in the 19th century, there were calls for making an effort to record the tombstone inscriptions of neglected cemeteries. This project got a boost when the Great Depression of 1929 occurred. The "New Deal" program of President Franklin D. Roosevelt was a massive effort to put Americans back to work by focusing on "public works" projects, including (as today) investments in infrastructure, e.g. the construction of public buildings and roads, schools, libraries, swimming pools and parks. The governmental unit that administered these resources was called the Works Progress Administration (or WPA). Almost every community in the United States could boast such a project and the benefits to local communities were remarkable. The WPA also invested in the arts, drama, media, literacy and local history projects. Under the final category listed above, were projects aimed at cataloguing local historical records, and oddly enough, some of the projects funded by the WPA were efforts to record the tombstone information in local cemeteries. I have no idea of how broad these efforts were or how much of an expenditure of resources this entailed, but we have several instances of a "cemetery project" aimed at recovering what many would consider to be vital information.[774]

---

[773] Ancestry.com. *Social Security Death Index* [database on-line]. Provo, UT, USA: Ancestry.com Operations Inc, 2010. The original data are from: Social Security Administration. *Social Security Death Index, Master File.* Social Security Administration.

[774] This information on the WPA cemetery project is drawn in part from the following
report: http://www.interment.net/column/records/wpa/wpa_history.htm.

After the WPA was dissolved, the records, now in the hands of state archives and historical societies, were microfilmed, indexed, and made available for use. However, many other records were placed into boxes and stored away. With the emergence of the internet, WPA records have found their way into mass distribution. Genealogists, who have long relied on microfilms of WPA records, are now finding the same records online. Many WPA cemetery recordings are also finding their way online. While no single WPA based project currently exists, hundreds of people across the United States have visited their local historical societies, copied some records, and published them to the internet on their own personal websites, or shared them with networks of web-based genealogists.

Of course, not everything is online, and in many cases one must navigate cemeteries on one's own. There are other important options for finding cemeteries, including street map books, cemetery records and cemetery lists from local libraries and historical societies. If the cemetery is there, one should normally be able to find it. Once there, the task is to find the family plot and the gravestones of interest. I do this part of the research the old-fashioned way. I enjoy wandering through cemeteries, with or without a cemetery map, looking for family gravestones. Of course, there are modern shortcuts. There are a number on online sources for photographs of grave markers and inscriptions. Some cemeteries organize online "virtual" cemeteries, for example, and there are websites like *Find A Grave*, that boast millions of gravestone photos. In addition, there are a number of genealogical websites that provide cemetery lists.

Primary Data on Residence

There are a number of potential sources of data on residence: Federal Census reports available from the National Archives, state level census data, county tax records, land records, land surveys and deeds, city/county directories and Social Security files. Several of these records are available online, through companies such as Ancestry.com for the price of a membership fee.

Census Reports

Census enumerations have been carried out at least since the time of the Roman Empire. Our Federal Census is provided for by Article I, Section 2 of the U.S. Constitution. It is the way in which our nation verifies representation in the House of Representatives. These federal censuses are conducted every 10 years—hence we call them "decennial" censuses. There are other censuses conducted by individual states, which have their own unique characteristics. One of the best sources of information on where people live are census reports, and these are readily available from *Ancestrycom*. Such census materials are generally a primary source of data that modern-day genealogists and family historians use to document the presence of a family and its members.

The first U.S. Federal Census was conducted in 1790, based on legislation passed at the second session of the First Congress, and was signed into law by President Washington on March 1, 1790.[775] In March of 1790, the United States was made up of twelve states, with Rhode Island, the last of the original thirteen colonies being admitted to the Union in May of that year. The 1790 Census enumerated the inhabitants of the present states (17 states in all) of Connecticut, Delaware, Georgia, Kentucky, Maine, Maryland, Massachusetts, New Hampshire, New Jersey, New York, North Carolina, Pennsylvania, Rhode Island, South Carolina, Tennessee, Vermont and Virginia.[776]

---

[775] "Introduction" to *Heads of Families at the First Census of the United States Taken in the Year 1790: Pennsylvania*, Baltimore MD: Genealogical Publishing Company, Inc., 1977, page 4.

[776] Complete sets of census schedules exist for the areas mentioned above, except for Delaware, Georgia, Kentucky, New Jersey, Tennessee, and Virginia, whose returns were lost when the British burned the U.S. Capital in Washington D.C. during the War of 1812. See "Introduction" to *Heads of Families at the First Census of the United States Taken in the Year 1790: Pennsylvania*, Baltimore MD: Genealogical Publishing Company, Inc., 1977, page 3.

The census taking was supervised by the marshals of several judicial districts in seventeen states, the original thirteen, plus those located in the northwest and southwest territories. In the original census, and those immediately following, the focus was on the number of people inhabiting the households within each township of a particular county. Only the heads of households are named, but numbers of others residing there are recorded in specific categories. For example, in the first Census, in addition to the name of the household head, the census schedules give counts of persons in the following categories:

Free white males of 16 years and upward, including heads of families.
Free white males under 16 years.
Free white females, including heads of families.
All other free persons.
Slaves.

The federal censuses of 1800 and 1810 were much the same as the first census in terms of information collected, although these censuses allowed for more categories for recording the age of household members. The 1820 through 1840 Censuses were also quite similar. The 1850 Federal Census vastly changed the scope and utility of federal census data for genealogical research, in that it was the first to list the name of each (free) person in a household, not simply the name of the head of household as was true in the earlier censuses. Each census schedule, thus, provided the name, age, sex, color (white, black, or mulatto), occupation for (free) persons fifteen years and older, value of the real estate owned, place of birth, and whether the person had been married within the census year. The 1860 and 1870 Federal Censuses were much the same as the 1850 Census, but it is worth noting that there was no such thing as "slave" status in the U.S. after the Emancipation Proclamation of 1863, and the 1870 census was the first decennial census to list African-, Chinese-, and Native Americans by name. The 1870 census was also quite innovative, in that it records the month of birth of all citizens born within the census year, and the month of marriage, if the person was married within the year.

The 1880 Federal Census was the first to provide information on the relationship of family members to the head of household, as well as the birthplace of the parents of each person listed. The 1890 Federal Census was almost completely destroyed by a fire in the basement of the Commerce Department building in Washington D.C. in 1921. Although some census schedules were saved, for all practical purposes the 1890 Federal Census records do not exist.

The 1900 Federal Census was the first census to give the exact month and year of birth for every person in the United States. These records are an invaluable complement to other primary data on date-of-birth information for family members. The 1910 through 1930 Federal Censuses gathered even further information that is of use to family historians.

All of these census materials are available in digitized form online.[777] However, it is important to know that information provided to the federal government is protected by law, as in the case of information available on the U.S. Census schedules. Information provided to the Bureau of the Census will be held in confidence and protected for 72 years. The 1930 Census enumeration records are now available to interested persons, and in 2012, the 1940 Census records became publicly available. This present volume relies extensively on information on the Allwein families taken from the Federal Census enumerations beginning in 1870 and continuing through 1940. More recent information of place of residence must rely on other sources, such as city directories.

City Directories

City directories are a useful supplement to census data, especially in years where census reports are unavailable. One such period is the 20-year period between the 1880 and 1900 Federal Censuses, due to the fact that the census materials for the 1890 Federal Census were destroyed by fire. In addition, city directories for the 1930s

---

[777] The source of all census information used in this volume is Ancestry. com and the Church of Jesus Christ of Latter-day Saints, Provo, Utah.

and 1940s are especially valuable, given that at the time of this writing there were no available census records beyond the Federal Census of 1940. Throughout the volume, I make use of whatever city directories are available for these years.

County Atlases

In addition to the Federal Census information and city directories, another important source of information used in this volume were the county atlases published in the latter part of the 19th century. For the present volume, I found several county atlases which contained information on Allwein families. The first of these was the 1875 *County Atlas of Lebanon*, published by F.W. Beers.[778] There was a second atlas of Lebanon County, produced in 1888 in conjunction with the charter of Lebanon as a city in 1885.[779] These documents are useful because they provide maps designating the residences of individuals and provide indexing by surname. I reference these maps in the discussion of each of the Allwein families in Lebanon during this period where it is relevant. In addition, there were county atlases for Adams, Dauphin and Lancaster, and York Counties that came in quite useful in researching some of these families.

Primary Data on Marriage

In 1885, the Commonwealth of Pennsylvania enacted legislation that required counties to keep records of marriage applications, and for this volume of *Familie Allwein* we have consulted available records. The 1885 law has been continuously applied to marriages at the county level, and county clerks have virtually 100 percent coverage of legal marriages. Although the nature of the information collected by Pennsylvania counties in this marriage certification process varies, the basic information is highly consistent across counties: names of parties, ages, residences, occupations, names of

---

[778] F.W. Beers, *County Atlas of Lebanon Pennsylvania from Recent and Actual Surveys and Records*, Reading & Philadelphia: F.A. Davis, 1875.
[779] Frederick B. Roe, *Atlas of the City of Lebanon, Lebanon County, Pennsylvania / Compiled, drawn and published from official plans and actual surveys*. Philadelphia: F.B. Roe, 1888.

parents, date and place of marriage, and marital history. Counties vary with respect to what they obtain from applicants about their parents. Some counties require the name, residence, occupation, and place of birth of the parents, and it is important to bear in mind that the county-level practices changed over time. In Lebanon County, as in most all other counties, the 1885 law was closely followed and excellent records exist today. I report marriage information whenever I have it.

I should add that in two census years, 1900 and 1910, the Federal Census enumerations included a question asking married respondents how many years they had been married. In the absence of other primary data, such as the county marriage records mentioned above, this is useful information, and usually remarkably accurate, despite its reliance on self-reports.

Finally, for marriages occurring prior to 1885 in Pennsylvania, there are three additional potential sources of marriage information: genealogies, church records, and local histories. These are often useful as well. Of the three, church records are probably the most reliable.

Primary Data on Military Service

Revolutionary War Service

In the case of Revolutionary War service, there are a number of secondary sources for service in the military, for example, the *Abstract of Graves of Revolutionary War Patriots*, but it is generally better to find primary data if at all possible.[780] The National Archive and many state archives maintain databases concerning persons who served in the Revolutionary War and the Civil War.

The National Archives and Record Administration (NARA) in Washington D.C. hold records relating to military service during the Revolutionary War, 1775-1783. These records include both

---

[780] Patricia Law Hatcher, *Abstract of Graves of Revolutionary War Patriots*, Dallas, Texas: Pioneer Heritage Press, 1987-1988, page 83.

Continental troops and state troops that served as Continental units. There are two sets of records: military service records and pension & land warrant records. We do not know how good the Archives' military service records are for the Revolutionary War period. The Revolutionary War service records were destroyed by fire in 1800 and 1814 and the collection of records now present at the National Archives resulted from the War Department's efforts to obtain substitutes for the original records. They admit that the War Department was not able to reconstruct every record, but they give no indication about how complete the current set of records is. I have examined the "Index to Compiled Military Service Records of Volunteers Who Served in the Revolutionary War" in several instances, and was not always able to find what I was looking for.

In the case of Pennsylvania, records pertaining to service in the Revolutionary War are available in the Archive of the Commonwealth of Pennsylvania. These records exist as card files containing transcriptions of data extracted from the original provincial records concerning service in the Pennsylvania Line, Pennsylvania Militia, and the Navy.[781] The abstract card file contains transcriptions of data extracted from original records in the custody of the State Archives concerning Revolutionary War service in the Pennsylvania Militia, Pennsylvania Line, and the Navy. Information is provided on the name and rank of soldier, whether his military service involved active or inactive duty, his county of residence, the battalion in which he served, and the record from which information was extracted. Typically, the source of the information is from the military accounts records in the *Records of the Comptroller General*, listed under militia service. It also notes whether the soldier was delinquent and fined or whether militia fines were abated.

There are other secondary sources that contain information similar to that presented above. For example, the *Pennsylvania*

---

[781] "Revolutionary War Military Abstract Card File," available online through the Pennsylvania State Archives web-based Archives Records Information Access System (ARIAS), available at http://www. digitalarchives.state.pa.us/archive.asp.

Archives, as they are known, consist of a total of 138 volumes of material published in nine series over the period 1838 to 1935. Across a period of nearly one hundred years, this series presents a wealth of information across a number of domains on the public activities of Pennsylvanians, for example, land ownership, church records on baptisms and marriages, military service, and the activities of government. Some of these volumes are indexed, while some are not. Some of these volumes contain primarily information of general historical relevance, while others contain information of prime interest to genealogists. There is information in these sources on Revolutionary War enlistments and participation.

The quality of the information included in the *Pennsylvania Archives* and its presentation is quite variable, and probably should not be considered a primary source. The initial period of publication of 28 volumes, between 1838-1860, edited by Samuel Hazard, in two parts—first, early *Colonial Records* (issued 1838-1853) containing such things as the minutes of the Provincial Council, the Council of Safety and those of the Supreme Executive Council of the Commonwealth, and second, the *First Series* (issued 1852-1856), containing records of the Secretary of the Commonwealth. During the period 1874-1899, the *Second* and *Third* series, containing a total of 45 volumes, issued under the editorship of John Blair Linn and William Henry Egle (Egle handling the *Third* series on his own), contain a variety of materials that are relevant to the Revolutionary War period. As a secondary source, the information provided in the *Pennsylvania Archives* is a valuable resource for corroborating what is found elsewhere for this period.]

The volumes in the *Third* series, edited by Dr. William Henry Egle, covering the period 1874-1899 are of particular interest to us here. During this period, Egle published a total of forty-five volumes dating prior to 1815, which contain materials varying widely in their degree of importance, but contains information on Revolutionary War soldiers.

Civil War Service

Information on Civil War service is much more abundant—and again, information is available from the National Archive and state archives. As with Revolutionary War service, compiled service records on Civil War service consist of an envelope containing card abstracts taken from muster rolls, returns, pay vouchers, and other records. They will provide you with your ancestor's rank, unit, date mustered in and mustered out, basic biographical information, medical information, and military information.

The National Archives also has pension applications and records of pension payments for veterans, their widows, and other heirs. The pension records in the National Archives Building in Washington, D.C. are based on service in the armed forces of the United States between 1775 and 1916. Pension application files usually provide the most genealogical information. These files often contain supporting documents such as: narratives of events during service, marriage certificates, birth records, death certificates, pages from family Bibles, family letters, depositions of witnesses, affidavits, discharge papers and other supporting papers. I have made great use of the Civil War pension application records and find them quite valuable.

Draft Registration Cards[782]

On April 6, 1917, the United States declared war on Germany and officially entered World War I (hereafter WWI). Six weeks later, on May 18, 1917, the Selective Service Act was passed, which authorized the president to increase the military establishment of the United States. As a result, every male living within the United States between the ages of eighteen and forty-five, whether native born, naturalized or alien, was required to register for the draft. Put another way, any male residing in the United States born between 1873 and 1900, and not already a part of the military, was required

---

[782] The following discussion relies heavily on the description of the World War I draft registration cards provided on the website Ancestry.com.

to find the draft board in their local community and register for the draft. These records are valuable for establishing place of residence.

The Selective Service System was responsible for establishing a process for selecting men for induction into the military service, from the initial registration to the actual delivery of men to military training camps. Under the office of the Provost Marshal General, the Selective Service System was made up of 52 state offices (one for each of the 48 states; the territories of Alaska, Hawaii, and Puerto Rico; and the District of Columbia), 155 district boards, and 4648 local boards. These organizations were responsible for registering men, classifying them, considering needs for manpower in certain industries and agriculture, as well as family situations of the registrants; handling appeals of these classifications; determining the medical fitness of individual registrants; determining the order in which registrants would be called; calling registrants; and placing them on trains to training centers.

The actual WWI draft registrations were completed in three parts: (1) the registration on June 5, 1917, was for men aged twenty-one to thirty-one—men born between June 6, 1886 and June 5, 1896; (2) the registration on June 5, 1918 was for men who had turned twenty-one years of age since the previous registration—men born between June 6, 1896 and June 5, 1897—men who had not previously registered and were not already in the military also registered, and in addition, a supplemental registration on 24 August 1918, was for men who turned twenty-one years of age since 5 June 1918; (3) this registration, held on September 12, 1918, was for men aged eighteen to twenty-one and thirty-one to forty-five—men born between September 11, 1872 and September 12, 1900.

As a consequence, in 1917 and 1918, approximately 24 million men living in the United States completed a WWI draft registration card. These registration cards represent approximately 98% of the men under the age of 46 in 1918. The total U.S. population in 1917-1918 was about 100 million individuals. In other words, close to one-quarter of the total population, and about one-half of the male population, is represented in these records. The original records are kept at the National Archives and Records

Administration (NARA)—Southeast Region in East Point, Georgia. Microfilm copies are at the National Archives regions that serve their respective states. In addition, some large libraries have the film of these cards for their own state. In addition, these records are available online—subscribers to Ancestry.com can obtain access to the World War I Draft Cards online as part of the U.S. Records Collection.

The WWI draft registration cards database can be an extremely useful resource because it covers a significant portion of the U.S. male population in the early twentieth-century. If one had family in the United States during WWI, they are likely to find at least one relative's information within this large collection. In addition to recording the location of the actual draft registration, these cards contain more than just names and dates; they contain significant genealogical information such as birthplace, citizenship status, and information on the individual's nearest relative, either their biological family members or their spouse. Draft registration cards for World War II, as well as military service records exist at Ancestry.com as well.

Newspaper Archives

Information available through local newspapers is often valuable for family research. Newspapers are especially a good source for obituaries, but other information as well. There are three online sources of newspaper archives that I have relied on to gather information on Allwein families, especially information on births, marriages and deaths, which include Ancestry.com, NewspaperArchives.com and GenealogyBank.com. Of course, there are often other online sources for obituaries as well, and microfilm records of local newspapers are often available at county and state historical libraries.

APPENDIX B

Cemetery Abbreviations

- A

AB—Annunciation of Blessed Virgin Mary Cemetery, McSherrystown, Pennsylvania

AG—Saint Augustine's Cemetery, Pleasanton, Alameda County, California

AK—East Akron Cemetery, Akron, Ohio

AN—Arlington National Cemetery, Arlington, Arlington County, Virginia

AU—Annville United Brethren Cemetery—Annville, Lebanon County, Pennsylvania

AR—Arlington Cemetery, Drexel Hill, Delaware County, Pennsylvania

AT—Antis Cemetery, Antis Township, Blair County, Pennsylvania

AZ—National Memorial Cemetery of Arizona, Phoenix, Maricopa County, Arizona

- B

BA—St. Bartholomew's Church Cemetery, Hanover, York County, Pennsylvania

BB—Most Blessed Sacrament Church Cemetery, Bally, Berks County, Pennsylvania

BC—Bowne Center Mennonite Cemetery, Bowne Center, Michigan

BF—Grandview Cemetery, Beaver Falls, Beaver County, Pennsylvania

BH—Berkeley Hills Cemetery, Johnstown, Cambria County, Pennsylvania

BI—Beth Israel Cemetery, Lebanon, Lebanon County, Pennsylvania

BK—Bismarck Cemetery, Quentin, Lebanon County, Pennsylvania

BL—Hempfield Church of the Brethren Cemetery, Manheim, Lancaster County, Pennsylvania

BM—Blough Mennonite Cemetery, Somerset County, Pennsylvania

BR—Blue Ridge Memorial Gardens, Harrisburg, Dauphin County, Pennsylvania

BS—Benshoff Hill Cemetery, Cambria County, Pennsylvania

BT—Baintertown Cemetery, Goshen, Elkhart County, Indiana

BV—Biglerville Cemetery, Biglerville, Adams County, Pennsylvania

BW—Burwood Cemetery, Escalon, California

- C

CA—Calvary Catholic Cemetery, Altoona, Pennsylvania

CB—Holy Trinity Catholic Cemetery, Bucyrus, Ohio

CC—Conewago Cemetery, Hanover, Pennsylvania

CD—Cathedral Cemetery, Wilmington, Delaware

CE—Cedar Lawn Cemetery, Lancaster, Pennsylvania

CG—Covenant Greenwood (Ebenezer) Cemetery, Ebenezer, Lebanon County, Pennsylvania

CH—Chestnut Hill Convent Cemetery, Philadelphia, Pennsylvania

CK—Colebrook Lutheran Cemetery, Colebrook, Lebanon County, Pennsylvania

CJ—Conejo Mountain Memorial Park, Camarillo, Ventura County, California

CL—Columbia City Cemetery, Whitley County, Indiana

CM—Calvary Cemetery, West Conshohocken, Montgomery County, Pennsylvania

CN—Conestoga Memorial Park, Lancaster, Lancaster County, Pennsylvania

CR—Mt. Carmel Cemetery, Littlestown, Adams County, Pennsylvania

CS—Most Pure Heart of Mary Catholic Cemetery, Shelby, Ohio

CU—Custer Cemetery, Somerset County, Pennsylvania
CV—Cleveland Catholic Cemeteries, Cleveland, Ohio
CW—Cornwall Cemetery, Cornwall, Lebanon County,
    Pennsylvania
CY—St. Patrick's Catholic Cemetery, York, Pennsylvania

- D

DC—Daughterty Cemetery, Rochester, Beaver County,
    Pennsylvania
DD—Dierdorff Cemetery—Elkhart Township, Elkhart, Indiana
DM—Woodlawn Cemetery of Denmark Manor—Penn Township,
    Westmoreland County
DP—Deppen Cemetery, Berks County, Pennsylvania
DV—Spring Hill Cemetery, Danville, Vermillion County, Illinois

- E

EA—Evergreen Cemetery, Annville, Lebanon County, Pennsylvania
EB—Ebenezer's Cemetery, Lancaster, Pennsylvania
EC—Ebenezer Cemetery, East Peru, Madison County, Iowa
ED—Ebenezer Cemetery, Harrisburg, Pennsylvania
EH—East Harrisburg Cemetery, Harrisburg, Pennsylvania
EL—Zion Lutheran and Reformed Cemetery (EL), East Hanover
    Township, Lebanon County, Pennsylvania
EN—Enola Cemetery, Enola, Cumberland County, Pennsylvania
EM—East Petersborough Mennonite Church, Petersborough,
    Pennsylvania
EP—Elkhart Prairie Cemetery, Elkhart Township, Elkhart, Indiana
EV—Evergreen Home Cemetery, Beatrice, Gage County, Nebraska
EU—Eastview Union Cemetery, Delmont, Pennsylvania

- F

FA—Fairview Cemetery, Altoona, Blair County, Pennsylvania
FC—New Calvary Catholic Cemetery, Flint, Michigan
FD—Fairview Cemetery, Arendtsville, Adams County, Pennsylvania
FH—Forest Hills Memorial Park, Exeter Township, Berks County,
    Pennsylvania

FL—Forest Lawn Memorial Park, Omaha, Nebraska
FM—Fairmont Cemetery, Tiffin, Ohio
FR—Fairland Cemetery, Cleona, Lebanon County, Pennsylvania
FV—Fairview Cemetery, Red Bank, New Jersey

- G

GA—Grandview Cemetery, Altoona, Pennsylvania
GC—Greensburg Catholic Cemetery, Greensburg, Pennsylvania
GD—Goods Mennonite Church Cemetery—Elizabethtown, Pennsylvania
GE—Saint Gertrude's Catholic Cemetery, Lebanon, Pennsylvania
GH—Geyer's Hillside Cemetery, Royalton, Pennsylvania
GL—Greenlawn Cemetery, Tiffin, Ohio
GM—Greenmount Cemetery, York, Pennsylvania
GN—Gettysburg National Cemetery, Gettysburg, Pennsylvania
GP—Grandview Memorial Park, Annville, Pennsylvania
GR—Gravel Hill Cemetery, Palmyra, Lebanon County, Pennsylvania
GS—Goshert's Cemetery, Mt. Zion, Lebanon County, Pennsylvania
GT—Gethsemane Cemetery, Laureldale, Berks County, Pennsylvania
GU—Greensburg Union Cemetery, Greensburg, Pennsylvania
GV—Grandview Cemetery, Johnstown, Pennsylvania
GW—Greenwood Cemetery, Tuckerton, Ocean County, New Jersey

- H

HA—Haag's Cemetery, Bernville, Berks County, Pennsylvania
HB—Harker Cemetery, Bloomington Township, Muscatine, Iowa
HC—Holy Cross Cemetery, Lebanon, Pennsylvania
HD—Hanoverdale Church of the Brethren Cemetery, Hanoverdale, Pennnsylvania
HE—Hershey Cemetery, Hershey, Dauphin County, Pennsylvania
HF—Heidelberg Cemetery, Heidelberg Township, Berks County, Pennsylvania
HG—Harmony Grove Cemetery, Lockeford, California
HH—Holy Cross Cemetery, Harrisburg, Dauphin County, Pennsylvania

HI—Highland Cemetery, What Cheer, Keokuk County, Iowa

HK—Hoyt City Cemetery, Hoyt, Jackson County, Kansas

HL—Holton City Cemetery, Holton, Jackson County, Kansas

HM—Harmony Cemetery, Milton, Northumberland Co.,
     Pennsylvania

HO—Hollidaysburg Presbyterian Cemetery, Hollidaysburg, Blair
     County, Pennsylvania

HP—Holtzschwamm Cemetery, Paradise Township, York Co.,
     Pennsylvania

HR—Harrison City Cemetery, Westmoreland Co., Pennsylvania

HS—St. Mary's Catholic Cemetery, Herman, Butler Co.,
     Pennsylvania

HT—Hummelstown Cemetery, Hummelstown, Pennsylvania

HV—Holy Savior Cemetery, Cornwall, Lebanon Co, Pennsylvania

- **I**

IC—Immaculate Conception Catholic Cemetery, New Oxford,
     Pennsylvania

IG—Indiantown Gap National Cemetery, East Hanover Township,
     Lebanon County, Pennsylvania

IR—Irwin Cemetery, Rochester, Beaver County, Pennsylvania

- **J**

JE—Jacob Eash Cemetery, Somerset County, Pennsylvania

- **K**

KC—Kochenderfer's Cemetery, Lebanon County, Pennsylvania

KD—Kriders Lutheran Church Cemetery, Westminster, Carroll
     County, Maryland

KM—Kaufman Mennonite Cemetery, Somerset County,
     Pennsylvania

KN—St. Peter's UCC Church Cemetery, Knauertown, Chester
     County, Pennsylvania

KR—Kimmerling's Reformed Cemetery, Lebanon County,
     Pennsylvania

- L

LA—St. John's Lutheran Cemetery, Abbottstown, Pennsylvania
LC—St. Mary's Church Cemetery, Lancaster, Pennsylvania
LH—West Laurel Hill Cemetery, Bala Cynwyd, Montgomery
   County, Pennsylvania
LI—Long Island National Cemetery, Farmingdale, New York
LJ—St. Joseph's Church Cemetery, Lancaster, Pennsylvania
LL—Lakeview Cemetery, Laramie, Wyoming
LM—Lakemont Memorial Gardens, Davidsonville, Maryland
LN—St. Joseph's New Catholic Cemetery, Lancaster, Lancaster
   County
LO—Our Lady of Lourdes Cemetery, Trenton, Mercer County, New
   Jersey
LV—Logan Valley Cemetery, Blair County, Pennsylvania
LM—Logan Memorial Cemetery, Blair County, Pennsylvania
LW—Laurel Wood Cemetery, Stroudsburg, Pennsylvania

- M

MA—Mount Annville Cemetery, Annville, Lebanon County,
   Pennsylvania
MB—Maple Spring Brethren Cemetery, Somerset County,
   Pennsylvania
MC—Mount Rose Cemetery, York, Pennsylvania
MD—Middletown Cemetery, Middletown, Dauphin County,
   Pennsylvania
ME—St. Mary's Catholic Cemetery, Beaver Falls, Pennsylvania
MF—Mount Vernon Memorial Park, Fair Oaks, Sacramento County,
   California
MG—Marburg Memorial Gardens, Hanover, York County,
   Pennsylvania
MH—Mount Hope Cemetery, Adams Township, Cambria Co.,
   Pennsylvania
MI—Millersville Mennonite Cemetery, Lancaster County,
   Pennsylvania
ML—Mount Lebanon Cemetery, Lebanon, Pennsylvania
MM—Mount Hope Cemetery, Myerstown, Lebanon County,
   Pennsylvania

MN—Massachusetts National Cemetery, Bourne, Massachusetts

MO—Mount Olive Cemetery, Abbottstown, Adams County,
Pennsylvania

MP—Marietta City Cemetery, Marietta, Pennsylvania

MR—Meuse-Argonne Cemetery, Romagne, France

MS—St. Mary's Cemetery, Tiffin, Ohio

MT—Mount Tunnel Cemetery, Elizabethtown, Pennsylvania

MU—Union Cemetery, Myerstown, Pennsylvania

MV—Mountain View Cemetery, Marriottsville, Howard County,
Maryland

MY—Maytown Union Cemetery, Maytown, Lancaster County,
Pennsylvania

MZ—Mount Zion Campground Cemetery, Morven, Brooks County,
Georgia

- N

NB—St. Peter Cemetery, West New Brighton, Richmond County,
New York

NC—National Cemetery, City Point, Virginia

NF—North Fork Cemetery, Franklin Township, Morrow County,
Ohio

NM—Newmanstown Memorial Cemetery, Newmanstown, Lebanon
County, Ohio

NO—New Oxford Cemetery, New Oxford, Adams County,
Pennsylvania

NP—New Paris Cemetery, New Paris, Elkhart County, Indiana

NR—New Freedom Cemetery, New Freedom, York County,
Pennsylvania

NW—New Cathedral Catholic Cemetery, Philadelphia,
Pennsylvania

- O

OA—Olinger Highland Mortuary and Cemetery, Thornton, Adams
County, Colorado

OB—Mount Ober Cemetery, Elizabethtown, Pennsylvania

OH—Oak Hill Cemetery, Coralville, Iowa

OJ—Old St. Joseph's Church Cemetery, Lancaster, Pennsylvania

OL—Oakland Cemetery, Shelby, Richland County, Ohio
OM—Mount Olivet Cemetery, Hanover, York County, Pennsylvania
OP—Oak Hill Cemetery, Plattsmouth, Cass County, Nebraska
OR—Oakridge Cemetery, Goshen, Elkhart County, Indiana
OV—Mount Olivet Cemetery, Hanover, York County, Pennsylvania
OZ—Ozone Cemetery, Johnson County, Arkansas

- P

PC—Immaculate Heart of Mary Catholic Cemetery, York County,
Pennsylvania
PH—Prospect Hill Cemetery, York, Pennsylvania
PL—St. Paul's Lutheran Cemetery, Zelienople, Butler County,
Pennsylvania
PR—Prospect Hill Cemetery, Omaha, Nebraska
PV—Pleasant View Cemetery, Little Rock, Lyon County, Iowa

- Q

QC—Quickel's Church Cemetery, Conewago Township, York
County, Pennsylvania
QH—Queen of Heaven Cemetery, Rapids, Niagara County, New
York

- R

RB—Most Holy Redeemer Cemetery, Baltimore, Maryland
RC—Rice Cemetery, Elkhart, Elkhart County, Indiana
RE—Rest Haven Cemetery, Penn Township, York County,
Pennsylvania
RG—Rolling Green Memorial Park, Camp Hill, Cumberland
County, Pennsylvania
RH—Rose Hills Memorial Park, Los Angeles, California
RI—Sunset Memorial Garden, Richland, Washington
RM—Rockaway Valley United Methodist Church Cemetery,
Boonton, Morris County, New Jersey
RN—Riverside Cemetery, Norristown, Montgomery County,
Pennsylvania
RV—Riverside Cemetery, Hastings, Barry County, Michigan

▪ S

SA—St. Anthony's Catholic Cemetery, Lancaster, Pennsylvania
SB—Solomon Creek Cemetery, Benton Township, Elkhart County, Indiana
SC—St. Clair Cemetery, Greensburg, Pennsylvania
SD—St. Mary's Catholic Cemetery, Dodgeville, Franklin Township, Des Moines County, Iowa
SE—Salem Evangelical Cemetery, Ono, Lebanon County, Pa.
SF—St. Francis Xavier Cemetery, Gettysburg, Pennsylvania
SG—Spring Grove Cemetery, Spring Grove, Pennsylvania
SH—Shauck Cemetery, Perry Township, Morrow County, Ohio
SI—St. Joseph Cemetery, Iowa City, Iowa
SJ—St. Joseph Cemetery, Tiffin, Ohio
SK—Sem K. Johns Cemetery, Somerset County, Pennsylvania
SL—Sala-Livingston Cemetery, Somerset County, Pennsylvania
SM—St. Mary's Cemetery, Lebanon, Pennsylvania
SN—St. Joseph's Catholic Cemetery, Taneytown, Maryland
SO—South Annville Cemetery, Lebanon County, Pennsylvania
SP—St. Peter Cemetery, Elizabethtown, Pennsylvania
SQ—Spring Creek Church of the Brethren Cemetery, Hershey, Dauphin County, Pennsylvania
SR—Salem (Reformed) United Church of Christ Cemetery, Campbelltown, Lebanon County, Pennsylvania
SS—Sunset Hills Memorial Park, Bellvue, Washington
ST—Stahl Mennonite Cemetery, Somerset County, Pennsylvania
SU—St. Michael's Union Cemetery, Berks County, Pennsylvania
SV—St. Vincent de Paul Catholic Cemetery, Hanover, York County, Pennsylvania
SX—Saxonburg Memorial Church Cemetery, Butler Co., Pennsylvania
SY—Sunnyside Cemetery, York Springs, Adams County, Pennsylvania
SZ—Susquehanna Memorial Gardens, York County, Pennsylvania

- T

TM—Thomas Mennonite Cemetery, Somerset County, Pennsylvania
TU—Toronto Union Cemetery, Toronto, Jefferson County, Ohio

- U

UR—Union Ridge Cemetery, Union Township, Houston County, Minnesota
US—United-Salem Evangelical Congregational Cemetery, Lickdale, Pennsylvania
UT—Uniontown Church of God Cemetery, Uniontown, Carroll County, Maryland

- V

VC—Violett Cemetery, Goshen, Elkhart County, Indiana
VH—Violet Hill Cemetery, Perry, Dallas County, Iowa

- W

WC—Highland Park Cemetery, Wyandotte County, Kansas
WG—West Goshen Cemetery, Goshen, Elkhart County, Indiana
WH—Whitehead/Maple Grove Cemetery, Elkhart County, Indiana
WK—City Cemetery, Washington, Kansas
WL—Westlawn-Hillcrest Memorial Park, Omaha, Nebraska
WM—Westminster Memorial Park, Westminster, Orange County, California

- Z

ZJ—Zion Lutheran Cemetery, Jonestown, Lebanon County, Pennsylvania
ZL—Zoar Lutheran Cemetery, Mount Zion, Pennsylvania

SOURCES CITED

Books and articles

Adams, Edmund and Barbara Brady O'Keefe, *Catholic Trails West: The Founding Catholic Families of Pennsylvania*, vol. 2, Baltimore, Maryland: Gateway Press, Inc., 1989.

Ahlstrom, Sydney, *A Religious History of the American People*, New Haven: Yale University Press, 1972.

Alwin, Duane F., "On Sacred Ground: Exploring Goshenhoppen Churches," *Journal of the Berks County Historical Society*, December, 2000, pages 14-19.

Alwin, Duane F., *Familie Allwein—Hans Jacob and Catharina Allwein and their Descendants*. Volume 1: *An Early History of the Allwein Family in America*. Bloomington, IN: Xlibris, 2009.

Alwin, Duane F., "Msgr. Charles Leo Allwein (1904-1995)—Bally, Berks County, Pennsylvania," *Journal of the Berks County Genealogical Society*, Winter, 2009, pages 8-12.

Alwin, Duane F., "The Dower Chest of Johannes Alweins," *Journal of the Berks County Genealogical Society*, Vol. 32, Spring, 2012, pages 7-11.

Alwin, Duane F., *A Soldier's Tale—A Biography of Lawrence Allwine, Philadelphia Chairmaker and Ohio Pioneer.* Unpublished monograph.

Bates, Samuel P., *History of Pennsylvania Volunteers 1861-65*, edited by Janet Hewett, Wilmington NC: Broadfoot Publishing Co., 1994.

Beidler, James M., "Genealogy," in Randall M. Miller and William Pencak (Eds.), *Pennsylvania: A History of the Commonwealth*, pages 481-500, University Park, Pa.: Pennsylvania State University Press, 2002.

Britt, Kent, "Pennsylvania's Old-Time Dutch Treat," *National Geographic*, April, 1973.

Brumbaugh, Martin Grove, *History of the Brethren in Europe and America*. Elgin, IL: Brethren Publishing House, 1899.

Dobyns, Kenneth W., "List of All U.S. Patents and Patentees (1790-1829)," *History of the United States Patent Office*, 1994. See: http://www.myoutbox.net/poinvtrs.htm

Eastern Pennsylvania Mennonite Church, *The American Mennonites: Tracing the Development of the (Old) Mennonite Church*, Eastern Pennsylvania Mennonite Church, Ephrata, Pa., 1998.

Egle, William Henry (Ed.), "Names of Foreigners Who Took the Oath of Allegiance in the Province and State of Pennsylvania, 1727-1775, with Foreign Arrivals 1786-1808," *Pennsylvania Archives*, Second Series, Volume 17, Harrisburg, Pa., E.K. Meyers, State Printer, 1892.

Egle, William Henry (Ed.), "Proprietary and State Tax Listsof the County of Berks, for the Years 1767, 1768, 1779, 1780, 1781, 1784, 1785," *Pennsylvania Archives*, Third Series, Volume 18, Harrisburg PA: W.S. Ray, State Printer of Pennsylvania, 1898.

Espenshade, A. Howry, *Pennsylvania Place Names*, State College, Pennsylvania: The Pennsylvania State College, 1925. [Reprinted by the Gale Research Company, 1969.]

Evans, Nancy Goyne, *Windsor-Chair Making in America—From Craft Shop to Consumer*, Hanover, New Hampshire: University Press of New England, 2006.

Fales, Dean A., Jr., *American Painted Furniture 1660-1880*. New York: E.P. Dutton, 1979.

Fink, Leo Gregory, *From Bally to Valley Forge: Historical Monograph of the Catholic Church in the Perkiomen Valley from 1741 to 1952*, No publisher given, 1953.

Fink, Leo Gregory, "The First Catholics in Reading," *Historical Review of Berks County*, vol. 33, No. 3, Summer, 1968, pages 93-95, 111-115.

Fogelman, Aaron, *Hopeful Journeys: German Immigration, Settlement, and Political Culture in Colonial America, 1717-1775*, Philadelphia: University of Pennsylvania Press, 1996.

Foster, John J., *The Story of Assumption of Blessed Virgin Mary Church, Lebanon, Pennsylvania*, Lebanon Pennsylvania: Sowers Printing Company, 1951.

Glatfelter, Charles. *Pastors and People: German Lutheran and Reformed Churches in the Pennsylvania Field, 1717—1793,* Volume I: Pastors and Congregations. Breinigsville, Pennsylvania, The Pennsylvania German Society, 1980.

Glatfelter, Charles. *Pastors and People: German Lutheran and Reformed Churches in the Pennsylvania Field, 1717—1793,* Volume II: The History. Breinigsville, Pennsylvania, The Pennsylvania German Society, 1981.

Hammond, James Sidney, "The Alwine Line," in Wilbert Jordan (Editor), *Colonial and Revolutionary Families of Pennsylvania—Genealogical and Personal Memoirs.* New Series, Volume XI. New York: Lewis Historical Publishing Co., Inc., 1948.

Hernandez, Donald J., *America's Children—Resources from Family, Government and the Economy.* New York, NY: Russell Sage Foundation, 1993.

Hinke, William J., "Introduction," *Pennsylvania German Pioneers: A Publication of the Original Lists of Arrivals in the Port of Philadelphia From 1727 to 1808* (pages xxxix-xlv), published by Ralph B. Strassberger for the Pennsylvania German Society. Baltimore, Maryland: Genealogical Publishing Co., 1980.

Hostetter, C. Nelson, *Anabaptist-Mennonites Nationwide USA.* Morgantown, Pa: Mastoff Press, 1997.

Isele, Evelyn L., *One Hundred Years of History—The Church Home, 1881-1981,* Jonestown Lutheran Church Home, Jonestown, Pennsylvania.

Kauffman, Stanley Duane, *Mifflin County Amish and Mennonite Story 1791-1991,* Mifflin County Historical Society, 1991.

Kerchner, Charles F., Jr., "Pennsylvania Dutch Are of German Heritage, Not Dutch," at the following website—http://www. kerchner.com/padutch.htm.

McCrea, Kenneth D., *Pennsylvania Land Applications—Volume 1: East Side Applications, 1765-1769,* Strasburg, Pennsylvania: McCrea Research, Inc., 2002.

Melcher, Bill, "Msgr. Charles L. Allwein, Pre-eminent Bally Genealogist and Chruchman," Berks County Historical Society, circa 1993.

Musser, Edgar A., "St. Mary's Church, Lancaster, 1785-1877," *Journal of the Lancaster County Historical Society,* 1969, vol. 73, pages 97-98.

Nolt, Steven M., *Foreigners in Their Own Land—Pennsylvania Germans in the Early Republic,* University Park, Pa.: Pennsylvania State University Press, 2002.

Quinter, Edward H., in collaboration with Charles L.Allwein, *Most Blessed Sacrament Church Bally, Pennsylvania, originally known as St. Paul's Chapel of Goshenhoppen, Berks County, Pennsylvania,* Publisher unknown, 1976.

Roan, Donald F., "The Goschenhoppen Historians: Preserving and Celebrating Pennsylvania German Folk Culture," *Pennsylvania Folklife Magazine,* Spring, 1996.

Schuyler, William Bishop, "Memoirs of the Rev. Augustin Bally, S.J.," *Records of the American Catholic Historical Society,* September, 1909, pp. 209-249.

Shelly, Donald, *The Fractur Writings or Illuminated Manuscripts of the Pennsylvania Germans,* Allentown, Pennsylvania: Pennsylvania German Folklore Society, 1961.

Shenk, Hiram H. and Esther Shenk (Editors), *Encyclopedia of Pennsylvania,* Harrisburg, Pennsylvania: National Historical Association, Inc., 1932.

Strassburger, Ralph B. and William John Hinke. *Pennsylvania German Pioneers: A Publication of the Original Lists of Arrivals in the Port of Philadelphia from 1727 to 1808.* Camden, ME: Picton Press, 1992.

Stryker, William S., *Official Register of the Officers and Men of New Jersey in the Revolutionary War,* published by William T. Nicholson & Co., Printers, Trenton NJ, 1872.

U.S. Department of Labor, *Dictionary of Occupational Titles,* Washington, D.C., U.S. Government Printing Office, 4th edition, 1977.

Waldenrath, Alexander, "Goshenhoppen (Bally), Early Center of Roman Catholicism in Berks County," *Historical Review of Berks County,* Vol. 39, No. 3, 1974, pages 92-97, 109.

Miscellaneous Publications

Alumni Association of the University of Pennsylvania, *General Alumni Catalogue of the University of Pennsylvania,* Philadelphia, Pennsylvania: Alumni Association of the University of Pennsylvania, 1917.

Coffin, Seldin J., *Men of Lafayette, 1826-1893,* Easton, Pennsylvania: George W. West, 1891.

Hafner, Arthur Wayne (Ed.), *The Directory of Deceased American Physicians, 1804-1929,* Chicago, IL: American Medical Association, 1993.

Hurd, Henry M. (Ed.), "State Hospital for the Insane, Warren, Pa." *The Institutional Care of the Insane in the United States and Canada,* Volume 3, Baltimore, Maryland: Johns Hopkins University Press, 1916.

Marquis, Albert Nelson, *Who's Who in Pennsylvania,* Volume 1, Chicago: The Albert Nelson Marquis Company, 1939.

Maxwell, W.J., *General Alumni Catalogue of the University of Pennsylvania,* Philadelphia, Pennsylvania: Alumni Association of the University of Pennsylvania, 1922.

Stonecipher, John Franklin, *Biographical Catalogue of Lafayeete College, 1832-1912,* Easton, Pennsylvania: Chemical Publishing Company, 1913.

University of Pennsylvania, *Catalogue of the Trustees, Officers and Students of the University of Pennsylvania.* One Hundred and Eighteenth Session, 1867-1868.

County Atlases

Beers, F.W., *County Atlas of Lebanon Pennsylvania from Recent and Actual Surveys and Records*, Reading & Philadelphia: F.A. Davis, 1875.

Roe, Frederick B., *Atlas of the City of Lebanon, Lebanon County, Pennsylvania / Compiled, drawn and published from official plans and actual surveys*, Philadelphia: F.B. Roe, 1888.

Local / County Histories and Biographies of Prominent Persons

Biographical and Historical Memoirs of Muskingum County, Ohio, Chicago: The Goodspeed Publishing Co., 1892.

Biographical Annals of Lebanon County, Pennsylvania, Containing Biographical Sketches of Prominent and Representative Citizens and of Many of the Early Settled Families, J.H. Beers & Company, Chicago, 1904, page 635-636.

Egle, William Henry (Ed.), *History of the County of Lebanon in the Commonwealth of Pennsylvania*, Philadelphia, Pennsylvania: Everts & Peck, 1883.

Ellis, Franklin and Samuel Evans (Eds.), *History of Lancaster County, Pennsylvania, with Biographical Sketches of Many of Its Pioneers and Prominent Men*. Philadelphia, Pennsylvania: Everts & Peck, 1883.

Goodspeed, Weston A. and Charles Blanchard, Editors, *Counties of Whitley and Noble, Indiana—Historical and Biographical*, Chicago: F.A. Battey & Co., Publishers, 1882, page 238

Historical Papers of Lancaster County, Historical Society of Pennsylvania, 1300 Locust Street, Philadelphia, Pennsylvania, No date.

Montgomery, Morton L., *Historical and Biographical Annals of Berks County Pennsylvania Embracing a Concise History of the County and a Genealogical and Biographical Record of Representative Families*. Volume I. Chicago: J.H. Beers & Co.

Runk, J.M., *Commemorative Biographical Encyclopedia of Dauphin County, Pennsylvania*, Chambersburg, Pennsylvania: J.M. Runk and Company, Publishers, 1896.

Sutor, J. Hope, *Past and Present of the City of Zanesville and Muskingum County, Ohio*, Chicago: Arke Publishing Co., 1905.

Waterman, Watkins and Company, *History of Bedford, Somerset and Fulton Counties, Pennsylvania with Illustrations and Biographical Sketches of some of its Pioneers and Prominent Men*, Chicago, IL: Waterman, Watkins & Co., 1884.

Genealogies

Allwein, Jerome Adam, *Genealogy of the Allwein-Arnold Families*, Philadelphia, Pennsylvania, 1902.

Egle, William Henry, *Notes and Queries: Historical, Biographical and Genealogical for Interior Pennsylvania*. Fourth Series, Volume 1, Harrisburg, Pennsylvania: Harrisburg Publishing Co., 1893 [reprinted by Genealogical Publishing Company, Baltimore, Maryland, 1970].

Jordan, Wilbert (Ed.), "James Sidney Hammond," *Colonial and Revolutionary Families of Pennsylvania—Genealogical and*

Personal Memoirs. New Series, Volume XI. New York: Lewis Historical Publishing Co., Inc., 1948.

Lau, Michael, *Alwine Families of York County, Pennsylvania and Surrounding Areas*, York County Historical Library, 1996-1999.

Biographical Records

American Catholic Historical Society of America. *The Goshenhoppen Registers 1741-1819: Registers of Baptisms, Marriages, and Deaths of the Catholic Mission at Goshenhoppen (Bally), Washington Township, Berks County, Pennsylvania,* Baltimore: Genealogical Publishing Company, Inc., 1984. [Reprinted by Clearfield Publishers, Baltimore, MD, 2002].

Berks County Estate Records for Jacob Allwein, Berks County Register of Wills and Clerk of the Orphan's Court, Reading, Pennsylvania.

California Death Index, 1940-1997. Ancestry.com.

Civil War Pension Records, National Archive and Records Administration, Washington, D.C.

Florida Marriage Records, 1927-2001. Ancestry.com

Hatcher, Patricia Law, *Abstract of Graves of Revolutionary War Patriots*, Dallas, Texas: Pioneer Heritage Press, 1987-88.

Irish, Donna R., *Pennsylvania German Marriages: Marriages and Marriage Evidence in Pennsylvania German Churches*, Baltimore, Maryland: Genealogical Publishing Company, Inc., 1982.

Lebanon County Estate Records for Peter Allwein. Clerk of Courts, Lebanon, Pennsylvania. Available from the Pennsylvania State Archives, Harrisburg, Pennsylvania.

Marriage records, Morrow County Historical Library, Mt. Gilead, Ohio.

Ohio Births and Christenings Index, 1800-1962. Ancestry.com.

Pennsylvania Department of Health, "Public Death Records," http://www.health. State.pa.us.

Raber, Nellie M., *Marriage Records of Whitley County, Indiana 1860-1884*. Fort Wayne Public Library, 1973.

Revolutionary War Pension and Bounty-Land Warrant Application Files. National Archive and Records Administration. Washington DC.

Saint Michael's Union Church, Upper Bern Township, "List of
Burials, 1769-1847," Historical Society of Pennsylvania, 1300
Locust Street, Philadelphia, Pennsylvania, No date.
Social Security Administration, "Social Security Death Index,
Master File," Ancestry.com.
State of Ohio Death Index—1908-1932. Ancestry.com.
U.S. World War I Draft Registration Cards, 1917-1918. Ancestry.com
U.S. World War II Draft Registration Cards, 1942. Ancestry.com.
Will of Johannes Alwein, February 21, 1809 [Codicil, October
30, 1809], Berks County Register of Wills and Clerk of the
Orphan's Court, Reading, Pennsylvania.

Cemetery Records

Berks County Heritage Center, "Deppen Cemetery," County of
Berks, Parks and Recreation Department, 2201 Tulpehocken
Road, Wyomissing, Pennsylvania, 19610.
Long, Kenneth, *Kimmerling's Cemetery, North Lebanon Township,
Lebanon County, Pennsylvania*. [Available at the Lebanon
County Historical Society, 924 Cumberland Street, Lebanon,
Pennsylvania 17042.]
Pennsylvania Veterans Burial Cards, 1777-1999, Ancestry.com.
Seaman, Luann and Betty Seaman, *St. Michael's Cemetery Burials
1766-1991*, St. Michael's Church and Cemetery, 529 St.
Michael's Road, Tilden Township, Hamburg, Pennsylvania.
St. Mary's Catholic Cemetery Records, Lebanon, Pennsylvania.
[Available at the Lebanon County Historical Society, 924
Cumberland Street, Lebanon, Pennsylvania 17042.]
Zion Evangelical Lutheran Church, Parish Register. Book II.
Jonestown, Lebanon County, Pennsylvania. [Available at the
Lebanon County Historical Society, 924 Cumberland Street,
Lebanon, Pennsylvania 17042.]

Newspapers

Allentown Morning Call, Allentown, Pennsylvania.
Altoona Mirror, Altoona, Pennsylvania.
Capital, Annapolis, Maryland.
Daily News, Huntingdon, Pennsylvania.

The Evening News, Harrisburg, Pennsylvania.
Getttysburg Compiler, Gettysburg, Pennsylvania.
The Gettysburg Times, Gettysburg, Pennsylvania.
Kent & Sussex Crossroads, The News Journal, Wilmington, Delaware.
Lake Zurich Courier, Lake Zurich, Illinois.
Lebanon Courier, Lebanon, Pennsylvania.
Lebanon Daily News, Lebanon, Pennsylvania.
Lebanon Semi-Weekly News, Lebanon, Pennsylvania.
Nashua Telegraph, Nashua, New Hampshire.
New York Times, New York, New York.
Palm Beach Post, Palm Beach, Florida.
Patriot-News, Harrisburg, Pennsylvania.
The Harrisburg Patriot, Harrisburg, Pennsylvania.
Reading Eagle, Reading, Pennsylvania.
The Pilot, Southern Pines, North Carolina.
Sun-Sentinel, Broward and Palm Beach Counties, Florida.
Tooele Transcript Bulletin Online, Tooele County, Utah.

Census Enumerations

First Census of the United States (1790)

Heads of Families at the First Census of the United States Taken in the Year 1790, Pennsylvania. Washington, D.C.: Government Printing Office, 1908.

Second Census of the United States (1800)

Inhabitants of Walnut Ward, Philadelphia, Philadelphia County, Pennsylvania, page 76.

Sixth Census of the United States (1840)

Inhabitants of Annville Township, Lebanon County, Pennsylvania, page 53.
Inhabitants of Swatara Township, Lebanon County, Pennsylvania, page 27.

Seventh Census of the United States (1850)

Inhabitants of Bethel Township, Lebanon County, Pennsylvania, page 207.

Inhabitants of North Annville Township, Lebanon County, Pennsylvania, page 266;

Inhabitants of North Lebanon Township, Lebanon County, Pennsylvania, page 44 and 153.

Inhabitants of South Lebanon Township, Lebanon County, Pennsylvania, page 104.

Inhabitants of Swatara Township, Lebanon County, Pennsylvania, page 189.

Eighth Census of the United States (1860)

Inhabitants of Conemaugh Borough, Cambria County, Pennsylvania, page 23.

Inhabitants of Elizabeth Township, Lancaster County, Pennsylvania, page 376.

Inhabitants of Bethel Township, Lebanon County, Pennsylvania, page 10.

Inhabitants of Lebanon Borough, Lebanon County, Pennsylvania, page 395.

Inhabitants of North Lebanon Borough, Lebanon County, Pennsylvania, page 406

Inhabitants of North Lebanon Township, Lebanon County, Pennsylvania, pages 419 and 454.

Inhabitants of South Annville Township, Lebanon County, Pennsylvania, page 649.

Inhabitants of Union Township, Lebanon County, Pennsylvania, page 798.

Ninth Census of the United States (1870)

Inhabitants of Conemaugh Borough, Cambria County, page 170.

Inhabitants of Bethel Township, Lebanon County, Pennsylvania, page 13.

Inhabitants of Borough of Lebanon, Lebanon County, Pennsylvania, pages 322, 323, 326, 331, 335, 337, 340, 344, and 371.

Inhabitants of Cornwall Township, Lebanon County, Pennsylvania, page 56.

Inhabitants of North Lebanon Township, Lebanon County, Pennsylvania, pages 234B, 236 and 242.

Inhabitants of South Lebanon Township, Lebanon County, Pennsylvania, page 407.

Inhabitants of Swatara Township, Lebanon County, Pennsylvania, pages 399, 407 and 408.

Tenth Census of the United States (1880)

Inhabitants of Richland Township, Whitley County, Indiana, page 418.

Inhabitants of Derry Township, Dauphin County, Pennsylvania, page 21.

Inhabitants of Middle Paxton Township, Dauphin County, Pennsylvania, page 71B.

Inhabitants of Susquehanna Township, Dauphin County, Pennsylvania, page 130D.

Inhabitants of Elizabeth Township, Lancaster County, Pennsylvania, page 349.

Inhabitants of Upper Rapho Township, Lancaster County, Pennsylvania, pages 195C and 195D.

Inhabitants of Bethel Township, Lebanon County, Pennsylvania, pages 16, 16D and 333.

Inhabitants of Borough of Lebanon, Lebanon County, Pennsylvania, pages 285B, 321D, 325, 325C, 328A, 331, 331C, 334, 338C, 345, 349, 350C, 352 and 364.

Inhabitants of Ward 1 Lebanon, Lebanon County, Pennsylvania, page 265.

Inhabitants of Ward 5, Lebanon Township, Lebanon County, Pennsylvania, page 329D.

Inhabitants of Londonderry Township, Lebanon County, Pennsylvania, page 404.

Inhabitants of North Lebanon Township, Lebanon County, Pennsylvania, pages 234, 236C, 240, 249 and 350.

Inhabitants of South Annville Township, Lebanon County, Pennsylvania, page 371.

Inhabitants of South Lebanon Township, Lebanon County, Pennsylvania, page 389C.

Inhabitants of Swatara Township, Lebanon County, Pennsylvania,
    page 404.
Inhabitants of Philadelphia, Philadelphia County, Pennsylvania,
    page 189.

Twelfth Census of the United States (1900)

Inhabitants of Portage Township, St. Joseph County, Indiana, E.D.
    No. 121, page 312B.
Inhabitants of Gibbon Township, Buffalo County, Nebraska, E.D.
    No. 29, page 137A.
Inhabitants of Rockaway, Morris County, New Jersey, E.D. No. 79,
    page 166B.
Inhabitants of Reading Ward 9, Berks County, Pennsylvania, E.D.
    No. 77, page 246A;
Inhabitants of West Reading, Cumru Township, Berks County,
    Pennsylvania, E.D. No. 13, 175B.
Inhabitants of Jefferson Township, Butler County, Pennsylvania,
    E.D. No. 29, page 179B.
Inhabitants of Harrisburg Ward 5, Dauphin County, Pennsylvania,
    E.D. No. 56, pages 2B and 3A.
Inhabitants of City of Harrisburg, Dauphin County, Pennsylvania,
    E.D. No. 77, page 9B.
Inhabitants of Mt. Zion, Bethel Township, Lebanon County,
    Pennsylvania, E.D. No. 113, page 23B.
Inhabitants of East Hanover Township, Lebanon County,
    Pennsylvania, E.D. No. 116, page 73B.
Inhabitants of Lebanon Borough, Lebanon County, Pennsylvania,
    E.D. No. 128, pages 250A and 252B.
Inhabitants of Lebanon Borough, Lebanon County, Pennsylvania,
    E.D. No. 129, pages 270A and 274A.
Inhabitants of Lebanon Borough, Lebanon County, Pennsylvania,
    E.D. No. 131, page 20A.
Inhabitants of Lebanon Ward 1, Lebanon County, Pennsylvania,
    E.D. No. 123, pages 167A and 173A.
Inhabitants of Lebanon Ward 2, Lebanon County, Pennsylvania,
    E.D. No. 125, pages 203B and 204A.
Inhabitants of Lebanon Ward 5, Lebanon County, Pennsylvania, E.D.
    No. 128, pages 244A, 244B, 246B, 247A, 248A, 248B, and 256B.

Inhabitants of Lebanon Ward 5, Lebanon County, Pennsylvania, E.D. No. 129, pages 5A, 270A, 272B, 273A, 284A, 286B, 287A and 289A.

Inhabitants of Lebanon Ward 6, Lebanon County, Pennsylvania, E.D. No. 130, pages 16A and 203B.

Inhabitants of Lebanon Ward 7, Lebanon County, Pennsylvania, E.D. No. 131, page 37B.

Inhabitants of North Lebanon Township, East Election District, Lebanon County, Pennsylvania, E.D. No. 137, pages 120B, 121A, 123B, 127B, 129A and 133B.

Inhabitants of North Lebanon Township, West Precinct, Lebanon County, Pennsylvania, E.D. No. 138, pages 127B, 152A, 153A, 154B, and 156A.

Inhabitants of South Annville Township, Lebanon County, Pennsylvania, E.D. No. 140, page 196A.

Inhabitants of South Lebanon Township, Lebanon County, Pennsylvania, E.D. No. 141, page 218B.

Inhabitants of Swatara Township, Lebanon County, Pennsylvania, E.D. No. 144, page 247B.

Inhabitants of West Lebanon Township, Lebanon County, Pennsylvania, E.D. No. 146, page 273B.

Inhabitants of Philadelphia Ward 26, Philadelphia County, Pennsylvania, E.D. No. 639, page 2B.

Inhabitants of Philadelphia Ward 31, Philadelphia County, Pennsylvania, E.D. No. 780, pages 154B and 155A.

Inhabitants of Conewango Township, Warren County, Pennsylvania, E.D. No. 132, page 81A.

Thirteenth Census of the United States (1910)

Inhabitants of Evanston Ward 1, Cook County, Illinois, E.D. No. 98, page 30A.

Inhabitants of Gibbon Township, Buffalo County, Nebraska, E.D. No. 37, page 100B.

Inhabitants of Rockaway Township, Morris County, New Jersey, E.D. No. 41, page 102B.

Inhabitants of Reading Ward 13, Berks County, Pennsylvania, E.D. No. 93, page 137A.

Inhabitants of Scranton Ward 9, Lackawana County, Pennsylvania,
    E.D. No. 35, page 28B.
Inhabitants of East Donegal Township, Lancaster County,
    Pennsylvania, E.D. No. 28, page 211A.
Inhabitants of Bethel Township, Lebanon County, Pennsylvania,
    E.D. No. 137, page 234A.
Inhabitants of East Hanover Township, Lebanon County, E.D. 140,
    page 276B.
Inhabitants of Lebanon Ward 1, Lebanon County, Pennsylvania,
    E.D. No. 147, pages 6B and 90A.
Inhabitants of Lebanon Ward 2, Lebanon County, Pennsylvania,
    E.D. No. 148, pages 105A, 116A and 117B.
Inhabitants of Lebanon Ward 3, Lebanon County, Pennsylvania,
    E.D. No. 151, page 144B.
Inhabitants of Lebanon Ward 4, Lebanon, County, Pennsylvania,
    E.D. No. 152, page 155B.
Inhabitants of Lebanon Ward 4, Lebanon County, Pennsylvania,
    E.D. No. 153, page 166A.
Inhabitants of Lebanon Ward 5, Lebanon County, Pennsylvania,
    E.D. No. 154, pages 186B, 188B,198B, 199B, 201B, 202A,
    202B, 205B and 212A.
Inhabitants of Lebanon Ward 5, Lebanon County, Pennsylvania,
    E.D. No. 155, pages 210B, 214B, 215B, 218B, 220A, 223B and
    228B.
Inhabitants of Lebanon Ward 6, Lebanon, County, Pennsylvania,
    E.D. No. 156, pages 233A, 236B and 244A.
Inhabitants of Lebanon Ward 7, Lebanon County, Pennsylvania,
    E.D. No. 147, pages 92B and 93A.
Inhabitants of Lebanon Ward 7, Lebanon County, Pennsylvania,
    E.D. No. 157, page 252B.
Inhabitants of Lebanon Ward 7, Lebanon County, Pennsylvania,
    E.D. No. 158, page 263B;
Inhabitants of North Lebanon Township, Lebanon County, E.D. 157,
    page 253B.
Inhabitants of North Lebanon Township, Lebanon County,
    Pennsylvania, E.D. No. 163, pages 75A, 75B, 78A, 86A, 101A
    and 106A.
Inhabitants of North Lebanon, Lebanon County, Pennsylvania, E.D.
    No. 164, page 133A.

Inhabitants of South Lebanon Township, Lebanon County, E.D. No. 167, pages 183A and 190A.

Inhabitants of Swatara Township, Lebanon County, Pennsylvania, E.D. No. 170, pages 235A and 238A.

Inhabitants of Philadelphia Ward 5, Philadelphia County, Pennsylvania, E.D. No. 67, page 28A.

Inhabitants of Philadelphia Ward 23, Philadelphia County, Pennsylvania, E.D. No. 462, page 255B.

Inhabitants of Philadelphia Ward 24, Philadelphia County, Pennsylvania, E.D. No. 490, page 36A.

Inhabitants of Philadelphia Ward 24, Philadelphia County, Pennsylvania, E.D. No. 501, page 262B.

Inhabitants of Philadelphia Ward 42, Philadelphia County, Pennsylvania, E.D. No. 1059, page 100A.

Inhabitants of Philadelphia Ward 44, Philadelphia County, Pennsylvania, E.D. No. 11-42, page 20A.

Inhabitants of Philadelphia Ward 47, Philadelphia County, Pennsylvania, E.D. No. 1201, page 50A.

Fourteenth Census of the United States (1920)

Inhabitants of Cambridge Ward 5, Middlesex County, Massachusetts, E.D. No. 53, page 144A.

Inhabitants of Reading Ward 13, Berks County, Pennsylvania, E.D. No. 103, page 116B;

Inhabitants of West Reading, Berks County, Pennsylvania, E.D. No. 149, page 260A;

Inhabitants of Harrisburg Ward 4, Dauphin County, Pennsylvania, E.D. No. 69, page 20B.

Inhabitants of the Pennsylvania State Lunatic Hospital, Susquehanna Township, Dauphin County, Pennsylvania, E.D. No. 144, page 236A.

Inhabitants of East Donegal Township, Lancaster County, Pennsylvania, E.D. No. 30, page 43B.

Inhabitants of Bethel Township, Lebanon County, Pennsylvania, E.D. No. 157, page 43A.

Inhabitants of Cornwall Township, Lebanon County, Pennsylvania, E.D. No. 160, page 69A;

Inhabitants of Jackson Township, Lebanon County, Pennsylvania,
    E.D. No. 165, page 49A;
Inhabitants of Lebanon Ward 1, Lebanon County, Pennsylvania,
    E.D. No. 167, page 87B.
Inhabitants of Lebanon Ward 1, Lebanon County, Pennsylvania,
    E.D. No. 168, pages 112B and 124A.
Inhabitants of Lebanon Ward 1, Lebanon County, Pennsylvania,
    E.D. No. 168, page 112B.
Inhabitants of Lebanon Ward 2, Lebanon County, Pennsylvania,
    E.D. No. 169, pages 137B and 139A.
Inhabitants of Lebanon Ward 4, Lebanon County, Pennsylvania,
    E.D. No. 172, pages 186B, 188B and 190B.
Inhabitants of Lebanon Ward 5, Lebanon County, Pennsylvania,
    E.D. No. 173, pages 202B, 209A, 210A, 210B, 211A, 217B,
    218B, 221B, 222B and 226A.
Inhabitants of Lebanon Ward 5, Lebanon County, Pennsylvania,
    E.D. No. 174, pages 242B, 248A, 251B, 253A, 253B and 259B.
Inhabitants of Lebanon Ward 6, Lebanon County, Pennsylvania,
    E.D. No. 175, pages 265B and 274A.
Inhabitants of Lebanon Ward 7, Lebanon County, Pennsylvania,
    E.D. No. 176, pages 283A, 296B and 299B.
Inhabitants of Lebanon Ward 8, Lebanon County, Pennsylvania,
    E.D. No. 177, pages 304A and 306A.
Inhabitants of Lebanon Ward 9, Lebanon County, Pennsylvania,
    E.D. No. 178, pages 310B, 312B, and 313A.
Inhabitants of North Lebanon Township, Lebanon County,
    Pennsylvania, E.D. No. 186, page 167B and 168A.
Inhabitants of North Lebanon Township, Lebanon County,
    Pennsylvania, E.D. No. 188, page 184A;
Inhabitants of North Lebanon Township West Precinct, Lebanon
    County, Pennsylvania, E.D. No. 167, page 89A.
Inhabitants of North Lebanon Township West Precinct, Lebanon
    County, Pennsylvania, E.D. No. 187, page 176B.
Inhabitants of Swatara Township, Lebanon County, Pennsylvania,
    E.D. No. 197, page 301B.
Inhabitants of Union Township, Lebanon County, E.D. No. 159,
    page 63B.
Inhabitants of Philadelphia Ward 22, Philadelphia County,
    Pennsylvania, E.D. No.614, page 98B.

Inhabitants of Philadelphia Ward 23, Philadelphia County, Pennsylvania, E.D. No. 661, page 251A;

Inhabitants of Philadelphia Ward 34, Philadelphia County, Pennsylvania, E.D. No. 1173, page 235A.

Inhabitants of Philadelphia Ward 34, Philadelphia County, Pennsylvania, E.D. No. 1217, page 232A.

Inhabitants of Philadelphia Ward 38, Philadelphia County, Pennsylvania, E.D. No. 1354, page 189A.

Inhabitants of Philadelphia Ward 44, Philadelphia County, Pennsylvania, E.D. No. 1643, page 78A.

Inhabitants of Philadelphia Ward 44, Philadelphia County, Pennsylvania, E.D. No. 1679, page 155B.

Inhabitants of Philadelphia Ward 47, Philadelphia County, Pennsylvania, E.D. No. 1784, page 242A.

Fifteenth Census of the United States (1930)

Inhabitants of Borough of Yeadon, Delaware County, Pennsylvania, E.D. 23-179, page 248A.

Inhabitants of Cambridge, Middlesex County, Massachusetts, E.D. No. 9-66, page 83B.

Inhabitants of City of Elizabeth, Union County, New Jersey, E.D. No. 20-20, page 12B.

Inhabitants of Akron, Summit County, Ohio, E.D. No. 77-47, page 127A.

Inhabitants of Aliquippa, Beaver County, Pennsylvania, E.D. No. 4-11, page 216B;

Inhabitants of Reading, Berks County, Pennsylvania, E.D. No. 6-11, page 40A.

Inhabitants of Reading, Berks County, Pennsylvania, E.D. No. 6-45, page 264A.

Inhabitants of Reading, Berks County, Pennsylvania, E.D. No. 6-62, page 181A.

*Inhabitants of Derry Township, Dauphin County, Pennsylvania,*E.D. No. 22-6, page 238A.

Inhabitants of Harrisburg, Dauphin County, Pennsylvania, E.D. No. 22-21, page 16B.

Inhabitants of the Pennsylvania State Lunatic Hospital, Susquehanna Township, Dauphin County, Pennsylvania, E.D. No. 22-102, page 66A.

*Inhabitants of Upper Darby Township, Delaware County,
   Pennsylvania,* E.D. No. 23-170, page 247B;

*Inhabitants of East Donegal Township, Lancaster County,
   Pennsylvania,* E.D. No. 36-27, page 16B.

Inhabitants of Bethel Township, Lebanon County, Pennsylvania,
   E.D. No. 38-5, page 45A.

Inhabitants of Cornwall Township, Lebanon County, Pennsylvania,
   E.D. No. 38-7, page 78B;

Inhabitants of Jackson Township, Lebanon County, Pennsylvania,
   E.D. No. 38-11, page 119A;

Inhabitants of Lebanon, Lebanon County, Pennsylvania, E.D. No.
   38-14, page 4B;

Inhabitants of Lebanon, Lebanon County, Pennsylvania, E.D. No.
   38-15, pages 46A and 241A.

Inhabitants of Lebanon, Lebanon County, Pennsylvania, E.D. No.
   38-16, page 56A.

Inhabitants of Lebanon, Lebanon County, Pennsylvania, E.D. No.
   38-17, page 77A.

Inhabitants of Lebanon, Lebanon County, Pennsylvania, E.D. No.
   38-19, pages 107A and 124A.

Inhabitants of Lebanon, Lebanon County, Pennsylvania, E.D. 38-20,
   pages 146A, 146B, 150A, 150B and 159A.

Inhabitants of Lebanon, Lebanon County, Pennsylvania, E.D. No.
   38-21, pages 157B and 162A

Inhabitants of Lebanon, Lebanon County, Pennsylvania, E.D. No.
   38-22, pages 138A, 186B, 190A, and 191B.

Inhabitants of Lebanon, Lebanon County, Pennsylvania, E.D. No.
   38-23, pages 202A, 206A, 207A and 210A.

Inhabitants of Lebanon, Lebanon County, Pennsylvania, E.D. No.
   38-24, page 217B and 236A.

Inhabitants of Lebanon, Lebanon County, Pennsylvania, E.D. No.
   38-25, pages 243B and 244B.

Inhabitants of Lebanon, Lebanon County, Pennsylvania, E.D. No.
   38-26, pages 264A, 265A and 266B.

Inhabitants of Lebanon, Lebanon County, Pennsylvania, E.D. No.
   38-27, pages 160A and 164B.

*Inhabitants of North Annville Township, Lebanon County,
   Pennsylvania,* E.D. No. 38-32, pages 224A and 228B.

Inhabitants of North Cornwall Township, Lebanon County, Pennsylvania, E.D. No. 38-33, pages 241A, 249A and 249B.

Inhabitants of North Lebanon Township, Lebanon County, Pennsylvania, E.D. No. 38-34, pages 256A, 256B, 262A and 265B.

Inhabitants of North Lebanon Township, Lebanon County, Pennsylvania, E.D. No. 38-35, page 276B.

Inhabitants of Borough of Lansdale, Montgomery County, Pennsylvania, E.D. No. 53, Page 15A.

Inhabitants of Germantown Township, Philadelphia County, Pennsylvania, E.D. No. 628, page 207A. *Inhabitants of Philadelphia, Philadelphia County, Pennsylvania*, E.D. No. 51-85, page 159A.

Inhabitants of Philadelphia, Philadelphia County, Pennsylvania, E.D. No. 51-445, page 126B;

Inhabitants of Philadelphia, Philadelphia County, Pennsylvania, E.D. No.51-848, page 157B.

Inhabitants of Philadelphia, Philadelphia County, Pennsylvania, E.D. No. 351, page 1A.

Inhabitants of Philadelphia, Philadelphia County, Pennsylvania, E.D. No. 625, page 19A.

Inhabitants of Philadelphia, Philadelphia County, Pennsylvania, E.D. No. 878, page 26B.

Inhabitants of Philadelphia Ward 38, Philadelphia County, Pennsylvania, E.D. 1325, page 171A.

Inhabitants of City of York, York County, Pennsylvania, E.D. No. 99, page 81B.

Sixteenth Census of the United States (1940)

Inhabitants of City of Elizabeth, Union County, New Jersey, E.D. No. 23-06, page 314B.

Inhabitants of Akron, Summit County, Ohio, E.D. No. 89-109, page 1532B.

Inhabitants of Aliquippa, Beaver County, Pennsylvania, E.D. No. 4-11, page 216A.

Inhabitants of Reading, Berks County, Pennsylvania, E.D. No. 70-35, Page 496A.

Inhabitants of Reading, Berks County, Pennsylvania, E.D. No. 70-106, page 1425A.

Inhabitants of Upper Darby Township, Delaware County, Pennsylvania, E.D. No. 23-202, page 3621A.

Inhabitants of East Donegal Township, Lancaster County, Pennsylvania, E.D. No. 36-27, page 499A.

Inhabitants of Bethel Township, Lebanon County, Pennsylvania, E.D. No. 38-4, page 69B.

Inhabitants of Cornwall, Lebanon County, Pennsylvania, E.D. 38-7, page 93A.

Inhabitants of Lebanon, Lebanon County, Pennsylvania, E.D. No. 38-14A, pages 202B and 206B.

Inhabitants of Lebanon, Lebanon County, Pennsylvania, E.D. No. 38-15, pages 226A and 244B.

Inhabitants of Lebanon, Lebanon County, Pennsylvania, E.D. No. 38-17, page 269A.

Inhabitants of Lebanon, Lebanon County, Pennsylvania, E.D. No. 38-18, page 292B.

Inhabitants of Lebanon, Lebanon County, Pennsylvania, E.D. 38-20, pages 326B and 327A.

Inhabitants of Lebanon, Lebanon County, Pennsylvania, E.D. 38-23A, pages 374A and 375B.

Inhabitants of Lebanon, Lebanon County, Pennsylvania, E.D. 38-24, page 393A.

Inhabitants of Lebanon, Lebanon County, Pennsylvania, E.D. No. 38-25, pages 413A and 418A. Inhabitants of Lebanon, Lebanon County, Pennsylvania*, E.D. 38-26, page 434A.

Inhabitants of Lebanon, Lebanon County, Pennsylvania, E.D. 38-27, page 444A.

Inhabitants of Lebanon, Lebanon County, Pennsylvania, E.D. No. 38-28, pages 417A, 461A and 468B.

Inhabitants of Lebanon, Lebanon County, Pennsylvania, E.D. No. 38-29, pages 489A and 495A.

Inhabitants of Lebanon, Lebanon County, Pennsylvania, E.D. 38-30, page 519A.

Inhabitants of Lebanon, Lebanon County, Pennsylvania, E.D. No. 38-34, pages 576A and 578B.

Inhabitants of Lebanon, Lebanon County, Pennsylvania, E.D. 38-35, page 589A.

Inhabitants of Lebanon, Lebanon County, Pennsylvania, E.D. No. 38-45, page 793A.

Inhabitants of North Annville Township, Lebanon County, Pennsylvania, E.D. No. 38-40, page 701B.

Inhabitants of North Lebanon Township, Lebanon County, Pennsylvania, E.D. No. 38-42, pages 738B and 742B.

Inhabitants of North Lebanon, Lebanon County, Pennsylvania, E.D. No. 38-43, page 761A.

Inhabitants of South Lebanon Township, Lebanon County, Pennsylvania, E.D. No. 38-51, page 889B.

Inhabitants of Lower Merion Township, Montgomery County, Pennsylvania, E.D. No. 46-86, page 1510A.

Inhabitants of Philadelphia, Philadelphia County, Pennsylvania, E.D. No. 51-462, page 5389A.

Inhabitants of Philadelphia, Philadelphia County, Pennsylvania E.D. No. 51-485, page 5628A.

Inhabitants of Philadelphia, Philadelphia County, Pennsylvania, E.D. No. 51-486, page 5644B.

Inhabitants of Philadelphia, Philadelphia County, Pennsylvania, E.D. No. 51-564, page 6612B.

Inhabitants of Philadelphia, Philadelphia County, Pennsylvania, E.D. No. 51-623, page 7338A.

Inhabitants of Philadelphia, Philadelphia County, Pennsylvania, E.D. No. 51-1136, page 13862A.

Inhabitants of Washington, District of Columbia, E.D. No. 1-339, page 587A.

Inhabitants of Hanover, York County, Pennsylvania, E.D. No. 67-39, page 502A.

Inhabitants of Jackson Township, York County, Pennsylvania, E.D. No. 67-45, page 597A.

City Directories

Harrisburg

Boyd's Directory of Harrisburg and Steelton, 1897, Harrisburg: W.H. Boyd Co, Publisher.

Boyd's Directory of Harrisburg and Steelton, 1898, Harrisburg: W.H. Boyd Co, Publisher.

Boyd's Directory of Harrisburg and Steelton, 1899, Harrisburg: W.H. Boyd Co, Publisher.

Boyd's Harrisburg (Pennsylvania) City Directory, 1932, volume 57, Philadelphia, Pa.: R.L. Polk & Co, Publishers.

Boyd's Harrisburg (Dauphin County, Pa.) City Directory, 1933, volume 58, Philadelphia, Pa.: R.L. Polk & Co., Publishers.

Boyd's Harrisburg (Dauphin County, Pa.) City Directory, 1934, volume 59, Philadelphia, Pa.: R.L. Polk & Co., Publishers.

Boyd's Harrisburg (Dauphin County, Pa.) City Directory, 1935, volume 60, Philadelphia, Pa.: R.L. Polk & Co., Publishers.

Polk's Greater Harrisburg (Dauphin County, Pa.) City Directory, 1936-37, volume 61, Philadelphia, Pa.: R.L. Polk & Co., Publishers.

Polk's Greater Harrisburg (Dauphin County, Pa.) City Directory, 1938, volume 62, Philadelphia, Pa.: R.L. Polk & Co., Publishers.

Polk's Greater Harrisburg (Dauphin County, Pa.) City Directory, 1939, volume 63, Philadelphia, Pa.: R.L. Polk & Co., Publishers.

Polk's Greater Harrisburg (Dauphin County, Pa.) City Directory, 1940, volume 64, Philadelphia, Pa.: R.L. Polk & Co., Publishers.

Polk's Greater Harrisburg (Dauphin County, Pa.) City Directory, 1941, volume 65, Philadelphia, Pa.: R.L. Polk & Co., Publishers.

Polk's Greater Harrisburg (Dauphin County, Pa.) City Directory, 1942, volume 66, Philadelphia, Pa.: R.L. Polk & Co., Publishers.

Polk's Greater Harrisburg (Dauphin County, Pa.) City Directory, 1943, volume 67, Boston, Mass.: R.L. Polk & Co., Publishers.

Polk's Greater Harrisburg (Dauphin County, Pa.) City Directory, 1944, volume 68, Boston, Mass.: R.L. Polk & Co., Publishers.

Polk's Greater Harrisburg (Dauphin County, Pa.) City Directory, 1945, volume 69, Boston, Mass.: R.L. Polk & Co., Publishers.

Polk's Greater Harrisburg (Dauphin County, Pa.) City Directory, 1946, volume 70, Boston, Mass.: R.L. Polk & Co., Publishers.

Polk's Greater Harrisburg (Dauphin County, Pa.) City Directory, 1947, volume 71, Boston, Mass.: R.L. Polk & Co., Publishers.

Polk's Greater Harrisburg (Dauphin County, Pa.) City Directory, 1949, volume 72, Boston, Mass.: R.L. Polk & Co., Publishers.

Lebanon

Directory of Lebanon City and County, 1889-90, Lebanon, Pa: The Lebanon Directory Company.

Boyd's Directory of Lebanon City, Names of the Citizens, 1891-1893, Reading, Pa.: W.H. Boyd.

Boyd's Directory of Lebanon City, Names of the Citizens, 1895-1896, Reading, Pa.: W.H. Boyd.

Shaffer and Company's Complete Directory of Lebanon City and Suburbs, 1897. Compiled and Published by Chas. C. Shaffer & Co., Lebanon, Pa.: Report Publishing Company.

Shaffer's Directory of Lebanon City and Suburbs, 1899. Compiled and Published by Chas. C. Shaffer, Lebanon, Pa.: Report Publishing Company.

Shaffer's Directory of City of Lebanon and Suburbs, 1901. Compiled and Published by Chas. C. Shaffer, Lebanon, Pa.: Report Publishing Company.

Shaffer's Directory of City of Lebanon, Pa., and Suburbs, 1903. Compiled and Published by Chas. C. Shaffer, Lebanon, Pa.: Report Publishing Company.

R.L. Polk and Company's Lebanon Directory, 1905. Pittsburgh, Pa.: R.L. Polk & Co., Publishers.

R.L. Polk and Company's Lebanon Directory, 1907. Pittsburgh, Pa.: R.L. Polk & Co., Publishers.

R.L. Polk and Company's Lebanon Directory, 1909. Pittsburgh, Pa.: R.L. Polk & Co., Publishers.

R.L. Polk and Company's Lebanon Directory, 1911. Pittsburgh, Pa.: R.L. Polk & Co., Publishers.

R.L. Polk and Company's Lebanon Directory, 1913, including Annville, Myerstown, West Myerstown and Palmyra. Pittsburgh, Pa.: R.L. Polk & Co., Publishers.

R.L. Polk and Company's Lebanon Directory, 1915, including Annville, Myerstown, West Myerstown and Palmyra. Pittsburgh, Pa.: R.L. Polk & Co., Publishers.

R.L. Polk and Company's Lebanon Directory, 1917, including Annville, Myerstown, and Palmyra. Pittsburgh, Pa.: R.L. Polk & Co., Publishers.

R.L. Polk and Company's Lebanon Directory, including Annville, Myerstown, and Palmyra, 1919-1920, volume 7, Pittsburgh, Pa.: R.L. Polk & Co., Publishers.

R.L. Polk and Company's Lebanon Directory, including Annville, Myerstown, and Palmyra, 1921-1922, volume 8, New York, NY: R.L. Polk & Co., Publishers.

R.L. Polk and Company's Lebanon, Pa. City Directory, including Annville, Myerstown and Palmyra, 1923-24, volume 9, New York, NY: R.L. Polk & Co., Publishers.

Polk's Lebanon Pennsylvania Directory, including Annville, Myerstown and Palmyra, 1925-26, volume 10, New York, NY: R.L. Polk & Co.

Polk's Lebanon (Pennsylvania) Directory, including Annville, Myerstown and Palmyra, 1928-29, volume 11, Philadelphia, Pa.: R.L. Polk & Co.

Polk's Lebanon (Pennsylvania.) City Directory, including Annville, Myerstown and Palmyra, 1930-31, volume 12, Philadelphia, Pa.: R.L. Polk & Co.

Polk's Lebanon (Lebanon County, Pa.) City Directory, including Annville, Cleona, Myerstown and Palmyra, 1933-34, volume 13, Philadelphia, Pa.: R.L. Polk & Co.

Polk's Lebanon (Lebanon County, Pa.) City Directory, including Annville, Cleona, Myerstown and Palmyra, 1936, volume 14, Philadelphia, Pa.: R.L. Polk & Co.

Polk's Lebanon (Lebanon County, Pa.) City Directory, including Annville, Cleona, Myerstown and Palmyra, 1938, volume 15, Philadelphia, Pa.: R.L. Polk & Co.

Polk's Lebanon (Lebanon County, Pa.) City Directory, including Annville, Cleona, Myerstown and Palmyra, 1940, volume 16, Philadelphia, Pa.: R.L. Polk & Co.

Polk's Lebanon (Lebanon County, Pa.) City Directory, including Annville, Cleona, Myerstown and Palmyra, 1942, volume 17, Philadelphia, Pa.: R.L. Polk & Co.

Polk's Lebanon (Lebanon County, Pa.) City Directory, including Annville, Cleona, Myerstown and Palmyra, 1945-46, volume 18, Philadelphia, Pa.: R.L. Polk & Co.

Polk's Lebanon (Lebanon County, Pa.) City Directory, including Annville, Cleona, Myerstown and Palmyra, 1948, volume 19, Philadelphia, Pa.: R.L. Polk & Co.

Philadelphia

McElroy's Philadelphia Directory for 1844, Philadelphia: Edward C. and John Biddle.

McElroy's Philadelphia Directory for 1847, Philadelphia: Edward C. and John Biddle.

McElroy's Philadelphia Directory for 1848, Philadelphia: Edward C. and John Biddle.

McElroy's Philadelphia Directory for 1850, Philadelphia: Edward C. and John Biddle.

McElroy's Philadelphia Directory for 1855, Philadelphia: Edward C. and John Biddle.

McElroy's Philadelphia Directory for 1857, Philadelphia: Edward C. and John Biddle.

McElroy's Philadelphia Directory for 1858, Philadelphia: Edward C. and John Biddle.

McElroy's Philadelphia Directory for 1860, Philadelphia: Edward C. and John Biddle.

McElroy's Philadelphia Directory for 1865, Philadelphia: A. McElroy.

Gopsill's Philadelphia City Directory for 1870, Philadelphia: James Gopsill's Sons.

Gopsill's Philadelphia City Directory for 1875, Philadelphia: James Gopsill's Sons.

Gopsill's Philadelphia City Directory for 1880, Philadelphia: James Gopsill's Sons.

Gopsill's Philadelphia City Directory for 1885, Philadelphia: James Gopsill's Sons.

Gopsill's Philadelphia City Directory for 1890, Philadelphia: James Gopsill's Sons.

Gopsill's Philadelphia City Directory for 1895, Philadelphia: James Gopsill's Sons.

Gopsill's Philadelphia City Directory for 1900, Philadelphia: James Gopsill's Sons.

Gopsill's Philadelphia City Directory for 1905, Philadelphia: James Gopsill's Sons.

Boyd's City Directory of Philadelphia 1910, Philadelphia: C.E. Howe Company.

Boyd's City Directory of Philadelphia 1915, Philadelphia: C.E. Howe Company;

Boyd's Combined City and Business Directory of Philadelphia 1919-1920, Philadelphia: C.E. Howe Company;

Polk's Philadelphia Directory 1925, Philadelphia: R.L. Polk & Company;

Polk's Philadelphia City Directory 1930, Philadelphia: R.L. Polk & Company;

Polk's Philadelphia City Directory, 1935-36, Philadelphia: R.L. Polk & Company.

Polk's Philadelphia Directory 1925, Philadelphia: R.L. Polk & Company;

Polk's Philadelphia City Directory 1930, Philadelphia: R.L. Polk & Company;

Polk's Philadelphia City Directory, 1935-36, Philadelphia: R.L. Polk & Company.

Reading

Boyd's Directory of Reading, 1895, Reading, Pa.: W.H. Boyd Co, Compilers and Publishers.

Boyd's Directory of Reading, 1896, Reading, Pa.: W.H. Boyd Co, Compilers and Publishers.

Boyd's Directory of Reading, 1897, Reading, Pa.: W.H. Boyd Co, Compilers and Publishers.

Boyd's Directory of Reading, 1898, Reading, Pa.: W.H. Boyd Co, Compilers and Publishers.

Boyd's Directory of Reading, 1900, Reading, Pa.: W.H. Boyd Co, Compilers and Publishers.

Boyd's Directory of Reading, 1903, Reading, Pa.: W.H. Boyd Co, Compilers and Publishers.

Boyd's Directory of Reading, 1907, Reading, Pa.: W.H. Boyd Co, Compilers and Publishers.

Boyd's Directory of Reading, 1908, Reading, Pa.: W.H. Boyd Co, Compilers and Publishers.

Boyd's Directory of Reading, 1909, Reading, Pa.: W.H. Boyd Co, Compilers and Publishers.

Boyd's Directory of Reading, 1910, Reading, Pa.: W.H. Boyd Co, Compilers and Publishers.

Boyd's Directory of Reading, 1911, Reading, Pa.: W.H. Boyd Co, Compilers and Publishers.

Boyd's Directory of Reading, 1926, Reading, Pa.: W.H. Boyd Co, Compilers and Publishers.

Boyd's Reading (Berks County, Pa.) City Directory, 1937, volume 75, Boston, Mass.: R.L. Polk & Co.

Boyd's Reading (Berks County, Pa.) City Directory, 1938, volume 76, Boston, Mass.: R.L. Polk & Co.

Boyd's Reading (Berks County, Pa.) City Directory, 1942, volume 80, Boston, Mass.: R.L. Polk & Co.

Boyd's Reading (Berks County, Pa.) City Directory, 1950, volume 86, Boston, Mass.: R.L. Polk & Co.

Scranton

R.L. Polk & Company's Scranton (Pennsylvania) City Directory, 1920, volume 17, Scranton, Pa.: R.L. Polk & Co., Publishers.

R.L. Polk & Company's Scranton (Pennsylvania) City Directory, 1921, volume 18, Scranton, Pa.: R.L. Polk & Co., Publishers.

R.L. Polk & Company's Scranton (Pennsylvania) City Directory, 1923, volume 19, Scranton, Pa.: R.L. Polk & Co., Publishers.

Polk's Scranton City Directory, 1924, volume 20, Scranton, Pa.: R.L. Polk & Co., Publishers.

Polk's Scranton City Directory, 1925, volume 21, Scranton, Pa.: R.L. Polk & Co., Publishers.

Polk's Scranton City Directory, 1926, volume 22, Scranton, Pa.: R.L. Polk & Co., Publishers.

Polk's Scranton (Pennsylvania) City Directory, 1927, volume 23, Scranton, Pa.: R.L. Polk & Co., Publishers.

Polk's Scranton (Pennsylvania) City Directory, 1928, volume 24, Scranton, Pa.: R.L. Polk & Co., Publishers.

York

Polk's York Pennsylvania City Directory, volume 18 (1931-32), Philadelphia: R.L. Polk & Co.

Polk's York Pennsylvania City Directory, volume 19 (1933-34), Philadelphia: R.L. Polk & Co.

Polk's York Pennsylvania City Directory, volume 20 (1935-36), Philadelphia: R.L. Polk & Co.

Polk's York Pennsylvania City Directory, volume 21 (1937-38), Philadelphia: R.L. Polk & Co.

Polk's York Pennsylvania City Directory, volume 22 (1939-40), Philadelphia: R.L. Polk & Co.

Polk's York Pennsylvania City Directory, volume 23 (1942), Philadelphia: R.L. Polk & Co.

Polk's York Pennsylvania City Directory, volume 24 (1943), Philadelphia: R.L. Polk & Co.

Miscellaneous

Akron Official City Directory, including Barberton and Cuyahoga Falls, 1931, Akron, Ohio: The Burch Directory Company.

Akron, Cuyahoga Falls and Barberton Official City Directory, 1933, Akron, Ohio: The Burch Directory Company.

Akron, Barberton and Cuyahoga Falls Official City Directory, 1934-35, Akron, Ohio: The Burch Directory Company.

Akron, Portage Lakes, Barberton and Cuyahoga Falls Official City Directory, 1941. Akron, Ohio: Burch Directory Company.

Akron, Tallmadge, Portage Lakes, Barberton and Cuyahoga Falls Official City Directory, 1943. Akron, Ohio: Burch Directory Company.

Akron, Tallmadge, Portage Lakes, Barberton and Cuyahoga Falls Official City Directory, 1948-49. Akron, Ohio: Burch Directory Company.

Hoye's Twelfth Volume Kansas City Directory, 1882, Kansas City, Missouri: Hoye City Directory Company.

Hoye's Kansas City Directory for 1883, Thirteenth Volume, Kansas City, Missouri: Hoye City Directory Company.

Hoye's City Directory of Kansas City, including Kansas City, Kansas, Wyandotte etc., 1884, Kansas City, Missouri: Hoye City Directory Company.

Hoye's City Directory of Kansas City, including Kansas City, Kansas, Wyandotte etc., 1885, Kansas City, Missouri: Hoye City Directory Company.

Hoye's City Directory of Kansas City, Mo., including Kansas City, Kansas [Consolidated cities] and Westport, Mo., 1886-1887, Kansas City, Missouri: Hoye Directory Company.

Hoye's City Directory of Kansas City, Mo., including Kansas City, Kansas [Consolidated cities] and Westport, Mo., 1887-1888, Kansas City, Missouri: Hoye Directory Company.

Swank, George, *General and Business Directory of Johnstown including Conemaugh, Cambria, Millville, Woodvale, Coopersdale, East Conemaugh, Franklin and Prospect*, 1869.

Additional online sources

Bingham's Line: <http://www.pghbridges.com/articles/canals/canal_
history_wilson.htm>

Bingham's Line: <http://www.pghbridges.com/articles/canals/canal_
history_boucher.htm>

New York Passenger Lists, 1820-1957. Ancestry.com

Pennsylvania Department of Health: <http://www.health.state.
pa.us>

Pennsylvania Germans: <http://www.kutztownfestival.com>

Pennsylvania State Archives, Revolutionary War Military Abstract
Card File <http://www.digitalarchives.state.pa.us/archive.asp.>

Pow Wow Doctors: <http://www.berkshistory.org/articles/pow-wow.
html> <http://www.esoteric.msu.edu/VolumeIV/Powwow.htm

Reading Central Catholic High School, URL: < http://www.cchsbc.
pvt.k12.pa.us/ >

Spanish American War Rosters: <http://www.paspanishamericanwar.
com/rosters.html>

State hospitals: <http://www.rootsweb.ancestry.com/~asylums/>

Thompson Funeral Home, Lebanon, Pennsylvania: URL:
<http://www.thompsonfuneralhomelebanon.com/?page=history>

U.S. National Homes for Disabled Volunteer Soldiers, 1866-1938.
Ancestry.com.

World War II Army Enlistment Records, 1938-1946. Ancestry.com.

Works Progress Administration Cemetery Project: <http://www.
interment.net/column/records/wpa/wpa_history.htm>

INDEX

SUBJECT INDEX

This index covers all persons mentioned in this book, as well as historical events, geographical locations, and information sources relevant to the narrative. Although every effort has been undertaken to make this index as complete as possible, it does not, however, cover all of the content contained in the appendices. Specifically, not all cemeteries listed in Appendix B are indexed here—some that are noteworthy are mentioned, but that appendix provides an alphabetical list of cemeteries and their locations. Also, in general, the index does not cover the information contained in the footnotes. For example, the locations given in the Federal Census enumerations cited in footnotes are not covered by this index, although many of the locations mentioned in those citations are indexed here, if they are specifically mentioned in the text. In this index, all women are listed according to their family names—and if married, their married names are given in parentheses. A few women are listed according to both their family and married names, but this practice is not generally followed.

A

B

C

D

G

I

J

L

Y

ACKNOWLEDGMENTS

Although it is a remarkable turn of events to have acquired a passion for my family history and to have been blessed with talents for research and bringing the results to the printed page, I wish to acknowledge that a project such as this requires the guidance, cooperation, and contributions of numerous people. In this space I wish to express my debt of gratitude to all of those people, named and unnamed. Most of all, I am indebted to my wife, Linda, and my three daughters—Heidi, Abby and Becky—who have been an unending source of love and support throughout my work on this project, but, of course, not only during this period. None of the work reported here would have been possible without their encouragement and their confidence in me.

There are other people who contributed in important ways to this endeavor. I acknowledged the major contributors to the work on this volume on the title page of this book, but they deserve further mention here as well. Nancy Allwein Nebiker is simply amazing— not only did she generously provide considerable information on which parts of this book are based (especially obituaries from the Lebanon newspapers), she provided tireless support in other ways. Nancy proof-read parts of the manuscript on more than one occasion, nailing down errors of commission and omission, and she communicated her findings with grace and aplomb. Patti Keefer Billow similarly proof-read parts of the manuscript and especially helped craft the section on John Henry Allwein and his descendants. Madeline Paine Moyer, Donna Wagner Koons, and Peter Hill Byrne continually provided encouragement and moral support along the way, for which I am deeply grateful. Along with all of them, others—Tommy Sims, Edward F. Allwein, Douglas Owen Alwine, Jim Hoffheins, Leonard Alwine, Thom Dunn Marti, Mary Simoni, Teri Whitridge, Cheryl Alwine Lutz, Kathleen Hoover, Patricia Alwine Lawver, Dan Hecker, Joel Keefer, Darla Alwine Grenewalt, and Thomas A. Stobie—provided valuable information on their family lines and, in many cases, old photographs of family members. They are all my cousins—in varying degrees of relationship—and my heartfelt gratitude goes to all of them. I apologize if I have left out mention of anyone else.

I want to especially thank Madeline Moyer for the photograph of the priceless Fractur drawing commemorating the birth of William Allwein, son of Philip Allwein and Barbara Frantz, which I used for the cover art. Also, I want to thank Simon Zimmerman of Lancaster, Pennsylvania, who owns the Johannes Alweins dower chest, for allowing us to make a photograph of it. In addition to the photographs already mentioned, I acknowledge the staff of the Thompson Funeral Home in Lebanon for the photograph of Pierce Henry Thompson, their founder. Although virtually all of the gravestone photographs were supplied by me, there was one (for Elizabeth Allwein Francis) which I obtained from Find-a-grave. com, and I wish to acknowledge that source here.

Finally, my thanks goes out to all the people, too numerous to mention, from historical societies, archives, libraries, cemeteries, and churches, as well as all of the descendants of the Allwein (Allwine, Alwine, etc.) families who have followed the research I presented in the first volume of *Familie Allwein*, and who have offered additional information and perspectives at family reunions and through e-mail exchanges.